SO-BRC-829

MAY 20 1987

LIFE IN MEXICO

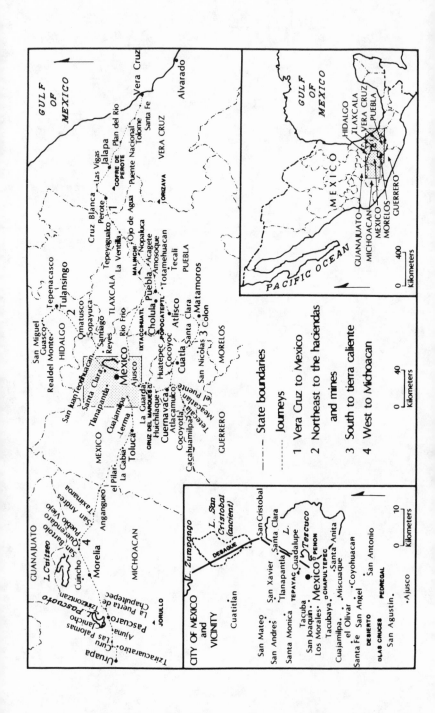

LIFE IN MEXICO

FRANCES CALDERÓN DE LA BARCA

University of California Press
Berkeley, Los Angeles, London

F
1213
C238
1982

University of California Press
Berkeley and Los Angeles, California

University of California Press, Ltd.
London, England

First California Edition 1982
ISBN 0-520-04662-5 paper
      0-520-04661-7 cloth
Printed in the United States of America

1 2 3 4 5 6 7 8 9

TABLE OF CONTENTS

Holyoke Community College Library

PREFACE

The present work is the result of observations made during a two years' residence in Mexico, by a lady, whose position there made her intimately acquainted with its society, and opened to her the best sources of information in regard to whatever could interest an enlightened foreigner. It consists of letters written to the members of her own family, and, *really*, not intended originally—however incredible the assertion—for publication. Feeling a regret that such rich stores of instruction and amusement, from which I have so much profited, myself, should be reserved for the eyes of a few friends only, I strongly recommended that they should be given to the world. This is now done, with a few such alterations and omissions as were necessary in a private correspondence; and although the work would derive more credit from the author's own name, than from anything which I can say, yet as she declines prefixing it, I feel much pleasure in making this statement by way of introduction to the public.

WILLIAM H. PRESCOTT.

Boston, December 20, 1842.

GLOSSARY

SPANISH OR MEXICAN WORDS

Which occur in the course of the work, which are generally explained when first used, but which being repeated, the reader might forget and wish to refer to.

Administrador—Agent.

Alameda—Public walk with trees.

Aquador—Water-carrier.

Alacran—Scorpion.

Anquera—Coating of stamped gilt leather, edged with little bells, which covers the back of the horses.

Arriero—Muleteer.

Arroba—Spanish weight of twenty-five pounds.

Azotea—The flat roof of a house.

Barranca—Ravine.

Botica—Apothecary's shop.

Calle—Street.

Cargadores—Men who carry loads.

Chinguirito—Spirit made from sugar-cane.

Chile—Hot peppers.

Compadre and *Comadre*—Godfather and Godmother; names by which two persons address each other, who have held the same child at the baptismal font, or have been sponsors together at a marriage, etc.

Canónigo—Canon or prebendary.

Cómicos—Actors.

Camarista—Lady of honour.

Dia de Años—Birthday.

Dulces—Sweetmeats.

Diário—Daily newspapers.

Frisones—Large horses from the north.

Funcion—Solemnity—festival.

Frijoles—Brown beans.

Galopina—Kitchen-girl.

Garbanzos—Chick-peas, *Cicer Arietinum.*

Gachupin—Name given to the Spaniards in Mexico.

Garita—City-gate.

Goleta—Schooner.

Gentuza—Rabble.

Honras—Funeral honours.

Hacienda—Country-place.

Ingenio de Azucar—Sugar plantation.

Inválidos—Disabled soldiers.

Jarro—Earthen jar.

Ladrones—Robbers.

Léperos—Beggars, low persons.

Litera—Litter.

Monte Pio—Office where money is lent on security.

Mezcal—Brandy distilled from pulque.

Manga—Cloak made of cloth, with a hole in the middle for putting the head through.

Novios—Betrothed persons.

Nuestro Amo—*Our Master,* used in speaking of the Host.

Ojo de Agua—Spring of water.

Portales—Covered portico supported by columns.

Pulqueria—Shop where pulque is sold.

Paséo—Public walk.

Paso—Pace, pacing.

Padrino—Godfather.

Plaza—Square.

Patio—Courtyard.

Petate—Matting.

Poblana—Woman of Puebla.

Pronunciamiento—A revolution in Mexico.

Pronunciados—Those who revolt.

Rancho—A farm.

Ranchero—Farmer.

Reboso—A scarf that goes over the head.

Reja—Iron grate.

Sopilote—Species of carrion vulture.

Sarape—A woollen blanket more or less fine, with a hole for the head to go through.

Traspaso—Conveyance, transfer.

Tilma—Indian cloak.

Tierra caliente—The hot land.

Tertulia—An evening party.

Toreador—Bull-fighter.

Tortilla—Species of thin cake.

Tortillera—Woman who bakes tortillas.

Vaca—Joint stock in gambling.

Vomito—Name given to the yellow fever.

Venta—Inn.

INTRODUCTION

Life in Mexico, by Fanny Calderón de la Barca, belongs to the accounts of travel and residence by foreigners which have furnished our most informative and perceptive reports on periods and countries. At their best, written by keen observers, endowed with incisive style and humor, they bring the objectivity and comparative point of view— at times the prejudices—of people bred and educated in another country. The foibles and oddities, the peculiarities of the country observed relative to others, stand out clearly as they could not in the observations of a native unless he were truly unusual. In *Life in Mexico*, the splendor, the misery, the political posturing and chronic instability of Mexican politics in 1839–1842 are sketched thoughtfully and incisively. So too are the luxury and crudity of a Mexican life which had not changed greatly from that of the eighteenth century and before which lay the immense changes of the decades to follow.

The author, who placed her name on the title page as Fanny Calderón de la Barca, was born Frances Erskine Inglis in Edinburgh on December 23, 1804, the fifth in what was to be a family of ten children. Her father, William Inglis, a well-to-do landowner, was a Writer to the Signet, in Scotland a special part of the legal profession; her mother, an Erskine, was related to the Earls of Buchan and other noble Scottish families. Frances, or Fanny as she preferred to be called, received a careful education including travel in Italy. In 1828, when her father was forced into bankruptcy, the family removed to Normandy, where in 1830 he died. Thereupon the widowed Mrs. Inglis, four of her daughters, including Fanny, and a number of grandchildren moved to Boston, where they opened a school. Scotland was then a prized source of school teachers, and they were well prepared for the role. The school enjoyed considerable success until it was involved in a scandal involving an anonymous satire on a charity bazaar of which Fanny was supposed to be co-author. Whatever the right of that story, the Inglis family moved in 1835 to the village of New Brighton on Staten Island, then a rural area of stately villas and farms

5

and a vacation retreat from the tropical summers of Washington, D.C.

On Staten Island, Fanny met her future husband, Angel Calderón de la Barca. Born in 1790 in Buenos Aires to a career Spanish civil servant and educated in England, Don Angel fought for his country against the French invaders of Spain during the Napoleonic Wars and fell prisoner. In 1819, some years after the conclusion of peace and his release, he entered his country's diplomatic service, where despite political upheavals at home he served with distinction and won steady promotion. In 1835 he came to the United States as the Spanish minister. He made the acquaintance of Fanny Inglis some time after his arrival, and on September 24, 1838 the two were married in New York. Don Angel was 48; his bride, 33. The couple spent the winter of 1838–1839 in Washington, and in the following summer began to prepare for Don Angel's new diplomatic assignment as the first Spanish minister to Mexico.

Mexico had declared its independence from Spain in 1821 and maintained it because the mother country was unable to muster the military force for invasion and repression. In 1825 the last fortress held by Spanish forces within Mexico, the island of San Juan de Ulúa in the harbor of Veracruz, surrendered to the Mexicans; but Spanish acceptance of Mexican independence and the establishment of peaceful relations foundered upon the steady refusal of the Spanish king, Ferdinand VII, to accept what was clearly an irreversible fact. Upon the death of Ferdinand in 1833 and the accession of his daughter, an infant, to the throne as Isabella II, negotiation became possible. In December 1836 the Spanish Cortes authorized the opening of relations upon the basis of recognition of Mexican independence, and two days after the promulgation of the law the Spanish Prime Minister and Minister for Foreign Affairs and the Mexican plenipotentiary to London signed a treaty of peace and amity in Madrid. The following day the Spanish government issued a decree declaring Mexico a friendly nation. Consular relations were established quickly; more formal diplomatic ones waited until 1839.

In those leisurely days, the Calderón de la Barca couple could prepare at some length for the new assignment. One arrangement they made was an agreement to search in Mexico for sources and information for William Hickling Prescott, then known as the author of a well-received life of Ferdinand and Isabella, who was planning a history of the conquest of Mexico. The book, when published, was to make him famous. Don Angel, who knew and admired Prescott, readily placed himself at the disposal of the author and not only located materials for him in Mexico but also served as intermediary in opening relations for Prescott with eminent and knowledgeable Mexicans, such as Lucas Alamán, the administrator of what remained of the Cortés Estate. The relations between Prescott and both Don Angel and Fanny lasted long after the couple left Mexico.

In Mexico, where they arrived in 1839, the new Spanish minister and his wife received a cordial welcome and mixed freely in Mexican society. The tact and good sense of Don Angel earned substantial success for a difficult assignment despite the number and variety of claims by Spanish subjects against the Mexican Republic. The diplomat and his wife were able to travel widely. Fanny recorded travels and events in her letters to her family and in three volumes of journal, of which two are extant.

When Don Angel's assignment in Mexico ended and the couple returned to the United States for reassignment, Prescott, who seems to have read many of the letters, urged Fanny to publish them. *Life in Mexico*, published under the date of 1843 although actually printed in December 1842, and issued with a short preface by Prescott warmly recommending the book, is an edited version of the letters, selecting those of greater interest and deleting passages or comments that Fanny decided most likely to cause serious offence or about which she had changed her mind. In the fashion of the time, people were referred to by the initial letter of their surnames, followed by a blank. No one has much trouble today identifying the people, nor for that matter did knowledgeable people at the time.

The book was issued in American and British editions. That in the United States was an instant success; that in the United Kingdom met a more varied reception, one reviewer even suggesting that the author had never been in Mexico. With time the book won universal favor. Publication in Spanish had a more varied history. Shortly after the appearance of the American edition, the Mexico City newspaper, *El siglo diez y nueve*, began to publish some of the letters. An initial uproar in the form of a bitter editorial in the official government newspaper soon subsided and a number of the letters were printed, although not those sketching in caustic terms General Santa Anna, then president. Publication of a complete translation waited until the twentieth century, when there have been two, in 1920 and 1959. In 1944 the Mexican government reissued in a special series of classics for the Mexican public the letters as they had been made available in *El siglo diez y nueve*. Both in the English-speaking world and in Mexico the book is now recognized as a classic, fixing on paper in sharply etched sketches a society and period now gone.

The life of Don Angel and Fanny after leaving Mexico continued to be notable. Don Angel served again as Spanish minister to the United States and completed his diplomatic career with a short term as Minister of State for Foreign Affairs. The fall of the government in July 1854 led to a period of exile in Paris. When the pair returned to Madrid, Don Angel became a senator in the Cortes. He died in 1861. Fanny remained in Spain and at the urgent invitation of Queen Isabella II became tutor and governess of Princess Isabella, then 7. Her service to the royal family continued through the revolution of 1868, which deposed Isabella II, and the restoration of her son as Alfonso XII in 1874. In 1876, in recognition of her services and those of Don Angel, she was created marquesa de Calderón de la Barca in her own right. Unfortunately, the couple had no children to inherit the title. In 1882 after a late supper in the royal palace, for which she had dressed in customary decolletage, she took cold, rapidly grew worse, and on February 6, died. She was 77.

For the rest, the letters speak for themselves.

Berkeley, California   —Woodrow Borah
August 1981

LIFE IN MEXICO

LETTER THE FIRST

Departure of the Norma—Last look of New York Bay—Fellow-passengers—Contrary Winds—Deceitful Appearances—Sunset in Southern Latitudes—Seas passed over by Columbus—Varied Occupations on Shipboard—Berry Islands—Bahama Banks—Evening in a Tropical Sea—L. E. L.—Pan of Matanzas—Morro Castle—Bay of Havana—Arrival—Handsome House in Havana—Sights and Sounds.

PACKET SHIP "NORMA," Oct. 27th, 1839.

This morning, at ten o'clock, we stepped on board the steamboat Hercules, destined to convey us to our packet with its musical name. The day was foggy and gloomy, as if refusing to be comforted, even by an occasional smile from the sun. All prognosticated that the Norma would not sail to-day, but "where there's a will," etc. Several of our friends accompanied us to the wharf; the Russian Minister, the Minister of Buenos Ayres, Mr. ——, who tried hard to look sentimental, and even brought tears into his eyes by some curious process; Judge ——, Mr. ——, and others, from whom we were truly sorry to part.

The Norma was anchored in one of the most beautiful points of the bay, and the steamboat towed us five miles, until we had passed the Narrows. The wind was contrary, but the day began to clear up, and the sun to scatter the watery clouds.

Still there is nothing so sad as a retreating view. It is as if time were visibly in motion; and as here we had to part from ——, we could only distinguish, as through a misty veil, the beauties of the bay; the shores covered to the water's edge with trees rich in their autumnal colouring; the white houses on Staten Island—the whole gradually growing fainter, till, like a dream, they faded away.

The pilot has left us, breaking our last link with the land. We still see the mountains of Neversink, and the lighthouse of Sandy Hook. The sun is setting, and in a few minutes we must take our leave, probably for years, of places long familiar to us.

Our fellow-passengers do not appear very remarkable. There

is Madame A——, returning from being prima donna in Mexico, in a packet called after the opera in which she was there a favourite, with her husband Señor V—— and her child. There is M. B—— with moustaches like a bird's nest; a pretty widow in deep affliction, at least in deep mourning; a maiden lady going out as a governess, and every variety of Spaniard and Havanero. So now we are alone, C——n and I, and my French femme-de-chambre, with her air of Dowager Duchess, and moreover sea-sick.

28th.—When I said I liked a sea life, I did not mean to be understood as liking a merchant ship, with an airless cabin, and with every variety of disagreeable odour. As a French woman on board, with the air of an afflicted porpoise, and with more truth than elegance, expresses it: "Tout devient puant, même l'eau-de-cologne."

The wind is still contrary, and the Norma, beating up and down, makes but little way. We have gone seventy-four miles, and of these advanced but forty. Every one being sick to-day, the deck is nearly deserted. The most interesting object I have discovered on board is a pretty little deaf and dumb girl, very lively and with an intelligent face, who has been teaching me to speak on my fingers. The infant heir of the house of —— has shown his good taste by passing the day in squalling. M. B——, pale, dirty, and much resembling a brigand out of employ, has traversed the deck with uneasy footsteps and a cigar appearing from out his moustaches, like a light in a tangled forest, or a jack-o'-lantern in a marshy thicket. A fat Spaniard has been discoursing upon the glories of olla podrida. *Au reste,* we are slowly pursuing our way, and at this rate might reach Cuba in three months.

And the stars are shining, quiet and silvery. All without is soft and beautiful, and no doubt the Norma herself looks all in unison with the scene, balancing herself like a lazy swan, white and graciously. So it is without, and within, there is miserable sea-sickness, bilge-water, and all the unavoidable disagreeables of a small packet.

31st.—Three days have passed without anything worthy of notice having occurred, except that we already feel the difference of temperature. The passengers are still enduring sea-sickness in all its phases.

This morning opened with an angry dispute between two of the gentlemen, on the subject of Cuban lotteries, and they ended by applying to each other epithets which, however much they might be deserved, were certainly rather strong;

but by dinner time, they were amicably engaged in concocting together an enormous tureen of *gaspachos,* a sort of salad, composed of bread, oil, vinegar, sliced onion and garlic—and the fattest one declares that in warm weather, a dish of *gaspachos,* with plenty of garlic in it, makes him feel as fresh as a rose. He must indeed be a perfect bouquet.

The opening of morning is dramatic in our narrow cabin. About twenty voices in Spanish, German, Italian, and broken English, strike up by degrees. From a neighbouring state room, *Nid d'oiseau* puts forth his head. "Stooar! a toomlar! here is no vater!" "Comin, sir, comin." *"Caramba!* Stooard!" "Comin, sir, comin!" "Stuart? vasser und toel!" "Here, sir." "Amigo! how is the wind?" (This is the waking up of el Señor Ministro, putting his head half suffocated out of his berth.) "Oh steward! steward!" "Yes, miss," "Come here, and look at *this!"* "I'll fix it, miss,"—etc.

1st November.—A fair wind after a stifling night, and strong hopes of seeing the Bahama Banks on Sunday. Most people are now gradually ascending from the lower regions, and dragging themselves on deck with pale and dejected countenances. Madame A—— has such a sweet-toned voice in speaking, especially in her accents of her *bella Italia,* that it is refreshing to listen to her. I have passed all day in reading, after a desultory fashion, "Les Enfants d'Edouard," by Casimir Delavigne, Washington Irving, D'Israeli's "Curiosities of Literature," etc.; and it is rather singular that while there is a very tolerable supply of English and French books here, I see but one or two odd volumes in Spanish, although these packets are constantly filled with people of that nation, going and coming. Is it that they do not care for reading, or that less attention is paid to them than to the French or American passengers? One would think Cervantes, Lope de Vega, Calderon, or Moratin, better worth buying than many commonplace novels which I find here.

3rd.—Yesterday the wind blew soft as on a summer morning. A land-bird flew into the ship. To-day the wind has veered round, but the weather continues charming. The sea is covered with multitudes of small flying-fish. An infantile waterspout appeared, and died in its birth. Mr. ——, the consul, has been giving me an account of the agreeable society in the Sandwich Islands! A magnificent sunset, the sight of which compensates for all the inconveniences of the voyage. The sky was covered with black clouds lined with silver, and surrounded by every variety of colour; deep blue, fleecy, rose, violet, and orange. The heavens are now thickly studded with stars, numbers shooting across the blue expanse like messengers of light, glancing and disappearing as if extinguished.

It is well to read the History of Columbus at sea, but especially in these waters, where he wandered in suspense, high-wrought expectation, and firm faith; and to watch the signs which the noble mariner observed in these latitudes; the soft serenity of the breezes, the clear blue of the heavens, the brilliancy and number of the stars, the sea-weeds of the gulf, which always drift in the direction of the wind, the little land-birds that come like harbingers of good tidings, the frequency of the shooting stars, and the multitude of flying-fish.

As the shades of evening close around, and the tropical sky glitters with the light of innumerable stars, imagination transports us back to that century which stands out in bold relief amidst other ages rolling by comparatively undistinguished, and we see as in a vision the Discoverer of a World, standing on the deck of his caravel, as it bounded over the unknown and mysterious waste of waters, his vigilant eyes fixed on the west, like a Persian intently watching the rising of his god; though his star was to arise from whence the day-god sets. We see him bending his gaze on the first dark line that separated the watery sea from the blue of the heavens, striving to penetrate the gloom of night, yet waiting with patient faith until the dawn of day should bring the long-wished for shores in sight.

6th.—For three days, three very long and uncomfortable days, the wind, with surprising constancy, has continued to blow dead ahead. In ancient days, what altars might have smoked to Æolus! Now, except in the increased puffing of consolatory cigar-smoke, no propitiatory offerings are made to unseen powers. There are indeed many mourning signs amongst the passengers. Every one has tied up his head in an angry-looking silken bandana, drawn over his nose with a dogged air. Beards are unshaven, a black stubble covering the lemon-coloured countenance, which occasionally bears a look of sulky defiance, as if its owner were, like Juliet, "past hope, past cure, past help."

7th.—This morning the monotony of fine weather was relieved by a hearty squall, accompanied by torrents of rain, much thunder, and forked lightning. The ship reeled to and fro like a drunken man, and the passengers, as usual in such cases, performed various involuntary evolutions, cutting right angles, sliding, spinning round, and rolling over, as if Oberon's magic horn were playing an occasional blast amidst the roaring winds; whilst the stewards alone, like Horace's good man, walked serene amidst the wreck of crockery and the fall of plates. Driven from our stronghold on deck, indiscriminately crammed in below like figs in a drum; "weltering," as Carlyle has it, "like an Egyptian pitcher of tamed vipers," the cabin windows all shut in, we tried to take it coolly, in spite of the suffocating heat.

There is a child on board who is certainly possessed, not by a witty malicious demon, a *diable boiteux,* but by a teasing, stupid, wicked imp, which inspires him with the desire of tormenting everything human that comes within his reach. Should he escape being thrown overboard, it will show a wonderful degree of forbearance on the part of the passengers.

8th.—The weather is perfect, but the wind inexorable; and the passengers, with their heads tied up, look more gloomy than ever. Some sit dejected in corners, and some quarrel with their neighbours, thus finding a safety-valve by which their wrath may escape.

9th.—There is no change in the wind, yet the gentlemen have all brightened up, taken off their handkerchiefs and shaved, as if ashamed of their six days' impatience, and making up their minds to a sea-life. This morning we saw land; a long, low ridge of hills on the island of Eleuthera, where they make salt, and where there are many negroes. Neither salt nor negroes visible to the naked eye; nothing but the gray outline of the hills, melting into the sea and sky; and having tacked about all day, we found ourselves in the evening precisely opposite to this same island. There are Job's comforters on board, who assure us that they have been thirty-six days between New York and "la joya mas preciosa de la corona de Espana."[1]

For my part, I feel no impatience, having rather a dislike to changing my position when tolerable, and the air is so fresh and laden with balm, that it seems to blow over some paradise of sweets, some land of fragrant spices. The sea also is a mirror, and I have read Marryat's "Pirate" for the first time.

Thus then we stand at eight o'clock, P.M.; wind ahead, and little of it, performing a zigzag march between Eleuthera and Abaco. On deck, the pretty widow lies in an easy chair, surrounded by her countrymen, who discourse about sugar, molas-

---

[1] The most precious jewel in the Spanish crown, the name given to Cuba.

ses, chocolate, and other local topics, together with the relative merits of Cuba as compared with the rest of the known world. Madame A—— is studying her part of Elizabetta in the opera of Roberto Devereux, which she is to bring out in Havana, but the creaking of the Norma is sadly at variance with harmony. A pale German youth, in dressing-gown and slippers, is studying Schiller. An ingenious youngster is carefully conning a well-thumbed note, which looks like a milliner's girl's last billet-doux. The little *possédé* is burning brown paper within an inch of the curtains of a state-room, while the steward is dragging it from him. Others are gradually dropping into their berths, like ripe nuts from a tree. Thus are we all pursuing our vocations.

9th.—Wind dead ahead! I console myself with Cinq-Mars and Jacob Faithful. But the weather is lovely. A young moon in her first quarter, like a queen in her minority, glitters like a crescent on the brow of night.

Towards evening the long-wished for lighthouse of Abaco (built by the English) showed her charitable and revolving radiance. But our ship, Penelope-like, undoes by night what she has performed by day, and her course is backward and crabbish. A delicious smell of violets is blowing from the land.

10th.—A fair wind. The good tidings communicated by the A——, *toute rayonnante de joie*. A fair wind and a bright blue sea, cool and refreshing breezes, the waves sparkling, and the ship going gallantly over the waters. So far, our voyage may have been tedious, but the most determined landsman must allow that the weather has been charming.

Sunday at sea; and though no bells are tolling, and no hymns are chanted, the blue sky above and the blue ocean beneath us, form one vast temple, where, since the foundations of the earth and sea were laid, *Day unto day uttereth speech, and night unto night showeth knowledge.*

This morning we neared the Berry Islands, unproductive and rocky, as the geography books would say. One of these islands belongs to a coloured man, who bought it for fifty dollars—a cheaply-purchased sovereignty. He, his wife and children, with their *negro slaves!* live there, and cultivate vegetables to sell at New York, or to the different ships that pass that way. Had the wind been favourable, they would probably have sent us out a boat with fresh vegetables, fish, and fruit, which would have been very acceptable. We saw, not far from the shore, the wreck of a two-masted vessel; sad sight to those who pass over the same waters to see

> "*A brave vessel,*
> *Who had, no doubt, some noble creatures in her,*
> *Dashed all to pieces!*"

Who had, at least, some of God's creatures in her. Anything but that! I am like Gonzalo, and "would fain die a dry death."

We are now on the Bahama Banks, the water very clear and blue, with a creamy froth, looking as if it flowed over pearls and turquoises. An English schooner man-of-war (a *boy*-of-war in size) made all sail towards us, doubtless hoping we were a slaver; but, on putting us to the test of his spy-glass, the captain, we presume, perceived that the general tinge of countenance was lemon rather than negro, and so abandoned his pursuit.

This evening on the Banks. It would be difficult to imagine a more placid and lovely scene. Everything perfectly calm, all sail set, and the heavens becoming gradually sprinkled with silver stars. The sky blue, and without a cloud, except where the sun has just set, the last crimson point sinking in the calm sea and leaving a long retinue of rainbow-coloured clouds, deep crimson tinged with bright silver, and melting away into gray, pale vapour.

On goes the vessel, stately and swanlike; the water of the same turquoise blue, covered with a light pearly froth, and so clear that we see the large sponges at the bottom. Every minute they heave the lead. "By the mark three." "By the mark three, less a quarter." "By the mark twain and a half," (fifteen feet, the vessel drawing thirteen,) two feet between us and the bottom. The sailor sings it out like the first line of a hymn in short metre, doled out by the parish clerk. I wish Madame A—— were singing it instead of he. "By the mark three, less a quarter." To this tune, the only sound breaking the stillness of the night, I dropped to sleep. The captain passed the night anxiously, now looking out for lights on the Banks, now at the helm, or himself sounding the lead:

> "*For some must watch whilst others sleep;*
> *Thus wags the world away.*"

11th.—Beautiful morning, and fair wind. About eight we left the Banks. Just then we observed, that the sailor who sounded, having sung out five, then six, then in a few minutes seven, suddenly found no bottom, as if we had fallen off all at once from the brink of the Bank into an abyss.

A fellow-captain, and passenger of our captain's, told me

this morning, that he spoke the ship which carried out Governor and Mrs. McLean to Cape-Coast Castle—the unfortunate L. E. L. It does not seem to me at all astonishing that the remedies which she took in England without injury, should have proved fatal to her in that wretched climate.

We have been accompanied all the morning by a fine large ship, going full sail, the Orleans, Captain Sears, bound for New Orleans. . . . A long semicircular line of black rocks in sight; some of a round form, one of which is called the Death's Head; another of the shape of a turtle, and some two or three miles long. At the extremity of one of these the English are building a lighthouse.

12th.—We are opposite the Pan of Matanzas, about sixty miles from Havana. Impatience becomes general, but the breeze rocks up and down, and we gain little. This day, like all last days on board, has been remarkably tedious, though the country gradually becomes more interesting. There is a universal brushing-up amongst the passengers; some shaving, some with their heads plunged into tubs of cold water. So may have appeared Noah's ark, when the dove did not return, and the passengers prepared for *terra firma*, after a forty days' voyage. Our Mount Ararat was the Morro Castle, which, dark and frowning, presented itself to our eyes, at six o'clock, P.M.

Nothing can be more striking than the first appearance of this fortress, starting up from the solid rock, with its towers and battlements, while here, to remind us of our latitude, we see a few feathery cocoas growing amidst the herbage that covers the banks near the castle. By its side, covering a considerable extent of ground, is the fortress called the *Cabaña*, painted rose-colour, with the angles of its bastions white.

But there is too much to look at now. I must finish my letter in Havana.

HAVANA, 13th November.

Last evening, as we entered the beautiful bay, everything struck us as strange and picturesque. The soldiers of the garrison, the prison built by General Tacon, the irregular houses with their fronts painted red or pale blue, and with the cool but uninhabited look produced by the absence of glass windows; the merchant ships and large men-of-war; vessels from every port in the commercial world, the little boats gliding amongst them with their snow-white sails, the negroes on the wharf—nothing European. The heat was great, that of a July day, without any freshness in the air.

As we approached the wharf the noise and bustle increased. The passengers all crowded upon deck, and we had scarcely anchored, when various little boats were seen making for the Norma. First boat brought an officer with the salutations of the Captain-General to his Excellency, with every polite offer of service; second boat brought the Administrador of the Yntendente (the Count de Villa Neuva), with the same civilities; the third, the master of the house where we now are, and whence I indite these facts; the fourth, the Italian Opera, which rushed simultaneously into the arms of the A——i; the fifth, prosaic custom-house officers; the sixth, a Havana count and marquis; the seventh, the family of General M——o. Finally, we were hoisted over the ship's side in a chair, into the government boat, and rowed to the shore. As it was rather dark when we arrived, and we were driven to our destination in a volante, we did not see much of the city. We could but observe that the streets were narrow, the houses irregular, most people black, and the volante, an amusing-looking vehicle, looking behind like a black insect with high shoulders, and with a little black postilion on a horse or mule, with an enormous pair of boots and a fancy uniform.

The house in which, by the hospitality of the H——a family we are installed, has from its windows, which front the bay, the most varied and interesting view imaginable. As it is the first house, Spanish fashion, which I have entered, I must describe it to you before I sleep. The house forms a great square, and you enter the court, round which are the offices, the rooms for the negroes, coal-house, bath-room, etc., and in the middle of which stand the volantes. Proceed upstairs, and enter a large gallery which runs all round the house. Pass into the *Sala*, a large cool apartment, with marble floor and tables, and *chaise-longues* with elastic cushions, chairs, and arm-chairs of cane. A drapery of white muslin and blue silk divides this from a second and smaller drawing-room, now serving as my dressing-room, and beautifully fitted up, with Gothic toilet-table, inlaid mahogany bureau, marble centre and side-tables, fine mirrors, cane sofas and chairs, green and gold paper. A drapery of white muslin and rose-coloured silk divides this from a bedroom, also fitted up with all manner of elegances. French beds with blue silk coverlids and clear mosquito curtains, and fine lace. A drapery divides this on one side from the gallery; and this room opens into others which run all round the house. The floors are marble or stucco—the roofs beams of pale blue wood placed transversely, and the whole has an air of agreeable coolness. Everything is handsome without being gaudy, and admirably adapted for the climate. The sleeping apartments have no windows, and are dark and cool, while the drawing-rooms have large windows down to the floor, with green shutters kept closed till the evening.

The mosquitoes have now commenced their evening song, a signal that it is time to put out the lights. The moon is shining on the bay, and a faint sound of military music is heard in the distance, while the sea moans with a sad but not unpleasing monotony. To all these sounds I retire to rest.

LETTER THE SECOND

Havana Aristocracy—"Lucia de Lammermoor"—La Rossi and Montresor—Brig-of-war—Countess de V——a—Dinner at H——a's—Southerly Winds—View from the Balcony—Quinta of Count V——a—San Cristobal—Mass at San Felipe—Erard Harp—Dinner at General M——o's—A Dessert at Havana—Queen of Spain's Birthday—Dinner at the Yntendencia—La Pantanelli—Theatre of Tacon—Railroad—Cure by Lightning —Shops—Ball at the Countess F——a's—Last Visit—Souvenirs.

15th.—We expected hospitality and a good reception, but certainly all our expectations have been surpassed, and the last few days have been spent in such a round of festivity, that not a moment has been left for writing. At home we have held a levee to all that is most distinguished in Havana. Counts, marquesses, and generals, with stars and crosses, have poured in and poured out ever since our arrival. I do not pretend to form any judgment of Havana. We have seen it too much *en beau.*

Last evening we found time to go to the theatre. The opera was "Lucia de Lammermoor." The *prima donna*, La Rossi, has a voice of much sweetness, sings correctly and with taste, is graceful in her movements, but sadly deficient in strength. Still she suits the character represented, and comes exactly up to my idea of poor Lucy, devoted and broken-hearted, physically and morally weak. Though the story is altered, and the interest weakened, how graceful the music is! how lovely and full of melody! The orchestra is good, and composed of blacks and whites, like the notes of a piano, mingled in harmonious confusion.

The theatre is remarkably pretty and airy, and the pit struck us as being particularly clean and respectable. All the seats are red leather arm-chairs, and all occupied by well-dressed people.

At the end of the first act, we went round to the Countess F——a's box, to return a visit which she had made me in the morning. We found her extremely agreeable and full of intelligence, also with a very decided air of fashion. She was dressed in fawn-coloured satin, with large pearls. At the end of the second act, Lucia was taken ill, her last aria missed out, and her monument driven on the stage without further ceremony. Montresor, the Ravenswood of the piece, came in, sung, and stabbed himself with immense enthusiasm. It is a pity that his voice is deserting him, while his taste and feeling remain. The house has altogether a French look. The boxes are private —that is, the property of individuals, but are not shut in, which in this climate would be suffocating. We passed out through a long file of soldiers. The sudden transition from Yankee land to this military Spanish negro-land is *dreamy*.

The General de la Marina (*Anglicè*, admiral of the station) called some days ago, and informed us that there is a brig of war destined to convey us to Vera Cruz.

Amongst the ladies who have called on me, I find none more charming than the Countess de V——a. Her voice is agreeable, her manners cordial and easy, her expression beautiful from goodness, with animated eyes and fine teeth, her dress quiet and rich. She is universally beloved here. I received from her, nearly every morning, a bouquet of the loveliest flowers from her quinta—roses, carnations, heliotrope, etc. The dinner at H——a's to-day was a perfect feast. I sat between the Count de F——a and the Count de S—— V——, a millionaire. Everything was served in French white and gold porcelain, which looks particularly cool and pretty in this climate. The Count de P——r was there and his brother; the latter a gentlemanly and intelligent man, with a great taste for music, and whose daughter is a first-rate singer and a charming person. After dinner we rose, according to custom, and went into an adjoining room while they arranged the dessert, consisting of every imaginable and unimaginable sweetmeat, with fruit, ices, etc. The fruits I have not yet learned to like. They are certainly wonderful and delicious productions of nature; but to eat eggs and custards and butter off the trees, seems unnatural.

The heat to-day is terrible; with a suffocating south wind blowing, and were the houses not built as they are, would be unbearable. The dinner is served in the gallery, which is spacious and cool.

After dinner, Señor Don P——o H——a rose, and, addressing C——n, pronounced a poetical impromptu, commemorating the late victory of Espartero, and congratulating C——n on his mission to the Mexican republic. We then adjourned to the balcony, where the air was delightful, a cool evening breeze having suddenly sprung up. A large ship, full sail, and various barks, passed the Morro. There were negroes with bare legs walking on the wall, carrying parcels, etc.; volantes passing by with their black-eyed occupants, in full dress, short sleeves, and flowers in their hair; well-dressed, martial-looking Spanish soldiers marching by, and making tolerably free remarks on the ladies in the volantes. . . . We had a visit from the Captain-General.

In the evening we went out to see the Countess de V——a, at her pretty quinta, a short way out of town, and walked in the garden by moonlight, amongst flowers and fountains. The little count is already one of the chamberlains to the Queen, and a diamond key has been sent him by Queen Christina in token of her approbation of his father's services. These country retreats are delightful after the narrow streets and impure air of the city. . . . We saw there a good engraving of Queen Victoria, with the Duchess of Sutherland and Lady Normanby.

17th.—Yesterday we went to see the procession of the patron saint, San Cristobal, from the balconies of the Yntendencia. It is a fine spacious building, and, together with the Captain-General's palace, stands in the Plaza de Armas, which was crowded with negroes and negresses, all dressed in white, with white muslin and blonde mantillas, framing and showing off their dusky physiognomies.

Two regiments, with excellent bands of music, conducted the procession, composed of monks and priests. San Cristobal, a large figure with thick gold legs, surrounded by gold angels with gold wings, was carried by to the music of "*Suoni la tromba*," to which were adapted the words of a hymn in praise of Liberty.

We attended mass in the morning in the church of San Felipe, and entered, preceded, according to custom, by a little negro footman carrying a piece of carpet. There were few people in church, but the grouping was picturesque. The black faces of the negresses, with their white mantillas and white satin shoes; the black silk dresses and black lace mantillas of the Havana ladies, with their white faces and black eyes, and little liveried negroes standing behind them; the officers, music, and long-bearded priests—all were very effective.

Found, on my return, an excellent Erard harp, sent me by the Marquesa de A——s, a pretty woman and female Crœsus.

A splendid entertainment was given us to-day by General M——o. His house is large and cool; the dinner, as usual, in the gallery; and although there were ninety-seven guests, and as many negroes in waiting, the heat was not oppressive. The jewels of the ladies were superb, especially the diamonds of the M—— family; sprays, necklaces, earrings, really beautiful. The Marquesa de A—— wore a set of emeralds the size of small eggs. She had a pretty, graceful-looking daughter with her, with beautiful eyes. Even the men were well sprinkled with diamonds and rubies.

The dessert, from variety and quantity, was a real curiosity. Immense vases and candelabras of alabaster were placed at different distances on the table, and hundreds of porcelain dishes were filled with sweetmeats and fruits—sweetmeats of every description, from the little meringue called "mouthful for a queen," to the blancmanger made of suprême de volaille and milk.

After dinner our health was drank, and another poetical address pronounced. The evening concluded with music and the Havana country-dances.

20th.—Yesterday being the Queen of Spain's birthday, a dinner was given to us at the Yntendencia. The house in size is a palace, and the apartments innumerable. The dinner very elegant, and the dessert arranged in another room, a curiosity as usual for profusion and variety. Her Majesty's health was proposed by Don B——o H——a, and so well-timed, that all the guns of the forts fired a salute, it being sunset, just as the toast was concluded, which was drank with real enthusiasm and hearty good will. According to Spanish custom, the aristocracy generally *se tutoient*, and call each other by their Christian names; indeed, they are almost all connected by intermarriages. You may guess at an inferior in rank, only by their increased respect towards him.

We stood on the balcony in the evening. The scene was beautiful, the temperature rather warm, yet delicious from the softness of the breeze. The moon rose so bright that she seemed like the sun shining through a silvery veil. Groups of figures were sauntering about in the square, under the trees, and two bands having stationed themselves with lamps and music, played alternately pieces from Mozart and Bellini. We regretted leaving so delightful a scene for the theatre, where we arrived in time to hear La Pantanelli sing an aria, dressed in helmet and tunic, and to see La Jota Arragonesa danced by two handsome Spanish girls in good style.

One evening we went to the theatre of Tacon, to the Captain-General's box. It is certainly a splendid house, large, airy, and handsome. The play was the "Campanero de San Pablo," which, though generally liked, appears to me a complicated and unnatural composition, with one or two interesting scenes. The best actor was he who represented the blind man. The chief actress is an overgrown dame, all fat and dimples, who kept up a constant sobbing and heaving of her chest, yet never getting rid of an eternal smirk upon her face. A bolero, danced afterwards by two Spanish damsels in black and silver, was very refreshing.

23rd.—To-morrow we sail in the Jason, should the wind not prove contrary. Visits, dinners, and parties have so occupied our time, that to write has been next to impossible. Of the country we have, from the same reason, seen little, and the people we are only acquainted with in full dress, which is not the way to judge of them truly. One morning, indeed, we dedicated to viewing the works of the Yntendente, the railroad, and the water-filterers. He and the Countess, and a party of friends, accompanied us.

The country through which the railroad passes is flat and rather monotonous; nevertheless, the quantity of wild flowers, which appeared for the most part of the convolvulus species, as we glanced past them—the orange-trees, the clumps of palm and cocoa, the plantain with its gigantic leaves, the fresh green coffee-plant, the fields of sugar-cane of a still brighter green, the half-naked negroes, the low wooden huts, and, still more, the scorching sun in the month of November,—all was new to us, and sufficient to remind us of the leagues of ocean we had traversed, though this is but a halt on our voyage.

At the village where the cars stopped, we listened with much amusement to the story of a fat, comfortable-looking individual, who was cured by lightning in the following manner:—He was in the last stage of a decline, when, one hot July morning, he was knocked down by a thunderbolt, a ball of fire, which entered his side, ran all through his body, and came out at his arm. At the place where the ball made its exit, a large ulcer was formed, and when it dispersed he found himself in perfect health, in which he has continued ever since! In such cases the "bottled lightning," demanded by Mrs. Nickleby's admirer, might be a valuable remedy.

Of course I could not leave Havana without devoting one morning to shopping. The shops have most seducing names —Hope, Wonder, Desire, etc. The French modistes seem to be wisely improving their time, by charging respectable prices for their work. The shopkeepers bring their goods out to the volante, it not being the fashion for ladies to enter the shops, though I took the privilege of a foreigner to infringe this rule occasionally. Silks and satins very dear—lace and muslin very reasonable, was, upon the whole, the result of my investigation; but as it only lasted two hours, and that my sole purchases of any consequence, were an indispensable mantilla, and a pair of earrings, I give my opinion for the present with due diffidence.

I can speak with more decision on the subject of a great ball given us by the Countess F——a, last evening, which was really superb. The whole house was thrown open—there was a splendid supper, quantities of refreshment, and the whole select aristocracy of Havana. Diamonds on all the women, jewels and orders on all the men, magnificent lustres and mirrors, and a capital band of music in the gallery.

The Captain-General was the only individual in a plain dress. He made himself very agreeable, in good French. About one hundred couple stood up in each country-dance, but the rooms are so large and so judiciously lighted, that we did not feel at all warm. Waltzes, quadrilles, and these long Spanish dances, succeeded each other. Almost all the girls have fine eyes and beautiful figures, but without colour, or much animation. The finest diamonds were those of the Countess F——a, particularly her necklace, which was *undeniable*.

Walking through the rooms after supper, we were amused to see the negroes and negresses helping themselves plentifully to the sweetmeats, uncorking and drinking fresh bottles of Champagne, and devouring everything on the supper tables, without the slightest concern for the presence either of their master or mistress; in fact, behaving like a multitude of spoilt children, who are sure of meeting with indulgence, and presume upon it. ° ° °

Towards morning we were led downstairs to a large suite of rooms, containing a library of several thousand volumes; where coffee, cakes, etc., were prepared in beautiful Sêvres porcelain and gold plate. We left the house at last to the music of the national hymn of Spain, which struck up as we past through the gallery.

Should the north wind, the dreaded *Norte,* not blow, we sail to-morrow, and have spent the day in receiving farewell visits. We also went to the theatre, where every one predicts we shall not get off to-morrow. The play was "Le Gamin de Paris," translated. After our return, I paid a very late visit to the P——r family, who live close by us, and now, at two in the morning, I finish my letter sleepily. Many beautiful *souvenirs*

have been sent us, and amongst others, the Count de S—— V——
has just sent C——n a model of the palace of Madrid, one of
the most beautiful and ingenious pieces of workmanship possible. It is carved in wood, with astonishing accuracy and
delicacy.

My next letter will be dated on board the Jason.

LETTER THE THIRD

Departure in the Jason—Spanish Captain and Officers—Life on board a Man-of-War—"Balances"—Fishing—"Le Petit Tambour"—Cocoa-nuts—A Norte—Spanish Proverb—Peak of Orizava—Theory and Practice—Norte Chocolatero—Contrary Winds—Chain of Mountains—Goleta.

JASON, 24th November.

This morning, at six o'clock, we breakfasted, together with Captain Estrada, the commander of the Jason, at the *Casa H——a;* and the wind being fair, repaired shortly after in volantes to the wharf, accompanied by our hospitable host, and several of our acquaintances; entered the boat, looked our last of the Palace and the Yntendencia, and of Havana itself, where we had arrived as strangers, and which now, in fifteen days, had begun to assume a familiar aspect, and to appear interesting in our eyes, by the mere force of human sympathy; and were transported to the ship, where a line of marines, drawn up to receive us, presented arms as we entered. The morning was beautiful; little wind, but fair. We took leave of our friends, waved our handkerchiefs to the balconies in return for signals from scarcely-distinguishable figures, passed between the red-tinted Cabana and the stately Morro, and were once more upon the deep, with a remembrance behind, and a hope before us. Our *Bergantina* is a handsome vessel, with twenty-five guns, five officers, a doctor, chaplain, and purser, and one hundred and fifty men.

We find the commander very attentive, and a perfect gentleman, like almost all of his class, and though very young in appearance, he has been twenty-nine years in the service.

25th.—The weather delightful, and the ship going at the rate of five knots an hour. The accommodations in a brig not destined for passengers are of course limited. There is a large cabin for the officers, separated by a smaller one, belonging to the captain, which he has given up to us.

At seven o'clock C——n rises, and at eight, a marine sentinel, transformed into a lady's page, whom we are taking to Mexico as porter, brings us some very delicious chocolate. He is followed by the Captain's familiar, an unhappy-looking individual, pale, lank, and lean, with the physiognomy of a methodist parson, and in general appearance like a weed that has grown up in one night. He tremblingly, and with most rueful countenance, carries a small plate of sugar-biscuits. These originals having vacated the cabin, I proceed to dress, an operation of some difficulty, which being performed *tant bien que mal,* I repair upstairs, armed with book and fan, and sit on deck till ten o'clock, when the familiar's lamentable announcement of breakfast takes us down again. The cook being French, the *comestibles* are decidedly good, and were the artist a little less of an oil, and more of a water painter, I individually would prefer his style. We have every variety of fish, meat, fowl, fruit, *dulces,* and wines.

A very long interval has to be filled up by reading, writing, sitting, or walking upon deck, as suits the taste of the individual, or by drinking orangeade, or by sleeping, or by any other ingenious resource for killing time. At five, dinner, at which no one joins us but the captain and one officer; and after dinner on deck till bed-time, walking about, or gazing on the sky or sea, or listening to the songs of the sailors.

26th.—Little wind, but a day of such abominably cruel *"balances,"* as they call them, that one is tempted to find rest by jumping overboard. Everything broken or breaking. Even the cannons disgorge their balls, which fall out by their own weight.

28th.—We have had two days of perfect weather though very warm; the sky blue, without one cloud. To-day we are on the sound, and have lain to, about noon, to let the sailors fish, thereby losing an hour or so of fair wind, and catching a preposterous number of fish of immense size. The water was so clear, that we could see the fish rush and seize the bait as fast as it was thrown in. Sometimes a huge shark would bite the fish in two, so that the poor finny creature was between Scylla and Charybdis. These fish are called *cherne* and *pargo,* and at dinner were pronounced good. At length a shark, in its wholesale greediness, seized the bait, and feeling the hook in his horrid jaw, tugged most fiercely to release himself, but in vain. Twelve sailors hauled him in, when, with distended jaws, he seemed to look out for the legs of the men, whereupon they rammed the butt-end of a harpoon down his throat, which put a stop to all further proceedings on his part. He was said to be quite young, perhaps the child of doting parents. The juvenile monster had, however, already cut three rows of teeth.

We are sometimes amused in the evening, when upon deck, by a little drummer, who invariably collects all the sailors round him, and spins them long, endless stories of his own invention, to which they listen with intense interest. On he goes, without a moment's hesitation, inventing everything most improbable and wonderful; of knights and giants and beautiful princesses, and imprisoned damsels, and poor peasants becoming great kings. He is a little ugly, active fellow, with a turned-up nose, a merry eye, and a laughing mouth. Amongst his axioms is the following verse, which he sings with great expression.

> *Hasta los palos del monte*
> *Tienen su destinacion*
> *Unos nacen para santos*
> *Y otros para hacer carbon.*

which may be translated so:

> *Even the mountain-trees*
> *Have their allotted goal,*
> *For some are born for saints*
> *Whilst others serve for coal.*

29th.—Beautiful day, fair wind, great heat, and more fishing. At least thirty large fish were caught this morning, also an infant shark, a grandchild who had wandered forth to nibble, and met an untimely grave. We have seen several alacrans or scorpions on board, but these are said not to be poisonous. The ship is the perfection of cleanness. No disagreeable odour affects the olfactory nerves, in which it has a singular advantage over all packets. This, and having it all to ourselves, and the officers being such perfect gentlemen, and all so kind and attentive, makes our voyage so far a mere pleasure trip.

We had some of the Countess de V——'s cocoa-nuts, of which she sent us a great supply, pierced this morning, each containing three tumblers of fresh and delicious water.

1st December.—We are now about thirty leagues from Vera Cruz, and if the wind blows a little fresher, may reach it tomorrow. This is Sunday, but the chaplain is too sick to say mass, and the heat is intense.

2nd.—An unpleasant variety—a *Norte!* I knew it was coming on, only by the face of the first lieutenant when he looked at the barometer. His countenance fell as many degrees as the instrument. It is very slight, but our entry into port will be delayed, for, on the coast, these winds are most devoutly

dreaded. It has rained all day, and, notwithstanding the rolling of the ship, we attempted a game at chess, but after having tried two games, abandoned it in despair, a "*balance*" having, at the most interesting period of each, overturned the
board, and left the victory undecided, somewhat after the
fashion of Homer's goddess, when she enveloped the contending armies in a cloud.

4th.—Yesterday evening a south wind, and the Spanish
proverb says truly

> "*Sur duro,*
> *Norte seguro.*"

> "*A south wind strong,*
> *The norther ere long.*"

This morning the sky is covered with watery clouds, yet
we can see the Cofre de Perote and the peak of Orizava, which
are thirty leagues inland! The latter, called by the Mexicans,
Citlal Tepetl, or the mountain of the star, from the fire which
used to burn on its lofty summit, rises nineteen thousand five
hundred and fifty-one feet above the level of the sea. Covered
with perpetual snows, and rising far above clouds and tem-
pests, it is the first mountain which the navigator discovers
as he approaches these shores.

But the south wind continues and we are obliged to turn
our back to the coast. There is much impatience on board.
A—— was taken ill, and declared she had got the yellow fever.
The doctor was sent for, who, very sick himself, and holding
by the table to keep himself from falling, told her, without
looking at her very particularly, that there was nothing the
matter, only to keep yourself "*quite quiet and still;*" and the
ship rolling at the same moment, he pitched head-foremost out
of the cabin, showing practically how much easier precept is
than example. As we shall no doubt have a norther after this,
which may last three days, our promised land is still at some
distance.

5th.—The weather is charming, but the south-west wind
holds most implacably, and the barometer has fallen five or
six degrees, which, added to other signs of the times known
to navigators, causes all hands to prepare for the dreaded
enemy.

6th.—Job never was on board a ship. A norther, not a very
severe one, but what they call a *Norte chocolatero,* that is, its
shock tore a sail in two, as I tear this sheet of paper. The

most ingenious person I see is "the master of the sails." He sews most excessively quick and well. Towards evening the wind calmed, but the ship, tossed upon a horribly swelled sea, became a mortal purgatory. Still the wind is lulled, though Humboldt and others say a Norte must last forty-eight hours, and we have only had it for twenty-four. We shall see.

7th.—A most horrible night! My hammock, which I had foolishly preferred to a bed, not having room to swing in, threw me furiously against the wall, till fearing a broken head, I jumped out and lay on the floor. To-day there is a comparative calm, a faint continuation of the Norte, which is an air with variations. Everything now seems melancholy and monotonous. We have been tossed about during four days in sight of Vera Cruz, and are now further from it than before. The officers begin to look miserable; even the cook with difficulty preserves his equilibrium.

Sunday, 8th.—A Norte! The sky is watery, and covered with shapeless masses of reddish clouds. This is a great day amongst all Spanish Catholics, *Le Virgen de la Concepcion,* the patroness of Spain and the Indies; but no mass to-day; the padre sick and the Norte blowing. What a succession of long faces—walking barometers!

9th.—Yesterday evening the wind held out false hopes, and every one brightened up with caution, for the wind, though faintly, blew from the right quarter. The rain ceased, the weather cleared, and "hope, the charmer," smiled upon us. The greater was our disappointment when the breeze died away, when the wind veered to the north, and when once more the most horrible rolling seized the unfortunate Jason, as if it were possessed by a demon. Finding it impossible to lie in my hammock, I stretched myself on the floor; where, during a night that seemed interminable, we were tossed up and down, knocked against the furniture, and otherwise maltreated.

This morning there is little wind, but that little from the north, so that the termination of our voyage appears as far off now as it did eight days ago. The faces of all on board are calmly lugubrious. Little said. A few Spanish shrugs interchanged with ominous significance.

10th.—As there is only one particular wind during which it is not dangerous to approach the coast, namely, *"la brisa,"* the breeze which usually follows the norther, we may spend our Christmas here. The weather is beautiful, though very sultry, especially during the calms which intervene between the

nortes. With books one might take patience, but I read and
re-read backwards and forwards everything I possess, or can
find—reviews, magazines, a volume of Humboldt, even an odd
volume of the "Barber of Paris"—"Turkish Letters," *purporting*
to be the translation of a continuation of the Montesquieu's
"Lettres Persanes," and in which the hero, disguised as a gardener, brings the Visier's daughter a bouquet, which she condescendingly receives, lying in bed *à l'Espagnole!* I am now
reduced to a very serious Spanish work on the truth of Christianity.

This evening, to the joy of all on board, arose the long-
desired breeze. The ship went slowly and steadily on her
course, at first four, then eight knots an hour. The captain,
however, looked doubtingly, and, indeed, towards morning,
the wind changed to the south, and our hopes died away.

11th.—Contrary wind. A south, expected to be followed by
a "norte seguro." But now, at eleven, A.M., it is quite calm,
and very sultry, whilst to increase, if possible, our weariness,
a long range of lofty mountains stretches along the horizon,
from Punta Delgada to the Cofre de Perote, and on till they
seem to sink in the ocean. Behind the Cofre rises Orizava, now
like a white cloud, but this morning tinged with a rosy light
by the rays of the rising sun. The sea is tranquil and the horizon clear, nevertheless the enemy is looked for. There are a
few white and feathery clouds flickering about in the sky, and
there is an uneasy swell in the waves. . . . At three o'clock,
out burst the norther, which, like the flaming sword, guarding
the issues of paradise,

> "Waved over by that flaming brand, the gate
> With dreadful faces throng'd and fiery arms,"

seems to warn off all vessels from approaching these iron-
bound shores. Eleven days within a few hours' distance of the
coast!

16th.—Five days more passed with a continuation of contrary winds and constant rolling. We are further from hope
than we were fourteen days ago. Captain, officers, sailors, all
seem nearly disheartened. This morning they caught the most
beautiful fish I ever beheld, of the dolphin species—the Cleo-
patra of the ocean, about four feet long, apparently composed
of gold, and studded with turquoises. It changed colour in
dying. There is a proverb, which the sailors are repeating to
each other, not very encouraging: "Este es el viage del Orinoco. Que él que no se murió, se volvió loco." "This is the

voyage of the Orinoco, in which he who did not die, became crazy."

17th.—Spoke a goleta, who came close up by our vessel, and seemed to have a miserable set on board, amongst others, a worthy pair from Havana, who had just come out of prison, having been accused of murdering a negro. The wind continues contrary. I shall fold up this sea-scrawl, and write no more till we reach Vera Cruz.

LETTER THE FOURTH

Distant View of Vera Cruz—Pilots—Boat from the City—Mutual Salutes—Approach to Vera Cruz—Crowd on the Wharf—House of Dionisio V——o—Guard of Honour—German Piano—Supper—Madonna—Aspect of the City—Sopilotes—Deliberations—General Guadalupe Victoria—Two-headed Eagle—Dilapidated Saint—Harp—Theatre—Donna Inocencia Martinez—Invitation from General Santa Anna.

VERA CRUZ, 18th.

This morning, the sanguine hoped, and the desponding feared, for the wind, though inclined to *la brisa,* seemed unlikely to prove sufficiently strong to enable us to reach Vera Cruz—this being the twenty-fifth day since we left Havana; a voyage that, with a steamer, might be performed in three days, and with a sailing-vessel and a fair wind, is made in six or seven. About noon, the aspect of things became more favourable. The breeze grew stronger, and with it our hopes.

At last appeared in view, faintly, certain spires beside the low sandy land, which for some time we had anxiously watched, and at length we could distinguish houses and churches, and the fort of San Juan de Ulua, of warlike memory. By slow but sure degrees, we neared the shore, until Vera Cruz, in all its ugliness, became visible to our much-wearied eyes. We had brought a pilot from Havana to guide us to these dangerous coasts, but though a native of these parts, it seemed that a lapse of years had blunted his memory, for we had nearly run upon the rocks. A gun was therefore fired, and another pilot came out, who at sight of the Spanish flag waxed enthusiastic, and pointing out the castle to our ignorant friend, exclaimed, alluding to the desperate struggle made by the Spaniards to defend this their last stronghold at the end of the war, "*We,* although but a handful of men, defended ourselves for years like soldiers, and now these Frenchmen took it in three days!" and, walking about in a transport of patriotic despair, he seemed to forget his actual duty in the tide of remembrances which the sight of Spanish colours and a Spanish crew had called forth.

Anything more melancholy, *délabré* and forlorn, than the whole appearance of things as we drew near, cannot well be imagined. On one side, the fort, with its black and red walls: on the other, the miserable, black-looking city, with hordes of large black birds, called *sopilotes,* hovering over some dead carcass, or flying heavily along in search of carrion. Still, as the goal of our voyage, even its dreary aspect was welcome, and the very hills of red sand by which it is surrounded, and which look like the deserts of Arabia, appeared inviting.

A boat full of cocked hats was now seen approaching from the city, containing the Consul in full uniform, and other authorities. C——n having sent for and obtained permission from the Governor, to permit the Jason, contrary to established usages, to anchor beneath the castle, a salute of twenty guns was fired from our ship. Being upon deck, I was nearly suffocated with smoke and powder. A salute of the same number of cannon was then fired from the castle, in honour of the first Spanish man-of-war that has appeared in this port since the Revolution.

And now we prepared, before the sun went down, to leave our watery prison; and the captain's boat being manned, and having taken leave of the officers, we, that is, C——n, the commander, and I, and my French maid and her French poodle, got into it. Then came a salute of twenty guns from the Jason in our honour, and we rode off amidst clouds of smoke. Then the fort gave us welcome with the same number of guns, and, amidst all this cannonading, we were landed at the wharf.

A singular spectacle the wharf presented. A crowd, as far as the eye could reach, of all ages and sexes of Vera Cruzians (and a very curious set they seemed to be), were assembled to witness his Excellency's arrival. Some had no pantaloons; and others, to make up for their neighbours' deficiencies, had two pair—the upper slit up the side of the leg, Mexican fashion. All had large hats, with silver or bead rolls, and every tinge of dark complexion, from the pure Indian, upwards. Some dresses were entirely composed of rags, clinging together by the attraction of cohesion; others had only a few holes to let in the air. All were crowding, jostling, and nearly throwing each other into the water, and gazing with faces of intense curiosity.

But a plume of coloured feathers was seen towering above the copper-coloured crowd, and immediate passage was made for an aide-de-camp from the Governor, General Guadalupe Victoria. He was an immensely tall man, in a showy uniform all covered with gold, with colossal epaulets and a towering plume of rainbow-coloured feathers. He brought to C——n the welcome and congratulations of the General, and those Spanish offers of service and devotion which sound agreeably, whatever be their true value.

We now began to move through the crowd, which formed a line on either side to let us pass, and entered the streets of Vera Cruz, which were crowded, balconies and all, and even roofs with curious faces. The guard formed as we passed, and struck up a march. The principal street is wide and clean, and we reached the house of Señor V——o, a rich merchant, formerly consul, where we are to reside, followed to the door by the whole population. We were received with great hospitality, and found excellent rooms prepared for us. The house is immensely large and airy, built in a square as they all are, but with that unfurnished melancholy look, which as yet this style of house has to me, though admirably adapted to the climate.

A guard of honour sent by General Victoria, trotted into the courtyard, whose attendance C——n declined with thanks, observing that his mission had for object to terminate the coolness hitherto existing between two families of brothers; that between members of the same family there was nothing to fear, and all compliments were unnecessary.

I found a German piano in the drawing-room, on which I was glad to put my fingers after a month's abstinence. A number of gentlemen came in the evening to visit C——n. We were received by this family with so much real kindness, that we soon found ourselves perfectly at home. We had a plentiful supper—fish, meat, wine, and chocolate, fruit and sweetmeats; the cookery, Spanish *Vera-Cruzified*. A taste of the style was enough for me, garlic and oil enveloping meat, fish, and fowl, with pimentos and plantains, and all kinds of curious fruit, which I cannot yet endure. Bed was not unwelcome, and most comfortable beds we had, with mosquito curtains, and sheets and pillows all trimmed with rich lace, so universal in Spanish houses, that it is not, as with us, a luxury. But the mosquitoes had entered in some unguarded moment, and they and the heat were inimical to sleep.

19th.—I opened my eyes this morning on the painting of a very lovely Madonna, which hung unvalued and ill-framed, in one corner of the apartment. At eight, rose and dressed, and went to breakfast. Here, when there are two guests whom they wish to distinguish, the gentleman is placed at the head of the table, and *his* lady beside him.

To me nothing can exceed the sadness of the aspect of this city and of its environs—mountains of moving sand, formed by the violence of the north winds, and which, by the reflection of the sun's rays, must greatly increase the suffocating heat of the atmosphere. The scene may resemble the ruins of Jerusalem, though without its sublimity. The houses seemed blackened by fire; there is not a carriage on the streets—nothing but the men with the wide trousers slit up the side of the leg, immense hats, and blankets, or *sarapes*, merely a closed blanket, more or less fine, with a hole for the head to go through; and the women with *reboses*, long coloured cotton scarfs, or pieces of ragged stuff, thrown over the head and crossing over the left shoulder. Add to this, the sopilotes cleaning the streets, —disgusting, but useful scavengers. These valuable birds have black feathers, with gray heads, beaks, and feet. They fly in troops, and at night perch upon the trees. They are not republican, nor do they appear inclined to declare their independence, having kings, to whom it is said they pay so much respect, that if one of the royal species arrives at the same time with a plebeian sopilote, in sight of a dead body, the latter humbly waits till the sovereign has devoured his share, before he ventures to approach.

A few ladies in black gowns and mantillas called this morning, and various men. We find the weather sultry. In summer, with greater heat and the addition of the *vomito*, it must be a chosen city! The principal street, where we live, is very long and wide, and seems to have many good houses in it. Nearly opposite is one which seems particularly well kept and handsome, and where we saw beautiful flowers as we passed. I find it belongs to an English merchant.

There is much deliberation as to the mode in which we are to travel to Mexico. Some propose a coach, others a *litera;* others advise us to take the diligence. While in this indecision, we had a visit this morning from a remarkable-looking character, Don Miguel S——, agent for the diligence office in Mexico, a tall, dark, energetic-looking person. He recommends the diligence, and offers, by accompanying us, to ensure our safety from accidents. He appears right. The diligence goes in four days, if it does not break down. The coach takes any time we choose over that; the *literas* nine or ten days, going slowly on mules with a sedan-chair motion. The diligence has food and beds provided for it at the inns—the others nothing. I am in favour of the diligence.

The couple from Havana, whom we passed in the *goleta,*

have very coolly requested permission to accompany us to Mexico, "under the protection of the *Embajador de España*." We should set off in select company.

C——n called this morning on General Victoria. Found his excellency in a large hall without furniture or ornament of any sort, without even chairs, and altogether in a style of more than republican simplicity. He has just returned the visit, accompanied by his colossal aide-de-camp.

General Guadalupe Victoria is perhaps the last man in a crowd whom one would fix upon as being the owner of the above high-sounding cognomen, which in fact is not his original, but his assumed name, *Guadalupe* being adopted by him in honour of the renowned image of the virgin of that name, and *Victoria* with less humility to commemorate his success in battle. He is an honest, plain, down-looking citizen, lame and tall, somewhat at a loss for conversation, apparently amiable and good-natured, but certainly neither courtier nor orator; a man of undeniable bravery, capable of supporting almost incredible hardships, humane, and who has always proved himself a sincere lover of what he considered liberty, without ever having been actuated by ambitious or interested motives.

It is said that his defects were indolence, want of resolution, and too much reliance on his own knowledge. He is the only Mexican president who finished as chief magistrate, the term prescribed by the laws. It is alleged, in proof of his simplicity, though I think it is too absurd to be true, that having received a despatch with the two-headed eagle on the seal, he remarked to the astonished envoy who delivered it—"Our arms are very much alike, only I see that his majesty's eagles have two heads. I have heard that some of that species exist here, in *tierre caliente,* and shall have one sent for."

The general is not married, but appears rather desirous of entering the united state. He strongly recommends us to avoid broken bones by going it literas, at least as far as Jalapa. Having stumbled about for some time in search of his cocked-hat, it was handed to him by his aide-de-camp, and he took leave.

We walked out in the evening to take a look of the environs, with Señor V——o, the commander of the Jason, and several young ladies of the house. We walked in the direction of an old church, where it is or was the custom for young ladies desirous of being married to throw a stone at the saint, their fortune depending upon the stone's hitting him, so that he is in a lapidated and dilapidated condition. Such environs! the surrounding houses black with smoke of powder or with fire

—a view of bare red sandhills all round—not a tree, or shrub, or flower, or bird, except the horrid black sopilote, or police-officer. All looks as if the prophet Jeremiah had passed through the city denouncing woe to the dwellers thereof. Such a melancholy, wholly deserted-looking burial-ground as we saw!

War and revolutions have no doubt done their work, yet I find difficulty in believing those who speak of Vera Cruz as having been a gay and delightful residence in former days, though even now, those who have resided here for any length of time, even foreigners, almost invariably become attached to it; and as for those born here, they are the truest of patriots, holding up Vera Cruz as superior to all other parts of the world.

The city was founded by the Viceroy, Count de Monterey, at the end of the seventeenth century, and ought not to be confounded, as it sometimes is, with either of the two colonies founded by the first Spaniards. Built in front of the island of San Juan de Ulua, it has one interesting recollection attached to it, since on the same arid shores, Cortes disembarked more than three centuries ago. Unlike the green and fertile coast which gladdened the eyes of Columbus, the Spanish conqueror beheld a bleak and burning desert, whose cheerless aspect might well have deterred a feebler mind from going further in search of the paradise that existed behind.

We returned to the house, and heard some ladies play upon a harp, so called, a small, light instrument in that form, but without pedals, so light, that they can lift it with one hand; and yet the music they bring from it is surprising; one air after another, a little monotonously, but with great ease and a certain execution, and with the additional merit of being self-taught.

I imagine that there must be a great deal of musical taste thrown away here. There are pianos in almost every house, and one lady, who came to see me to-day, and whose mother was English, had been extremely well taught, and played with great taste. They attempted dancing, but having no masters, can only learn by what they *hear*. On the balcony this evening, it was delightful, and the moon is a universal beautifier.

21st.—We walked about the city yesterday, and returned visits. The streets are clean, and some few churches tolerably handsome.

The *Comicos* came in the morning to offer us the centre box in the theatre, it being the benefit night of Donna Inocencia Martinez from Madrid, a favourite of the public, and, in fact, a pretty woman and good comic actress. The theatre is small, and, they say, generally deserted, but last night it was crowded. The drop-scene represents the fine arts, who are so fat, that their condition here must be flourishing. We were, however, agreeably disappointed in the performance, which was the "Segunda Dama Duende," nearly a translation from the "Domino Noir," and very amusing; full of excellent *coups-de-théâtre*. Donna Inocencia in her various characters, as domino, servant-girl, abbess, etc., was very handsome, and acted with great spirit. Moreover, she and her sister, with two Spaniards, danced the Jota Aragonesa in perfection, so that we spent a pleasant evening, upon the whole, within the precincts of the city of the True Cross.

To-morrow is the day fixed for our departure, and we shall not be sorry to leave this place, although this house is excellent, a whole suite of rooms given to us, and neither ceremony nor *gêne* of any sort. The weather is certainly beautiful. The heat may be a little oppressive in the middle of the day, but the evenings are cool and delightful.

We had a visit yesterday from the English and French consuls. M. de —— prophesies broken arms and dislodged teeth, if we persist in our plan of taking the diligence,—but all things balanced, we think it preferable to every other conveyance. General Victoria returned to see us this morning, and was very civil and amiable, offering very cordially every service and assistance in his power. We are to rise to-morrow at two, being invited to breakfast with General Santa Anna, at his country-seat Manga de Clavo, a few leagues from this.

We have been sitting on the balcony till very late, enjoying the moonlight and refreshing breeze from the sea, and as we rise before daybreak, our rest will be but short.

LETTER THE FIFTH

JALAPA, 23rd December.

Yesterday morning at two o'clock we rose by candlelight, with
the pleasant prospect of leaving Vera Cruz and of seeing Santa
Anna. Two boxes, called carriages, drawn by mules, were
at the door, to convey us to Magna de Clavo. Señor V——o,
C——n, the commander of the Jason, and I being encased in
them, we set off half-asleep. By the faint light, we could just
distinguish as we passed the gates, and the carriages ploughed
their way along nothing but sand—sand—as far as the eye could
reach; a few leagues of Arabian desert.

At length we began to see symptoms of vegetation; occasional palm-trees and flowers, and by the time we had reached
a pretty Indian village, where we stopped to change mules,
the light had broke in, and we seemed to have been transported, as if by enchantment, from a desert to a garden. It
was altogether a picturesque and striking scene; the huts composed of bamboo, and thatched with palm-leaves, the Indian
women with their long black hair standing at the doors with
their half-naked children, the mules rolling themselves on the
ground, according to their favourite fashion, snow-white goats
browsing amongst the palm-trees, and the air so soft and
balmy, the first fresh breath of morning; the dew-drops still

glittering on the broad leaves of the banana and palm, and all around so silent, cool, and still.

The huts, though poor, were clean; no windows, but a certain subdued light makes its way through the leafy canes. We procured some tumblers of new milk, and having changed mules, pursued our journey, now no longer through hills of sand, but across the country, through a wilderness of trees and flowers, the glowing productions of *tierra caliente*. We arrived about five at Manga de Clavo, after passing through leagues of natural garden, the property of Santa Anna.

The house is pretty, slight-looking, and kept in nice order. We were received by an aide-de-camp in uniform, and by several officers, and conducted to a large, cool, agreeable apartment, with little furniture, into which shortly entered the Señora de Santa Anna, tall, thin, and, at that early hour of the morning, dressed to receive us in clear white muslin, with white satin shoes, and with very splendid diamond earrings, brooch, and rings. She was very polite, and introduced her daughter Guadalupe, a miniature of her mamma, in features and costume.

In a little while entered General Santa Anna himself; a gentlemanly, good-looking, quietly-dressed, rather melancholy-looking person, with one leg, apparently somewhat of an invalid, and to us the most interesting person in the group. He has a sallow complexion, fine dark eyes, soft and penetrating, and an interesting expression of face. Knowing nothing of his past history, one would have said a philosopher, living in dignified retirement—one who had tried the world, and found that all was vanity—one who had suffered ingratitude, and who, if he were ever persuaded to emerge from his retreat, would only do so, Cincinnatus-like, to benefit his country. It is strange, how frequently this expression of philosophic resignation, of placid sadness, is to be remarked on the countenances of the deepest, most ambitious, and most designing men. C——n gave him a letter from the Queen, written under the supposition of his being still President, with which he seemed much pleased, but merely made the innocent observation, "How very well the Queen writes!"

It was only now and then, that the expression of his eye was startling, especially when he spoke of his leg, which is cut off below the knee. He speaks of it frequently, like Sir John Ramorny of his bloody hand, and when he gives an account of his wound, and alludes to the French on that day, his countenance assumes that air of bitterness which Ramorny's may have exhibited when speaking of "Harry the Smith."

Otherwise, he made himself very agreeable, spoke a great deal of the United States, and of the persons he had known there, and in his manners was quiet and gentlemanlike, and altogether a more polished hero than I had expected to see. To judge from the past, he will not long remain in his present state of inaction, besides having within him, according to Zavala, "a principle of action for ever impelling him forward."

En attendant, breakfast was announced. The Señora de Santa Anna led me in. C——n was placed at the head of the table, I on his right, Santa Anna opposite, the Señora on my right. The breakfast was very handsome, consisting of innumerable Spanish dishes, meat and vegetables, fish and fowl, fruits and sweetmeats, all served in white and gold French porcelain, with coffee, wines, etc. After breakfast, the Señora having despatched an officer for her cigar-case, which was gold, with a diamond latch, offered me a cigar, which I having declined, she lighted her own, a little paper "cigarito," and the gentlemen followed her good example.

We then proceeded to look at the out-houses and offices; at the General's favourite war-horse, an old white charger, probably a sincerer philosopher than his master; at several game-cocks, kept with especial care, cock-fighting being a favourite recreation of Santa Anna's; and at his *litera,* which is handsome and comfortable. There are no gardens, but, as he observed, the whole country, which for twelve leagues square belongs to him, is a garden. The appearance of the family says little for the healthiness of the *locale;* and indeed its beauty and fertility will not compensate for its insalubrity.

As we had but a few hours to spare, the General ordered round two carriages, both very handsome, and made in the United States, one of which conveyed him and C——n, the Señora and me. In the other were the little girl and the officers; in which order we proceeded across the country to the high-road, where the diligence and servants, with our guide, Don Miguel S——, were to overtake us. The diligence not having arrived, we got down and sat on a stone bench, in front of an Indian cottage, where we talked, while the young lady amused herself by eating apples, and C——n and the General remained moralizing in the carriage.

Shortly after, and just as the sun was beginning to give us a specimen of his power, our lumbering escort of Mexican soldiers galloped up (orders having been given by the govern-

ment that a fresh escort shall be stationed every six leagues)
and announced the approach of the diligence. We were agreeably disappointed by the arrival of a handsome new coach,
made in the United States, drawn by ten good-looking mules,
and driven by a smart Yankee coachman. Our party consisted
of ourselves, Don Miguel, the captain of the Jason and his
first lieutenant, who accompany us to Mexico. The day was
delightful, and every one apparently in good-humour. We took
leave of General Santa Anna, his lady and daughter, also of
our hospitable entertainer, Señor V——o; got into the diligence
—doors shut—all right—lash up the mules, and now for Mexico!

Gradually, as in Dante's Commedia, after leaving Purgatory, typified by Vera Cruz, we seemed to draw nearer to Paradise. The road is difficult, as the approach to Paradise ought
to be, and the extraordinary jolts were sufficient to prevent
us from being too much enraptured by the scenery, which
increased in beauty as we advanced. At Santa Fé and Sopilote
we changed horses, and at Tolomé, one of the sites of the
civil war, came to the end of Santa Anna's twelve leagues of
property.

We arrived at Puente Nacional, formerly Puente del Rey,
celebrated as the scene of many an engagement during the
Revolution, and by occupying which, Victoria frequently prevented the passage of the Spanish troops, and that of the con-
voys of silver to the port. Here we stopped a short time to
admire the beautiful bridge thrown over the river Antigua,
with its stone arches, which brought Mrs. Ward's sketch to
my recollection, though it is very long since I saw the book.
We were accompanied by the commander of the fort. It is
now a peaceful-looking scene. We walked to the bridge, pulled
branches of large white flowers, admired the rapid river dashing over the rocks, and the fine, bold scenery that surrounds
it. The village is a mere collection of huts, with some fine trees.

It was difficult to believe, as we journeyed on, that we were
now in the midst of December. The air was soft and balmy.
The heat, without being oppressive, that of a July day in England. The road through a succession of woody country; trees
covered with every variety of blossom, and loaded with the
most delicious tropical fruits; flowers of every colour filling
the air with fragrance, and the most fantastical profusion of
parasitical plants intertwining the branches of the trees, and
flinging their bright blossoms over every bough. Palms, cocoas,
oranges, lemons, succeeded one another, and at one turn of
the road, down in a lovely green valley, we caught a glimpse

of an Indian woman, with her long hair, resting under the shade of a lofty tree—beside a running stream—an Oriental picture. Had it not been for the dust and the jolting, nothing could have been more delightful. As for Don Miguel, with his head out of the window, now desiring the coachman to go more quietly, now warning us to prepare for a jolt, now pointing out everything worth looking at, and making light of difficulties, he was the very best conductor of a journey I ever met with. His hat of itself was a curiosity to us; a white beaver with immense brim, lined with thick silver tissue, with two large silver rolls and tassels round it.

One circumstance must be observed by all who travel in Mexican territory. There is not one human being or passing object to be seen that is not in itself a picture, or which would not form a good subject for the pencil. The Indian women with their plaited hair, and little children slung to their backs, their large straw hats, and petticoats of two colours—the long strings of arrièros with their loaded mules, and swarthy, wild-looking faces—the chance horseman who passes with his *sarape* of many colours, his high ornamented saddle, Mexican hat, silver stirrups, and leathern boots—this is picturesque. Salvator Rosa and Hogarth might have travelled here to advantage, hand-in-hand; Salvator for the sublime, and Hogarth taking him up where the sublime became the ridiculous.

At La Calera we had a distant view of the sea. Occasionally we stopped to buy oranges fresh from the trees, pineapples, and granaditas, which are like Brobdinagian gooseberries, the pulp enclosed in a very thick yellow or green rind, and very refreshing.

It was about seven in the evening, when very dusty, rather tired, but very much enchanted with all we had seen, we arrived at Plan del Rio. Here the diligence passengers generally stop for the night; that is, sleep a few hours on a hard bed, and rise at midnight to go on to Jalapa. But to this arrangement, I for one made vociferous objections, and strongly insisted upon the propriety and feasibility of sleeping at Jalapa that night. Don Miguel, the most obsequious of dons, declared that it should be exactly as the Señora ordered.

Accordingly it was agreed that we should wait for the moon, and then pursue our journey; and meanwhile we walked out to a short distance, to see the bridge, the river, and the wood. The bridge consists of a single large arch thrown over the river, and communicating with a great high-road, formerly paved, but now going to ruin.

We returned to the inn, a long row of small rooms, built of brick and prettily situated, not far from the water. Here we had the luxury of water and towels, which enabled us to get rid of a certain portion of dust before we went to supper.

The diligence from Jalapa has just deposited at the inn, a German with his wife and child, he bearing so decidedly the stamp of a German musician, that we at once guessed his calling. They are from Mexico, from whence the fine arts seem to be taking their flight, and gave a most woeful account of the road between this and Jalapa.

We had a very tolerable supper; soup, fish, fowls, steak, and *frijoles*, all well seasoned with garlic and oil. The jolting had given me too bad a headache to care for more than coffee. We were strongly advised to remain the night there, but lazy people know too well what it is to rise in the middle of the night, especially when they are much fatigued; and when the moon rose, we packed ourselves once more into the diligence, sufficiently refreshed to encounter new fatigues. The moon was very bright, and most of the party prepared themselves for sleep with cigars in their mouths; not a very easy matter, for the roads were infamous, a succession of holes and rocks. As we were gradually ascending, the weather became cooler, and from cool began to grow cold, forcing us to look out for cloaks and shawls. We could now discern some change in the vegetation, or rather a mingling of the trees of a colder climate with those of the tropics, especially the Mexican oak, which begins to flourish here. Fortunately, at one part of the road, the moon enabled us to see the captain of the escort lying on the ground fast asleep, his horse standing quietly beside him, he having fallen off while asleep, and continued his nap. The soldiers shook him up with some difficulty.

At *Carral falso* we changed mules, and from the badness of the road, continued to go slowly.

The cold increased, and at last by the moonlight, we had a distinct view of the Peak of Orizava, with his white nightcap on (excuse the simile, suggested by extreme sleepiness), the very sight enough to make one shiver.

As we approached Jalapa, the scene was picturesque. The escort had put on their *sarapes*, and with their high helmets and feathers, went galloping along, and dashing amongst the trees and shrubs. Orizava and the Cofre de Perote shone white in the distance, while a delicious smell of flowers, particularly of roses, gave token of the land through which we were passing.

It was nearly two in the morning when we reached Jalapa,

tired to death, and shivering with cold. Greatly we rejoiced as we rattled through its mountainous streets, and still more when we found ourselves in a nice clean inn, with brick floors and decent small beds, and everything prepared for us. The sight of a fire would have been too much luxury; however, they gave us some hot tea, and very shortly after, I at least can answer for myself, that I was in bed, and enjoying the most delightful sleep that I have had since I left New York.

This morning the diligence being at our disposal we did not rise by break of day, but on the contrary, continued to sleep till eight o'clock. I was waited on by such a nice, civil, clean little old woman, that I should like to carry her off with me. Meanwhile, various authorities of the town were stationed at the door to give C——n welcome when he should appear.

Our breakfast was delicious. Such fresh eggs, and fresh butter, and good coffee and well-fried chickens; moreover, such good bread and peculiarly excellent water, that we fell very much in love with Jalapa.

After breakfast we walked out, accompanied by various gentlemen of the place. The town consists of little more than a few steep streets, very old, with some large and excellent houses, the best as usual belonging to English merchants, and many to those of Vera Cruz, who come to live in or near Jalapa, during the reign of the "*Vomito.*" There are some old churches, a very old convent of Franciscan monks, and a well-supplied market-place. Everywhere there are flowers—roses creeping over the old walls, Indian girls making green garlands for the virgin and saints, flowers in the shops, flowers at the windows, but, above all, everywhere one of the most splendid mountain views in the world.

The Cofre de Perote, with its dark pine forests and gigantic *chest* (a rock of porphyry which takes that form), and the still loftier snow-white peak of Orizava, tower above all the others, seeming like the colossal guardians of the land. The intervening mountains, the dark cliffs and fertile plains, the thick woods of lofty trees clothing the hills and the valleys; a glimpse of the distant ocean; the surrounding lanes shaded by fruit trees: aloes, bananas, chirimoyas, mingled with the green liquidambar, the flowering myrtle, and hundreds of plants and shrubs and flowers of every colour and of delicious fragrance, all combine to form one of the most varied and beautiful scenes that the eye can behold.

Then Jalapa itself, so old and gray, and rose-becovered, with a sound of music issuing from every open door and window, and its soft and agreeable temperature, presents, even in a few hours, a series of agreeable impressions not easily effaced.

But we are now returned to our inn, for it is near noon, and the veil of clouds, that earlier in the morning enveloped Orizava, has passed away, leaving its white summit environed by a flood of light. I shall probably have no opportunity of writing until we reach Puebla.

PUEBLA, 24th.

Yesterday morning we took leave of the *Jalapenos,* and once more found ourselves *en route.* Such a view of the mountains as we ascended the steep road! and such flowers and blossoming trees on all sides! Large scarlet blossoms, and hanging purple and white flowers, and trees covered with fragrant bell-shaped flowers like lilies, which the people here call the *floripundio,* together with a profusion of double pink roses that made the air fragrant as we passed; and here and there a church, a ruined convent, or a white hacienda. We had the advantage of clear weather, not always to be found at Jalapa, especially when the north wind, blowing at Vera Cruz, covers this city and its environs with a dense fog.

We stopped at a small village to change horses (for on leaving Jalapa, our mules were exchanged for eight strong white horses), and here Don Miguel made us enter a very pretty house belonging to some female friends of his, one of whom was very handsome, with a tasteful white turban. The curiosity of this place is a rock behind the house, covered with roses, clove-carnations, and every variety of bright flower-tree, together with oranges, lemons, limes, and cedrats, all growing out of the rock. The ladies were very civil, though I dare say surprised at our admiration of their December flowers, and gave us orangeade and cake, with large cedrats and oranges from the trees; but above all, the most delicious bouquet of roses and carnations; so that, together with the unknown scarlet and purple blossoms which the captain of the escort had gathered for me, the diligence inside looked like an arbour.

We continued our journey, the road ascending towards the tableland, and at one striking point of view we got out and looked back upon Jalapa, and round upon a panorama of mountains. Gradually the vegetation changed: fine, fresh-looking European herbage and trees succeeded the less hardy though more brilliant trees and flowers of the tropics; the banana and chirimoya gave place to the strong oak, and higher still, these were interspersed with the dark green of the pine.

At San Miguel de los Soldados we stopped to take some refreshment. The country became gradually more bleak, and before arriving at the village of Las Vigas, nearly all trees had disappeared but the hardy fir, which flourishes amongst the rocks. The ground for about two leagues was covered with lava, and great masses of black calcined rock, so that we seemed to be passing over the crater of a volcano. This part of the country is deservedly called the *Mal Pais*, and the occasional crosses with their faded garlands, that gleam in these bleak, volcanic regions, give token that it may have yet other titles to the name of "Evil Land." The roses and carnations that I had brought from Jalapa were still unwithered, so that in a few hours we had passed through the whole scale of vegetation.

The road became steep and dreary, and after passing *Cruz Blanca*, excepting occasional cornfields and sombre pine-forests, the scene had no objects of interest sufficient to enable us to keep our eyes open. The sun was set—it grew dusk, and by the time we reached Perote, where we were to pass the night, most of us had fallen into an uncomfortable sleep, very cold and quite stupefied, and too sleepy to be hungry, in spite of finding a large supper prepared for us.

The inn was dirty, very unlike that at Jalapa, the beds miserable, and we were quite ready to get up by the light of an unhappy specimen of tallow which the landlord brought to our doors at two in the morning.

There are some scenes which can never be effaced from our memory, and such a one was that which took place this morning at Perote at two o'clock, the moon and the stars shining bright and cold.

Being dressed, I went into the kitchen, where C——n, the officers of the Jason, Don Miguel, and the Mexican captain of the last night's escort, were assembled by the light of one melancholy sloping candle, together with a suspicious-looking landlord, and a few sleepy Indian women with bare feet, tangled hair, copper faces and reboses. They made us some chocolate with goat's milk, horrid in general, and rancid in particular.

It appeared that all parties were at a standstill, for, by some mistake in the orders, the new escort had not arrived, and the escort of the preceding night could go no further. Don Miguel, with his swarthy face, and great sarape, was stalking about, rather out of humour, while the captain was regretting,

in very polite tones, with his calm, Arab-looking, impassive
face, that his escort could proceed no further. He seemed to
think it extremely probable that we should be robbed, believed, indeed had just heard it asserted, that a party of *ladrones* were looking out for el Señor Ministro, regretted that
he could not assist us, though quite at our service, and recommended us to wait until the next escort should arrive.

To this advice our conductor would by no means listen.
He was piqued that any detention should occur, and yet aware
that it was unsafe to go on. He had promised to convey us
safely, and in four days, to Mexico, and it was necessary to
keep his word. Some one proposed that two of the men should
accompany the diligence upon mules, as probably a couple of
these animals might be procured. The captain observed, that
though entirely at our disposal, two men could be of no manner of use, as, in case of attack, resistance, except with a large
escort, was worse than useless. Nevertheless it was remarked
by some ingenious person, that the robbers seeing two, might
imagine that there were more behind. In short there were
various opinions. One proposed that they should go on the
coach, another that they should go *in* it. Here I ventured to
interpose, begging that they might ride on mules or go outside, but by no means within. As usual, it was as the Señora
pleased.

At length we all collected before the door of the inn, and
a queer group we must have made by the light of the moon,
and a nice caricature, I thought to myself, our friend Mr. G——
would have made of us, had he been there.

The diligence with eight white horses and a Yankee coachman, originally, no doubt, called Brown, but now answering
to the mellifluous appellation of *Bruno;* A—— with her French
cap, and loaded with sundry mysterious-looking baskets; I with
cloak and bonnet; C——n with Greek cap, cloak, and cigar;
the captain of the Jason also with cloak and cigar, and very
cold; the lieutenant in his navy uniform, taking it coolly; Don
Miguel, with his great sarape and silver hat—(six people belonging to five different countries); the Mexican captain, with
his pale impassive face and moustaches, enveloped in a very
handsome sarape, and surrounded by the sleepy escort of the
preceding night; dirty-looking soldiers lounging on the ground,
wrapped in their blankets; the Indian women and the host of
the inn, and a bright moon and starry sky lighting up the
whole—the figures in the foreground, and the lofty snow-clad
mountains, and the dismal old town of Perote itself, that

looked gray and sulky at being disturbed so early, with its old castle of San Carlos, and cold, sterile plains.

Meanwhile, two soldiers with cloaks and arms had climbed up outside of the coach. The captain remarked that they could not sit there. Bruno made some reply, upon which the captain very coolly drew his sword, and was about to put a very decided impediment to our journey by stabbing the coachman, when Don Miguel, his eyes and cigar all shining angrily, rushed in between them.

High words ensued between him and the captain, and the extreme coolness and precision with which the latter spoke, was very amusing. It was as if he were rehearsing a speech from a play. "I always speak frankly," said Don Miguel, in an angry tone. "And I," said the captain, in a polite, measured voice, "am also accustomed to speak my mind· with extreme frankness. I regret, however, that I did not at the moment perceive the Señora at the door, otherwise," etc.

At length the two little men, who with their arms and sarapes looked like bundles of ammunition, and who, half asleep, had been by some zealous person, probably by our friend Bruno, tumbled upon the diligence like packages, were now rolled off it, and finally tumbled upon mules, and we got into the coach. Don Miguel, with his head out of the window, and not very easy in his mind, called up the two bundles and gave them directions as to their line of conduct in a *stage* whisper, and they trotted off, primed with valour, while we very cold and (I answer for myself) rather frightened, proceeded on our way. The earliness of the hour was probably our salvation, as we started two hours before the usual time, and thus gained a march upon the gentlemen of the road.

We were not sorry, however, when at our first halting-place, and whilst we were changing horses, we descried a company of lancers at full gallop, with a very good-looking officer at their head, coming along the road; though when first I heard the sound of horses' hoofs, clattering along, and, by the faint light, discerned the horsemen enveloped as they were in a cloud of dust, I felt sure that they were a party of robbers. The captain made many apologies for the delay, and proceeded to inform us that the alcaldes of Tepeyagualco, La Ventilla, and of some other villages, whose names I forget, had for twenty days prepared a breakfast in expectation of his Excellency's arrival:—whether twenty breakfasts, or the same one cold, or *réchauffé*, we may never know.

The captain had a very handsome horse, which he caused

to *caracolear* by the side of the diligence, and put at my disposal with a low bow, every time I looked at it. He discoursed with C——n of robbers and wars, and of the different sites which these gentry most affected, and told him how his first wife had been shot by following him in some engagement, yet how his second wife invariably followed him also.

Arrived at Tepeyagualco, after having passed over a succession of sterile plains covered with scanty pasture, an alcalde advanced to meet the diligence, and hospitably made C——n an offer of the before-mentioned twenty days' entertainment, which he with many thanks declined. Who ate that breakfast, is buried in the past. Whether the alcalde was glad or sorry, did not appear. He vanished with a profusion of bows, and was followed by a large, good-looking Indian woman, who stood behind him while he made his discourse. Perhaps they eat together the long-prepared feast; which was at least one of the many tributes paid to the arrival of the first messenger of peace from the mother-country.

At La Ventilla, however, we descended with a good appetite, and found several authorities waiting to give C——n a welcome. Here they gave us delicious chirimoyas, a natural custard, which we liked even upon a first trial, also granaditas, bananas, sapotes, etc. Here also I first tasted *pulque;* and on a first impression it appears to me, that as nectar was the drink in Olympus, we may fairly conjecture that Pluto cultivated the maguey in his dominions. The taste and smell combined took me so completely by surprise, that I am afraid my look of horror must have given mortal offence to the worthy alcalde who considers it the most delicious beverage in the world; and in fact, it is said, that when one gets over the first shock, it is very agreeable. The difficulty must consist in getting over it.

After a tolerable breakfast, hunger making chile and garlic supportable, we continued our route; and were informed that the robbers, having grown very daring, and the next stage being very dangerous, our escort was to be doubled. Since we left Perote, the country had gradually become more dreary, and we had again got into the *"mal pais,"* where nothing is to be seen but a few fir-trees and pines, dark and stunted, black masses of lava, and an occasional white cross to mark either where a murder has been committed, or where a celebrated robber has been buried. Of each, Don Miguel gave us a succinct account. Some lines of Childe Harold suit this scene as if written for it:

"And here and there, as up the crags you spring,
  Mark many rude-carved crosses near the path:
Yet deem not these devotion's offering—
  These are memorials frail of murderous wrath;
For, wheresoe'er the shrieking victim hath
  Pour'd forth his blood beneath the assassin's knife,
Some hand erects a cross of mouldering lath;
  And grove and glen with thousand such are rife,
Throughout this purple land, where law secures not life."

The whole scene was wild and grand, yet dreary and monotonous, presenting the greatest contrast possible to our first day's
journey. The only signs of life to be met with were the long
strings of arrièros with their droves of mules, and an occasional Indian hut, with a few miserable half-naked women and
children.

At one small, wild-looking inn, where, very cold and miserable, we stopped, some hot wine was brought us, which was
very acceptable. The tavern-keeper, for it was no more than
a spirit-shop, if not a robber, had all the appearance of one;
wild, melancholy, and with a most sinister expression of countenance. Salvator never drew a more bandit-looking figure, as
he stood there with his blanket and slouched hat, and a knife
in his belt, tall and thin and muscular, with his sallow visage
and his sad, fierce eyes. However, he showed us the marks on
his door, where a band of twenty robbers had broken in one
night, and robbed some travellers, who were sleeping there,
of a large sum of money.

C——n asked him how the robbers treated the women when
they fell into their power. *"Las saludan,"* said he, "and sometimes carry them off to the mountains, but rarely, and chiefly
when they are afraid of their giving information against them."

At *Ojo de Agua,* where we changed horses, we saw the accommodations which those who travel in private coach or litera must submit to, unless they bring their own beds along
with them, and a stock of provisions besides—a common room
like a barn, where all must herd together; and neither chair,
nor table, nor food to be had. It was a solitary-looking house,
standing lonely on the plain, with a few straggling sheep nib-
bling the brown grass in the vicinity. A fine spring of water
from which it takes its name, and Orizava, which seems to
have travelled forward, and stands in bold outline against the
sapphire sky, were all that we saw there worthy notice.

We changed horses at Nopaluca, Acagete and Amosoque,

all small villages, with little more than the *posada*, and a few poor houses, and all very dirty. The country, however, improves in cultivation and fertility, though the chief trees are the sombre pines. Still accompanied by our two escorts, which had a very grandiloquent effect, we entered, by four o'clock, Puebla de los Angeles, the second city to Mexico (after Guadalajara) in the republic, where we found very fine apartments prepared for us in the inn, and where, after a short rest and a fresh toilet, we went out to see what we could of the city before it grew dusk, before it actually became what it now is, *Christmas-eve!*

It certainly does require some time for the eye to become accustomed to the style of building adopted in the Spanish colonies. There is something at first sight exceedingly desolate-looking in these great wooden doors, like those of immense barns, the great iron-barred windows, the ill-paved courtyards, even the flat roofs; and then the streets, where, though this is a fête-day, we see nothing but groups of peasants or of beggars—the whole gives the idea of a total absence of comfort. Yet the streets of Puebla are clean and regular, the houses large, the cathedral magnificent, and the plaza spacious and handsome.

The cathedral was shut, and is not to be opened till midnight mass, which I regret the less as we must probably return here some day.

The dress of the Poblana peasants is pretty, especially on fête-days. A white muslin chemise, trimmed with lace round the skirt, neck, and sleeves, which are plaited neatly; a petticoat shorter than the chemise, and divided into two colours, the lower part made generally of a scarlet and black stuff, a manufacture of the country, and the upper part of yellow satin, with a satin vest of some bright colour, and covered with gold or silver, open in front, and turned back. This vest may be worn or omitted, as suits the taste of the wearer. It is without sleeves, but has straps; the hair plaited in two behind, and the plaits turned up and fastened together by a diamond ring; long earrings, and all sorts of chains and medals and tinkling things worn round the neck. A long, broad, coloured sash, something like an officer's belt, tied behind after going twice or thrice round the waist, into which is stuck a silver cigar-case. A small coloured handkerchief like a broad ribbon, crossing over the neck, is fastened in front with a brooch, the ends trimmed with silver, and going through the sash. Over all is thrown a reboso, not over the head, but thrown on like a scarf; and they wear silk stockings, or more commonly no stockings, and white satin shoes trimmed with silver.

This is on holidays. On common occasions, the dress is the same, but the materials are more common, at least the vest with silver is never worn; but the chemise is still trimmed with lace, and the shoes are satin.

Christmas-eve in Puebla! The room is filled with visitors, who have come to congratulate C——n on his arrival, and a wonderfully handsome room it is, to do it justice, with chairs and sofas of scarlet stuff. But I was anxious to see *something*. As we are to leave Puebla very early, I am prohibited from going to the midnight mass. I proposed the theatre, where there is to be a *Nacimiento*, a representation in figures of various events connected with the Birth of Christ; such as the Annunciation, the Holy Family, the Arrival of the Wise Men of the East, etc. But after some deliberation, it was agreed that this would not do; so finding that there is nothing to be done, and tired of polite conversation, I betake myself to bed.

Christmas-day.

It is now about three o'clock, but I was awakened an hour ago by the sounds of the hymns which ushered in Christmas morning; and looking from the window, saw, by the faint light, bands of girls dressed in white, singing in chorus through the streets.

We have just taken chocolate, and, amidst a profusion of bows and civilities from the landlord, are preparing to set off for Mexico.

LETTER THE SIXTH

*Departure from Puebla — Chirimoyas — Rio Frio — Indian
Game—Black Forest—Valley of Mexico—Recollections of
Tenochtitlan—Mexican Officer—Reception—Scenery—Vari-
ety of Dresses—Cheers—Storm of Rain—Entry to Mexico—
Buenavista—House by Daylight—Sights from the Windows
—Visits—Mexican Etiquette—Countess C——a—Flowers in
December—Serenade—Patriotic Hymn.*

MEXICO, 26th December.

We left Puebla between four and five in the morning, as we
purposely made some delay, not wishing to reach Mexico too
early; and in so doing, acted contrary to the advice of Don
Miguel, who was generally right in these matters. The day was
very fine when we set off, though rain was predicted. Some of
the gentlemen had gone to the theatre the night before, to
see the *Nacimiento,* and the audience had been composed entirely of *Gentuza,* the common people, who were drinking
brandy and smoking; so it was fortunate that we had not
shown our faces there.

The country was now flat but fertile, and had on the whole
more of a European look than any we had yet passed through.

At Rio Prieto, a small village, where we changed horses,
I found that I had been sitting very comfortably with my feet
in a basket of chirimoyas, and that my bordequins, white
gown, and cloak, had been all drenched with the milky juice,
and then made black by the floor of the diligence.

With no small difficulty a trunk was brought down, and
another dress procured, to the great amusement of the Indian
women, who begged to know if my gown was the *last fashion,*
and said it was *"muy guapa,"* very pretty. Here we found
good hot coffee, and it being Christmas-day, every one was
cleaned and dressed for mass.

At Rio Frio, which is about thirteen leagues from Mexico,
and where there is a pretty good posada in a valley surrounded
by woods, we stopped to dine. The inn was kept by a Bordelaise and her husband, who wish themselves in Bordeaux
twenty times a day. In front of the house some Indians were

playing at a curious and very ancient game—a sort of swing, resembling *"El Juego de los Voladores,"* "The game of the flyers," much in vogue amongst the ancient Mexicans. Our French hostess gave us a good dinner, especially excellent potatoes, and jelly of various sorts, regaling us with plenty of stories of robbers and robberies and horrid murders all the while. On leaving Rio Frio, the road became more hilly and covered with woods, and we shortly entered the tract known by the name of the Black Forest, a great haunt for banditti, and a beautiful specimen of forest scenery, a succession of lofty oaks, pines, and cedars, with wild flowers lighting up their gloomy green. But I confess that the impatience which I felt to see Mexico, the idea that in a few hours we should actually be there, prevented me from enjoying the beauty of the scenery, and made the road appear interminable.

But at length we arrived at the heights looking down upon the great valley, celebrated in all parts of the world, with its framework of everlasting mountains, its snow-crowned volcanoes, great lakes, and fertile plains, all surrounding the favoured city of Montezuma, the proudest boast of his conqueror, once of Spain's many diadems the brightest. But the day had overcast, nor is this the most favourable road for entering Mexico. The innumerable spires of the distant city were faintly seen. The volcanoes were enveloped in clouds, all but their snowy summits, which seemed like marble domes towering into the sky. But as we strained our eyes to look into the valley, it all appeared to me rather like a vision of the Past than the actual breathing Present. The curtain of Time seemed to roll back, and to discover to us the great panorama that burst upon the eye of Cortes when he first looked down upon the table-land; the king-loving, God-fearing conqueror, his loyalty and religion so blended after the fashion of ancient Spain, that it were hard to say which sentiment exercised over him the greater sway. The city of Tenochtitlan, standing in the midst of the five great lakes, upon verdant and flower-covered islands, a western Venice, with thousands of boats gliding swiftly along its streets, long lines of low houses, diversified by the multitudes of pyramidal temples, the Teocalli, or houses of God—canoes covering the mirrored lakes—the lofty trees, the flowers, and the profusion of water now wanting to the landscape—the whole fertile valley enclosed by its eternal hills and snow-crowned volcanoes—what scenes of wonder and of beauty to burst upon the eyes of these wayfaring men!

Then the beautiful gardens surrounding the city, the profu-

sion of flowers, and fruit, and birds—the mild bronze-coloured
Emperor himself advancing in the midst of his Indian nobility,
with rich dress and unshod feet, to receive his unbidden and
unwelcome guest—the slaves and the gold and the rich plumes,
all to be laid at the feet of "His most sacred Majesty"—what
pictures are called up by the recollection of the simple narrative of Cortes, and how forcibly they return to the mind now,
when, after a lapse of three centuries, we behold for the first
time the city of palaces raised upon the ruins of the Indian
capital. It seemed scarcely possible that we were indeed so
near the conclusion of our journey, and in the midst of so different a scene, only two months minus two days since leaving
New York and stepping aboard the Norma. How much land
and sea we had passed over since then! How much we had
seen! How many different climates, even in the space of the
last four days!

But my thoughts which had wandered three centuries into
the past, were soon recalled to the present by the arrival of an
officer in full uniform at the head of his troop, who came out
by order of the government to welcome the bearer of the olive-
branch from ancient Spain, and had been on horseback since
the day before, expecting our arrival. As it had begun to rain,
the officer, Colonel Miguel Andrade, accepted our offer of taking shelter in the diligence. We had now a great troop galloping along with us, and had not gone far before we perceived
that in spite of the rain, and that it already began to grow
dusk, there were innumerable carriages and horsemen forming
an immense crowd, all coming out to welcome us. Shortly after
the diligence was stopped, and we were requested to get into
a very splendid carriage, all crimson and gold, with the arms
of the republic, the eagle and nopal, embroidered in gold on
the roof inside, and drawn by four handsome white horses. In
the midst of this immense procession of troops, carriages, and
horsemen, we made our entry into the city of Montezuma.

The scenery on this side of Mexico is arid and flat, and where
the waters of the Lagunas, covered with their gay canoes, once
surrounded the city, forming canals through its streets, we
now see melancholy marshy lands, little enlivened by great
flights of wild duck and waterfowl. But the bleakness of the
natural scenery was concealed by the gay appearance of the
procession—the scarlet and gold uniforms, the bright-coloured
sarapes, the dresses of the gentlemen (most, I believe, Spaniards), with their handsome horses, high Mexican saddles,
gold-embroidered *anqueras* generally of black fur, their Mexi-

can hats ornamented with gold, richly-furred jackets, pantaloons with hanging silver buttons, stamped-leather boots, silver
stirrups, and graceful mangas with black or coloured velvet
capes.

At the gates of Mexico the troops halted, and three enthusiastic cheers were given as the carriage entered. It was now
nearly dusk, and the rain was falling in torrents, yet we met
more carriages full of ladies and gentlemen, which joined the
others. We found that a house, in the suburbs at Buenavista,
had been taken for us *provisoirement* by the kindness of the
Spaniards, especially of a rich merchant who accompanied us
in the carriage, Don M——l M——z del C——o; consequently
we passed all through Mexico before reaching our destination,
always in the midst of the crowd, on account of which and
of the ill-paved streets we went very slowly. Through the rain
and the darkness we got an occasional faint lamp-light glimpse
of high buildings, churches, and convents. Arrived at length
in the midst of torrents of rain, C——n got out of the carriage
and returned thanks for his reception, giving some ounces to
the sergeant for the soldiers. We then entered the house, accompanied by the Mexican officer, and by a large party of
Spaniards.

We found the house very good, especially considering that
it had been furnished for us in eight-and-forty hours, and we
also found an excellent supper smoking on the table; after
doing justice to which we took leave of our friends, and, very
tired, prepared for sleep.

The servants and luggage arrived late. They had been left
with the diligence, under the guardianship of Don Miguel,
and it appeared that the robbers had mingled with the crowd,
and followed in hopes of plunder; insomuch that he had been
obliged to procure two carriages, one for the servants, while
into another he put the luggage, mounting in front himself to
look out. Tired enough the poor man was, and drenched with
rain; and we found that much of this confusion and difficulty,
which was chiefly caused by the storm and darkness, would
have been avoided had we left Puebla some hours sooner.

However, "All's well that ends well." I thought of Christmas in "Merrie England," and of our family gatherings in the
olden time, and as if one had not travelled enough in the body,
began travelling in the mind, away to far different, and distant, and long gone-by scenes, fell asleep at length with my
thoughts in Scotland, and wakened in Mexico!

By daylight we find our house very pretty, with a large

garden adjoining, full of flowers, and rosebushes in the court-yard, but being all on the ground-floor, it is somewhat damp, and the weather, though beautiful, is so cool in the morning, that carpets, and I sometimes think even a *soupçon* of fire, would not be amiss. The former we shall soon procure, but there are neither chimneys nor grates, and I have no doubt a fire would be disagreeable for more than an hour or so in the morning. The house stands alone, with a large court before it, and opposite to it passes the great stone aqueduct, a mag-nificent work of the Spaniards, though not more so, probably, than those which supplied the ancient Tenochtitlan with wa-ter. Behind it we see nothing but several old houses, with trees, so that we seem almost in the country. To the right is one large building, with garden and olive-ground, where the Eng-lish legation formerly lived, a palace in size, since occupied by Santa Anna, and which now belongs to Señor Perez Galvez; a house which we shall be glad to have, if the proprietor will consent to let it.

But what most attracts our attention are the curious and picturesque groups of figures which we see from the windows —men bronze-colour, with nothing but a piece of blanket thrown round them, carrying lightly on their heads earthen basins, precisely the colour of their own skin, so that they look altogether like figures of terra cotta: these basins filled with sweetmeats or white pyramids of grease (*mantequilla*); women with rebosos, short petticoats of two colours, generally all in rags, yet with a lace border appearing on their under garment: no stockings, and dirty white satin shoes, rather shorter than their small brown feet; gentlemen on horseback with their Mexican saddles and sarapes; lounging *léperos,* moving bundles of rags, coming to the windows and begging with a most piteous but false sounding whine, or lying under the arches and lazily inhaling the air and the sunshine, or sit-ting at the door for hours basking in the sun or under the shadow of the wall: Indian women, with their tight petticoat of dark stuff and tangled hair, plaited with red ribbon, laying down their baskets to rest, and meanwhile deliberately *examin-ing* the hair of their copper-coloured offspring. We have enough to engage our attention for the present.

Several visitors came early—gentlemen, both Spaniards and Mexicans. Señor A——z, decidedly the ugliest man I ever be-held, with a hump on his back, and a smile of most portentous hideosity, yet celebrated for his *bonnes fortunes;* Señor de G——a, Ex-Minister of the Treasury, extremely witty and

agreeable, and with some celebrity as a dramatic writer;
Count C——a, formerly attached to the bedchamber in Spain,
married to a pretty Andalusian, and entirely Mexicanized, his
heart where his interests are. He is very gentlemanlike and
distinguished-looking, with good manners, and extremely eloquent in conversation. I hear him called *"inconsecuente,"* and
capricious, but he has welcomed C——n, who knew him intimately in Madrid, with all the warmth of ancient friendship.

We are told that a great serenade has been for some time
in contemplation, to be given to C——n, the words, music, and
performance by the young Spaniards here.

27th.—A day or two must elapse before I can satisfy my
curiosity by going out, while the necessary arrangements are
making concerning carriage and horses, or mules, servants,
etc.; our vehicles from the United States not having yet arrived,—nor is it difficult to foresee, even from once passing
through the streets, that only the more solid-built English carriages will stand the wear and tear of a Mexican life, and that
the comparatively flimsy coaches which roll over the well-
paved streets of New York, will not endure for any length of
time.

Meanwhile we have constant visits, but chiefly from gentlemen and from Spaniards, for there is one piece of etiquette,
entirely Mexican, nor can I imagine from whence derived, by
which it is ordained that all new arrivals, whatever be their
rank, foreign ministers not excepted, must in solemn print give
notice to every family of any consideration in the capital, that
they have arrived, and offer themselves and their house to their
"disposicion;" failing in which etiquette, the newly-arrived
family will remain unnoticed and unknown. Our cards to this
effect are consequently being printed under the auspices of
Count C——a. I have, however, received the visits of some ladies who have kindly waived this ceremony in my favour; and
amongst others, from the Dowager and the young Countess of
C——a; the eldest a very distinguished woman, of great natural
talent, one of the true ladies of the old school, of whom not
many specimens now remain in Mexico; the other extremely
pretty, lively, and amiable, a true Andalusian both in beauty
and wit. The old Countess was dressed in black velvet, black
blonde mantilla, diamond earrings and brooch—her daughter-
in-law also in black, with a mantilla, and she had a pretty little daughter with her, whose eyes will certainly produce a
kindling effect on the next generation.

They were both extremely kind and cordial; if there are

many such persons in Mexico, we shall have no reason to complain. I hope I am not seeing the cream before the milk!

Some Mexican visits appear to me to surpass in duration all that one can imagine of a visit, rarely lasting less than one hour, and sometimes extending over a greater part of the day. And gentlemen, at least, arrive at no particular time. If you are going to breakfast, they go also—if to dinner, the same—if you are asleep, they wait till you awaken—if out, they call again. An indifferent sort of man, whose name I did not even hear, arrived yesterday, a little after breakfast, sat still, and walked in to a late dinner with us! These should not be called visits, but visitations,—though I trust they do not often occur to that extent. An open house and an open table for your friends, which includes every passing acquaintance; these are merely Spanish habits of hospitality transplanted.

Had a visit from Señor —— and his wife, very civil and obliging people, always agreeing with each other, and with you, and with all the world, almost to the extent of Polonius to Hamlet. Our conversation reminded me of that the whole time they were here.

I have just brought from the garden a lapful of pink roses, clove-carnations, and sweet-peas. Rosetta could not sing here—

"For June and December will never agree."

The weather is lovely, the air fresh and clear, the sky one vast expanse of bright blue, without a single cloud. Early this morning it was cool, but now, by ten o'clock, the air is as soft and balmy as on a summer-day with us.

28th.—Day of the memorable serenade. After dinner some ladies paid me a visit, amongst others the wife and daughter of the Spanish consul, Señor M——y, who were accompanied by the sister of Count A——a. They and a few gentlemen arrived about six o'clock, and it was said that the serenade would not begin till twelve. It may be supposed that our conversation, however agreeable it might be, would scarcely hold out that time. In fact, by nine o'clock, we were all nearly overcome by sleep, and by ten I believe we were already in a refreshing slumber, when we were awakened by the sound of crowds assembling before the door, and of carriages arriving and stopping. Not knowing who the occupants might be, we could not invite them in, which seemed very inhospitable, as the night, though fine, was cold and chilly. About eleven the Count and Countess C——a arrived, and the Señora de G——,

a remarkably handsome woman, a Spaniard, looking nearly as
young as her daughters; also the pretty daughters of the proprietress of this house, who was a beauty, and is married to
her third husband; and a lively little talkative person, the
Señora de L——n, all Spanish; and who, some on that account,
and others from their husbands having been former friends of
C——n's have not waited for the ceremony of receiving cards.
Gradually, however, several Mexican ladies, whom we had
sent out to invite, came in. Others remained in their carriages,
excusing themselves on the plea of their not being *en toilette*.
We had men *à discrétion*, and the rooms were crowded.

About midnight arrived a troop of Mexican soldiers, carrying torches, and a multitude of musicians, both amateur and
professional, chiefly the former, and men carrying music-
stands, violins, violoncellos, French horns, etc., together with
an immense crowd, mingled with numbers of léperos, so that
the great space in front of the house as far as the aqueduct,
and all beyond and along the street as far as we could see,
was covered with people and carriages. We threw open the
windows, which are on a level with the ground, with large
balconies and wide iron gratings, and the scene by the torch-
light was very curious. The Mexican troops holding lights for
the musicians, and they of various countries, Spanish, German,
and Mexican; the léperos, with their ragged blankets and wild
eyes, that gleamed in the light of the torches; the ladies within,
and the crowd without, all formed a very amusing *spectacle*.

At length the musicians struck up in full chorus, accompanied by the whole orchestra. The voices were very fine, and
the instrumental music so good, I could hardly believe that
almost all were amateur performers.

A hymn, which had been composed for the occasion, and
of which we had received an elegantly-bound copy in the
morning, was particularly effective. The music was composed
by Señor Retes, and the words by Señor Covo, both Spaniards. Various overtures from the last operas were played, and
at the end of what seemed to be the first act, in the midst
of deafening applause from the crowd, C——n made me return
thanks from the window in beautiful impromptu Spanish!
Then came shouts of "Viva la España!" "Viva Ysabel Segunda!" "Viva el Ministro de España!" Great and continued
cheering. Then C——n gave in return, "Viva la Republica Mexicana!" "Viva Bustamente!" and the shouting was tremendous.
At last an Andalusian in the crowd shouted out, "Viva todo

el Mundo!" (Long live everybody), which piece of wit was followed by general laughter.

After hot punch and cigars had been handed about out of doors, a necessary refreshment in this cold night, the music recommenced, and the whole ended with the national hymn of Spain, with appropriate words. A young Spanish girl, whose voice is celebrated here, was then entreated by those within, and beseeched by those without, to sing alone the hymn composed in honour of C——n, which she naturally felt some hesitation in doing before such an immense audience. However, she consented at last, and in a voice like a clarion, accompanied by the orchestra, sung each verse alone, joined in the chorus by the whole crowd. I give you a copy:

Himno Patriótico que varios Españoles, Residentes en México, dedican al Esmo. Sr. Don A—— C—— de la B——, Ministro Plenipotenciario de S. M. C. en lá República, con Motivo de su Llegada á dicha Capital.

Musica del Sr. J. N. de Retes; Palabras del Sr. Dn. Juan Covo.

CORO.

> *Triunfamos, amigos,*
> *Triunfamos enfin,*
> *Y libre respir*
> *La Patria del Cid.*

> *La augusta* Cristina,
> *De España embeleso,*
> *El mas tierno beso*
> *Imprime á* Ysabel:
> *Y "Reina," le dice,*
> *"No ia sobre esclavos;*
> *Sobre Iberos bravos,*
> *Sobre un pueblo fiel."*

> *Triunfamos, amigos, etc.*

> *Donde está de Carlos*
> *La perfida hueste?*
> *Un rayo celeste*
> *Polvo la tornó.*
> *Rayo que al malvado*
> *Hundió en el abismo—*

Rayo que al Carlismo
Libertad lanzó.

Triunfamos, amigos, etc.

Al bravo Caudillo,
Al bueno, al valiente,
Ciñamos la frente
De mirto y laurel.
Tu diestra animosa,
Heroico guerrero,
Tu diestra, Espartero,
Sojuzgó al infiel.

Triunfamos, amigos, etc.

Veranse acatadas
Nuestras santas leyes;
Temblaran los Reyes
De España al poder.
Y el cetro de oprobrio,
Si empuna un tirano,
De su infame mano
Le harémos cær.

Triunfamos, amigos, etc.

Salud á Ysabela,
Salud á Cristina,
Quel el cielo destina
La patria á salvar.
Y el libre corone
La candida frente
De aquella inocente
Que juró amparar.

Triunfamos, amigos, etc.

Y tu, mensagero
De paz y ventura,
Oye la voz pura
De nuestra lealtad.
Oye los acentos
Que al cielo elevamos,

Oye cual gritamos,
Patria! Libertad!

> *Triunfamos, amigos, etc.*

Tu el símbolo digno
Serás, C——n,
De grata reunion,
De eterna amistad,
Que ya, en ambos mundos,
La insana discordia
Trocóse en concordia
Y fraternidad.

> *Triunfamos, amigos, etc.*

TRANSLATION.

Patriotic Hymn which various Spaniards, resident in Mexico, dedicate to his Excellency Señor Don A—— C—— de la B——, Minister Plenipotentiary and Envoy Extraordinary from H. C. M. to the Republic, to celebrate his arrival in this Capital.

The music by Señor Don J. N. DE RETES; the words by Señor Don JUAN COVO.

CHORUS.

> Let us triumph, my friends,
> Let us triumph at length,
> And let the country of the Cid
> Breathe freely again.

The august Christina,
The ornament of Spain,
Imprinted the most tender kiss
On the cheek of Isabel.
And "Reign," she said to her,
"Not now over slaves,
But over brave Iberians,
Over a faithful people!"

> Let us triumph, my friends, etc.

Where is the perfidious
Army of Carlos?

A celestial thunderbolt
Has turned it to dust—
A thunderbolt which plunged
The wicked one into the abyss—
A thunderbolt which Liberty
Launched against Carlism.

    Let us triumph, my friends, etc.

Of the brave chief,
Of the good, the valiant,
Let us gird the forehead
With myrtle and laurel.
Thy brave right hand,
Heroic warrior,
Thy right hand, Espartero,
Subdued the disloyal one.

    Let us triumph, my friends, etc.

Our holy laws
Will be acknowledged,
And kings will tremble
At the power of Spain;
And should a tyrant grasp
The sceptre of opprobrium,
From his infamous hand
We shall cause it to fall.

    Let us triumph, my friends, etc.

Health to Isabella,
Health to Christina,
Whom Heaven has destined
To save the country;
And may he freely crown
The white forehead
Of the innocent princess
He swore to protect.

    Let us triumph, my friends, etc.

And thou, messenger
Of peace and joy,
Hear the pure voice
Of our loyalty;

Hear the accents
Which we raise to Heaven;
Hear what we cry,
Country! Liberty!

Let us triumph, my friends, etc.

Thou, C——n, shalt be
The worthy symbol
Of grateful reunion,
Of eternal friendship,
Which already has changed,
In both worlds,
Insane discord
Into concord and fraternity.

Let us triumph, my friends, etc.

The air was rent with vivas! and bravos! as the Señorita de F—— concluded. Her voice was beautiful, and after the first moment of embarrassment, she sang with much spirit and enthusiasm. This was the finale of the serenade, and then the serenaders were invited in, and were in such numbers that the room would scarcely hold them all. More cigars, more punch, more giving of thanks. About three o'clock the crowd began to disperse, and at length, after those Spanish leave-takings, which are really no joke, had ended, Captain E——, C——n, and I, all three excessively cold and shivering, having passed the night at the open windows, consoled ourselves with hot chocolate and punch, and went to dream of sweet-sounding harmonies. Altogether, it was a scene which I would not have missed for a great deal.

The enthusiasm caused by the arrival of the first minister from Spain seems gradually to increase. The actors are to give him a *"funcion extraordinaria,"* in the theatre—the matadors a bull-fight extraordinary, with fireworks. . . . But in all this you must not suppose there is any personal compliment. It is merely intended as a mark of good will towards the first representative of the Spanish monarchy who brings from the mother-country the formal acknowledgment of Mexican independence.

*Début in Mexico—Cathedral—Temple of the Aztecs—Congre-
gation—Stone of Sacrifices—Palace—Importunate Léperos—
Visit to the President—Countess C——a—Street-cries—Tortilleras—*Sartor Resartus.

I made my *début* in Mexico by going to mass in the cathedral.
We drove through the Alameda, near which we live, and admired its noble trees, flowers, and fountains, all sparkling in
the sun. We met but few carriages there, an occasional gentleman on horseback, and a few solitary-looking people resting
on the stone benches, also plenty of beggars, and the *forçats* in
chains, watering the avenues. We passed through the Calle
San Francisco, the handsomest street in Mexico, both as to
shops and houses (containing, amongst others, the richly-
carved but now half-ruined palace of Yturbide), and which
terminates in the great square where stand the cathedral and
the palace. The streets were crowded, it being a holiday; and
the purity of the atmosphere, with the sun pouring down upon
the bright-coloured groups, and these groups so picturesque,
whether of soldiers or monks, peasants or veiled ladies; the
very irregularity of the buildings, the number of fine churches
and old convents, and everything on so grand a scale, even
though touched by the finger of time, or crushed by the iron
heel of revolution, that the attention is constantly kept alive,
and the interest excited.

The carriage drew up in front of the cathedral, built upon
the site of part of the ruins of the great temple of the Aztecs;
of that pyramidal temple, constructed by *Ahuitzotli*, the sanctuary so celebrated by the Spaniards, and which comprehended with all its different edifices and sanctuaries, the
ground on which the cathedral now stands, together with part
of the plaza and streets adjoining.

We are told, that within its enclosure were five hundred
dwellings, that its hall was built of stone and lime, and ornamented with stone serpents. We hear of its four great gates,
fronting the four cardinal points of its stone-paved court, great
stone stairs, and sanctuaries dedicated to the gods of war; of
the square destined for religious dances, and the colleges for

the priests, and seminaries for the priestesses; of the horrible temple, whose door was an enormous serpent's mouth; of the temple of mirrors and that of shells; of the house set apart for the emperor's prayers; of the consecrated fountains, the birds kept for sacrifice, the gardens for the holy flowers, and of the terrible towers composed of the skulls of the victims—strange mixture of the beautiful and the horrible! We are told that five thousand priests chanted night and day in the Great Temple, to the honour and in the service of the monstrous idols, who were anointed thrice a day with the most precious perfumes; and that of these priests the most austere were clothed in black, their long hair dyed with ink, and their bodies anointed with the ashes of burnt scorpions and spiders; their chiefs were the sons of kings.

It is remarkable, by the way, that their god of war, *Mejitli*, was said to have been born of a woman, *a Holy Virgin*, who was in the service of the temple; and that when the priests, having knowledge of her disgrace, would have stoned her, a voice was heard, saying, "Fear not, mother, for I shall save thy honour and my glory," upon which the god was born, with a shield in his left hand, an arrow in his right, a plume of green feathers on his head, his face painted blue, and his left leg adorned with feathers! Thus was his gigantic statue represented.

There were gods of the Water, of the Earth, of Night, Fire, and Hell; goddesses of Flowers and of Corn: there were oblations offered of bread and flowers and jewels, but we are assured that from twenty to fifty thousand human victims were sacrificed annually in Mexico alone! That these accounts are exaggerated, even though a bishop is among the narrators, we can scarcely doubt; but if the tenth part be truth, let the memory of Cortes be sacred, who, with the cross, stopped the shedding of innocent blood, founded the cathedral on the ruins of the temple which had so often resounded with human groans, and in the place of these blood-smeared idols enshrined the mild form of the Virgin.

Meanwhile we entered the Christian edifice, which covers an immense space of ground, is of the Gothic form, with two lofty ornamented towers, and is still immensely rich in gold, silver, and jewels. A balustrade running through it, which was brought from China, is said to be very valuable, but seems to me more curious than beautiful. It is a composition of brass and silver. Not a soul was in the sacred precincts this morning but miserable *léperos*, in rags and blankets, mingled with women in ragged *rebosos;*—at least a sprinkling of ladies with mantillas was so very slight, that I do not think there were half a dozen in all. The floor is so dirty that one kneels with a feeling of horror, and an inward determination to effect as speedy a change of garments afterwards as possible. Besides, many of my Indian neighbours were engaged in an occupation which I must leave to your imagination; in fact, relieving their heads from the pressure of the colonial system, or rather, eradicating and slaughtering the colonists, who swarm there like the emigrant Irish in the United States. I was not sorry to find myself once more in the pure air after mass; and have since been told that, except on peculiar occasions, and at certain hours, few ladies perform their devotions in the cathedral. I shall learn all these particulars in time.

We saw, as we passed out, the Aztec Calendar,—a round stone covered with hieroglyphics, which is still preserved and fastened on the outside of the cathedral. We afterwards saw the Stone of Sacrifices, now in the courtyard of the university, with a hollow in the middle, in which the victim was laid, while six priests, dressed in red, their heads adorned with plumes of green feathers (they must have looked like macaws), with gold and green earrings, and blue stones in their upper lips, held him down while the chief priest cut open his breast, threw his heart at the feet of the idol, and afterwards put it into his mouth with a golden spoon. They then cut off his head, to make use of it in building the tower of skulls, ate some parts of him, and either burnt the rest, or threw it to the wild beasts who were maintained in the palace.

These interesting particulars occurred to us as we looked at the stone, and we were not sorry to think that it is now more ornamental than useful.

After leaving the cathedral, C——n fastened on his orders in the carriage, as this day was appointed for his presentation to the President, and we drove to the place, where I left him, and returned home. He was received with great etiquette, a band of music playing in the court, the President in full uniform, surrounded by all his ministers and aides-de-camp, standing before a throne, under a velvet dais, his feet upon a tabouret, the whole being probably the same as was used by the viceroys. *Viva la Republica!* C——n made a discourse to him, and he made one in return, both of which may be found by those who are curious in these matters, in the *Diario* of the 31st December. . . .

Whilst I am writing a horrible lépero, with great leering

eyes, is looking at me through the windows, and performing
the most extraordinary series of groans, displaying at the same
time a hand with two long fingers, probably the other three
tied in. "Señorita! Señorita! For the love of the most Holy Virgin! For the sake of the most pure blood of Christ! By the
miraculous Conception!——" The wretch! I dare not look up,
but I feel that his eyes are fixed upon a gold watch and seals
lying on the table. That is the worst of a house on the ground
floor. . . . There come more of them! A paralytic woman
mounted on the back of a man with a long beard. A sturdy-
looking individual, who looks as if, were it not for the iron
bars, he would resort to more effective measures, is holding up
a *deformed foot*, which I verily believe is merely fastened back
in some extraordinary way. What groans! what rags! what a
chorus of whining! This concourse is probably owing to our
having sent them some money yesterday. I try to take no notice, and write on as if I were deaf. I must walk out of the
room, without looking behind me, and send the porter to disperse them. There are no bell-ropes in these parts. . . .

I come back again to write, hardly recovered from the start
that I have just got. I had hardly written the last words, when
I heard a footstep near me, and, looking up, lo! there was my
friend with *the foot*, standing within a yard of me, his hand
stretched out for alms! I was so frightened, that for a moment
I thought of giving him my watch, to get rid of him. However,
I glided past him with a few unintelligible words, and rushed
to call the servants; sending him some money by the first person who came. The porter, who had not seen him pass, is now
dispersing the crowd. What vociferous exclamations! A—— has
come in and drawn the curtains, and I think they are going off.

Yesterday evening I was taken to visit the President. The
palace is an immense building, containing, besides the apartments of the President and his ministers, all the chief courts
of justice. It occupies one side of the square, but is no way
remarkable in its architecture. At the end of every flight of
steps that we mounted we came upon lounging soldiers, in
their yellow cloaks, and women in rebosos, standing about. We
passed through a hall filled with soldiers, into the antecham-
ber, where we were received by several aides-de-camp, who
conducted us into a very well-furnished room, where we sat a
few minutes, till an officer came to lead us into the reception-
room, which is a handsome apartment, about a hundred feet
long, and fitted up with crimson and gold, also well lighted.

General Bustamante, now in plain clothes, gave us a very cordial reception.

He looks like a good man, with an honest, benevolent face, frank and simple in his manners, and not at all like a hero. His conversation was not brilliant, indeed I do not know apropos to what, I suppose to the climate, but it chiefly turned on *medicine*. There cannot be a greater contrast, both in appearance and reality, than between him and Santa Anna. There is no lurking devil in his eye. All is frank, open, and unreserved. It is impossible to look in his face without believing him to be an honest and well-intentioned man. An unprincipled but clever writer has said of him, that he has no great capacity or superior genius; but that, whether from reflection or from slowness of comprehension, he is always extremely calm in his determinations: that, before entering into any project, he inquires and considers deeply as to whether it be just or not; but that once convinced that it is or appears to be so, he sustains his ground with firmness and constancy. He adds, that it suits him better to obey than to command; for which reason he was always so devoted a servant of the Spaniards and of Yturbide.

He is said to be a devoted friend, is honest to a proverb, and personally brave, though occasionally deficient in moral energy. He is therefore an estimable man, and one who will do his duty to the best of his ability, though whether he has severity and energy sufficient for those evil days in which it is his lot to govern, may be problematical.

Having made a sufficiently long visit to his Excellency, we went to return that of the Countess C——, who has a magnificent house, with suites of large rooms, of which the drawing-room is particularly handsome, of immense size, the walls beautifully painted, the subjects religious, and where I found one of Broadwood's finest grand pianos. But although there are cabinets inlaid with gold, fine paintings, and hundreds of rich and curious things, our European eyes are struck with numerous inconsistencies in dress, servants, etc., in all of which there is a want of keeping very remarkable. Yet this house, and the one adjoining, which also belongs to the family, are palaces in vastness, and the Countess receives me more as if I were her daughter, than a person with whom she has been acquainted but a few days.

There are an extraordinary number of street-cries in Mexico, which begin at dawn and continue till night, performed by hundreds of discordant voices, impossible to understand at first; but Señor —— has been giving me an explanation of them, until I begin to have some distinct idea of their meaning. At dawn you are awakened by the shrill and desponding cry of the Carbonero, the coalmen, "Carbon, Señor?" which, as he pronounces it, sounds like "Carbosiu?" Then the grease-man takes up the song, "Mantequilla! lard! lard! at one real and a half." "Salt beef! good salt beef!" ("Cecina buena!") interrupts the butcher in a hoarse voice. "Hay cebo-o-o-o-o-o?" This is the prolonged and melancholy note of the woman who buys kitchen-stuff, and stops before the door. Then passes by the *cambista,* a sort of Indian she-trader or exchanger, who sings out, "Tejocotes por venas de chile?" a small fruit which she proposes exchanging for hot peppers. No harm in that.

A kind of ambulating pedler drowns the shrill treble of the Indian cry. He calls aloud upon the public to buy needles, pins, thimbles, shirt-buttons, tape, cotton-balls, small mirrors, etc. He enters the house, and is quickly surrounded by the women, young and old, offering him the tenth part of what he asks, and which, after much haggling, he accepts. Behind him stands the Indian with his tempting baskets of fruit, of which he calls out all the names, till the cook or housekeeper can resist no longer, and putting her head over the balustrade, calls him up with his bananas, and oranges, and granaditas, etc.

A sharp note of interrogation is heard, indicating something that is hot, and must be snapped up quickly before it cools. "Gorditas de horna caliente?" "Little fat cakes from the oven, hot?" This is in a female key, sharp and shrill. Follows the mat-seller. "Who wants mats from Puebla? mats of five yards?" These are the most matinal cries.

At midday the beggars begin to be particularly importunate, and their cries, and prayers, and long recitations, form a running accompaniment to the other noises. Then above all rises the cry of "Honey-cakes!" "Cheese and honey?" "Requeson and good honey?" (*Requeson* being a sort of hard curd, sold in cheeses.) Then come the dulce-men, the sellers of sweetmeats, of meringues, which are very good, and of all sorts of candy. "Caramelos de esperma! bocadillo de coco!" Then the lottery-men, the messengers of Fortune, with their shouts of "The last ticket yet unsold, for half a real!" a tempting announcement to the lazy beggar, who finds it easier to gamble than to work, and who may have that sum hid about his rags.

Towards evening rises the cry of "Tortillas de cuajada?"

"Curd-cakes?" or, "Do you take nuts?" succeeded by the night-cry of "Chestnuts hot and roasted!" and by the affectionate vendors of ducks; "Ducks, oh my soul, hot ducks!" "Maize-cakes," etc., etc. As the night wears away, the voices die off, to resume next morning in fresh vigour.

Tortillas, which are the common food of the people, and which are merely maize cakes mixed with a little lime, and of the form and size of what we call *scones,* I find rather good when very hot and fresh-baked, but insipid by themselves. They have been in use all through this country since the earliest ages of its history, without any change in the manner of baking them, excepting that, for the noble Mexicans in former days, they used to be kneaded with various medicinal plants, supposed to render them more wholesome. They are considered particularly palatable with *chile,* to endure which, in the quantities in which it is eaten here, it seems to me necessary to have a throat lined with tin.

In unpacking some books to-day, I happened to take up "*Sartor Resartus,*" which, by a curious coincidence, opened of itself, to my great delight, at the following passage:

"The simplest costume," observes our Professor, "which I anywhere find alluded to in history, is that used as regimental by Bolivar's cavalry, in the late Columbian wars. A square blanket, twelve feet in diagonal, is provided, (some were wont to cut off the corners, and make it circular;) in the centre a slit is effected, eighteen inches long; through this the mother-naked trooper introduces his head and neck; and so rides, shielded from all weather, and in battle from many strokes (for he rolls it about his left arm); and not only dressed, but harnessed and draperied." Here then we find the true "Old Roman contempt of the superfluous," which seems rather to meet the approbation of the illustrious Professor Teufelsdroch.

LETTER THE EIGHTH

Ball in Preparation—Agreeable Family—Fine Voices—Theatre —Smoking—Castle of Chapultepec—Viceroy Galvez—Montezuma's Cypress—Vice-Queen—Valley of Mexico—New Year's Day—Opening of Congress—Visits from the Diplomatic Corps—Poblana Dress—"Function extraordinaria"— Theatre—Visit to the Cathedral of Guadalupe—Divine Painting—Bishop—Beggars—Mosquitoes' Eggs.

A great ball is to be given on the 8th of January, in the theatre, for the benefit of the poor, which is to be under the patronage of the most distinguished ladies of Mexico. After much deliberation amongst the patronesses, it is decided that it shall be a *bal costumé*, and I have some thoughts of going in the Poblana dress, which I before described to you. As I am told that the Señora G——a wore it at a ball in London, when her husband was minister there, I have sent my maid to learn the particulars from her.

We called to-day on a family nearly related to the C——as, and who have been already excessively kind to us; Señor A——d, who is married to a daughter of Don Francisco Tagle, a very distinguished Mexican. We found a very large, very handsome house, the walls and roof painted in the old Spanish style, which, when well executed, has an admirable effect. The lady of the house, who is only nineteen, I took a fancy to at first sight. She is not regularly beautiful, but has lovely dark eyes and eyebrows, with fair complexion and fair hair, and an expression of the most perfect goodness, with very amiable manners. I was surprised by hearing her sing several very difficult Italian songs with great expression and wonderful facility. She has a fine contralto, which has been cultivated; but some Spanish ballads, and little songs of the country, she sang so delightfully, and with so much good-nature and readiness, that had it not been a first visit, I should have begged her to continue during half the morning. Fine voices are said to be extremely common, as is natural in a country peopled from Spain; and the opera, while it lasted, contributed greatly to the cultivation of musical taste.

In the evening we went to the theatre. Such a theatre! Dark, dirty, redolent of bad odours; the passages leading to the boxes so ill-lighted, that one is afraid in the dark to pick one's steps through them. The acting was nearly of a piece. The first actress, who is a favourite, and who dresses well, and bears a high reputation for good conduct, is perfectly wooden, and never frightened out of her proprieties in the most tragical scenes. I am sure there is not a fold deranged in her dress when she goes home. Besides, she has a most remarkable trick of pursing up her mouth in a smile, and frowning at the same time with tears in her eyes, as if personifying an April day. I should like to hear her sing

"Said a smile to a tear."

There was no applause, and half the boxes were empty, whilst those who were there seemed merely to occupy them from the effect of habit, and because this is the only evening amusement. The prompter spoke so loud, that as

"Coming events cast their shadows before,"

every word was made known to the audience in confidence, before it came out upon the stage officially. The whole pit smoked, the galleries smoked, the boxes smoked, the prompter smoked, a long stream of smoke curling from his box, giving something oracular and Delphic to his prophecies.

"The force of smoking could no further go."

The theatre is certainly unworthy of this fine city.

31st.—We have spent the day in visiting the castle of Chapultepec, a short league from Mexico, the most haunted by recollections of all the traditionary sites of which Mexico can boast. Could these hoary cypresses speak, what tales might they not disclose, standing there with their long gray beards, and outstretched venerable arms, century after century: already old when Montezuma was a boy, and still vigorous in the days of Bustamante! There has the last of the Aztec emperors wandered with his dark-eyed harem. Under the shade of these gigantic trees he has rested, perhaps smoked his "tobacco mingled with amber," and fallen to sleep, his dreams unhaunted by visions of the stern traveller from the far-east, whose sails even then might be within sight of the shore. In these tanks he has bathed. Here were his gardens, and his aviaries, and his fish-ponds. Through these now tangled and deserted woods, he may have been carried by his young nobles in his open litter, under a splendid dais, stepping out upon the rich stuffs which his slaves spread before him on the green and velvet turf.

And from the very rock where the castle stands, he may have looked out upon his fertile valley and great capital, with its canoe-covered lakes and outspreading villages and temples, and gardens of flowers, no care for the future darkening the bright vision!

Tradition says, that now these caves and tanks and woods are haunted by the shade of the conqueror's Indian love, the far-famed Doña Marina, but I think she would be afraid of meeting with the wrathful spirit of the Indian emperor.

The castle itself, modern though it be, seems like a tradition! The Viceroy Galvez, who built it, is of a bygone race! The apartments are lonely and abandoned, the walls falling to ruin, the glass of the windows and the carved work of the doors have been sold; and standing at this great height, exposed to every wind that blows, it is rapidly falling to decay. We were accompanied by Count C——a, and received by a Mexican governor, who rarely resides there, and who very civilly conducted us everywhere. But Chapultepec is not a *show-place*. One must go there early in the morning, when the dew is on the grass, or in the evening, when the last rays of the sun are gilding with rosy light the snowy summits of the volcanoes; and dismount from your horse, or step out of your carriage and wander forth without guide or object, or fixed time for return.

We set off early, passing over a fine paved road, divided by a great and solid aqueduct of nine hundred arches, one of the two great aqueducts by which fresh water is conveyed to the city, and of which the two sources are in the hill of Chapultepec, and in that of Santa Fé, at a much greater distance. When we arrived, the sleepy soldiers, who were lounging before the gates, threw them open to let the carriage enter, and we drew up in front of the great cypress, known by the name of "Montezuma's Cypress," a most stupendous tree—dark, solemn, and stately, its branches unmoved as the light wind played amongst them, of most majestic height, and forty-one feet in circumference. A second cypress standing near, and of almost equal size, is even more graceful, and they, and all the noble trees which adorn these speaking solitudes, are covered with a creeping plant, resembling gray moss, hanging over every branch like long gray hair, giving them a most venerable and druidical look.

We wandered through the noble avenues, and rested under

the trees, and walked through the tangled shrubberies, bright with flowers and coloured berries, and groped our way into the cave, and stood by the large clear tank, and spent some time in the old garden; and then got again into the carriage, that we might be dragged up the precipitous ascent on which stands the castle, the construction of which aroused the jealousy of the government against the young count, whose taste for the picturesque had induced him to choose this elevated site for his summer palace.

The interior was never finished; yet, even as it stands, it cost the Spanish government three hundred thousand dollars. When we look at its strong military capabilities and commanding position, fortified with salient walls and parapets towards Mexico, and containing on its northern side great moats and subterraneous vaults, capable of holding a vast supply of provisions, the jealousy of the government, and their suspicions that it was a fortress masked as a summer retreat, are accountable enough.

The Vice-Queen Galvez, was celebrated for her beauty and goodness, and was universally adored in Mexico. A sister of hers, who still survives, and who paid me a visit the other day, says that her beauty chiefly consisted in the exceeding fairness of her complexion, very few *blondes* having then been seen in this part of the world.

From the terrace that runs round the castle, the view forms the most magnificent panorama that can be imagined. The whole valley of Mexico lies stretched out as in a map; the city itself, with its innumerable churches and convents; the two great aqueducts which cross the plain; the avenues of elms and poplars which lead to the city; the villages, lakes, and plains, which surround it. To the north, the magnificent cathedral of Our Lady of Guadalupe—to the south, the villages of San Augustin, San Angel, and Tacubaya, which seem imbosomed in trees, and look like an immense garden. And if in the plains below there are many uncultivated fields, and many buildings falling to ruin, yet with its glorious enclosure of mountains, above which tower the two mighty volcanoes, Popocatepetl and Iztaccihuatl, the Gog and Magog of the valley, off whose giant sides great volumes of misty clouds were rolling, and with its turquoise sky for ever smiling on the scene, the whole landscape, as viewed from this height, is one of nearly unparalleled beauty.

1st January, 1840.—New Year's Day! The birth of the young year is ushered in by no remarkable signs of festivity. More ringing of bells, more chanting of mass, gayer dresses amongst the peasants in the streets, and more carriages passing along, and the ladies within rather more dressed than apparently they usually are, when they do not intend to pay visits. In passing through the Plaza this morning, our carriage suddenly drew up, and the servants took off their hats. At the same moment, the whole population, men, women, and children, vendors and buyers, peasant and señora, priest and layman, dropped on their knees, a picturesque sight. Presently a coach came slowly along through the crowd, with the mysterious *Eye* painted on the panels, drawn by piebald horses, and with priests within, bearing the divine symbols. On the balconies, in the shops, in the houses, and on the streets, every one knelt while it passed, the little bell giving warning of its approach.

We were then at the door of the palace, where we went this morning to see the opening of Congress, the two houses being included in this building. The House of Representatives, though not large, is handsome, and in good taste. Opposite to the presidential chair is a full-length representation of Our Lady of Guadalupe. All round the hall, which is semi-circular, are inscribed the names of the heroes of independence, and that of the Emperor Augustin Yturbide is placed on the right of the presidential chair, with his sword hanging on the wall; while on the left of the chief magistrate's seat there is a vacant space; perhaps destined for the name of another emperor. The multitude of priests with their large shovel-hats, and the entrance of the president in full uniform, announced by music and a flourish of trumpets, and attended by his staff, rendered it as anti-republican-looking an assembly as one could wish to see. The utmost decorum and tranquillity prevailed. The president made a speech in a low and rather monotonous tone, which in the diplomate's seat, where we were, was scarcely audible. No ladies were in the house, myself excepted; which I am glad I was not aware of before going, or I should perhaps have stayed away.

Yesterday I received visits from the gentlemen of the diplomatic corps, who are not in great numbers here. England, Belgium, Prussia, and the United States, are the only countries at present represented, Spain excepted. The French minister has not arrived yet, but is expected in a few days. I was not sorry to hear English spoken once more, and to meet with so gentlemanly a person as the minister who for the last fourteen years has represented our island in the Republic. His visit and a large packet of letters just received from Paris and from the United States, have made me feel as if the distance from home were diminished by one-half.

This morning a very handsome dress was forwarded to me with the compliments of a lady whom I do not know, the wife of General ——; with a request that, if I should go to the fancy ball as a Poblana peasant, I may wear this costume. It is a Poblana dress, and very superb, consisting of a petticoat of maroon-coloured merino, with gold fringe, gold bands and spangles; an under-petticoat, embroidered and trimmed with rich lace, to come below it. The first petticoat is trimmed with gold up the sides, which are slit open, and tied up with coloured ribbon. With this must be worn a chemise, richly embroidered round the neck and sleeves, and trimmed with lace; a satin vest, open in front, and embroidered in gold; a silk sash tied behind, the ends fringed with gold, and a small silk handkerchief which crosses the neck, with gold fringe. I had already another dress prepared, but I think this is the handsomer of the two.

The actors have just called to inform C——n, that their *"funcion extraordinaria"* in his honour, is to be given on the third, that a box is prepared for us, and that the play is to be "Don John of Austria."[1]

4th.—Having sat through five acts last evening in the theatre, we came home very tired. The play was *awfully* long, lasting from eight o'clock till one in the morning. At the end of the first act, the prefect and other dignitaries came round with much precipitation and carried off C——n to a large box in the centre, intended for him; for, not knowing which it was, we had gone to that of the Countess C——a. The theatre looked much more decent than before; being lighted up, and the boxes hung with silk draperies in honour of the occasion. The ladies also were in full dress, and the boxes crowded, so that one could scarcely recognise the house.

This morning we drove out to see the cathedral of Our Lady of Guadalupe: C——n in one carriage with Count C——a, and the Señora C——a and I in another, driven by Señor A——d, who is a celebrated whip; the carriage open, with handsome white horses, *frisones,* as they here call the northern horses, whether from England or the United States, and which are much larger than the spirited little horses of the country. As usual, we were accompanied by four armed outriders.

We passed through miserable suburbs, ruined, dirty, and

[1] Translated from the French of Casimir Delavigne.

with a commingling of odours which I could boldly challenge those of Cologne to rival. After leaving the town, the road is not particularly pretty, but is for the most part a broad, straight avenue, bounded on either side by trees.

At Guadalupe, on the hill of Tepayac, there stood, in days of yore, the Temple of Tonantzin, the goddess of earth and of corn, a mild deity, who rejected human victims, and was only to be propitiated by the sacrifices of turtle-doves, swallows, pigeons, etc. She was the protectress of the Totonoqui Indians. The spacious church, which now stands at the foot of the mountain, is one of the richest in Mexico. Having put on veils, no bonnets being permitted within the precincts of a church, we entered this far-famed sanctuary, and were dazzled by the profusion of silver with which it is ornamented.

The divine painting of the Virgin of Guadalupe, represents her in a blue cloak covered with stars, a garment of crimson and gold, her hands clasped, and her foot on a crescent, supported by a cherub. The painting is coarse, and only remarkable on account of the tradition attached to it.

We afterwards visited a small chapel, covered by a dome, built over a boiling spring, whose waters possess miraculous qualities, and bought crosses and medals which have touched the holy image, and pieces of white ribbon, marked with the measure of the Virgin's hands and feet. We climbed (albeit very warm) by a steep path to the top of the hill, where there is another chapel, from which there is a superb view of Mexico; and beside it, a sort of monument in the form of the sails of a ship, erected by a grateful Spaniard, to commemorate his escape from shipwreck, which he believed to be owing to the intercession of Our Lady of Guadalupe. We then went to the village to call on the bishop, the Ylustrisimo Señor Campos, whom we found in his canonicals, and who seems a good little old man, but no conjurer; although I believe he had the honour of bringing up his cousin, Señor Posada, destined to be Archbishop of Mexico. We found him quietly seated in a large, simply-furnished room, and apparently buried over some huge volume, so that he was not at first aware of our entrance.

A picture of the Virgin of Guadalupe hung on the wall, which C——n having noticed, he observed that he could not answer for its being a very faithful resemblance, as Our Lady did not appear often, not so often as people supposed. Then folding his hands, and looking down, he proceeded to recount the history of the miraculous apparition, pretty much as follows:

In 1531, ten years and four months after the conquest of Mexico, the fortunate Indian whose name was Juan Diego, and who was a native of Cuatitlan, went to the suburb of Tlaltelolco to learn the Christian doctrine which the Franciscan monks taught there. As he was passing by the mountain of Tepeyac, the Holy Virgin suddenly appeared before him and ordered him to go, in her name, to the bishop, the Ylustrisimo D. Fr. Juan de Zumarraga, and to make known to him that she desired to have a place of worship erected in her honour, on that spot. The next day the Indian passed by the same place, when again the Holy Virgin appeared before him, and demanded the result of his commission. Juan Diego replied, that in spite of his endeavours, he had not been able to obtain an audience of the bishop. "Return," said the Virgin, "and say that it is I, the Virgin Mary, the Mother of God, who sends thee." Juan Diego obeyed the divine orders, yet still the bishop would not give him credence, merely desiring him to bring some sign or token of the Virgin's will. He returned with this message on the twelfth of December, when, for the third time, he beheld the apparition of the Virgin. She now commanded him to climb to the top of the barren rock of Tepeyac, to gather the roses which he should find there, and to bring them to her. The humble messenger obeyed, though well knowing that on that spot were neither flowers nor any trace of vegetation. Nevertheless, he found the roses, which he gathered and brought to the Virgin Mary, who, throwing them into his *tilma,* said, "Return, show these to the bishop, and tell him that these are the credentials of thy mission." Juan Diego set out for the episcopal house, which stood on the ground occupied by the hospital, now called San Juan de Dios, and when he found himself in the presence of the prelate, he unfolded his *tilma* to show him the roses, when there appeared imprinted on it the miraculous image which had existed for more than three centuries.

When the bishop beheld it, he was seized with astonishment and awe, and conveyed it in a solemn procession to his own oratory, and shortly after, this splendid church was erected in honour of the patroness of New Spain. "From all parts of the country," continued the old bishop, "people flocked in crowds to see Our Lady of Guadalupe, and esteemed it an honour to obtain a sight of her. What then must be *my* happiness, who can see her most gracious majesty every hour and every minute of the day! I would not quit Guadalupe for any other part of the world, nor for any temptation that could be held out to me;" and the pious man remained for a few minutes as if wrapt in ecstasy. That he was sincere in his assertions, there could be no doubt. As evening prayers were about to begin, we accompanied him to the cathedral. An old woman opened the door for us as we passed out. "Have my chocolate ready when I return," said the bishop. "Si, padrecito!" said the old woman, dropping upon her knees, in which posture she remained for some minutes. As we passed along the street, the sight of the reverend man had the same effect; all fell on their knees as he passed, precisely as if the host were carried by, or the shock of an earthquake were felt. Arrived at the door of the cathedral, he gave us his hand, or rather his pastoral amethyst, to kiss.

The organ sounded fine as it pealed through the old cathedral, and the setting sun poured his rays in through the Gothic windows with a rich and glowing light. The church was crowded with people of the village, but especially with *léperos,* counting their beads, and suddenly in the midst of an "Ave Maria Purisima," flinging themselves and their rags in our path with a "Por el amor de la Santisima Virgen!" and if this does not serve their purpose, they appeal to your domestic sympathies. From men they entreat relief "By the life of the Señorita." From women, "By the life of the little child!" From children it is "By the life of your mother!" And a mixture of piety and superstitious feeling makes most people, women at least, draw out their purses.

Count C——a has promised to send me to-morrow a box of mosquitoes' eggs, of which tortillas are made, which are considered a great delicacy. Considering mosquitoes as small winged *cannibals,* I was rather shocked at the idea, but they pretend that these which are from the Laguna, are a superior race of creatures, which do not sting. In fact the Spanish historians mention that the Indians used to eat bread made of the eggs which the fly called *agayacatl* laid on the rushes of the lakes, and which they (the Spaniards) found very palatable.

LETTER THE NINTH

5th January.

Yesterday (Sunday), a great day here for visiting after mass is over. We had a concourse of Spaniards, all of whom seemed anxious to know whether or not I intended to wear a Poblana dress at the fancy ball, and seemed wonderfully interested about it. Two young ladies or women of Puebla, introduced by Señor —— came to proffer their services in giving me all the necessary particulars, and dressed the hair of Josefa, a little Mexican girl, to show me how it should be arranged; mentioned several things still wanting, and told me that every one was much pleased at the idea of my going in a Poblana dress. I was rather surprised that *every one* should trouble themselves about it. About twelve o'clock the president, in full uniform, attended by his aides-de-camp, paid me a visit, and sat about half an hour, very amiable as usual. Shortly after came more visits, and just as we had supposed they were all concluded, and we were going to dinner, we were told that the secretary of state, the ministers of war and of the interior, and others, were in the drawing-room. And what do you think was the purport of their visit? To adjure me by all that was most alarming, to discard the idea of making my appearance in a Poblana dress! They assured us that Poblanas generally were *femmes de rien,* that they wore no stockings, and that the wife of the Spanish minister should by no means assume, even for one evening, such a costume. I brought in my dresses, showed their length and their propriety, but in vain; and, in fact, as to their being in the right, there could be no doubt, and nothing but a kind motive could have induced them to take this trouble; so I yielded with a good grace, and thanked the cabinet council for their timely warning, though fearing, that in this land of procrastination, it would be difficult to procure another dress for the fancy ball; for you must know, that our luggage is still toiling its weary way, on the backs of mules, from Vera Cruz to the capital. They had scarcely gone, when Señor — brought a message from several of the principal ladies here, whom we do not even know, and who had requested, that as a stranger, I should be informed of the reasons which rendered the Poblana dress objectionable in this country, especially on any public occasion like this ball. I was really thankful for my escape.

Just as I was dressing for dinner, a note was brought, marked *reservada* (private), the contents of which appeared to me more odd than pleasant. I have since heard, however, that the writer, Don José Arnaiz, is an old man, and a sort of privileged character, who interferes in everything, whether it concerns him or not. I translate it for your benefit.

"The dress of a Poblana is that of a woman of no character. The lady of the Spanish minister is a *lady* in every sense of the word. However much she may have compromised herself, she ought neither to go as a Poblana, nor in any other character but her own. So says to the Señor de C——n, José Arnaiz, who esteems him as much as possible."

6th.—Early this morning, this being the day of the "bull-fight extraordinary," placards were put up, as I understand, on all the corners of the streets, announcing it, accompanied by a portrait of C——n! Count C——a came soon after breakfast, accompanied by Bernardo, the first matador, whom he brought to present to us. I send you the white satin note of invitation, with its silver lace and tassels, to show you how beautifully they can get up such things here. The matador is a handsome but heavy-looking man, though said to be active and skilful. To-morrow I shall write you an account of my *first bull-fight.*

7th.—Yesterday, towards the afternoon, there were great fears of rain, which would have caused a postponement of the combat; however, the day cleared up, the bulls little knowing how much their fate depended upon the clouds. A box in the centre, with a carpet and a silver lamp, had been prepared for us; but we went with our friends, the C——as, into their box adjoining. The scene, to me especially, who have not seen the magnificence of the Madrid arena, was animating and brilliant in the highest degree. Fancy an immense amphitheatre, with four great tiers of boxes, and a range of uncovered seats in front, the whole crowded almost to suffocation; the boxes filled with ladies in full dress, and the seats below by gaily-dressed and most enthusiastic spectators; two military bands of music, playing beautiful airs from the operas; an extraordinary variety of brilliant costumes, all lighted up by the eternally deep-blue sky; ladies and peasants, and officers in full uniform,—and you may conceive that it must have been altogether a varied and curious spectacle.

About half-past six, a flourish of trumpets announced the president, who came in uniform with his staff, and took his seat to the music of "Guerra! Guerra! I bellici trombi." Shortly after the matadors and picadors, the former on foot, the latter on horseback, made their entry, saluting all around the arena, and were received with loud cheering.

Bernardo's dress of blue and silver was very superb, and cost him five hundred dollars. The signal was given—the gates were thrown open, and a bull sprang into the arena; not a great, fierce-looking animal, as they are in Spain, but a small, angry, wild-looking beast, with a troubled eye.

> "Thrice sounds the clarion; lo! the signal falls,
> The den expands, and expectation mute
> Gapes round the silent circle's peopled walls.
> Bounds with one lashing spring the mighty brute,
> And, wildly staring, spurns with sounding foot
> The sand, nor blindly rushes on his foe;
> Here, there, he points his threatening front, to suit
> His first attack, wide waving to and fro
> His angry tail; red rolls his eye's dilated glow."

A picture equally correct and poetical. That first *pose* of the bull is superb! Pasta, in her Medea, did not surpass it. Meanwhile the matadors and the *banderilleros* shook their coloured scarfs at him—the picadors poked at him with their lances. He rushed at the first, and tossed up the scarfs which they threw at him, while they sprung over the arena; galloped after the others, striking the horses, so that along with their riders they occasionally rolled in the dust; both, however, almost instantly recovering their equilibrium, in which there is no time to be lost. Then the matadors would throw fireworks, crackers adorned with streaming ribbons, which stuck on his horns, as he tossed his head, enveloped him in a blaze of fire. Occasionally the picador would catch hold of the bull's tail, and passing it under his own right leg, wheel his horse round, force the bullock to gallop backwards, and throw him on his face.

Maddened with pain, streaming with blood, stuck full of darts, and covered with fireworks, the unfortunate beast went galloping round and round, plunging blindly at man and horse, and frequently trying to leap the barrier, but driven back by the waving hats and shouting of the crowd. At last, as he stood at bay, and nearly exhausted, the matador ran up and gave him the mortal blow, considered a peculiar proof of skill. The bull stopped, as if he felt that his hour were come, staggered, made a few plunges at nothing, and fell. A finishing stroke, and the bull expired.

The trumpets sounded, the music played. Four horses galloped in tied to a yoke, to which the bull was fastened, and swiftly dragged out of the arena. This last part had a fine effect, reminding one of the Roman sacrifice. In a similar manner, eight bulls were done to death. The scene is altogether fine, the address amusing, but the wounding and tormenting of the bull is sickening, and as here the tips of his horns are blunted, one has more sympathy with him than with his human adversaries. It cannot be good to accustom a people to such bloody sights.

Yet let me confess, that though at first I covered my face and could not look, little by little I grew so much interested in the scene, that I could not take my eyes off it, and I can easily understand the pleasure taken in these barbarous diversions by those accustomed to them from childhood.

The bull-fight having terminated amidst loud and prolonged cheering from the crowd, a tree of fireworks, erected in the midst of the arena, was lighted, and amidst a blaze of coloured light, appeared, first the Arms of the Republic, the Eagle and Nopal; and above, a full-length portrait of C——n! represented by a figure in a blue and silver uniform. Down fell the Mexican eagle with a crash at his feet, while he remained burning brightly, and lighted up by fireworks, in the midst of tremendous shouts and cheers. Thus terminated this *"funcion extraordinaria;"* and when all was over, we went to dine at Countess C——a's; had some music in the evening, and afterwards returned home tolerably tired.

10th.—The fancy ball took place last evening in the theatre, and although, owing either to the change of climate, or to the dampness of the house, I have been obliged to keep my room since the day of the bull-fight, and to decline a pleasant dinner at the English Minister's, I thought it advisable to make my appearance there. Having discarded the costume of the light-headed Poblamanas, I adopted that of a virtuous Roman Contadina, simple enough to be run up in one day; a white skirt, red bodice, with blue ribbons, and lace veil put on square behind; *à propos* to which head-dress, it is very common amongst the Indians to wear a piece of stuff folded square, and laid flat upon the head, in this Italian fashion; and as it is not fastened, I cannot imagine how they trot along, without letting it fall.

We went to the theatre about eleven, and found the *entrée,* though crowded with carriages, very quiet and orderly. The *coup d'œil* on entering was extremely gay, and certainly very amusing. The ball, given for the benefit of the poor, was under the patronage of the ladies C——a, G——a, Guer——a, and others, but such was the original dirtiness and bad condition of the theatre, that to make it decent, they had expended nearly all the proceeds. As it was, and considering the various drawbacks, the arrangements were very good. Handsome lustres had superseded the lanterns with their tallow candles, the boxes were hung with bright silk draperies, and a canopy of the same drawn up in the form of a tent, covered the whole ball-room. The orchestra also was tolerably good. The boxes were filled with ladies, presenting an endless succession of China crape shawls of every colour and variety, and a monotony of diamond earrings; while in the theatre itself, if ever a ball might be termed a fancy-ball, this was that ball. Of Swiss peasants, Scotch peasants, and all manner of peasants, there were a goodly assortment; as also of Turks, Highlanders, and men in plain clothes. But being public, it was not, of course, select, and amongst many well-dressed people, there were hundreds who, assuming no particular character, had exerted their imagination to appear merely fanciful, and had succeeded. One, for example, would have a scarlet satin petticoat, and over it a pink satin robe, with scarlet ribbons to match. Another, a short blue satin dress, beneath which appeared a handsome purple satin petticoat; the whole trimmed with yellow bows. They looked like the signs of the zodiac. All had diamonds and pearls; old and young, and middle-aged; including little children, of whom there were many.

The lady patronesses were very elegant. The Señora de Gu——a, wore a head-dress in the form of a net, entirely composed of large pearls and diamonds; in itself a fortune. The Señora de C——a, as Madame de la Vallière, in black velvet

and diamonds, looking pretty as usual, but the cold of the
house obliged her to muffle up in furs and boas, and so to
hide her dress. The Señora de G——a, as Mary, Queen of
Scots, in black velvet and pearls, with a splendid diamond
necklace, was extremely handsome; she wore a cap, introduced
by the Albini, in the character of the Scottish Queen, but
which, though pretty in itself, is a complete deviation from
the beautiful simplicity of the real Queen-Mary cap. She certainly looked as if she had arrived at her prime without knowing Fotheringay.

Various ladies were introduced to me who are only waiting
to receive our cards of *faire part* before they call. Amongst
the girls, the best dresses that I observed were the Señoritas
de F——d, the one handsome, with the figure and face of a
Spanish peasant; the other much more graceful and intelligent-
looking, though with less actual beauty. However, so many of
the most fashionable people were in their boxes, that I am
told this is not a good occasion on which to judge of the beauty
or style of toilet of the Mexican women; besides which, these
fancy balls being uncommon, they would probably look better
in their usual costume. Upon the whole, I saw few striking
beauties, little grace, and very little good dancing. There was
too much velvet and satin, and the dresses were too much
loaded. The diamonds, though superb, were frequently ill-set.
The dresses, compared with the actual fashion, were absurdly
short, and the feet, naturally small, were squeezed into shoes
still smaller, which is destructive to grace, whether in walking
or dancing.

I saw many superb pairs of eyes, and beautiful hands and
arms, perfect models for a sculptor, the hands especially; and
very few good complexions.

There was a young gentleman pointed out to me as being
in the costume of a Highlander! How I wished that Sir William Cumming, Macleod of Macleod, or some veritable High-
land chieftain could suddenly have appeared to annihilate
him, and show the people here what the dress really is! There
were various unfortunate children bundled up in long satin
or velvet dresses, covered with blond and jewels, and with
artificial flowers in their hair.

The room was excessively cold, nor was the ancient odour
of the theatre entirely obliterated; nor indeed do I think that
all the perfumes of Arabia would overpower it. Having walked
about, and admired all the varieties of fancy costumes, I, being nearly frozen, went to the Countess C——a's box on the

pit tier, and enveloped myself in a cloak. They pointed out the most distinguished persons in the boxes, amongst others the family of the E——s, who seem very handsome, with brilliant colours and fine teeth. We remained until three in the morning, and declined all offers of refreshment, though, after all, a cup of hot chocolate would not have been amiss. There was supper somewhere, but I believe attended only by gentlemen. I had the satisfaction in passing out to see numerous ladies on their partners' arms, and all bedizened as they were with finery, stop under the lamps, and light their cigars,—cool and pretty.

16th.—I have passed nearly a week in a slight fever; shivering and hot. I was attended by a doctor of the country, who seems the most harmless creature imaginable. Every day he felt my pulse, and gave me some little innocent mixture. But what he especially gave me was a lesson in polite conversation. Every day we had the following dialogue, as he rose to take leave:

"Madam!" (this by the bedside) "I am at your service."

"Many thanks, sir."

"Madam!" (this at the foot of the bed) "know me for your most humble servant."

"Good morning, sir."

"Madam!" (here he stopped beside a table) "I kiss your feet."

"Sir, I kiss your hand."

"Madam!" (this near the door) "my poor house, and all in it, myself though useless, all I have, is yours."

"Many thanks, sir."

He turns round and opens the door, again turning round as he does so.

"Adieu, madam! your servant."

"Adieu, sir."

He goes out, partly reopens the door, and puts in his head—

"Good morning, madam!"

This civility so lengthened out, as if parting were such "sweet sorrow," between doctor and patient, seems rather misplaced. It is here considered more polite to say Señorita than Señora, even to married women, and the lady of the house is generally called by her servants, "La Niña," the little girl, even though she be over eighty. This last custom is still more common in Havana, where the old negresses, who have always lived in the family, and are accustomed to call their young mistress by this name, never change, whatever be her age.

I have received a packet of letters which have done me more good than the old doctor's visits. The captain left us yesterday, and took charge of a box of chocolate stamped with various figures, and of some curious *dulces* for you. Our cards, giving the Mexicans the tardy information of our arrival, were sent out some days ago. I copy one, that you may have a specimen of the style, which looks for all the world like that of a shop-advertisement, purporting that Don —— makes wigs, dresses hair, and so forth, while Doña —— washes lace, and does up fine linen.

"Don A—— C—— de la B——, Enviado Extraordinario y Ministro Plenipotenciario de S. M. C. cerca de la Republica Mexicana; y su Esposa, Doña F—— E—— C—— de la B——; Participan á su Llegada á este Capital y se afrecen á su disposicion, en la Plazuela de Buenavista, No. 2."[1]

18th.—For the last few days our rooms have been filled with visitors, and my eyes are scarcely yet accustomed to the display of diamonds, pearls, silks, satins, blondes, and velvets, in which the ladies have paid their first visits of etiquette. A few of the dresses I shall record for your benefit, not as being richer than the others, but that I happen to recollect them best.—The Marquesa de San Roman, an old lady who has travelled a great deal in Europe, and is very distinguished for talents and information. She has the Grand Cross of Maria Louisa of Spain, is of a noble Venetian family, and aunt to the Duke of Canizzaro. Her dress was a very rich black Genoa velvet, black blonde mantilla, and a very splendid parure of diamonds. She seems in exceedingly delicate health. She and her contemporaries are fast fading away, the last record of the days of Viceroyalty. In their place a new race have started up, whose manners and appearance have little of the *vieille cour* about them; chiefly, it is said, wives of military men, sprung from the hotbeds of the revolutions, ignorant and full of pretensions, as *parvenus* who have risen by chance and not by merit must be. I continue my list after the fashion of the Court Journal.

Countess de S——o. Under dress of rich violet satin, gown of black blonde, mantilla of black blonde, diamond earrings,

[1] Don A—— C—— de la B——, Envoy Extraordinary and Minister Plenipotentiary from H. C. M.; and his Lady, Doña F—— E—— C—— de la B——; Inform you of their arrival in this capital, and put themselves at your disposal, in the street of Buenavista, No. 2.

five or six large diamond brooches fastening the mantilla, necklace of large pearls and diamond sévigné. The Señora S——. Dress of white satin, gown of white blonde, white blonde mantilla, pearls, diamonds, and white satin shoes. Madame S——r. Black velvet dress, white blonde mantilla, pearls, diamonds, short sleeves, and white satin shoes. The Señora de A——d. Fawn-coloured satin dress, black blonde mantilla, diamonds, and black satin shoes.

The Señora B——a, the wife of a General, extremely rich, and who has the handsomest house in Mexico. Dress of purple velvet, embroidered all over with flowers of white silk, short sleeves, and embroidered corsage; white satin shoes and *bas à jour;* a deep flounce of Mechlin appearing below the velvet dress, which was short. A mantilla of black blonde, fastened by three diamond aigrettes. Diamond earrings of extraordinary size. A diamond necklace of immense value, and beautifully set. A necklace of pear pearls, valued at twenty thousand dollars. A diamond sévigné. A gold chain going three times round the neck, and touching the knees. On every finger two diamond rings, like little watches. As no other dress was equally magnificent, with her I conclude my description, only observing that no Mexican lady has yet paid me her first morning visit without diamonds. They have few opportunities for displaying their jewels, so that were it not on the occasion of some such morning visit of etiquette, the diamonds would lie in their cases, wasting their serene rays in darkness.

Last night an attempt was made to break into the house, but our fine little bull-dog Hercules, a present from Señor A——d, kept his ground so well, and barked so furiously, that the servants were awakened, even the porter, the soundest slumberer amongst them; and the robbers escaped without doing further mischief than inflicting a severe wound on the poor animal's paw, which has made him for the present quite lame.

A *propos* to which matters, a most cruel murder, of which I have just been hearing the particulars, was committed not very long ago in this neighbourhood, upon Mr. M——, the Swiss consul. He was also a leather-merchant, and one morning having sent out his porter on some commission, a carriage drove up to the door, and three gentlemen presented themselves to Mr. M——, requesting to speak to him on business. He begged them to walk in, and there entered a general in uniform, a young officer, and a monk. Mr. M—— requested to be informed of their business, when suddenly the general, seizing hold of him, whilst the others went to secure the door, exclaimed, "We have not come to hear about your goods, we want your money." The poor man, astounded at perceiving the nature of his customers, assured them he kept but little money in the house, but proceeded instantly to open his private drawers, and empty their contents, amounting, in fact, to a trifle of some few hundred dollars. Finding that he had indeed no more to give them they prepared to depart, when the *monk* said, "We must kill him, or he will recognise us." "No," said the officers, "leave him and come along. There is no danger." "Go on," said the monk, "I follow;" and, turning back, stabbed the consul to the heart. The three then reentered the carriage, and drove off at full speed. A few minutes afterwards the porter returning found his master bathed in blood, and rushing out to a neighbouring gambling-house, gave the alarm. Several gentlemen ran to his assistance, but he died in an hour after, having given all the particulars of the dress and appearance of his murderers, and that of their carriage. By these tokens they were soon afterwards discovered, and by the energy of the Governor, then Count C——a, they were arrested and hanged upon the trees in front of our house, together with the *real* Mexican colonel, who had kindly lent the ruffians his carriage for the occasion. It is seldom that crime here meets with so prompt a punishment.

Our friend, Count C——a, when Governor of Mexico, was celebrated for his energy in *"el persiguimiento de los ladrones,"* (persecuting the robbers,) as it is called. It is said upon one occasion his zeal carried him rather far. Various robberies having been committed in the city, he had received a hint from the government, that the escape of the perpetrators was considered by them as a proof that he had grown lukewarm in the public service. A few days afterwards, riding in the streets, he perceived a notorious robber, who, the moment he observed himself recognised, darted down another street with the swiftness of an arrow. The governor pursued him on horseback; the robber made all speed towards the Square, and rushed into the sanctuary of the cathedral. The count galloped in after him, and dragged him from his place of refuge near the altar. This violation of the church's sanctity was, of course, severely reprimanded, but, as the governor remarked, they could no longer accuse him of want of zeal in the discharge of his duty.

He took as his porter the captain of a gang of robbers, ordering him to stand at the door, and to seize any of his former acquaintances who might pass, his own pardon depending on his conduct in this respect. Riding out one day to his country place with his lady, this man accompanying them as a servant, they were overtaken by a messenger, who desired the return of the count to the city, upon some urgent and important business. It was already dusk, yet the count, trusting to the honour of the robber, ordered him to conduct his lady to the hacienda; and she alone, on horseback, with this alarming guide, performed her journey in safety.

Before I conclude this letter, I must tell you that I received a visit this morning from a very remarkable character, well known here by the name of *La Güera* (the fair) *Rodriguez,* said to have been many years ago celebrated by Humboldt as the most beautiful woman he had seen in the whole course of his travels. Considering the lapse of time which has passed since that distinguished traveller visited these parts, I was almost astonished when her card was sent up with a request for admission, and still more so to find that in spite of years and of the furrows which it pleases Time to plough in the loveliest faces, La Güera retains a profusion of fair curls without one gray hair, a set of beautiful white teeth, very fine eyes, and great vivacity.

Her sister, the Marquesa de Juluapa, lately dead, is said to have been also a woman of great talent and extraordinary conversational powers; she is another of the ancient noblesse who has dropped off. The physician who attended her in her last illness, a Frenchman of the name of Plan, in great repute here, has sent in a bill to her executors of ten thousand dollars, which, although it does not excite any great astonishment, the family refuse to pay, and there is a lawsuit in consequence. The extortions of medical men in Mexico, especially of foreign physicians, have arrived at such a height, that a person of moderate fortune must hesitate before putting himself into their hands.[1] A rich old lady in delicate health, and with no particular complaint, is a surer fund for them than a silver-mine.

I found La Güera very agreeable, and a perfect living chronicle. She is married to her third husband, and had three

[1] The Mexican Government has since taken this matter into consideration, and is making regulations which render it necessary for a medical man to possess a certain degree of knowledge, and to have resided a specified time in the city, before he is permitted to practise; they are also occupied in fixing a certain sum for medical attendance.

daughters, all celebrated beauties; the Countess de Regla, who died in New York, and was buried in the cathedral there; the Marquesa de Guadalupe, also dead, and the Marquesa de A——a, now a handsome widow. We spoke of Humboldt, and talking of herself as of a third person, she related to me all the particulars of his first visit, and his admiration of her; that she was then very young, though married, and the mother of two children, and that when he came to visit her mother, she was sitting sewing in a corner where the baron did not perceive her; until talking very earnestly on the subject of cochineal, he inquired if he could visit a certain district where there was a plantation of nopals. "To be sure," said La Güera from her corner; "we can take M. de Humboldt there;" whereupon he first perceiving her, stood amazed, and at length exclaimed, "*Valgame Dios!* who is that girl?" Afterwards he was constantly with her, and more captivated, it is said, by her wit than by her beauty, considering her a sort of western Madame de Staël; all which leads me to suspect that the grave traveller was considerably under the influence of her fascinations, and that neither mines nor mountains, geography nor geology, petrified shells nor *alpenkalkstein,* had occupied him to the exclusion of a slight *stratum* of flirtation. It is a comfort to think that "sometimes even the great Humboldt nods."

One of La Güera's stories is too original to be lost. A lady of high rank having died in Mexico, her relatives undertook to commit her to her last resting-place, habited according to the then prevailing fashion, in her most magnificent dress, that which she had worn at her wedding. This dress was a wonder of luxury, even in Mexico. It was entirely composed of the finest lace, and the flounces were made of a species of point which cost fifty dollars a *vara* (the Mexican yard). Its equal was unknown. It was also ornamented and looped up at certain intervals with bows of ribbon very richly embroidered in gold. In this dress, the Condesa de —— was laid in her coffin, thousands of dear friends crowding to view her beautiful *costume de mort,* and at length she was placed in her tomb, the key of which was intrusted to the sacristan.

From the tomb to the opera is a very abrupt transition; nevertheless, both have a share in this story. A company of French dancers appeared in Mexico, a twentieth-rate ballet, and the chief danseuse was a little French damsel, remarkable for the shortness of her robes, her coquetry, and her astonishing pirouettes. On the night of a favourite ballet, Mademoiselle Pauline made her *entrée* in a succession of pirouettes, and poising on her toe, looked round for approbation, when a sudden thrill of horror, accompanied by a murmur of indignation, pervaded the assembly. Mademoiselle Pauline was equipped in the very dress in which the defunct countess had been buried! Lace, point flounces, gold ribbons; impossible to mistake it. Hardly had the curtain dropped, when the little danseuse found herself surrounded by competent authorities, questioning her as to where and how she had obtained her dress. She replied that she had bought it at an extravagant price from a French *modiste* in the city. She had rifled no tomb, but honestly paid down golden ounces, in exchange for her lawful property. To the modiste's went the officers of justice. She also pleaded innocent. She had bought it of a man who had brought it to her for sale, and had paid him much more than *à poids d'or*, as indeed it was worth. By dint of further investigation, the man was identified, and proved to be the sacristan of San ——. Short-sighted sacristan! He was arrested and thrown into prison, and one benefit resulted from his cupidity, since in order to avoid throwing temptation in the way of future sacristans, it became the custom, after the body had lain in state for some time in magnificent robes, to substitute a plain dress previous to placing the coffin in the vault. A poor vanity after all.

I was told by a lady here, that on the death of her grandchild, he was not only enveloped in rich lace, but the diamonds of three condesas and four marquesas were collected together and put on him, necklaces, bracelets, rings, brooches and tiaras, to the value of several hundred thousand dollars. The street was hung with draperies, and a band of music played, whilst he was visited by all the titled relatives of the family in his dead splendour, poor little baby! Yet his mother mourned for him as for all her blighted hopes, and the last scion of a noble house. Grief shows itself in different ways; yet one might think that when it seeks consolation in display, it must be less profound than when it shuns it.

LETTER THE TENTH

San Fernando—House of Perez de Galvez—A Removal—Size of the Houses—Old Monastery—View by Sunset—Evening Visits—Mexican Etiquette—A Night-view from the Azotea —Tacubaya—Magueys—Making of Pulque—Organos and No-pal—Environs of Mexico—Miracle—Hacienda—View from the Countess C——a's House—Arzobispado—Anecdote— Comparative View of Beauty—Indians Rancheritas—Mexi-can Cordiality—Masses for the Dead—San Augustin—Form of Invitation—Death of a Senator—A Mistake.

SAN FERNANDO, 25th February.

We have been engaged for some time past in the disagreeable occupations, first of finding, then of furnishing, and lastly of entering into a new house. We were very anxious to hire that of the Marquesa de Juluapa, which is pretty, well situated, and has a garden; but the agent, after making us wait for his decision more than a fortnight, informed us that he had de-termined to sell it. House-rent is extremely high; nothing tolerable to be had under two thousand five hundred dollars per annum, unfurnished. There is also an extraordinary cus-tom of paying a sum called *traspaso*, sometimes to the amount of fourteen thousand dollars, taking your chance of having the money repaid you by the next person who takes the house. We next endeavoured to procure a house not far from our present residence,—a palace in fact, which I mentioned to you before as having been occupied at one time by Santa Anna, and at another by the English Legation, but the present pro-prietor cannot be prevailed upon to let it. It has a beautiful garden and olive-ground, but is not a very secure abode, except with a guard of soldiers. We at length came to the determina-tion of taking up our quarters here. It is a handsome new house, built by General G——, and has the fault of being only too large. Built in a square, like all Mexican houses, the ground-floor, which has a stone-paved court with a fountain in the middle, contains about twenty rooms, besides out-houses, coach-house, stables, pigeon-house, garden-house, etc. The second storey where the principal apartments are, the

first-floor being chiefly occupied by servants, has the same
number of rooms, with coal-room, wood-room, bath-room,
and water everywhere, in the court below, in the garden, and
on the azotea, which is very spacious, and where, were the
house our own, we might build a *mirador*, and otherwise ornament it; but to build for another is too heroic. The great
defect in all these houses is their want of finish; the great
doors that will not shut properly, and the great windows down
to the ground, which in the rainy season will certainly admit
water, making these residences appear something like a cross-
breed between a palace and a barn; the splendour of the one,
the discomfort of the other. I will not inflict upon you the
details of all our petty annoyances caused by procrastinating
tradesmen. Suffice it to say, that the Mexican *mañana* (to-
morrow), if properly translated, means *never*. As to prices, I
conclude we pay for being foreigners and diplomates, and will
not believe in a first experience. However, we are settled at
last, and find the air here much purer than in the heart of the
city, while the maladies and epidemics so common there, are
here almost unknown. Behind this house is a very small garden, bounded on one side by the great wall which encloses
the orchard of the old monastery of San Fernando, within
whose vast precincts only seven or eight monks now linger. It
is an immense building, old and gray, and time-worn, with
church adjoining, and spacious lands appertaining to it. At
all times it is picturesque, but by moonlight or sunset it forms
a most olden-time vision.

At that hour, standing alone in the high-walled garden when
the convent bells are tolling, and the convent itself, with its
iron-barred, Gothic windows, and its gray-green olive-trees that
look so unreal and lifeless, is tinged by the last rays of the sun,
the whole seems like a vision, or a half-remembered sketch,
or a memory of romance.

Then the sun sets behind the snow-crowned mountains
with a bright fiery red, covering their majestic sides with a
rosy glow, while great black clouds come sailing along like
the wings of night; and then is the hour for remembering that
this is Mexico, and in spite of all the evils that have fallen
over it, the memory of the romantic past hovers there still.
But the dark clouds sail on, and envelop the crimson tints
yet lingering and blushing on the lofty mountains, and like
monstrous night-birds brood there in silent watch; and gradually the whole landscape—mountains and sky, convent and

olive-trees, look gray and sad, and seem to melt away in the dim twilight.

Then the bright moon rises and flings her silver veil over the mountains, and lights up the plains, glittering and quivering upon the old gray stones, and a sound of military music is heard in the distance far and faint. And all the bells are tolling; from old San Fernando that repeats himself like a sexagenarian; from the towers of the cathedral, from many a distant church and convent; and above the rumbling of carriages and the hum of the city, are heard the notes of a hymn, now rising, now falling on the ear, as a religious procession passes along to some neighbouring temple. But it grows late— a carriage enters the courtyard—a visit. There is no romance here. Men and women are the same everywhere, whether enveloped in the graceful mantilla, or wearing *Herbault's last*, whether wrapped in Spanish cloak, or Mexican sarape, or Scottish plaid. The manners of the ladies here are extremely kind, but Spanish etiquette and compliments are beyond measure tiresome. After having embraced each lady who enters, according to the fashion, which after all seems cordial, to say the least of it, and seated the lady of most consequence on the right side of the sofa, a point of great importance, the following dialogue is *de rigueur*. "How are you? Are you well?" "At your service, and you?" "Without novelty (*sin novedad*) at your service." "I am rejoiced, and how are you, Señora?" "At your disposal, and you?" "A thousand thanks, and the Señor?" "At your service, without novelty," etc., etc., etc. Besides, before sitting down, there is, "Pray be seated." "Pass first, Señorita." "No, madam, pray pass first." "*Vaya*, well, to oblige you, without further ceremony; I dislike compliments and etiquette." And it is a fact that there is no real etiquette but the most perfect *laissez aller* in the world. All these are mere words, tokens of good will. If it is in the morning, there is the additional question of "How have you passed the night?" And the answer, "In your service." Even in Mexico the weather affords a legitimate opening for a conversation battery, but this chiefly when it rains or looks dull, which, occasioning surprise, gives rise to observation. Besides a slight change in the degree of heat or cold which we should not observe, they comment upon.

The visit over, the ladies re-embrace, the lady of the house following her guest to the top of the staircase, and again compliments are given and received. "Madam, you know that my house is at your disposal." "A thousand thanks, madam. Mine is at yours, and though useless, know me for your servant, and command me in everything that you may desire." "Adieu, I hope you may pass a good night," etc., etc., etc. At the bottom of the first landing-place the visitors again turn round to catch the eye of the lady of the house, and the adieus are repeated. All this, which struck me at first, already appears quite natural, and would scarce be worth mentioning, but as affording a contrast to our slight and indifferent manner of receiving and taking leave of our guests. All the ladies address each other, and are addressed by gentlemen, by their Christian names, and those who have paid me more than one or two visits, use the same familiar mode of address to me. Amongst women I rather like this, but it somewhat startles my ideas of the fitness of things to hear a young man address a married woman as Maria, Antonia, Anita, etc. However, things must be taken as they are meant, and as no familiarity is intended, none should be supposed. . . .

But these visitors are gone, and into the open court the consolatory moon is shining. All clouds have passed away, and the blue sky is so blue, as to dazzle the eyes even in the moonlight. Each star shines out bright, golden, and distinct, and it seems a sin to sleep and to lose so lovely a night. . . . But for a true night view, mount upon the Azotea, and see all Mexico sleeping at your feet; the whole valley and the city itself floating in moonlight; the blue vault above gemmed with stars, and the mountains all bathed in silver, the white volcanoes seeming to join earth and sky. Here even Salvator's genius would fail. We must evoke the ghost of Byron. The pencil can do nothing. Poetry alone might give a faint idea of a scene so wondrously beautiful.

26th.—We went yesterday with Mr. M——, his wife and daughter and a padre to visit the archbishop's palace at Tacubaya, a pretty village about four miles from Mexico, and a favourite ride of ours in the morning. The country round Mexico, if not always beautiful, has the merit of being original, and on the road to Tacubaya, which goes by Chapultepec, you pass large tracts of country, almost entirely uncultivated, though so near the city, or covered by the mighty maguey plant, the American agave, which will flourish on the most arid soil, and, like a fountain in a desert place, furnishes the poorest Indian with the beverage most grateful to his palate. It seems to be to them what the reindeer is to the Esquimaux, fitted by nature to supply all his wants. The maguey and its produce, *pulque*, were known to the Indians in the most ancient times, and the primitive Aztecs may have become as intoxicated on their favourite *octli,* as they called it, as the modern Mexicans do on their beloved pulque.

It is not often that we see the superb flower with its colossal stem, for the plant that is in blossom is a useless beauty. The moment the experienced Indian becomes aware that his maguey is about to flower, he cuts out the heart, covers it over with the side leaves of the plant, and all the juice which should have gone to the great stem of the flower, runs into the empty basin thus formed, into which the Indian, thrice a day, and during several months in succession, inserts his *acojote* or gourd, a kind of siphon, and applying his mouth to the other end, draws off the liquor by suction; a curious-looking process. First it is called honey-water, and is sweet and scentless; but easily ferments when transferred to the skins or earthen vases where it is kept. To assist in its fermentation, however, a little old pulque, *Madre pulque,* as it is called, which has fermented for many days, is added to it, and in twenty-four hours after it leaves the plant, you may imbibe it in all its perfection. It is said to be the most wholesome drink in the world, and remarkably agreeable when one has overcome the first shock occasioned by its rancid odour. At all events, the maguey is a source of unfailing profit, the consumption of pulque being enormous, so that many of the richest families in the capital owe their fortune entirely to the produce of their magueys. When the owners do not make the pulque themselves, they frequently sell their plants to the Indians; and a maguey, which costs a real when first planted, will, when ready to be cut, sell for twelve or eighteen dollars; a tolerable profit, considering that it grows in almost any soil, requires little manure, and, unlike the vine, no very special or periodical care. They are planted in rows like hedges, and though the individual plant is handsome, the general effect is monotonous. Of the fibres is made an excellent strong thread called *pita,* of which pita they make a strong brownish paper, and might make cloth if they pleased. There is, however, little improvement made by the Mexicans upon the ingenuity of their Indian ancestors, in respect to the maguey. Upon paper made of its fibres, the ancient Mexicans painted their hieroglyphical figures. The strong and pointed thorns which terminate the gigantic leaves, they used as nails and pins; and amongst the abuses, not the uses of these, the ancient sanguinary priests were in the habit of piercing their breasts and tearing their arms with them, in acts of expiation.

Besides, there is a very strong brandy distilled from pulque, which has the advantage of producing intoxication in an infinitely shorter period.

Together with the maguey, grows another immense production of nature, the *organos*, which resembles the barrels or pipes of an organ, and being covered with prickles, the plants growing close together, and about six feet high, makes the strongest natural fence imaginable, besides being covered with beautiful flowers. There is also another species of cactus, the nopal, which bears the tuna, a most refreshing fruit, but not ripe at this season. The plant looks like a series of flat green pin-cushions fastened together, and stuck full of diminutive needles.

But though the environs of Mexico are flat, though there are few trees, little cultivation, and uninhabited haciendas, and ruined churches in all directions, still, with its beautiful climate and ever-smiling sky, the profusion of roses and sweet-peas in the deserted gardens, the occasional clumps of fine trees, particularly the graceful Arbold de Peru (*shinum molle*, the Peruvian pepper-tree), its bending branches loaded with bunches of coral-coloured berries, the old orchards with their blossoming fruit-trees, the conviction that everything necessary for the use of man can be produced with scarcely any labour, all contributes to render the landscape one which it is impossible to pass through with indifference.

A magnificent ash-tree (the Mexican *fresno*), the pride of Tacubaya; which throws out its luxuriant branches, covering a large space of ground, was pointed out to us as having a tradition attached to it. It had nearly withered away, when the Ylustrisimo Señor Fonti, the last of the Spanish archbishops, gave it his solemn benediction, and prayed that its vigour might be restored. Heaven heard his prayer; new buds instantly shot forth, and the tree has since continued to thrive luxuriantly.

Tacubaya is a scattered village, containing some pretty country-houses, and some old gardens with stone fountains. The word country-house must not, however, be understood in the English acceptation of the word. The house, which is in fact merely used as an occasional retreat during the summer months, is generally a large empty building, with innumerable lofty rooms, communicating with each other, and containing the scantiest possible supply of furniture. One room will have in it a deal table and a few chairs; you will then pass through five or six quite empty; then you will arrive at two or three, with green painted bedsteads and a bench; the walls bare, or ornamented with a few old pictures of Saints and Virgins, and bare floors ornamented with nothing. To this add a kitchen and outhouses, a garden running to waste and overrunning with flowers, with stiff stone walks and a fountain in the middle, an orchard and an olive-ground; such are most of the haciendas that I have yet seen. That of the Countess C——a, which seems to be the handsomest in Tacubaya, is remarkable for commanding from its windows one of the most beautiful views imaginable of Mexico, the volcanoes and Chapultepec. From her azotea there is also a splendid view of the whole valley; and as her garden is in good order, that she has an excellent billiard-table, a piano, but above all, a most agreeable society in her own family, and that her house is the very centre of hospitality, one may certainly spend many pleasant hours there, without regretting the absence of the luxurious furniture, which, in Mexico, seems entirely confined to the town houses. The countess herself assured us that she had twice completely furnished the house, but as, in two revolutions, everything was thrown out of the windows and destroyed, she was resolved in future to confine herself to *le stricte nécessaire*.

We went to see a house and garden which has fallen, in chance succession, to a poor woman, who, not being able to occupy her unexpected inheritance, is desirous of selling it. The garden and grounds are a deserted wilderness of sweets. We were joined by several monks from a neighbouring convent, and with them went to visit the archbishop's palace. *Chemin faisant*, the padre informed us that he was formerly a merchant, a married man, and a friend of Yturbide's. He failed, his wife died, his friend was shot, and he joined a small community of priests who lived retired in the convent of La Profesa, which, with its church is one of the richest in Mexico.

The Arzobispado is a large, handsome, but deserted building, commanding the same fine view as from the house of the countess, and with a garden and fine olive-ground, of which the trees were brought from Europe. The garden was filled with large double pink roses, and bunches of the mille-fleur-rose, which are disposed in arches, a favourite custom here, also with a profusion of sweet-peas and jessamine, and a few orange-trees. The gardener gave us some beautiful bouquets, and we lingered here till sunset, admiring the view. There is no point from which Mexico is seen to such advantage. It is even a finer prospect than that from Chapultepec, since it embraces the castle itself, one of the most striking features in the landscape. But just as the sun sunk behind the mountains, a sudden change took place in the weather. The wind rose, great masses of dark clouds came driving over the sky, and the rain fell in torrents, forcing us to make a hasty retreat to our carriages, and having omitted to take any precautions, and this road not being particularly safe at night, we were probably indebted for our safe return more to "good luck than good guidance;" or, perhaps, we owed it in part to the *padre*, for the robbers are shy at attacking either soldiers or priests, the first from fear, and the second from awe.

Talking of robbers and robberies, rather a fertile theme of conversation, Señor —— told me the other day that, in the time of a former president, it came to pass, that a certain gentleman went to take his leave at the palace, previous to setting off for Vera Cruz. He was received by the president, who was alone with his aide-de-camp, General ——, and mentioned to him in confidence that he was about to take a considerable sum of money with him, but that it was so well concealed in the lining of a trunk, which he described, that even if attacked by robbers, it was impossible they should discover it, and that therefore he did not think it necessary to take an escort with him. The next day this confidential gentleman left Mexico, in the diligence. Not far from the gates the coach was attacked, and, strange to say, the robbers singled out the very trunk which contained the money, opened it, ripped up the lining, and having possessed themselves of the sum therein concealed, peaceably departed. It was a singular coincidence that the captain of the robbers, though somewhat disguised, bore a striking general resemblance to the president's aide-de-camp! These coincidences will happen. . . .

My chief occupation, lately, has consisted in returning visits; and it is certain that, according to our views of the case, there is too wide a distinction between the full-dress style of toilet adopted by the ladies when they pay visits, and the undress in which they receive their visitors at home. To this there are some, nay, many exceptions, but *en masse* this is the case. . . .

On first arriving from the United States, where an ugly woman is a phœnix, one cannot fail to be struck at the first glance with the general absence of beauty in Mexico. It is only by degrees that handsome faces begin to dawn upon us; but, however, it must be remarked that beauty without colour is apt to be less striking and to make less impression on us at

first. The brilliant complexion and fine figure of an Englishwoman strike every one. The beauty of expression and finely-
chiselled features of a Spaniard steal upon us like a soft moonlight, while a Frenchwoman, however plain, has so graceful a
manner of saying agreeable things, so charming a tournure,
such a piquant way of managing her eyes, and even her mouth,
that we think her a beauty after half an hour's acquaintance,
and even lose our admiration for the quiet and highbred, but
less graceful *Anglaise*. The beauty of the women here consist
in superb black eyes, very fine dark hair, a beautiful arm and
hand, and small, well-made feet. The defects are, that they
are frequently too short and too fat, that their teeth are often
bad, and their complexion not the clear olive of the Spaniards,
nor the glowing brown of the Italians, but a bilious-looking
yellow. Their notion of inserting the foot into a shoe half an
inch shorter, ruins the foot, and destroys their grace in walking, and, consequently, in every movement. This fashion is,
fortunately, beginning to fall into disuse. . . . It is therefore
evident that when a *Mexicana* is endowed with white teeth
and a fine complexion, when she has not grown too fat, and
when she does not torture her small foot to make it smaller,
she must be extremely handsome. . . . The general carelessness of their dress in the morning is, however, another great
drawback to beauty. A woman without stays, with uncombed
hair and *reboso*, had need to be very lovely, if she retain any
attraction at all. This indolence, indeed, is going out of fashion, especially among the younger part of the community,
owing, perhaps, to their more frequent intercourse with foreigners, though it will probably be long before the morning
at home is not considered a privileged time and place for
dishabille. Notwithstanding, I have made many visits where I
have found the whole family in a perfect state of order and
neatness, but I have observed that there the fathers, and what
is more important, the mothers, had travelled in Europe, and
established a new order of things on their return.

Upon the whole, the handsomest women here are not Mexicans, that is, not born in the capital, but in the provinces.
From Puebla, and Jalapa and Vera Cruz, we see many distinguished by their brilliant complexions and fine teeth, and
who are taller and more graceful than those born in the city
of Mexico; precisely as in Spain, where the handsomest
women in Madrid are said to be those born out of it.

The common Indians, whom we see every day bringing in
their fruit and vegetables to market, are, generally speaking,

very plain, with an humble, mild expression of countenance, very gentle, and wonderfully polite in their manners to each other; but occasionally, in the lower classes, one sees a face and form so beautiful, that we might suppose such another was the Indian who enchanted Cortes; with eyes and hair of extraordinary beauty, a complexion dark but glowing, with the Indian beauty of teeth like the driven snow, together with small feet and beautifully-shaped hands and arms, however imbrowned by sun and toil. In these cases it is more than probable that, however Indian in her appearance, there must have been some intermarriages in former days between her progenitors and the descendants of the conquerors. We also occasionally observe very handsome *Rancheritas*, wives or daughters of the farmers, riding in front of their farm-servants on the same horse, with the white teeth and fine figures which are preserved by the constant exercise that country women must perforce take, whatever be their natural indolence, while the early fading of beauty in the higher classes, the decay of teeth, and the over-corpulency so common amongst them, are no doubt the natural consequences of want of exercise and of injudicious food. There is no country in the world where so much animal food is consumed, and there is no country in the world where so little is required. The consumers are not the Indians, who cannot afford it, but the better classes, who generally eat meat three times a day. This, with the quantities of chile and sweetmeats, in a climate which every one complains of as being irritating and inflammatory, probably produces those nervous complaints which are here so general, and for which constant hot baths are the universal and agreeable remedy.

In point of amiability and warmth of manner, I have met with no women who can possibly compete with those in Mexico, and it appears to me that women of all other countries will appear cold and stiff by comparison. To strangers this is an unfailing charm, and it is to be hoped that whatever advantages they may derive from their intercourse with foreigners, they may never lose this graceful cordiality, which forms so agreeable a contrast with English and American frigidity.

C——n received an invitation some time ago to attend the *honras* of the daughter of the Marquis of S——a; that is, the celebration of mass for the repose of her soul. M—— was observing to-day, that if this Catholic doctrine be firmly believed, and that the prayers of the Church are indeed availing to shorten the sufferings of those who have gone before us; to relieve those whom we love from thousands of years of torture, it is astonishing how the rich do not become poor, and the poor beggars, in furtherance of this object; and that if the idea be purely human, it showed a wonderful knowledge of human nature, on the part of the inventor, as what source of profit could be more sure? . . . .

Certainly no expense was spared on this occasion. San Augustin, in itself a beautiful church, was fitted up with extraordinary splendour. The walls and pillars were covered with draperies of rich crimson velvet. Innumerable wax candles were lighted, and an invisible band of music played during the intervals of the deep-rolling organ. All the monks of San Augustin, with their white hoods and sandalled feet, and carrying lighted tapers, were ranged near the altar. All the male relatives of the family, dressed in deep mourning, occupied the high-backed chairs placed along one side of the church, the floor of which was covered with a carpet, on which various veiled and mourning figures were kneeling, whom I joined. The whole service, the chanting, the solemn music, and the prayers, were very impressive, yet more joyous than sad, perhaps from the pervading feeling that each note, as it rose to heaven, carried some alleviation to the spirit of the young and beloved one for whose repose they played, and brought her nearer to the gates of the Holy City.

She was but twenty when she died; and our first house is close to that of the Marquis de S——a, her father, so that we were shocked to learn that she had expired on the night of our great serenade (we, of course, not aware of her illness), actually to the sound of that gay music, and amidst the shouting and clapping of hands of the multitude. When the service was over the procession passed out, every one kissing the hand of the bishop as he went along, and we found some difficulty in making our way through the crowds of *léperos,* who, though not allowed to enter the church on this occasion, were swarming at the gates. Our carriage, as we returned home, formed one of a file of at least one hundred.

We found on our table another invitation to a very splendid mass, which is to be performed in San Francisco, on account of the death of a friend of ours, a senator of a distinguished family. The style of these invitations is as follows:—A device is engraved on the paper, such as a tomb and cypress, and below is printed,

"José Maria A——,
José G—— de la C——a, and Basilio G——,
brothers and uncle of the
Senator Don Augustin T——,
who died on the twenty-eighth of last month,
request you to assist at the suffrage of the funeral honours,
which, by the desire of his wife, Doña J—— A——, will be celebrated in the church of San Francisco on the morning of the
eighth of this month of February, 1840, at nine o'clock."

Beside this invitation, was a piece of information of a different description:

"General A—— and Anna R—— beg to inform you that they
have contracted matrimony, and have the honour of offering
themselves to your disposal.
"M—— Street, No. 24. Mexico, 1840."

Here, as in Spain, a lady, after her marriage, retains her
maiden name; and though she adds to it that of her husband,
she is more commonly known by her own.

From ignorance of another Mexican custom, I made rather
an awkward blunder the other day; though I must observe,
in my justification, that I had lately been in the agonies of
searching for servants, and had just filled all the necessary
departments pretty much to my satisfaction. Therefore, when
the porter of the Señora de —— brought me the compliments
of his mistress, and that she begged to inform me that she
had another servant at my disposal (*otra criada á mi disposicion*), I returned for answer, that I was greatly obliged,
but had just hired a *recamerera* (chambermaid). At this the
man, stupid as he was, opened his great eyes with a slight
expression of wonder. Fortunately, as he was turning away, I
bethought me of inquiring of the señora's health, and his reply,
that "she and the baby were coming on very well," brought
the truth suddenly before me, that the message was merely
the etiquette used on informing the friends of the family of
the birth of a child—a conviction which induced me slightly
to alter the style of my answer. *Experientia docet!*

LETTER THE ELEVENTH

Calle de Tacuba—The Leap of Alvarado—The "Noche Triste"
—Sale of a Curate's Goods—Padre Leon—Leprosy—Pictures
—The Annunciation—The Alameda—Paseo de Bucarelli—
The Viga—Indians in Canoes—A Murder—A Country Fête
—Visit to the Colegio Vizcaino—The Jota Arragonesa—Old
Soldiers.

The street in which we live forms part of the Calle de Tacuba, the ancient Tlacopan, one of the great causeways by which ancient Mexico communicated with the continent. The other two were Tepeyayac (now Guadalupe) and Iztapalapan, by which last the Mexican emperor and his nobles went out to receive Cortes on his entrance to Tenochtitlan. The ancient city was divided into four districts, and this division is still preserved, with a change from the Indian names to those of San Pablo, San Sebastian, San Juan, and Santa Maria. The streets run in the same direction as they did in former times. The same street frequently changes its name in each division, and this part of the Calle de Tacuba is occasionally called the "Plazuela del Sopilote," "San Fernando," and the "Puente de Alvarado," which is the more classic of the three, as celebrating the valour of a hero; while a ditch, crossed by a small bridge near this, still retains the name of "el Salto de Alvarado," in memory of the famous leap given by the valiant Spaniard, Pedro de Alvarado, on the memorable night called the *"noche triste,"* of the 1st of July, 1520, when the Spaniards were forced to retreat from Mexico to the mountains of Tepeyayac.

On that "sad night," the rain falling in torrents, the moon and the stars refusing their light, the sky covered with thick clouds, Cortes commanded the silent march of his troops. Sandoval, the unconquerable captain, led his vanguard; and the stern hero, Pedro de Alvarado, brought up the rear. A bridge of wood was carried by forty soldiers, to enable the troops to pass the ditches or canals, which must otherwise have impeded their retreat. It is said that in choosing the night for this march Cortes was guided by the counsels of an astrologer.

Be that as it may, the first canal was happily passed by means of the portable bridge. The sentinels who guarded that point were overcome; but the noise of the struggle attracted the attention of the vigilant priests, who in the silence of the night were keeping watch in the temple. They blew the holy trumpets, cried to arms, and awakened the startled inhabitants from their slumbers.

In a moment the Spaniards were surrounded by water and by land. At the second canal, which they had already reached, the combat was terrible. All was confusion, wounds, groans, and death; and the canal became so choked with dead bodies, that the rear-guard passed over them as over a bridge. We are told that Cortes himself swam more than once over the canal, regardless of danger, cheering on his men, giving out his orders, every blow aimed in the direction of his voice, yet cool and intrepid as ever, in the midst of all the clamour and confusion and darkness. But arrived at the third canal, Alvarado finding himself alone, and surrounded by furious enemies, against whom it was in vain for his single arm to contend, fixed his lance in the bottom of the canal, and leaning against it, gave one spring to the opposite shore.

An Aztec author, and contemporary of Cortes, says that when the Indians beheld this marvellous leap, and that their enemy was safe, they bit the dust (*comieron tierra*); and that the children of Alvarado, who was ever after known as "Alvarado of the leap," proved in the course of a lawsuit before the judges of Tezcuco, by competent witnesses, the truth of this prowess of their father.

In a hitherto unpublished manuscript which has come to light this year, in an annual called the "Mosaico Mexicano," there are some curious particulars concerning the "*noche triste.*" It is said that the alarm was given by an old woman who kept a stall; and mention is made of the extraordinary valour of a lady called Maria de Estrada, who performed marvellous deeds with her sword, and who was afterwards married to Don Pedro Sanchez Farfan. It is also said that when the Indians beheld the leap they called out, "Truly this man is the offspring of the sun;" and that this manner of tearing up the ground, and eating earth by handfuls, was a common Indian mode of expressing admiration. However, Mexico is so rich in traditions, that when I particularize this one it is only because we live on the site where the event took place. . . .

We went a few days ago to see some effects which are for sale, belonging to a *cura* who died lately, having heard that he has left some good paintings amongst them. We went in the evening, and found no one but the agent (an individual in the Daniel Lambert style), an old woman or two, and the Padre Leon, a Jesuit, *capellan* of the Capuchin nuns, and whose face, besides being handsome, looks the very personification of all that is good, and mild, and holy. What a fine study for a painter his head would be! The old priest who died, and who had brought over various valuables from Spain, had a sister who was a leper, and who died in the hospital of San Lazaro. This dreadful scourge is by no means wholly unknown here; and though it is ordained that all who are afflicted by it shall be shut up in this hospital, I have met two persons, and one of these in society, who have the disease.

For this house, which is very large, the executors ask a preposterous rent. The goods of the defunct, which were for sale, were ranged on long tables in a very large apartment. There were virgins and saints, surplices, candlesticks, and snuffer-trays; boxes of all sorts and sizes; an ill-set parure of emeralds and diamonds; several good paintings, especially one of the Annunciation. There was the death of San José, various saints, etc., all religious subjects, as may be supposed. Two C——n bought; one I greatly coveted. There were also two large pieces of embroidered velvet, on which were the arms of Castile, said to have been hung on a portrait of Queen Cristina when she entered Madrid. The agent begged C——n to buy them, asking at the same time an impossible price therefor.

There was moreover a large box full of relics from Jerusalem, which the padre told me could not be sold, but that I might choose whatever I liked; so that I returned home with various Agnus Deis, crucifixes, and rosaries. The next day a messenger from Padre Leon brought me the painting of the Annunciation, which I had admired so much, and which is a sketch of Bayeu, a Valencian painter, from his own painting of the Annunciation in the royal chapel of Aranjuez; also the embroidered velvet, begging my acceptance of both. We have since wished to show our sense of the padre's politeness, but he will neither accept presents, nor will he visit any one but such as in the hour of need require his spiritual services. In the house of sickness and by the bed of death he is ever to be found, but chiefly if it is also the abode of poverty. In the house of the rich man he rarely visits, and then only when his presence has been requested—when he has been called in to administer spiritual consolation to the sick or the dying. But in the dwelling of the lowly, in the meanest and most wretched hovels, he has never to be sought. The guardian and friend of the poor, his charities are equally extensive and judicious. . . .

Yesterday being a fête-day, the *Paséo* was very full of carriages, and consequently more brilliant and amusing than usual. This Paséo is the Mexican Prado or Hyde Park, while the *Viga* may be reckoned the Kensington Gardens of the metropolis, only however as succeeding to the other, for there is no walking, which in Mexico is considered wholly unfashionable; and though a few ladies in black gowns and mantillas do occasionally venture forth on foot very early to shop or to attend mass, the streets are so ill kept, the pavements so narrow, the crowd so great, and the multitude of *léperos* in rags and blankets so annoying, that all these inconveniences, added to the heat of the sun in the middle of the day, form a perfect excuse for their non-appearance in the streets of Mexico.

In the Alameda, however, which is so pretty and shady, it is very agreeable to walk; but though I have gone there frequently in the morning, I have met but three ladies on foot, and of these two were foreigners. After all, every one has feet, but ladies alone have carriages, and it may be a mixture of aristocracy and indolence which prevents the Mexican Doñas from profaning the soles of their feet by a contact with their mother earth.

The Paséo called *de Bucarelli*, after a viceroy of that name, is a long and broad avenue bounded by the trees which he planted, and where there is a large stone fountain, whose sparkling waters look cool and pleasant, ornamented by a gilded statue of Victory. Here, every evening, but more especially on Sundays and fête-days, which last are nearly innumerable, may be seen two long rows of carriages filled with ladies, crowds of gentlemen on horseback riding down the middle between these carriages, soldiers at intervals attending to the preservation of public order, and multitudes of common people and *léperos,* mingled with some well-dressed gentlemen on foot. The carriages are for the most part extremely handsome—European coaches with fine horses and odd liveries, mingled with carriages made in the country, some in the old Mexican fashion, heavy and covered with gilding, or a modern imitation of an English carriage, strong, but somewhat clumsy and ill-finished. Various hackney-coaches, drawn by mules, are seen among the finer equipages, some very tolerable, and others of extraordinary form and dimensions, which bear tokens of having belonged in former days to some noble Don.

Horses, as being more showy, are more fashionable in these public promenades than mules; but the latter animal requires less care, and is capable of undergoing more fatigue than the horse. Most families have both mules and horses in their stable, and for those who visit much this is necessary. The carriages, of which the most fashionable seems to be the *carratela,* open at the sides, with glass windows, are filled with ladies in full toilet, without mantillas, their heads uncovered, and, generally, *coiffées* with flowers or jewels; but the generality being close coaches, afford but an indistinct view of the inmates, as they pass along saluting each other with their fingers or fan. The whole scene, on the evening of a fête, is exceedingly brilliant, but very monotonous. The equestrians, with their fine horses and handsome Mexican dresses, apparently take no notice of the ladies as they pass, rarely salute them, and never venture to enter into conversation with them. But they are well aware to whom each carriage belongs, and consequently when it behoves them to make their horses curvet, and otherwise show off their horsemanship to advantage. Black eyes are upon them, and they know it. When the carriages have made two or three turns, they draw up at different stations in a semicircle a little off the road, and there the inmates sit and view the passers-by. Occasional streams of smoke may be seen issuing from the carriages, but chiefly, it must be confessed, from the most old-fashioned equipages, and from the hackney-coaches. Smoking amongst ladies in the higher classes is going very much out of fashion, and is rarely practised openly except by elderly, or at least by married ladies. In a secondary class, indeed, young and old inhale the smoke of their cigaritos without hesitation, but when a custom begins to be considered *vulgar,* it will hardly subsist another generation. Unfeminine as it is, I do not think it looks ungraceful to see a pretty woman smoke.

This Paséo commands a fine view of the mountains, but I greatly prefer the *Viga,* which now begins to be the fashionable promenade. It is bordered by a canal shaded by trees, which leads to the *Chinampas,* and is constantly covered with Indians in their canoes bringing in fruit and flowers and vegetables to the Mexican market. Early in the morning it is a pretty sight to see them in these canoes gliding along in a perfect bower of green branches and flowers.

Yesterday, on returning from an evening drive there, having left C——n and several gentlemen who had dined with us, taking coffee and smoking upon the balcony, I found that by good fortune I had escaped being witness of a murder which took place before our door. These gentlemen had observed, for some time, a group of persons, male and female, of the lower class, talking and apparently amusing themselves; sometimes laughing, and at other times disputing and giving each other blows. Suddenly, one of the number, a man, darted out from amongst the others, and tried to escape by clambering over the low wall which supports the arches of the aqueduct. Instantly, and quite coolly, another man followed him, drew his knife, and stabbed him in the back. The man fell backwards with a groan, upon which a woman of the party, probably the murderer's wife, drew out her knife, and stabbed the man several times to the heart, the others, meanwhile, neither speaking nor interfering, but looking on with folded arms, and their usual placid smile of indifference.

At the same time, some soldiers appeared in the distance, riding down the street; seeing which, the man and woman who had committed the murder, endeavoured to take shelter in our house. The porter had, fortunately, barred the doors, and the soldiers riding up, took them both into custody. No sensation was excited by this, which is an everyday occurrence. Yesterday I saw a dead man lying near the *Longa* (the Exchange) and nobody took any notice of him. "You have been engaged in a disagreeable business," said I to Colonel ——, who had come to pay us a visit, and was still *en grande tenue,* having just returned from the execution of one of his own soldiers, who had stabbed a comrade. "Yes," said he, with an air of peculiar gaiety; "we have just been shooting a little *tambour.*" . . . We were invited, lately, to a "dia de campo" (a day in the country), a very common amusement here, in which, without any peculiar arrangement or etiquette, a number of people go out to some country place in the environs, and spend the day in dancing, breakfasting, walking about, etc. This was given at Tacubaya by Don B——o G——a, a senator, and was amusing enough. The music consisted of a band of guitars, from which the performers, common men, and probably self-taught, contrived to draw wonderfully good music, and, in the intervals of dancing, played airs from the Straniera and Puritani. The taste for music is certainly universal, the facilities wonderful, the science nearly at zero.

The ladies in general wore neither diamonds nor pearls, but a sort of demi-toilet, which would have been pretty if their dresses had been longer and their shoes not so tight. Some wore bonnets, which are considered full dress. The E—— family, and the young Señora de C——, were beautifully dressed. Mexican women, when they sit, have an air of great dignity, and the most perfect repose of feature. They are always to be seen to most advantage on their sofas, in their carriages, or in their boxes at the theatre.

There were immensely long tables, covered with Mexican cookery, which I begin to get accustomed to; and a great many toasts were given and a great quantity of champagne drank. We danced a great deal, quadrilles, waltzes and Spanish country-dances, walked about in the garden and orchard in the evening, and returned to dance again to the music of the indefatigable guitars, so that it was dusk when all the carriages set off, much about the same time, to bear each other company. . . .

The following day, the Countess C——a having been kind enough to procure an order for permission to visit the *Colegio Vizcaino*, which I was anxious to see, we went there with a large party. This college, founded by the gratuitous charities of Spaniards, chiefly from the province of Biscay, is a truly splendid institution. It is an immense building of stone, in the form of a square, on the model, they say, of the palace of Madrid, and possesses in the highest degree that air of solidity and magnificence which distinguishes the Mexican edifices, and which, together with the width and regularity of the streets, the vastness of the public squares, the total absence of all paltry ornament, the balconies with their balustrades and window-gratings of solid iron and bronze, render Mexico, in spite of its insufficient police, one of the noblest-looking cities in the world. The object of this college is to provide for the education of the children of Spaniards, especially for the descendants of Biscayans, in Mexico; a certain number being admitted upon application to the directors. There are female teachers in all the necessary branches, such as reading, writing, sewing, arithmetic, etc.; but besides this, there is a part of the building with a separate entrance, where the children of the poor, of whatever country, are educated gratis. These spend the day there, and go home in the evening. The others are kept upon the plan of a convent, and never leave the institution while they belong to it; but the building is so spacious and airy, with its great galleries, and vast court and fine fountains, garden and spacious azotea, that the children are perfectly well off. There are *portières* and sisters, pretty much as in a convent; together with an old respectable *Rectora;* and the most perfect order and cleanliness prevails through the whole establishment.

We first visited the poor scholars, passing through the large halls where they sat with their teachers, divided into classes, sewing, writing, reading, embroidering, or casting up accounts, which last accomplishment must, I think, be sorely against the Mexican genius. One of the teachers made a little girl present me with a hair chain which she had just completed. Great order and decorum prevailed. Amongst the permanent scholars in the upper part of the institution, there are some who embroider astonishingly well—surplices, altar-hangings, in short, all the church vestments in gold or silk. In the room where these are kept are the confessionals for the pupils. The priests are in a separate room, and the penitents kneel before the grating which separates the two apartments. All the sleeping-rooms are scrupulously neat and clean, with two green painted beds in each, and a small parlour off it, and frequently ornamented with flowers and birds. The girls are taught to cook and iron, and make themselves generally useful, thus being fitted to become excellent wives to respectable men in their own rank of life.

We visited the chapel, which is extremely rich and handsome, incrusted with gilding, and very large. The pupils and their teachers attend mass in the gallery above, which looks down upon the chapel and has a grating before it. Here they have the organ, and various shrines, saints, *nacimientos*, etc. We were afterwards shown into a great hall devoted to a different purpose, containing at one end a small theatre for the pupils to act plays in. All the walls of the long galleries are covered with old paintings on holy subjects, but many of them falling to pieces from damp or want of care. The building seems interminable, and after wandering all through it for several hours, and visiting everything—from the garden below where they gave me a large bunch of roses and carnations, to the azotea above, which looks down upon every street and church and convent in Mexico—we were not sorry to rest on the antique, high-backed chairs of a handsome apartment, of which the walls were hung with the portraits of the different Spanish directors of the college in an ancient court costume. Here we found that the directors had prepared a beautiful collation for us—fruit, ices, cakes, custards, jellies, wines, etc., in great profusion.

Rested and refreshed, we proceeded to visit the pupils at their different classes. At the writing-class various specimens of that polite art were presented to us. That of the elder girls was generally bad, probably from their having entered the college late in life. That of the younger ones was much more tolerable. We saw some really beautiful specimens of embroidery. Having returned to the hall where there was a piano, some of our party began to sing and play. The Señora G——o sang an Italian air beautifully. She is evidently a scientific musician. The Señorita H——s played one of Herz's most difficult *combinations* with great execution, and a pretty girl, who is living in a convent, having been placed there by her *novio*, to keep her out of harm's way till he is prepared to give her his hand, sang a duet with another young lady, which I accompanied. Both had fine voices, but no notion of what they were singing. My friend the Señora C—— delighted us with some of the innumerable and amusing verses of the *Jota Arragonesa*, which seem to have neither end nor beginning, all gay and all untranslatable, or at least losing their point and wit when put into an English dress. Such as

> *A poor man met with a sixpence,*
> *And for joy he gave up the ghost,*
> *And in the troubles of death,*
> *Even his sixpence was lost.*

> *The woman who loves two at once,*
> *Knows what is discreet and right*
> *Since if one of her candles goes out,*
> *Still the other remains alight, etc. . . .*

It is impossible to see any building of this size kept more perfectly clean and neat; generally the case here in all establishments which are under petticoat government. These old Spanish institutions are certainly on a magnificent scale, though now for the most part neglected and falling to ruin; nor has any work of great consequence been attempted since the independence. . . .

After various alarms and rumours in our house concerning robbers, some true, some exaggerated, and some wholly false, we have at length procured two old Spanish soldiers of the *Invalidos*, who have taken up their quarters downstairs, and spend their time in cleaning their guns, making shoes, eating and sleeping, but as yet have had no occasion to prove their valour. Perhaps the fact of there being soldiers in the house will be sufficient to keep off the more ordinary robbers.

LETTER THE TWELFTH

The Viga during the Carnival—Variety of Equipages—The Millionaires—The Monks—Masked Ball—An Alarming Sight —Medical Students—Dinner at the Prussian Minister's—Rides on Horseback—Indian Love of Flowers—Santa Anita—The Chinampas—Their Origin—Indians in Canoes—Song of "El Palomo"—Fighting—The Great Lakes—The Drain of Huehuetoca—The great Market of Tlatelolco.

16th March.

We are now in Lent in the midst of prayer, church-going, and fasting. The carnival was not very gay, with the exception of a few public masked balls and very brilliant *paséos*. The Viga is one of the most beautiful promenades imaginable, though it might easily be rendered still more so; but even as it is, with its fine shady trees and canal, along which the lazy canoes are constantly gliding, it would be difficult, on a fine evening, just before sunset, especially on the evening of a fête-day, to find anywhere a prettier or more characteristic scene. Which rank of society shows the most taste in their mode of enjoyment, must be left to the scientific to determine; the Indians, with their flower-garlands and guitars, lying in their canoes, and dancing and singing after their own fashion as they glide along the water, inhaling the balmy breezes; or the ladies, who shut up in their close carriages, promenade along in full dress and silence for a given space of time, acknowledging by a gentle movement of their fan, the salutations of their fair friends from the recesses of their coaches, and seeming to dread lest the air of heaven should visit them too roughly; though the soft breeze, laden with balm, steals over the sleepy water, and the last rays of the sun are gilding the branches of the trees with a broken and flickering light. . . .

Then at certain intervals of time each carriage slowly draws up beside its neighbour (as in the other paséo); the elegant *carratela* beside the plebeian hackney-coach; the splendid equipage of the millionaire beside the lumbering and antique vehicle whose fashion hath now departed. There sit the inmates in silence, as if the business of life were over, and it was now their part to watch the busy world from the loopholes of their retreat, and see it rolling along whilst they take their rest. The gentlemen also draw up their prancing steeds, though not within hail of the carriages, but they in the fresh air and under the green trees have as much advantage over the Señoras as the wandering friar has over the cloistered nun.

Yet enter the Viga about five o'clock, when freshly watered, and the soldiers have taken their stand to prevent disturbance, and two long lines of carriages are to be seen going and returning as far as the eye can reach, and hundreds of gay plebeians are assembled on the sidewalks with flowers and fruit and *dulces* for sale, and innumerable equestrians in picturesque dresses, and with spirited horses, fill up the interval between the carriages, and the canoes are covering the canal, the Indians singing and dancing lazily as the boats steal along, and the whole under a blue and cloudless sky, and in that pure clear atmosphere: and could you only shut your eyes to the one disagreeable feature in the picture, the number of léperos busy in the exercise of their vocation, you would believe that Mexico must be the most flourishing, most enjoyable, and most peaceful place in the world, and moreover the wealthiest; not a republic, certainly, for there is no well-dressed *people;* hardly a connecting link between the blankets and the satins, the poppies and the diamonds. As for the carriages, many would not disgrace Hyde Park, though there are some that would send a shiver all along Bond-street; but the very contrast is amusing, and upon the whole, both as to horses and equipages, there is much more to admire than to criticise. . . .

There, for example, is the handsome carriage of the rich —— ——, who has one of the finest houses in Mexico; his wife wears a velvet turban twisted with large pearls, and has at this moment a cigar in her mouth. She is not pretty, but her jewels are superb. How he made his fortune, partly by gambling, and partly by even less honourable means, let some abler chronicler relate. Or look at this elegant *carratela,* with its glass sides all open, giving to view a constellation of fair ones, and drawn by handsome gray *frisones.* These ladies are remarkable as having a more European air than most others, brighter colours, longer and simpler dresses, and Paris bonnets. Perhaps they have been in Europe. It is remarkable that the horses of the gentlemen all appear peculiarly unmanageable every time they pass this carriage. Another handsome, plain carriage, containing the family of one of the ministers; mother and daughters all beautiful, with Spanish eyes and dark glowing complexions, followed close by a hackney-coach containing women with rebosos, and little children, with their faces and fingers all bedaubed with candy. . . . Some of the coachmen and footmen wear Mexican dresses, and others have liveries. . . . But here come three carriages *en suite,* all with the same crimson and gold livery, all luxurious, and all drawn by handsome white horses. It is the President? Certainly not; it is too ostentatious. Even royalty goes in simpler guise, when it condescends to mingle in the amusements of its subjects. In the first carriage appear the great man himself and his consort, rather withdrawing from the plebeian gaze. There is here much crimson and gold, much glass and well-stuffed cushions, much comfort and magnificence combined. Two handsome northern steeds, white and prancing, draw this commodious equipage. The next is a splendid coach containing the children and servants, while in the third, equally magnificent, are the babies and nurses. By the side of the first carriage rides an elderly gentleman, who, were his seat firmer, might be mistaken for a *picador.* He wears a rich Mexican dress, all covered with gold embroidery; his hat with gold rolls is stuck jauntily on one side, contrasting oddly enough with his uneasy expression of countenance, probably caused by the inward trepidation of which he cannot wholly repress the outward sign while managing his highbred steed, and with his feet pressing his silver stirrups, cautiously touching him with a whip which has a large diamond in the handle.

But the chief wonder of his equipment, and that which has procured him such a retinue of little ragged and shouting boys, is his saddle. This extraordinary piece of furniture, which cost the owner five thousand dollars, is entirely covered with velvet, richly embossed in massive gold; he sometimes appears with another, inlaid with pure silver.

His whole appearance is the most singular imaginable, and the perturbation of spirit in which he must return when it begins to grow dusk, and he reflects at once upon his own value, and his countrymen's taste for appropriation, must balance the enjoyment which his vanity receives from the admiration of the little boys in the Paseo.

Just as these millionaires pass by, an old hackney-coach in their wake, attracts our attention, exactly the sort of quaint old vehicle in which it sometimes pleases Lady Morgan to introduce her heroines. In it are six figures, closely masked, their faces covered with shawls. After many conjectures, it is impossible to guess whether they are men or women. It *was* impossible, but as the carriages return, the wind suddenly blows aside the shawls of two of the party, and discloses the gowns and hoods of the—friars! *O tempora! O Mores!*

There were three masked balls at the theatre, of which we only attended one. We went about ten o'clock to a box on the pit tier, and although a *pronunciamento* (a fashionable term here for a revolution) was prognosticated, we found everything very quiet and orderly, and the ball very gay and crowded. As we came in, and were giving our tickets, a number of masks came springing by, shrieking out our names in their unearthly voices. Captain G——, brother of Lord ——, came to our box; also a scion of *La jeune France,* M. de C——, who condescendingly kept his hat on during the whole evening. In a box directly above us were the French legation who arrived lately. Amongst the women, the dresses were for the most part dominoes, adopted for greater concealment, as it was not considered very creditable to be there.

There were also several in men's attire, chiefly French modistes, generally a most disreputable set here, and numerous men dressed as women. There were masked Poblanas without stockings, and with very short petticoats; knights in armour; innumerable dresses probably borrowed from the theatre, and even more than the usual proportion of odd figures. The music was very good, and the dancers waltzed and *galloped,* and flew round the room like furies. There was at least no want of animation. Hundreds of masks spoke to us, but I discovered no one. One in a domino was particularly anxious to direct my attention to the Poblana dress, and asked me if it would have done for me to attend a fancy ball in such a costume. Very angry at his absurdity, I began to explain how I should have dressed, when I recollected the folly of explaining anything to a creature whom I did not know. C——n stepped out of the box, to walk amongst the crowd, at which various masks showed great signs of joy, surrounding and shaking hands with him.

The boxes were filled with ladies, and the scene was very amusing. Señor M——, whose box we occupied, ordered in cakes and wine, and about one o'clock we left the ball-room and returned home, one of our soldiers acting as lackey. . . .

I paid a visit the other day, which merits to be recorded. It was to the rich Señora ——, whose first visit I had not yet returned. She was at home, and I was shown into a very large drawing-room, where, to my surprise, I found the lamps, mirrors, etc., covered with black crape, as in cases of mourning here. I concluded that some one of the family was dead, and that I had made a very ill-timed first visit. However I sat down, when my eyes were instantly attracted by *something awful,* placed directly in front of the sofa where I sat. There were six chairs ranged together, and on these lay stretched out a figure, apparently a dead body, about six feet long, enveloped in black cloth, the feet alone visible, from their pushing up the cloth. Oh, horror! Here I sat, my eyes fixed upon this mysterious apparition, and lost in conjecture as to whose body it might be. The master of the house? He was very tall, and being in bad health might have died suddenly. My being received, argued nothing against this, since the first nine days after a death, the house is invariably crowded with friends and acquaintances, and the widow, or orphan, or childless mother must receive the condolences of all and sundry, in the midst of her first bitter sorrow. There seems to be no idea of grief wishing for solitude.

Pending these reflections, I sat uneasily, feeling or fancying a heavy air in the apartment, and wishing, most sincerely, that some living person would enter. I thought even of slipping away, but feared to give offence, and in fact began to grow so nervous, that when the Señora de —— entered at length, I started up as if I had heard a pistol. She wore a coloured muslin gown and a blue shawl; no signs of mourning!

After the complimentary preface, I asked particularly after her husband, keeping a side glance on the mysterious figure. He was pretty well. Her family? Just recovered from the small-pox, after being severely ill. "Not dangerously?" said I, hesitatingly, thinking she might have *a tall son,* and that she alluded to the recovery of the others. "No;" but her sister's children had been alarmingly ill. "Not *lost* any, I hope?"— "None." Well, so taken up was I, that conversation flagged, and I answered and asked questions at random, until, at last, I happened to ask the lady if she were going to the country soon. "Not to remain. But to-morrow we are going to convey a *Santo Cristo* (a figure of the Crucifixion) there, which has just been made for the chapel;" glancing towards the figure; "for which reason this room is, as you see, hung with black." I never felt so relieved in my life, and thought of the Mysteries of Udolpho.

The houses being so large, and the servants not drilled to announce visitors; besides that the entresols are frequently let to other families, it is a matter of no small difficulty for a stranger to pioneer him or herself into the presence of the people of the house. The mistakes that I have made! for not being aware of this fact concerning the entresols, which are often large and handsome, and the porter having begged me to walk up, I generally stopped at the first landing-place, and then *walked up* to the first door that I saw. I did walk in one morning upon two gentlemen who seemed marvellously startled by my visit. They looked like two medical students, and were engaged before a table, Heaven knows how; dissecting, I imagine. I inquired for the Señora ——, which astonished them still more, as well it might. However, they were very civil, and rushed downstairs to call up the carriage. After that adventure I never entered a house unaccompanied by a footman, until I had learnt my way through it.

We had a pleasant dinner-party a few days ago at the Prussian Minister's, and met the C——s family there. The Condesa de C—— has been a long while in Europe, and in the best society, and is now entirely devoted to the education of her daughters, giving them every advantage that Mexico can afford in the way of masters, besides having at home a Spanish governess to assist her, an excellent woman, whom they regard as a second mother.

Though there is very little going on in Mexico at present, I amuse myself very well; there is so much to see, and the people are so kind and friendly. Having got riding-horses we have been making excursions all round the country, especially early in the morning, before the sun is high, when the air is delightfully cool and refreshing. Sometimes we go to the Viga at six in the morning, to see the Indians bringing in their flowers and vegetables by the canal. The profusion of sweet-peas, double poppies, blue bottles, stock gillyflower, and roses, I never saw equalled. Each Indian woman in her canoe looks as if seated in a floating flower-garden. The same love of flowers distinguishes them now as in the time of Cortes; the same which Humboldt remarked centuries afterwards. In the evening these Indian women, in their canoes, are constantly crowned with garlands of roses or poppies. Those who sit in the market, selling their fruit or their vegetables, appear as if they sat in bowers formed of fresh green branches and coloured flowers. In the poorest village church the floor is strewed with flowers, and before the service begins fresh nosegays are brought in and arranged upon the altar. The baby at its christening, the bride at the altar, the dead body in its bier, are all adorned with flowers. We are told that in the days of Cortes a bouquet of rare flowers was the most valuable gift presented to the ambassadors who visited the court of Montezuma, and it presents a strange anomaly, this love of flowers having existed along with their sanguinary worship and barbarous sacrifices.

We went the other evening on the canal, in a large canoe with an awning, as far as the little village of Santa Anita, and saw, for the first time, the far-famed Chinampas, or floating gardens, which have now become fixtures, and are covered with vegetables, intermingled with flowers, with a few poor huts beside them, occupied by the Indians, who bring these to the city for sale. There were cauliflowers, chile, tomatoes, cabbages, and other vegetables, but I was certainly disappointed in their beauty. They are however curious, on account of their origin. So far back as 1245, it is said the wandering Aztecs or Mexicans arrived first at Chapultepec, when, being persecuted by the princes of Taltocan, they took refuge in a group of islands to the south of the lake of Tezcuco. Falling under the yoke of the Tezcucan kings, they abandoned their island home and fled to Tezapan, where, as a reward for assisting the chiefs of that country in a war against other petty princes, they received their freedom, and established themselves in a city to which they gave the name of Mexicalsingo, from Mejitli, their god of war—now a collection of strong barns and poor huts. But they did not settle there, for to obey an oracle they transported themselves from this city to the islands east of Chapultepec to the western side of the lake of Tezcuco. An ancient tradition had long been current amongst them, that wherever they should behold an eagle seated upon a nopal whose roots pierced a rock, there they should found a great city. In 1325 they beheld this sign, and on the spot, in an island in the lake, founded the first house of God—the Teocalli, or Great Temple of Mexico. During all their wanderings, wherever they stopped, the Aztecs cultivated the earth, and lived upon what nature gave them. Surrounded by enemies and in the midst of a lake where there are few fish, necessity and industry compelled them to form floating fields and gardens on the bosom of the waters.

They weaved together the roots of aquatic plants, intertwined with twigs and light branches, until they had formed a foundation sufficiently strong to support a soil formed of the earth which they drew from the bottom of the lake; and on it they sowed their maize, their chile, and all other plants necessary for their support. These floating gardens were about a foot above the water, and in the form of a long square. Afterwards, in their natural taste for flowers, they not only cultivated the useful but the ornamental, and these small gardens multiplying were covered with flowers and aromatic herbs, which were used in the worship of the gods, or were sent to ornament the palace of the emperor. The Chinanpas along the canal of the Viga are no longer floating gardens, but fixed to the mainland in the marshy grounds lying between the two great lakes of Chalco and Tezcuco. A small trench full of water separates each garden; and though now in this marshy land they give but a faint idea of what they may have been when they raised their flower-crowned heads above the clear waters of the lake, and when the Indians, in their barks, wishing to remove their habitations, could tow along their little islands of roses, it is still a pretty and a pleasant scene.

We bought numerous garlands of roses and poppies from the Indian children, both here and at Santa Anita, a little village where we landed, and as we returned towards evening we were amused by the singing and dancing of the Indians. One canoe came close up to ours, and kept beside it for some time. A man was lying lazily at the bottom of the boat tingling his guitar, and one or two women were dancing monotonously and singing at the same time to his music. Sundry jars of pulque and earthen dishes with tortillas and chile and pieces of *tasajo*, long festoons of dried and salted beef, proved that the party were not without their solid comforts, in spite of the romantic guitar and the rose and poppy garlands with which the dancing nymphs were crowned. Amongst others they performed the *Palomo*, the Dove, one of their most favourite dances. The music is pretty, and I send it to you with the words, the music from ear; the words are given me by my friend the Señora A——d, who sings all these little Indian airs in perfection. If we may form some judgment of a people's civilization by their ballads, none of the Mexican songs give us a very high idea of theirs. The words are generally a tissue of absurdities, nor are there any patriotic songs which their new-born freedom might have called forth from so musical a people. At least I have as yet only discovered one air of which the words bear reference to the glorious "Grito de Dolores," and which asserts in rhyme that on account of that memorable event, the Indian was able to get as drunk as a Christian! The translation of the Palomo is as follows:

"What are you doing, little dove, there in the wineshop? Waiting for my love until Tuesday, my life. A dove in flying hurt her little wing. If you have your dove I have my little dove too. A dove in flying all her feathers fell off. Women pay badly; not all, but some of them. Little dove of the barracks, you will tell the drummers when they beat the retreat to strike up the march of my loves. Little dove, what are you doing there leaning against that wall? Waiting for my dove till he brings me something to eat." At the end of each verse the chorus of "Palomita, palomo, palomo."

Yet, monotonous as it is, the air is so pretty, the women sang so softly and sleepily, the music sounded so soothingly as we glided along the water, that I felt in a pleasant half-dreamy state of perfect contentment, and was sorry when, arriving at the landing-place, we had to return to a carriage and civilized life, with nothing but the garlands of flowers to remind us of the Chinampas.

Unfortunately these people generally end by too frequent applications to the jarro of pulque, or what is worse to the pure spirit known by the name of *chinguirite;* the consequence of which is, that from music and dancing and rose-becrowning, they proceed to quarrelling and jealousy and drunkenness, which frequently terminates in their fighting, stabbing each other, or throwing each other into the canal. "The end crowns the work."

Noble as this present city of Mexico is, one cannot help thinking how much more picturesque the ancient Tenochtitlan was, and how much more fertile its valley must have been, on account of the great lakes. Yet even in the time of Cortes these lakes had no great depth of water, and still further back, in the time of the Indian Emperors, navigation had been so frequently interrupted in seasons of drought, that an aqueduct had been constructed in order to supply the canals with water.

After this, the Spaniards, like all new settlers, hewed down the fine trees in this beautiful valley, both on plain and mountain, leaving the bare soil exposed to the vertical rays of the sun. Then their well-founded dread of inundation caused them to construct the famous *Desagüe* of Huehuetoca, the drain or subterranean conduit or channel in the mountain for drawing off the waters of the lakes; thus leaving marshy lands or sterile plains covered with carbonate of soda, where formerly were silver lakes covered with canoes. This last was a necessary evil, since the Indian emperors themselves were sensible of its necessity and had formed great works for draining the lakes, some remains of which works still exist in the vicinity of the Penon. The great Desagüe was begun in 1607, when the Marquis of Salinas was viceroy of Mexico; and the operations were commenced with great pomp, the viceroy assisting in person, mass being said on a portable altar, and fifteen hundred workmen assembled, while the marquis himself began the excavation by giving the first stroke with a spade. From 1607 to 1830, eight millions of dollars were expended, and yet this great work was not brought to a conclusion. However, the limits of the two lakes of Zumpango and San Cristobal, to the north of the valley, were thus greatly reduced, and the lake of Tezcuco, the most beautiful of all the five, no longer received their contributions. Thus the danger of inundations has diminished, but water and vegetation have diminished also, and the suburbs of the city, which were formerly covered with beautiful gardens, now present to the eye an arid expanse of efflorescent salt. The plains near San Lazaro especially, in their arid whiteness, seem characteristic of the unfortunate victims of leprosy enclosed in the walls of that hospital.

We rode out the other day by the *barrio,* or ward of Santiago, which occupies part of the ancient Tlatelolco, which once constituted a separate state, had kings of its own, and was conquered by a Mexican monarch, who made a communication by bridges between it and Mexico. The great market mentioned by Cortes was held here, and its boundaries are still pointed out, whilst the convent chapel stands on the height where Cortes erected a battering engine, when he was besieging the Indian Venice.

LETTER THE THIRTEENTH

Convent of San Joaquin—Mexico in the Morning—Tacuba—
Carmelite Prior—Convent Garden—Hacienda of Los Mo-
rales—El   Olivar—A   Huacamaya—Humming-birds—Corre-
spondence—Expected Consecration—Visit to the Mineria—
Botanic Garden—Arbol de las Manitas—The Museum—
Equestrian Statue—Academy of Painting and Sculpture—
Disappointment.

Early this morning we rode to the convent of San Joaquin,
belonging to friars of the Carmelite order, passing through
Tacuba, the ancient Tlacopan, once the capital of a small
kingdom, and whose monarch, *Tetlepanquetzaltzin* (short and
convenient name), Cortes caused to be hung on a tree for a
supposed or real conspiracy. The number of carts, the innumerable Indians loaded like beasts of burden, their women
with baskets of vegetables in their hands and children on their
backs, the long strings of *arrièros* with their loaded mules, the
droves of cattle, the flocks of sheep, the herds of pigs, render
it a work of some difficulty to make one's way on horseback
out of the gates of Mexico at an early hour of the morning,
but it must be confessed, that the whole scene is lively and
cheerful enough to make one forget that there is such a thing
as care in the world. There is an indifferent, placid smile on
every face, and the bright blue sky smiling over them all; dogs
bark, and asses bray, and the Indian, with near a mule's load
on his back, drags his hat off to salute a bevy of his bronze-
coloured countrymen, nearly equally laden with himself, and
they all show their teeth and talk their liquid Indian and
pass on.

These plains of Tacuba, once the theatre of fierce and
bloody conflicts, and where, during the siege of Mexico, Alvarado of the Leap fixed his camp, now present a very tranquil
scene. Tacuba itself is now a small village of mud huts, with
some fine old trees, a few very old ruined houses, a ruined
church, and some traces of a building which —— assured us
had been the palace of their last monarch; whilst others declare it to have been the site of the Spanish encampment.

San Joaquin, also a poor village, contains the fine convent

and immense walled garden and orchard belonging to the rich monks of the Carmelite order. As C——n knows the prior, he sent in our names, and I was admitted as far as the sacristy of the convent church. The prior received us with the utmost kindness: he is a good-looking man, extremely amiable and well-informed, and still young. The gentlemen were admitted into the interior of the convent, which they describe as being a very large handsome building, clean and airy, with a fine old library, chiefly composed of theological works; to the garden, which is immensely large, and though not much cultivated, full of flowers; and to the great orchard, celebrated for the profusion and excellence of its fruit. There is a mirador in the garden which can be seen from the road, and from which there is a very extensive view. I was very anxious for admission only to the garden, and pleaded the *manly* appearance of my riding-hat, which would prevent all scandal were I seen from a distance; but the complaisance of the good prior would not go quite so far as that, so I sat in the sacristy and conversed with a good-natured old monk with a double chin, whilst the others wandered through the grounds. They afterwards gave us a very nice breakfast, simple but good; fish from the lake, different preparations of eggs, *riz-ou-lait*, coffee, and fruit. The monks did not sit down with us, nor would they partake of anything themselves.

We went in the evening to see a pretty hacienda called Los Morales (the mulberry-tree) belonging to a Spaniard, which has a nice garden with a bath in it, and where they bestowed a quantity of beautiful flowers on us.

The other day we set off early, together with the Belgian and French ministers and their families, in carriages, to visit a beautiful deserted hacienda, called *el Olivar*, belonging to the Marquis of Santiago. The house is perfectly bare, with nothing but the walls; but the grounds are a wilderness of tangled flowers and blossoming trees, rose-bushes, sweet-peas, and all manner of fragrant flowers. We passed an agreeable day, wandering about, breakfasting on the provisions brought with us, arranging large bouquets of flowers, and firing at a mark, which must have startled the birds in this solitary and uncultivated retreat. We had a pleasant family dinner at the E——'s, and passed the evening at the Baron de ——'s. The gentlemen returned late, it being the day of a diplomatic dinner at the English minister's.

The Countess del V——e has just sent me a beautiful bird with the most gorgeous plumage of the brightest scarlet and

blue. It is called a *huacamaya*, and is of the parrot species,
but three times as large, being about two feet from the beak
to the tip of the tail. It is a superb creature but very wicked,
gnawing not only its own pole, but all the doors, and committing great havoc amongst the plants, besides trying to bite
every one who approaches it. It pronounces a few words very
hoarsely and indistinctly, and has a most harsh, disagreeable
cry. In fact it presumes upon its beauty to be as unamiable
as possible.

I prefer some beautiful little humming-birds (*chupamirtos*
as they are called here) which have been sent me, and which
I am trying to preserve alive, but I fear the cold will kill
them, for though we see them occasionally here, hanging by
their beaks upon the branches of the flowers, like large butterflies, and shaking their brilliant little wings so rapidly that
they seem to emit sparkles of coloured light; still this is not
their home; properly speaking, they belong to the *tierra
caliente*. These little birds are of a golden green and purple,
and are so tame, that whilst I am writing I have two on my
shoulder and one perched on the edge of a glass, diving out
its long tongue for sugar and water. Our live stock is considerable: we have Guinea fowls, who always remind me of
old maiden ladies in half-mourning, and whose screaming
notes match those of the huacamaya; various little green parrots; a scarlet cardinal, one hundred and sixty pigeons in the
pigeon-house, and three fierce dogs in conspicuous situations.

I received a very polite letter to-day from the Señora de
Santa Anna, and as it was enclosed in a few lines from Santa
Anna himself, I send you his *autograph*, for I doubt much
whether we have seen the last of that illustrious personage,
or whether his philosophic retirement will endure for ever.

I have been endeavouring lately to procure permission from
Señor Posada, who is shortly to be consecrated archbishop,
to visit the convents of nuns in Mexico. Señor C——o, secretary
of state, our particular friend, has been kind enough to interest
himself in the matter, though with indifferent hopes of success. A few days ago he sent me his correspondence with
Señor Posada, who observes that the vice-queens alone had
the privilege of the *entrée*, and seems to hesitate a good deal
as to the advisableness of granting a permission which might
be considered a precedent for others. However, I think he is
too amiable to resist our united entreaties. I hold out as an
argument, that C——n, being the *duplicado* of the queen herself, my visit is equal to that of the vice-queen, which argu-

ment has at least amused him. His consecration is fixed for the 31st of May.

Don Pedro Fonti, the last archbishop named in the time of the Spanish dominion, having renounced the mitre, three illustrious churchmen were proposed to fill the vacant place: this Don Manuel Posada, Don Antonio Campos, and Dr. Don José Maria de Santiago. The first was chosen by the Mexican government, and was afterwards proclaimed in the Roman Consistory last December, with the approbation of Gregory XVI. They are now only waiting for the pontifical bulls, which are daily expected from Rome; and it is said that the ceremony, which will take place in the cathedral, will be very magnificent.

April 3rd.—Accompanied by the —— minister, we spent yesterday in visiting the Mineria, the Botanic Garden, the Museum, etc., all which leave a certain disagreeable impression on the mind, since, without having the dignity of ruins, they are fine buildings neglected. The Mineria, or School of Mines, the work of the famous architect and sculptor Tolsa, is a magnificent building, a palace whose fine proportions would render it remarkable amongst the finest edifices of any European country. All is on a great scale, its noble rows of pillars, great staircases, large apartments and lofty roofs, but it reminds one of a golden aviary, containing a few common sparrows. Several rich Spaniards contributed more than six hundred thousand dollars to its construction. We were shown through the whole of this admirable building by the director, who occupies a very handsome house attached to it. But however learned the professors may be,—and amongst them is the scientific Señor del Rio, now very old, but a man of great learning and research,—the collection of minerals, the instruments and models, are all miserable and ill kept.

The Botanic Garden, within the palace, is a small ill-kept enclosure, where there still remain some rare plants of the immense collection made in the time of the Spanish government, when great progress was made in all the natural sciences, four hundred thousand dollars having been expended in botanical expeditions alone. Courses of botanical lectures were then given annually by the most learned professors, and the taste for natural history was universal.

El Arbol de las Manitas (the tree of the small hands) was the most curious which we saw in the garden. The flower is of a bright scarlet, in the form of a hand, with five fingers and a thumb; and it is said that there are only three of these trees in the republic. The gardener is an old Italian, who came over with one of the viceroys, and though now one hundred and ten years old, and nearly bent double, possesses all his faculties. The garden is pretty from the age of the trees, and luxuriance of the flowers, but melancholy as a proof of the decay of the science in Mexico. The palace itself, now occupied by the president, formerly belonged to Cortes, and was ceded by his descendants to the government. In exchange they received the ground formerly occupied by the palace of the Aztec kings, and built on it a very splendid edifice, where the state archives are kept, and where the *Monte Pio* (the office where money is lent on plate, jewels, etc.) now is, the director of which is Don Francisco Tagle, whose apartments within the building are very elegant and spacious.

The Museum within the University, and opposite the palace, in the plaza called del Volador, contains many rare and valuable works, many curious Indian antiquities, but they are ill arranged. On the walls are the portraits of the vice-kings, beginning with Hernan Cortes. We spent a long while here examining these antiquities; but we have seen nothing in Mexico to equal the beauty of the colossal equestrian statue in bronze of Charles IV, placed on a pedestal of Mexican marble, which stands in the court of the University, but formerly adorned the middle of the square. It is a magnificent picture of sculpture, the masterpiece of Tolosa, remarkable for the noble simplicity and purity of its style, and was made at the expense of an ex-viceroy, the Marquis of Branciforte. We also saw the goddess of war lying in a corner of the court, beside the stone of sacrifices, which we had already been shown.

To-day we have been visiting the Academy of painting and sculpture, called the Academy of Fine Arts, of which I unfortunately recollected having read Humboldt's brilliant account, in my forcibly prolonged studies on board the Jason, and that he mentions its having had the most favourable influence in forming the national taste. He tells us that every night, in these spacious halls, well illumined by Argand lamps, hundreds of young men were assembled, some sketching from the plaster-casts, or from life, and others copying designs of furniture, candelabras and other bronze ornaments; and that here all classes, colours, and races, were mingled together; the Indian beside the white boy, and the son of the poorest mechanic beside that of the richest lord. Teaching was gratis, and not limited to landscape and figures, one of the principal objects being to propagate amongst the artists a general taste for elegance and beauty of form, and to enliven the national industry. Plaster-casts, to the amount of forty thousand dollars, were sent out by the King of Spain, and as they possess in the academy various colossal statues of basalt and porphyry, with Aztec hieroglyphics, it would have been curious, as the same learned traveller remarks, to have collected these monuments in the courtyard of the Academy, and compared the remains of Mexican sculpture, monuments of a semi-barbarous people, with the graceful creations of Greece and Rome.

Let no one visit the Academy with these recollections or anticipations in his mind. . . . That the simple and noble taste which distinguishes the Mexican buildings, their perfection in the cutting and working of their stones, the chaste ornaments of the capitals and relievoes, are owing to the progress they made in this very Academy is no doubt the case. The remains of these beautiful but mutilated plaster-casts, the splendid engravings which still exist, would alone make it probable; but the present disorder, the abandoned state of the building, the nonexistence of these excellent classes of sculpture and painting, and, above all, the low state of the fine arts in Mexico, at the present day, are amongst the sad proofs, if any were wanting, of the melancholy effects produced by years of civil war and unsettled government. . . .

The Holy Week is now approaching, and already Indians are to be seen bringing in the palm-branches and the flowers for the altars, and they are beginning to erect booths and temporary shops, and to make every preparation for the concourse of people who will arrive next Sunday from all the different villages and ranchoes, far and near.

LETTER THE FOURTEENTH

Palm Sunday—Holy Thursday—Variety of Costumes—San Francisco — Santo Domingo — Santa Teresa — Nuns — Stone Bust—The Academy—Religious Procession—Pilgrimage to the Churches—Santa Clara—Nun's Voice—Orange-trees and Rose-bushes—The Cathedral Illuminated—Our Saviour in Chains—Good Friday—The great Square towards Evening —Dresses of Men, Women, and Children—Approach of the Host—Judas—Great Procession—Miserere—The Square by Moonlight—A Lonely Walk—Sabado de Gloria—Ball in Contemplation—Weekly Soirées—Embroidered Muslins—A Tertulia at Home.

21st April.

On the morning of Palm Sunday, I went to the Cathedral, accompanied by Mademoiselle de ——, daughter of the —— Minister. We found it no easy matter to make our way through the crowd; but at last, by dint of patience and perseverance, and changing our place very often, we contrived to arrive very near the great altar; and there we had just taken up our position, when a disinterested man gave us a friendly hint, that as the whole procession, with their branches, must inevitably squeeze past the spot where we were, we should probably be crushed or suffocated; consequently we followed him to a more convenient station, also close to the altar and defended by the railing, where we found ourselves tolerably well off. Two ladies, to whom he made the same proposition, and who rejected it, we afterwards observed in a sad condition, their mantillas nearly torn off and the palm-branches sweeping across their eyes.

In a short time, the whole cathedral presented the appearance of a forest of palm-trees, (*à la* Birnam wood) moved by a gentle wind; and under each tree a half-naked Indian, his rags clinging together with wonderful pertinacity; long, matted, dirty black hair both in men and women, bronze faces with mild unspeaking eyes, or all with one expression of eagerness to see the approach of the priests. Many of them had probably travelled a long way, and the palms were from *tierra caliente,* dried and plaited into all manner of ingenious ways. Each palm was about seven feet high, so as far to overshadow the head of the Indian who carried it; and whenever they are blessed, they are carried home to adorn the walls of their huts. The priests arrived, at length, in great pomp; and also carrying palm-branches. For four mortal hours, we remained kneeling or sitting on the floor, and thankful we were when it was all over, and we could make our way once more into the fresh air.

From this day, during the whole week, all business is suspended, and but one train of thought occupies all classes, from the highest to the lowest. The peasants flock from every quarter, shops are shut, churches are opened; and the Divine Tragedy enacted in Syria eighteen hundred years ago, is now celebrated in land then undiscovered, and by the descendants of nations sunk in Paganism for centuries after that period.

But amongst the lower classes, the worship is emphatically the worship of Her who Herself predicted, "From henceforth all nations shall call me blessed." Before her shrines, and at all hours, thousands are kneeling. With faces expressive of the most intense love and devotion, and with words of the most passionate adoration, they address the mild image of the Mother of God. To the Son their feelings seem composed of respectful pity, of humble but more distant adoration; while to the Virgin they appear to give all their confidence, and to look up to her as to a kind and bountiful Queen, who, dressed in her magnificent robes and jewelled diadem, yet mourning in all the agony of her divine sorrows, has condescended to admit the poorest beggar to participate in her woe, whilst in her turn she shares in the afflictions of the lowly, feels for their privations, and grants them her all-powerful intercession.

On Holy Thursday nothing can be more picturesque than the whole appearance of Mexico. No carriages are permitted and the ladies, being on foot, take the opportunity of displaying all the riches of their toilet. On this day velvets and satins are your only wear. Diamonds and pearls walk the streets. The mantillas are white or black blonde; the shoes white or coloured satin. The petticoats are still rather short, but it would be hard to hide such small feet, and such still smaller shoes. "Il faut souffrir pour être belle," but *à quoi bon être belle?* if no one sees it. As for me, I *ventured* upon a lilac silk of Palmyre's, and a black mantilla.

The whole city was filled with picturesque figures. After the higher Señoras were to be remarked the common women, chiefly in clear white, very stiffly starched muslins, some very richly embroidered, and the petticoat trimmed with lace, white satin shoes, and the dresses extremely short, which in them looks very well. A reboso is thrown over all. Amongst these were many handsome faces, but in a still lower and more Indian class, with their gay-coloured petticoats, the faces were sometimes beautiful, and the figures more upright and graceful; also they invariably walk well whilst many of the higher classes, from tight shoes and want of custom, seem to feel pain in putting their feet to the ground.

But none could vie with the handsome Poblana peasants in their holiday dresses, some so rich and magnificent, that, remembering the warning of our ministerial friends, I am inclined to believe them more showy than respectable. The pure Indians, with whom the churches and the whole city is crowded, are as ugly as can be imagined; a gentle, dirty, and much-enduring race. Still, with their babies at their backs, going along at their usual gentle trot, they add much to the general effect of the *coup-d'œil*.

We walked to San Francisco about ten o'clock, and the body of the church being crowded, went upstairs to a private gallery with a gilded grating, belonging to the Countess de Santiago, and here we had the advantage of seats, besides a fine view of the whole. This church is very splendid, and the walls were hung with canvas paintings representing different passages of our Saviour's life; his entry into Jerusalem, the woman of Samaria at the well, etc., which, with the palm-trees had a cool and oriental effect.

Before the altar, which was dazzling with jewels, was a representation of the Lord's Supper, not in painting, but in sculptured figures as large as life, habited in the Jewish dresses. The bishops and priests were in a blaze of gold and jewels. They were assisted during the ceremony by the young Count of Santiago. The music was extremely good, and the whole effect impressive. We visited several churches in the course of the day, and continued walking until four o'clock, when we went to dine with our friends the A——s. After dinner one of their coachmen, a handsome Mexican, in a superb dress, all embroidered in gold, was called upstairs to dance the *Jarabe* to us with a country girl. The dance is monotonous, but they acquitted themselves to perfection.

We then continued our pilgrimage through the city, though, as the sun had not yet set, we reserved our chief admiration until the churches should be illuminated. One, however, we entered at sunset, which is worthy of remark—Santo Domingo. It looked like a little Paradise, or a story in the Arabian Nights. All the steps up the altar were covered with pots of beautiful flowers; orange-trees, loaded with fruit and blossom, and rose-bushes in full bloom, glasses of coloured water, and all kinds of fruit. Cages full of birds, singing delightfully, hung from the wall, and really fine paintings filled up the intervals. A gay carpet covered the floor, and in front of the altar, instead of the usual representation of the Saviour crucified, a little infant Jesus, beautifully done in wax, was lying amidst flowers with little angels surrounding him. Add to this, the music of Romeo and Juliet, and you may imagine that it was more like a scene in an opera, than anything in a church. But certainly, as the rays of the setting sun streamed in with a rosy light through the stained windows, throwing a glow over the whole; birds, and flowers, and fruit, paintings and angels, it was the prettiest and most fantastic scene I ever beheld, like something expressly got up for the benefit of children.

We did not kneel before each altar for more than three minutes, otherwise we should never have had time even to enter the innumerable churches which we visited in the course of the night. We next went to Santa Teresa la Nueva, a handsome church, belonging to a convent of strict nuns, which was now brilliantly illuminated; and here, as in all the churches, we made our way through the crowd with extreme difficulty. The number of *léperos* was astonishing, greatly exceeding that of well-dressed people. Before each altar was a figure, dreadful in the extreme, of the Saviour, as large as life, dressed in purple robe and crown of thorns, seated on the steps of the altar, the blood trickling from his wounds; each person, before leaving the church, devoutly kneeling to kiss his hands and feet. The nuns, amongst whom is a sister of Señor A——, sung behind the grating of the gallery above, but were not visible.

One of the churches we visited, that of Santa Teresa, called the *Antigua,* stands upon the site formerly occupied by the palace of the father of the unfortunate Montezuma. It was here that the Spaniards were quartered when they took Montezuma prisoner, and here Cortes found and appropriated the treasures of that family. In 1830 a bust of stone was found in the yard of the convent, which the workmen were digging up. Don Lucas Alaman, then Minister of Exterior Relations, offered a compensation to the nuns for the curious piece of antiquity which they gladly gave up to the government, on whose account he acted. It is said to be the idol goddess of the Indians, *Centeotl*, the goddess of medicine and medicinal herbs, also known by the name of *Temaz calteci*, or the "Grandmother of the Baths." A full account is given of her in one of the numbers of the "Mosaico Megicano," as also of a square stone found in the same place, beautifully carved, and covered with hieroglyphical characters.

In the evening, towards the hour when the great procession was expected, we went to the balconies of the Academia, which command a fine view of the streets by which it was to pass. Till it arrived we amused ourselves by looking over the *beaux restes* of former days, the collections of painting and sculpture, the fine plaster-casts that still remain, and the great volumes of fine engravings. It was dark when the procession made its appearance, which rendered the effect less gaudy and more striking. The Virgin, the Saints, the Holy Trinity, the Saviour in different passages of his life, imprisonment and crucifixion, were carried past in succession, represented by figures magnificently dressed, placed on lofty scaffoldings of immense weight, supported by different bodies of men. One is carried by the coachmen, another by the aguadores (water-carriers), a third by the cargadores (porters), a Herculean race.

First arrived the favourite protectress of all classes, the Virgin of Dolores, surmounted by a velvet canopy, seated on a glittering throne, attired in her sable robes, her brow surmounted by glittering rays, and contracted with an expression of agony; of all representations of the Virgin, the only one which is always lovely, however rudely carved, with that invariably beautiful face of terrible anguish. Then followed the Saviour bearing the cross; the Saviour crucified, the Virgin supporting the head of her dying son; the Trinity (the Holy Spirit represented by a dove); all the apostles, from St. Peter with the keys to Judas with the money-bag; and a long train of saints, all brilliantly illuminated and attended by an amazing crowd of priests, monks, and laymen. However childish and superstitious all this may seem, I doubt whether it be not as well thus to impress certain religious truths on the minds of a people too ignorant to understand them by any other process. By the time the last saint and angel had vanished, the hour was advanced, and we had still to visit the illuminated churches. Being recommended to divest ourselves of our ornaments before wandering forth amongst the crowd, a matter of some moment to the Señora A——, who wore all

her diamonds, we left our earrings, brooches, etc., in charge
of the person who keeps the Academia, and recommenced our
pilgrimage.

Innumerable were the churches we visited that evening;
the Cathedral, La Ensenanza, Jesus Maria, Santa Clara, Santa
Brigida, San Hipolito, La Encarnacion, the five churches of
San Francisco, etc., etc., a list without an end, kneeling for a
short space of time before each blazing altar, for the more
churches one visits, the more meritorious is the devotion. The
cathedral was the first we entered, and its magnificence struck
us with amazement. Its gold and silver and jewels, its innumerable ornaments and holy vessels, the rich dresses of the
priests, all seemed burning in almost intolerable brightness.
The high altar was the most magnificent; the second, with its
pure white marble pillars, the most imposing.

The crowd was immense, but we made our way slowly
through it to the foot of each altar, where the people were
devoutly kissing the Saviour's hand or the hem of his garment;
or beating their breasts before the mild image of Our Lady
of Grief. Each church had vied with the other in putting
forth all its splendour of jewellery, of lights, of dresses, and
of music.

In the church of Santa Clara, attached to the convent of
the same name, small but elegant, with its pillars of white
marble and gold, one voice of angelic sweetness was singing
behind the grating alone, and in the midst of a most deathlike
stillness. It sounded like the notes of a nightingale in a cage.
I could have listened for hours, but our time was limited, and
we set off anew. Fortunately the evening was delightful, and
the moon shining brightly. We visited about twenty churches
in succession. In all the organ was pealing, the blaze of light
overpowering, the magnificence of jewels and crimson velvet
and silver and gold dazzling, the crowd suffocating, the incense blinding.

The prettiest effect in every church was caused by the
orange-trees and rose-bushes, which covered the steps of the
altars, up to where the magnificence of the altar itself blazed
out; and the most picturesque effect was produced by the
different orders of monks in their gowns and hoods, either
lying on their faces or standing ranged with torches like figures
carved in stone.

In the passage leading to most of the churches was a table,
at which several ladies of the highest rank sat collecting alms
for the poor. The fair *quêteuses* had not been very successful,

and that chiefly amongst the lower classes. The fatigue was terrible, walking for so many hours on that bad pavement with thin satin shoes, so that at length our feet seemed to move mechanically, and we dropped on our knees before each altar like machines touched by a spring, and rose again with no small effort. Of all the churches we entered that night, the cathedral was the most magnificent, but the most beautiful and tasteful was San Francisco. The crowd there was so dense, that we were almost carried off our feet, and were obliged, in defiance of all rule, to take the arms of our *caballeros*. Still it was worth the trouble of making our way through it to see such a superbly illuminated altar. It was now eleven o'clock, and the crowd were breaking up as the churches are shut before midnight. In one corner of the middle aisle, near the door, was the representation of a prison from which issued a stream of soft music, and at the window was a figure of Christ in chains, his eyes bandaged, and a Jew on each side; the chains hanging from his hands, and clanking as if with the motion of his arms. The rush here was immense. Numbers of people were kneeling before the window of the prison, and kissing the chains and beating their breasts with every appearance of contrition and devotion. This was the night before the Crucifixion, and the last scene of the Holy Thursday.

We reached home hardly able to stand. I never felt more dazzled, bewildered, and sleepy; but I was wakened by finding a packet of letters from home, which brought back my thoughts, or rather carried them away to very different lands.

On Good Friday, a day of sorrow and humiliation, the scene in the morning is very different. The great sacrifice is complete—the Immortal has died a mortal death. The ladies all issue forth in mourning, and the churches look sad and wan after their last night's brilliancy. The heat was intense. We went to San Francisco, again to the Tribuna of the Countess de Santiago, to see the Adoration and Procession of the Cross, which was very fine.

But the most beautiful and original scene was presented towards sunset in the great square, and it is doubtful whether any other city in the world could present a *coup-d'œil* of equal brilliancy. Having been offered the *entrée* to some apartments in the palace, we took our seats on the balconies, which commanded a view of the whole. The Plaza itself, even on ordinary days, is a noble square, and but for its one fault, a row of shops called the Parian, which breaks its uniformity, would be nearly unrivalled. Every object is interesting. The eye wanders from the cathedral to the house of Cortes (the Monte Pio), and from thence to a range of fine buildings with lofty arcades to the west. From our elevated situation, we could see all the different streets that branch out from the square, covered with gay crowds pouring in that direction to see another great procession, which was expected to pass in front of the palace. Booths filled with refreshments, and covered with green branches and garlands of flowers, were to be seen in all directions, surrounded by a crowd who were quenching their thirst with orgeat, *chia*,[1] lemonade, or pulque. The whole square, from the cathedral to the Portales, and from the Monte Pio to the palace, was covered with thousands and tens of thousands of figures, all in their gayest dresses, and as the sun poured his rays down upon their gaudy colours, they looked like armies of living tulips. Here was to be seen a group of ladies, some with black gowns and mantillas; others, now that their church-going duty was over, equipped in velvet or satin, with their hair dressed,—and beautiful hair they have; some leading their children by the hand, dressed . . . alas! how they were dressed! Long velvet gowns trimmed with blonde, diamond earrings, high French caps befurbelowed with lace and flowers, or turbans with plumes of feathers. Now and then the head of a little thing that could hardly waddle alone, might have belonged to an English dowager-duchess in her opera-box. Some had extraordinary bonnets, also with flowers and feathers, and as they toddled along, top heavy, one would have thought they were little old women, till a glimpse was caught of their lovely little brown faces and black eyes. Now and then a little girl, simply dressed with a short frock, and long black hair plaited down and uncovered, would trip along, a very model of grace amongst the small caricatures. The children here are generally beautiful, their features only too perfect and regular for the face "to fulfil the promise of its spring." They have little colour, with swimming black or hazel eyes, and long lashes resting on the clear pale cheek, and a perfect mass of fine dark hair of the straight Spanish or Indian kind plaited down behind.

As a contrast to the Señoras, with their over-dressed beauties, were the poor Indian women, trotting across the square, their black hair plaited with dirty red ribbon, a piece of woollen cloth wrapped about them, and a little mahogany baby hanging behind, its face upturned to the sky, and its

---

[1] A drink made of the seed of the plant of that name.

head going jerking along, somehow without its neck being dislocated. The most resigned expression on earth is that of an Indian baby. All the groups we had seen promenading the streets the day before were here collected by hundreds; the women of the shopkeeper class, or it may be lower, in their smart white embroidered gowns, with their white satin shoes, and neat feet and ankles, and rebosos or bright shawls thrown over their heads; the peasants and countrywomen, with their short petticoats of two colours, generally scarlet and yellow (for they are most anti-quakerish in their attire), thin satin shoes and lace-trimmed chemises, or bronze-coloured damsels, all crowned with flowers, strolling along with their admirers, and tingling their light guitars. And above all, here and there a flashing Poblana, with a dress of real value and much taste, and often with a face and figure of extraordinary beauty, especially the figure; large and yet *élancée*, with a bold coquettish eye, and a beautiful little brown foot, shown off by the white satin shoe; the petticoat of her dress frequently fringed and embroidered in real massive gold, and a reboso either shot with gold, or a bright-coloured China crape shawl, coquettishly thrown over her head. We saw several whose dresses could not have cost less than five hundred dollars.

Add to this motley crowd, men dressed *à la Mexicaine*, with their large ornamented hats and sarapes, or embroidered jackets, sauntering along, smoking their cigars, *léperos* in rags, Indians in blankets, officers in uniform, priests in their shovel hats, monks of every order; Frenchmen exercising their wit upon the passers-by; Englishmen looking cold and philosophical; Germans gazing through their spectacles, mild and mystical; Spaniards seeming pretty much at home, and abstaining from remarks; and it may be conceived that the scene at least presented variety. Sometimes the tinkling of the bell announced the approach of *Nuestro Amo*. Instantly the whole crowd are on their knees, crossing themselves devoutly. Two men who were fighting below the window suddenly dropped down side by side. Disputes were hushed, flirtations arrested, and to the busy hum of voices succeeded a profound silence. Only the rolling of the coach-wheels and the sound of the little bell were heard.

No sooner had it passed than the talkers and the criers recommenced with fresh vigour. The vendors of hot chestnuts and cooling beverages plied their trade more briskly than ever. A military band struck up an air from Semiramis: and the noise of the innumerable *matracas* (rattles), some of wood and some of silver, with which every one is armed during the last days of the holy week, broke forth again as if by magic, while again commenced the sale of the *Judases*, fireworks in the form of that arch-traitor, which are sold on the evening of Good Friday, and let off on Saturday morning. Hundreds of these hideous figures were held above the crowd, by men who carried them tied together on long poles. An ugly misshapen monster they represent the betrayer to have been. When he sold his master for thirty pieces of silver, did he dream that in the lapse of ages his effigies should be held up to the execration of a Mexican mob, of an unknown people in undiscovered countries beyond the seas?—A secret bargain, perhaps made whisperingly in a darkened chamber with the fierce Jewish rulers; but now shouted forth in the ears of the descendants of Montezuma and Cortes!

But the sound of a distant hymn rose on the air, and shortly after there appeared, advancing towards the square, a long and pompous retinue of mitred priests, with banners and crucifixes and gorgeous imagery, conducting a procession in which figures representing scenes concerning the death of our Saviour, were carried by on platforms, as they were the preceding evening. There was the Virgin in mourning at the foot of the cross—the Virgin in glory—and more saints and more angels —St. Michael and the dragon, etc., etc., a glittering and innumerable train. Not a sound was heard as the figures were carried slowly onwards in their splendid robes, lighted by thousands of tapers, which mingled their unnatural glare with the fading light of day.

As the *Miserere* was to be performed in the cathedral late in the evening, we went there, though with small hopes of making our way through the tremendous crowd. Having at length been admitted through a private entrance, *per favour*, we made our way into the body of the church; but the crowd was so intolerable, that we thought of abandoning our position, when we were seen and recognised by some of the priests, and conducted to a railed-off enclosure near the shrine of the Virgin, with the luxury of a Turkey carpet. Here, separated from the crowd, we sat down in peace on the ground. The gentlemen were accommodated with high-backed chairs, beside some ecclesiastics; for men may sit on chairs or benches in church, but women must kneel or sit on the ground. Why? "*Quien sabe?*" (Who knows?) is all the satisfaction I have ever obtained on that point.

The music began with a crash that wakened me out of an

agreeable slumber into which I had gradually fallen; and such discordance of instruments and voices, such confusion worse confounded, such inharmonious harmony, never before deafened mortal ears. The very spheres seemed out of tune, and rolling and crashing over each other. I could have cried *Miserere!* with the loudest; and in the midst of all the undrilled band was a *music-master,* with violin-stick uplifted, rushing desperately from one to the other, in vain endeavouring to keep time, and frightened at the clamour he himself had been instrumental in raising, like Phaeton intrusted with his unmanageable coursers. The noise was so great as to be really alarming; and the heat was severe in proportion. The calm face of the Virgin seemed to look reproachfully down. We were thankful when, at the conclusion of this stormy appeal for mercy, we were able to make our way into the fresh air and soft moonlight, through the confusion and squeezing at the doors, where it was rumoured that a soldier had killed a baby with his bayonet. A bad place for poor little babies—decidedly.

Outside, in the square, it was cool and agreeable. A military band was playing airs from Norma, and the womankind were sitting on the stones of the railing, or wandering about and finishing their day's work by a quiet flirtation *au clair de la lune.*

It was now eleven o'clock, and the pulquerias were thrown open for the refreshment of the faithful, and though hitherto much order had prevailed, it was not likely to endure much longer; notwithstanding which, we had the imprudence to walk unattended to our own house, at San Fernando. In the centre of the city there seemed no danger. People were still walking, and a few still drinking at the lighted booths; but when arrived at the lower part of the Alameda, all was still, and as we walked outside, under the long shadows of the trees, I expected every moment to be attacked, and wished we were anywhere, even on the silvery top of Popocatepetl! We passed several crowded pulquerias, where some were drinking and others drunk. Arrived at the arches, we saw from time to time a suspicious blanketed figure half hid by the shadow of the wall. A few doors from our own domicile was a pulque-shop filled with léperos, of whom some were standing at the door, shrouded in their blankets. It seemed to me we should never pass them, but we walked fast, and reached our door in safety. Here we thundered in vain. The porter was asleep, and for nearly ten minutes we heard voices within, male and female, ineffectually endeavouring to persuade the heavy-headed Cerberus to relinquish his keys. It would have been a choice moment for our friends, had any of them wished to accost us; but either they had not observed us, or perhaps they thought that C——n walking so late must have been armed; or perhaps, more charitable construction, they had profited by the solemnities of the day.

We got in at last, and I felt thankful enough for shelter and safety, and as wearied of the day's performances as you may be in reading a description of them.

Next morning, Sabado de Gloria, I could not persuade myself to go as far as the Plaza, to see the Iscariots explode. At a distance we listened to the hissing and crackling of the fireworks, the ringing of all the bells, and the thundering of artillery; and knew by the hum of busy voices, and the rolling of carriages, that the Holy Week was numbered with the past. . . .

We hear that it is in contemplation amongst the English here, headed by their Minister, to give a ball in the Mineria, to celebrate the Marriage of Queen Victoria, which will be turning these splendid halls to some account.

I have some intention of giving a series of weekly soirées, but am assured that they will not succeed, because hitherto such parties have failed. As a reason, is given the extravagant notions of the ladies in point of dress, and it is said that nothing but a ball where they can wear jewels, and a toilet therewith consistent, will please them; that a lady of high rank who had been in Madrid, having proposed simple tertulias and white muslin dresses, half the men in Mexico were ruined that year by the embroidered French and India muslins bought by their wives during this reign of simplicity; the idea of a plain white muslin, a dress worn by any *lépera,* never having struck them as possible. Nevertheless we can but make the attempt.

We propose going next week to Tulansingo, where our friends the —— have a country place, from thence we proceed to visit the mines of Real del Monte.

23rd.—On Monday we gave a Tertulia, which, notwithstanding all predictions, went off remarkably well, and consisted of nearly all the pleasantest people in Mexico. We had music, dancing, and cards, and at three in the morning the German cotillon was still in full vigour. Every one was disposed to be amused, and, moreover, the young ladies were dressed very simply; most of them in plain white muslins.

There was but a small sprinkling of diamonds, and that chiefly among the elderly part of the community. Still it is said that the novelty alone induced them to come, and that weekly soirées will not succeed. We shall try. Besides which, the Lady of the —— Minister proposes being *At home* on Wednesday evenings; the Lady of the —— Minister takes another evening; I, a third, and we shall see what can be effected.

LETTER THE FIFTEENTH

Letter from the Archbishop—Visit to the "Encarnacion"—Reception—Description—The Novices—Convent-supper—Picturesque Scene—Sonata on the Organ—Attempt at Robbery—Alarms of the Household—Visit to San Agustin—Anonymous Letter—The Virgin de los Remedios—Visit to the Chapel—The Padre—The Image—Anecdote of the large Pearl—A Mine.

24th.

The Archbishop has not only granted me permission to visit the convents, but permits me to take two ladies along with me, of which I have been informed by the Minister, Señor C——o, in a very amiable note just received, enclosing one from Señor Posada, which I translate for your edification.

To His Excellency, Señor Don J. de D. C——o.
April 24th, 1842.

My dear Friend and Companion:
    The Abbess and Nuns of the Convent of the Encarnacion are now prepared to receive the visit of our three pilgrims, next Sunday, at half-past four in the afternoon, and should that day not suit them, let them mention what day will be convenient.

    Afterwards we shall arrange their visit to the Concepcion, Enseñanza Antigua, and Jesus Maria, which are the best, and I shall let you know, and we shall agree upon the days and hours most suitable. I remain your affectionate friend and *Capellan,*

MANUEL POSADA.

27th.—Accordingly, on Sunday afternoon, we drove to the *Encarnacion,* the most splendid and richest convent in Mexico, excepting perhaps la Concepcion. If it were in any other country, I might mention the surpassing beauty of the evening, but as except in the rainy season, which has not yet begun, the evenings are always beautiful, the weather leaves no room for description. The sky always blue, the air always soft, the flowers always blossoming, the birds always singing; Thomson never could have written his "Seasons" here. We descended at the convent gate, were admitted by the portress, and received by several nuns, their faces closely covered with a double crape veil. We were then led into a spacious hall, hung with handsome lustres, and adorned with various Virgins and Saints magnificently dressed; and here the eldest, a very dignified old lady, lifted her veil, the others following her example, and introduced herself as the *Madre Vicaria;* bringing us many excuses from the old abbess, who having an inflammation in her eyes, was confined to her cell. She and another reverend mother, and a group of elderly dames, tall, thin, and stately, then proceeded to inform us, that the archbishop had, in person, given orders for our reception, and that they were prepared to show us the whole establishment.

The dress is a long robe of very fine white casimere, a thick black crape veil, and long rosary. The dress of the novices is the same, only that the veil is white. For the first half-hour or so, I fancied, that along with their politeness, was mingled a good deal of restraint, caused perhaps by the presence of a foreigner, and especially of an Englishwoman. My companions they knew well; the Señorita having even passed some months there. However this may have been, the feeling seemed gradually to wear away. Kindness or curiosity triumphed; their questions became unceasing; and before the visit was concluded, I was addressed as *"mi vida"* (my life), by the whole establishment. Where was I born? Where had I lived? What convents had I seen? Which did I prefer, the convents in France, or those in Mexico? Which were largest? Which had the best garden? etc., etc. Fortunately, I could, with truth, give the preference to their convent, as to spaciousness and magnificence, over any I ever saw.

The Mexican style of building is peculiarly advantageous for recluses; the great galleries and courts affording them a constant supply of fresh air, while the fountains sound so cheerfully, and the garden in this climate of perpetual spring affords them such a constant source of enjoyment all the year round, that one pities their secluded state much less here than in any other country.

This convent is in fact a palace. The garden, into which they led us first, is kept in good order, with its stone walks, stone benches, and an ever-playing and sparkling fountain. The trees were bending with fruit, and they pulled quantities of the most beautiful flowers for us; sweet-peas and roses, with which all gardens here abound, carnations, jasmine, and heliotrope. It was a pretty picture to see them wandering about, or standing in groups in this high-walled garden, while the sun was setting behind the hills, and the noise of the city was completely excluded, everything breathing repose and contentment. Most of the halls in the convent are noble rooms. We visited the whole, from the refectory to the *botica,* and admired the extreme cleanness of everything, especially of the immense kitchen, which seems hallowed from the approach even of a particle of dust; this circumstance is partly accounted for by the fact that each nun has a servant, and some have two; for this is not one of the strictest orders. The convent is rich; each novice at her entrance pays five thousand dollars into the common stock. There are about thirty nuns and ten novices.

The prevailing sin in a convent generally seems to be pride;

"The pride that apes humility;"

and it is perhaps nearly inseparable from the conventual state. Set apart from the rest of the world, they, from their little world, are too apt to look down with contempt which may be mingled with envy, or modified by pity, but must be unsuited to a true Christian spirit.

The novices were presented to us—poor little entrapped things! who really believe they will be let out at the end of the year if they should grow tired, as if they would ever be permitted to grow tired! The two eldest and most reverend ladies are sisters, thin, tall, and stately, with high noses, and remains of beauty. They have been in the convent since they were eight years old (which is remarkable, as sisters are rarely allowed to profess in the same establishment), and consider *La Encarnacion* as a small piece of heaven upon earth. There were some handsome faces amongst them, and one whose expression and eyes were singularly lovely, but truth to say, these were rather exceptions to the general rule.

Having visited the whole building, and admired one virgin's blue satin and pearls, and another's black velvet and diamonds, sleeping holy infants, saints, paintings, shrines, and confessionals,—having even climbed up the Azotea, which commands a magnificent view, we came at length to a large hall, decorated with paintings and furnished with antique high-backed arm-chairs, where a very elegant supper, lighted up and ornamented, greeted our astonished eyes; cakes, choco-late, ices, creams, custards, tarts, jellies, blancmangers, orange and lemonade, and other profane dainties, ornamented with gilt paper cut into little flags, etc. I was placed in a chair that might have served for a pope under a holy family; the Señora —— and the Señorita —— on either side. The elder nuns in stately array, occupied the other arm-chairs, and looked like statues carved in stone. A young girl, a sort of *pensionnaire*, brought in a little harp without pedals, and while we dis-cussed cakes and ices, sung different ballads with a good deal of taste. The elder nuns helped us to everything, but tasted nothing themselves. The younger nuns and the novices were grouped upon a mat *à la Turque*, and a more picturesque scene altogether one could scarcely see.

The young novices in their white robes, white veils, and black eyes, the severe and dignified *madres* with their long dresses and mournful-looking black veils and rosaries, the veiled figures occasionally flitting along the corridor;—our-selves in contrast, with our *worldly* dresses and coloured rib-bons; and the great hall lighted by one immense lamp that hung from the ceiling—I felt transported three centuries back, and half afraid that the whole would flit away, and prove a mere vision, a waking dream.

A gossiping old nun, who hospitably filled my plate with everything, gave me the enclosed *flag* cut in gilt paper, which, together with her custards and jellies, looked less unreal. They asked many questions in regard to Spanish affairs, and were not to be consoled for the defeat of Don Carlos, which they feared would be an end of the true religion in Spain.

After supper we proceeded upstairs to the choir (where the nuns attend public worship, and which looks down upon the handsome convent church) to try the organ. I was set down to a Sonata of Mozart's, the servants blowing the bellows. It seems to me that I made more noise than music, for the organ is very old, perhaps as old as the convent, which dates three centuries back. However, the nuns were pleased, and after they had sung a hymn, we returned below. I was rather sorry to leave them, and I felt as if I could have passed some time there very contentedly; but it was near nine o'clock, and we were obliged to take our departure; so having been embraced very cordially by the whole community, we left the hospitable walls of the Encarnacion.

28th.—Last evening we were sitting at home very quietly about ten o'clock, C——n, Monsieur de ——, of the —— Legation, and I, when A—— rushed into the room all dishevelled. "Come quickly, sir! Robbers are breaking open the kitchen-door!" A succession of feminine shrieks in the distance, added effect to her words. C——n jumped up, ran for his pistols, gave one to Monsieur de ——, called up the soldiers, but no robbers appeared. The kitchen-door was indeed open, and the trembling *galopina* attested, that being in the kitchen alone, dimly lighted by one small lamp, three men, all armed, had entered, and had rushed out again on hearing her give the alarm. We somewhat doubted her assertions, but the next morning found that the men had in fact escaped by the Azotea, a great assistance to all Mexican depredators. At the end of this row of houses the people ran out and fired upon them, but without effect. The house of the old Countess of S—— F—— had been broken into, her porter wounded, report says killed, and her plate carried off. In the meantime our soldiers watch in the kitchen, a pair of loaded pistols adorn the table, a double-barrelled gun stands in the corner, and a bull-dog growls in the gallery. This little passing visit to us was probably caused by the arrival of some large boxes from London, especially of a very fine harp and piano, both *Erard's,* which I had the pleasure of seeing unpacked this morning, and which, in spite of jolting and bad roads, have arrived in perfect condition. . . .

Thus far I had written, it being now the evening, and I sitting alone, when a succession of shrieks arose, even more awful than those which alarmed us last night. At the same time the old *galopina*, her daughter, and a French girl who lives here, rushed shouting along the gallery; not a word they said comprehensible, but something concerning "a robber in black, with men at his back, who had burst open the door." At the noise the whole household had assembled. One ran this way, one ran that. A little French *teinturier,* who it appeared had been paying the maids a polite visit, seized the loaded gun; the footman took a pistol and hid himself behind the porter; A——, like a second Joan of Arc, appeared, with a rusty sabre; the soldiers rushed up with their bayonets; the coachman stood aloof with nothing; the porter led up the rear, holding a large dog by the collar; but no robber appears; and the girls are all sobbing and crying because we doubt their having seen one. Galopina the younger shedding tears in torrents, swears to the man. Galopina the elder, enveloped in her reboso, swears to any number of men; and the *reca-*

merera has cried herself into a fit between fear and indignation.

Such is the agreeable state of things about nine o'clock this evening, for one real attempt to enter the house, invariably gives rise to a thousand imaginary attacks and fanciful alarms. . . .

After many attempts at walking, I have very nearly abandoned it, but take a great deal of exercise both on horseback and in the carriage; which last, on account of the ill-paved condition of the streets, affords rather more exercise than the former. I drove out this morning in an open carriage with the Señorita E—— to her country-house at San Agustin, the gambling emporium. But the famous annual fête does not take place till Whitsunday, and the pretty country villas there are at present abandoned. We walked in the garden till the sun became insupportable. The fragrance of the roses and jasmine was almost overpowering. There are trees of millefleur roses; heliotrope and honeysuckle cover every pillar, and yellow jasmine trails over everything. . . .

Found on my return an anonymous letter, begging me to "beware of my cook!" and signed *Fernandez*. Having shown it to some gentlemen who dined here, one thought it might be a plan of the robbers to get rid of the cook, whom they considered in their way; another, with more probability, that it was merely a plan of the attentive Señor Fernandez to get the cook's place for himself.

We went lately to pay a visit to the celebrated Virgen de los Remedios, the *Gachupina*, the Spanish patroness, and rival of Our Lady of Guadalupe. This Virgin was brought over by Cortes, and when he displaced the Indian idols in the great Temple of Mexico, caused them to be broken in pieces, and the sanctuary to be purified, he solemnly placed there a crucifix and this image of the Virgin; then kneeling before it, gave solemn thanks to Heaven, which had permitted him thus to adore the Most High in a place so long profaned by the most cruel idolatries.

It is said that this image was brought to Mexico by a soldier of Cortes's army called Villafuerte, and that the day succeeding the terrible *Noche Triste*, it was concealed by him in the place where it was afterwards discovered. At all events, the image disappeared, and nothing further was known of it until, on the top of a barren and treeless mountain, in the heart of a large maguey, she was found by a fortunate Indian. Her restoration was joyfully hailed by the Spaniards. A church was erected on the spot. A priest was appointed to take charge of the miraculous image. Her fame spread abroad. Gifts of immense value were brought to her shrine. A treasurer was appointed to take care of her jewels; a camarista to superintend her rich wardrobe. No rich dowager died in peace until she had bequeathed to Our Lady of Los Remedios her largest diamond, or her richest pearl. In seasons of drought she is brought in from her dwelling in the mountain, and carried in procession through the streets. The viceroy himself on foot used to lead the holy train. One of the highest rank drives the chariot in which she is seated. In succession she visits the principal convents, and as she is carried through the cloistered precincts, the nuns are ranged on their knees in humble adoration. Plentiful rains immediately follow her arrival. ——, who accompanied us, has on several occasions filled the office of her coachman, by which means he has seen the interior of most of the convents in Mexico. It is true that there came a time when the famous curate Hidalgo, the prime mover of the Revolution, having taken as his standard an image of the Virgin of Guadalupe, a rivalry arose between her and the Spanish Virgin; and Hidalgo having been defeated and forced to fly, the image of the Virgen de los Remedios was conducted to Mexico dressed as a general, and invoked as the patroness of Spain. Later still, the Virgin herself was denounced as a Gachupina! her general's sash boldly torn from her by the valiant General ——, who also signed her passport, with an order for her to leave the republic. However, she was again restored to her honours, and still retains her treasurers, her camarista, and sanctum sanctorum.

Being desirous of seeing this celebrated image, we set off one fine afternoon in a carriage of ——'s, drawn by six unbroken horses, accompanied by him and his lady, and performed four leagues of bad road in an incredibly short space of time. The horses themselves were in an evident state of astonishment, for after kicking and plunging, and, as they imagined, running away, they found themselves driven much faster than they had the slightest intention of going: so after a little while they acknowledged, in ——'s capital coachman, *une main de maître.*

The mountain is barren and lonely, but the view from its summit is beautiful, commanding the whole plain. The church is old and not very remarkable, yet a picturesque object, as it stands in its gay solitariness, with one or two trees beside it, of which one without leaves was entirely covered with the most brilliant scarlet flowers. Señor —— having been the Virgin's coachman, the Señora —— being the daughter of her camarista, and C——n the minister from the land of her predilection, we were not astonished at the distinguished reception which we met with from the reverend padre, the guardian of the mountain. The church within is handsome; and above the altar is a copy of the original Virgin. After we had remained there a little while, we were admitted into the Sanctum, where the identical Virgin of Cortes, with a large silver maguey, occupies her splendid shrine. The priest retired and put on his robes, and then returning, and all kneeling before the altar, he recited the *credo*. This over, he mounted the steps, and opening the shrine where the Virgin was encased, knelt down and removed her in his arms. He then presented her to each of us in succession, every one kissing the hem of her satin robe. She was afterwards replaced with the same ceremony.

The image is a wooden doll about a foot high, holding in its arms an infant Jesus, both faces evidently carved with a rude penknife; two holes for the eyes and another for the mouth. This doll was dressed in blue satin and pearls with a crown upon her head and a quantity of hair fastened on to the crown. No Indian idol could be much uglier. As she has been a good deal scratched and destroyed in the lapse of ages, C——n observed that he was astonished they had not tried to restore her a little. To this the padre replied, that the attempt had been made by several artists, each one of whom had sickened and died. He also mentioned as one of her miracles, that living on a solitary mountain she had never been robbed; but I fear the good padre is somewhat *oblivious*, as this sacrilege has happened more than once. On one occasion a crowd of léperos being collected, and the image carried round to be kissed, one of them, affecting intense devotion, bit off the large pearl that adorned her dress in front, and before the theft was discovered, he had mingled with the crowd and escaped. When reminded of the circumstance, the padre said it was true, but that the thief was a *Frenchman*. After taking leave of the Virgin, we visited the padre in his own old house, attached to the church, where his only attendant, as usual among padres, is an old woman.

We then made our way on foot down a steep hill, stopping to admire some noble stone arches, the remains of an aqueduct built by the Spaniards for conveying water from one mountain to the other; and with an Indian for our guide, vis-

LIFE IN MEXICO 159

ited a newly-discovered, though anciently-opened mine, said
to be of silver, and which had until lately been covered with
rubbish. We groped through it, and found vaults and excavations and a deep pit of water. C——n got some Indians to break
off pieces of stone for him, which were put into a sack and
sent home for examination. We were so tired of our walk
down this steep and mountainous path, that on our return,
I mounted a horse with a man's saddle, belonging to one of
the servants, and contrived to keep on, while it climbed up
the perpendicular ascent. As this seemed rather a selfish proceeding while the others walked, I invited the Señora —— to
mount also in front; which she did, and the path being almost
perpendicular, my head nearly touched the ground, which certainly made the seat not over safe or easy. However, we reached
the top of the mountain in safety, though somewhat exhausted
with laughing, and were driven home with the speed of a
rail-car.

LETTER THE SIXTEENTH

Mexico in May—Leave Mexico for Santiago—Coach of Charles X—Mexican Travelling—General Aspect of the Country—Village of Santa Clara—Robbers' House—Temples of the Sun and Moon—San Juan—Mexican Posada—School-house —Skulls—Hard Fare—Travelling Dress—Sopayuca—Military Administrador—Santiago—Matadors and Picadors—Evenings in the Country—Dances—Mexican Songs—Cempoala—Plaza de Toros—Skill of the Horsemen—Omatusco—Accident—Tulansingo—Beautiful Garden—Mexican Dishes—Fruits—Horses—Games of Forfeits—Ranchera's Dress—Young Girls and their Admirers—Verses—Knowledge of Simple Medicine—Indian Baths—Hidden Treasures—Anecdote.

SANTIAGO, May 6th.

Before the setting in of the rainy season, we accepted of the invitation of our friends the ——s, to visit the different haciendas, as in a short time the roads will become nearly impassable. The country in May is perhaps at its highest beauty, or even a little earlier, as already the great blow of roses is nearly over; *au reste* there are roses all the year round, though more in December than in July. And this, by the way, is rather a source of disappointment to the unwary traveller. He arrives in December, and finds the gardens full of flowers. "If this be the case in December," says he to himself, "what will it be in May?" May comes—the roses are over, and the chief flowers in the gardens are dahlias and marigolds, our autumnal flowers—September, and these autumnal flowers still bloom, and with them you have mignonette and roses, and then pinks and jasmine, and other flowers. In fact there seems to be no particular season for anything.

The weather at present is neither warm nor cold, but colder here than in Mexico, and when it does not rain it is lovely. Already there has been much rain, and the torrents are so swelled, that there was some doubt as to whether our carriages could pass them.

Yesterday, at five in the morning we left Mexico, in a coach once the property of Charles X. "Sic transit," etc.; and a most luxurious travelling-carriage is that of his ex-majesty, entirely covered with gilding, save where the lilies of France surmount the crown, (sad emblems of the fallen dynasty!) lined with white satin with violet-coloured binding, the satin cushions most excellently stuffed: large, commodious, and with a movement as soft as that of a gondola.

A Frenchman bought it on a speculation, and brought it here for sale. In former days, from its gilded and showy appearance, it would have brought any price; but the taste for gaudy equipages has gone by since the introduction of foreign, and especially of English carriages; and the present proprietor, who bought it for its intrinsic good qualities, paid but a moderate sum for it. In this carriage, drawn by six strong horses, with two first-rate coachmen and several outriders well-armed, we went along at great speed. The drivers, dressed Mexican fashion, with all their accoutrements smart and new, looked very picturesque. Jackets and trousers of deerskin, and jackets embroidered in green, with hanging silver buttons, the trousers also embroidered and slit up the side of the leg, trimmed with silver buttons, and showing an under pair of unbleached linen; these, with the postilions' boots, and great hats with gold rolls, form a dress which would *faire fureur,* if some adventurous Mexican would venture to display it on the streets of London.

We left the city by the gate of Guadalupe, and passed by the great cathedral, our road lying over the marshy plains once covered by the waters of Lake Tezcuco.

To the east lay the great lake, its broad waters shining like a sheet of molten silver, and the two great volcanoes: the rising sun forming a crown of rays on the white brow of Popocatepetl.

To describe once for all the general aspect of the country on this side of the valley of Mexico, suffice it to say, that there is a universal air of dreariness, vastness, and desolation. The country is flat, but always enlivened by the surrounding mountains, like an uninteresting painting in a diamond frame; and yet it is not wholly uninteresting. It has a character peculiar to itself, great plains of maguey, with its huts with uncultivated patches, that have once been gardens, still filled with flowers and choked with weeds; the huts themselves, generally of mud, yet not unfrequently of solid stone, roofless and windowless, with traces of having been fine buildings in former days; the complete solitude, unbroken except by the passing Indian, certainly as much in a state of savage nature as the lower class of Mexicans were when Cortes first traversed these plains—with the same character, gentle and cowardly, false and cunning, as weak animals are apt to be by nature, and indolent and improvident as men are in a fine climate; ruins every-where—here a viceroy's country palace serving as a tavern, where the mules stop to rest, and the drivers to drink pulque —there, a whole village crumbling to pieces; roofless houses, broken down walls and arches, an old church—the remains of a convent. . . . For Leagues scarcely a tree to be seen; then a clump of the graceful Arbol de Peru, or one great cypress —long strings of mules and asses, with their drivers—pasture-fields with cattle—then again whole tracts of maguey, as far as the eye can reach; no roads worthy of the name, but a pas-sage made between fields of maguey, bordered by crumbling-down low stone walls, causing a jolting from which not even the easy movement of Charles X's coach can save us. But the horses go at full gallop, accustomed to go through and over everything.

The first village we saw was Santa Clara, to our left, lying at the foot of some dark hills, with its white church and flat-roofed or no-roofed houses. There being no shade, frequently not a tree for leagues, the sun and dust very disagreeable, and became more so as the day advanced. Here it came to pass, that, travelling rapidly over the hot and dusty plains, the wheels of our carriage began to smoke. No house in sight —no water within ken. It was a case of difficulty; when sud-denly —— recollected that not far from thence was an old rancho, a deserted farmhouse at present occupied by robbers; and having ordered the coachman to drive to within a few hundred yards of this house, he sent a servant on horseback with a *medio* (fourpence) to bring some water, which was treating the robbers like honourable men. The man galloped off, and shortly returned with a can full of water, which he carried back when the fire was extinguished.

Meanwhile we examined, as well as we could, the external appearance of the robbers' domicile, which was an old half-ruined house, standing alone on the plain, with no tree near it. Several men, with guns, were walking up and down before the house—sporting-looking characters, but rather dirty—appar-ently either waiting for some expected *game,* or going in search of it. Women with rebosos, were carrying water, and walking amongst them. There were also a number of dogs. The well-armed men who accompanied us, and the name of ——, so well known in these parts, that once when his carriage was surrounded by robbers, he merely mentioned who he was, and they retreated with many apologies for their mistake, precluded all danger of an attack; but woe to the solitary horseman or the escorted carriage that should pass thereby! Nor, indeed, are they always in the same mood, for Señor ——'s houses have been frequently attacked in his absence, and his hacienda at Santiago once stood a regular siege, the robbers being at length repulsed by the bravery of his servants.

We set off again *au grand galop*, drivers and outriders giving, from time to time, the most extraordinary shrieks to encourage the horses and to amuse themselves, wild and shrill enough to frighten any civilized quadruped. The road grew more picturesque as we advanced, and at length our attention was arrested by the sight of the two great pyramids, which rise to the east of the town of San Juan Teotihuacan, which are mentioned by Humboldt, and have excited the curiosity and attention of every succeeding traveller. The huge masses were consecrated to the sun and moon, which, in the time of Cortes, were there represented by two vast stone idols, covered with gold. The conquerors made use of the gold, and broke the idols in pieces, by order of the first bishop of Mexico. Unfortunately, our time was too limited to give them more than a passing observation. Fragments of obsidian, in the form of knives and of arrows, with which the priests opened the breasts of their human victims, are still to be found there; and numerous small idols, made of baked clay, are to be seen both there and in the plains adjoining. The Indians rather dislike to guide travellers to these pyramids, and their reluctance to do so has increased the popular belief of the existence of great concealed treasures near or in them.

The whole plain on which these great pyramids stand was formerly called Micoatl, or the Pathway of the Dead; and the hundreds of smaller pyramids which surround the larger ones (the Temples of the Sun and Moon) are symmetrically disposed in wide streets, forming a great burial-plain, composed perhaps of the dust of their ancient warriors, an Aztec or Toltec Père-la-Chaise, or rather a roofless Westminster Abbey. So few of the ancient *teocallis* now remain, and these being nearly the only traces now existing of that extraordinary race, we regretted the more not being able to devote some time to their examination. Fanaticism and policy induced the Spanish conquerors to destroy these heathen temples; and when we recollect that at the time of the Reformation in civilized England, the most splendid Catholic edifices were made level with the ground, in compliance with the ferocious edict of John Knox,

"Ding down the nests, and the rooks will fly off," we can have little wonder or blame to bestow upon Cortes, who, in the excitement of the siege, gave orders for the destruction of these blood-stained sanctuaries. In the afternoon we arrived at San Juan, a pretty village, boasting of an inn, a school-house, an avenue of fine trees, and a stream of clear water. It is true that the inn is a Mexican posada, bearing as much resemblance to what is generally called an inn, as an hacienda does to an English country-house; the school-house, a room with a mud floor and a few dirty benches, occupied by little ragged boys and girls; but the avenue is pretty, the grass as green as emeralds, and the water crystal. We walked out while they changed horses, of which Señor —— had fresh relays of his own prepared all along the road; and entered the school-house, attracted by the noise and the invitingly open door. The master was a poor, ragged, pale, careworn looking young man, seemingly half-dinned with the noise, but very earnest in his work. The children, all speaking at once, were learning to spell out of some old bills of Congress. Several moral sentences were written on the wall in very independent orthography. C——n having remarked to the master that they were ill-spelt, he seemed very much astonished, and even inclined to doubt the fact. I thought it was one of those cases where ignorance is bliss, and fear the observation may have cost the young man a night's rest.

A row of grinning skulls was ranged round the wall of the churchyard, and the sexton, who gave us admittance to the church, taking up one to show it off, it all crumbled into dust, which filled the air like a cloud.

At the posada they gave us rancid sheep's milk, cheese, and biscuits so hard, that C——n asked the host if they were made in the same year with the church; at which he seemed mightily pleased, and could not stop laughing till we got into the carriage.

Soon after leaving San Juan we were met by the Señora de ——, in an open carriage, coming with her children to meet us; and though she had travelled since sunrise from her hacienda, she appeared as if freshly dressed for an evening party; her dress, amber-coloured crape, trimmed with white blonde, short sleeves and *décolletée;* a set of beautiful Neapolitan strawberry-coral, set in gold, straw-coloured satin shoes, and a little China crape shawl, embroidered in bright flowers; her hair dressed and uncovered.

We stopped at their hacienda of Sopayuca, an old house,

standing solitary in the midst of great fields of maguey. It has a small deserted garden adjoining, amongst whose tangled bushes a pretty little tame deer was playing, with its half-startled look and full wild eye. We found an excellent breakfast prepared, and here, for the first time, I conceived the possibility of not disliking *pulque*. We visited the large buildings where it is kept, and found it rather refreshing, with a sweet taste and a creamy froth upon it, and with a much less decided odour than that which is sold in Mexico.

This hacienda is under the charge of an administrador, to whom —— pays a large annual sum, and whose place is by no means a sinecure, as he lives in perpetual danger from robbers. He is captain of a troop of soldiers, and as his life has been spent in "persecuting robbers," he is an object of intense hatred to that free and independent body, and has some thoughts of removing to another part of the country, where he may be more tranquil. He gave us a terrible account of these night attacks, of the ineffectual protection afforded him by the government, and of the nearly insuperable difficulties thrown in the way of any attempt to bring these men to justice. He lately told the president that he had some thoughts of joining the robbers himself, as they were the only persons in the republic protected by the government. The president, however, is not to blame in this matter. He has used every endeavour to check these abuses; and difficulties have been thrown in his way from very unexpected sources. . . .

A propos to which, the —— consul told us the other day, that some time ago, having occasion to consult Judge —— upon an affair of importance, he was shown into an apartment where that functionary was engaged with some suspicious-looking individuals, or rather who were above suspicion, their appearance plainly indicating their calling. On the table before him lay a number of guns, swords, pistols, and all sorts of arms. The Judge requested Monsieur de —— to be seated, observing that he was investigating a case of robbery committed by these persons. The robbers were seated, smoking very much at their ease, and the Judge was enjoying the same innocent recreation; when his cigar becoming extinguished, one of these gentlemen taking his from his mouth, handed it to the magistrate, who relighted his *puro* (cigar) at it, and returned it with a polite bow. In short, they were completely *hand in glove*.

In the evening we reached Santiago, where we now are, about eighteen leagues from Mexico, a large house in a wild-looking country, standing in solitary state, with hills behind, and rocks before it, and surrounded by great uncultivated plains and pasture-fields. Everything is *en grande* in this domain. There is a handsome chapel and sacristy; a plaza de toros; hundreds of horses and mules; and between *dependientes* and hangers-on, we sat down, thirty or forty people, to dinner.

7th.—The very day of our arrival, Bernardo the Matador, with his men, arrived from Mexico, bringing their superb dresses with them, for the purpose of giving us a country bull-fight. As an hacienda of this kind is an immense empty house, without furniture or books, all the amusement is to be found either out of doors, or in large parties in the house; and the unostentatious hospitality which exists in this and some other of the old families, is a pleasing remnant of Spanish manners and habits, now falling into disuse, and succeeded by more pretension to refinement, and less of either real wealth or sociability.

In the evening here, all assemble in a large hall; the Señora de —— playing the piano; while the whole party, agents, dependientes, major-domo, coachmen, matadors, picadors, and women-servants, assemble, and perform the dances of the country; *jarabes, aforrados, enanos, palomos, zapateros,* etc., etc. It must not be supposed that in this apparent mingling of ranks between masters and servants, there is the slightest want of respect on the part of the latter; on the contrary, they seem to exert themselves, as in duty bound, for the amusement of their master and his guests. There is nothing republican in it; no feeling of equality; as far as I have seen, that feeling does not exist here, except between people of the same rank. It is more like some remains of the feudal system, where the retainers sat at the same table with their chief, but below the salt. The dances are monotonous, with small steps and a great deal of shuffling, but the music is rather pretty, and some of the dancers were very graceful and agile; and if it were not invidious to make distinctions, we *might* particularize Bernardo the Matador, the head coachman, and a handsome peasant-girl, with a short scarlet and yellow petticoat, and a foot and ankle *à la Vestris*. They were all very quiet, but seemed in a state of intense enjoyment; and some of the men accompanied the dancers on the guitar.

First the player strikes up in quick time, and the dancer performs a quick movement; then the musician accompanies the music with his voice, and the dancer goes through some slow steps. Such is the case in the *Aforrado* or *Lining,* a curious *nom de tendresse*, expressive, I suppose, of something soft and well wadded. The words are as follow:

1.

Aforrado de mi vida!
Come estás, como te va?
Como has pasado la noche,
No has tenido novedad?

2.

Aforrado de mi vida!
Yo te quisiera cantar,
Pero mis ojos son tiernos,
Y empazaran á llorar.

3.

De Guadalajara vengo,
Lideando con un soldado,
Solo por venir a ver
A mi jarabe aforrado.

4.

Y vente con migo,
Y yo te daré
Zapatos de raso
Color de café.

Of these poetical sublimities, a translation at once literal and metrical, would, we think, damp the spirit of a Coleridge.

1.

Lining of my life!
How are you? how do you do?
How have you passed the night?
Have you met with nothing new?

2.

Lining of my life!
To you I should like to sing;
But that my eyes are weak,
And tears might begin to spring.

3.

From Guadalajara fighting,
With a soldier I came on,
My well-lined sweet syrup!
I came to see you alone.

4.
And come then with me,
And I will give thee
Such fine shoes of satin,
The colour of tea.

It is *coffee*, but you will excuse the poetical licence. The music married to this "immortal verse," I have learned by ear, and shall send you. In the *"enanos"* (the dwarfs) the dancer *makes himself little*, every time the chorus is sung.

1.
Ah! que bonitos
Son los enanos,
Los chiquititos
Y Mejicanos.

2.
Sale la linda,
Sale la fea,
Sale el enano,
Con su zalea.

3.
Los enanitos
Se enojaron,
Porque á las enanas
Les pellizcaron.

There are many more verses, but I think you will find these quite satisfactory, "Ah! how pretty are the dwarfs, the little ones, the Mexicans! Out comes the pretty one, out comes the ugly one, out comes the dwarf with his jacket of skin. The little he-dwarfs were angry, because some one pinched the she-dwarfs." There is another called the *Toro*, of which the words are not very interesting; and the *Zapatero*, or shoe-maker, was very well danced by a gentleman who accompanied himself, at the same time, on the guitar.

Yesterday morning we set off in a burning sun, over a perfect Egyptian desert, to visit the famous arches of Cempoala, a magnificent work, which we are told had greatly excited the admiration of Mr. Poinsett when in this country. This aqueduct, the object of whose construction was to supply these arid plains with water, was the work of a Spanish Franciscan friar, and has never been entirely concluded. We travelled about six leagues, and sat there for hours, looking up at the great stone arches, which seem like a work of giants.

In the afternoon we all rode to the Plaza de Toros. The evening was cool, and our horses good, the road pretty and shady, and the plaza itself a most picturesque enclosure, surrounded by lofty trees. Chairs were placed for us on a raised platform; and the bright green of the trees, the flashing dresses of the *toreadors,* the roaring of the fierce bulls, the spirited horses, the music and the cries; the Indians shouting from the trees up which they had climbed; all formed a scene of savage grandeur, which for a short time at least is interesting. Bernardo was dressed in blue satin and gold; the picadors in black and silver; the others in maroon-coloured satin and gold; all those on foot wear knee-breeches and white silk stockings, a little black cap with ribbons, and a plait of hair streaming down behind. The horses were generally good, and as each new adversary appeared, seemed to participate in the enthusiasm of their riders. One bull after another was driven in roaring, and as here they are generally fierce, and their horns not blunted as in Mexico, it is a much more dangerous affair. The bulls were not killed, but were sufficiently tormented. One stuck full of arrows and fireworks, all adorned with ribbons and coloured paper, made a sudden spring over an immensely high wall, and dashed into the woods. I thought afterwards of this unfortunate animal, how it must have been wandering about all night, bellowing with pain, the concealed arrows piercing its flesh, and looking like gay ornaments;

> "So, when the watchful shepherd, from the blind,
> Wounds with a random shaft the careless hind,
> Distracted with her pain, she flies the woods,
> Bounds o'er the lawn, and seeks the silent floods—
> With fruitless care; for still the fatal dart
> Sticks in her side, and rankles in her heart."

If the arrows had stuck too deep, and that the bull could not rub them off against the trees, he must have bled to death. Had he remained, his fate would have been better, for when the animal is entirely exhausted they throw him down with a lazo, and pulling out the arrows put ointment on the wounds.

The skill of the men is surprising; but the most curious part of the exhibition was when a coachman of ——'s, a strong, handsome Mexican, mounted on the back of a fierce bull, which plunged and flung himself about as if possessed by a legion of demons, and forced the animal to gallop round and round the arena. The bull is first caught by the lazo, and thrown on his side, struggling furiously. The man mounts while he is still on the ground. At the same moment the lazo is withdrawn, and the bull starts up, maddened by feeling the weight of his unusual burden. The rider must dismount in the same way, the bull being first thrown down, otherwise he would be gored in a moment. It is terribly dangerous, for if the man were to lose his seat, his death is nearly certain; but these Mexicans are superb riders. A monk, who is attached to the establishment, seems an ardent admirer of these sports, and his presence is useful, in case of a dangerous accident occurring, which is not unfrequent.

The amusement was suddenly interrupted by sudden darkness, and a tremendous storm of rain and thunder, in the midst of which we mounted our horses, and galloped home.

TULANSINGO ——, 8th.

Another bull-fight last evening! It is like pulque; one makes wry faces at it at first, and then begins to like it. One thing we soon discovered; which was, that the bulls, if so inclined, could leap upon our platform, as they occasionally sprang over a wall twice as high. There was a part of the spectacle rather too horrible. The horse of one of the picadors was gored, his side torn up by the bull's horns, and in this state, streaming with blood, he was forced to gallop round the circle.

We spent one day in visiting Omatusco, an hacienda belonging to the Señora T——a, situated in the plains of Apan, and famous for the superior excellence of its pulque. The organas, the nopal, and great fields of maguey, constitute the chief vegetation for many miles round. The hacienda itself, a fine large building, stands lonely and bleak in the midst of magueys. A fine chapel, left unfinished since her husband's death, attracted our attention by its simple architecture and unpretending elegance. It is nearly impossible to conceive anything more lonely than a residence here must be; or in fact in any of the haciendas situated on these great plains of Otumba and Apan.

This morning we set off for Tulansingo, in four carriages-and-six, containing the whole family, ourselves, maids, and children, padre and nursery governess; relays being placed all along the road, which we traversed at full gallop. But in crossing some great pasture-fields, the drivers of two of the carriages began to race; one of the horses fell and threw the postilion; the carriage itself was overturned, and though none of the inmates were injured, the poor *mozo* was terribly wounded in his head and legs. No assistance being near, he changed places with one of the men on horseback, and was brought on slowly.

About three in the afternoon we arrived at Tulansingo, rather an important city in its way, and which has been the theatre of many revolutionary events; with various streets and shops, a handsome church; alcaldes, a prefect, etc. There appear to be some few good houses and decent families, and clean, small shops, and there are pretty, shady walks in the environs; and though there are also plenty of miserable dwellings and dirty people, it is altogether rather a civilized place. The house of ——, which stands within a courtyard, and is *the* house *par excellence*, is very handsome, with little furniture, but with some remnants of luxury. The dining-hall is a noble room, with beautiful Chinese paper, opening into a garden, which is the boast of the republic, and is indeed singularly pretty, and kept in beautiful order, with gravel walks and fine trees, clear tanks and sparkling fountains, and an extraordinary profusion of the most beautiful flowers, roses especially. There is something extremely oriental in its appearance, and the fountains are ornamented with China vases and Chinese figures of great value. Walking along under arches formed by rose-bushes, a small column of water spouted forth from each bush, sprinkling us all over with its showers. But the prettiest thing in the garden is a great tank of clear water, enclosed on three sides by a Chinese building, round which runs a piazza with stone pillars, shaded by a drapery of white curtains. Comfortable well-cushioned sofas are arranged along the piazza, which opens into a large room, where one may dress after bathing. It is the prettiest and coolest retreat possible, and entirely surrounded by trees and roses. Here one may lie at noonday, with the sun and the world completely shut out. They call this an English garden, than which it rather resembles the summer retreat of a sultan.

When we arrived, we found dinner laid for forty persons, and the table ornamented by the taste of the gardener, with pyramids of beautiful flowers.

I have now formed acquaintance with many Mexican dishes; *molé* (meat stewed in red chile), boiled nopal, fried bananas, green chile, etc. Then we invariably have *frijoles* (brown beans stewed), hot tortillas—and this being in the country, pulque is the universal beverage. In Mexico, tortillas and pulque are considered unfashionable, though both are to be met with occasionally, in some of the best old houses. They have here a most delicious species of cream cheese made by the Indians, and ate with virgin honey. I believe there is an intermixture of goats' milk in it; but the Indian families who make it, and who have been offered large sums for the receipt, find it more profitable to keep their secret.

Every dinner has *puchero* immediately following the soup; consisting of boiled mutton, beef, bacon, fowls, garbanzos (a white bean), small gourds, potatoes, boiled pears, greens, and any other vegetables; a piece of each put on your plate at the same time, and accompanied by a sauce of herbs or tomatoes.

As for fruits, we have mameys, chirimoyas, granaditas, white and black zapotes; the black, sweet, with a green skin and black pulp, and with black stones in it; the white resembling it in outward appearance and form, but with a white pulp, and the kernel, which is said to be poisonous, is very large, round, and white. It belongs to a larger and more leafy tree than the black zapote, and grows in cold or temperate climates; whereas the other is a native of *tierra caliente.* Then there is the chicozapote, of the same family, with a whitish skin, and a white or rose-tinged pulp; this also belongs to the warm regions. The capulin, or Mexican cherry; the mango, of which the best come from Orizaba and Cordova; the cayote, etc. Of these I prefer the chirimoya, zapote blanco, granadita, and mango; but this is a matter of taste.

12th.—We have spent some days here very pleasantly; riding amongst the hills in the neighbourhood, exploring caves, viewing waterfalls, and climbing on foot or on horseback, wherever foot or horse could penetrate. No habits to be worn in these parts, as I found from experience, after being caught upon a gigantic maguey, and my gown torn in two. It is certainly always the wisest plan to adopt the customs of the country one lives in. A dress either of stuff, such as merino, or of muslin, as short as it is usually worn, a reboso tied over one shoulder, and a large straw hat, is about the most convenient costume that can be adopted. The horses are small, but strong, spirited, and well-made; generally unshod, which they say makes the motion more agreeable; and almost all, at least all ladies' horses, are taught the *paso,* which I find tiresome for a continuance, though a good paso-horse will keep up with others that gallop, and for a longer time.

The great amusement here in the evening is playing at *juegos de prendas,* games with forfeits, which I recommend to all who wish to make a rapid improvement in the Spanish tongue. Last night, being desired to name a forfeit for the padre, I condemned him to dance the *jarabe,* of which he performed a few steps in his long gown and girdle, with equal awkwardness and good nature. We met to-day the prettiest little ranchera, a farmer's wife or daughter, riding in front of a *mozo* on the same horse, their usual mode, dressed in a short embroidered muslin petticoat, white satin shoes, a pearl necklace, and earrings, a reboso, and a large round straw hat. The ladies sit their horse on a contrary side to our fashion. They have generally adopted English saddles, but the farmers' wives frequently sit in a sort of chair, which they find much more commodious.

Some country ladies, who attended mass in the chapel this morning, were dressed in very short clear white muslin gowns, very much starched, and so disposed as to show two under-petticoats, also stiffly starched, and trimmed with lace, their shoes coloured satin. Considered as a costume of their own, I begin to think it rather pretty. The oldest women here or in Mexico never wear caps; nothing but their own gray hair, sometimes cut short, sometimes turned up with a comb, and not unusually tied behind in a pigtail. There is no attempt to conceal the ravages of time. . . .

It appears to me, that amongst the young girls here there is not that desire to enter upon the cares of matrimony, which is to be observed in many other countries. The opprobious epithet of "old maid" is unknown. A girl is not the less admired because she has been ten or a dozen years in society; the most severe remark made on her is that she is "hard to please." No one calls her *passée,* or looks out for a new face to admire. I have seen no courting of the young men either in mothers or daughters; no match-making mammas, or daughters looking out for their own interests. In fact, young people have so few opportunities of being together, that Mexican marriages must be made in heaven; for I see no opportunity of bringing them about upon earth! The young men when they do meet with young ladies in society, appear devoted to and very much afraid of them. I know but one lady in Mexico who has the reputation of having manœuvred all her daughters into great marriages; but she is so clever, and her daughters were such beauties, that it can have cost her no trouble; as for flirtation, the name is unknown, and the thing.

I have been taking lessons in the Indian dances from

Doña R——a; they are not ungraceful, but lazy and monotonous. . . .

On every door in this house there is a printed paper to the
following effect:

> *"Quien á esta casa da luz? Jesus.*
> *Quien la llena de alegria? Maria.*
> *Y quien la abraza en la fé? José.*
> *Luego bien claro se vé*
> *Que siempre habrá contricion,*
> *Teniendo en la corazon,*
> *A Jesus, Maria, y José."*

> *"Who gives light to this house? Jesus.*
> *Who fills it with joy? Mary.*
> *Who kindles faith in it? Joseph.*
> *Then we see very clearly*
> *That there will always be contrition,*
> *Keeping in our hearts,*
> *Jesus, Mary, and Joseph."*

These are written in verse, and below: "The most illustrious
Bishop of Monte-Rey, Don Fray José de Jesus Maria Balaun-
zaran, hereby ordains and grants, along with the Bishops of
Puebla, Durango, Valladolid and Guadalajara, two hundred
days of indulgence to all those who devoutly repeat the above
ejaculation, and invoke the sweet names of Mary, Jesus, and
Joseph." . . . The people here have certainly a poetical vein in
their composition. Everything is put into verse—sometimes
doggerel, like the above (in which *luz* rhyming with *Jesus,*
shows that the *z* is pronounced here like an *s*), occasionally
a little better, but always in rhyme.

We went this evening to visit the Countess del ——, who
has a house in the village. Found her in bed, feverish, and
making use of simple remedies, such as herbs, the knowledge
and use of which have descended from the ancient Indians to
the present lords of the soil. The Spanish historians who have
written upon the conquest of Mexico, all mention the knowledge which the Mexican physicians had of herbs. It was supposed by these last, that for every infirmity there was a remedy in the herbs of the field; and to apply them according to
the nature of the malady, was the chief science of these primitive professors of medicine. Much which is now used in European pharmacy is due to the research of Mexican doctors; such

as sarsaparilla, jalap, friars' rhubarb, *mechoacan*, etc.; also various emetics, antidotes to poison, remedies against fever, and an infinite number of plants, minerals, gums, and simple medicines. As for their infusions, decoctions, ointments, plasters, oils, etc., Cortes himself mentions the wonderful number of these which he saw in the Mexican market for sale. From certain trees they distilled balsams; and drew a balsamic liquid both from a decoction of the branches, and from the bark steeped in water. Bleeding and bathing were their other favourite remedies. The country-people breathed a vein with a maguey-point, and when they could not find leeches, substituted the prickles of the American hedgehog.

Besides bathing in the rivers, lakes, tanks, and fountains, they used a bath which is still to be seen in many Indian villages, and which they call the temezcalli. It is made of unbaked bricks; its form is that of a baker's oven, about eight feet wide and six high; the pavement rather convex, and lower than the surface of the soil. A person can enter this bath only on his knees. Opposite the entry is a stone or brick stove, its opening towards the exterior of the bath, with a hole to let out the smoke. Before the bath is prepared, the floor inside is covered with a mat, on which is placed a jar of water, some herbs and leaves of corn. The stove is then heated until the stones which unite it with the bath become red-hot. When the bather enters the entry is closed, and the only opening left is a hole at the top of the vault, which, when the smoke of the oven has passed through, is also shut. They then pour water upon the red-hot stones, from which a thick vapour arises, which fills the temezcalli. The bather then throws himself on the mat, and drawing down the steam with the herbs and maize, wets them in the tepid water of the jar, and if he has any pain, applies them to the part affected. This having produced perspiration, the door is opened and the well-baked patient comes out and dresses. For fevers, for bad colds, for the bite of a poisonous animal, this is said to be a certain cure; also for acute rheumatism.

For the cure of wounds, the Spaniards found the Mexican remedies most efficacious. Cortes himself was cured by one of their doctors of a severe wound in the head, received at Otumba, through which we lately passed. For fractures, for humours, for everything they had their remedy; sometimes pulverizing the seeds of plants, and attributing much of their efficacy to the superstitious ceremonies and prayers which they used while applying them, especially those which they offered up to *Tzapotlatenan*, the goddess of medicine.

A great deal of this knowledge is still preserved amongst their descendants, and considered efficacious. For every illness there is an herb, for every accident a remedy. Baths are in constant use, although these temezcallis are confined to the Indians. In every family there is some knowledge of simple medicine, very necessary, in *haciendas* especially, where no physician can possibly be procured.

There is a hill upon ——'s property, said to contain much buried treasure. There are many traditions here of this concealed Indian wealth, but very little gold has been actually recovered from these mountain-tombs. Buried gold has occasionally come to light; not by researches in the mountains, for few are rash enough to throw away their money in search of what would probably prove an imaginary treasure; but by accident—in the ruins of old houses, where the proprietors had deposited it for safety in some period of revolution; perhaps no later than at the time of the Spanish expulsion.

Some years ago, an old and very poor woman rented a house in the environs of Mexico, as old and wretched as herself, for four reals a week. It had an old broken-up stone *patio* (inner courtyard), which she used occasionally to sweep with a little old broom. One day she observed two or three stones in this patio larger and more carefully put together than the others, and the little old woman, being a daughter of Eve by some collateral branch, poked down and worked at the stones until she was able to raise them up—when lo and behold, she discovered a can full of treasure; no less than five thousand dollars' in gold! Her delight and her fright were unbounded; and, being a prudent old lady, she determined, in the first place, to leave the house, and next to bring in her treasure, *poquito á poquito* (little by little), to a room in Mexico, keeping the old house as a sort of bank. She did so; took a nice room, and instead of sleeping on a *petate* (mat), as she had hitherto done, bought herself a little bedstead, and even a mattress; treated herself not only to chocolate, but a few bottles of good wine! Such extraordinary luxury could not fail to create suspicion. She was questioned by her neighbours, and at length intrusted her secret to their keeping. History says, that notwithstanding this, she was not robbed, and was allowed to enjoy her good fortune in peace. It is difficult to credit such a miracle in this land of picking and stealing, but my authority is beyond impeachment.

. . . Whilst I write on these irrelevant matters, I am warned that the coaches are at the door, and that we are about setting off for Tepenacasco, another hacienda of Señor ——'s, a few leagues from this.

LETTER THE SEVENTEENTH

*Arrival at Tepenacasco—Lake with Wild-duck—Ruined Ha-
cienda—Sunset on the Plains—Troop of Asses—Ride by
Moonlight—Leave Tepenacasco—San Miguel—Description—
Thunderstorm—Guasco—Journey to Real del Monte—Eng-
lish Road—Scenery—Village of Real—Count de Regla—Di-
rector's House—English Breakfast—Visit to the Mines—The
Cascade—The Storm—Loneliness—A Journey in Storm and
Darkness—Return to Tepenacasco—Journey to Sopayuca—
Narrow Escape—Famous Bull—Return to Mexico.*

TEPENACASCO.

This is a fine wild scene. The house stands entirely alone; not
a tree near it. Great mountains rise behind it, and in every
other direction, as far as the eye can reach, are vast plains,
over which the wind comes whistling fresh and free, with
nothing to impede its triumphant progress. In front of the
house is a clear sheet of water, a great deep square basin for
collecting the rain. These *jagueys*, as they are called, are very
common in Mexico, where there are few rivers, and where the
use of machines for raising water is by no means general as
yet. There is no garden here, but there are a few shrubs and
flowers in the inner courtyard. The house inside is handsome,
with a chapel and a patio, which is occasionally used as a
plaza de toros. The rooms are well fitted up, and the bedroom
walls covered with a pretty French paper, representing scenes
of Swiss rural life. There are great outhouses, stables for the
mules and horses, and stone barns for the wheat and barley,
which, together with pulque, form the produce of this hacienda.

We took a long ride this morning to visit a fine lake where
there are plenty of wild-duck and turtle. The gentlemen took
their guns and had tolerable sport. The lake is very deep, so
that boats have sailed on it, and several miles in circumference,
with a rivulet flowing from it. Yet with all this water the surrounding land, not more than twenty feet higher, is dry and
sterile, and the lake is turned to no account, either from want
of means, or of hydraulic knowledge. However, C——n having

made some observation on this subject, the proprietor of the lake and of a ruined house standing near, which is the very picture of loneliness and desolation, remarked in reply, that from this estate to Mexico, the distance is thirty-six leagues; that a load of wheat costs one real a league, and moreover the *alcaba*, the duty which has to be paid at the gates of Mexico, so that it would bring no profit if sent there; while in the surrounding district there is not sufficient population to consume the produce; so that these unnecessary and burdensome taxes, the thinness of the population, and the want of proper means of transport, impede the prosperity of the people, and check the progress of agriculture. . . .

I had a beautiful horse, but half-broke, and which took fright and ran off with me. I got great credit for keeping my seat so well, which I must confess was more through good fortune than skill. The day was delightful, the air exhilarating, and the blue sky perfectly cloudless as we galloped over the plains; but at length the wind rose so high that we dismounted, and got into the carriage. We sat by the shores of the lake, and walked along its pebbly margin, watching the wild-duck as they skimmed over its glassy surface, and returned home in a magnificent sunset; the glorious god himself a blood-red globe, surrounded by blazing clouds of gold and crimson.

In the evening a troop of asses were driven across the plain, and led round to the back of the house; and we were all called out in haste, and each desired to choose one of the long-eared fraternity for our particular use. Some had saddles and some had none, but we mounted to the number of thirty persons, followed by a cavalcade of little ragged boys armed with sticks and whips. My ass was an obstinate brute, whom I had mistakenly chosen for his sleek coat and open countenance; but by dint of being lashed up, he suddenly set off at full gallop, and distanced all the others. Such screaming and laughing and confusion! and so much difficulty in keeping the party together? It was nearly dark when we set off; but the moon rose, the silver disc lighting up the hills and the plains; the wind fell, and the night was calm and delightful. We rode about six miles to a pretty little chapel with a cross, that gleamed amongst the trees in the moonlight, by the side of a running stream. Here we dismounted, and sat by the brink of the little sparkling rivulet, while the deep shadows came stealing over the mountains, and all around was still, and cool, and silent; all but the merry laughter of our noisy cavalcade. We returned about eleven o'clock, few accidents having occurred.

Doña R——a had fallen once. Doña M—— had crushed her foot against her neighbour's ass. The padre was shaken to a jelly, and the learned senator, who was of the party, declared he should never recover from that night's jolting. To-morrow we shall set off for Real del Monte.

17th.—After mass in the chapel we left Tepenacasco about seven o'clock, and travelled (I believe by a short cut) over rocks and walls, torrents and fields of maguey, all in a heavy carriage with six horses. Arriving in sight of walls, the mozos gallop on and tear them down. Over the mountain-torrents or *barrancas,* they dash boldly, encouraging the horses by the wildest shrieks.

We stopped at San Miguel, a country-house belonging to the Count de Regla, the former proprietor of the mines which we were about to visit; the most picturesque and lovely place imaginable, but entirely abandoned; the house comfortless and out of repair. We wandered through paths cut in the beautiful woods, and by the side of a rivulet that seems to fertilize everything through which it winds. We climbed the hills, and made our way through the tangled luxuriance of trees and flowers, and in the midst of hundreds of gaudy blossoms, I neglected them all upon coming to a grassy slope covered with daisies and buttercups. We even found some hawthorn-bushes. It might be English scenery, were it not that there is a richness in the vegetation unknown in England. But all these beautiful solitudes are abandoned to the deer that wander fearlessly amongst the woods, and the birds that sing in their branches. While we were still far from the house, a thunderstorm came on. When it rains here, the windows of heaven seem opened, and the clouds pour down water in floods; the lightning also appears to me peculiarly vivid, and many more accidents occur from it here than in the north. We were drenched in five minutes, and in this plight resumed our seats in the carriage, and set off for *Guasco* (a village where we were to pass the night) in the midst of the pelting storm. In an hour or two the horses were wading up to their knees in water, and we arrived at the pretty village of Guasco in a most comfortless condition. There are no inns in these parts, but we were hospitably received by a widow-lady, a friend of ——'s.

The Señora de ——, in clear muslin and lace, with satin shoes, was worse than I in mousseline-de-laine and brodequins; nevertheless, I mean to adopt the fashion of the country tomorrow, when we are to rise at four to go on to Real del

Monte, and try the effect of travelling with clear gown, satin petticoat, and shoes ditto; because "when one is in Rome," etc. The storm continues with such unabated violence, that we must content ourselves with contemplating the watery landscape from the windows.

TEPENACASCO.

Rose in Guasco at four o'clock; dressed by candle-light, took chocolate, and set off for Real del Monte. After we had travelled a few leagues, tolerably cold, we rejoiced when the sun rose, and dispelling the mist, threw his cheerful light over mountain and wood. The trees looked green and refreshing after their last night's bath; the very rocks were sparkling with silver. The morning was perfectly brilliant, and every leaf and flower was glittering with the rain-drops not yet dried. The carriage ascended slowly the road cut through the mountains by the English company; a fine and useful enterprise; the first broad and smooth road I have seen as yet in the republic. Until it was made, hundreds of mules daily conveyed the ore from the mines over a dangerous mountain-path, to the hacienda of Regla, a distance of six or seven leagues. We overtook wagons conveying timber to the mines of Real, nine thousand feet above the level of the sea.

The scenery was magnificent. On one side mountains covered with oak and pine, and carpeted by the brightest-coloured flowers; goats climbing up the perpendicular rocks, and looking down upon us from their vantage-ground; fresh clear rivulets, flinging themselves from rock to rock, and here and there little Indian huts perched amongst the cliffs; on the other, the deep valley with its bending forests and gushing river; while far above, we caught a glimpse of Real itself, with its sloping roofs and large church, standing in the very midst of forests and mountains. We began to see people with fair hair and blue eyes, and one individual, with a shock of fiery red hair and an undeniable Scotch twang, I felt the greatest inclination to claim as a countryman. The Indians here looked cleaner than those in or near Mexico, and were not more than half naked. The whole country here, as well as the mines, formerly belonged to the Count de Regla, who was so wealthy, that when his son, the present count, was christened, the whole party walked from his house to the church upon ingots of silver. The countess having quarrelled with the vice-queen, sent her, in token of reconciliation, a white satin slipper, entirely covered with large diamonds. The count invited the King of Spain to visit his Mexican territories, assuring him that the hoofs of his majesty's horse should touch nothing but solid silver from Vera Cruz to the capital. This might be a bravado; but a more certain proof of his wealth exists in the fact, that he caused two ships of the line, of the largest size, to be constructed in Havana at his expense, made of mahogany and cedar, and presented them to the king. The present count was, as I already told you, married to the beautiful daughter of the *Güerra Rodriguez.*

We arrived at Real del Monte about nine o'clock, and drove to the director's house, which is extremely pretty, commanding a most beautiful and extensive view, and where we found a large fire burning in the grate—very agreeable, as the morning was still somewhat chill, and which had a look of home and comfort that made it still more acceptable. We were received with the greatest cordiality by the director, Mr. Rule, and his lady, and invited to partake of the most delicious breakfast that I have seen for a long while; a happy *mélange* of English and Mexican. The snow-white table-cloth, smoking tea-urn, hot rolls, fresh eggs, coffee, tea, and toast looked very much *à l'Anglaise,* while there were numbers of substantial dishes *à l'Espagnole,* and delicious fresh cream-cheeses, to all which our party did ample justice.

After breakfast, we went out to visit the mines, and it was curious to see English children, clean and pretty, with their white hair and rosy cheeks, and neat straw bonnets, mingled with the little copper-coloured Indians. We visited all the different works; the apparatus for sawing, the turning-lathe, foundry, etc.; but I regretted to find that we could not descend into the mines. We went to the mouth of the shaft called the Dolores, which has a narrow opening, and is entered by perpendicular ladders. The men go down with conical caps on their heads, in which is stuck a lighted tallow candle. In the great shaft, called Terreros, they descend, by means of these ladders, to the depth of a thousand feet, there being platforms at certain distances, on which they can rest. We were obliged to content ourselves with seeing them go down, and with viewing and admiring all the great works which English energy has established here; the various steam-engines, the buildings for the separation and washing of the ore; the great stores, workshops, offices, etc. Nearly all the workmen are British, and of these the Scotch are preferred. Most of the miners are Indians, who work in companies, and receive in payment the eighth part of the proceeds. The director gave us some specimens of silver from the great heaps where they lie, sparkling like genii's treasure.

Although I have not descended into these mines, I might give you a description of them by what I have heard, and fill my paper with arithmetical figures, by which you might judge of the former and the present produce. I might tell you how Don Lucas Alaman went to England, and raised, as if by magic, the enthusiasm of the English; how one fortune after another has been swallowed up in the dark, deep gulf of speculation; how expectations have been disappointed; and how the great cause of this is the scarcity of quicksilver, which has been paid at the rate of one hundred and fifty dollars per quintal in real cash, when the same quantity was given at credit by the Spanish government for fifty dollars; how heaps of silver lie abandoned, because the expense of acquiring quicksilver renders it wholly unprofitable to extract it; and I might repeat the opinion of those persons by whom I have heard the subject discussed, who express their astonishment that, such being the case, an arrangement is not made with the country which is the almost exclusive possessor of the quicksilver-mines, by which it might be procured at a lower rate, and this great source of wealth not thrown away. But for all these matters I refer you to *Humboldt* and *Ward,* by whom they are scientifically treated, and will not trouble you with superficial remarks on so important a subject. In fact, I must confess that my attention was frequently attracted from the mines, and the engines, and the works of man, and the discussions arising therefrom, to the stupendous natural scenery by which we were surrounded; the unexplored forests that clothe the mountains to their very summits, the torrents that leaped and sparkled in the sunshine, the deep ravines, the many-tinted foliage, the bold and jutting rocks. All combine to increase our admiration of the bounties of nature to this favoured land, to which she has given "every herb bearing seed, and every tree that is pleasant to the sight and good for food," while her veins are rich with precious metals; the useful and the beautiful offered with unsparing hand.

We were obliged to leave Real about two o'clock, having a long journey to perform before night, as we had the intention of returning to sleep at Tepenacasco. We took leave of our hospitable entertainers, and again resumed our journey over these fine roads, many parts of which are blasted from the

great rocks of porphyry; and as we looked back at the picturesque colony glistening in the sun, could hardly believe the
prophecies of our more experienced drivers, that a storm was
brewing in the sky, which would burst forth before evening.
We were determined not to believe it, as it was impossible
to pass by the famous hacienda and ravine of Regla without
paying them at least a short visit.

This stupendous work of the Mexican miners in former
days, is some leagues to the south of Real del Monte, and
is said to have cost many millions of dollars. One should view
it as we did, in a thunderstorm, for it has an air of vastness
and desolation, and at the same time of grandeur, that shows
well amidst a war of the elements. Down in a steep barranca,
encircled by basaltic cliffs, it lies; a mighty pile of building,
which seems as if it might have been constructed by some
philosophical giant or necromancer;—so that one is not prepared to find there an English director and his wife, and the
unpoetic comforts of roast mutton and potatoes!

All is on a gigantic scale: the immense vaulted storehouses
for the silver ore; the great smelting-furnaces and covered
buildings where we saw the process of amalgamation going
on; the water-wheels; in short, all the necessary machinery for
the smelting and amalgamation of the metal. We walked to
see the great cascade, with its row of basaltic columns, and
found a seat on a piece of broken pillar beside the rushing
river, where we had a fine view of the lofty cliffs, covered with
the wildest and most luxuriant vegetation: vines trailing themselves over every broken shaft; moss creeping over the huge
disjointed masses of rock; and trees overhanging the precipitous ravine. The columns look as if they might have been the
work of those who, on the plains of Shinar, began to build
the city, and the tower whose top was to reach to heaven.

But, as we sat here, the sky suddenly became overcast; great
black masses of cloud collected over our heads, and the rumbling of thunder in the distance gave notice of an approaching
storm. We had scarcely time to get under shelter of the director's roof, when the thunder began to echo loudly amongst
the rocks, and was speedily followed by torrents of rain. It
was a superb storm: the lightning flashed amongst the trees,
the wind howled furiously, while

"*Far along
From peak to peak, the rattling crags among,*
Leapt *the live thunder.*"

After resting and dining amidst a running accompaniment of plashing rain, roaring wind, and deep-toned thunder, we found that it was in vain to wait for a favourable change in the weather; and certainly, with less experienced drivers, it would have been anything but safe to have set off amidst the darkness of the storm, down precipitous descents and over torrents swelled by the rain. The Count de Regla, who, attracted by the plentiful supply of water in this ravine, conceived the idea of employing part of his enormous fortune in the construction of these colossal works, must have had an imagination on a large scale. The English directors, whose wives bury themselves in such abysses, ought to feel more grateful to them than any other husbands towards their sacrificing better halves. For the men, occupied all day amongst their workmen and machinery, and returning late in the evening to dine and sleep, there is no great self-immolation; but a poor woman, living all alone, in a house fenced in by gigantic rocks; with no other sound in her ears from morning till night but the roar of thunder or the clang of machinery, had need for her personal comfort, to have either a most romantic imagination, so that she may console herself with feeling like an enchanted princess in a giant's castle, or a most commonplace spirit, so that she may darn stockings to the sound of the waterfall, and feel no other inconvenience from the storm, but that her husband will require dry linen when he comes home.

As for us, we were drenched before we reached the carriage, into which the water was pouring, and when we set off once more amidst the rapidly-increasing darkness, and over these precipitous roads, we thought that our chance of reaching the proposed haven that night was very small. After much toil to the horses, we got out of the ravines and found ourselves once more on the great plains, where the tired animals ploughed their way over fields and ditches and great stones, and among trees and tangled bushes; an occasional flash of lightning our only guide. Great was our joy, when, about eleven o'clock, a man riding on in advance shouted out that the lights of Tepenacasco were in sight; and still more complete our satisfaction when we drove round the tank into the courtyard of the hacienda. We were received with great applause by the inmates, and were not sorry to rest after a very fatiguing yet agreeable day.

We left Tepenacasco the day before yesterday. Our journey was very dangerous, in consequence of the great rains, which had swelled the torrents; especially as we set off late, and most of it was performed by night. In these barrancas, carriages and horsemen have been frequently swept away and dashed in pieces over the precipices. But to make our situation more disagreeable, we had scarcely set off, before a terrible storm of thunder and rain again came on with more violence than the night preceding. It grew perfectly dark, and we listened with some alarm to the roaring torrents, over which, especially over one, not many leagues from Sopayuca, where we were to spend the night, it was extremely doubtful whether we could pass. The carriage was full of water, but we were too much alarmed to be uneasy about trifles. Amidst the howling of the wind and the pealing of thunder, no one could hear the other speak. Suddenly, by a vivid flash of lightning, the dreaded barranca appeared in sight for a moment, and almost before the drivers could stop them, the horses had plunged in.

It was a moment of mortal fear such as I shall never forget. The shrieks of the drivers to encourage the horses, the loud cries of Ave Maria! the uncertainty as to whether our heavy carriage could be dragged across, the horses struggling and splashing in the boiling torrent, and the horrible fate that awaited us should one of them fall or falter! . . . The Señora —— and I shut our eyes and held each other's hands, and certainly no one breathed till we were safe on the other side. We were then told that we had crossed within a few feet of a precipice over which a coach had been dashed into fifty pieces during one of these swells, and of course every one killed; and that if instead of horses we had travelled with mules, we must have been lost. You may imagine that we were not sorry to reach Sopayuca; where the people ran out to the door at the sound of carriage-wheels, and could not believe that we had passed the barranca that night; as two or three horsemen who had rode in that direction had turned back, and pronounced it impassable.

Lights and supper were soon procured, and by way of interlude a monstrous bull, of great fame in these parts, was led up to the supper-table for our inspection with a rope through his nose, a fierce brute, but familiarly called "el chato" (the flatnose), from the shortness of his horns. The lightning continued very vivid, and they told us that a woman had been struck there some time before, while in the chapel by night.

We rose at four o'clock the next morning and set off for Mexico. The morning, as usual after these storms, was peculiarly fresh and beautiful; but the sun soon grew oppressive on the great plains. About two o'clock we entered Mexico by the Guadalupe gate. We found our house *in statu quo*,—agreeable letters from Europe,—great preparations making for the English ball, to assist at which we have returned sooner than we otherwise should, and for which my *femme-de-chambre* has just completed a dress for me, very much to her own satisfaction.

LETTER THE EIGHTEENTH

English Ball—Dresses—Diamonds—Mineria—Arrival of the Pope's Bull—Consecration of the Archbishop—Foreign Ministers—Splendour of the Cathedral—Description of the Ceremony.

25th.

The English ball at the Mineria has passed off with great *éclat*. Nothing could be more splendid than the general effect of this noble building, brilliantly illuminated and filled with a well-dressed crowd. The president and corps diplomatique were in full uniform, and the display of diamonds was extraordinary. We ladies of the corps diplomatique tried to flatter ourselves that we made up in elegance what we wanted in magnificence! for in jewels no foreign ladies could attempt to compete with those of the country. The daughter of Countess ——, just arrived from Paris, and whose acquaintance I made for the first time, wore pale blue, with garlands of pale pink roses, and a parure of most superb brilliants. The Señora de A——'s head reminded me of that of the Marchioness of Londonderry, in her opera-box. The Marquesa de Vivanco had a rivière of brilliants of extraordinary size and beauty, and perfectly well set. Madame S——r wore a very rich blonde dress, *garnie* with plumes of ostrich feathers, a large diamond fastening each plume. One lady wore a diadem which —— said could not be worth less than a hundred thousand dollars. Diamonds are always worn plain or with pearls; coloured stones are considered trash, which is a pity, as I think rubies and emeralds set in diamonds would give more variety and splendour to their jewels. There were a profusion of large pearls, generally of a pear shape. The finest and roundest were those worn by the Señora B——a. There were many blonde dresses, a great fashion here. I know no lady without one. Amongst the prettiest and most tastefully-dressed girls were the E——s, as usual. Many dresses were overloaded, a common fault in Mexico; and many of the dresses, though rich, were old-fashioned; but the *coup d'œil* was not the less brilliant, and it was somewhat astonishing, in such a multitude, not to see a single objectionable person. To be sure the company were all invited.

On entering the noble court, which was brilliantly illuminated with coloured lamps, hung from pillar to pillar, and passing up the great staircase, we were met at the first landing by Mr. P——, in full uniform, and other English gentlemen, the directors of the ball, who stood there to receive the ladies. His excellency led me upstairs to the top of the ball-room, where chairs were placed for the president, ladies of the *diplomaties*, cabinet ministers, etc. The music was excellent, and dancing was already in full force. And though there were assembled what is called *all Mexico*, the rooms are so large, that the crowd was not disagreeable, nor the heat oppressive. Pictures of Queen Victoria were hung in the different large halls. The supper-tables were very handsome; and in fact the ball altogether was worthy of its object; for Messieurs les Anglais always do these things well when they attempt them.

The president took me to supper. The company walked in to the music of "God save the Queen." After we had sat a little while the president demanded silence, and, in a short speech, proposed the health of Her Majesty Queen Victoria, which was drank by all the company standing. After supper we continued dancing till nearly six in the morning; and when we got into the carriage it was broad daylight, and all the bells were ringing for mass.

This is the best ball we have seen here, without any exception; and it is said to have cost eleven thousand dollars. There were certainly a great number of pretty faces at this fête, many pretty girls whom we had not seen before, and whom the English secretaries have contrived to *unearth*. Fine eyes are a mere *drug*—every one has them; large, dark, full orbs, with long silken lashes. As for diamonds, no man above the rank of a *lépero* marries in this country without presenting his bride with at least a pair of diamond earrings, or a pearl necklace with a diamond clasp. They are not always a proof of wealth, though they constitute it in themselves. Their owners may be very poor in other respects. They are considered a necessary of life; quite as much so as shoes and stockings.

June 2nd.—On the 15th of April, the pontifical bulls arrived from Rome, confirming the election of the Señor Posada to the Archiepiscopal dignity; and on Saturday last, the 31st of May, the consecration took place in the cathedral with the greatest pomp. The presiding bishop was the Señor Belaunzaran, the old Bishop of Linares; the two assistant bishops were

the Señor Madrid, a young, good-looking man, who having
been banished from Mexico during the revolution, took refuge
in Rome, where he obtained the favour of the Pope, who
afterwards recommended him to an episcopal see in Mexico;
and the Doctor Morales, formerly Bishop of Sonora. His *padrino* was the President, General Bustamante, who in his capacity presented his godson with the splendid pastoral ring,
a solitary diamond of immense size. All the diplomatic body
and the cabinet went in full uniform; chairs being placed for
them on each side of the *crugia* (the passage leading to the
altar). A dispute upon the subject of precedence arose between an excellency of the diplomatic corps, and the secretary
of state, which seems likely to have disagreeable consequences.
I had the pleasure of kneeling beside these illustrious persons
for the space of three or four hours, for no seats were placed
for the wives either of the diplomates or of the cabinet.

But the ceremony, though long, was very superb, the music
fine, the quantity of jewels on the dresses of the bishops and
priests, and on the holy vessels, etc., enormous. The bishops
were arrayed in white velvet and gold, and their mitres were
literally covered with diamonds. The gold candlesticks and
golden basins for holy water, and golden incensories, reminded
me of the description of the ornaments of the Jewish tabernacle in the days of Moses; of the "candlesticks of pure gold,
with golden branches;" and "the tongs and snuff-dishes of pure
gold:" or of the temple of Solomon, where the altar was of
gold, and the table of gold, and the candlesticks and the snuff-
ers, and the basins, and the spoons, and the censors were of
pure gold. The pontifical vestments destined for the elected
primate, were all prepared;—sandals, amice, surplice, girdle,
pectoral cross, stole, gown, vestment, with open sleeves (the
dalmatica), crosier, mitre, pontifical ring, etc. Magnificent
chairs were prepared for the bishops near the altar, and the
president in uniform took his place amongst them. The presiding bishop took his seat alone, with his back to the altar,
and the Señor Posada was led in by the assisting bishops, they
with their mitres, he with his priest's cap on. Arrived before
the presiding bishop, he uncovered his head, and made a profound obeisance. These three then took their places on chairs
placed in front; and the ceremony having begun, in case you
should wish to have some idea of it, I shall endeavour to give
it you, for I was so situated, that although the cathedral was
crowded to excess, I could see and hear all that passed. Let

me premise, however, that there was not one *lépero,* as they are always excluded on such occasions.

Posada and his assisting bishops rose, and uncovered their heads; and the Bishop Morales turning to the presiding bishop, said, "Most reverend father, the holy Catholic Mother Church requests you to raise this Presbyter to the charge of the archbishopric."

"Have you an apostolical mandate?"

"We have."

"Read it."

An assistant priest then read the mandate in a loud voice; upon which they all sat down, and the consecrator saying, "Thanks be to God!" Then the Posada kneeling before him, took an oath, upon the Bible, which the bishop held, concluding with these words—"So may God help me, and these his holy gospels." Then sitting down, and resuming their mitres, the examination of the future archbishop took place. It was very long, and at its conclusion, Posada knelt before the presiding bishop and kissed his hand. To this succeeded the confession, every one standing uncovered before the altar, which was then sprinkled with incense. Then followed the mass, chanted.

The assisting bishops then led out the Señor Posada to the chapel, where they put on his sandals, and where he assumed the pectoral cross, amice, surplice, etc.; and arriving at the altar read the office of the mass. He was then conducted again before the consecrating bishop, who was seated with his mitre, and after saluting him reverently, he sat down. Then the bishop, addressing him said: "It is the duty of the bishop to judge, interpret, consecrate, ordain, offer, baptize, and confirm."

All then rose, and the bishop prayed that the newly-elected primate might receive the grace of heaven. All the bishops and priests then prostrated themselves while the Litanies were sung. The presiding bishop, rising, took the crosier, and prayed three times for a blessing on the Chosen One; thrice making on him the sign of the cross; and they continued to sing the Litanies; at the conclusion of which they all arose, took their seats and resumed their mitres, Posada alone kneeling before the bishop.

The Bible was then placed upon his shoulders, while he remained prostrated, and the bishop rising up, pronounced a solemn benediction upon him, while the hymn of "Veni Creator Spiritus," was sung in full chorus. Then the bishop, dipping his hand in the holy chrism, anointed the primate's head, making on it the sign of the cross, saying, "Let thy head be anointed and consecrated with the celestial benediction, according to the pontifical mandate." The bishop then anointed his hands, making in the same manner the sign of the cross, and saying, "May these hands be anointed with holy oil; and as Samuel anointed David a king and a prophet, so be thou anointed and consecrated." This was followed by a solemn prayer.

Then the crosier was blessed, and presented to the elected archbishop with these words. "Receive the pastoral crosier, that thou mayest be humanely severe in correcting vices, exercising judgment without wrath," etc. The blessing of the ring followed with solemn prayer, and being sprinkled with holy water, it was placed on the third finger of the right hand, the bishop saying, "Receive the ring, which is a sign of faith; that, adorned with incorruptible faith, thou mayest guard inviolably the spouse of God, his Holy Church."

The Bible being then taken off the shoulders of the prostrate prelate, was presented to him with an injunction to receive and to preach the gospel. Finally, the bishop bestowed on him the kiss of peace; and all the other bishops did so in their turn. Posada then retired, and his head and hands being washed, he soon after returned with the assistant bishops, carrying two lighted wax tapers, which he presented to the presiding bishop, together with two loaves and two small barrels of wine, reverently kissing his hand. After this, the presiding bishop washed his hands and mounted the steps of the altar, and the new primate received the sacrament.

The mitre was then blessed and placed upon his head, with a prayer by the bishop, that thus, with his head armed and with the staff of the gospels, he might appear terrible to the adversaries of the True Faith. The gloves were next consecrated and drawn on his hands, the bishop praying that his hands might be surrounded by the purity of the new man; and that as Jacob, when he covered his hands with goat-skins, offered agreeable meats to his father, and received his paternal benediction, so he, in offering the Holy Sacrament, might obtain the benediction of his Heavenly Father. The archbishop was then seated by the consecrating bishop on his pontifical throne, and at the same moment, the hymn "Te Deum laudamus" was chanted. During the hymn, the bishops, with their jewelled mitres, rose, and passing through the church, blessed the whole congregation, the new archbishop still remaining near the altar, and without his mitre. When he returned to his seat, the assistant bishops, including the consecrator, remained standing till the hymn was concluded.

The presiding bishop then advancing, without his mitre, to the right hand of the archbishop, said, "May thy hand be strengthened! May thy right hand be exalted! May justice and judgment be the preparation of thy see!" Then the organ pealed forth, and they chanted the hymn of "Gloria Patri." Long and solemn prayer followed; and then, all uncovered, stood beside the gospels, at the altar.

The archbishop rose, and with mitre and crosier, pronounced a solemn blessing on all the people assembled. Then, while all knelt beside the altar, he said—"For many years." This he repeated thrice; the second time, in the middle of the altar, the third at the feet of the presiding bishop. Then all rising, the archbishop bestowed on each the kiss of peace, and the ceremony concluded.

When everything was over, our carriage not being visible amongst the crowd of vehicles, I returned home in that of the —— Minister, with him and his attachés; after which, they and C——n returned to dine with the new archbishop in his palace. A dish of sweetmeats was sent me from his table, which are so pretty, (probably the chef-d'œuvre of the nuns,) that I send them to you, to preserve as a memorial of the consecration of the first Mexican archbishop—perhaps of the last!

LETTER THE NINETEENTH

*Mexican Servants—Anecdotes—Remedies—An unsafe Porter—
Galopinas—The Reboso—The Sarape—Women Cooks—Foreign Servants—Characteristics of Mexican Servants—Servants' Wages—Nun of the Santa Teresa—Motives for taking
the Veil.*

June 3rd.

You ask me to tell you how I find the Mexican servants. Hitherto I had avoided the ungrateful theme, from very weariness
of it. The badness of the servants, is an unfailing source of
complaint even amongst Mexicans; much more so amongst
foreigners, especially on their first arrival. We hear of their
addiction to stealing, their laziness, drunkenness, dirtiness,
with a host of other vices. That these complaints are frequently just, there can be no doubt, but the evil might be
remedied to a great extent. In the first place servants are constantly taken without being required to bring a recommendation from their last place; and in the next, recommendations
are constantly given, whether from indolence or mistaken
kindness, to servants who do not deserve them. A servant who
has lived in a dozen different houses, staying about a month
in each, is not thought the worse of on that account. As the
love of finery is inherent in them all, even more so than in
other daughters of Eve, a girl will go to service merely to earn
sufficient to buy herself an embroidered chemise; and if, in
addition to this, she can pick up a pair of small old satin
shoes, she will tell you she is tired of working, and going home
to rest, *"para descansar."* So little is necessary, when one can
contentedly live on tortillas and chile, sleep on a mat, and
dress in rags!

A decent old woman, who came to the house to wash shortly
after our arrival in this country, and left us at the end of the
month, *"para descansar."* Soon after, she used to come with
her six children, they and herself all in rags, and beg the gardener to give her any *odds and ends* of vegetables he could
spare. My maid asked her, why, being so poor, she had left
a good place, where she got twelve dollars a month. "Jesus!"

said she, "if you only knew the pleasure of doing nothing."

I wished to bring up a little girl as a servant, having her taught to read, sew, etc. A child of twelve years old, one of a large family, who subsisted upon charity, was procured for me; and I promised her mother that she should be taught to read, taken regularly to church, and instructed in all kinds of work. She was rather pretty, and very intelligent, though extremely indolent; and though she had no stockings, would consent to wear nothing but dirty white satin shoes, too short for her foot. Once a week, her mother, a tall, slatternly woman, with long tangled hair, and a cigar in her mouth, used to come to visit her, accompanied by a friend, a friend's friend, and a train of girls, her daughters. The housekeeper would give them some dinner, after which they would all light their cigars, and, together with the little Josefita, sit, and howl, and bemoan themselves, crying and lamenting her sad fate in being obliged to go out to service. After these visits, Josefita was fit for nothing. If desired to sew, she would sit looking so miserable, and doing so little, that it seemed better to allow her to leave her work alone. Then, tolerably contented, she would sit on a mat, doing nothing, her hands folded, and her eyes fixed on vacancy.

According to promise, I took her several times to see her mother, but one day being occupied, I sent her alone in the carriage, with charge to the servants to bring her safely back. In the evening she returned, accompanied by the whole family, all crying and howling; "For the love of the Most Holy Virgin, Señora mia! Por la purissima concepcion!" etc., etc., etc. I asked what had happened, and after much difficulty discovered that their horror was occasioned by my having sent her alone in the carriage. It happened that the Countess S——was in the drawing-room, and to her I related the cause of the uproar. To my astonishment, she assured me that the woman was in this instance right, and that it was very dangerous to send a girl of twelve years of age from one street to another, in the power of the coachman and footman. Finding from such good authority that this was the case, I begged the woman to be contented with seeing her daughter once a month, when, if she could not come herself, I would send her under proper protection. She agreed; but one day having given Josefita permission to spend the night at her mother's, I received next morning a very dirty note, nearly illegible, which, after calling down the protection of the Virgin upon me, concluded—"but with much sorrow I must take my child from the most illustrious protection of your excellency, for she needs to rest herself, (es preciso que descanse,) and is tired for the present of working." The woman then returned to beg, which she considered infinitely less degrading.

Against this nearly universal indolence and indifference to earning money, the heads of families have to contend; as also against thieving and dirtiness; yet I think the remedy much easier than it appears. If on the one hand, no one were to receive a servant into their house, without respectable references, especially from their last place, and if their having remained one year in the same house were considered necessary to their being received into another, unless from some peculiar circumstances; and if on the other hand it were considered as unjust and dangerous, as it really is, to recommend a servant who has been guilty of stealing, as being "*muy honrado,*" very honest, some improvement might soon take place.

A porter was recommended to us as "muy honrado;" not from his last place, but from one before. He was a well-dressed, sad-looking individual; and at the same time we took his wife as washerwoman, and his brother as valet to our attaché, thus having the whole family under our roof, wisely taking it for granted that he being recommended as particularly honest, his relations were "all honourable men." An English lady happened to call on me, and a short time after I went to return her visit; when she informed me that the person who had opened the door for her was a notorious thief; whom the police had long been in search of; that she had feared sending a servant to warn us of our danger, lest guessing the purport of her message, he might rob the house before leaving it. We said·nothing to the man that evening, but he looked paler and more miserable than usual, probably foreseeing what would be the result of Mrs. ——'s visit. The next morning C——n sent for him and dismissed him, giving him a month's wages, that he might not be tempted to steal from immediate want. His face grew perfectly livid, but he made no remark. In half an hour he returned and begged to speak with C——n. He confessed that the crime of which he concluded he was accused, he had in fact committed; that he had been tempted to a gambling house, while he had in his pocket a large sum of money belonging to his master. After losing his own money, he tried his fortune with what was not his own; lost the whole sum, then pawned a valuable shawl worth several hundred dollars, with which also he had been entrusted; and having lost everything, in despair made his escape from Mexico. He remained in concealment for some time, till hearing that we wanted a porter, he ventured to present himself to the house-keeper with his former certificate. He declared himself thoroughly repentant—that this was his first, and would be his last crime—but who can trust the good resolutions of a gambler! We were obliged to send him away, especially as the other servants already had some suspicions concerning him; and everything stolen in the house would in future have been attributed to him. The gentleman who had recommended him, afterwards confessed that he always had strong suspicions of this man's honesty, and knew him to be so determined a gambler, that he had pawned all he possessed, even his wife's clothes, to obtain money for that purpose. Now as a porter in Mexico has pretty much at his disposal the property and even the lives of the whole family, it is certainly most blameable to recommend to that situation a man whose honesty is more than doubtful. We afterwards procured two soldiers from the *Invalidos,* old Spaniards, to act in that capacity, who had no other foiblesse but that of being constantly drunk. We at length found two others, who only got tipsy alternately, so that we considered ourselves very well off.

We had a long series of *galopinas,* kitchen-maids, and the only one who brought a first-rate character with her, robbed the housekeeper. The money, however, was recovered, and was found to have been placed by the girl in the hands of a rich and apparently respectable coachmaker. He refunded it to the rightful owner, and the galopina was punished by a month's imprisonment, which he should have shared with her. One of the most disagreeable customs of the women servants, is that of wearing their long hair hanging down at its full length, matted, uncombed, and always in the way. I cannot imagine how the Mexican ladies, who complain of this, permit it. Flowing hair sounds very picturesque, but when it is very dirty, and suspended over the soup, it is not a pretty picture.

The reboso, in itself graceful and convenient, has the disadvantage of being the greatest cloak for all untidiness, uncombed hair and raggedness, that ever was invented. Even in the better classes, it occasions much indolence in the toilet, but in the common people, its effect is overwhelming. When the reboso drops off, or is displaced by chance, we see what they would be without it! As for the sarape, it is both convenient and graceful, especially on horseback; but though Indian in its origin, the custom of covering the lower part of the face with it, is taken from the Spanish cloak; and the

opportunity which both sarape and reboso afford for concealing large knives about the person, as also for enveloping both
face and figure so as to be scarcely recognizable, is no doubt
the cause of the many murders which take place amongst the
lower orders, in moments of excitement and drunkenness. If
they had not these knives at hand, their rage would probably
cool, or a fair fight would finish the matter, and if they could
not wear these knives concealed, I presume they would be
prohibited from carrying them.

As for taking a woman-cook in Mexico, one must have strong
nerves and a good appetite to eat what she dresses, however
palatable, after having seen her. One look at her flowing locks,
one glance at her reboso, *et c'est fini*. And yet the Mexican
servants have their good qualities, and are a thousand times
preferable to the foreign servants one finds in Mexico; especially the French. Bringing them with you is a dangerous experiment. In ten days they begin to fancy themselves ladies
and gentlemen—the men have *Don* tacked to their name; and
they either marry and set up shops, or become unbearably
insolent. A tolerable French cook may occasionally be had,
but you must pay his services their weight in gold, and wink
at his extortions and robberies. There are one or two French
restaurans, who will send you in a very good dinner at an extravagant price: and it is common in foreign houses, especially
amongst the English, to adopt this plan whenever they give
a large entertainment.

The Mexican servants have some never-failing good qualities. They are the perfection of civility—humble, obliging, excessively good-tempered, and very easily attached to those with
whom they live; and if that *rara avis*, a good Mexican housekeeper, can be found, and that such may be met with I from
experience can testify, then the troubles of the menage rest
upon her shoulders, and accustomed as she is to the amiable
weaknesses of her *compatriotes*, she is neither surprised nor
disturbed by them.

As for wages, a good porter has from fifteen to twenty dollars per month; a coachman from twenty to thirty—many
houses keep two or even three coachmen; one who drives from
the box, one who rides postilion, and a third for emergencies.
Our friend ——, who has many horses, mules, and carriages,
has four; and pays forty dollars per month to his head coachman; the others in proportion. A French cook has about thirty
dollars—a housekeeper from twelve to fifteen; a major-domo
about twenty or more; a footman six or seven; galopine and

chambermaid five or six; a gardener from twelve to fifteen. Sewing-girls have about three reals per diem. Porter, coach-men, and gardener, have their wives and families in the house, which would be an annoyance, were the houses not so large. The men-servants generally are much cleaner and better dressed than the women.

One circumstance is remarkable; that, dirty as the women-servants are, and notwithstanding the enormous size of Mexi-can houses, and Mexican families, the houses themselves are, generally speaking, the perfection of cleanliness. This must be due either to a good housekeeper, which is rarely to be found, or to the care taken by the mistress of the house herself. That private houses should have this advantage over churches and theatres, only proves that ladies know how to manage these matters better than gentlemen, so that one is inclined to wish à la Martineau, that the Mexican police were entirely com-posed of old women.

12th.—I have formed an acquaintance with a very amiable and agreeable nun in the convent of Santa Teresa, one of the strictest orders. I have only seen her twice, through a grating. She is a handsome woman of good family, and it is said of a remarkably joyous disposition; fond of music and dancing, and gay society, yet at the age of eighteen, contrary to the wishes of all her family, she took the veil, and declares she has never repented of it. Although I cannot see her, I can hear her voice, and talk to her through a turning wooden screen, which has a very mysterious effect. She gives me an account of her oc-cupations and of the little events that take place in her small world within; whilst I bring her news from the world with-out. The common people have the greatest veneration for the holy sisterhood, and I generally find there a number of women with baskets, and men carrying parcels or letters; some asking their advice or assistance, others executing their commissions, bringing them vegetables or bread, and listening to the sound of their voice with the most eager attention. My friend, the Madre ——, has promised to dress a number of wax figures for me, in the exact costume of all the different nuns in Mexico, beginning with that of her own convent.

I have now seen three nuns take the veil; and, next to a death, consider it the saddest event that can occur in this nether sphere; yet the frequency of these human sacrifices here is not so strange as might at first appear. A young girl, who knows nothing of the world, who, as it too frequently happens, has at home neither amusement nor instruction, and no society abroad, who from childhood is under the dominion of her confessor, and who firmly believes that by entering a convent she becomes sure of heaven; who moreover finds there a number of companions of her own age, and of older women who load her with praises and caresses—it is not, after all, astonishing that she should consent to insure her salvation on such easy terms.

Add to this the splendour of the ceremony, of which she is the sole object; the cynosure of all approving eyes. A girl of sixteen finds it hard to resist all this. I am told that more girls are smitten by the ceremony, than by anything else, and am inclined to believe it, from the remarks I have heard made on these occasions by young girls in my vicinity. What does she lose? A husband and children? Probably she has seen no one who has touched her heart. Most probably she has hitherto seen no men, or at least conversed with none but her brothers, her uncles, or her confessor. She has perhaps also felt the troubles of a Mexican ménage. The society of men! She will still see her confessor, and she will have occasional visits from reverend padres and right reverend bishops.

Some of these convents are not entirely free from scandal. Amongst the monks, there are many who are openly a disgrace to their calling, though I firmly believe that by far the greater number lead a life of privation and virtue. Their conduct can, to a certain extent, be judged of by the world; but the pale nuns, devout and pure, immured in the cloister for life, kneeling before the shrine, or chanting hymns in the silence of the night, a veil both truly and allegorically must shade their virtues or their failings. The nuns of the Santa Teresa and of other strict orders, who live sparingly, profess the most severe rules, and have no servants or boarders, enjoy a universal reputation for virtue and sanctity. They consider the other convents worldly, and their motto is, "All or nothing; the world or the cloister." Each abbess adds a stricter rule, a severer penance than her predecessor, and in this they glory. My friend the Madre —— frequently says—"Were I to be born again, I should choose, above every lot in life, to be a nun of the Santa Teresa, but of no other convent." . . .

It is strange how, all the world over, mankind seems to expect from those who assume religion as a profession a degree of superhuman perfection. Their failings are insisted upon. Every eye is upon them to mark whatsoever may be amiss in their conduct. Their virtues, their learning, their holy lives—nothing will avail them, if one blot can be discovered in their character. There must be no moral blemish in the priesthood. In the Catholic religion, where more is professed, still more is demanded, and the errors of one padre or one ecclesiastic seem to throw a shade over the whole community to which they belong.

LETTER THE TWENTIETH

4th June.

Some days ago, having received a message from *my nun* that a girl was about to take the veil in her convent, I went there about six o'clock, and knowing that the church on these occasions is apt to be crowded to suffocation, I proceeded to the *reja*, and speaking to an invisible within, requested to know in what part of the church I could have a place. Upon which a voice replied—

"Hermanita (my sister), I am rejoiced to see you. You shall have a place beside the godmother."

"Many thanks, Hermanita. Which way shall I go?"

Voice.—"You shall go through the sacristy. José Maria!"

José Maria, a thin, pale, lank individual, with hollow cheeks, who was standing near like a page in waiting, sprang forward —"*Madrecita*, I am here!"

Voice.—"José Maria—That lady is the Señora de C——n. You will conduct her excellency to the front of the grating, and give her a chair."

After I had thanked the *voice* for her kindness in attending to me on a day when she was so much occupied with other affairs, the obsequious José Maria led the way, and I followed him through the sacristy into the church, where there were already a few kneeling figures; and thence into the railed-off enclosure destined for the relatives of the future nun, where I was permitted to sit down in a comfortable velvet chair. I had been there but a little while when the aforesaid José Maria reappeared, picking his steps as if he were walking upon eggs in a sick-room. He brought me a message from the Madre

—— that the nun had arrived, and that the madrecita wished to know if I should like to give her an embrace before the ceremony began. I therefore followed my guide back into the sacristy, where the future nun was seated beside her godmother, and in the midst of her friends and relations, about thirty in all.

She was arrayed in pale blue satin, with diamonds, pearls, and a crown of flowers. She was literally smothered in blonde and jewels; and her face was flushed as well it might be, for she had passed the day in taking leave of her friends at a fête they had given her, and had then, according to custom, been paraded through the town in all her finery. And now her last hour was at hand. When I came in she rose and embraced me with as much cordiality as if we had known each other for years. Beside her sat the Madrina, also in white satin and jewels; all the relations being likewise decked out in their finest array. The nun kept laughing every now and then in the most unnatural and hysterical manner, as I thought, apparently to impress us with the conviction of her perfect happiness; for it is a great point of honour amongst girls similarly situated to look as cheerful and gay as possible; the same feeling, though in a different degree, which induces the gallant highwayman to jest in the presence of the multitude when the hangman's cord is within an inch of his neck, the same which makes the gallant general whose life is forfeited, command his men to fire on him; the same which makes the Hindoo widow mount the funeral pile without a tear in her eye, or a sigh on her lips. If the robber were to be strangled in a corner of his dungeon; if the general were to be put to death privately in his own apartment; if the widow were to be burnt quietly on her own hearth; if the nun were to be secretly smuggled in at the convent gate like a bale of contraband goods,—we might hear another tale. This girl was very young, but by no means pretty; on the contrary, rather *disgraciée par la nature;* and perhaps a knowledge of her own want of attraction may have caused the world to have few charms for her.

But José Maria cut short my train of reflections, by requesting me to return to my seat before the crowd arrived, which I did forthwith. Shortly after, the church doors were thrown open, and a crowd burst in, every one struggling to obtain the best seat. Musicians entered, carrying desks and music-books, and placed themselves in two rows, on either side of the enclosure where I was. Then the organ struck up its solemn psalmody, and was followed by the gay music of the band.

Rockets were let off outside the church, and, at the same time, the Madrina and all the relations entered and knelt down in front of the grating which looks into the convent, but before which hung a dismal black curtain. I left my chair and knelt down beside the godmother.

Suddenly the curtain was withdrawn, and the picturesque beauty of the scene within baffles all description. Beside the altar, which was in a blaze of light, was a perfect mass of crimson and gold drapery; the walls, the antique chairs, the table before which the priests sat, all hung with the same splendid material. The bishop wore his superb mitre and robes of crimson and gold; the attendant priests also glittering in crimson and gold embroidery.

In contrast to these, five-and-twenty figures, entirely robed in black from head to foot, were ranged on each side of the room prostrate, their faces touching the ground, and in their hands immense lighted tapers. On the foreground was spread a purple carpet bordered round with a garland of freshly-gathered flowers, roses and carnations and heliotrope, the only thing that looked real and living in the whole scene; and in the middle of this knelt the novice, still arrayed in her blue satin, white lace veil and jewels, and also with a great lighted taper in her hand.

The black nuns then rose and sang a hymn, every now and then falling on their faces and touching the floor with their foreheads. The whole looked like an incantation, or a scene in Robert le Diable. The novice was then raised from the ground and led to the feet of the bishop, who examined her as to her vocation, and gave her his blessing, and once more the black curtain fell between us and them.

In the *second act*, she was lying prostrate on the floor, disrobed of her profane dress, and covered over with a black cloth, while the black figures kneeling round her chanted a hymn. She was now dead to the world. The sunbeams had faded away, as if they would not look upon the scene, and all the light was concentrated in one great mass upon the convent group.

Again she was raised. All the blood had rushed into her face, and her attempt at a smile was truly painful. She then knelt before the bishop and received the benediction, with the sign of the cross, from a white hand with the pastoral ring. She then went round alone to embrace all the dark phantoms as they stood motionless, and as each dark shadow clasped her in its arms, it seemed like the dead welcoming a new arrival to the shades.

But I forget the sermon, which was delivered by a fat priest, who elbowed his way with some difficulty through the crowd to the grating, panting and in a prodigious heat, and ensconced himself in a great arm-chair close beside us. He assured her that she "had chosen the good part, which could not be taken away from her;" that she was now one of the elect, "chosen from amongst the wickedness and dangers of the world;"—(picked out like a plum from a pie). He mentioned with pity and contempt those who were "yet struggling in the great Babylon;" and compared their miserable fate with hers, the Bride of Christ, who, after suffering a few privations here during a short term of years, should be received at once into a kingdom of glory. The whole discourse was well calculated to rally her fainting spirits, if fainting they were, and to inspire us with a great disgust for ourselves.

When the sermon was concluded, the music again struck up—the heroine of the day came forward, and stood before the grating to take her last look of this wicked world. Down fell the black curtain. Up rose the relations, and I accompanied them into the sacristy. Here they coolly lighted their cigars, and very philosophically discoursed upon the exceeding good fortune of the new-made nun, and on her evident delight and satisfaction with her own situation. As we did not follow her behind the scenes, I could not give my opinion on this point. Shortly after, one of the gentlemen civilly led me to my carriage, and *so it was*.

As we were returning home, some soldiers rode up and stopped the carriage, desiring the coachman to take to the other side of the aqueduct, to avoid the body of a man who had just been murdered within a few doors of our house.

In the Convent of the Incarnation, I saw another girl sacrificed in a similar manner. She was received there without a dowry, on account of the exceeding fineness of her voice. She little thought what a fatal gift it would prove to her. The most cruel part of all was, that wishing to display her fine voice to the public, they made her sing a hymn alone, on her knees, her arms extended in the form of a cross, before all the immense crowd; "Ancilla Christi sum," "The Bird of Christ I am." She was a good-looking girl, fat and comely, who would probably have led a comfortable life in the world, for which she seemed well fitted; most likely without one touch of romance or enthusiasm in her composition; but having the unfortunate

honour of being niece to two chanoines, she was thus honoura-
bly provided for without expense in her nineteenth year. As
might be expected, her voice faltered, and instead of singing,
she seemed inclined to cry out. Each note came slowly, heavily,
tremblingly; and at last she nearly fell forward exhausted,
when two of the sisters caught and supported her.

I had almost made up my mind to see no more such scenes,
which, unlike pulque and bull-fights, I dislike more and more
upon trial; when we received an invitation, which it was not
easy to refuse, but was the more painful to accept, being acquainted, though slightly, with the victim. I send you the
printed note of invitation.

"On Wednesday, the —— of this month, at six o'clock in
the evening, my daughter, Doña Maria de la Concepcion,
P——e——, will assume the habit of a nun of the choir and the
black veil in the Convent of Our Lady of the Incarnation. I
have the honour to inform you of this, entreating you to co-
operate with your presence in the solemnity of this act, a favour which will be highly esteemed by your affectionate servant, who kisses your hand.

"MARIA JOSEFA DE ——.
"Mexico, June ——, 1840."

Having gone out in the carriage to pay some visits, I suddenly recollected that it was the very morning of the day in
which this young girl was to take the veil, and also that it
was necessary to inquire where I was to be placed; for as to
entering the church with the crowd on one of these occasions,
it is out of the question; particularly when the girl being, as
in the present case, of distinguished family, the ceremony is
expected to be peculiarly magnificent. I accordingly called at
the house, was shown upstairs, and to my horror, found myself in the midst of a "goodlie companie," in rich array, consisting of the relations of the family, to the number of about a
hundred persons; the bishop himself in his purple robes and
amethysts, a number of priests, the father of the young lady
in his general's uniform; she herself in purple velvet, with diamonds and pearls, and a crown of flowers; the *corsage* of her
gown entirely covered with little bows of ribbon of divers colours, which her friends had given her, each adding one, like
stones thrown on a cairn in memory of the departed. She had
also short sleeves and white satin shoes.

Being very handsome, with fine black eyes, good teeth, and
fresh colour, and above all with the beauty of youth, for she

is but eighteen, she was not disfigured even by this overloaded dress. Her mother, on the contrary, who was to act the part of Madrina, who wore a dress fac-simile, and who was pale and sad, her eyes almost extinguished with weeping, looked like a picture of misery in a ball-dress. In the adjoining room, long tables were laid out, on which servants were placing refreshments for the fête about to be given on this joyous occasion. I felt somewhat shocked, and inclined to say with Paul Pry, "Hope I don't intrude." But my apologies were instantly cut short, and I was welcomed with true Mexican hospitality; repeatedly thanked for my kindness in coming to see the nun, and hospitably pressed to join the family feast. I only got off upon a promise of returning at half-past five to accompany them to the ceremony, which, in fact, I greatly preferred to going there alone.

I arrived at the hour appointed, and being led upstairs by the Senator Don —— ——, found the morning party, with many additions, lingering over the dessert. There was some gaiety, but evidently forced. It reminded me of a marriage feast previous to the departure of the bride, who is about to be separated from her family for the first time. Yet how different in fact is this banquet, where the mother and daughter met together for the last time on earth!

At stated periods, indeed, the mother may hear her daughter's voice speaking to her as from the depths of the tomb; but she may never more fold her in her arms, never more share in her joys or in her sorrows, or nurse her in sickness; and when her own last hour arrives, though but a few streets divide them, she may not give her dying blessing to the child who has been for so many years the pride of her eyes and heart.

I have seen no country where families are so knit together as in Mexico, where the affections are so concentrated, or where such devoted respect and obedience are shown by the married sons and daughters to their parents. In that respect they always remain as little children. I know many families of which the married branches continue to live in their father's house, forming a sort of small colony, and living in the most perfect harmony. They cannot bear the idea of being separated, and nothing but dire necessity ever forces them to leave their *fatherland*. To all the accounts which travellers give them of the pleasures to be met with in the European capitals, they turn a deaf ear. Their families are in Mexico—their parents, and sisters, and relatives—and there is no happiness for them elsewhere. The greater therefore is the sacrifice which those parents make, who from religious motives devote their daughters to a conventual life.

——, however, was furious at the whole affair, which he said was entirely against the mother's consent, though that of the father had been obtained; and pointed out to me the confessor whose influence had brought it about. The girl herself was now very pale, but evidently resolved to conceal her agitation, and the mother seemed as if she could shed no more tears—quite exhausted with weeping. As the hour for the ceremony drew near, the whole party became more grave and sad, all but the priests, who were smiling and talking together in groups. The girl was not still a moment. She kept walking hastily through the house, taking leave of the servants, and naming probably her last wishes about everything. She was followed by her younger sisters, all in tears.

But it struck six, and the priests intimated that it was time to move. She and her mother went downstairs alone, and entered the carriage which was to drive them through all the principal streets, to show the nun to the public according to custom, and to let them take their last look, they of her, and she of them. As they got in, we all crowded to the balconies to see her take leave of her house, her aunts saying, "Yes, child, *despidete de tu casa*, take leave of your house, for you will never see it again!" Then came sobs from the sisters, and many of the gentlemen, ashamed of their emotion, hastily quitted the room. I hope, for the sake of humanity, I did not rightly interpret the look of constrained anguish which the poor girl threw from the window of the carriage at the home of her childhood.

They drove off, and the relations prepared to walk in procession to the church. I walked with the Count S——o, the others followed in pairs. The church was very brilliantly illuminated, and as we entered, the band was playing one of *Strauss's* waltzes! The crowd was so tremendous that we were nearly squeezed to a jelly in getting to our places. I was carried off my feet between two fat Señoras in mantillas and shaking diamond pendants, exactly as if I had been packed between two moveable feather-beds.

They gave me, however, an excellent place, quite close to the grating, beside the Countess de S——o, that is to say, a place to kneel on. A great bustle and much preparation seemed to be going on within the convent, and veiled figures were flitting about, whispering, arranging, etc. Sometimes a skinny old dame would come close to the grating, and lifting up her veil, bestow upon the pensive public a generous view of a very haughty and very wrinkled visage of some seventy years standing, and beckon into the church for the major-domo of the convent (an excellent and profitable situation by the way), or for padre this or that. Some of the holy ladies recognised and spoke to me through the grating.

But at the discharge of fireworks outside the church the curtain was dropped, for this was the signal that the nun and her mother had arrived. An opening was made in the crowd as they passed into the church, and the girl, kneeling down, was questioned by the bishop, but I could not make out the dialogue, which was carried on in a low voice. She then passed into the convent by a side door, and her mother, quite exhausted and nearly in hysterics, was supported through the crowd to a place beside us, in front of the grating. The music struck up; the curtain was again drawn aside. The scene was as striking here as in the convent of the Santa Teresa, but not so lugubrious. The nuns, all ranged around, and carrying lighted tapers in their hands, were dressed in mantles of bright blue, with a gold plate on the left shoulder. Their faces, however, were covered with deep black veils. The girl, kneeling in front, and also bearing a heavy lighted taper, looked beautiful, with her dark hair and rich dress, and the long black lashes resting on her glowing face. The churchmen near the illuminated and magnificently-decked altar formed, as usual, a brilliant background to the picture. The ceremony was the same as on the former occasion, but there was no sermon.

The most terrible thing to witness was the last, straining, anxious look which the mother gave her daugher through the grating. She had seen her child pressed to the arms of strangers, and welcomed to her new home. She was no longer hers. All the sweet ties of nature had been rudely severed, and she had been forced to consign her, in the very bloom of youth and beauty, at the very age in which she most required a mother's care, and when she had but just fulfilled the promise of her childhood, to a living tomb. Still, as long as the curtain had not fallen, she could gaze upon her, as upon one on whom, though dead, the coffin-lid is not yet closed.

But while the new-made nun was in a blaze of light, and distinct on the foreground, so that we could mark each varying expression of her face, the crowd in the church, and the comparative faintness of the light, probably made it difficult for her to distinguish her mother; for, knowing that the end was at hand, she looked anxiously and hurriedly into the church, without seeming able to fix her eyes on any particular object; while her mother seemed as if her eyes were glazed, so intently were they fixed upon her daughter.

Suddenly, and without any preparation, down fell the black curtain like a pall, and the sobs and tears of the family broke forth. One beautiful little child was carried out almost in fits. Water was brought to the poor mother; and at last, making our way with difficulty through the dense crowd, we got into the sacristy. "I declare," said the Countess —— to me, wiping her eyes, "it is worse than a marriage!" I expressed my horror at the sacrifice of a girl so young, that she could not possibly have known her own mind. Almost all the ladies agreed with me, especially all who had daughters, but many of the old gentlemen were of a different opinion. The young men were decidedly of my way of thinking; but many young girls, who were conversing together, seemed rather to envy their friend, who had looked so pretty and graceful, and "so happy," and whose dress "suited her so well," and to have no objection to "go, and do likewise."

I had the honour of a presentation to the bishop, a fat and portly prelate, with good manners, and well besuiting his priestly garments. I amused myself, while we waited for the carriages, by looking over a pamphlet which lay on the table, containing the ceremonial of the veil-taking. When we rose to go, all the ladies of the highest rank devoutly kissed the bishop's hand; and I went home, thinking by what law of God a child can thus be dragged from the mother who bore and bred her, and immured in a cloister for life, amongst strangers, to whom she has no tie, and towards whom she owes no duty. That a convent may be a blessed shelter from the calamities of life, a haven for the unprotected, a resting-place for the weary, a safe and holy asylum, where a new family and kind friends await those whose natural ties are broken and whose early friends are gone, I am willing to admit; but it is not in the flower of youth that the warm heart should be consigned to the cold cloister. Let the young take their chance of sunshine or of storm: the calm and shady retreat is for helpless and unprotected old age.

——, to whom I described one of these ceremonies, wrote some verses, suggested by my account of them, which I send you.

In tropic gorgeousness, the Lord of Day
   To the bright chambers of the west retired,
And with the glory of his parting ray
   The hundred domes of Mexico he fired,
When I, with vague and solemn awe inspired,
   Entered the Incarnation's sacred fane.
The vaulted roof, the dim aisle far retired,
   Echoed the deep-toned organ's holy strain,
   Which through the incensed air did mournfully complain.

The veiling curtain suddenly withdrew,
   Op'ning a glorious altar to the sight,
Where crimson intermixed its regal hue
   With gold and jewels that outblazed the light
Of the huge tapers near them flaming bright
   From golden stands—the bishop, mitre-crowned,
Stood stately near—in order due around
   The sisterhood knelt down, their brows upon the ground.

The novice entered: to her doom she went,
   Gems on her robes, and flowers upon her brow.
Virgin of tender years, poor innocent!
   Pause, ere thou speak th' irrevocable vow.
What if thy heart should change, thy spirit fail?
   She kneels. The black-robed sisters cease to bow.
They raise a hymn which seems a funeral wail,
While o'er the pageant falls the dark, lugubrious veil.

Again the veil is up. On earth she lies,
   With the drear mantle of the pall spread o'er,
The new-made nun, the living sacrifice,
   Dead to this world of ours for evermore!
The sun his parting rays has ceased to pour,
   As loth to lend his light to such a scene. . . .
The sisters raise her from the sacred floor,
   Supporting her their holy arms between;
   The mitred priest stands up with patriarchal mien.

And speaks the benediction; all is done.
   A life-in-death must her long years consume
She clasped her new-made sisters one by one.
   As the black shadows their embraces gave
They seemed like spectres from their place of doom,
   Stealing from out eternal night's blind cave,
   To meet their comrade new, and hail her to the grave.

The curtain fell again, the scene was o'er,
   The pageant gone—its glitter and its pride,
And it would be a pageant and no more,
   But for the maid miscalled the Heavenly Bride.
If I, an utter stranger, unallied
   To her by slightest ties, some grief sustain,
What feels the yearning mother, from whose side
   Is torn the child whom she hath reared in vain,
   To share her joys no more, no more to sooth her pain!

LETTER THE TWENTY-FIRST

*San Agustin—The Gambling Fête—The Beauties of the Village
—The Road from Mexico—Entry to San Agustin—The Gam-
bling Houses—San Antonio—The Pedregal—Last Day of the
Fête—The Cock-pit—The Boxes—The Cock-fight—Decorum
—Comparisons—Dinner—Ball at Calvario—House of General
Moran—View of the Gambling-tables—The Advocate—Ball
at the Plaza de Gallos—Return to Mexico—Reflections—Con-
versation between two Ministers.*

15th June.

Since my last letter we have been at San Agustin de las Cuevas,
which, when I last saw it, was a deserted village, but which
during three days in the year presents the appearance of a
vast bee-hive or ant-hill. San Agustin! At the name how
many hearts throb with emotion! How many hands are mechanically thrust into empty pockets! How many visions of
long-vanished golden ounces flit before aching eyes! What
faint crowing of wounded cocks! What tinkling of guitars and
blowing of horns come upon the ear! Some, indeed, there be,
who can look round upon their well-stored hacienda and easy-
rolling carriages, and remember the day, when with thread-
bare coat, and stake of three modest ounces, they first courted
Fortune's favours, and who, being then indigent, and enjoying
an indifferent reputation, found themselves, at the conclusion
of a few successive San Agustins, the fortunate proprietors of
gold, and land, and houses; and, moreover, with an unimpeachable fame; for he who can fling gold-dust in his neighbour's eyes, prevents him from seeing too clearly. But these
favourites of the blind goddess are few and far between; and
they have for the most part, with a view to greater security,
become holders or sharers of banks at San Agustin, thus in-
vesting their fortune in a secure fund; more so decidedly, if
we may believe the newspaper reports, than in the bank of
the United States at this present writing.

Time, in its revolutions whirling all things out of their places,
has made no change in the annual fête of San Agustin. Fashions alter. The graceful mantilla gradually gives place to the

ungraceful bonnet. The old painted coach, moving slowly like a caravan, with Guido's Aurora painted on its gaudy panels, is dismissed for the London-built carriage. Old customs have passed away. The ladies no longer sit on the door-sills, eating roast duck with their fingers, or with the aid of tortillas. Even the Chinampas have become stationary, and have occasionally joined the continent. But the annual fête of San Agustin is built on a more solid foundation than taste or custom, or floating soil. It is founded upon that love of gambling, which is said to be a passion inherent in our nature, and which is certainly impregnated with the Mexican constitution, in man, woman, and child. The beggars gamble at the corners of the streets or under the arches; the little boys gamble in groups in the villages; the coachmen and footmen gamble at the doors of the theatre while waiting for their masters.

But while their hand is thus *kept in* all the year round, there are three days sacredly set apart annually, in which every accommodation is given to those who are bent upon ruining themselves or their neighbours; whilst every zest that society can afford, is held out to render the temptation more alluring. As religion is called in to sanctify everything, right or wrong; as the robber will plant a cross at the mouth of his cave, and the pulque-shops do occasionally call themselves "Pulquerias of the Most Holy Virgin," so this season of gambling is fixed for the fête of *Pascua* (Whitsunday), and the churches and the gambling-houses are thrown open simultaneously.

The village is in itself pretty and picturesque; and, as a stone at its entry informs us, was built by the active Viceroy Revillagigedo, with the product, as —— assured us, of two lotteries. It is charmingly situated, in the midst of handsome villas and orchards, whose high walls, overtopped by fruit-trees, border the narrow lanes. At this season the trees are loaded with the yellow *chabacano* and the purple plum, already ripe; while the pear-trees are bending under the weight of their fruit. The gardens are full of flowers; the roses in their last bloom, covering the crowd with their pink leaves, and jasmine and sweet-peas in profusion, making the air fragrant. The rainy season has scarce set in, though frequent showers have laid the dust, and refreshed the air. The country villas are filled with all that is gayest and most distinguished in Mexico, and every house and every room in the village has been hired for months in advance. The ladies are in their most elegant toilets, and looking forward to a delightful whirl of dancing, cock-fighting, gambling, dining, dressing, and driving about.

The high-road leading from Mexico to San Agustin is covered with vehicles of every description; carriages, diligences, hackney-coaches, carts, and carratelas. Those who are not fortunate enough to possess any wheeled conveyance, come out on horse, ass, or mule; single, double, or treble, if necessary; and many hundreds, with visions of silver before their eyes, and a few *clacos* (pence), hid under their rags, trudge out on foot. The President himself, in carriage-and-six, and attended by his aides-de-camp, sanctions by his presence the amusements of the fête. The Mexican generals and other officers follow in his wake, and the gratifying spectacle may not unfrequently be seen, of the president leaning from his box in the *plaza de gallos,* and betting upon a cock, with a coatless, bootless, hatless, and probably worthless ragamuffin in the pit. Every one, therefore, however humble his degree, has the pleasure, while following his speculative inclinations, of reflecting that he treads in the steps of the magnates of the land; and, as Sam Weller would say, "Vot a consolation that must be to his feelings!"

At all events, nothing can be gayer than the appearance of the village, as your carriage makes its way through the narrow lanes into the principal plaza, amidst the assembled crowd of coaches and foot-passengers; though the faces of the people bear evidence that pleasure alone has not brought them to San Agustin. All round the square are the gambling-houses, where for three nights and three days every table is occupied. At the principal *montes* nothing is played but gold, but as there is accommodation for all classes, so there are silver tables in the inferior houses, while outside are rows of tables on which are heaps of copper, covered with a rugged awning, and surrounded by léperos and blanketed Indians, playing monta in imitation of their betters, though on a scale more suited to their finances.

Having left Mexico early in the morning, we stopped to breakfast at San Antonio, a noble hacienda, about four leagues from Mexico, belonging to the Dowager Marquesa de Vivanco, where we breakfasted with a large party. It is a fine solid mass of building, and as you enter the courtyard, through a deep archway, the great outhouses, stables, and especially the granary, look like remains of feudalism, they are on so large and magnificent a scale. It is an immense and valuable property, producing both maize and maguey, and the hospitality of the family, who are amongst our earliest friends here, is upon as large a scale as everything that belongs to them. We had a splendid breakfast, in a fine old hall, and stayed but a short time to visit the gardens and the chapel, as we were anxious to arrive at San Agustin in time for the cock-fight.

It is singular, that while San Agustin is situated in the midst of the most fertile and productive country, there should lie opposite to it, and bounded as it were by the graceful Peruvian trees and silver poplars which surround a small church on the other side of the high-road, a great tract of black lava, steril, bleak, and entirely destitute of vegetation, called the *Pedregal*. This covers the country all along to San Agustin and to the base of the mountain of Ajusco, which lies behind it, contrasting strangely with the beautiful groves and gardens in its neighbourhood, and looking as if it had been cursed for some crime committed there. The high-road, which runs nearly in a direct line from the hacienda to San Agustin, is broad and in tolerable repair; but before arriving there, it is so little attended to, that during the rainy season it might be passed in canoes; yet this immense formation of ferruginous larva and porphyritic rock lies conveniently in its vicinity. A large sum, supposed to be employed in mending the road, is collected annually at the toll, close to San Antonio. For each carriage two dollars are asked, and for carts and animals in proportion. The proprietor of this toll or *postazgo* is also the owner of the plaza de gallos, where a dollar is paid for entry, the sums produced by which go exclusively to enrich the same individual. The government has no advantage from it. . . .

The last day of the fête is considered the best, and it is most crowded on that day, both by families from Mexico and by foreigners who go solely for pleasure, though not unfrequently tempted to do a little business on their own account. In fact, the temptations are great; and it must be difficult for a young man to withstand them.

We went to the *gallos* about three o'clock. The plaza was crowded, and the ladies in their boxes looked like a parterre of different-coloured flowers. But whilst the Señoras in their boxes did honour to the fête by their brilliant toilet, the gentlemen promenaded round the circle in jackets, high and low being on the same *curtailed* footing, and certainly in a style of dress more befitting the exhibition. The president and his suite were already there, also several of the foreign ministers.

Meanwhile, the cocks crowed valiantly, bets were adjusted, and even the women entered into the spirit of the scene, taking bets with the gentlemen *sotto voce* in their boxes, upon such and such favourite animal. As a small knife is fastened to the leg of each cock, the battle seldom lasted long, one or other falling every few minutes in a pool of blood. Then there was a clapping of hands, mingled with the loud crowing of some unfortunate cock, who was giving himself airs previous to a combat where he was probably destined to crow his last. It has a curious effect to European eyes, to see young ladies of good family, looking peculiarly feminine and gentle, sanctioning, by their presence, this savage diversion. It is no doubt the effect of early habit, and you will say that at least it is no worse than a bull-fight; which is certain—yet cruel as the latter is, I find something more *en grande,* more noble, in the

> "*Ungentle sport, that oft invites*
> *The Spanish maid, and cheers the Spanish swain;*"

in the roaring of the "lord of lowing herds," the galloping of the fine horses, the skill of the riders, the gay dresses, the music, and the agile matador; in short, in the whole pomp and circumstances of the combat, than when one looks quietly on to see two birds peck each other's eyes out, and cut each other to pieces. Unlike cock-pits in other countries, attended by blacklegs and pickpockets and gentlemanly *roués,* by far the largest portion of the assembly in the pit was composed of the first young men in Mexico, and for that matter, of the first old ones also. There was neither confusion, nor noise, nor even loud talking, far less swearing, amongst the lowest of those assembled in the ring; and it is this quiet and orderly behaviour which throws over all these incongruities a cloak of decency and decorum, that hides their impropriety so completely, that even foreigners who have lived here a few years, and who were at first struck with astonishment by these things, are now quite reconciled to them.

As far as the company went, it might have been the House of Representatives in Washington; the ladies in the gallery listening to the debates, and the members in the body of the house surrounding Messrs. —— and ——, or any other two vehement orators; applauding their biting remarks and cutting sarcasms, and encouraging them to crow over each other. The president might have been the speaker, and the corps diplomatique represented itself.

We had an agreeable dinner at the E——s, and afterwards accompanied them to the Calvario, a hill where there was a ball *al fresco,* which was rather amusing, and then paid a visit to the family of General Moran, who has a beautiful house and gardens in the neighbourhood. We found a large party assembled, and amongst them the president. Afterwards, accompanied by the —— minister, and the ladies of our party, we went to take a view of the gambling-tables, and opened our eyes at the heaps of gold, which changed owners every minute. I saw C——a, a millionaire, win and lose a thousand ounces apparently with equal indifference. A little advocate having won two thousand five hundred ounces, wisely ordered his carriage and set off for Mexico, with the best *fee* he had ever received in his life. Ladies do not generally look on at the tables, but may if they please, and especially if they be strangers. Each gambling-room was well fitted up, and looked like a private apartment.

We then returned home and dressed for the ball, which was given in the evening in the plaza de gallos. We first went upstairs to a box, but I afterwards took the advice of M. de —— and came down to see the dancers. There were ladies in full dress, and gentlemen in white jackets—rather inconsistent. The company, though perfectly quiet and well-behaved, were not very select, and were, on that account, particularly amusing. Madame de —— and I walked about, and certainly laughed much more than we should have done in a more distinguished society.

About two in the morning we returned to Mexico, and as I this moment receive a note from the American minister, informing me that the packet from Vera Cruz is about to sail, I shall send off my letters now; and should we still be here next year, I shall then give you a more detailed description of the fête, of the ball, both at Calvario and in the cock-pit, and also of the "high life below stairs" gambling, at which the scenes are *impayable*. In one respect the fashions of San Agustin are altered from what they were a few years ago, when the Señoras used to perform five elaborate and distinct toilets daily; the first in the morning, the second for the cock-fight, the third for the dinner, the fourth for the ball on the hill of Calvary, and the fifth for the ball in the evening. I am told that as they danced in the open air, on the hill, with all their diamonds and pearls on, in the midst of an immense concourse of people, a great many jewels were constantly lost, which the *léperos* used afterwards to search for, and pick up from the grass; a rich harvest. Though they still dress a great deal, they are contented with changing their toilet twice, or at the most, three times in the course of the day.

Upon the whole, these three days are excessively amusing,

and as all ranks and conditions are mingled, one sees much more variety than at a ball in the city.

On their way home, C——n and Señor —— discussed the effects likely to be produced on the morals of the people by this fête. Señor ——, like nearly all the wisest men here, persists in considering gambling an innocent amusement, and declares, that at all events, this fête ought never to be done away with. In his opinion, it conduces to the happiness of the people, gives them an annual pleasure to look forward to, and by the mingling of all ranks which then takes place, keeps up a good feeling between the higher and lower orders. C——n asked him why, if such was the case, the government did not at least endeavour to draw some advantage from it, after the manner of the Count de Revillagigedo—why, as the bank, by the nature of the game, has, besides a great capital, which swallows up all the smaller ones, an immense profit, amounting to twenty-five per cent., they do not make the bankers pay four or five per cent., and charge half a dollar or more to each individual who enters to gamble; with which money they might beautify the village, make a public *pasoe*, a good road, a canal to Mexico, etc.

I thought that whatever the government might feel on this subject, neither the bankers nor the gamblers would relish the insinuation. I shall write in a few days by the Baron de ——, minister from ——, who leaves Mexico in a fortnight.

LETTER THE TWENTY-SECOND

Countess C——a—Gutierrez Estrada—Dinner at General Mo-
ran's—Dowager Marquesa—Fête at San Antonio—Approach
of the Rainy Season—Diamonds and Plate—Great Ball—
Night Travelling—Severe Storm—Chapter of Accidents—
Corpus Christi—Poblana Dress—Book-club—Ball—Hum-
ming-bird—Franciscan Friar—Missions to Old and New
California—Zeal and Endurance of the Missionaries—Pres-
ent Condition—Convent Gardener.

17th June.

As we dine nearly every Sunday with the Countess de la C——a
at Tacubay, where she keeps open house to all her friends,
we have had the pleasure of becoming intimately acquainted
with her son-in-law, Señor Gutierrez Estrada, who, with his
amiable wife, has lately returned from Europe.

A great dinner was given us the other day by General Moran and his lady the Marquesa de Vivanco, at San Agustin.
We went early that we might have time to walk about the
garden, which is beautiful, and to visit an artificial cave there,
which we found lighted up with coloured lamps, and where
a most fascinating species of cold milk punch, with cakes, was
served to the company. The dinner would certainly have been
superb in any country; the family have travelled a great deal
in Europe, (*per force*, the general having been exiled for several years,) and are amongst the oldest and richest in Mexico.
The dowager marquesa has a most patriarchal family of daughters and grand-daughters, and of the large party assembled at
table, nearly all were composed of its different members. In
the evening we had a pleasant dance under the trees.

20th.—Being invited yesterday to a fête at San Antonio, we
left Mexico about eight o'clock, by the great causeway leading
to San Agustin. The day was peculiarly brilliant, but the
rainy season is now announcing its approach by frequent showers towards evening. We found a large party assembled, and
about twelve o'clock sat down to a most magnificent breakfast of about sixty persons. Everything was solid silver; even
the plates. A vast capital is sunk in diamonds and plate in

this country, no good sign of the state of commerce. The ladies
in general were dressed in white embroidered muslins, over
white or coloured satin, and one or two Paris dresses shone
conspicuous. There was one specimen of real Mexican beauty;
the Señora ——, a face perhaps more Indian than Spanish,
very dark, with fine eyes, beautiful teeth, very long dark hair,
and full of expression. The house, which is immensely large,
is furnished, or rather unfurnished, in the style of all Mexican
haciendas. After breakfast, we had music, dancing, walking,
and billiard-playing. Some boleros were very gracefully danced
by a daughter of the marquesa's, and they also showed us
some dances of the country. The fête terminated with the
most beautiful supper I almost ever saw. A great hall was
lighted with coloured lamps, the walls entirely lined with
green branches, and hung with fresh garlands of flowers most
tastefully arranged. There was a great deal of gaiety and cordiality, of magnificence without ceremony, and riches without
pretension.

Although warned by various showers that a bad night would
probably set in, and although it was too likely that the hospitality within the house would be extended to our coachmen,
and even though the whole party were strongly pressed by the
marquesa to pass the night there, so that it was with difficulty
we resisted her entreaties to remain, we did, in the face of
all this, set off at twelve o'clock at night to return to Mexico;
about seven carriages together, with various gentlemen riding.
Though very dark there was no rain, and we flattered ourselves
it would keep fair till we reached the city. The minister of
the interior, who is married to a daughter of the marquesa,
C——n and I, and La Güera Rodriguez, set off in one carriage.
Some carriages had lamps, others had none. Some had six
horses; we had six mules, and an escort of dragoons. We had
not gone two miles before a thunderstorm came on; and the
black clouds which had been gathering above our heads burst
forth in torrents of rain. The wind was tremendous. All the
lamps were extinguished. The horses waded up to their knees
in mud and water. Suddenly there was a crash, followed by
loud cries. A carriage was overturned, in which were the Señora
L—— and a party of gentlemen. In the midst of this awful
storm, and perhaps still more bewildered by generous liquor,
their coachman had lost his way, and lodged them all in a
ditch. The poor Señora was dreadfully bruised, her head cut,
and her wrist dislocated. In the darkness and confusion she
was extricated with difficulty, and placed in another carriage.

Our mules stood still. As far as the noise of the storm would allow us to hear, we made out that our coachman also had lost the road. Two dragoons rode up to direct him. One fell, horse and all, into a deep ditch, where he remained till the next morning. Another carriage came ploughing its way behind us. Another exclamation in the darkness! A mule had fallen and broken his traces, and plunged into the water. The poor animal could not be found. Never was there such a chapter of accidents. We were the only carriage-load which escaped entirely, owing chiefly to the sobriety of the coachman. Very slowly and after sundry detentions, we arrived in Mexico towards morning, very tired, but with neither broken bones nor bruises.

24th.—Day of the Corpus Christi, in which the host is carried through the city in great procession at which the president, in full uniform, the archbishop, and all the ministers, etc., assist. In former days this ceremony took place on Holy Thursday; but finding that, on account of the various ceremonies of the holy week, it could not be kept with due solemnity, another day was set apart for its celebration. We went to a window in the square, to see the procession, which was very brilliant; all the troops out, and the streets crowded. Certainly, a stranger entering Mexico on one of these days would be struck with surprise at its apparent wealth. Everything connected with the church is magnificent.

This evening the Señora A—— came after it was dark, in a Poblana dress, which she had just bought to wear at a *Jamaica,* which they are going to have in the country—a sort of fair, where all the girls disguise themselves in peasants' dresses, and go about selling fruit, lemonade, vegetables, etc., to each other—a very ancient Mexican amusement. This dress cost her some hundred dollars. The top of the petticoat is yellow satin; the rest, which is of scarlet cashmere, is embroidered in gold and silver. Her hair was fastened back with a thick silver comb, and her ornaments were very handsome, coral set in gold. Her shoes white satin, embroidered in gold; the sleeves and body of the chemise, which is of the finest cambric, trimmed with rich lace; and the petticoat, which comes below the dress, shows two flounces of Valenciennes. She looks beautiful in this dress, which will not be objected to in the country, though it might not suit a fancy ball in Mexico.

June 27th.—I was awakened this morning by hearing that two boxes had arrived from New York, containing books, letters, etc.; all very acceptable. We also received a number of old newspapers by post, for which we had to pay eighteen dollars! Each sheet costs a real and a half—a mistaken source of profit in a republic, where the general diffusion of knowledge is of so much importance, for this not only applies to the introduction of French and English, but also of Spanish newspapers. Señors Gutierrez Estrada and Canedo used every effort to reduce this duty on newspapers, but in vain. The post-office opposes its reduction, fearing to be deprived of an imaginary rent—imaginary, because so few persons, comparatively, think it worth their while to go to this expense.

There is but one daily newspaper in Mexico, "La Gazeta del Gobierno" (the government paper), and it is filled with orders and decrees. An opposition paper, the "Cosmopolita," is published twice a week; also a Spanish paper, the "Hesperia;" both (especially the last) are well written. There is also the "Mosquito," so called from its stinging sarcasms. Now and then another with a new title appears, like a shooting star, but, from want of support, or from some other motive, is suddenly extinguished.

Enlightened individuals like Don Lucas Alaman and Count Cortina have published newspapers, but not for any length of time. Count Cortina, especially, edited a very witty and brilliant paper called the "Zurriago," the "Scourge," and another called the "Mono," the "Ape;" and in many of his articles he was tolerably severe upon the incorrect Spanish of his brother editors, of which no one can be a better judge, he having been a member of the "Academia de la Lengua," in Spain.

The only kind of monthly review in Mexico is the "Mosaico Megicano," whose editor has made his fortune by his own activity and exertions. Frequently it contains more translations than original matter; but from time to time it publishes scientific articles, said to be written by Don J. M. Bustamante, which are very valuable, and occasionally a brilliant article from the pen of Count Cortina. General Orbegoso, who is of Spanish origin, is also a contributor. Sometimes, though rarely, it publishes "documentos ineditos" (unedited documents), connected with Mexican antiquities, and Mexican natural history and biography, which are very important; and now and then it contains a little poetical gem, I know not whether original or not, but exceedingly beautiful. So far as it goes, this review is one great means of spreading knowledge, at least amongst the better classes; but I understand that the editor, Don Ygnacio Cumplido, a very courteous, intelligent man, complains that it does not pay.

There are no circulating libraries in Mexico. Books are at least double the price that they are in Europe. There is no diffusion of useful knowledge amongst the people; neither cheap pamphlets nor cheap magazines written for their amusement or instruction; but this is less owing to want of attention to their interests on the part of many good and enlightened men, than to the unsettled state of the country; for the blight of civil war prevents the best systems from ripening.

Fortunately, there is an English society here, a kind of book-club, who, with their minister, have united in a subscription to order from England all the new publications, and as C——n is a member of this society, we are not so *arrierés* in regard to the literature of the day as might be supposed. Like all English societies, its basis is a good dinner, which each member gives in turn, once a month, after which there is a sale of the books that have been read, and propositions for new books are given in to the president. It is an excellent plan, and I believe is in part adopted by other foreigners here. But Germans of a certain class do not seem to be sufficiently numerous for such an undertaking, and the French in Mexico, barring some distinguished exceptions, are apt to be amongst the very worst specimens of that people which "le plaisant pays de France" can furnish forth.

We went lately to a ball given by a young Englishman, which was very pretty, and where nearly all the English were collected. Of families, there are not more than half a dozen resident here, the members of whom form a striking contrast in complexion to the *Mexicanas*. With very few exceptions (and these in the case of English women married to foreigners, they keep themselves entirely aloof from the Mexicans, live quietly in their own houses, into which they have transplanted as much English comfort as possible, rarely travel, and naturally find Mexico the dullest of cities. C——n has gone to dine with the English minister, and I am left alone in this large room, with nothing but a humming-bird to keep me company; the last of my half-dozen. It looks like a large blue fly, and is perfectly tame, but will not live many days.

I was startled by a solemn voice, saying, "Ave Maria Purissima!" And looking up there stood in the doorway a "friar of orders gray," bringing some message to C——n from the head of the convent of San Fernando, with which monks C——n has formed a great intimacy, chiefly in consequence of the interest which he has taken in the history of their missions to California.

In fact, when we hear the universal cry that is raised against these communities for the inutility of their lives, it is but just that exceptions should be made in favour of those orders, who, like the monks of San Fernando, have dispersed their missionaries over some of the most miserable parts of the globe, and who, undeterred by danger, and by the prospect of death, have carried light to the most benighted savages. These institutions are of a very remote date. A learned Jesuit monk, Eusebio Kuhn, is said to have been the first who discovered that California was a peninsula. In 1683 the Jesuits had formed establishments in old California, and for the first time it was made known that the country which had until then been considered an El Dorado, rich in all precious metals and diamonds, was arid, stony, and without water or earth fit for vegetation; that where there is a spring of water it is to be found amongst the bare rocks, and where there is earth there is no water. A few spots were found by these industrious men, uniting these advantages, and there they founded their first missions.

But the general hatred with which the Jesuits were regarded, excited suspicion against them, and it was generally supposed that their accounts were false, and that they were privately becoming possessed of much treasure. A *visitador* (surveyor) was sent to examine into the truth, and though he could discover no traces of gold or silver, he was astonished by the industry and zeal with which they had cultivated the barren and treeless waste. In a few years they had built sixteen villages, and when they were expelled, in 1767, the Dominican friars of Mexico took their place.

Until these missions were established, and in every part of the peninsula which is not included in the territory of the missions, the savages were the most degraded specimens of humanity existing. More degraded than the beasts of the field, they lay all day upon their faces on the arid sand, basking in the heat; they abhorred all species of clothing, and their only religion was a secret horror that caused them to tremble at the idea of three divinities, belonging to three different tribes, and which divinities were themselves supposed to feel a mortal hatred, and to wage perpetual war against each other.

Undeterred by the miserable condition both of human and of vegetable nature, these missionaries cultivated the ground, established colonies, made important astronomical observations, and devoted themselves to science, to agriculture, and to the amelioration of the condition of these wretched savages.

In New California, the missions were under the charge of thirty-six Franciscan friars, under whom the most extraordinary progress in civilization took place; since in little more than thirty years, upwards of thirty-three thousand Indians were baptized, and eight thousand marriages had taken place. The soil being fertile and the climate more benign than in the other California, in eighteen missions established there, they cultivated corn, wheat, maize, etc., and introduced vegetables and fruit-trees from Spain; amongst these the vine and the olive, from which excellent wine and oil were made all through that part of the country.

Amongst the monks destined to these distant missions were those of San Fernando. There, banished from the world, deprived of all the advantages of civilization, they devoted themselves to the task of *taming* the wild Indians, introduced marriage amongst them, taught them to cultivate the ground, together with some of the most simple arts; assisted their wants, reproved their sins, and transplanted the beneficent doctrines of Christianity amongst them, using no arms but the influence which religion and kindness, united with extreme patience, had over their stubborn natures; and making what Humboldt, in speaking of the Jesuit missions, calls "a pacific conquest" of the country.

Many were the hardships which these poor men endured; changed from place to place; at one time ordered to some barren shore, where it was necessary to recommence their labours,—at another, recalled to the capital by orders of the prelate, in conjunction with the wishes of their brethren, among whom there was a species of congress, called by them a *capitulo*. No increase of rank, no reward, no praise, inspired their labours; their only recompense was their intimate conviction of doing good to their fellow-creatures.

In the archives of the convent there still exist papers, proving the hardships which these men underwent; the zeal with which they applied themselves to the study of the languages of the country; (and when we are informed that in the space of one hundred and eighty leagues, nineteen different languages are spoken, it was no such easy task;) and containing their descriptions of its physical and moral state, more or less well written, according to their different degrees of instruction or talent.

It frequently happened that marketable goods and even

provisions had to be sent by sea to those missionaries who lived in the most savage and uncultivated parts of the peninsula; and a curious anecdote on this subject was related to C——n by one of these men, who is now a gardener by profession. It happened that some one sent to the monks, amongst other things, a case of fine Malaga raisins; and one of the monks, whose name I forget, sowed a number of the dried seeds. In process of time they sprouted up, became vines, and produced fine grapes, from which the best wine in California was made.

When the independence was declared, and that revolutionary fury which makes a merit of destroying every establishment, good or bad, which is the work of the opposite party, broke forth; the Mexicans, to prove their hatred to the mother-country, destroyed these beneficent institutions; thus committing an error as fatal in its results as when in 1828 they expelled so many rich proprietors, who were followed into exile by their numerous families and by their old servants, who gave them in these times of trouble proofs of attachment and fidelity belonging to a race now scarcely existing here, except amongst a few of the oldest families.

The result has been, that the frontiers, being now unprotected by the military garrisons or *presidios*, which were established there, and deserted by the missionaries, the Indians are no longer kept under subjection, either by the force of arms or by the good counsels and persuasive influence of their padres. The Mexican territory is, in consequence, perpetually exposed to their invasions—whole families are massacred by the savages, who exchange guns for rifles, which they already know how to use, and these evil consequences are occasionally and imperfectly averted at a great expense to the republic. Bustamante has indeed been making an investigation lately as to the funds and general condition of these establishments, with the intention of re-establishing some similar institutions; but as yet I believe that nothing decisive has been done in this respect. . . .

Near the convent there is a beautiful garden, where we sometimes walk in the morning, cultivated by an old monk, who, after spending a laborious life in these distant missions, is now enjoying a contented old age among his plants and flowers. Perhaps you are tired of my *prosing* (caused by the apparition of the old lay-brother), and would prefer some account of him in verse.

An aged monk in San Fernando dwells,
  An innocent and venerable man;
His earlier days were spent within its cells,
  And end obscurely as they first began.
Manhood's career in savage climes he ran,
  On lonely California's Indian shore—
Dispelling superstition's deadly ban,
  Or teaching (what could patriot do more?)
Those rudiments of peace, the gardener's humble store.

Oft have I marked him, silent and apart,
  Loitering near the sunny convent-gate,
Rewarded by tranquillity of heart
  For toils so worthy of the truly great;
And in my soul admired, compared his state
  With that of some rude brawler, whose crude mind
Some wondrous change on earth would fain create;
  Who after flatt'ring, harassing mankind,
Gains titles, riches, pomp, with shame and scorn combined.

LETTER THE TWENTY-THIRD

The President—Yturbide—Visit from the Archbishop—Señor Cañedo—General Almonte—Señor Cuevas—Situation of an Archbishop in Mexico—Of Señor Posada—His Life—Mexican Charity—Wax Figures—Anecdote—Valuable Present—Education — Comparison — Schools — Opportunities — Natural Talent—Annual—Compliments to the Mexican Ladies by the Editor—Families of the Old School—Morals—Indulgence—Manners—Love of Country—Colleges.

5th July.

Yesterday morning we had a visit from the president, with two of his officers. He was riding one of the handsomest black horses I ever saw. On going out we stopped to look at a wax figure of Yturbide on horseback, which he considers a good resemblance, and which was sent me as a present some time ago. He ought to be a good judge, as he was a most devoted friend of the unfortunate Agustin I., who, whatever were his faults, seems to have inspired his friends with the most devoted and enthusiastic attachment. In the prime of life, brave and active, handsome and fond of show, he had all the qualities which render a chief popular with the multitude; "but popularity, when not based upon great benefits, is transient; it is founded upon a principle of egotism, because a whole people cannot have personal sympathies." Ambition led him to desert the royal cause which he had served for nine years; and vanity blinded him to the dangers that surrounded him in the midst of his triumphs, even when proclaimed emperor by the united voice of the garrison and city of Mexico—when his horses were taken from his carriage, and when, amidst the shouts of the multitude, his coach was dragged in triumph to the palace. His great error, according to those who talk of him impartially, was indecision in the most critical emergencies, and his permitting himself to be governed by circumstances, instead of directing these circumstances as they occurred.

I could not help thinking, as the general stood there looking at the waxen image of his friend, what a stormy life he himself has passed; how little real tranquillity he can ever have enjoyed, and wondering whether he will be permitted to finish his presidential days in peace, which, according to rumour, is doubtful.

8th.—I had the honour of a long visit this morning from his grace the archbishop. He came about eleven o'clock, after mass, and remained till dinner-time, sitting out all our Sunday visitors, who are generally numerous, as it is the only day of rest for *employés*, and especially for the cabinet. Amongst our visitors were Señor Cañedo, who is extremely agreeable in conversation, and as an orator famed for his sarcasm and cutting wit. He has been particularly kind and friendly to us ever since our arrival—General Almonte, Minister of War, a handsome man and pleasant, and an officer of great bravery—very unpopular with one party and especially disliked by the English, but also a great friend of ours. Señor Cuevas, Minister of the Interior, married to a daughter of the Marquesa de Vivanco, an amiable and excellent man, who seems generally liked, and is also most friendly to us. All these gentlemen are praised or abused according to the party of the person who speaks of them; but I not interfering in Mexican politics, find them amongst the most pleasant of our acquaintances.

However, were I to choose a situation here, it would undoubtedly be that of Archbishop of Mexico, the most enviable in the world to those who would enjoy a life of tranquillity, ease, and universal adoration. He is a pope without the trouble, or a tenth part of the responsibility. He is venerated more than the Holy Father is in enlightened Rome, and, like kings in the good old times, can do no wrong. His salary amounts to about one hundred thousand dollars, and a revenue might be made by the sweetmeats alone which are sent him from all the nuns in the republic. His palace in town, his well-cushioned carriage, well-conditioned horses, and sleek mules, seem the very perfection of comfort. In fact, *comfort,* which is unknown amongst the profane of Mexico, has taken refuge with the archbishop; and though many drops of it are shed on the shaven heads of all bishops, curates, confessors, and friars, still in his illustrious person it concentrates as in a focus. He himself is a benevolent, good-hearted, good-natured, portly, and jovial personage, with the most *laissez-aller* air and expression conceivable. He looks like one on whom the good things of this world have fallen in a constant and benignant shower, which shower hath fallen on a rich and fertile soil. He is generally to be seen leaning back in his carriage, dressed in purple, with amethyst cross, and giving his benediction to the people as he passes. He seems engaged in a pleasant revery, and his countenance wears an air of the most placid and *insouciant* content. He enjoys a good dinner, good wine, and ladies' society, but just sufficiently to make his leisure hours pass pleasantly, without indigestion from the first, headaches from the second, or heartaches from the third. So does his life seem to pass on like a deep untroubled stream, on whose margin grow sweet flowers, on whose clear waters the bending trees are reflected, but on whose placid face no lasting impression is made.

I have no doubt that his charities are in proportion to his large fortune; and when I say that I have no doubt of this, it is because I firmly believe there exists no country in the world where charities, both public and private, are practised on so noble a scale, especially by the women under the direction of the priests. I am inclined to believe that, generally speaking, charity is a distinguishing attribute of a Catholic country.

The archbishop is said to be a man of good information, and was at one time a senator. In 1833, being comprehended in the law of banishment, caused by the political disturbances which have never ceased to afflict this country since the independence, he passed some time in the United States, chiefly in New Orleans; but this, I believe, is the only cloud that has darkened his horizon, or disturbed the tranquil current of his life. His consecration, with its attendant fatigues, must have been to him a wearisome overture to a pleasant drama, a hard stepping-stone to glory. As to the rest, he is very unostentatious, and his conversation is far from austere. On the contrary, he is one of the best-tempered and most cheerful old men in society that it is possible to meet with. . . .

I send you, by the Mexican commissioners, who are kind enough to take charge of a box for me, the figure of a Mexican *tortillera,* by which you may judge a little of the perfection in which the commonest *lépero* here works in wax. The incredible patience which enabled the ancient Mexicans to work their statues in wood or stone with the rudest instruments, has descended to their posterity, as well as their extraordinary and truly Chinese talent for imitation. With a common knife and a piece of hard wood, an uneducated man will produce a fine piece of sculpture. There is no imagination. They do not leave the beaten track, but continue on the models which the Spanish conquerors brought out with them, some of which, however, were very beautiful.

In wax, especially, their figures have been brought to great perfection. Everything that surrounds them they can imitate, and their wax portraits are sometimes little gems of art; but in this last branch, which belongs to a higher order of art, there are no good workmen at present.

A *propos* to which, a poor artist brought some tolerable wax portraits here for sale the other day, and, amongst others, that of a celebrated general. C——n remarked that it was fairer than the original, as far as he recollected. "Ah!" said the man, "but when his excellency *washes his face*, nothing can be more exact." A valuable present was sent lately by a gentleman here, to the Count de —— in Spain; twelve cases, each case containing twelve wax figures; each figure representing some Mexican trade, or profession or employment. There were men drawing the pulque from the maguey, Indian women selling vegetables, tortilleras, venders of ducks, fruitmen, lard-sellers, the postman of Guachinango, loaded with parrots, monkeys, etc.,—more of everything than of letters—the Poblana peasant, the rancherita on horseback before her farm-servant, the gaily-dressed ranchero, in short, a little history of Mexico in wax. . . .

You ask me how Mexican women are educated. In answering you, I must put aside a few brilliant exceptions, and speak *en masse*, the most difficult thing in the world, for these exceptions are always rising up before me like accusing angels, and I begin to think of individuals, when I should keep to generalities. Generally speaking, then, the Mexican Señoras and Señoritas write, read, and play a little, sew, and take care of their houses and children. When I say they read, I mean they know how to read; when I say they write, I do not mean that they can always spell; and when I say they play, I do not assert that they have generally a knowledge of music. If we compare their education with that of girls in England, or in the United States, it is not a comparison, but a contrast. Compare it with that of Spanish women, and we shall be less severe upon their *far niente* descendants. In the first place, the climate inclines every one to indolence, both physically and morally. One cannot pore over a book when the blue sky is constantly smiling in at the open windows; then, out of doors after ten o'clock, the sun gives us due warning of our tropical latitude, and even though the breeze is so fresh and pleasant, one has no inclination to walk or ride far. Whatever be the cause, I am convinced that it is impossible to take the same exercise with the mind or with the body in this country, as in Europe or in the northern states. Then as to schools, there are none that can deserve the name, and no governesses. Young girls can have no emulation, for they never meet. They have no public diversion, and no private amusement. There are a few good foreign masters, most of whom have come to Mexico for the purpose of making their fortune, by teaching, or marriage, or both, and whose object, naturally, is to make the most money in the shortest possible time, that they may return home and enjoy it. The children generally appear to have an extraordinary disposition for music and drawing, yet there are few girls who are proficient in either.

When very young, they occasionally attend the schools, where boys and girls learn to read in common, or any other accomplishment that the old women can teach them; but at twelve they are already considered too old to attend these promiscuous assemblages, and masters are got for drawing and music to finish their education. I asked a lady the other day if her daughter went to school. "Good heavens!" said she, quite shocked, "she is past eleven years old!" It frequently happens that the least well-informed girls are the children of the cleverest men, who, keeping to the customs of their forefathers, are content if they confess regularly, attend church constantly, and can embroider and sing a little. Where there are more extended ideas, it is chiefly amongst families who have travelled in Europe, and have seen the different education of women in foreign countries. Of these the fathers occasionally devote a short portion of their time to the instruction of their daughters, perhaps during their leisure evening moments, but it may easily be supposed that this desultory system has little real influence on the minds of the children. I do not think there are above half-a-dozen married women, or as many girls above fourteen, who, with the exception of the mass-book, read any one book through in the whole course of the year. They thus greatly simplify the system of education in the United States, where parties are frequently divided between the advocates for solid learning and those for superficial accomplishments; and according to whom it is difficult to amalgamate the solid beef of science with the sweet sauce of *les beaux arts.*

But if a Mexican girl is ignorant, she rarely shows it. They have generally the greatest possible tact; never by any chance wandering out of their depth, or betraying by word or sign that they are not well informed of the subject under discussion. Though seldom graceful, they are never awkward, and always self-possessed. They have plenty of natural talent, and where it has been thoroughly cultivated, no women can surpass them. Of what is called literary society, there is of course none—

> "No bustling Botherbys have they to show 'em
> That charming passage in the last new poem."

There is a little annual lying beside me called "*Calendario de las Señoritas Mejicanas*," of which the preface, by Galvan, the editor, is very amusing.

"To none," he says, "better than to Mexican ladies, can I dedicate this mark of attention—(*obsequio*). Their graceful attractions well deserve any trouble that may have been taken to please them. Their bodies are graceful as the palms of the desert; their hair black as ebony, or golden as the rays of the sun, gracefully waves over their delicate shoulders; their glances are like the peaceful light of the moon. The Mexican ladies are not so white as the Europeans, but their whiteness is more agreeable to our eyes. Their words are soft, leading our hearts by gentleness, in the same manner as in their moments of just indignation they appal and confound us. Who can resist the magic of their song, always sweet, always gentle, and always natural? Let us leave to foreign ladies (*las ultramarinas*) these affected and scientific manners of singing; here nature surpasses art, as happens in everything, notwithstanding the cavillings of the learned.

"And what shall I say of their souls? I shall say that in Europe the minds are more cultivated, but in Mexico the hearts are more amiable. Here they are not only sentimental, but tender; not only soft, but virtuous; the body of a child is not more sensitive, (*no es mas sensible el cuerpo de un niño*), nor a rose-bud softer. I have seen souls as beautiful as the borders of the rainbow, and purer than the drops of dew. Their passions are seldom tempestuous, and even then they are kindled and extinguished easily; but generally they emit a peaceful light, like the morning star, Venus. Modesty is painted in their eyes, and modesty is the greatest and most irresistible fascination of their souls. In short, the Mexican ladies, by their manifold virtues, are destined to serve as our support whilst we travel through the sad desert of life.

"Well do these attractions merit that we should try to please them; and in effect a new form, new lustre, and new graces have been given to the 'Almanac of the Mexican Ladies,' whom the editor submissively entreats to receive with benevolence this small tribute due to their enchantments and their virtues!"

There are in Mexico a few families of the old school, people of high rank, but who mingle very little in society; who are little known to the generality of foreigners, and who keep their daughters entirely at home, that they may not be contaminated by bad example. These select few, rich without ostentation, are certainly doing everything that is in their power to remedy the evils occasioned by the want of proper schools, or of competent instructresses for their daughters. Being nearly all allied by birth, or connected by marriage, they form a sort of *clan;* and it is sufficient to belong to one or other of these families, to be hospitably received by all. They meet together frequently, without ceremony, and whatever elements of good exist in Mexico, are to be found amongst them. The fathers are generally men of talent and learning, and the mothers, women of the highest respectability, to whose name no suspicion can be attached.

But, indeed, it is long before a stranger even suspects the state of morals in this country, for whatever be the private conduct of individuals, the most perfect decorum prevails in outward behaviour. But indolence is the mother of vice, and not only to little children might Doctor Watts have asserted that

> *"Satan finds some mischief still,*
> *For idle hands to do."*

They are besides extremely *leal* to each other, and with proper *esprit de corps,* rarely gossip to strangers concerning the errors of their neighbours' ways;—indeed, if such a thing is hinted at, deny all knowledge of the fact. So long as outward decency is preserved, habit has rendered them entirely indifferent as to the *liaisons* subsisting amongst their particular friends; and as long as a woman attends church regularly, is a patroness of charitable institutions, and gives no scandal by her outward behaviour, she may do pretty much as she pleases. As for flirtations in public, they are unknown.

I must, however, confess that this indulgence on the part of women of unimpeachable reputation is sometimes carried too far. We went lately to a breakfast, at which was a young and beautiful countess, lately married, and of very low birth. She looked very splendid, with all the —— diamonds, and a dress of rose-coloured satin. After breakfast we adjourned to another room, where I admired the beauty of a little child who was playing about on the floor, when this lady said, "Yes, she is very pretty—very like my little girl, who is just the same age." I was rather surprised, but concluded she had been a widow, and made the inquiry of an old French lady who was sitting near me. "Oh, no!" said she—"she was never married before; she alludes to the children she had before the count became acquainted with her!" And yet the Señora de ——, the strictest woman in Mexico, was loading her with attentions and caresses. I must say, however, that this was a singular instance. . . .

There are no women more affectionate in their manners than those of Mexico. In fact, a foreigner, especially if he be an Englishman, and a shy man, and accustomed to the coolness of his fair countrywomen, need only live a few years here, and understand the language, and become accustomed to the peculiar style of beauty, to find the Mexican Señoritas perfectly irresistible.

And that this is so, may be judged of by the many instances of Englishmen married to the women of this country, who *invariably* make them excellent wives. But when an Englishman marries here, he ought to settle here, for it is very rare that a *Mexicaine* can live out of her own country. They miss the climate—they miss that warmth of manner, that universal cordiality by which they are surrounded here. They miss the *laissez-aller* and absence of all etiquette in habits, toilet, etc. They find themselves surrounded by women so differently educated, as to be doubly strangers to them, strangers in feeling as well as in country. A very few instances there are of girls, married very young, taken to Europe, and introduced into good society, who have acquired European ways of thinking, and even prefer other countries to their own; but this is so rare, as scarcely to form an exception. They are true patriots, and the visible horizon bounds their wishes. In England especially, they are completely out of their element. A language nearly impossible for them to acquire, a religion which they consider heretical, outward coldness covering inward warmth, a perpetual war between sun and fog, etiquette carried to excess, an insupportable stiffness and order in the article of the toilet; rebosos unknown, *cigaritos* considered barbarous. . . . They feel like exiles from paradise, and live but in hopes of a speedy return.

As to the colleges for young men, although various projects of reform have been made by enlightened men in regard to them, especially by Don Lucas Alaman, and afterwards by

Señor Gutierrez Estrada, and though to a certain extent many of the plans were carried into effect, it is a universal source of complaint among the most distinguished persons in Mexico, that in order to give their sons a thorough education, it is necessary to send them abroad.

LETTER THE TWENTY-FOURTH

*Revolution in Mexico—Gomez Farias and General Urrea—
The Federalists—The President Imprisoned—Firing—Cannon
—First News—Escape—Proclamation of the Government—
Cannonading—Count C——a—Houses deserted—Countess del
V——e—Proclamation of the Federalists—Circular of the
Federalists—Scarcity of Provisions—Bursting of a Shell—Ref-
ugees—Dr. Plan—Young Lady Shot—Gomez Farias—Ru-
mours—Address of Gomez Farias—Balls and Bullets—Visit
from the —— Minister—Arrival of Monsieur de —— —Ex-
pected Attack—Skirmish—Appearance of the Street—San
Cosmé—General —— —The Count de B—— —More Rumours
—Suspense—Cannonading—Government Bulletin—Plan of
the Rebels defeated—Proclamation of the President—Of
General Valencia—Maternal Affection—Fresh Reports—
Families leaving the City—Letter from Santa Anna—Busta-
mante's Letter when Imprisoned—Propositions—Refusal—
Tacubaya—Archbishop—Fresh Proposals—Refusal—Second
Letter from Santa Anna—Government Bulletin—Proclama-
tions—An awkward Mistake—The Archbishop visits the
President—Conclusion of the Revolution—Government
Newspapers—Circulars.*

July 15th.

Revolution in Mexico! or *Pronunciamiento,* as they call it. The
storm which has for some time been brewing, has burst forth
at last. Don Valentin Gomez Farias and the banished General
Urrea have pronounced for federalism. At two this morning,
joined by the fifth battalion and the regiment of *comercio,* they
took up arms, set off for the palace, surprised the president
in his bed, and took him prisoner. Our first information was a
message, arriving on the part of the government, desiring the
attendance of our two old soldiers, who put on their old uniforms, and set off quite pleased. Next came our friend Don
M—— del C——o, who advised us to haul out the Spanish colours, that they might be in readiness to fly on the balcony in
case of necessity. Little by little, more Spaniards arrived with
different reports as to the state of things. Some say that it will

end in a few hours—others, that it will be a long and bloody contest. Some are assured that it will merely terminate in a change of ministry—others that Santa Anna will come on directly and usurp the presidency. At all events, General Valencia, at the head of the government troops, is about to attack the pronunciados, who are in possession of the palace. . . .

The firing has begun! People come running up the street. The Indians are hurrying back to their villages in double-quick trot. As we are not in the centre of the city, our position for the present is very safe, all the cannon being directed towards the palace. All the streets near the square are planted with cannon, and it is pretended that the revolutionary party are giving arms to the *léperos*. The cannon are roaring now. All along the street people are standing on the balconies, looking anxiously in the direction of the palace, or collected in groups before the doors, and the azoteas, which are out of the line of fire, are covered with men. They are ringing the tocsin—things seem to be getting serious.

Nine o'clock, P.M.—Continuation of firing without interruption. I have spent the day standing on the balcony, looking at the smoke, and listening to the different rumours. Gomez Farias has been proclaimed president by his party. The streets near the square are said to be strewed with dead and wounded. There was a terrible thunderstorm this afternoon. Mingled with the roaring of the cannon, it sounded like a strife between heavenly and earthly artillery. We shall not pass a very easy night, especially without our soldiers. Unfortunately there is a bright moon, so night brings no interruption to the firing and slaughter.

16th.—Our first news was brought very early this morning by the wife of one of our soldiers, who came in great despair, to tell us that both her husband and his comrade are shot, though not killed—that they were amongst the first who fell; and she came to entreat C——n to prevent their being sent to the hospital. It is reported that Bustamante has escaped, and that he fought his way, sword in hand, through the soldiers who guarded him in his apartment. Almonte at all events is at the head of his troops. The balls have entered many houses in the square. It must be terribly dangerous for those who live there, and amongst others, for our friend Señor Tagle, Director of the Monte Pio, and his family.

They have just brought the government bulletin, which gives the following statement of the circumstances:—"Yesterday, at midnight, Urrea, with a handful of troops belonging to the garrison and its neighbourhood took possession of the National Palace, surprising the guard, and committing the *incivility* of imprisoning His Excellency the President, Don Anastasio Bustamante, the commander-in-chief, the *Mayor de la Plaza,* and other chiefs. Don Gabriel Valencia, chief of the *plana mayor* (the staff), General Don Antonio Mozo, and the Minister of War, Don Juan Nepomuceno Almonte, re-united in the citadel, prepared to attack the *pronunciados,* who, arming the lowest populace, took possession of the towers of the cathedral, and of some of the highest edifices in the centre of the city. Although summoned to surrender, at two in the afternoon firing began, and continued till midnight, recommencing at five in the morning, and only ceasing at intervals. The colonel of the sixth regiment, together with a considerable part of his corps, who were in the barracks of the palace, escaped and joined the government troops, who have taken the greatest part of the positions near the square and the palace. His Excellency the President, with a part of the troops which had *pronounced* in the palace, made his escape on the morning of the sixteenth, putting himself at the head of the troops who have remained faithful to their colours, and at night published the following proclamation:"

"*The President of the Republic to the Mexican Nation.*

"Fellow-Citizens:—The seduction which has spread over a very small part of the people and garrison of this capital; the forgetfulness of honour and duty, have caused the defection of a few soldiers, whose misconduct up to this hour has been thrown into confusion by the valiant behaviour of the greatest part of the chiefs, officers, and soldiers, who have intrepidly followed the example of the valiant general-in-chief of the *plana mayor* of the army. *The government was not ignorant of the machinations that were carrying on; their authors were well known to it, and it foresaw that the gentleness and clemency which it had hitherto employed in order to disarm them, would be corresponded to with ingratitude.*

"This line of policy has caused the nation to remain *headless* (*acéfala*) for some hours, and public tranquillity to be disturbed; but my liberty being restored, the dissidents, convinced of the evils which have been and may be caused by these tumults, depend upon a reconciliation for their security. The government will remember that they are misled men, belonging to the great Mexican family, but not for this will it forget how much they have forfeited their rights to respect; nor what is due to the great bulk of the nation. Public tranquillity will be restored in a few hours; the laws will immediately recover their energy, and the government will see them obeyed.

"ANASTASIO BUSTAMANTE.

"Mexico, July 16th, 1840."

A roar of cannon from the Palace, which made the house shake and the windows rattle, and caused me to throw a blot over the President's good name, seems the answer to this proclamation.

17th.—The state of things is very bad. Cannon planted all along the streets, and soldiers firing indiscriminately on all who pass. Count C——a slightly wounded, and carried to his country-house at Tacubaya. Two Spaniards have escaped from their house, into which the balls were pouring, and have taken refuge here. The E—— family have kept their house, which is in the very centre of the affray, cannons planted before their door, and all their windows already smashed. Indeed, nearly all the houses in that quarter are abandoned. We are living here like prisoners in a fortress. The Countess del V——e, whose father was shot in a former revolution, had just risen this morning, when a shell entered the wall close by the side of her bed, and burst in the mattress.

As there are two sides to every story, listen to the proclamation of the chief of the rebels.

"Señor Valentin Gomez Farias to the Mexican People.

"Fellow-Citizens:—We present to the civilized world two facts, which, while they will cover with eternal glory the Federal army and the heroic inhabitants of this capital, will hand down with execration and infamy, to all future generations, the name of General Bustamante; this man without faith, breaking his solemnly-pledged word, after being put at liberty by an excess of generosity; for having promised to take immediate steps to bring about a negotiation of peace, upon the honourable basis which was proposed to him, he is now converted into the chief of an army, the enemy of the Federalists; and has beheld, with a serene countenance, this beautiful capital destroyed, a multitude of families drowned in tears, and the death of many citizens; not only of the combatants, but of those who have taken no part in the struggle. Amongst these must be counted an unfortunate woman *enceinte,* who was killed as she was passing the palace gates under the belief that a parley having come from his camp, the firing would be suspended, as in fact it was on our side. This government, informed of the misfortune, sent for the husband of the deceased, and ordered twenty-five dollars to be given him; but the unfortunate man, though plunged in grief, declared that twelve were sufficient to supply his wants. Such was the horror inspired by the atrocious conduct of the ex-government of Bustamante, that this sentiment covered up and suffocated all the others.

"Another fact, of which we shall with difficulty find an example in history, is the following. The day that the firing began, being in want of some implements of war, it was necessary to cause an iron case to be opened, belonging to Don Stanislaus Flores, in which he had a considerable sum of money in different coin, besides his most valuable effects. Thus, all that the government could do, was to make this known to the owner, Señor Flores, in order that he might send a person of confidence to take charge of his interests, making known what was wanting, that he might be immediately paid. The pertinacity of the firing prevented Señor Flores from naming a commissioner for four days, and then, although the case has been open, and no one has taken charge of it, the commissioner has made known officially that nothing is taken from it but the implements of war which were sent for. Glory in yourselves, Mexicans! The most polished nation of the earth, illustrious France, has not presented a similar fact. The Mexicans possess heroic virtues, which will raise them above all the nations in the world. This is the only ambition of your fellow-citizen,

"VALENTIN GOMEZ FARIAS.
"God, Liberty, and Federalism.
"Mexico, July 17th, 1840."

Besides this, a circular has been sent to all the governors and commandants of the different departments, from the "Palace of the Federal Provisional Government," to this effect:

"The Citizen José Urrea, with the greater part of the garrison of the capital, and the whole population, pronounced early on the morning of this day, for the re-establishment of the Federal system, adopting in the interim the Constitution of 1824, whilst it is reformed by a Congress which they are about to convoke to that effect; and I, having been called, in order that at this juncture I should put myself at the head of the government, communicate it to your Excellency, informing you at the same time, that the object of the Citizen Urrea, instead of re-establishing the Federal system, has been to re-unite all the Mexicans, by proclaiming toleration of all opinions, and respect for the lives, properties, and interests of all.

"God, Liberty, and Federalism.

"VALENTIN GOMEZ FARIAS.

"National Palace of Mexico, 15th July, 1840."

18th.—There is a great scarcity of provisions in the centre of the city, as the Indians, who bring in everything from the country, are stopped. We have laid in a good stock of *comestibles*, though it is very unlikely that any difficulties will occur in our direction. While I am writing, the cannon are roaring almost without interruption, and the sound is anything but agreeable, though proving the respect entertained by Farias for "the lives, properties, and interests of all." We see the smoke, but are entirely out of the reach of the fire.

I had just written these words, when the Señora ——, who lives opposite, called out to me that a shell has just fallen in her garden, and that her husband had but time to save himself. The cannon directed against the palace kill people in their beds, in streets entirely out of that direction, while this ball, intended for the citadel, takes its flight to San Cosmé! Both parties seem to be *fighting the city* instead of each other; and this manner of firing from behind parapets, and from the tops of houses and steeples, is decidedly safer for the soldiers than for the inhabitants. It seems also a novel plan to keep up a continual cannonading by night, and to rest during a great part of the day. One would think that were the guns brought nearer the palace, the affair would be sooner over.

Late last night, a whole family came here for protection; the Señora —— with ——, nurse, and baby, etc. She had remained very quietly in her own house, in spite of broken windows, till the bullets whizzed past her baby's bed. This morning, everything remains as it was the first day—the president in the citadel, the rebels in the palace. The government are trying to hold out until troops arrive from Puebla. In an interval of firing, the —— Secretary contrived to make his way here this morning. The English Minister's house is also filled with families, it being a little out of the line of fire. Those who live in the Square, and in the Calle San Francisco are most exposed, and the poor shopkeepers in the *Parian* are in a state of great'and natural trepidation. I need not say that the shops are all shut.

19th.—Dr. Plan, a famous French physician, was shot this morning, as he was coming out of the palace, and his body has just been carried past our door into the house opposite.

The Señorita —— having imprudently stepped out on her balcony, her house being in a very exposed street, a pistol-ball entered her side, and passed through her body. She is still alive, but it seems impossible that she can recover. The Prior of San Joaquin, riding by just now, stopped below the windows to tell us that he fears we shall not remain long here in safety, as the pronunciados have attacked the Convent of La Concepcion, at the end of the street.

My writing must be very desultory. Impossible to fix one's attention on anything. We pass our time on the balconies, listening to the thunder of the cannon, looking at the different parties of troops riding by, receiving visitors, who, in the intervals of the firing, venture out to bring us the last reports—wondering, speculating, fearing, hoping, and excessively tired of the whole affair.

Gomez Farias, the prime mover of this revolution, is a distinguished character, one of the *notabilities* of the country, and has always maintained the same principles, standing up for "rapid and radical reform." He is a native of Guadalajara, and his literary career is said to have been brilliant. He is also said to be a man of an ardent imagination and great energy. His name has appeared in every public event. He first aided in the cause of Independence, then, when deputy for Zacatecas, showed much zeal in favour of Yturbide—was afterwards a warm partisan of the federal cause—contributed to the election of General Victoria; afterwards to that of Pedraza—took an active part in the political changes of '33 and '34; detests the Spaniards, and during his presidency endeavoured to abolish the privileges of the clergy and troops—suppressed monastic institutions—granted absolute liberty of opinion—abolished the laws against the liberty of the press—created many literary institutions; and whatever were his political errors, and the ruthlessness with which in the name of liberty and reform he marched to the attainment of his object, without respect for the most sacred things, he is generally allowed to be a man of integrity, and even by his enemies, an enthusiast, who deceives himself as much as others. Now in the hopes of obtaining some uncertain and visionary good, and even while declaring his horror of civil war and bloodshed, he has risen in rebellion against the actual government, and is the cause of the cruel war now raging, not in the open fields or even in the scattered suburbs, but in the very heart of a populous city.

This morning all manner of opinions are afloat. Some believe that Santa Anna has started from his retreat at Manga de Clavo, and will arrive to-day—will himself swallow the disputed oyster (the presidential chair), and give each of the combatants a shell apiece; some that a fresh supply of troops for the government will arrive to-day, and others that the rebels must eventually triumph. Among the reports which I trust may be classed as doubtful, is, that General Urrea has issued a proclamation, promising *three hours' pillage* to all who join him. Then will be the time for testing the virtues of all the diplomatic *drapeaux*. In the midst of all, here comes another.

"Address of His Excellency, Señor Don Valentin Gomez Farias, charged provisionally with the government of Mexico, and of the General-in-Chief of the Federal army, to the troops under his command.

"Companions in arms:—No one has ever resisted a people who fight for their liberty and who defend their sacred rights. Your heroic endeavours have already reduced *our unjust aggressors* almost to complete nullity. Without infantry to cover their parapets, without artillery to fire their pieces, without money, without credit, and without support, they already make their last useless efforts. On our side, on the contrary, all is in abundance (*sobra*), men, arms, ammunition, and money, and above all, the invincible support of opinion;— while the parties which adhere to our *pronunciamiento* in all the cities out of the capital, and the assistance which within this very city is given by every class of society to those who are fighting for the rights of the people, offer guarantees which they will strictly fulfil to all the inhabitants of the country, natives as well as foreigners. Our enemies, in the delirium of their impotence, have had recourse to their favourite weapon, calumny. In a communication directed to us, they have had the audacity to accuse you of having attacked some property. Miserable wretches! No, the soldiers of the people are not robbers; the cause of liberty is very noble, and its defence will not be stained by a degrading action. This is the answer given to your calumniators by your chiefs, who are as much interested in your reputation as in their own. Soldiers of the people! let valour, as well as all other civic virtues, shine in your conduct, that you may never dim the renown of valiant soldiers and of good citizens.

> "VALENTIN GOMEZ FARIAS.
> "JOSÉ URREA."

We hear that two shells have fallen into the house of Señor ——, who has a pretty wife and a number of children, and that his azotea is occupied by the federalist troops. Fortunately, these grenades burst in the *patio* of his house, and no one was injured. The chief danger to those who are not actually engaged in this affair, is from these bullets and shells, which come rattling into all the houses. We have messages from various people whom we invited to come here for safety, that they would gladly accept our offer, but are unwilling to leave their houses exposed to pillage, and do not dare to pass through the streets. So our numbers have not increased as yet.

You may suppose, that although this is Sunday, there is no mass in the churches. The Prior of San Fernando, who has just sent us round some colossal cauliflowers and other fine vegetables from his garden, permits us to come to his convent for safety, should anything occur here. . . . I am afraid he would lodge the women-kind in some outhouse.

I had written thus far, when we received a visit from the Baron de ——, —— Minister, who, living in a very exposed situation, near the palace, requests us to receive his secretary of legation, M. de ——, who is dangerously ill of typhus fever, as the doctors, no doubt warned by the fate of poor Dr. Plan, fear to pass into that street which is blocked up by troops and cannon. Some people fear a universal sacking of the city, especially in the event of the triumph of the federalist party. The ministers seem to have great confidence in their *flags*— but I cannot help thinking that a party of armed *léperos* would be no respecters of persons or privileges! As yet our position continues very safe. We have the Alameda between us and the troops; the palace, the square, and the principal streets being on the other side of the Alameda; and this street, a branch of the great Calle de Tacuba, stretching out beyond it. I write more to occupy my thoughts than in hopes of interesting you; for I am afraid that you will almost be tired of this *revolutionary* letter. As a clever Mexican, the Marquis of ——, says—"Some years ago we gave forth cries (*gritos*)—that was in the infancy of our independence—now we begin to *pronounce* (pronuncianos). Heaven knows when we shall be old enough to speak plain, so that people may know what we mean!"

Sunday Evening.—Monsieur de —— has arrived, and is not worse. We have unexpectedly had twelve persons to dinner to-day. The news to-night is, that the government troops have arrived, and that a great attack will be made by them to-morrow on the rebels in the palace, which will probably bring matters to a conclusion. Some of our guests are sitting up, and others lying down on the sofa without undressing. I prefer being comfortable, so good-night.

20th.—We were astonished this morning at the general tranquillity, and concluded that, instead of having attacked the rebels, the government was holding a parley with them, but a note from the English minister informs us that a skirmish has taken place between the two parties at one of the gates of the city, in which the government party has triumphed. So far the news is good.

Our street has a most picturesque and lively appearance this morning. It is crowded with Indians from the country, bringing in their fruit and vegetables for sale, and establishing a temporary market in front of the church of San Fernando. Innumerable carriages, drawn by mules, are passing along, packed inside and out, full of families hurrying to the country with their children and moveables. Those who are poorer, are making their way on foot—men and women carrying mattresses, and little children following with baskets and bird-cages—carts are passing, loaded with chairs and tables and beds, and all manner of old furniture, uprooted for the first time no doubt since many years—all are taking advantage of this temporary cessation of firing to make their escape. Our stables are full of mules and horses sent us by our friends in the centre of the city, where all supplies of water are cut off. Another physician, a Spaniard, has just been shot!

Every room at San Cosmé and in all the suburbs is taken. In some rooms are numbers of people, obliged to sleep upon mats, too glad to have escaped the danger to care for any inconvenience. A quantity of plate and money and diamonds were sent here this morning, which we have been hiding in different parts of the house; but they say that in cases of pillage the plunderers always search the most *impossible* places,

pulling up the boards, brick floors, etc., ripping up the mattresses, and so on; so I believe there is no use in concealing
anything. Near us lives a celebrated general, on whose political
opinions there seems much doubt, as he has joined neither
party, and has become invisible ever since this affair commenced. He is a showy, handsome man, with a good deal of
superficial instruction, and exceedingly vain of his personal
advantages. I am quite sure that, having allowed him to be a
fine-looking man, he would forgive me for saying that his character is frivolous, and that his principles, both moral and political, are governed entirely by that which best suits his own
advantage.

The Count de B——, secretary to the French Legation,
mounted his horse last evening, and, like a true young Frenchman, set off to pay a visit to a pretty girl of his acquaintance,
passing through the most dangerous streets, and particularly
conspicuous by his singular dress, good looks, and moustaches.
He had not gone far before he was surrounded by some dozen
of *léperos* with knives, who would, no doubt, have robbed and
despatched him, but that in tearing off his sarape they discovered his uniform, and not being very skilled in military accoutrements, concluded him to be an officer on the part of the
government. They being on the federalist side, hurried with
their prize to the palace, where he was thrown into prison,
and obliged to remain until some of the officers came to see
the prisoner, and recognized him, much to their astonishment.

We are now going to dine with what appetite we may,
which is generally pretty good.

Ten o'clock, P.M.—We ventured out after dinner to take a
turn in the direction opposite the city, and met various parties
of ladies, who, as they cannot use their carriages at present,
were thankful to escape from their temporary and crowded
dwellings, and were actually taking exercise on foot; when we
were encountered by people full of the intelligence that the
great attack on the palace is to be made this evening, and
were advised to hurry home. We were also assured that a
party of *léperos*, headed by their long-bearded captain, an old
robber of the name of Castro, had passed the night before our
door. Before we could reach home the firing began, and we
have passed several hours in a state of great suspense, amidst
the roaring of the cannon, the shouting of the troops, the occasional cries of those who are wounded, and, to make everything appear more lugubrious, the most awful storm of thunder and rain I almost ever heard. The Señora de ——'s brother

is a captain in the government service, and he and his regiment have distinguished themselves very much during these last few days; consequently she is dreadfully uneasy to-night.

The gentlemen seem inclined to pass the night in talking. We think of lying down, and sleeping if we can. I hope nothing will happen in the night, for everything seems worse in the darkness and consequent confusion.

21st.—After passing a sleepless night, listening to the roaring of cannon, and figuring to ourselves the devastation that must have taken place, we find to our amusement that nothing decisive has occurred. The noise last night was mere skirmishing, and half the cannons were fired in the air. In the darkness there was no mark. But though the loss on either side is so much less than might have been expected, the rebels in the palace cannot be very comfortable, for they say that the air is infected by the number of unburied dead bodies lying there; indeed there are many lying unburied on the streets, which is enough to raise a fever, to add to the calamitous state of things.

The government bulletin of to-day expresses the regret of the supreme magistrate at seeing his hopes of restoring peace frustrated, and publishes the assurances of fidelity which they have received from all the departments, especially from Puebla, Querétaro, and Vera Cruz, in spite of the extraordinary despatches which had there been received from Farias, desiring them to recognize Urrea as minister of war, and Don Manuel Crecencio Rejon as minister of the interior; "which communications," says the commandant of Querétaro, "produced in my soul only indignation and contempt towards their miserable authors."

The account of the yesterday's affair is as follows. "The *pronunciados* in the palace, knowing that the infantry which was to come from Puebla to the assistance of the government, was expected to arrive yesterday, endeavoured to surprise it near the gate of Saint Lazarus, with a column of infantry of two hundred in number, and some cavalry; but the brave Colonel Torrejon, with eighty dragoons, beat them completely, killing, wounding, and taking many prisoners, and pursuing them as far as the archbishop's palace. The supreme government, appreciating the distinguished services and brilliant conduct of the aforesaid colonel, have given him the rank of general of brigade."

The president in to-day's proclamation, after declaring that "the beautiful capital of the republic is the theatre of war," says "that nothing but consideration for the lives and properties of the inhabitants has been able to restrain the enthusiasm of the soldiers of the nation, and to prevent them from putting forth their whole force to dislodge the rebels from the different points of which they have possessed themselves." The president adds, "that this revolt is the more inexcusable, as his administration has always been gentle and moderate; that he has economized the public treasure, respected the laws, and that citizens of whatever opinion had always enjoyed perfect tranquillity under his rule—that constitutional reforms were about being realized, as well as the hopes of forming by them a bond of union between all Mexicans. He concludes by reproaching those revolutionary men who thus cause the shedding of so much innocent blood.

The commander-in-chief, General Valencia, writing perhaps under some inspiring influence, is more figurative in his discourse. "Soldiers of Liberty!" he exclaims; "Anarchy put out its head, and your arms drowned it in a moment." This would have been a finer figure in the days of the great lakes. And again he exclaims—"Mexicans! my heart feels itself wounded by the deepest grief, and all humanity shudders in contemplating the unsoundable chaos of evils in which the authors of this rebellion have sunk the incautious men whom they have seduced, in order to form with their dead bodies the bloody ladder which was to raise them to their aggrandizement! Already the Mexican people begin to gather the bitter fruits with which these men who blazon forth their humanity and philanthropy have always allured them, feeding themselves on the blood of their brothers, and striking up songs to the sad measure of sobs and weeping!" These tropes are very striking. All is brought before us as in a picture. We see anarchy raising his rascally head above the water (most likely adorned with a liberty cap), and the brave soldiers instantly driving it down again. We behold Gomez Farias and Urrea rushing up a ladder of dead bodies. And then the Lucrezia Borgia kind of scene that follows!—alluring their victims with bitter fruit (perhaps with sour grapes), drinking blood, and singing horridly out of tune to a running bass of sobs! The teeth of humanity are set on edge only by reading it. Well may his Excellency add—"I present them to the nations of the world as an inimitable model of ferocity and barbarity!"

This morning General —— sent a few lines from the citadel, where he and the president are, in which he speaks with confidence of speedily putting down the rebels. C——n returned many affectionate messages, accompanied by a supply of cigars. They say that the greatest possible bravery is shown by the boys of the Military College, who are very fine little fellows, and all up in arms on the side of the government. A strong instance of maternal affection and courage was shown by the Señora G— this morning. Having received various reports concerning her son, who belongs to this college; first that he was wounded; then that the wound was severe; then that it was slight—and being naturally extremely uneasy about him, she set off alone, and on foot, at five o'clock in the morning, without mentioning her intention to any one, carrying with her a basket of provisions; passed across the square, and through all the streets planted with cannon, made her way through all the troops into the citadel; had the satisfaction of finding her son in perfect health, and returned home, just as her husband and family had become aware of her absence.

General Valencia is said to have a large party amongst the soldiers, who are in favour of his being named president. It is said that he was seen riding up and down in the lines in a most *spirited* manner, and rather unsteady in his saddle. Some rumours there are that Santa Anna has arrived at Perote; but, as he travels in a litter, he cannot be here for some days, even should this be true. There seems no particular reason to believe that this will end soon, and we must remain shut up here as patiently as we can. In the intervals of firing the gentlemen go out, but they will not hear of our doing so, except sometimes for a few minutes in the evening, and then either firing or thunder sends us back. Various people, and especially the Countess C——a, have invited us to their country places; but, besides that we are in the safest part of the city, and have several guests, C——n does not think it right for him to leave Mexico. They say that house-rents will rise hereabouts, on account of the advantages of the *locale* in cases of this sort.

Amongst other announcements, the government have published, that the rebels have demanded that the jewels, together with the service of gold and silver belonging to the Holy Cathedral Church, shall be given up to them, and threaten to seize the whole by force, should their demand not be acceded to within two hours. "It is very probable that they will do so," adds the bulletin; thus adding a new crime to all they have committed.

It is now evening, and again they announce an attack upon the palace, but I do not believe them, and listen to the cannon with tolerable tranquillity. All day families continue to pass by, leaving Mexico. The poor shopkeepers are to be pitied. Besides the total cessation of trade, one at least has been shot, and others plundered. A truce of two hours was granted this afternoon, to bury the dead, who were carried out of the palace. Two of our colleagues ventured here this morning.

22nd.—The government bulletin of this morning contains a letter from Santa Anna, dated Mango de Clavo, 19th of July, informing the president, with every expression of loyalty and attachment to the government, that according to his desire he will set off this morning in the direction of Perote, "at the head of a respectable division." Various other assurances of fidelity from Victoria, from Galindo, etc., are inserted, with the remark that the Mexican public will thus see the uniformity and decision of the whole republic in favour of order, and especially will receive in the communication of his Excellency, General Santa Anna, an equivocal proof of this unity of sentiment, notwithstanding the assurances given by the rebels to the people, that Santa Anna would either assist them, or would take no part at all in the affair. It must be confessed, however, that his Excellency is rather a dangerous umpire.

The Governor Vieyra published a proclamation to-day, declaring "Mexico in a state of siege." It seems to me that we knew that already! Upon the whole, things are going on well for the government. Parties of *pronunciados* have been put down in various places. The wounded on both sides have been carried to the hospital of San Andrés. A battery is now planted against the palace, in the Calle de Plateros, where they are at least near enough to do more execution than before.

One circumstance worthy of notice has been published to-day. The rebels, as you may recollect, declared that they had permitted the president to leave the palace, on condition of his taking conciliatory measures, and that he had agreed to favour their pretensions. Now here is Bustamante's own letter, written in the palace, when surrounded by his enemies; a proof, if any were wanting, of his exceeding personal bravery, and perfect coolness in the midst of danger. There is something rather *Roman* in these few lines:

"Ministers,—I protest that I find myself without liberty and without defence, the guards of the palace having abandoned me. Under these circumstances, let no order of mine, which is contrary to the duties of the post I occupy, be obeyed. Since, although I am resolved to die before failing in my obligations, it will not be difficult to falsify my signature. Let this be made known by you to the Congress, and to those generals and chiefs who preserve sentiments of honour and fidelity.

"National Palace, July 15th, 1840.
"ANASTASIO BUSTAMANTE."

The following propositions are made to the government by the rebels:

"Article 1st. It not having been the intention of the citizen José Urrea, and of the troops under his command, to attack in any way the person of the president of the republic, General Anastasio Bustamante, he is replaced in the exercise of his functions.

"2nd. Using his faculties as president of the republic, he will cause the firing to cease on the part of the troops opposed to the citizen Urrea; who on his side will do the same.

"3rd. The president shall organize a ministry deserving of public confidence, and shall promise to re-establish the observance of the constitution of 1824, convoking a congress immediately, for the express purpose of reform.

"4th. Upon these foundations, peace and order shall be re-established, and no one shall be molested for the opinions which he has manifested, or for the principles he may have supported, all who are in prison for political opinions being set at liberty."

Almonte, in the name of the president, rejected these conditions, but offered to spare the lives of the pronunciados, in case they should surrender within twenty-four hours. The chiefs of the opposite party hereupon declared the door shut to all reconcilement, but requested a suspension of hostilities, which was granted.

A—— is going to drive me out during this suspension, in an open cab, to call on the C——a family. The ——s have left their house, their position having become too dangerous. Another letter from General Almonte this morning. Nothing decisive. The streets continue blocked up with cannon, the roofs of the houses, and churches are covered with troops, the shops remain closed, and the streets deserted. People are paying ounces for the least morsel of room in the suburbs, on the San Cosmé side of the city.

23rd.—Yesterday the archbishop invited the chiefs of the pronunciados to a conference in his archiepiscopal palace, in order that he might endeavour, in his apostolical character, to check the effusion of blood. The conference took place, and the rebels requested a suspension of hostilities, whilst the prelate should communicate its results to the president, which was granted by the general-in-chief. But the *pronunciados* broke the truce, and endeavoured to surprise the president and Almonte in the citadel, passing over the parapets in the *Calle de Monterilla*. They were repulsed with slaughter, and a fierce cannonading was kept up all night. They have now requested a parley, which is granted them. . . .

In the midst of all, there is a communication from the Governor of Morelia, giving an account of the routing of a band of robbers who had attacked an hacienda.

We went to Tacubaya, and met with no other danger but that of being drenched wet; as a daily watering of the earth, short, but severe, now takes place regularly. The new propositions of the *pronunciados* are these:

1st. "The forces of both armies shall retire to occupy places out of the capital.

2nd. "Both the belligerent parties shall agree that the constitutional laws of 1836 shall remain without force.

3rd. "A convention shall be convoked, establishing the new constitution, upon the basis fixed in the Constitutive Act, which will begin to be in force directly.

4th. "The elections of the members of the convention, will be verified according to the laws by which the deputies of the Constituent Congress were directed.

5th. "His actual Excellency, the President, will form a provisional government, he being the chief, until the foregoing articles begin to take effect.

6th. "No one shall be molested for political opinions manifested since the year '21 until now: consequently the persons, employments and properties of all who have taken part in this or in the past revolutions shall be respected.

7th. "That the first article may take effect, the government will facilitate all that is necessary to both parties."

The government have refused these second propositions; and at the same time made known to the Mexican world that various deserters from the opposite party assure them, that the *pronunciados*, including the principal chiefs, are occupied in destroying everything within the palace—that the general archives and those of the ministers are torn in pieces, and that the despatches are taken to make cartouches, and so on. They end by accusing them of being all united with the most noted robbers and public highwaymen, such as a *Ricardo Teo*, a *José Polvorilla*, a *Roman Chavez*, a *Juan Vega*, a *Rosas*, a *Garcilazo*, and others. I put down the names of these Mexican Dick Turpins and Paul Cliffords, in case we should meet them some *beau jour.*

More forces have arrived from Puebla and Toluca. Santa Anna is expected to reach Puebla to-night, and again General Valencia holds out an invitation to repentance to the "deceived men in the palace."

25th.—A letter is published to-day from Santa Anna to General Victoria, assuring him that whatever personal considerations might have detained him in his countryseat, he accepts with pleasure the command of the division going to Perote, and will in this, as in all things, obey the orders of the supreme government. Firing, with short intervals, continued all yesterday, during the night, and this morning. Two mortars are placed in front of the old *Acordada,* in the direction of the palace, but as yet they have not been used. There are a crowd of people examining them.

Things remain nearly in the same position as before, except that there are more deserters from the revolted party. A proclamation was issued by Urrea, accusing the government of all the evils that afflict the city, and of all the bloodshed caused by this civil war. Amongst other things, they complain of the death of Dr. Plan, who was shot in the Calle de Seminario, and, according to them, by the government troops. General Valencia answers this time without figures, and with good reason, that the responsibility of these misfortunes must be with those who have provoked the war.

In the bulletin of to-day, the government praise their own moderation in having taken off the duties from all provisions entering the capital, in order that the price might not become too high, an advantage in which the *pronunciados* themselves participate—mention their exertions to supply the city with water, and their permission given to the *pronunciados* to send their wounded to the hospital of San Andrés. They deny that the government has any share in the evils that afflict the whole population, their endeavour having ever been to preserve tranquillity and order; "but when a handful of factious men have taken possession of part of the city, no choice is left them but to besiege and combat them until they surrender, and not to abandon the peaceful citizens to pillage and vengeance." They declare that they might already have subdued them, and are only held back by the fear of involving in their ruin the number of innocent persons who occupy the circumjacent houses. The policy of this moderation seems doubtful, but the sincerity of the president is unimpeachable. They continue to observe upon the absurdity of this handful of men pretending to impose laws upon the whole republic, when already the body of the nation have given unequivocal proofs that they have no desire that the questions relative to their political institutions should be decided by the force of arms.

While the *pronunciados* declare on their side that "information of *pronunciamientos* everywhere" has been received by them; the government remarks that eleven days have now elapsed, which has given full time for all the departments to declare themselves in favour of those who call themselves their representatives; but on the contrary, nothing has been received but assurances of fidelity, and of support to the government cause. I believe that the English packet will be detained till the conclusion of this affair, but should it not be so, you need not feel any uneasiness in regard to us. Our house is full of people, money, jewels, and plate—our stables of horses and mules. Amongst the diamonds are those of the Señora L——, which are very fine, and there are gold rouleaus enough to set up a bank at San Agustin. Santa Anna seems in no hurry to arrive. People expect him to-morrow, but perhaps he thinks the hour has not come for him.

26th.—The proclamation of the governor of the department of Jalisco is published to-day, in which he observes: "The nation cannot forget that this Urrea, who has brought so many evils upon his country, this faithful friend of *Mr. Carlos Baudin*, and of the French squadron which invaded our territory, for whom he procured all the fresh provisions which they required, is the same man who now escapes from prison, to figure at the head of a tumultuous crowd, whose first steps were marked by the capture of his Excellency the President." Firing continues, but without any decided result. It is a sound that one does not learn to hear with indifference. There seems little doubt that ultimately the government will gain the day, but the country will no doubt remain for some time in a melancholy state of disorder. Bills are fastened to-day on the corners of the streets, forbidding all ingress or egress through the military lines, from six in the evening till eight in the morning. Gentlemen who live near us now venture in towards evening, to talk politics or play at whist; but generally, in the middle of a game, some report is brought in, which drives them back to their houses and families with all possible haste. Señor ——, a young Spaniard who is living with us, returning here late last night, was challenged by the sentinels at the corner of the street, with the usual *"Quien viva?"* to which, being in a brown study, he mechanically replied, *"Spain!"* Fortunately, the officer on duty was a man of common sense and humanity, and instead of firing, warned him to take better care for the future.

Last night the archbishop paid a visit to the president, in the convent of San Agustin, to intercede in favour of the *pronunciados*. The mortars have not yet played against the palace, owing, it is said, to the desire of the general-in-chief to avoid the further effusion of blood.

The tranquillity of the sovereign people during all this period, is astonishing. In what other city in the world would they not have taken part with one or other side? Shops shut, workmen out of employment, thousands of idle people, subsisting, Heaven only knows how, yet no riot, no confusion, apparently no impatience. Groups of people collect on the streets, or stand talking before their doors, and speculate upon probabilities, but await the decision of their military chiefs, as if it were a judgment from Heaven, from which it were both useless and impious to appeal.

27th.—"Long live the Mexican Republic! Long live the Supreme Government!" Thus begins the government bulletin of to-day, to which I say Amen! with all my heart, since it ushers in the news of the termination of the revolution. And what particularly attracts my attention is, that instead of the usual stamp, the eagle, serpent, and nopal, we have to-day, a shaggy pony, flying as never did mortal horse before, his tail and mane in a most violent state of excitement, his four short legs all in the air at once, and on his back a man in a jockey-cap, furiously blowing a trumpet, from which issues a white flag, on which is printed "News!" *in English!* and apparently in the act of springing over a milestone, on which is inscribed, also in English—"100 *to New York!"*

"We have," says the government, "the grateful satisfaction of announcing, that the revolution of this capital has terminated happily. The rebellious troops having offered, in the night, to lay down arms upon certain conditions, his Excellency the Commander-in-Chief, has accepted their proposals with convenient modifications, which will be verified to-day; the empire of laws, order, tranquillity, and all other social guarantees being thus re-established," etc. Cuevas, Minister of the Interior, publishes a circular addressed to the governors of the departments to the same effect, adding, that "in consideration of the inhabitants and properties which required the prompt termination of this disastrous revolution, the guarantees of personal safety solicited by the rebels have been granted, but none of their pretensions have been acceded to; the conspiracy of the fifteenth having thus had no other effect but to make manifest the general wish and opinion in favour of the government, laws, and legitimate authorities." A similar circular is published by General Almonte.

Having arrived at this satisfactory conclusion, which must be as agreeable to you as it is to us, I shall close this long letter, merely observing, in apology, that as Madame de Staël said, in answer to the remark, that "Women have nothing to do with politics;"—"That may be, but when a woman's head is about to be cut off, it is natural she should ask *why?*" so it appears to me, that when bullets are whizzing about our ears, and shells falling within a few yards of us, it ought to be considered extremely natural, and quite feminine, to inquire into the cause of such *phenomena*.

LETTER THE TWENTY-FIFTH

Plan of the Federalists—Letter from Farias—Signing of Articles —Dispersion of the "Pronunciados"—Conditions—Orders of General Valencia—Of the Governor—Address of General Valencia—Departure of our Guests—The Cosmopolite— State of the Palace and Streets—Bulletin of the Firing— Interior of Houses—Escape of Families—Conduct of the Troops—Countess del V——e—Santa Anna—Congress—Anecdote—Discussion in Congress—Leprosy.

28th July.

To-day is published the plan which was formed by the federalists for the "political regeneration of the republic." They observe, that it is six years since the federal plan, adopted freely by the nation in 1824, was replaced by a system which monopolizes all advantages in favour of a few; that evils had now arrived at that height, in which the endeavours of a few men, however illustrious, could have no effect in remedying them; rendering it necessary for all Mexicans to unite in one combined and energetic force to better their situation; that salvation can only be hoped for from the nation itself, etc. They then proceed to lay their plan, consisting of ten articles, before the public.

The first restores the constitution of '24, the national interests to be reformed by a congress, composed of four deputies from each state. By the second, the reformed constitution is to be submitted to the legislatures of the states for approbation. By the third, they engage to respect the Catholic religion, the form of popular government, representative and federal, the division of powers, political liberty of the press, the organization of a military and naval force, and the equality of rights between all the inhabitants of the nation. By the fourth article, a provisional government is to be established in the capital, whose functions are to be limited exclusively to the direction of the external relations of the republic. By the fifth, this provisional government is to be vested in a Mexican, reuniting the requisites for this employment, as established in the constitution of '24. By the sixth, the republic promises to give back the ten per cent. added to the duties of consumption, to those who have paid it until now. By the seventh, in eight months after the triumph of the present revolution, all interior custom-houses are to be suppressed, and henceforth no contributions shall be imposed upon the internal circulation of goods, whether foreign or domestic. By the eighth, they promise to confirm all the civil and military employments of those who do not oppose this political regeneration. By the ninth, the army is to be paid with great punctuality. By the tenth, a general amnesty is promised to all who have committed political errors since the Independence; and the names of Farias and Urrea are followed by a goodly list of major-generals, colonels, etc.

There is also published a letter from Farias, indignantly denying the report of the federal party's having threatened to seize the cathedral jewels and plate; accompanied by one from the archbishop himself, not only denying the circumstances, but expressing his satisfaction with the conduct of the federalist party in regard to all the convents which they had occupied, and the respect which they had shown towards all things pertaining to the church.

On the night of the twenty-sixth, the articles of capitulation were signed on both sides; a letter from General Andrade having been received by General Valencia, to the effect that as General Urrea had abandoned the command of the troops and left it in his hands, he, in the name of the other chiefs and officers, was ready to ratify the conditions stipulated for by them on the preceding night. This was at three in the morning; and about eight o'clock, the capitulation was announced to the *pronunciados* in the different positions occupied by them; and they began to disperse in different directions, in groups of about a hundred, crying, "Vive la Federacion!" At a quarter before two o'clock, General Manuel Andrade marched out, with all the honours of war, to Tlanapantla, followed by the *pronunciados* of the palace.

This morning, at eleven, *Te Deum*, was sung in the cathedral, there being present, the archbishop, the president, and all the authorities. The bells, which have preserved an ominous silence during these events, are now ringing forth in a confusion of tongues. The palace being crippled with balls, and in a state of utter confusion, the president and his ministers occupy cells in the convent of San Agustin.

The Federalists have marched out upon the following conditions: 1st, Their lives, persons, and employments, and properties are to be inviolably preserved. 2nd, General Valencia engages to interpose his influence with the government by all legal means, that they may request the chambers to proceed to reform the constitution. 3rd, All political events, which have occurred since the fifteenth, up to this date, are to be totally forgotten, the forces who adhered to the plan of the fifteenth being included in this agreement. 4th, A passport out of the republic is to be given to whatever individual, comprehended in this agreement, may solicit it. 5th, The troops of the *pronunciados* are to proceed to wherever General Valencia orders them, commanded by one of their own captains, whom he shall point out, and who must answer for any disorders they may commit. 6th, General Valencia and all the other generals of his army, must promise on their honour, before the whole world, to keep this treaty, and see to its exact accomplishment. 7th, It only applies to Mexicans. 8th, Whenever it is ratified by the chiefs of both parties, it is to be punctually fulfilled, hostilities being suspended until six in the morning of the twenty-seventh, which gives time to ratify the conditions.

The president may exclaim, "One such victory more, and I am undone!" Orders are issued by General Valencia to the effect, that until the Federalist troops have marched out of the city, no group passing five in number will be permitted in the streets; that until then, there is to be no trading through the streets; that at three o'clock the eating-houses may be thrown open, but not the taverns till the next day; and that the police and alcaldes of the different wards are held responsible for the accomplishment of these orders, and may make use of armed force to preserve order.

The governor enforces these orders with additions. People must turn in at nine o'clock, or give an account of themselves —must give up all their guns, carbines, etc., to the alcalde, under a heavy penalty; and none, excepting military men, may go on horseback from five in the evening until six in the morning, during five days.

General Valencia makes a pathetic address to his soldiers, and foretells that henceforth all mothers, wives, and old men, will point them out as they pass, saying, "There go our deliverers!" and adds—"I grow proud in speaking to you." "Inhabitants of this beautiful capital!" he says again, "the aurora of the 15th of July was very different from that of the 27th; *that* prognosticated destruction, *this* rises announcing happiness. *Never again will you hear the crash of cannon but to celebrate the triumphs of your country, or to solemnize your civic functions.*" May your words be prophetic, and especially may you yourself assist in their accomplishment.

29th.—Our guests have left us, all but Monsieur ——, who, although recovered, cannot yet be moved. All money, plate, and jewels in our charge, are restored to their rightful owners; and the Spanish colours, which have never been hoisted, return to their former obscurity. I reopen the piano, uncover and tune the harp, and as we have been most entirely shut up during thirteen days of heavenly weather, feel rejoiced at the prospect of getting out again. As yet, I have not seen the state of things in the city, but the "Cosmopolite" of to-day says—"I should wish to have the pen of Jeremiah, to describe the desolation and calamities of this city, which has been the mistress of the new world. In the days of mourning that have passed, we have not been able to fix our eyes on any part of it where we have not encountered desolation, weeping, and death. The palace has become *a sieve*, and the southern bulwark is destroyed; that part of the *portal* which looks towards the *Monterilla* is ruined; the finest buildings in the centre have suffered a great deal; innumerable houses at great distances from it have been also much injured by stray balls. Persons of all ages, classes, and conditions, who interfered in nothing, have been killed, not only in the streets, but even in their own apartments. The balls crossed each other in every direction, and the risk has been universal. The city has been in the dark during these days, without patrol or watch; and many malefactors have taken advantage of this opportunity to use the murderous poniard without risk, and with the utmost perfidy. At the break of day horrible spectacles were seen, of groups of dogs disputing the remains of a man, a woman, and a child." The "Cosmopolite" goes on to insist upon the necessity of forming a new ministry and of a reform in the two houses.

August 1st.—Have just come in from a drive through the city. The palace and houses near it are certainly in a melancholy condition. The palace, with its innumerable smashed windows and battered walls, looks as if it had become stone blind in consequence of having the smallpox. Broken windows and walls full of holes characterize all the streets in that direction, yet there is less real damage done than might have been expected, after such a furious firing and cannonading.

To read the accounts published, and of the truth of which we had auricular demonstration, one would have expected to find half the city in ruins. Here is the sum total of the firing, as published:—"On the 15th, firing from two o'clock till the next day. On the 16th, continual firing till one o'clock. Suspension till four o'clock. Firing from that hour, without intermission, till the following day. 17th, firing from morning till night. 18th, firing from before daybreak till the evening. 19th, continual firing. Constant emigration of families these last four days. 20th, continual firing all day. Skirmish at the gate of San Lazaro. 21st, firing continued, though less hotly, but in the night with more vigour than ever. 22nd, day of the Junta in the archbishop's palace. Firing began at eleven at night, and lasted till morning. 23rd, firing till midday. Parley. 24th, formidable firing, terrible attack, and firing till morning. 25th, firing till the evening. 26th, firing from six in the morning till two o'clock. Capitulation that night."

As "every bullet has its billet," they must all have lodged somewhere. Of course, nothing else is talked of as yet, and every one has his own personal experiences to recount. Some houses have become nearly uninhabitable—glass, pictures, clocks, plaster, all lying in morsels about the floor, and airholes in the roofs and walls, through which these winged messengers of destruction have passed. Ladies and children escaped, in many instances, by the azoteas, going along the street from one roof to another, not being able to pass where the cannon was planted. The Señora ——, with her six beautiful boys, escaped in that way to her brother's house, in the evening, and in the very thick of the firing. I was in her drawing-room to-day, which has a most forlorn appearance; the floor covered with heaps of plaster, broken pictures, bullets, broken glass, etc., the windows out, and holes in the wall that look as if they were made for the pipe of a stove to fit into.

The soldiers of both parties, who have occupied the roofs of the houses, behaved with great civility; their officers, on many occasions, sending to the family with a request that they would complain of any insolence that might be shown by their men. But no civility could ensure the safety of the dwellers in these houses.

The poor nuns have been terribly frightened, and have passed these stormy nights in prayers and hymns, which those who live near their convents say were frequently heard at midnight, in the intervals of firing.

I went to see the Countess de V——e, and she showed me the great hole in the wall by her bedside, through which the shell made its *entrée*. The fragments are still lying there, so heavy that I could not lift them. All the windows at the head of that street are broken in pieces. The shops are reopened, however, and people are going about their usual avocations, pretty much as if nothing had happened; and probably the whole result of all this confusion and destruction will be—a change of ministry.

Santa Anna, finding that he was not wanted, has modestly retired to Manga de Clavo, and has addressed the following letter to the Minister of War:

"The triumph which the national arms have just obtained over the horrible attempts at anarchy, communicated to me by your Excellency, in your note of the 27th, is very worthy of being celebrated by every citizen who desires the welfare of his country, always supposing that public vengeance (*la vindicta publica*) has been satisfied; and in this case, I offer you a thousand congratulations. This division, although filled with regret at not having participated on this occasion in the risks of our companions in arms, are rejoiced at so fortunate an event, and hope that energy and a wholesome severity will now strengthen order for ever, and will begin an era of felicity for the country. The happy event has been celebrated here, in the fortress, and in Tepeyahualco, where the first brigade had already arrived (and whom I have ordered to countermarch), with every demonstration of joy. I anxiously desire to receive the details which your Excellency offers to communicate to me, so that if the danger has entirely ceased, I may return to my *hacienda*, and may lay down the command of those troops which your Excellency orders me to preserve here.

"With sentiments of the most lively joy for the cessation of the misfortunes of the capital, I reiterate to your Excellency those of my particular esteem.

"God and Liberty.

"ANTONIO LOPEZ DE SANTA ANNA.

"Perote, July 29, 1840."

The houses of Congress are again opened. The ministers presented themselves in the Chamber of Deputies, and a short account of the late revolution was given by General Almonte, who, by the way, was never taken prisoner, as was at first reported. He had gone out to ride early in the morning, when General Urrea, with some soldiers, rode up to him and demanded his sword; telling him that the president was arrested. For all answer, Almonte drew his sword, and fighting his way through them, galloped to the citadel. Urrea, riding back, passed by Almonte's house, and politely taking off his hat, saluted the ladies of the family, hoped they were well, and remarked on the fineness of the weather. They were not a little astonished when, a short time after, they heard what had happened.

Madame de C—— and her daughter were out riding when the firing began on the morning of the revolution, and galloped home in consternation.

7th.—A long discussion to-day in Congress on the propriety of granting extraordinary powers to the president; also a publication of the despatches written by Gomez Farias during the revolution. He speaks with the utmost confidence of the success of his enterprise. In his first letter, he observes, that General Urrea, with the greater part of the garrison and people of the capital, have pronounced for the re-establishment of the federal system, and have, by the most fortunate combination of circumstances, got possession of the palace, and arrested the president. That troops have been passing over to them all day, and that the triumph of the federalists is so sure, he has little doubt that the following morning will see tranquillity and federalism re-established. The different accounts of the two parties are rather amusing. It is said that Gomez Farias is concealed in Mexico. . . .

8th.—Paid a visit to-day, where the lady of the house is a leper; though it is supposed that all who are afflicted with this scourge are sent to the hospital of San Lazaro. . . .

We rode before breakfast this morning to the old church of *La Piedad,* and, on our return, found a packet containing letters from London, Paris, New York, and Madrid. The arrival of the English packet, which brings all these *nouveautés,* is about the most interesting event that occurs here.

LETTER THE TWENTY-SIXTH

August 30th.

In the political world nothing very interesting has occurred, and as yet there is no change of ministry. Yesterday morning C——n set off in a coach-and-six for the valley of Toluca, about eighteen leagues from Mexico, with a rich Spaniard, Señor M——r y T——n, who has a large hacienda there.

Last Sunday morning, being the first Sunday since the revolution, we had forty visitors—ladies and gentlemen, English, French, Spanish, and Mexican. Such varieties of dresses and languages I have seldom seen united in one room; and so many anecdotes connected with the *pronunciamiento* as were related, some grave, some ludicrous, that would form a volume! The Baron de —— having just left this for your part of the world, you will learn by him the last intelligence of it and of us.

As there is a want of rain, the Virgen de los Remedios was brought into Mexico, but as there is still a slight ripple on the face of the lately-troubled waters, she was carried in privately—for all reunions of people are dreaded at this juncture, I had just prepared pieces of velvet and silk to hang on the balconies, when I found that the procession had gone by a back street after sunset.

I went lately to visit the nuns of the *Encarnacion*, to inquire how they stood their alarms, for their convent had been filled with soldiers, and they had been in the very heart of the firing. I was welcomed by a figure covered from head to foot with a double black crape veil, who expressed great joy at *seeing* me again, and told me she was one of the madres who received us before. She spoke with horror of the late revolution, and of the state of fear and trembling in which they had passed their time; soldiers within their very walls, and their prayers interrupted by volleys of cannon. Thanks to the intercession of the Virgin, no accident had occurred; but she added, that had the Virgin of los Remedios been brought in sooner, these disorders might never have taken place.

I went from thence to the convent of Santa Teresa, where I saw no one, but discoursed with a number of *voices*, from the shrill treble of the old *Madre Priora*, to the full cheerful tones of my friend the Madre A——. There is something rather awful in sending one's voice in this way into an unknown region, and then listening for a response from the unseen dwellers there. I have not yet been inside this convent, but now that affairs are settled for the present, I trust that the archbishop will kindly grant his permission to that effect.

The rainy season is now at its height; that is, it rains severely every evening, but in the morning it is lovely. The disagreeable part of it is, that the roads are so bad, it is difficult to continue our rides in the environs. Horse and rider, after one of these expeditions, appear to have been taking a mud-bath. It is very amusing to stand at the window about four o'clock, and see every one suddenly caught in the most tremendous shower. In five minutes the streets become rivers; and canoes would be rather more useful than carriages. Strong porters (*cargadores*) are in readiness to carry well-dressed gentlemen or women who are caught in the deluge, across the streets. Coachmen and footmen have their great-coats prepared to draw on; and all horsemen have their sarapes strapped behind their saddles, in which, with their shining leather hats, they can brave the storm. Trusting to an occasional cessation of rain, which sometimes takes place, people continue to go out in the evening, but it is downright cruelty to coachmen and animals, unless the visit is to a house with a *porte-cochère*, which many of the houses have—this amongst others.

September 1st.—Had a dispute this morning with an Englishman, who complains bitterly of Mexican insincerity. I believe the chief cause of this complaint amongst foreigners consists in their attaching the slightest value to the common phrase, "*Está à la disposicion de V.*" Everything is placed at your disposal—house, carriage, servants, horses, mules, etc.—the lady's earrings, the gentleman's diamond pin, the child's frock. You admire a ring—it is perfectly at your service; a horse—*ditto.* Letters are dated "from your house;" (*de la casa de V.*) Some from ignorance of the custom, and others from knavery, take advantage of these offers, which are mere expressions of civility, much to the confusion and astonishment of the polite *offerer,* who has no more intention of being credited, than you have when, from common etiquette, you sign yourself the very humble servant of the very greatest bore. It is a mere habit, and to call people who indulge in it insincere, reminds me of the Italian mentioned somewhere by Lady Blessington, who thought he had made a conquest of a fair Englishwoman, though somewhat shocked by her forwardness, because, in an indifferent note to him, she signed herself "*Truly yours.*" Shall I ever forget the crestfallen countenance of a Mexican gentleman who had just purchased a very handsome set of London harness, when hearing it admired by a Frenchman, he gave the customary answer, "It is quite at your disposal," and was answered by a profusion of bows, and a ready acceptance of the offer! the only difficulty with the Frenchman being as to whether or not he could carry it home under his cloak, which he did.

If all these offers of service, in which it is Mexican etiquette to indulge, be believed in—"Remember that I am here but to serve you"—"My house and everything in it is quite at your disposal"—"Command me in all things;" we shall of course be disappointed by finding that, notwithstanding these reiterated assurances, we must hire a house for ourselves, and even servants to wait on us; but take these expressions at what they are worth, and I believe we shall find that people here are about as sincere as their neighbours.

8th.—A good deal of surmise, because four Texian vessels are cruising in the bay off Vera Cruz. There is also a good deal of political talk, but I have no longer Madame de Staël's excuse for intefering in politics, which, by the way, is a subject on which almost all Mexican women are well informed; possessing practical knowledge, the best of all, like a lesson in geography given by travelling. I fear we live in a Paradise Lost, which will not be regained in our day. . . .

My attention is attracted, while I write, by the apparition of a beautiful girl in the opposite balcony, with hair of a golden brown hanging in masses down to her feet. This is an uncommon colour here; but the hair of the women is generally very long and fine. It rarely or never curls. We were amused the other day in passing by a school of little boys and girls, kept in a room on the first-floor of Señor ——'s house, to see the schoolmistress, certainly not in a very elegant *dishabille,* marching up and down with a spelling-book in her hand, her long hair hanging down, and trailing on the floor a good half-yard behind her; while every time she turned, she switched it round like a court-train. . . .

You ask me about this climate, for ——. For one who, like her, is in perfect health, I should think it excellent; and even an invalid has only to travel a few hours, and he arrives at *tierra caliente.* This climate is that of the tropics, raised some thousand feet above the level of the sea; consequently there is an extreme purity and thinness of the atmosphere, which generally affects the breathing at first. In some it causes an oppression on the chest. On me, it had little effect, if any; and at all events, the feeling goes off, after the first month or so. There is a general tendency to nervous irritation, and to inflammatory complaints, and during September and October, on account of the heavy rains and the drained lakes on which part of the city is built, there is said to be a good deal of ague. Since the time of the cholera in 1833, which committed terrible ravages here, there has been no other epidemic. The smallpox indeed has been very common lately, but it is owing to the carelessness of the common people, or rather to their prejudice against having their children vaccinated.

The nervous complaints of the ladies are an unfailing source of profit to the sons of Galen, for they seem to be incurable. Having no personal experience in these evils, I speak only from what I see in others. It appears to me that the only fault of the climate consists in its being monotonously perfect, which is a great drawback to easy and polite conversation. The evening deluge is but a periodical watering of the earth, from which it rises like Venus from the sea, more lovely and refreshed than ever.

C——n has returned from Toluca, after an absence of eight days. Every one is hurrying to the theatre just now, in spite of the rain, to see some Spaniards, who are performing *tours de force* there.

16th.—Celebration of the Day of Independence, Anniversary of the *"Glorioso Grito de Dolores,"* of September the 16th, 1810; of the revolution begun thirty years ago, by the curate of the village of Dolores in the province of Gunanajuato. "It is very easy," says Zavala, it is about the most sensible remark, "to put a country into combustion, when it possesses the elements of discord; but the difficulties of its re-organization are infinite."

A speech was made by General Tornel in the Alameda. All the troops were out—plenty of officers, monks, priests, and ladies, in full dress. We did not go to hear the speech, but went to the E——'s house to see the procession, which was very magnificent. The line of carriages was so deep, that I thought we should never arrive. After all was over, we walked in the Alameda, where temporary booths were erected, and the trees were hung with garlands and flowers. The paseo in the evening was extremely gay; but I cannot say that there appeared to be much enthusiasm or public spirit. They say that the great difficulty experienced by the *Junta*, named on these occasions for the preparation of these festivities, is to collect sufficient funds.

19th.—We went yesterday to San Angelo, one of the prettiest villages in the environs of Mexico, and spent the day at the hacienda of Señor T——e, which is in the neighbourhood. The rain has rendered the roads almost impassable, and the country round Mexico must be more like Cortes's description of it at this season, than at any other period. One part of the road near the hacienda, which is entirely destroyed, the owner of the house wished to repair; but the Indians, who claim that part of the land, will not permit the innovation, though he offered to throw a bridge over a small stream which passes there, at his own expense.

24th.—We passed a pleasant day at Tacubaya, and dined with Monsieur S——, who gave a fête in consequence of its being his wife's saint's day.

27th.—Great fête; being the anniversary of the day on which the army called the *trigarante* (the three guarantees) entered Mexico with Yturbide at their head. The famous plan of Iguala, (so called from having been first published in that city,) was also called the plan of the three guarantees; freedom, union, and religion, which were offered as a security to the Spaniards, against whom so many cruelties had been exercised. We have had ringing of bells and firing all the morning, and in the evening there is to be a bull-fight, followed by the exhibition of the *tours de force* of these Spaniards, commonly called here "*los Hercules*," who have just come to offer us a box in the Plaza.

This plan of the Iguala was certainly the only means by

which Spain could have continued to preserve these vast and distant possessions. The treaty of Cordova, which confirmed it, was signed in that city between the Spanish General O'Donoju and Don Agustin Yturbide, in August 1821, and consisted of seventeen articles.

By the first, Mexico was to be acknowledged as a free and independent nation, under the title of the Mexican empire.

By the second, its government was to be a constitutional monarchy.

By the third, Ferdinand VII, Catholic King of Spain, was called to the throne of Mexico; and should he renounce or refuse the throne, it was offered to his brother the Infant Don Carlos, and under the same circumstances, to each brother in succession.

By the fourth, the emperor was to fix his court in Mexico, which was to be considered the capital of the empire.

By the fifth, two commissioners named by O'Donoju were to pass over to the Spanish court, to place the copy of the treaty and of the accompanying exposition in his majesty's hands, to serve him as an antecedent, until the Cortes should offer him the crown with all formality; requesting him to inform the Infantes of the order in which they were named; interposing his influence in order that the Emperor of Mexico should be one of his august house, for the interest of both nations, and that the Mexicans might add this link to the chain of friendship which united them with the Spaniards.

By the sixth, a *Junta* of the first men in Mexico; first by their virtues, position, fortune, etc., was to be named, sufficient in number to ensure success in their resolutions by the union of so much talent and information.

By the seventh, this Junta takes the name of the Administrative Provincial Junta.

By the eighth, O'Donoju was named member of this Junta.

By the ninth, this Junta was to name a president.

By the tenth, it was to inform the public of its installation, and of the motives which had caused it to meet.

By the eleventh, this assembly was to name a regency, composed of three persons, to compose the executive power, and to govern in the name of the monarch, until his arrival.

By the twelfth, the Junta was then to govern conformably to the laws, in everything which did not oppose the plan of Iguala, and till the Cortes had formed the constitution of the state.

By the thirteenth, the regency, as soon as they were named,

were to proceed to the convocation of the Cortes, according to the method decreed by the provisional Junta.

By the fourteenth, the executive power was to reside in the regency—the legislative in the Cortes—but until the reunion of the Cortes, the legislative power was to be exercised by the Junta.

By the fifteenth, all persons belonging to the community, the system of government being changed, or the country passing into the power of another prince, were perfectly at liberty to transport themselves and their fortunes wherever they chose, etc., etc.

By the sixteenth, this does not hold good in regard to the military or public *employés* disaffected to the Mexican independence; they will leave the empire within the term prescribed by the regency, etc., etc.

By the seventeenth and last, as the occupation of the capital by the peninsula troops is an obstacle to the realization of the treaty, this difficulty must be vanquished; but as the chief of the imperial army desires to bring this about, not by force, but by gentler means, General O'Donoju offers to employ his authority with the troops, that they may leave the capital without any effusion of blood, and by an honourable treaty. This treaty was signed by Yturbide and O'Donoju.

Had this plan of Iguala taken effect, what would have been the result in Mexico?—what its present condition? . . .

This being Sunday, and a fête-day, a man was murdered close by our door, in a quarrel brought about probably through the influence of pulque, or rather of *chinguirite*. If they did not so often end in deadly quarrel, there would be nothing so amusing as to watch the Indians gradually becoming a little intoxicated. They are at first so polite—handing the pulque-jar to their fair companions (fair being taken in the general or *Pickwickian* sense of the word); always taking off their hats to each other, and if they meet a woman, kissing her hand with an humble bow as if she were a duchess;—but these same women are sure to be the cause of a quarrel, and then out come these horrible knives—and then, *Adios!*

It is impossible to conceive anything more humble and polite than the common country-people. Men and women stop and wish you a good day, the men holding their hats in their hands, and all showing their white teeth, and faces lighted up by careless good-nature. I regret to state, however, that to-day there are a great many women quite as tipsy as the men, returning home after the fête, and increasing the distance to their village, by taking a zigzag direction through the streets. . . .

Señor Cañedo, Secretary of State, has formally announced his intention of resigning. Certainly the situation of premier in Mexico, at this moment is far from enviable, and the more distinguished and clear-headed the individual, the more plainly he perceives the impossibility of remedying the thickly-gathering evils which crowd the political horizon. "Revolution," says Señor de ——, "has followed revolution since the Independence; no stable government has yet been established. Had it been so, Mexico would have offered to our eyes a phenomenon unknown until now in the world—that of a people, without previous preparation, passing at once to govern themselves by democratical institutions."

28th.—We drove out to the *Peñon*, a natural boiling fountain, where there are baths, which are considered a universal remedy, a pool of Bethesda, but an especial one for rheumatic complaints. The baths are a square of low stone buildings, with a church—each building containing five or six empty rooms, in one of which is a square bath. The idea seems to have been to form a sort of dwelling-house for different families, as each bath has a small kitchen attached to it. Like most *great ideas* of Spanish days, it is now in a state of perfect desolation, though people still flock there for various complaints. When one goes there to bathe, it is necessary to carry a mattress, to lie down on when you leave the bath, linen, a bottle of cold water, of which there is not a drop in the place, and which is particularly necessary for an invalid in case of faintness—in short everything that you may require. A poor family live there to take charge of the baths, and there is a small tavern where they sell spirits and pulque; and occasionally a padre comes on Sunday to say mass in the old church.

We were amused by meeting there with General —— and his family, who had brought with them a whole coach-load of provisions, besides mattresses, sheets, etc. The road to the Peñon crosses the most dreary plain imaginable. Behind the baths are two volcanic hills; and the view of Mexico and of the great volcanoes from this is magnificent. It is the most solitary of buildings; not a tree to be seen in its environs; these volcanic rocks behind—Mexico fronting it—the great lakes near it—to the right Guadalupe—to the left San Angel, San Agustin, and the mountains which bound the valley. The Indian family who live there are handsome savages; and the girl who attended me at the bath spoke an extraordinary jargon, half

Spanish, half Indian, but was a fine specimen of savage good looks. The water is extremely warm, and my curiosity to try its temperature was very soon satisfied.

These boiling springs are said to contain sulphate of lime, carbonic acid, and muriate of soda, and the Indians make salt in their neighbourhood, precisely as they did in the time of Montezuma, with the difference, as Humboldt informs us, that then they used vessels of clay, and now they use copper caldrons. The solitary-looking baths are ornamented with odd-looking heads of cats or monkeys, which grin down upon you with a mixture of the sinister and facetious rather appalling.

The Señora de —— insisted on my partaking of her excellent luncheon after the bath. We could not help thinking, were these baths in the hands of some enterprising and speculative Yankee, what a fortune he would make; how he would build an hotel à la Sarratoga, would paper the rooms, and otherwise beautify this uncouth temple of boiling water.

There is an indescribable feeling of solitude in all houses in the environs of Mexico, a vastness, a desolation, such as I never before experienced in the most lonely dwellings in other countries. It is not sad—the sky is too bright, and nature too smiling, and the air we inhale too pure for that. It is a sensation of being entirely out of the world, and alone with a giant nature, surrounded by faint traditions of a bygone race; and the feeling is not diminished, when the silence is broken by the footstep of the passing Indian, the poor and debased descendant of that extraordinary and mysterious people, who came, we know not whence, and whose posterity are now "hewers of wood and drawers of water," on the soil where they once were monarchs.

In Chapultepec especially, near as it is to a large and populous city, the traditions of the past come so strongly upon the mind, that one would rather look for the apparition of a whole band of these inky-haired adder-anointed priests of Montezuma, than expect to meet with the benevolent-looking archbishop, who, in purple robes, occasionally walks under the shade of the majestic cypresses.

All Mexicans at present, men and women, are engaged in what are called the *desagravios,* a public penance performed at this season in the churches, during thirty-five days. The women attend church in the morning, no men being permitted to enter, and the men in the evening, when women are not admitted. Both rules are occasionally broken. The penitence of the men is most severe, their sins being no doubt proportionably greater than those of the women; though it is one of the few countries where they suffer for this, or seem to act upon the principle, that "if all men had their deserts, who should escape whipping?"

To-day we attended the morning penitence at six o'clock, in the church of San Francisco; the hardest part of which was their having to kneel for about ten minutes with their arms extended in the form of a cross, uttering groans; a most painful position for any length of time. It is a profane thought, but I dare say so many hundreds of beautifully-formed arms and hands were seldom seen extended at the same moment before. Gloves not being worn in church, and many of the women having short sleeves, they were very much seen.

But the other night I was present at a much stranger scene, at the discipline performed by the men; admission having been procured for us, by certain means, *private but powerful*. Accordingly, when it was dark, enveloped from head to foot in large cloaks, and without the slightest idea of what it was, we went on foot through the streets to the church of San Agustin. When we arrived, a small side-door apparently opened of itself, and we entered, passing through long vaulted passages, and up steep winding stairs, till we found ourselves in a small railed gallery, looking down directly upon the church. The scene was curious. About one hundred and fifty men, enveloped in cloaks and sarapes, their faces entirely concealed, were assembled in the body of the church. A monk had just mounted the pulpit, and the church was dimly lighted, except where he stood in bold relief, with his gray robes and cowl thrown back, giving a full view of his high bald forehead and expressive face.

His discourse was a rude but very forcible and eloquent description of the torments prepared in hell for impenitent sinners. The effect of the whole was very solemn. It appeared like a preparation for the execution of a multitude of condemned criminals. When the discourse was finished, they all joined in prayer with much fervour and enthusiasm, beating their breasts and falling upon their faces. Then the monk stood up, and in a very distinct voice, read several passages of scripture descriptive of the sufferings of Christ. The organ then struck up the *Miserere*, and all of a sudden the church was plunged in profound darkness; all but a sculptured representation of the Crucifixion, which seemed to hang in the air illuminated. I felt rather frightened, and would have been very glad to leave the church, but it would have been impossible in the darkness. Suddenly, a terrible voice in the dark cried, "My brothers! when Christ was fastened to the pillar by the Jews, he was *scourged!*" At these words, the bright figure disappeared, and the darkness became total. Suddenly, we heard the sound of hundreds of scourges descending upon the bare flesh. I cannot conceive anything more horrible. Before ten minutes had passed, the sound became *splashing*, from the blood that was flowing.

I have heard of these penitences in Italian churches, and also that half of those who go there do not really scourge themselves; but here where there is such perfect concealment, there seems no motive for deception. Incredible as it may seem, this awful penance continued, without intermission, for half an hour! If they scourged *each other*, their energy might be less astonishing.

We could not leave the church, but it was perfectly sick-ening; and had I not been able to take hold of the Señora ——'s hand, and feel something human beside me, I could have fancied myself transported into a congregation of evil spirits. Now and then, but very seldom, a suppressed groan was heard, and occasionally the voice of the monk encouraging them by ejaculations, or by short passages from Scripture. Sometimes the organ struck up, and the poor wretches, in a faint voice, tried to join in the *Miserere*. The sound of the scourging is indescribable. At the end of half an hour a little bell was rung, and the voice of the monk was heard, calling upon them to desist; but such was their enthusiasm, that the horrible lashing continued louder and fiercer than ever.

In vain he entreated them not to kill themselves; and as-sured them that heaven would be satisfied, and that human nature could not endure beyond a certain point. No answer, but the loud sound of the scourges, which are many of them of iron, with sharp points that enter the flesh. At length, as if they were perfectly exhausted, the sound grew fainter, and little by little ceased altogether. We then got up in the dark, and, with great difficulty, groped our way in the pitch darkness through the galleries and down the stairs, till we reached the door, and had the pleasure of feeling the fresh air again. They say that the church-floor is frequently covered with blood after one of these penances, and that a man died the other day in consequence of his wounds.

I then went to the house of the —— minister, where there was a *reunion*, and where I found the company comfortably engaged in eating a very famous kind of German salad, composed of herrings, smoked salmon, cold potatoes, and apples; (salmagundi?) and drinking hot punch. After the cold, darkness, and horrors of the church, this formed rather a contrast; and it was some time before I could shake off the disagreeable impression left by the *desagravios,* and join in the conversation. . . .

Along with this you will receive some Mexican airs, which I have written by ear from hearing them played, and of some of which I gave you the words in a former letter.

MEXICAN AIRS
(Letters 12 and 16)
PERICO

EL AFORRADO

JARAVE PALAMO

LOS ENANOS

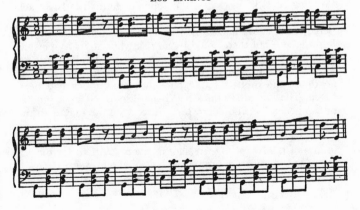

LETTER THE TWENTY-SEVENTH

*Fête-day—Friendly Hint—Precautions—General Tranquillity—
President in San Agustin—Revisit Museum—Ancient Manu-
scripts—Sculpture—Bronze Bust, etc.—Freshness after Rain—
Ball at the French Minister's—Pamphlet—Gutierrez Estrada
—His Character—Concealment—Mexicalsingo—Minister of
the Treasury—Archbishop's Permission—Paintings—Mexican
Painters—Santa Teresa—Description of the Interior—The
Penitences — Tortures — Disciplines, etc.— Supper — Profane
Ballads—Monasteries—San Francisco—Padre Prior—Soldiers
and Friars.*

October 3rd.

Yesterday being C——n's fête-day, we had a dinner and small
soirée, and according to custom, visits the whole day. A very
agreeable guest from Havana, Don J—— A——, arrived to
spend a few weeks with us. We had rather a pleasant party,
and some good singing; but just as dancing had begun, C——n
took me aside, and showed me a little friendly note which he
had received while at dinner, from General ——, in which he
informs him that the robbers would in all probability attack
our respective houses that night; that he had taken his precautions, and advises C——n to do the same, in the understanding that, if necessary, they should mutually assist each
other. A pleasant piece of intelligence! The thing got whispered about, and some of the ladies looked a little blank at the
information; but there could be no risk while so many persons
were collected. About one they went away, and C——n sent for
some soldiers to keep watch all night. Nothing happened, as
no doubt the robbers found out what precautions had been
taken. The intended attack had been discovered by a servant
of the general's, who heard them discussing the matter in the
back-room of a pulque-shop.

We have been obliged to procure two old soldiers as porters,
in lieu of the two who were shot in the revolution; for though
not killed, they are entirely disabled for the present.

Mexico appears particularly quiet just now; and whatever
storms may be preparing, no symptoms are visible to the un-

initiated eye. The palace has got in its glass eyes again, and externally is almost entirely repaired; but it is not yet fit for the residence of the president, who still *holds his court* in the convent of San Agustin. I have been driving about with our Havana friend, like an old resident, showing the beauties of Mexico to a stranger. We have been in the Mineria, Museum, Botanical Garden, Biscay College, etc., all of which can bear revision.

The Museum especially, which, owing to the want of arrangement and classification in the antiquities, and the manner in which they are crowded together in the different rooms of the university, appears at first undeserving of much attention, improves upon acquaintance. It is only since the year '25 that it was established by the government, and various plans have been since made for enriching and arranging it, and also for transporting it to the old building of the Inquisition. But as yet nothing essential has been carried into effect.

It contains upwards of two hundred historical manuscripts, some in hieroglyphical characters anterior to the conquest, and many in the different ancient languages of the country. Of the ancient sculpture, it possesses two colossal statues and many smaller ones, besides a variety of busts, heads, figures of animals, masks, and instruments of music or of war, curiously engraved, and indicating the different degrees of civilization of the different nations to whom they belonged. A great many of the vases of *tecal,* and of the candlesticks in clay, curiously worked, were drawn from excavations in the Isle of Sacrifices, near Vera Cruz, from Oajaca, etc., and from the suburbs of Mexico. There is also a collection of very ancient medals to the number of six hundred, a bronze bust of Philip V, and about two hundred Mexican paintings, comprehending two collections of the portraits of the Spanish viceroys, many of the celebrated Cabrera's, and various dresses, arms, and utensils, from both the Californias. In the cabinet of natural history there is a good collection of minerals, and some very fine specimens of gold and silver. But in the animal or vegetable branch of natural history there is a great deficiency, and altogether the museum is not worthy of a country which seems destined by nature to be the great emporium of all natural science.

Of course we have revisited old Chapultepec and Our Lady of Guadalupe, with her Legend and Holy Well. In the morning we have rode to Tacubaya and the environs, and the weather at that early hour has the most indescribable freshness, caused by the evening rains. Everything looks bright and sparkling. The Peruvian trees, with their bending green branches and bunches of scarlet berries, glitter with the heavy rain-drops, and even the hoary cypresses of Chapultepec sparkle with water in all their gigantic branches. Little pools have become ponds, and ditches rivulets, and frequently it is rather wading than riding, which is not so pleasant.

24th.—Last evening we had a very pretty ball in the house of the French minister, where all the Paris furniture was very effective. There were as usual plenty of diamonds, and some handsome dresses—mine white satin, with flowers.

25th.—The whole world is talking of a pamphlet written by Señor Gutierrez Estrada, which has just appeared, and seems likely to cause a greater sensation in Mexico than the discovery of the gunpowder plot in England. Its sum and substance is the proposal of a constitutional Monarchy in Mexico, with a foreign prince (not named) at its head, as the only remedy for the evils by which it is afflicted. The pamphlet is written merely in a speculative form, inculcating no sanguinary measures, or sudden revolution; but the consequences are likely to be most disastrous to the fearless and public-spirited author. Even those who most question his prudence in taking this step, agree that in this, as well as in every other political action of his life, he has acted from thorough conviction and from motives of the purest patriotism, unalloyed by one personal feeling; indeed, entirely throwing behind him every consideration of personal or family interest, which even the best men allow to have some weight with them on such occasions.

In a political review of Mexico, written some years ago by a Mexican who deals fearlessly, and it would seem impartially, with the characters of all the leading men of that period, I find some remarks on Señor Gutierrez Estrada, which you will place more faith in, as coming from a less partial source than from persons so attached as we are to him and his family. In speaking of the conduct of the administration, he says—"Señor Gutierrez Estrada was one of the few who remained firm in his ideas, and above all, true to his political engagements. This citizen is a native of the State of Yucatan, where his family, who are distinguished in every point of view, reside. It is unnecessary to say that Gutierrez received a thorough and brilliant education, as it is sufficient to have conversed with him to discover this fact; nor that he knew how to turn it to account in the career of public service to which he devoted himself, and in which he has remained pure and unblemished in the midst of a corrupt class. From the first he was destined to the

European legations, on account of his fluency in speaking and writing both English and French; and he is one of the few who have employed their time usefully in the capitals of the Old World. Flexible by nature, honourable by education, and expeditious in business, his services have been perfect, and above all, loyal and conscientious." He goes on to say that, "notwithstanding the gentleness of his temper, his political conscience is so firm and pure, that he will never yield in what he considers his obligation, *even when it interferes with the most intimate friendships,* or most weighty considerations." One would think that the writer had foreseen the present emergency. I have not yet read the pamphlet which the friends of the author consider an equal proof of his noble independence, bold patriotism, and vast information; being, to say the truth, much more interested in its domestic effects than in its public results, or even its intrinsic merits.

26th.—Soldiers were sent to the house of the Countess de la C——a, to arrest her son-in-law, but in compliance with the entreaties of his family, he had gone into concealment. I found them in great affliction, but they are so accustomed to political persecution from one party or another, particularly the countess, that her courage has never deserted her for a moment. He is accused in Congress—in the senate-house—a proclamation is made by the president, anathematizing his principles—even the printer of the pamphlet is thrown into prison. Nothing else is spoken of, and the general irritation is so terrible, that it is to be hoped his place of concealment is secure; otherwise the consequences may be fatal.

On pretend that many distinguished men here hold the same opinions, but their voices, even were they to venture to raise them, could not stem the tide of public indignation. The most offended are naturally the military men. . . . In short, Señor Gutierrez, who has been passing four years abroad, in countries where hundreds of obscure scribblers daily advocate republicanism or any wild theory that strikes their fancy, with the most perfect security, was probably hardly aware of the extraordinary ferment which such a pamphlet was likely to produce at the present juncture.

27th.—A few days before Señor A—— left us, we went up the canal in a canoe, as far as Santa Anita, to show him all that remains of the Chinampas. It is as pleasant a way of passing an evening as any that I know of here.

We drove lately to Mexicalsingo, where there is a cave in

which there is a figure of our Saviour, which they pretend has lately appeared there.

The excitement concerning the pamphlet seems rather to increase than diminish, but Señor Gutierrez has many devoted friends, and the place of his retreat is secure. There is little doubt that he will be forced to fly the country.

29th. Señor Don Xavier Hechavarria, Minister of the Treasury, has sent in his resignation. Being a man of large private fortune, extremely simple in his habits, and the most amiable of men in domestic life, I believe that no minister has ever thrown off with more unaffected satisfaction the burden of state affairs, or will enjoy his retreat from public life with more true philosophy.

I have been so much interested in the affairs of the C——a family, that I have forgotten to tell you of my having obtained permission from the archbishop to visit the Santa Teresa, accompanied by one young married lady, who has a sister there. The archbishop desired that our visit should be kept a secret; but it has *oozed* out by some means or other, probably through the nuns themselves, and exposed him to so much inconvenience and such a torrent of solicitations from those ladies who, having daughters or sisters amongst the nuns, are naturally most desirous to see them, that I fear, notwithstanding his good nature, he will put a veto on all my future applications. You will think I pass my time in convents, but I find no other places half so interesting, and you know I always had a fancy that way.

In some of these convents there still exist, buried alive like the inmates, various fine old paintings; amongst others, some of the Flemish school, brought to Mexico by the monks, at the time when the Low Countries were under Spanish dominion. Many masters also of the Mexican school, such as Enriquez, Cabrera, etc., have enriched the cloisters with their productions, and employed their talent on holy subjects, such as the lives of the saints, the martyrs, and other Christian subjects. Everywhere, especially, there are *Cabreras,* an artist somewhat in the Luca Giordano style; the same monotony, facility, and "*fa presto Luca!*" All his pictures are agreeable, and some strikingly beautiful. Occasionally he copies from the old masters, but rarely. Ximenes and Enriquez are not so common, and some of their productions are very good, and deserve to be better known than I imagine they are in Europe. They are a branch of the Spanish school, and afford striking proofs of the extraordinary talent of the Mexicans for the fine arts, as well as of the facilities which the mother-country afforded them.

But it is in the convent of the Profesa that the finest paintings are, and there I cannot enter! The galleries are full of paintings, the most part by Cabrera; and C——n speaks with enthusiasm of one exceedingly beautiful painting, in the sacristy of the chapel, said to be an original Guido, being a representation of Christ tied to the pillar and scourged; in which the expression of pure divinity and suffering humanity is finely blended, and well contrasted with savage cruelty in the countenances of his executioners. But most of these paintings are neglected, and so falling to decay that it is pitiable to look at them.

The Santa Teresa, however, has few ornaments. It is not nearly so large as the *Encarnacion,* and admits but twenty-one nuns. At present there are, besides these, but three novices. Its very atmosphere seems holy, and its scrupulous and excessive cleanness makes all profane dwellings appear dirty by comparison. We were accompanied by a bishop, Señor Madrid, the same who assisted at the archbishop's consecration—a good-looking man, young and tall, and very splendidly dressed. His robes were of purple satin, covered with fine point-lace, with a large cross of diamonds and amethysts. He also wore a cloak of very fine purple cloth, lined with crimson velvet, crimson stockings, and an immense amethyst ring.

When he came in we found that the nuns had permission to put up their veils, rarely allowed in this order in the presence of strangers. They have a small garden and fountain, plenty of flowers, and some fruit, but all is on a smaller scale, and sadder than in the convent of the Incarnation. The refectory is a large room, with a long narrow table running all round it—a plain deal table, with wooden benches; before the place of each nun, an earthen bowl, an earthen cup with an apple in it, a wooden plate and a wooden spoon; at the top of the table a grinning skull, to remind them that even these indulgences they shall not long enjoy.

In one corner of the room is a reading-desk, a sort of elevated pulpit, where one reads aloud from some holy book, whilst the others discuss their simple fare. They showed us a crown of thorns, which, on certain days, is worn by one of their number, by way of penance. It is made of iron, so that the nails entering inwards, run into the head, and make it bleed. While she wears this on her head, a sort of wooden bit is put into her mouth, and she lies prostrate on her face till dinner is ended; and while in this condition her food is given her, of which she eats as much as she can, which probably is none.

We visited the different cells, and were horror-struck at the self-inflicted tortures. Each bed consists of a wooden plank raised in the middle, and on days of penitence crossed by wooden bars. The pillow is wooden, with a cross lying on it, which they hold in their hands when they lie down. The nun lies on this penitential couch, embracing the cross, and her feet hanging out, as the bed is made too short for her upon principle. Round her waist she occasionally wears a band with iron points turning inwards; on her breast a cross with nails, of which the points enter the flesh, of the truth of which I had melancholy ocular demonstration. Then, after having scourged herself with a whip covered with iron nails, she lies down for a few hours on the wooden bars, and rises at four o'clock. All these instruments of discipline, which each nun keeps in a little box beside her bed, look as if their fitting place would be in the dungeons of the Inquisition. They made me try their *bed and board*, which I told them would give me a very decided taste for early rising.

Yet they all seem as cheerful as possible, though it must be confessed that many of them look pale and unhealthy. It is said, that when they are strong enough to stand this mode of life, they live very long; but it frequently happens that girls who come into this convent, are obliged to leave it from sickness, long before the expiration of their novitiate. I met with the girl whom I had seen take the veil, and cannot say that she looked either well or cheerful, though she assured me, that "of course, in doing the will of God," she was both. There was not much beauty amongst them generally, though one or two had remains of great loveliness. My friend, the Madre A——, is handsomer on a closer view than I had supposed her, and seems an especial favourite with old and young. But there was one whose face must have been strikingly beautiful. She was as pale as marble, and though still young, seemed in very delicate health; but her eyes and eyebrows as black as jet, the eyes so large and soft, the eyebrows two pencilled arches; and her smiles so resigned and sweet, would have made her the loveliest model imaginable for a Madonna.

Again, as in the Incarnation, they had taken the trouble to prepare an elegant supper for us. The bishop took his place in an antique velvet chair, the Señor —— and I were placed on each side of him. The room was very well lighted, and there was as great a profusion of custards, jellies, and ices, as if we had been supping at the most profane *café*. The nuns did not sit down, but walked about, pressing us to eat, the bishop now and then giving them cakes, with permission to eat them, which they received laughing. They have the most humble and caressing manners, and really appear to be the most amiable and excellent women in the world. They seem to make no ostentation of virtue, but to be seriously impressed with the conviction that they have chosen the true road to salvation; nor are there in them any visible symptoms of that spiritual pride from which few devotees are exempt.

After supper a small harp was brought in, which had been sent for by the bishop's permission. It was terribly out of tune, with half the strings broken; but we were determined to grudge no trouble in putting it in order, and giving these poor recluses what they considered so great a gratification. We got it into some sort of condition at last, and when they heard it played, they were vehement in their expressions of delight. The Señora ——, who has a charming voice, afterwards sang to them, the bishop being very indulgent, and permitting us to select whatever songs we chose, so that when rather a profane canticle, "The Virgin of the Pillar" (La Virgen del Pilar), was sung, he very kindly turned a deaf ear to it, and seemed busily engaged in conversation with an old madre, till it was all over.

We were really sorry to leave them; particularly as it is next to impossible that we shall ever see them again; and it seemed as if in a few hours a friendship had been formed between us and these recluses, whose sensations are so few, they must be the more lasting. The thoughts of these poor women cost me a sad and sleepless night. They have sent me some wax figures, dressed in the costumes of the different orders, beginning with their own. They wear the coarsest and hardest stuff next their skin, in itself a perpetual penance.

In these robes they are buried; and one would think that if any human being can ever leave this world without a feeling of regret, it must be a nun of the Santa Teresa, when, her privations in this world ended, she lays down her blameless life, and joins the pious sisterhood who have gone before her; dying where she has lived, surrounded by her companions, her last hours soothed by their prayers and tears, sure of their vigils for the repose of her soul, and above all, sure that neither pleasure nor vanity will ever obliterate her remembrance from their hearts.

At matins, at vespers, at the simple board, at the nightly

hymn, she will be missed from their train. Her empty cell will recall her to their eyes; her dust will be profaned by no stranger's footstep, and though taken away she still seems to remain amongst them. . . .

As for the monasteries, not only no woman can enter, but it is said, with what truth I know not, that a vice-queen having insisted on the privilege of her vice-royalty to enter, the gallery and every place which her footsteps desecrated were unpaved. This was very Saint Senanus like, and *peu galant*, to say the least.

The finest convent of monks in Mexico is that of San Francisco, which from alms alone has an immense annual rent. According to Humboldt, it was to have been built upon the ruins of the temple of Huitzilopoclitli, the god of war; but these ruins having been destined for the foundation of the cathedral, this immense convent was erected where it now stands, in 1531. The founder was an extraordinary man, a great benefactor of the Indians, and to whom they owed many useful mechanical arts which he brought them from Europe. His name was Fray Pedro de Gante—his calling that of a lay-friar —and his father was the Emperor Charles V!

Of the interior of this convent I am enabled to give you a partial description, but whether from hearsay, in a vision, or by the use of my natural eyes, I shall not disclose. It is built in the form of a square, and has five churches attached to it. You enter a gate, pass through the great, silent, and grass-grown court—up the broad staircase, and enter the long, arched cloisters, lighted by one dim lamp, where everything seems to breathe a religious repose. . . .

The padre prior, seated alone in his cell, with a thick and richly-clasped volume before him, a single lamp on his table, on the wall a crucifix, plain but decent furniture, with his bald head, and pale, impressive face, would have made a fine study for a painter. By such men, the embers of learning and of science were nursed into a faint but steady flame, burning through the long, gloomy night of the dark ages, unseen by profane eyes, like the vestal fire in pagan temples. . . .

A small room, opening into his little parlour, contains his bed, on which is a mattress; for the padres do not perform such acts of self-denial and penitence as the cloistered nuns —and I am assured that his cigars are genuine Havana. . . .

Beggars lounging in the courtyard—a group of monks talking together within the walled enclosure. . . .

Change the scene to the monastery of San Agustin, and you

might fancy yourself in the days of one of Walter Scott's ro-
mances, in the *mélange* of soldiers and friars; for here his Excellency the President has his temporary abode; and the torch-
light gleams brightly on the swarthy faces of the soldiers, some
lying on the ground enveloped in their cloaks; others keeping
guard before the convent gate. This convent is also very large,
but not so immense as that of San Francisco. The padre prior
is a good little old man, but has not the impressive, ascetic
visage of the guardian of the other convent. His room is as
simple, though not in such perfect order; and his bed is also
furnished with a comfortable mattress. An air half military,
half monkish, pervades the convent—aides-de-camp of the
president passing along the galleries, their uniforms contrasting with the dark robe of a passing monk, returning at nightfall to his cell.

The president had an alarm the night preceding, the prisoners in the jail having broken out. A serious affray had been
expected, and everything was prepared for putting the person
of the president in safety. The back stairs and secret passages
in these old convents lead to excellent hiding-places, and have
been put to frequent use during the revolutions. In the old
Monte Pio there is a communication with a convent of nuns,
and in cases of pillage, the jewels used to be carried by a
private staircase out of Monte Pio, and placed under the care
of the nuns of Santa Brigida.

The convent of La Profesa is also a fine and spacious building, but excepting that it has a greater number of good paintings than the others, when you have seen one, you have seen
all, and I believe none are as large as that founded by the
illegitimate scion of the Imperial Charles, who himself ended
his days in a similar retreat.

LETTER THE TWENTY-EIGHTH

Dia de Muertos—*Leave Mexico*—Herraderos—*San Cristobal*—*Tunas*—*Plaza de Toros*—*Throwing the* Lazo—*Accidents*—*Rustic Breakfast*—*Country Fare*—*Baked Meat*—*Indian Market*—*Buried Bull*—*Mountain*—*Solitary* Hacienda—Reyes—*Mules marked*—*Return*—*Queen of Spain's Birthday*—*Diplomatic Dinner.*

SANTIAGO, November 3rd.

Yesterday, the second of November, a day which for eight centuries has been set apart in the Catholic Church for commemorating the dead, the day emphatically known as the *"Dia de Muertos,"* the churches throughout all the Republic of Mexico present a gloomy spectacle; darkened and hung with black cloth, while in the middle aisle is a coffin, covered also with black, and painted with skulls and other emblems of mortality. Every one attends church in mourning, and considering the common lot of humanity, there is, perhaps, not one heart over the whole Catholic world, which is not wrung that day, in calling up the memory of the departed.

After early mass, we set off for Santiago, where we intend to spend a week, to be present at the *Herraderos*—the marking of the bulls with a hot iron with the initials of the proprietor's name; stamping them with the badge of slavery—which is said to be an extraordinary scene; to which all rancheros and Indians look forward with the greatest delight. We had a very pleasant journey here, leaving Mexico at six in the morning, and travelling at the usual rate, with *seven* horses and plenty of *mozos*. Indeed, no one attempts a journey of any length into the country, without at least six horses or mules.

Near Sopayuca, while they were changing horses, we went to mass, in the picturesque church of San Cristobal. The magnificence of these places of worship is extraordinary. Here was this country church crowded with léperos, the officiating priests, Indians with bare feet; yet the building large and rich, hung with black cloth, and lighted with great tapers which threw their gloomy rays on as much of the rich gilding that encrusted the walls, as the dark pall left visible.

We got into the carriage a basket of that most refreshing of fruits, the *tuna*, which grow wild in abundance all over the country. The first time I unwarily pulled them off the trees, I got my fingers full of the innumerable little prickles which cover the skin, and which it is very difficult to get rid of. The Indians have great dexterity in gathering and peeling them. There is the green and the red tuna; the last the prettiest to look at, but not nearly so agreeable a fruit as the other.

When we arrived at Santiago, we sat down to a dinner to the number of about fifty persons, and in the room next to us was a party still larger, of lower degree, for all the world has come to be present at this annual festivity.

6th.—The next morning we set off early to the *plaza de toros*. The day was fresh and exhilarating. All the country people from several leagues round were assembled, and the trees up to their very topmost branches presented a collection of bronze faces and black eyes, belonging to the Indians, who had taken their places there as comfortably as spectators in a one-shilling gallery. A platform opposite ours was filled with the wives and daughters of agents and small farmers, little *rancheras*, with short white gowns and rebosos. There was a very tolerable band of music, perched upon a natural orchestra. Bernardo and his men were walking and riding about, and preparing for action. Nothing could be more picturesque than the whole scene.

Seven hundred bulls were driven in from the plains, bellowing loudly, so that the air was filled with their fierce music. The universal love which the Mexicans have for these sports, amounts to a passion. All their money is reserved to buy new dresses for this occasion, silver rolls or gold linings for their hats, or new deerskin pantaloons and embroidered jackets with silver buttons. The accidents that happen are innumerable, but nothing damps their ardour. *It beats fox-hunting.* The most striking part of the scene is the extraordinary facility which these men show in throwing the lazo. The bulls being all driven into an enclosure—one after another, and sometimes two or three at a time, were chosen from amongst them, and driven into the plaza, where they were received with shouts of applause, if they appeared fierce, and likely to afford good sport; or of irony, if they turned to fly, which happened more than once.

Three or four bulls are driven in. They stand for a moment, proudly reconnoitring their opponents. The horsemen gallop up, armed only with the lazo, and with loud insulting cries of "*Ah toro!*" challenge them to the contest. The bulls paw the ground, then plunge furiously at the horses, frequently wounding them at the first onset. Round they go in fierce gallop, bulls and horsemen, amidst the cries and shouts of the spectators. The horseman throws the lazo. The bull shakes his head free of the cord, tosses his horns proudly, and gallops on. But his fate is inevitable. Down comes the whirling rope, and encircles his thick neck. He is thrown down struggling furiously, and repeatedly dashes his head against the ground in rage and despair. Then, his legs being also tied, the man with the hissing red-hot iron in the form of a letter, brands him on the side with the token of his dependence on the lord of the soil. Some of the bulls stand this martyrdom with Spartan heroism and do not utter a cry; but others, when the iron enters their flesh, burst out into long bellowing roars, that seem to echo through the whole country. They are then loosened, get upon their legs again, and like so many branded Cains, are driven out into the country, to make way for others. Such roaring, such shouting, such an odour of singed hair and *biftek au naturel*, such playing of music, and such wanton risks as were ran by the men!

I saw a toreador, who was always foremost in everything, attempting to drag a bull by the horns, when the animal tossed his head, and with the jerk of one horn, tore all the flesh off his finger to the very bone. The man coolly tore a piece off a handkerchief, shook the blood off his finger with a slight grimace, bound it up in a moment, and dashed away upon a new venture. One Mexican, extraordinarily handsome, with eyes like an eagle, and very thin and pale, is, they say, so covered from head to foot with wounds received in different bull-fights, that he cannot live long; yet this man was the most enthusiastic of them all. His master tried to dissuade him from joining in the sport this year; but he broke forth into such pathetic entreaties, conjuring him "by the life of the Señorita," etc., that he could not withhold his consent.

After an enormous number of bulls had been caught and *labelled*, we went to breakfast. We found a tent prepared for us, formed of bows of trees intertwined with garlands of white moss, like that which covers the cypresses of Chapultepec, and beautifully ornamented with red blossoms and scarlet berries. We sat down upon heaps of white moss, softer than any cushion. The Indians had cooked meat under the stones for us, which I found horrible, smelling and tasting of smoke. But we had also boiled fowls, and quantities of burning chile, hot tortillas, atole, or *atolli*, as the Indians call it, a species of cakes made of very fine maize and water, and sweetened with sugar or honey; *embarrado*, a favourite composition of meat and chile, very like *mud*, as the name imports, which I have not yet made up my mind to endure; quantities of fresh tunas, granaditas, bananas, aguacates, and other fruits, besides pulque, *à discrétion.*

The other people were assembled in circles under the trees, cooking fowls and boiling eggs in a gipsy fashion, in caldrons, at little fires made with dry branches; and the band, in its intervals of tortilla and pulque, favoured us with occasional airs. After breakfast, we walked out amongst the Indians, who had formed a sort of temporary market, and were selling pulque, chia, roasted chestnuts, yards of baked meat, and every kind of fruit. We then returned to see a great bull-fight, which was followed by more *herraderos*—in short, spent the whole day amongst the *toros*, and returned to dinner at six o'clock, some in coaches, some on horseback. In the evening, all the people danced in a large hall; but at eleven o'clock I could look on no longer, for one of these days in the hot sun is very fatiguing. Nevertheless, at two in the morning, these men, who had gone through such violent exercise, were still dancing jarabes.

8th.—For several days we lived amongst bulls and Indians, the *herraderos* continuing, with variation of *colear*, riding the bulls, etc. Not the slightest slackening in the eagerness of the men. Even a little boy of ten years old mounted a young bull one day, and with great difficulty and at a great risk succeeded in forcing him to gallop round the circle. His father looked on, evidently frightened to death for the boy, yet too proud of his youthful prowess to attempt to stop him.

At night, when I shut my eyes, I see before me visions of bulls' heads. Even when asleep I hear them roaring, or seem to listen to the shouts of *"Ah toro!"* The last day of the *herraderos*, by way of winding up, a bull was killed in honour of C——n, and a great flag was sent streaming from a tree, on which flag was inscribed in large letters, "Gloria al Señor Ministro de la Augusta Cristina!" a piece of gallantry which I rewarded with a piece of gold.

The animal, when dead, was given as a present to the *toreadores;* and this bull, cut in pieces, they bury with his skin on, in a hole in the ground previously prepared with fire in it, which is then covered over with earth and branches. During a certain time, it remains baking in this natural oven, and the common people consider it a great delicacy, (in which I differ from them).

Yesterday, we climbed to the top of a steep mountain, which cost us as much labour as if it had been that steep path which "leads to fame." Fortunately, it has a good deal of wood, and we had an occasional rest in the shade. We mounted the hill on horseback as far as horses could go, but the principal part could only be performed on foot. Most of the party remained half way. We reached the top, swinging ourselves up by the branches, in places where it was nearly perpendicular. We were rewarded, first by the satisfaction one always has in making good one's intentions, and next, by a wonderfully fine and extensive view. Our return was more agreeable, as the weather, except in the heat of the noonday sun, is very cold in this part of the country. The hills are covered chiefly with tunas, low firs, and numbers of shrubs, with flowers and berries. . . . Met on our return a horseman who came to announce the arrival of a guest, Señor H——, from Puebla, who proved a pleasant addition to our society.

15th.—We went out early this morning on horseback, and breakfasted at an·*hacienda*, five leagues distant from Santiago, belonging to the widow of ——'s agents, a good-looking, respectable woman, who, alone, in this solitary place, brings up her eight children as she best can. This may really be called solitude. From one year to another she never sees a human being, except an occasional Indian. She is well off, and everything in her house is clean and comfortable. She herself manages the farm, and educates her children to the best of her abilities, so that she never finds time to be dull. She expected us, and gave us breakfast (we being about twenty in number), consisting of everything which that part of the country can afford; and the party certainly did justice to her excellent fare. She gave us pulque, fermented with the juice of the pineapple, which is very good.

When the sun had gone down a little, we rode to the fine *hacienda* of Reyes, belonging to Señor A——, where he is making and projecting alterations and improvements. When we left Reyes it began to rain, and we were glad to accept the covering of *sarapes*, as we galloped over the plains. We had a delightful ride. Towards evening the rain ceased, and the moon rose brightly and without a cloud; but we were certainly tired enough when we got home, having rode in all ten leagues.

17th.—These two days have been passed in seeing the mules

marked. They are even more dangerous than the bulls, as they bite most ferociously while in their wild state. When thrown down by the lazo, they snore in the most extraordinary manner, like so many aldermen in an apoplectic nap.

This is, perhaps, the most useful and profitable of all Mexican animals. As beasts of burden and for draught, they are in use over the whole republic, and are excellent for long journeys, being capable of immense fatigue, particularly in those arid, hilly parts of the country, where there are no roads. Those which go in droves, can carry about five hundred pounds weight, going at the rate of twelve or fourteen miles a day, and in this way they can perform journeys of more than a thousand miles. For constant use they are preferable to horses, being so much less delicate, requiring less care, and enduring more fatigue. A good pair of carriage mules will cost from five hundred to a thousand dollars.

After dinner we saw some of these wild creatures, that had just been caught, put into a carriage, each wild mule harnessed with a civilized one, and such kicking and flinging up of heels I never witnessed. However, the *mozos* can manage anything, and in about half an hour, after much alternate soothing and lashing, they trotted along with the heavy coach after them, only rearing and plunging at decent intervals.

MEXICO, 12th.

We have passed ten days in the country, taking constant exercise, and have been obliged to return home rather sooner than we should have wished, in order to mark Queen Ysabel's ,Day with a diplomatic dinner.

Though less is now said on the subject of the pamphlet than when we left this, the irritation seems to continue as before. Señor Gutierrez remains concealed, communicating only with his family and a few devoted friends; a most disagreeable position, and one which it is impossible for him to endure long.

20th.—Our dinner has *gone off* as well as could be expected. The party were twenty-six in number, consisting of His Grace the Archbishop, their Excellencies of the Cabinet and *Corps Diplomatique,* together with Count Cortina, the Valencias, and Gorostizas. The gentlemen were in full uniform—the ladies *en grande toilette*—the archbishop in his robes. We had a band of music in the gallery, and walked in to the sound of Norma, precedence being given to the archbishop, who took me, or rather whom I took, as I found some difficulty in getting my arm into his robes. I believe no blunders in etiquette were committed. The dinner lasted three and a half mortal hours. The archbishop proposed the health of Her Majesty the Queen, which was drank standing, the band performing God save the queen. I was dreadfully tired (though in a very agreeable position), and have no doubt every one else was the same, it being eleven when we returned to the drawing-room.

The archbishop's familiars, two priests who always accompany him, respectable *black guards*, were already in waiting. As for him, he was as kind and agreeable as usual, and, after coffee, took his departure to the sound of music.

LETTER THE TWENTY-NINTH

Virgin of Cavadonga—*Santo Domingo—Decorations and Music—Daguerreotype—Weekly Soirées—An Arrival—An Earthquake—Honourable Mr. —— —Broken Furniture—*Dias—*Day
of the Virgin of Guadalupe—Party of the* Desierto—Itzcuintepotzotli—*Inn of* Guajimaclo—*Ruined Convent—Its Origin
—*Déjeuné à la Fourchette—*Splendid Scenery—Vow to the
Virgin—Musical Mass—Tacuba—Ride with the Prior.*

21st.

We received a few days since an invitation to attend the sumptuous mass, annually given by the Asturian Brotherhood, in
honour of the Virgin of Cavadonga, in the church of Santo
Domingo. The invitation being printed on blue satin, with
gold lace and tassels, seems worthy of a place in a box of wax
figures, which will be sent by the next packet.

The church was superbly decorated, and only well-dressed
people were admitted. C——n was carried off to a post of honour near the altar, and a padre gave me a velvet chair. The
music was beautiful, but too gay for a church. There were
violins and wind instruments, and several amateur players.
Some pieces from the *Cheval de Bronze* were very well played.
The sermon, preached by Guerrero, a chanoine who has some
reputation as an orator, contained a prudent degree of praise
of the Spaniards, and even of a king, could that king be a
pelayo.

In the evening we dined at the Prussian minister's—a pleasant party.

Yesterday we went to Chapultepec, C——n and I, M. de
G——t, and M. de N——, to take views with the Daguerreotype, which C——n had the pleasure of receiving some time
ago from Boston, from our friend, Mr. Prescott. While they
were working in the sun, I, finding that the excessive heat had
the effect of cooling my enthusiasm, established myself with
a book under Montezuma's cypress, which felt very romantic.
The poetry of the scene, however, was greatly weakened by
the arrival of a party of *forçats* in chains, who are working in
the castle, which I believe there is some intention of having

transformed into a military college. They are so insolent, that forgetting they are guarded and chained in couples, I felt glad to see that the servants were within call.

Our weekly *soirées* have begun, and, so far, are very successful. There are now three tertulias in the week at the houses of the diplomates. We have generally music, cards, and plenty of dancing, and every one seems pleased, the best proof of which they give by generally staying till two or three in the morning.

28th.—You may imagine my joy at the arrival of K—— and A—— in health and safety at three o'clock to-day. They have had a good journey from Vera Cruz, suffering from nothing but the cold, which they felt especially at Perote. As they arrived on the day of a *soirée*, they did not make their appearance, being tired. I have now an excuse for revisiting all my old haunts, and the first week or two must pass in sightseeing.

30th.—We dined yesterday at Tacubaya; where the C——a family, particularly the ladies of the family, are in a state of the greatest uneasiness.

I had just written these words, when I began, to my great astonishment, to rock up and down, chair, table, and myself. Suddenly, the room, the walls, all began to move, and the floor to heave like the waves of the sea! At first, I imagined that I was giddy, but almost immediately saw that it was an earthquake. We all ran, or rather staggered as well as we could, into the gallery, where the servants were already arranged on their knees, praying and crossing themselves with all their might. The shock lasted above a minute and a half, and I believe has done no injury, except in frightening the whole population, and cracking a few old walls. All Mexico was on its knees while it lasted, even the poor madmen in San Hepolito, which A—— had gone to visit in company with Señor ——. I have had a feeling of sea-sickness ever since. They expect a return of the shock in twenty-four hours. How dreadful a severe earthquake must be! how terrible it is to feel this heaving of the solid earth, to lose our confidence in its security, and to be reminded that the elements of destruction which lurk beneath our feet, are yet swifter and more powerful to destroy, than those which are above us.

I cannot help laughing yet at the recollection of the face of a poor little clerk who had just entered the house with a packet of letters for C——n. He did not kneel, but sat down upon the steps as pale as death, looking as "creamed faced" as the messenger to Macbeth; and when the shock was over, he was so sick, that he ran out of the house without making any remarks. The scarlet *hucamaya,* with a loud shriek, flew from its perch, and performed a zig-zag flight through the air, down to the troubled fountain in the court.

Your friend, the Honourable Mr. ——, arrived the other day, looking very ill, having had the yellow fever at Havana very severely, a peculiar piece of bad fortune at this season.

All the furniture we ordered from the United States, arrived some time ago, a mass of legs and arms. Tables, wardrobes, etc., were, I believe, all sold for the mahogany at Vera Cruz. The mirrors also arrived *in powder.* This must be owing to bad packing, since our most delicate things from London, such as crystal, porcelain, etc., have arrived in excellent condition.

December 3rd.—Have had many visits to-day, this being my *dia de fiesta.* Amongst others the president was here. This custom of keeping people's *dias* gives one a great deal of trouble, but the omission is considered rather a breach of politeness.

12th.—This being the anniversary of the day of the miraculous apparition of our Lady of Guadalupe, the cathedral and village will be crowded with Indians from all parts of the country. A—— and Mr. B—— have driven over there; but, from all accounts, the crowd will be so great, that we are not tempted to accompany them. We have a *soirée* this evening, and have had two pleasant parties this week at the other houses. To-morrow we intend going with a large party to the *Desierto,* where some gentlemen are to give a breakfast. I understand that there are to be twenty-three people on horseback, and eighteen in carriages, and our *trysting-place* is by the great fountain with the gilt statue, in the Paseo de Bucarelli; the hour, half-past seven. They say the Desierto is a beautiful place, but being seven leagues from Mexico, we shall probably all return as tired as possible.

15th.—The morning of our party to the Desierto was beautiful. Here one need not fear those *contretemps* in regard to the weather, which in England so often render a party of pleasure painful; unless, indeed, one chooses to select an evening in the rainy season for an expedition. We met by the fountain at the hour appointed, some in carriages, and some on horseback. Of the latter I formed part. The road leads along the aqueduct by Chapultepec, and through Tacubaya, and is the high-road that goes to Toluca. The first part, after

passing Tacubaya, is steep, bleak, and uninteresting. Planta-
tions of maguey and occasional clumps of Peruvian trees are
the only vegetation, and Indian huts the only traces of human
life. But after a tedious ascent, the view looking back upon
Mexico, with all her churches, lakes, and mountains is truly
magnificent. The road also begins to wind through a fertile
and wooded country. About noon we reached an inn, where
travellers stop who are going to Toluca, and where we
halted to collect our scattered forces. Hanging up by a hook
in the entry, along with various other dead animals, polecats,
weasels, etc., was the ugliest creature I ever beheld. It seemed
a species of dog, with a hunch back, a head like a wolf, and
no neck, a perfect monster. As far as I can make out it must
be the *itzcuintepotzotli*, mentioned by some old Mexican
writers. The people had brought it up in the house, and killed
it on account of its fierceness. This inn stands in the valley
of Guajimalco, and is about a league from the Desierto.

There is no longer any road there, but a steep and winding
path through the beautiful woods. Therefore those who had
come in coaches were now obliged to proceed on donkeys,
with Indian guides. The beauty of the scenery is indescribable.
The path winds, ascending through a wilderness of trees and
flowering shrubs, bathed by a clear and rapid rivulet; and every now and then, through the arched forest-trees, are glimpses
of the snowy volcanoes and of the distant domes and lakes
of Mexico.

The ruins of the old Carmelite convent, standing on the
slope of a hill, are surrounded by noble forests of pine, and
oak, and cedar; long and lofty forest-aisles, where the monks
of former days wandered in peaceful meditation. But they removed from this beautiful site to another, said to be equally
beautiful and wilder, also called the Desierto, but much farther from Mexico; and this fertile region (which the knowing
eye of a Yankee would instantly discover to be full of capabilities in the way of machinery), belongs to no one, and lies
here deserted, in solitary beauty. Some poor Indians live
amongst the ruins of the old cloisters, and the wild deer possess the undisputed sovereignty of the woods.

It is said that a benighted traveller, who had lost his way
in these solitudes, and was miraculously saved from dying of
cold, founded this rich convent of Carmelite monks, in gratitude to Heaven for his deliverance, bequeathing his desire,
that all travellers who passed that way should receive hospitality from the convent. Certainly no place more fitted for

devotion could have been selected than this mountain retreat; and when the convent bell tolled at evening, calling the monks to prayer, and wakening the echoes of the silent hills, its deep notes must have been all in unison with the solemn scene.

But the sight of a very magnificent *déjeuné à la fourchette*, spread under the pine-trees, the uncorking of champagne bottles and Scotch ale, the savoury odour of soups and fricandeaus, the bustling attendance of English waiters, put to flight all romantic fancies. We remembered that we were hungry, that we had ridden seven miles and had not breakfasted; and no order of friars could have done more justice to the repast than we did. . . . But the component parts of a party of pleasure must be very curiously selected, the mosaic of the society very nicely fitted, or it will inevitably terminate unpleasantly; and the elements of discord are more dangerous, their effects more lasting, than even the coughs and colds and rheumatisms produced by those watery elements, sworn foes to all picnics and gipsy parties in our foggy island.

About four o'clock we remounted our horses, and retraced our path through the woods; and who could ruminate on petty disputes, or complain of trifling accidents, or not forget any disagreeable individuals who might have been found among our numerous party, when the splendid panorama of Mexico burst upon us, with all its mountains, lakes, and plains, its churches, and towers, and gardens, bathed in a flood of golden light, the rich crimson clouds of sunset resting upon the snow of the volcanoes, while the woods through which our horses picked their steps, over stones and streamlets, were fragrant with blossoming shrubs and wild roses?

When we reached the inn where the carriages had been left, we remounted our horses, and as it was growing dusk, and the whole party had not yet collected together, we thought it advisable for the equestrian part of the expedition to ride forward; so leaving the carriages with their escort, we set off for Mexico; C——n, I, A——, and a servant, at full gallop, and hardly drew our bridles till we reached the city; tired, as you may suppose, after our fourteen leagues' ride.

20th.—Our yesterday evening's tertulia was very crowded; and there was a great deal of music and dancing. These weekly *soirées* are decidedly successful, and the best families in Mexico unite there without etiquette, which we were told it was impossible to bring about. . . .

Perhaps it is that I am getting accustomed to the Mexican style of face, but it appeared to me that there was a great deal of beauty assembled; and as for fine voices, they are as common in Mexico as they are rare in England. . . .

A rich senator, Don B—— G——, made a vow to the Virgin some years ago, that he would cause a splendid mass to be performed annually in the cathedral, at his own expense, in honour of our Saviour's birth, on the morning of Christmas-eve. This mass is performed entirely by amateurs, most of the young ladies in Mexico, who have fine voices, taking a part in it. I was *drawn in,* very unwillingly, to promise to take a trifling part on the harp, the accompaniment to the *Incarnatus.*

Preparations have long been going on for this solemnization, and various rehearsals have taken place amongst the amateur singers, in the evening, before large audiences in the Mineria. The whole thing promises well.

24th.—C——n has gone with Señor Zurutuza (a Spanish gentleman), to Cuernavaca, in *tierra caliente,* to spend a few days at his estate in the neighbourhood; which at this season will be delightful.

This morning we rode to San Joaquin, where we met the prior on horseback, on his way to Mexico to confess the old prioress of the convent of Santa Teresa. He turned back, and accompanied us during the rest of our ride. He rode with us to Tacuba, round the traces of the ruins, and to the fine old church and dismantled convent, where we dismounted, and having taken off our riding-hats, accompanied the prior through the deserted cloisters into the old church; and I imagine we must have looked very picturesque; I in my riding-habit, and the sandalled friar in his white robes, kneeling side by side, on the broken steps of the altar. He is so pleasant and well-informed, that he is a particularly agreeable companion.

LETTER THE THIRTIETH

Christmas-day—Kalends and Mass—Amateur Performances— Solo—Posadas—Wandering of the Holy Family—Nacimiento —Crowded Party—French Cooks—Mexican Cook—State of Household — New Year's Day — Mass — Dirtiness of the Churches, etc. — Comparisons — Private Chapels — English Club—Preparations for Journey.

25th.

Christmas-day! One year this evening since we made our entry into Mexico. What a different aspect everything has assumed to us in one year! Then every object was new, every face that of a stranger. Now we are surrounded by familiar sights and sounds, and above all by friendly faces. But though novelty, which has its charms and its *désagrémens*, has gone, nothing in Mexico even appears commonplace. Everything is on so large a scale, and everything so picturesque. Then there is so much interest attached to its old buildings, so much to see, even though there are no *sights* and no show-places, unless we are to put in that class the Minera, Museum, Cathedral, University, and Botanic Garden, usually visited by travellers, that at whatever period we may leave it, I feel convinced we shall regret some point of interest, that we have left unvisited. . . .

Some days ago coloured cards, printed in gilt letters, were sent round, inviting all the senator's friends to the mass, in this form:—

"J——é B——o G—— requests that you will honour him with your presence and that of your family, in the solemn function of Kalends and Mass, with which he annually makes an humble remembrance of the Birth of the Saviour, which festivity will take place on the morning of the 24th of this month, at nine o'clock in the Parish Church of the *Sagrario* of the Holy Cathedral.
"Mexico, December, 1840."

By nine we were all assembled in the choir; Don B——o in his uniform, dark blue and gold, we in mantillas. The church looked very splendid, and, as usual on these occasions, no *léperos* were admitted, therefore the crowd was very elegant and select. The affair went off brilliantly. Four or five of the girls, and several of the married women, have superb voices; and not one of all those who sang in chorus had a bad voice. The finest I almost ever heard is that of the Señorita C——. Were she to study in Italy, I venture to predict that she might rival Grisi. Such depth, power, extension, and sweetness, with such richness of tone in the upper notes, are very rarely united. She sang a solo in such tones that I thought the people below must have been inclined to applaud. There are others whose voices are much more cultivated, and who have infinitely more science. I speak only of the raw material. The orchestra was really good, and led by a first-rate musician. I was thankful when my part of the entertainment was over, and I could give an individual attention to the others. The celebration lasted four hours, but there was rather a long sermon. You will shortly receive a detailed account of the whole, which is to be published in the Mexican Annual, called "The Ladies' Guide."

In the evening we went to the house of the Marquesa de V——o, to spend the Christmas-eve. On this night all the relations and intimate friends of each family assemble in the house of the *head of the clan*, a real gathering, and in the present case to the number of fifty or sixty persons.

This is the last night of what are called the *Posadas*, a curious mixture of religion and amusement, but extremely pretty. The meaning is this: At the time when the decree went forth from Cæsar Augustus, that "all the world should be taxed," the Virgin and Joseph having come out of Galilee to Judæa to be inscribed for the taxation, found Bethlehem so full of people, who had arrived from all parts of the world, that they wandered about for nine days, without finding admittance in any house or tavern, and on the ninth day took shelter in a manger, where the Saviour was born. For eight days this wandering of the Holy Family to the different *Posadas* is represented, and seems more intended for an amusement to the children than anything serious. We went to the Marquesa's at eight o'clock, and about nine the ceremony commenced. A lighted taper is put into the hand of each lady, and a procession was formed, two by two, which marched all through the house, the corridors and walls of which were all decorated with evergreens and lamps, the whole party singing the Litanies. K—— walked with the dowager marquesa; and a group of little children, dressed as angels, joined the procession. They wore little robes of silver or gold lama, plumes of white feathers, and a profusion of fine diamonds, and pearls, in *bandeaux*, brooches, and necklaces, white gauze wings, and white satin shoes, embroidered in gold.

At last the procession drew up before a door, and a shower of fireworks was sent flying over our heads, I suppose to represent the descent of the angels; for a group of ladies appeared, dressed to represent the shepherds who watched their flocks by night upon the plains of Bethlehem. Then voices, supposed to be those of Mary and Joseph, struck up a hymn, in which they begged for admittance, saying that the night was cold and dark, that the wind blew hard, and that they prayed for a night's shelter. A chorus of voices from within refused admittance. Again those without entreated shelter, and at length declared that she at the door, who thus wandered in the night, and had not where to lay her head, was the Queen of Heaven! At this name the doors were thrown wide open, and the Holy Family entered singing. The scene within was very pretty: a *nacimiento*. Platforms, going all round the room, were covered with moss, on which were disposed groups of wax figures, generally representing passages from different parts of the New Testament, though sometimes they begin with Adam and Eve in paradise. There was the Annunciation —the Salutation of Mary to Elizabeth—the Wise Men of the East—the Shepherds—the Flight into Egypt. There were green trees and fruit trees, and little fountains that cast up fairy columns of water, and flocks of sheep, and a little cradle in which to lay the Infant Christ. One of the angels held a waxen baby in her arms. The whole was lighted very brilliantly, and ornamented with flowers and garlands. A padre took the baby from the angel, and placed it in the cradle, and the posada was completed.

We then returned to the drawing-room—angels, shepherds, and all, and danced till supper-time. The supper was a show for sweetmeats and cakes.

To-day, with the exception of there being no service in all the churches, Christmas is not kept in any remarkable way. We are spending this evening alone, and very quietly. To-morrow we have a *soirée*. I have letters from C——n, from Cuernavaca, delighted with the beauties of *tierra caliente,* and living amongst roses and orange trees. I hope that in January we shall be able to go there, in case anything should occur to induce us to leave Mexico before next winter.

27th.—We had a very crowded party last evening, I think the best we have had yet, a fact which I mention, because I triumph in my opinion that these weekly parties would succeed in Mexico having proved correct.

I have lately been engaged in search of a *cook,* with as much pertinacity as Japhet in search of his father, and with as little success as he had in his preliminary inquiries. One, a Frenchman, I found out had been tried for murder—another was said to be deranged—a third, who announced himself as the greatest *artiste* who had yet condescended to visit Mexico, demanded a salary which he considered suitable to his abilities. I tried a female Mexican, in spite of her flowing hair. She seemed a decent woman and tolerable cook; and, although our French housekeeper and prime minister had deserted us at our utmost need, we ventured to leave the house, and to spend the day at Tacubaya. On our return, found the whole establishment unable to stand! Cook tipsy—soldiers ditto—galopine slightly intoxicated—in short, the house taking care of itself—no *standing force* but the coachman and footman, who have been with us some time, and appear to be excellent servants. I am, however, promised a good Mexican housekeeper, and trust that some order will be established under her government; also, a Chinese cook, with a *celestial* character. . . .

Letters from Spain, announcing the speedy arrival of a Secretary of Legation and another attaché.

1st January, 1841.—A happy New Year to all! We began it by attending early mass in San Francisco, about the cleanest church in Mexico, and most frequented by the better classes. There you may have the good fortune to place yourself between two well-dressed women, but you are equally likely to find your neighbour a beggar with a blanket; besides, the floor is nearly as dirty as that of the cathedral. This dirtiness is certainly one of the greatest drawbacks to human felicity in this beautiful country, degrading the noble edifices dedicated to the worship of God, destroying the beautiful works destined for the benefit of his creatures. The streets, the churches, the theatres, the market-place, the people, all are contaminated by this evil. The market-place is indeed full of flowers and green branches and garlands—but those who sell the flowers and weave the wreaths are so dirty, that the effect of what would otherwise be the prettiest possible picture, is completely destroyed. In the theatre there is a series of suffocating odours, especially in the dimly-lighted corridors, which is anything but agreeable. The custom of kneeling on the floor in church seems

fitting and devout, but there surely can be no reason why the
floor of a sacred building should not be kept scrupulously
clean, or why the lower classes should not be obliged to dress
themselves with common decency. Those who are unable to
do so, though probably there are not half a dozen people in
Mexico who do not wear rags merely from indolence, should
certainly have a place set apart for them, in which case this
air of squalid poverty would no doubt disappear. On occasion
of any peculiar fête, the church is washed and beggars are
excluded, and then indeed these noble edifices seem fitting
temples wherein to worship the Most High.

On other days, in addition to the léperos (especially in the
cathedral), the Indian women are in the habit of bringing their
babies and baskets of vegetables to church, and the babies on
their part are in the habit of screaming, as babies will when
they consider themselves neglected. This may be difficult to
amend, the poor woman having come in from her village, and
perforce brought her progeny with her; but the strong, stout
man in rags, who prefers begging to working—the half-naked
woman who would consider herself degraded by doing anything to better her condition, except asking for alms—the dogs
which wander up and down during divine service,—all these
might be brought to order by proper regulations.

Notwithstanding all these drawbacks, I have sometimes
compared, in my own mind, the appearance of a fashionable
London chapel with that of a Mexican church, on the occasion
of a solemn fête, and the comparison is certainly in favour of
the latter. The one, light, airy, and gay, with its velvet-lined
pews, its fashionable preacher, the ladies a little sleepy after
the last night's opera, but dressed in the most elegant morning
toilet, and casting furtive glances at Lady ——'s bonnet and
feathers, and at Mrs. ——'s cashmere shawl or lovely ermine
pelisse, and exchanging a few fashionable nothings at the door,
as the footmen let down the steps of their gay equipages—
the other, solemn, stately, and gloomy, and showing no distinction of rank. The floor covered with kneeling figures—some
enveloped in the reboso, others in the mantilla, and all alike
devout, at least in outward seeming. No showy dress, or gay
bonnet, or fashionable mantle to cause the eye of the poor to
wander with envy or admiration. Apparently considering
themselves alike in the sight of Heaven, the peasant and the
marquesa kneel side by side, with little distinction of dress;
and all appear occupied with their own devotions, without

observing either their neighbour's dress or degree of devout-
ness. Religious feeling may be equally strong in the frequenters
of both places of worship; but as long as we possess senses
which can be affected by external objects, the probabilities of
the most undivided devotional feeling are in favour of the latter. The eye will wander—the thoughts will follow where it
leads. In the one case it rests on elegant forms and fashionable
toilets—in the other, it sees nothing but a mass of dark and
kneeling figures, or a representation of holy and scriptural
subjects.

However, one consequence of the exceeding dirtiness of the
Mexican churches, and the number of léperos who haunt
them, as much in the way of their calling as from devotion, is
that a great part of the principal families here, having oratorios
in their houses, have engaged the services of a padre, and
have mass at home. There is a small chapel in the house of
General B——a, the handsomest house in Mexico, where there
is a virgin carved in wood, one of the most exquisite pieces
of sculpture that can be seen. The face is more than angelic
—it is divine; but a divine nature, suffering mortal anguish.

27th.—On the first of February we hope to set off on an expedition to *tierra caliente,* from which C——n returned some
time ago. We have, by good fortune, procured an excellent
Mexican housekeeper, under whose auspices everything has
assumed a very different aspect, and to whose care we can
intrust the house when we go. Nothing remarkable has occurred here lately—the usual routine of riding on horseback,
visiting in carriage, walking very rarely in the Alameda, driving in the Paséo, dining at Tacubaya, the three weekly *soirées,*
varied by a diplomatic dinner in the house of the —— minister,
and by the dinner of the English club who met here yesterday
—by a sale of books after dinner, in which the president of the
society fined me five dollars for keeping a stupid old poem past
the time, upon which I *moved* that the poem should be presented to me, which was carried *nem. con.*

We have been strongly advised not to attempt this journey,
and the stories of robbers and robberies, related by credible
persons, are not encouraging. Robbers, bad roads, horrible
heat, poisonous animals; many are the difficulties prognosticated to us. The season is already rather advanced, but it has
been impossible for us to set off sooner. Our next letters will
be written either during our journey, should we find the opportunity, or after our return.

LETTER THE THIRTY-FIRST

Leave Mexico — Cuernavaca — Tierra Caliente — Atlacamulco —Orange Groves—Sugar-cane—Annual Produce—Will of Cortes—Description—Coffee Plantation—Scorpions—List of Venemous Reptiles—Acapansingo—Doubts and Difficulties —A Decision.

ATLACAMULCO, February 2nd.

A quiet day in a hospitable country-house, too sunny to go out, and nothing else to do, are temptations sufficient to induce me to sit down and give you an account of our proceedings during these last two days. Yesterday, the first of February, at four in the morning, very sleepy, we set off in the diligence which we had taken for ourselves; our sole luggage, two portmanteaus and a carpet bag; our dresses, dark strong calico gowns, large Panama hats, rebosos tied on like scarfs, and thick green barége veils. A government escort of four soldiers with a corporal, renewed four times, accompanied us as far as Cuernavaca, which is about eighteen leagues from Mexico, and the entrance as it were to *tierra caliente*. These are supposed sufficient to frighten away three times the number of robbers, whose daring, however, has got to such a height, that no diligence now arrives from Puebla without being robbed. Six robberies have happened there in the last fortnight, and the road to Cuernavaca is said to be still more dangerous. We took chocolate before starting, and carried with us a basket of cold meat and wine, as there is nothing on the road that can be called an inn. When we set off it was cool, almost cold; the astral lamps were out, and the great solar lamp was not yet lighted.

> *"But soon, like lobster boiled, the morn,*
> *From black to red began to turn."*

By the time we had reached San Agustin, where we changed horses, the sun had risen, enabling us to see all the horrors of the road, which, after leaving that beautiful village with its trees and gardens, winds over the mountain, amongst great volcanic rocks, a toilsome ascent; and passes by the village of Ajusco, a miserable robber's nest. Yet the view, as we looked back from this barren tract, while the sun was breaking over the summits of the mountains, was very grand in its mixture of fertility and wildness, in its vast extent of plains and villages with their groves and gardens, and in its fine view of Mexico itself, white and glittering in the distance. The mountain of Ajusco, clothed with dark forests of pine, frowned on our right, and looked worthy of its brigand haunted reputation. At La Guarda, a collection of miserable huts, we changed horses, and declined some suspicious-looking frijoles in dirty saucers, which were offered to us; a proof both that we were young travellers in this country, and that we had not exhausted our basket of civilized provender.

The road wound round through a succession of rocks and woods till we reached *Cruz del Marques*—the Marquis being of course Cortes, while the cross, it is said, was planted there by him to mark the limits of his territory, or rather of that which the Indian Emperor had assigned him. About two o'clock the heat became intense, and we began to see and to feel symptoms of our approach to *tierra caliente*.

We arrived at the Indian village of *Huichilaque*, which is rather pretty, with cane cottages and a good many flowering trees; and from the eminence on which it is situated, the *hot land* is visible.

The diligence now began galloping down the rocky and stony descent. The country looked even more arid than before; the vegetation more dried up. Not a tree—but here and there, at long intervals, a feathery cocoa or a palm, and occasionally some beautiful, unknown wild flowers. But the heat, the dust, the jolting! When at length we rattled through Cuernavaca, and stopped before the quiet-looking inn, it was with joy that we bade adieu, for some time at least, to all diligences, coaches, and carriages; having to trust for the future to four-legged conveyances, which we can guide as we please.

Cuernavaca (*cow's horn*), the ancient Quauhnahuac, was one of the thirty cities which Charles the Fifth gave to Cortes, and afterwards formed part of the estates of the Duke of Monteleone, representative of the family of Cortes, as Marquis of the Valley of Oajaca. It was celebrated by the ancient writers for its beauty, its delightful climate, and the strength of its situation; defended on one side by steep mountains, and on the other by a precipitous ravine, through which ran a stream which the Spaniards crossed by means of two great trees that had thrown their branches across the barranca, and formed a natural bridge. It was the capital of the Tlahuica nation, and, after the conquest, Cortes built here a splendid palace, a church, and a convent of Franciscans, believing that he had laid the foundation of a great city. And in fact, its delicious climate, the abundance of the water, the minerals said to exist in the neighbourhood, its fine trees, delicious fruits, and vicinity to the capital, all combined to render it a flourishing city. It is, however, a place of little importance, though so favoured by nature; and the conqueror's palace is a half-ruined barrack, though a most picturesque object, standing on a hill, behind which starts up the great white volcano. There are some good houses, and the remains of the church which Cortes built, celebrated for its bold arch; but we were too tired to walk about much, and waited most anxiously for the arrival of horses and men from the sugar estate of Don Anselmo Zurutuza, at Atlacamulco, where we were to pass the night. The house where the diligence stopped was formerly remarkable for the fine garden attached to it, and belonged to a wealthy proprietor. We sat down amongst the fruit trees, by the side of a clear tank, and waited there till the arrival of our horses and guides. It was nearly dusk when they came— the sun had gone down, the evening was cool and agreeable, and after much kicking and spurring and loading of mules and barking of dogs, we set off over hill and dale, through pretty wild scenery, as far as we could distinguish by the faint light, climbing hills and crossing streams for two leagues; till at length the fierce fires, pouring from the sugar oven chimneys of Atlacamulco, gave us notice that we were near our haven for the night. We galloped into the courtyard, amongst dogs and negroes and Indians, and were hospitably received by the administrador (the agent). Greatly were we divided between sleep and hunger; but hunger gained the victory, and an immense smoking supper received our most distinguished attention.

This morning, after a refreshing sleep, we rose and dressed at eight o'clock—late hours for *tierra caliente*—and then went out into the coffee plantation and orange walk. Anything so lovely! The orange-trees were covered with their golden fruit and fragrant blossom; the lemon-trees, bending over, formed a natural arch, which the sun could not pierce. We laid ourselves down on the soft grass, contrasting this day with the preceding. The air was soft and balmy, and actually heavy with the fragrance of the orange blossom and starry jasmine.

All round the orchard ran streams of the most delicious clear water, trickling with sweet music, and now and then a little cardinal, like a bright red ruby, would perch on the trees. We pulled bouquets of orange blossom, jasmines, lilies, double red roses, and lemon leaves, and wished we could have transported them to you, to those lands where winter is now wrapping the world in his white winding-sheet.

The gardener, or coffee-planter—such a gardener!—Don Juan by name, with an immense black beard, Mexican hat, and military sash of crimson silk, came to offer us some orange-ade; and having sent to the house for sugar and tumblers, pulled the oranges from the trees, and drew the water from a clear tank overshadowed by blossoming branches, and cold as though it had been iced. There certainly is no tree more beautiful than the orange, with its golden fruit, shining green leaves and lovely white blossom with so delicious a fragrance. We felt this morning as if Atlacamulco was an earthly paradise.

It belongs in fact to the Duke of Monteleone, and is let by his agent, Don Luis Alaman, to Señor Zurutuza. Its average annual produce of silver is about thirty thousand *arrobas,* (an arroba containing twenty-five pounds). The sugar-cane was unknown to the ancient Mexicans, who made syrup of honey, and also from the maguey, and sugar from the stalk of maize. The sugar-cane was introduced by the Spaniards from the Canary Islands to Santo Domingo, from whence it passed to Cuba and Mexico. The first sugar-canes were planted in 1520, by Don Pedro de Atienza. The first cylinders were constructed by Gonzalo de Velosa, and the first sugar mills built by the Spaniards at that time were worked by hydraulic wheels and not by horses. M. de Humboldt, who examined the will of Cortes, informs us that the conqueror had left sugar planta-tions near Cuyoacan, in the valley of Mexico, where now, owing, it is supposed, to the cutting down of the trees, the cold is too great for sugar-cane or any other tropical produc-tion to thrive. There are few negroes on these sugar planta-tions. Their numbers have not increased since their introduc-tion. We observed but one old negro, said to be upwards of a hundred, who was working in the courtyard as we passed; the generality of the workmen are Indians.

As for the interior of these haciendas, they are all pretty much alike, so far as we have seen; a great stone building, which is neither farm nor country-house (according to our notions), but has a character peculiar to itself—solid enough to stand a siege, with floors of painted brick, large deal tables, wooden benches, painted chairs, and whitewashed walls; one or two painted or iron bedsteads, only put up when wanted; numberless empty rooms; kitchen and outhouses; the court-yard a great square, round which stand the house for boiling the sugar, whose furnaces blaze day and night; the house, with machinery for extracting the juice from the cane, the refining rooms, the places where it is dried, etc., all on a large scale. If the hacienda is, as here, a coffee plantation also, then there is the great mill for separating the beans from the chaff, and sometimes also there are buildings where they make brandy. Here there are four hundred men employed, exclusive of boys, one hundred horses, and a number of mules. The property is generally very extensive, containing the fields of sugar-cane, plains for cattle, and the pretty plantations of coffee, so green and spring-like, this one containing upwards of fifty thousand young plants, all fresh and vigorous, besides a great deal of uncultivated ground, abandoned to the deer and hares and quails, of which there are great abundance. For four months in the year, *tierra caliente* must be a paradise, and it has the advantage over the coasts, in being quite free from yellow fever. But the heat in summer, and the number of poisonous insects, are great drawbacks. Of these, the *alacrans*, or scor-pions, which haunt all the houses, are amongst the worst. Their bite is poisonous, and, to a child, deadly, which is one of the many reasons why these estates are left entirely to the charge of an agent, and though visited occasionally by the proprietor, rarely lived in by the family. The effects are more or less violent in different constitutions. Some persons will re-main for eight days in convulsions, foaming at the mouth, and the stomach swelled, as if by dropsy; others, by immediate remedies, do not suffer much. The chief cures are brandy, taken in sufficient quantities to stupefy the patient, guyacum and boiled silk, which last is considered most efficacious. In Durango they are particularly numerous and venomous, so that a reward is given for so many *head* of scorpions to the boys there, to encourage them to destroy them. The Señora ——, who lives there, feels no inconvenience from their bite, but the scorpion who bites her immediately dies! It is pre-tended that they prefer dark people to fair, which is to sup-pose them very discriminating. Though as yet there have been few seen in the houses, I must confess that we feel rather un-easy at night, and scrupulously examine our beds and their environs before venturing to go to sleep. The walls being pur-posely whitewashed, it is not difficult to detect them; but where the roofs are formed of beams, they are very apt to drop through.

There are other venomous reptiles, for whose sting there is no remedy, and if you would like to have a list of these interesting creatures, according to the names by which they are known in these parts, I can furnish you with one from the best authority. These, however, are generally to be found about outhouses, and only occasionally visit your apartments. There is the *chicaclina,* a striped viper, of beautiful colours—the *coralillo,* a viper of a coral colour, with a black head—the *vinagrillo,* an animal like a large cricket. You can discover it, when in the room, by its strong smell of vinegar. It is orange-coloured, and taps upon the person whom it crawls over, without giving any pain, but leaving a long train of deadly poison —I have fancied that I smelt vinegar in every room since hearing this—the *salamanquesa,* whose bite is fatal: it is shaped like a lizard—the *eslaboncillo,* which throws itself upon you, and if prevented from biting you, dies of spite—the *cencoatl,* which has five feet, and shines in the dark; so that fortunately a warning is given of the vicinity of these animals in different ways; in some by the odour they exhale, in some by the light they emit, and in others, like the rattlesnake, by the sound they give out.

Then there is a beautiful black and red spider, called the *chinclaquili,* whose sting sends a pain through all your bones; the only cure for which is to be shut up for several days in a room thick with smoke. There are also the *tarantula* and *casampulga* spiders. Of the first, which is a shocking-looking soft fat creature, covered with dark hair, it is said that the horse which treads on it instantly loses its hoof—but this wants confirmation. Of the scorpions, the small yellowish coloured ones are the most dangerous, and it is pretended that their bite is most to be apprehended at midday. The workmen occasionally eat them, after pulling out the sting. The flesh of the viper is also eaten roasted, as a remedy against eruptions of the skin. Methinks the remedy is worse than the disease. . . .

But to banish this *creeping* subject, which seems not at all in unison with the lovely scenes that surround us—an Eden where no serpent should enter—we have been riding this evening to a beautiful little Indian village called *Acapansingo,* than which I never beheld anything prettier in its way. Some few houses there are of stone, but the generality are of cane, and each cottage is surrounded by its fruit-trees, and by others covered with lilac or white blossoms, and twined with creepers. The lanes or streets of the village are cleanly swept, and shaded by the blossoming branches that overhang them; while every now and then they are crossed by little streams of the purest water. I think I never knew what really delicious water was till I came here. The Indians, both men and women, looked clean, and altogether this is the prettiest Indian village we have yet seen.

As we are very anxious to visit the celebrated cave of Cacauamilpa, near the city of Cautlamilpa, and also to see as much of *tierra caliente* as possible, we have determined, though with regret, to leave our present quarters at Atlacamulto to-morrow morning, at two o'clock A.M. As there are no inns, we are furnished with letters of recommendation to the proprietors of the chief haciendas in these parts. Formerly there was so much hospitality here, that an annual sum (three thousand dollars it is said) was assigned by the proprietors to their agents, for the reception of travellers, whether rich or poor, and whether recommended or not. . . .

Our plan of visiting the cave has been nearly frustrated by the arrival of General C——s, a neighbouring proprietor, who assured us that we were going to undertake an impossibility; that the barrancas, by which we must pass to arrive at the cave, were impassable for women, the mountain paths being so steep and perpendicular, that men and horses had frequently fallen backwards in the ascent, or been plunged forward over the precipices, in attempting to descend. We were in despair, when it was suggested that there was another, though much longer road to the cave, by which we might ride; and though our time is at present very precious, we were too glad to agree to this compromise.

C——n and A—— have returned from a shooting expedition, in which they have not been very successful; and though I have only recounted to you the beginning of our adventures, I must stop here, and take a few hours' rest before we set off on our *matinal* expedition.

LETTER THE THIRTY-SECOND

Leave Atlacamulco—*Assemble by Starlight—Balmy Atmos-phere—Flowers and Trees of the Tropics—The Formidable* Barrancas—*Breakfast under the Trees—Force of the Sun—* Meacatlan—*Hospitality—Profitable Estate—Leave Meacat-lan—Beautiful Village—Musical Bells—Ride by Moonlight—Sugar Fires—Cocoyotla—Old Gentleman—Supper—Orange-trees and Cocoas—Delicious Water—Sugar Estates—A Scor-pion—Set off for the Cave—Morning Ride—Dangerous Path.*

COCOYOTLA, 5th.

On the morning of the third of February we rose about half-past two, and a little after three, by the light of the stars and the blaze of the sugar fires, our whole party were assembled on horseback in the courtyard. We were about twelve in number. Don Juan, the coffee-planter, and Don Pedro, a friend of his, were deputed by the agent to act as our guides. Four or five well-armed *mozos*, farm-servants, were our escort, together with our Mexican boy; and we had mules to carry our luggage, which was compressed into the smallest possible compass. The morning was perfectly enchanting, and the air like balm, when we set off by this uncertain light; not on roads (much to our satisfaction), but through fields, and over streams, up hills and down into valleys, climbing among stones, the horses picking their way like goats. I certainly never felt or imagined such an atmosphere. The mere inhaling it was sufficient pleasure.

When the light gradually began to dawn, so that we could discern each other's faces, and made sure that we were not a party of shadows, for besides the obscurity, a mixture of sleepi-ness and placid delight had hitherto kept us all silent, we looked round on the landscape, as little by little it assumed form and consistency. The fires from the hacienda were still visible, but growing pale in the beams of morning, vanishing like false visions from before the holy light of truth. As we rode along, we found that the scenery on the hilly parts was generally bleak and sterile, the grass dried up, and very little vegetation; but wherever we arrived at a valley sheltered from the sun's rays, there we found a little rivulet trickling through it, with water like liquid diamonds, bathing the trees and the flowers—the loveliest blossoming trees, mingled with bananas, oranges, and lemons, and interspersed with bright flowers, forming a natural garden and orchard.

One tree, with no leaves on it, is covered with white starry flowers, and looks at a distance as if it had been covered with snow, which had melted off the branches, leaving only occasional white tufts. Another is bending with lilac blossoms, which hang in graceful clusters—another with flowers like yellow balls. Then there are scarlet wild flowers, that seem as if they were made of wax or shining coral, and quantities of white jasmine, trailing on the grass, and throwing itself over the branches of the trees. There is one beautiful tree, with flowers like immense white lilies, and buds that look like shut lily blossoms in white wax.

Leaving these beautiful and fertile lands that adorn the slopes and bases of the hills, you mount again up the steep paths, and again you find the grass dried up, and no vegetation but stunted nopals or miserable-looking blue-green magueys. Yet sometimes in the most desert spot, a little sheltered by a projecting hill, you come upon the most beautiful tree, bending with rich blossoms, standing all alone, as if through ambition it had deserted its lowly sisters in the valley, and stood, in its exalted station, solitary and companionless.

As for the names of these tropical trees, they are almost all Indian, and it is only *botanically* that they can be properly distinguished. There is the *floripundio,* with white odoriferous flowers hanging like bells from its branches, with large pointed pale-green leaves—the *yollojochitl,* signifying flower of the heart, like white stars with yellow hearts, which when shut have the form of one, and the fragrance of which is delicious —the *izgujochitl,* whose flowers look like small white musk-roses—another with a long Indian name, and which means the flower of the raven, and is white, red, and yellow. The Indians use it to adorn their altars, and it is very fragrant as well as beautiful.

After six hours' good riding, our guides pointed out to us the formidable barrancas at some distance, and expressed their opinion, that, with great caution, our horses being very sure-footed, we might venture to pass them, by which means we should save three leagues, and be enabled to reach an hacienda within six leagues of the cave that night; and after some deliberation, it was agreed that the attempt should be made. These barrancas (the word literally means a ravine or mountain gully) are two mountains, one behind the other, which it is necessary to cross by a narrow path, that looks like a road for goats. We began the ascent in silence, and some fear, one by one till the horses were nearly perpendicular. It lasted about twenty minutes; and we then began to descend slowly, certainly not without some danger of being thrown over our horses' heads. However, we arrived in safety at the end of the first mountain, and this being accomplished, drew up to rest our horses and mules beside a beautiful clear stream, bordered by flowering trees. Here some clear-headed individual of the party proposed that we should open our hamper, containing cold chicken, hard eggs, sherry, etc.; observing, that it was time to be hungry. His suggestion was agreed to without a dissenting voice, and a napkin being spread under a shady tree, no time was lost in proving the truth of his observation. A very ingenious contrivance for making a wine-glass, by washing an egg-shell in the stream, is worthy of record. When we had demolished the cold chicken, the *mozos* surrounded the cold meat, and after gathering branches covered with beautiful flowers, with which we ornamented our horses' heads and our own hats, we prepared to ascend the second mountain. This is as steep, or nearly as steep as the first; but we were already confident in the sure-footedness of our horses, and even able to admire the view as we ascended single file. After much rain, this path must of course be completely impassable. The day had now become oppressively warm, though it was not later than eleven o'clock; and having passed the hills, we came to a dusty high-road, which, about twelve, brought us to the hacienda of Meacatlan, belonging to the family of Perez Palacio. We were overtaken on the road by the eldest son of the proprietor, who cordially invited us in, and introduced us to the ladies of his family, and to his father, a fine, noble-looking old gentleman. As we were excessively tired, hot, and dusty, we were very glad to spend a few hours here during the heat of the sun; and after joining the family at breakfast, consisting of the most extraordinary variety of excellent dishes, with a profusion of fine fruits and curious sweetmeats (amongst which was that ethereal-looking production, called *angel's hair, cabella de angel*), we were glad to lie down and rest till four o'clock.

This hacienda is very productive and valuable, and has a silver mine on it.

There is also every variety of fine fruit, especially the largest *cedrats* I ever saw; which, although they have not a great deal of flavour, are very refreshing. With all their beauty and fertility, there is something very lonely in a residence on these estates, which are so entirely shut out of the world; not so much for the proprietors themselves, who are occupied in the care of their interests, but for the female part of the family.

We left this hospitable mansion about four o'clock, rested and refreshed, the proprietor giving K—— a horse of his, instead of her own, which was tired. The sun was still powerful, when we and our train remounted, but the evening had become delightfully cool, by the time that we had reached the beautiful village of San Francisco de Tetecala, lying amongst wooded hills, its white houses gleaming out from amidst the orange-trees, with a small river crossed by bridges running through it. Many of the houses were tolerably large and well built. It was a fête-day, and the musical bells ringing merrily; the people were clean and well dressed, and were assembled in crowds in an enclosure, looking at a bull-fight, which must be hot work in this climate, both for man and beast.

But when the moon rose serenely, and without a cloud, and a soft breeze, fragrant with orange blossom, blew gently over the trees, I felt as if we might have rode on for ever, without fatigue, and in a state of the most perfect enjoyment. It were hard to say whether the first soft breath of morning, or the languishing and yet more fragrant airs of evening were most enchanting. Sometimes we passed through a village of scattered Indian huts, with little fires of sticks lighted in their courts, glowing on the bronze faces of the women and children; and at the sound of our horses' hoofs, a chorus of dogs, yelping with most discordant fury, would give us loud notice of their total disapprobation of all night travellers. Sometimes a decided smell of boiled sugar was mingled with the fragrance of the orange blossom and jasmine; reminding us of those happy days of yore, when the housekeeper in all her glory, was engaged in making her annual stock of jellies and jams.

Once we were obliged to dismount, that our horses might make an *ugly leap* over a great ditch guarded by thorny bushes, and amongst trees where the moon gave us no light.

About ten o'clock symptoms of weariness began to break out amongst us, spite of moonbeams and orange-buds; when down in a valley we saw the sugar fires of *Cocoyotla*, the hacienda to which we trusted for our next place of shelter, darting out their fierce red tongues amongst the trees. We knocked for admittance at the great gate, and it was some time before the people within would undo the fastenings, which they did with great caution, and after carefully reconnoitring us; afterwards giving for excuse, that a party of thirty robbers had passed by the night before, and that they thought we might have been some of these *night-errants*. We sent in our credentials to the proprietor, an old gentleman married to a young wife, who, living on the road to the cave, is by no means pleased at his house being turned into a posada for all and sundry, and complained bitterly of a party of Englishmen who had passed by some time before, "and the only *Spanish* word they could say, was *Vater*, by which they meant *Agua*, Caramba!" However, he was very hospitable to us, and pressed us to remain there the following day, and rest ourselves and our horses after our fourteen leagues march, previous to going on to the cave.

A very good supper and a very sound sleep were refreshing, and the whole of the next day we spent in wandering about or sitting lazily amongst the magnificent orange-trees and cocoas of this fine hacienda. Here the orange-trees are the loftiest we had yet seen; long ranges of noble trees, loaded with fruit and flowers. At the back of the house is a small grove of cocoas, and a clear running stream passing through beautiful flowers, and refreshing everything in its course. Indeed all through *tierra caliente*, except on the barren hills, there is a profusion of the most delicious water, here at once a necessity and a luxury.

These sugar estates are under high cultivation, the crops abundant, the water always more than sufficient both for the purposes of irrigation and for machinery, which A—— considers equal to anything he has seen in Jamaica. They produce annually from thirty to fifty thousand *arrobas* of sugar. The labourers are free Indians, and are paid from two and a half to six and a half reals per day. I believe that about one hundred and fifty are sufficient for working on a large estate. Bountiful nature, walking on the traces of civil war, fills up the ravages caused by sanguinary revolutions, and these estates in the valley of Cuernavaca, which have so frequently been theatres of bloodshed, and have so often changed proprietors, remain in themselves as fertile and productive as ever.

In the evening we visited the *trapiche*, as they call the sugar-works, the sugar-boilers, warehouses, store-rooms, and engines. The heat is so intense among these great boilers, that we could not endure it for more than a few minutes, and pitied the men who have to spend their lives in this work. They make *panoja* on this estate, cakes of coarse sugar, which the common people prefer to the refined sugar.

Just as we were preparing to retire for the night, an animal on the wall attracted our attention, close by K——'s bed—and, gentle reader! it was a scorpion! We gave a simultaneous cry, which brought Señor —— into the room, who laughed at our fears, and killed our foe; when lo! just as our fright had passed away, another, a yellowish-coloured, venomous-looking creature, appeared stealing along the wall. The lady of the house came this time, and ordered the room and the beds to be searched. No more could be discovered, but it was difficult to sleep in peace after such an apparition.

At three the next morning we rose, and set off by moon and starlight for the cave. The morning was lovely as usual, and quite cool. We passed a great deal of barren and hilly road, till we reached some plains, where we had a delightful gallop, and arrived early at a small rancho, or farmhouse, where we were to procure guides for the cave. Here we added four Indians, and the master of the house, *Benito,* to our party, which was afterwards increased by numbers of men and boys, till we formed a perfect regiment. This little rancho, with its small garden, was very clean and neat. The woman of the house told us she had seen no ladies since an English *Ministra* had slept there two nights. We concluded that this must have been Mrs. Ashburnham, who spent two days in exploring the cave. We continued our ride over loose stones, and dry, rocky hills, where, were the horses not sure-footed, and used to climb, the riders' necks would no doubt suffer. Within about a quarter of a mile of the cave, after leaving on our right the pretty village of Cautlamilpas, we found ourselves in a place which I consider much more dangerous than even the barrancas near *Meacatlan;* a narrow path, overhanging a steep precipice, and bordering a perpendicular hill, with just room for the horses' feet, affording the comfortable assurance that one false step would precipitate you to the bottom. I confess to having held my breath, as one by one, and step by step, no one looking to the right or the left, our gowns occasionally catching on a bush, with our whole train we wound slowly down this narrow descent. Arrived near the mouth of the cave, we dismounted, and climbed our way among stones and gravel to the great mountain opening. But an account of the cave itself must be reserved till our return to Atlacamulco.

LETTER THE THIRTY-THIRD

Cave of Cacahuamilpa—*Superstition*—*Long-bearded Goat* — *Portal* — *Vestibule* — *Fantastic Forms* — *Breakfast* — *Pine Torches*—*Noble Hall*—*Stalactites and Stalagmites*—*Egyptian Pyramids*—*Double Gallery*—*Wonderful Formations*— *Corridor* — *Frozen Landscape* — *Amphitheatre* — *World in Chaos*—*Skeleton*—*Wax Lights*—*Hall of Angels*—*Return*— *Distant Light*—*Indian Alcalde*—Cautlamilpas—*Rancho*—*Return to Cocoyotla*—*Chapel*—*Meacatlan*—*Eclipse of the Moon* —*Benighted Travellers*—*Indian Village*—El Puente—*Return to* Atlacamulco.

The cave of Cacahuamilpa, whose actual wonders equal the fabled descriptions of the palaces of Genii, was, until lately, known to the Indians alone, or if the Spaniards formerly knew anything about it, its existence was forgotten amongst them. But although in former days it may have been used as a place of worship, a superstitious fear prevented the more modern Indians from exploring its shining recesses, for here it was firmly believed the evil spirit had his dwelling, and in the form of a goat, with long beard and horns, guarded the entrance of the cave. The few who ventured there and beheld this apparition, brought back strange tales to their credulous companions, and even the neighbourhood of the enchanted cave was avoided, especially at nightfall.

The chain of mountains, into whose bosom it leads, is bleak and bare, but the ravine below is refreshed by a rapid stream, that forms small waterfalls as it tumbles over the rocks, and is bordered by green and flowering trees. Amongst these, is one with a smooth, satin-like bark, of a pale golden colour, whose roots have something snakish and witch-like in their appearance, intertwining with each other, grappling as it were with the hard rock, and stretching out to the most extraordinary distance.

We arrived at the entrance of the cave, a superb portal, upwards of seventy feet high, and one hundred and fifty wide, according to the computation of a learned traveller—the rocks which support the great arch so symmetrically disposed as to resemble a work of art. The sun was already high in the heavens, shining with intense brightness on the wild scenery that surrounded us, the rocks and trees and rushing waters; a sensation of awe came over us as we stood at the mouth of the cave, and, turning from day to night, strained our eyes to look down a deep descent into a gigantic vaulted hall, faintly lighted by the red embers of a fire which the Indians had kindled near the entrance. We made our way down a declivity of, it may be, one hundred and fifty feet, surrounded by blocks of stone and rock, and remained lost in astonishment at finding ourselves in this gloomy subterranean palace, surrounded by the most extraordinary, gigantic, and mysterious forms, which it is scarcely possible to believe are the fantastic productions of the water which constantly trickles from the roof.

I am shocked to confess it—I would prefer passing it over —but we had tasted nothing that morning, and we had rode for eight hours, and were dying of hunger! Moreover we travelled with a cook, a very tolerable native artist, but without sentiment—his heart in his stew-pan; and he, without the least compunction, had begun his frying and broiling operations in what seemed the very vestibule of Pharaoh's palace. Our own *mozos* and our Indian guides were assisting in its operations with the utmost zeal; and in a few minutes, some sitting round the fire, and others upon broken pyramids, we refreshed ourselves with fried chicken, bread, and hard eggs, before proceeding farther on our exploring expedition. Unromantic as this proceeding was, we looked, Indians and all, rather awful, with no other light than the ruddy glare of the fire, flickering upon the strange, gigantic forms in that vast labyrinth; and as to what we felt, our valour and strength of mind were increased sevenfold.

Twenty-four huge pine torches were then lighted, each man carrying one. To K—— and me were given lighted wax candles, in case by accident any one should go astray from his companions, and lose his way, as would too certainly happen, in the different windings and galleries and compartments of the cave, and be alone in the darkness! We walked on in awe and wonder, the guides lighting up the sides of the cavern with their torches. Unfortunately, it is indescribable; as in the fantastic forms of the clouds, every one sees some different creation of his fancy in these stupendous masses. It is said that the first *sala*, for travellers have pretended to divide it into halls, and a very little imagination may do so, is about two hundred feet long, one hundred and seventy wide, and one hundred and fifty in height—a noble apartment. The walls are shaded with different colours of green and orange; great sheets of stalactites hang from the roof: and white phantoms, palm-trees, lofty pillars, pyramids, porches, and a thousand other illusions, surround us on all sides. One figure, concerning which all agree, is a long-haired goat, the Evil One in that form. But some one has broken the head, perhaps to show the power-lessness of the enchanted guardian of the cave. Some say that there are no living animals here, but there is no doubt that there are bats; and an exploring party, who passed the night here, not only heard the hissing of the rattlesnake, but were startled by the apparition of a fierce leopard, whose loud roar-ings were echoed amongst the vaults, and who, after gazing at them by the light of the torches, stalked majestically back into the darkness.

We passed on to the second *sala,* collecting as we went fragments of the shining stones, our awe and astonishment in-creasing at every step. Sometimes we seemed to be in a sub-terranean Egyptian temple. The architecture was decidedly Egyptian, and the strange forms of the animals resembled those of the uncouth Egyptian idols; which, together with the pyramids and obelisks, made me think, that perhaps that an-cient people took the idea of their architecture and of many of their strange shapes from some natural cave of this descrip-tion, just as nature herself suggested the idea of the beautiful Corinthian pillar.

Again we seemed to enter a tract of country which had been petrified. Fountains of congealed water, trees hung with frozen moss, pillars covered with gigantic acanthus leaves, pyramids of ninety feet high losing their lofty heads in the darkness of the vault, and looking like works of the pre-Adamites; yet no being but He who inhabits eternity could have created them. This second hall, as lofty as the other, may be nearly four hundred feet in length.

We then passed into a sort of double gallery, separated by enormous pyramidal formations—*stalagmites,* those which are formed by water dropping on the earth. The ground was damp, and occasionally great drops trickled on our heads from the vaults above. Here Gothic shrines, odd figures; some that look like mummies, others like old men with long beards, ap-pal us like figures that we see in some wild dream. These are intermingled with pyramids, obelisks, baths that seem made of the purest alabaster, etc. A number of small round balls, petrifactions of a dead white, lie about here, forming little hollows in the ground. Here the cave is very wide—about two hundred feet, it is said.

When we left this double gallery, we came to another vast corridor, supported by lofty pillars, covered with creeping plants, but especially with a row of the most gigantic cauliflowers, each leaf delicately chiseled, and looking like a fitting food for the colossal dwellers of the cavern. But to attempt anything like a regular description is out of the question. We gave ourselves up to admiration, as our torches flashed upon the masses of rock, the hills crowned with pyramids, the congealed torrents that seem to belong to winter at the north pole, and the lofty Doric columns that bring us back to the pure skies of Greece. But amongst all these curious *accidents* produced by water, none is more curiously exquisite than an amphitheatre, with regular benches, surmounted by a great organ, whose pipes, when struck, give forth a deep sound. It is really difficult not to believe that some gigantic race once amused themselves in these petrified solitudes, or that we have not invaded the sanctuary of some mysterious and superhuman beings. It is said that this cavern has been explored for four leagues, and yet that no exit has been discovered. As for us, I do not know how far we went: our guides said a league. It seemed impossible to think of time when we looked at these great masses, formed drop by drop, slowly and rarely and at distant intervals falling, and looked back upon the ages that must have elapsed since these gigantic formations began.

At length, on account of the loose stones, the water, and the masses of crystal rock that we had to climb over, our guides strongly recommended us to return. It was difficult to turn away our eyes from the great unformed masses that now seemed to fill the cave as far as the eye could reach. It looked like the world in chaos—nature's vast workshop, from which she drew the materials which her hand was to reduce to form and order. We retraced our steps slowly and lingeringly through these subterranean palaces, feeling that one day was not nearly sufficient to explore them, yet thankful that we had not left the country without seeing them. The skeleton of a man was discovered here by some travellers, lying on his side, the head nearly covered with crystallization. He had probably entered these labyrinths alone, either from rash curiosity or to escape from pursuit; lost his way and perished from hunger. Indeed to find the way back to the entrance of the cave is nearly impossible, without some clue to guide the steps amongst these winding galleries, halls, and issues and entries, and divided corridors.

Though there are some objects so striking that they may immediately be recognised, such as the amphitheatre for instance, there is a monotony even in the variety! and I can imagine the unfortunate man wandering amongst obelisks and pyramids and alabaster baths and Grecian columns—amongst frozen torrents that could not assuage his thirst, and trees with marble fruit and foliage, and crystal vegetables that mocked his hunger: and pale phantoms with long hair and figures in shrouds, that could not relieve his distress—and then his cries for help, where the voice gives out an echo, as if all the pale dwellers in the cave answered in mockery—and then, his torch becoming extinguished, and he lying down exhausted and in despair near some inhospitable marble porch, to die.

As we went along, our guides had climbed up and placed wax candles on the top of all the highest points, so that their pale glimmering light pointed out the way to us on our return. The Indians begged they might be left there "on account of the blessed souls in purgatory," which was done. As we returned, we saw one figure we had not observed before, which looks something like a woman mounted on an enormous goat. To one hall, on account of its beauty, some travellers have given the name of the "Hall of Angels." It is said that, by observation, the height of the stalagmites might determine the age of their formation, but where is the enterprising geologist who would shut himself up in these crystal solitudes sufficiently long for correct observation?

I never saw or could have imagined so beautiful an effect as that of the daylight in the distance, entering by the mouth of the cave; such a faint misty blue, contrasted with the fierce red light of the torches, and broken by the pillars through which its pale rays struggled. It looked so pure and holy, that it seemed like the light from an angel's wings at the portals of the "*città dolente.*" What would that poor traveller have given to have seen its friendly rays! After climbing out and leaving the damp, cool subterraneous air, the atmosphere felt dry and warm, as we sat down to rest at the mouth of the cavern, surrounded by our Indian torch-bearers. Truly, nature is no coquette. She adorns herself with greater riches in the darkest mountain cave, than on the highest mountain top.

We were sitting in thoughtful silence, ourselves, Indians and all, in a circle, when we saw, stumping down the hill, in great haste, and apparently in great wrath, an Indian alcalde, with a thick staff in his hand, at whose approach the Indians looked awe-struck. He carried in his brown hand a large letter, on which was written in great type; "*Al Señor dominante de esta caravana de gente.*" "To the Commander of this caravan of people!" This missive set forth that the justice of peace of the city of Cuautla Amilpas, begged to know by what right, by whose authority, and with what intentions we had entered this cave, without permission from government; and desired the "Señor dominante" to appear forthwith before the said justice for contempt of his authority. The spelling of the letter was too amusing. The Indians looked very much alarmed, and when they saw us laugh, still more astonished. C——n wrote with a pencil in answer to the summons, that he was the Spanish Minister, and wished good day to the alcalde, who plodded up the hill again, very ill pleased.

We now took leave of this prodigious subterranean palace, and again put ourselves *en route.* Once more we wound our way round the brink of the precipice, and this time it was more dangerous for us than before, for we rode on the side next it, our gowns overhanging the brink, and if caught by a branch there, might have been dragged over. Our two guides afterwards said that if alone, they would have dismounted; but that as the ladies said nothing, they did not like to propose it.

Some day, no doubt, this cave will become a show-place, and measures will be taken to render the approach to it less dangerous; but as yet, one of its charms consists in its being unhackneyed. For, long after, its recollection rests upon the mind, like a marble dream. But, like Niagara, it cannot be described; perhaps even it is more difficult to give an idea of this underground creation, than of the emperor of cataracts; for there is nothing with which the cave can be compared.

Meanwhile, we had rather a disagreeable ride, in all the force of the sun's last rays, back to the rancho. No one spoke —all our thoughts were wandering amongst marble palaces, and uncouth, gigantic, half-human forms.

But our attention was again attracted by the sudden reappearance of our friend, the alcalde, on the brow of the hill, looking considerably indignant. He came with a fresh summons from the judge of Cuautla Amilpas, which lay white and glittering in the valley below. C——n endeavoured gravely to explain to him that the persons of ambassadors were not subject to such laws, which was Greek and Hebrew to him of the bronze countenance. "If it were a *Consul* indeed, there might be something in that." At last our guide, the ranchero, promised to call upon the judge in the evening, and explain the matter to his satisfaction; and again our alcalde departed upon his bootless errand—bootless in every sense, as he stalked down the hill with his bare bronze supporters. As we passed along, a parcel of soldiers in the village were assembled in haste, who struck up an imposing military air, to give us some idea of their importance.

Politically speaking, Cuautla Amilpas has been the theatre of important events. It was there that the curate Morelos shut himself up with a troop of insurgents, until the place being besieged by the Spaniards under Calleja, and the party of Morelos driven to extremity for want of food, he secretly abandoned his position, drawing off his forces in the night.

When we arrived at the rancho, we found that a message had come from the judge, prohibiting Don Benito from accompanying strangers to the cave in future, which would be hard upon the old man, who makes a little money by occasionally guiding strangers there. C——n has therefore written on the subject to the *prefect* of the department.

In the cool of the evening, we had a delightful ride to Cocoyotla. The air was soft and fragrant—the bells of the villages were ringing amongst the trees, for every village, however poor, has at least one fine church, and all the bells in Mexico, whether in the city or in the villages, have a mellow and musical sound, owing, it is said, to the quantity of silver that enters into their composition.

It was late when we arrived at Cocoyotla, but we did not go to rest without visiting the beautiful chapel, which we had omitted to do on our last visit; it is very rich in gilding and ornaments, very large and in good taste. We supped, and threw ourselves down to rest for a few hours, and set off again at three o'clock, by the light of a full moon. Our greatest difficulty in these hurried marches is to get our things in and out of our portmanteaus, and to dress in time in the dark. No looking-glasses of course—we arrange our hair by our imagination. Everything gets broken, as you may suppose; the mules that carry our trunks cantering up and down the hills to keep up with us, in most unequal measure.

The moon was still high, though pale, when the sun rose, like a youthful monarch impatient to take the reins from the hands of a mild and dying queen. We had a delightful gallop, and soon left the fires of Cocoyotla far behind us. After riding six leagues, we arrived at six in the morning at the house of the Perez Palacios. We should have gone further while it was cool; but their hospitality, added to a severe fit of toothache which had attacked C——n, induced us to remain till four o'clock, during which time we improved our acquaintance with the family. How strange and even melancholy are those glimpses which travellers have of persons whom they will probably never meet again; with whom they form an intimacy, which owing to peculiar circumstances seems very like friendship—much nearer it certainly, than many a long acquaintanceship which we form in great cities, and where the parties go on *knowing each other* from year to year, and never exchanging more than a mere occasional and external civility.

It was four o'clock when we left Meacatlan, and we rode hard and fast till it grew nearly dark, for our intention was to return to our head-quarters at Atlacamulco that night, and we had a long journey before us, especially as it was decided that we should by no means attempt to recross the barrancas by night, which would have been too dangerous. Besides an eclipse of the moon was predicted, and in fact, as we were riding across the fields, she appeared above the horizon, half in shadow, a curious and beautiful spectacle. But we should have been thankful for her entire beams, for after riding for hours we discovered that we had lost our way, and worse still, that there were no hopes of our finding it. Not a hut was in sight—darkness coming on—nothing but great plains and mountains to be distinguished, and nothing to be heard but bulls roaring round us. We went on, trusting to chance, and where chance would have led us it is hard to say; but by good fortune our advanced guard stumbled over two Indians, a man and a boy, who agreed to guide us to their own village, but nowhere else.

After following them a long and weary way, all going at a pretty brisk trot, the barking of hundreds of dogs announced an Indian village, and by the faint light we could just distinguish the cane huts snugly seated amongst bananas and with little enclosed gardens before each. Our cavalcade drew up before a hut, a sort of tavern or spirit-shop, where an old half-naked hag, the *beau idéal* of a witch, was distributing *fire-water* to the Indians, most of whom were already drunk. We got off our horses and threw ourselves down on the ground too tired to care what they were doing, and by some means a cup of bad chocolate was procured for us. We found that we had entirely lost our way, and it was therefore agreed, that instead of attempting to reach Atlacamulco that night, we should ride to the village of el Puente, where our conductors knew a Spanish family of bachelor brothers, who would be glad to *harbour* us for the remainder of the night. We then remounted and set off somewhat refreshed by our rest and by the bad chocolate.

It was late at night when we entered el Puente, after having crossed in pitch darkness a river so deep that the horses were nearly carried off their feet; yet they were dancing in one place, playing cards on the ground in another, dogs were barking as usual, and candles lighted in the Indian huts. We were very well received by the Spaniards, who gave us supper and made us take their room, all the rest of the party sleeping upon mattresses placed on the floor of a large empty apartment. We slept a few hours very soundly, rose before daylight, wakened the others, who, lying on the ground, rolled up in their sarapes, seemed to be sleeping for a wager, and remounted our horses, not sorry at the prospect of a day's rest at Atlacamulco. It was dark when we set off; but the sun had risen and had lighted up the bright green fields of sugar-cane, and the beautiful coffee-plantations that look like flowering myrtles, by the time we reached the hacienda of Señor Neri del Barrio, whose family is amongst the most distinguished of the old *Spanish Mexican* stock. We stopped to take a tumbler of milk fresh from the cow; declined an invitation to go in, as we were anxious to finish our journey while it was cool; and after a hard ride galloped into the courtyard of Atlacamulco, which seemed like returning home. We spent a pleasant, idle day, lying down and reading while the sun was high, and in the evening sauntering about under the orange-trees. We concluded with a hot bath.

7th.—Before continuing our journey, we determined to spend one more day here, which was fortunate, as we received a large packet of letters from home, forwarded to this place, and we have been reading them, stretched under the shade of a natural bower formed by orange-boughs, near a clear, cold tank of water in the garden. To-morrow we shall set off betimes for the hacienda of Cocoyoc, the property of Don Juan Goriva, with whom C——n was acquainted in Mexico. After visiting that and some other of the principal estates, we shall continue our ride to Puebla, and as we shall pass a few days there, hope to have leisure to write again from that city.

LETTER THE THIRTY-FOURTH

On the 9th of February we took leave of Atlacamulco and the
hospitable administrador, and our party being diminished by
the absence of Don Pedro, who was obliged to go to Mexico,
we set off as usual by starlight, being warned of various *bad
bits* on the road, where the ladies at least were advised to dismount. The country was wild and pretty, mountainous and
stony. When the light came in we separated and galloped
about in all directions. The air was cool and laden with sweetness. We came, however, to a pretty lane, where those of our
escort who were in front stopped, and those who were behind
rode up and begged us to keep close together, as for many
leagues the country was haunted by robbers. Guns and pistols
being looked to, we rode on in serried ranks, expecting every
moment to hear a bullet whizz over our heads.

Here were the most beautiful wild flowers we have yet seen;
some purple, white, and rose-colour in one blossom; probably
the flower called *ocelojo-chitl*, or viper's head, others bright
scarlet, others red, with white and yellow stripes, and with an
Indian name, signifying the tiger's flower; some had rose-
coloured blossoms, others were of the purest white.

We came at last to a road over a mountain, about as bad as
anything we had yet seen. Our train of horses and mules, and
men in their Mexican dresses, looked very picturesque winding up and down these steep crags; and here again, forgetful
of robbers, each one wandered according to his own fancy,
some riding forward, and others lingering behind to pull

branches of these beautiful wild blossoms. The horses' heads were covered with flowers of every colour, so that they looked like victims adorned for sacrifice. C——n indulged his botanical and geological propensities, occasionally to the great detriment of his companions, as we were anxious to arrive at some resting-place before the sun became insupportable. As for the robbers, these gentlemen, who always keep a sharp look-out, and rarely endanger their precious persons without some sufficient motive, and who, moreover, seem to have some magical power of seeing through stone walls and into portmanteaus, were no doubt aware that our luggage would neither have replenished their own nor their *ladies'* wardrobes, and calculated that people who travel for pleasure are not likely to carry any great quantity of superfluous coin. Besides this, they are much more afraid of these honest, stout, well-armed farm servants, who are a fine race of men, than even soldiers.

We arrived about six o'clock at the village of Hautepec, remarkable for its fine old church and lofty trees, especially for one magnificent wide-spreading ash-tree in the churchyard. There were also many of those pretty trees with the silvery bark, which always look as if the moon were shining on them. The road began to improve, but the sun became very oppressive about nine o'clock, when we arrived at a pretty village, which had a large church and a *venta* (tavern), where we stopped to refresh ourselves with water and some very well-baked small cakes. The village was so pretty that we had some thoughts of remaining there till the evening, but as Don Juan assured us that one hour's good gallop would carry us to Cocoyoc, the hacienda of Don Juan Gorivar, we determined to continue. We had a dreadful ride in the hot sun, till we arrived at a pretty Indian village on the estate, and shortly after entered the courtyard of the great hacienda of Cocoyoc, where we were most hospitably welcomed by the proprietor and his family.

We were very tired owing to the extreme heat, and white with dust. A fresh toilet, cold water, an hour's rest, and an excellent breakfast, did wonders for us. Soon after our arrival, the sugar-house, or rather the cane rubbish, took fire, and the great bell swung heavily to and fro, summoning the workmen to assist in getting it under. It was not extinguished for some time, and the building is so near the house, that the family were a little alarmed. We stood on the balcony, which commands a beautiful view of Popocatepetl, watching the blaze.

After a hard battle between fire and water, water carried the day.

In the evening we drove to the orange grove, where three thousand lofty trees are ranged in avenues, literally bending under the weight of their golden fruit and snowy blossom. I never saw a more beautiful sight. Each tree is perfect, and lofty as a forest tree. The ground under their broad shadows is strewed with thousands of oranges, dropping in their ripeness, and covered with the white, fragrant blossoms. The place is lovely, and everywhere traversed by streams of the purest water. We ate a disgraceful number of oranges, limes, guayavas, and all manner of fruits, and even tasted the sweet beans of the coffee-plants.

We spent the next morning in visiting the coffee-mills, the great brandy-works, sugar-houses, etc., all which are in the highest order; and in strolling through the orange groves, and admiring the curious and beautiful flowers, and walking among orchards of loaded fruit-trees—the calabash, papaw, mango, tamarind, citron—also mameys, chirimoyas, custard apples, and all the family of the zapotes, white, black, yellow, and *chico;* cayotes, cocoas, cacahuates, aguacates, etc., etc., etc., a list without an end.

Besides these are an infinity of trees covered with the brightest blossoms; one, with large scarlet flowers, most gorgeous in their colouring, and one whose blossoms are so like large pink silk tassels, that if hung to the cushions of a sofa, you could not discover them to be flowers. What prodigality of nature in these regions! With what a lavish hand she flings beauty and luxury to her tropical children!

In the evening we drove to Casasano, an hacienda about three leagues from Cocoyoc, and passed by several other fine estates, amongst others, the hacienda of Calderon. Casasano is an immense old house, very dull-looking, the road to which lies through a fine park for cattle, dotted with great old trees, but of which the grass is very much burnt up. Each hacienda has a large chapel attached to it, at which all the workmen and villagers in the environs attend mass; a padre coming from a distance on Sundays and fête-days. Frequently there is one attached to the establishment. We went to see the celebrated water-tank of Casasano, the largest and most beautiful reservoir in this part of the country; the water so pure, that though upwards of thirty feet deep, every blade of grass at the bottom is visible. Even a pin, dropped upon the stones below, is seen shining quite distinctly. A stone wall, level with the water, thirty feet high, encloses it, on which I ventured to walk all round the tank, which is of an oval form, with the assistance of our host, going one by one. A fall would be sufficiently awkward, involving drowning on one side and breaking your neck on the other. The water is beautiful—a perfect mirror, with long green feathery plants at the bottom.

The next morning we took leave of our friends at three o'clock, and set off for Santa Clara, the hacienda of Don Eusebio Garcia. Señor Goriva made me a present of a very good horse, and our ride that day was delightful, though the roads led over the most terrible barrancas. For nine long leagues, we did nothing but ford rivers and climb steep hills, those who were pretty well mounted beating up the tired cavalry. But during the first hours of our ride, the air was so fresh among the hills, that even when the sun was high, we suffered little from the heat; and the beautiful and varied views we met at every turn were full of interest.

Santa Clara is a striking, imposing mass of building, beautifully situated at the foot of three bold, high rocks, with a remarkably handsome church attached to it. The family were from home, and the agent was a philosopher, living upon herb-tea, quite above the common affairs of life. It is a fine hacienda, and very productive, but sad and solitary in the extreme, and as K—— and I walked about in the courtyard after supper, where we had listened to frightful stories of robbers and robberies, we felt rather uncomfortably dreary, and anxious to change our quarters. We visited the sugar-works, which are like all others, the chapel, which is very fine, and the shop where they sell spirituous liquors and calicoes.

The hills looked gray and solemn. The sun sank gloomy behind them, his colour a turbid red. So much had been said about robbers, that we were not sure how our next day's journey might terminate. The administrador's own servant had turned out to be the captain of a band! whom the robbers, from some mysterious motive, had murdered a few days before.

As we intended to rise before dawn, we went to bed early, about nine o'clock, and were just in the act of extinguishing a melancholy-looking candle, when we were startled by the sight of an alacran on the wall. A man six feet high came at our call. He looked at the scorpion, shook his head, and ran out. He came back in a little while with another large man, he with a great shoe in his hand, and his friend with a long pole. While they were both hesitating how to kill it, Don Juan came in, and did the deed. We had a melancholy night after this, afraid of everything, with a long unsnuffed candle illuminating the darkness of our large and lonely chamber.

The next morning, the 11th of February, before sunrise, we took our leave, in the darkness, of Santa Clara and the philosopher. The morning, wonderful to relate, was windy, and almost cold. The roads were frightful, and we hailed the first gray streak that appeared in the eastern sky, announcing the dawn, which might enable us at least to see our perils. Fortunately it was bright daylight when we found ourselves crossing a barranca, so dangerous, that after following for some time the precipitous course of the mountain path, we thought it advisable to get off our horses, who were pawing the slippery rock, without being able to find any rest for the soles of their feet. We had a good deal of difficulty in getting along ourselves on foot among the loose, sharp stones, and the horses, between sliding and stumbling, were a long while in accomplishing the descent. After climbing up the barranca, one of them ran off along the edge of the cliff, as if he were determined to cut the whole concern, and we wasted some time in catching him.

It was the afternoon when we rode through the lanes of a large Indian village, and shortly after arrived at Colon, an hacienda belonging to Don Antonio Orria. He was from home, but the good reception of the honest administrador, the nice, clean, cheerful house, with its pretty painted chairs, good beds, the excellent breakfasts and dinners, and the *good will* visible in the whole establishment, delighted us very much, and decided us to pitch our tent here for a day or two. Some Spaniards, hearing of C——n's arrival, rode over from a distance to see him, and dined with us. There was a capital housekeeper, famous for her excellent cakes and preserves. We had also the refreshment of a warm bath, and felt ourselves as much at home as if we had been in our own house.

The next morning we rode through the great sugar-cane fields to the hacienda of San Nicolas, one of the finest estates in the republic, eighteen leagues long and five wide, belonging to Señor Zamora, in right of his wife. It is a productive place, but a singularly dreary residence. We walked out to see all the works, which are on a great scale, and breakfasted with the proprietor, who was there alone. We amused ourselves by seeing the workmen receive their weekly pay (this being Saturday), and at the mountains of copper piled up on tables in front of the house. There is a feeling of vastness, of solitude, and of dreariness in some of these great haciendas, which is oppressive. Especially about noon, when everything is still, and there is no sound except the incessant buzz of myriads of insects, I can imagine it like what the world must have been before man was created.

Colon, which is not so large as San Nicolas, has a greater air of life about it; and in fact we liked it so well, that, as —— observed, we seemed inclined to consider it, not as a *colon,* but a *full stop.* You must not expect more vivacious puns in *tierra caliente.* We rode back from San Nicolas in the afternoon, accompanied by the proprietor, and had some thoughts of going to *Matamoras* in the evening, to see the "Barber of Seville" performed by a strolling company in the open air, under a tree! admittance twenty-five cents. However, we ended by remaining where we were, and spent the evening in walking about through the village, surrounded by barking dogs, the greatest nuisance in these places, and pulling wild flowers, and gathering castor-oil nuts from the trees. A begging Franciscan friar, from the convent of San Fernando, arrived for his yearly supply of sugar which he begs from the different haciendas, for his convent, a tribute which is never refused.

We left our hospitable entertainer the next morning, with the addition of sundry baskets of cake and fruit from the housekeeper. As we were setting off, I asked the administrador if there were any barrancas on this road. "No," said he, "but I have sent a basketful with one of the boys, as they are very refreshing." I made no remark, concluding that I should find out his meaning in the course of the journey, but keeping a sharp look-out on the mysterious *mozo,* who was added to our train. When the light became stronger, I perceived that he carried under his sarape a large basket of fine *naranjas* (oranges), which no doubt the honest administrador thought I was inquiring after. It rained, when we left Colon, a thick misty drizzle, and the difference of the temperature gave us notice that we were passing out of *tierra caliente.* The road was so straight and uninteresting, though the surrounding country was fertile, that a few barrancas would really have been enlivening.

At Colon we took leave of our conductor, Don Juan, who returned to Atlacamulco, and got a new director of our forces, a handsome man, yclept Don Francisco, who had been a Spanish soldier. We had an uncomfortable ride in a high wind and hard rain, the roads good, but devoid of interest, so that we were glad when we learnt that *Atlisco,* a town where we were to pass the night, was not far off. Within a mile or two of the city we were met by a tall man on horseback, with a pink turban, and a wild, swarthy face, who looked like an Abencerrage, and who came with the compliments of his master, a Spanish gentleman, to say that a house had been prepared for us in the town.

Atlisco is a large town, with a high mountain behind it, crowned by a white chapel, a magnificent church at the base; the whole city full of fine churches and convents, with a plaza and many good houses. The numerous pipes, pointed all along from the roofs, have a very threatening and warlike effect; one seems to ride up the principal street under a strong fire. We found that Don Fernando ——, pink turban's master, not considering his own house good enough, had, on hearing of our expected arrival, hired another, and furnished part of it for us! This is the sort of wholesale hospitality one meets with in this country. Our room looked out upon an old Carmelite monastery, where C——n, having a recommendation to the prior, paid a visit, and found one or two good paintings. Here also we saw the famous cypress mentioned by Humboldt, which is seventy-three feet in circumference. The next morning we set out with an escort of seven *mozos,* headed by Don Francisco, and all well armed, for the road from Atlisco to Puebla is the robbers' highway, *par excellence.*

This valley of Atlisco, as indeed the whole department of Puebla, is noted for its fertility, and its abundant crops of maguey, wheat, maize, frijoles, garbanzos, barley, and other vegetables, as well as for the fineness of its fruits, its chirimoyas, etc. There is a Spanish proverb which says,

> *"Si a morar en Indias feures,*
> *Que sea doude los volcanes vieres."*

"If you go to live in the Indias, let it be within sight of the volcanoes;" for it appears that all the lands surrounding the different volcanoes are fertile, and enjoy a pleasant climate. The great Cordilleras of Anahuac cross this territory, and amongst these are the Mountain of the Malinchi, Ixtaccihuatl, Popocatepetl, and the Peak of Orizava. The Malinchi, a corruption by the Spaniards of the Indian name Malintzin, signifying Doña Maria or Marina, is supposed to be called after Cortes's Indian Egeria, the first Christian woman of the Mexican empire.

Though given to Cortes by the Tabascan Indians, it seems

clear that she was of noble birth, and that her father was the lord of many cities. It is pretended that she fell into a tributary situation, through the treachery of her mother, who remarried after the death of her first husband, and who, bestowing all her affection on the son born of this second marriage, determined, in concert with her husband, that all their wealth should pass to him. It happened, in furtherance of their views, that the daughter of one of their slaves died, upon which they gave out that they had lost their own daughter, affected to mourn for her, and, at the same time, privately sold her, after the fashion of Joseph's brethren, to some merchants of Gicalanco, who in their turn disposed of her to their neighbours, the Tabascans, who presented her to Cortes. That she was beautiful and of great talent, versed in different dialects, the devoted friend of the Spaniards, and serving as their interpreter in their negotiations with the various Indian tribes, there seems no doubt. She accompanied Cortes in all his expeditions—he followed her advice; and in the whole history of the conquest, Doña Marina (the name given to the beautiful slave at her Christian baptism) played an important part. Her son, Martin Cortes, a knight of the order of Santiago, was put to the torture in the time of Philip II., on some unfounded suspicion of rebellion. It is said that when Cortes, accompanied by Doña Marina, went to Honduras, she met her guilty relatives, who, bathed in tears, threw themselves at her feet, fearful lest she might avenge herself of their cruel treatment; but that she calmed their fears, and received them with much kindness. The name of her birthplace was Painala, a village in the province of Cuatzacualco. After the conquest, she was married to a Spaniard, named Juan de Jaramillo.

But I have wandered a long way from the Sierra Malinchi. The two great volcanoes, but especially Popocatepetl, the highest mountain in New Spain, seem to follow the traveller like his guardian spirit, wherever he goes. Orizava, which forms a boundary between the departments of Puebla and Vera Cruz, is said to be the most beautiful of mountains on a near approach, as it is the most magnificent at a distance; for while its summit is crowned with snow, its central part is girded by thick forests of cedar and pine, and its base is adorned with woods and sloping fields covered with flocks, and dotted with white ranchos and small scattered villages; forming the most agreeable and varied landscape imaginable. Ixtaccihuatl means white woman; Popocatepetl the mountain that throws out smoke. They are thus celebrated by the poet Heredia:

Nieve eternal corona las cabezas
De Ixtaccihuatl puríssimo, Orizava
Y Popocatepetl; sin que el invierno
Toque jamas con destructora mano
Los campos fertillísimos do ledo
Los mira el indio en purpura ligera
Yoro teñirse, reflejando el brillo
Del sol en Occidente, que sereno
En yelo eterno y perennal verdura
A torrentes versió su luz dorada,
Y vió a naturaleza conmovida
Con su dulce calor, hervir en vida.

TRANSLATION

Eternal snow crowns the majestic heads
Of Orizava, Popocatepetl,
And of Ixtaccihuatl the most pure.
Never does winter with destructive hand
Lay waste the fertile fields where from afar
The Indian views them bathed in purple light
And dyed in gold, reflecting the last rays
Of the bright sun, which, sinking in the west,
Poured forth his flood of golden light, serene
Midst ice eternal, and perennial green;
And saw all nature warming into life,
Moved by the gentle radiance of his fires.

The morning was really cold, and when we first set out, Popocatepetl was rolled up in a mantle of clouds. The road led us very near him. The wind was very piercing, and K—— was mounted on a curate's pony, evidently accustomed to short distances and easy travelling. We had been told that it was "muy proprio para Señora," very much suited to a lady, an encomium always passed upon the oldest, most stupid, and most obstinate quadruped that the haciendas can boast. We overtook and passed a party of cavalry, guarding some prisoners, whom they were conducting to Puebla.

As the sun rose, all eyes were turned with amazement and admiration to the great volcano. The clouds parted in the middle, and rolled off in great volumes, like a curtain withdrawn from a high altar. The snowy top and sides of the mountain appeared, shining in the bright sun, like a grand dome of the purest white marble. But it cannot be described. I thought of Sinai, of Moses on the Mount, when the glory of the Lord

was passing by; of the mountain of the Transfiguration, something too intolerably bright and magnificent for mortal eye to
look upon and live. We rode slowly, and in speechless wonder, till the sun, which had crowned the mountain like a
glory, rose slowly from its radiant brow, and we were reminded
that it was time to ride forwards.

We were not far from the ancient city of Cholula, lying
on a great plain at a short distance from the mountains,
and glittering in the sunbeams, as if it still were the city of
predilection as in former days, when it was the sacred city,
"the Rome of Anahuac." It is still a large town, with a spacious
square and many churches, and the ruins of its great pyramid
still attest its former grandeur; but of the forty thousand
houses and four hundred churches mentioned by Cortes, there
are no traces. The base of this pyramid, which at a distance
looks like a conical mountain, is said by Humboldt to be
larger than that of any discovered in the old continent, being
double that of Cheops. It is made of layers of bricks mixed
with coats of clay and contains four stories. In the midst of the
principal platform, where the Indians worshipped Quetzal-
coatl, the god of the air (according to some the patriarch
Noah, and according to others the apostle Saint Thomas! for
doctors differ), rises a church dedicated to the Virgen de los
Remedios, surrounded by cypresses, from which there is one
of the most beautiful views in the world. From this pyramid,
and it is not the least interesting circumstance connected with
it, Humboldt made many of his valuable astronomical observations.

The treachery of the people and priests of Cholula, who,
after welcoming Cortes and the Spaniards, formed a plan for
exterminating them all, which was discovered by Doña Marina, through the medium of a lady of the city, was visited by
him with the most signal vengeance. The slaughter was dreadful; the streets were covered with dead bodies, and houses
and temples were burnt to the ground. This great temple was
afterwards purified by his orders, and the standard of the cross
solemnly planted in the midst. Cholula, not being on the direct road to Puebla, is little visited, and as for us our time
was now so limited, that we were obliged to content ourselves
with a mere passing observation of the pyramid, and then to
hurry forward to Puebla.

We entered that city to the number of eighteen persons,
eighteen horses, and several mules, and passed some people
near the gates who were carrying blue-eyed angels to the

chosen city, and who nearly let them drop, in astonishment, on seeing such a cavalcade. We were very cold, and felt very tired as we rode into the courtyard of the hotel, yet rather chagrined to think that the remainder of our journey was now to be performed in a diligence. Having brought my story up to civilized life, and it being late, I conclude.

LETTER THE THIRTY-FIFTH

PUEBLA.

You will be surprised when I tell you that, notwithstanding our fatigue, we went to the theatre the evening we arrived, and sat through a long and tragical performance, in the box of Don A——o H——o, one of the richest citizens of Puebla, who, hearing of our arrival, instantly came to invite us to his house, where he assured us rooms were prepared for our reception. But being no longer in savage parts, where it is necessary to throw yourself on the hospitality of strangers or to sleep in the open air, we declined his kind offer, and remained in the inn, which is very tolerable, though we do not see it now *en beau* as we did last year, when we were expected there. The theatre is clean and neat, but dull, and we were much more looked at than the actors, for few foreigners (ladies especially) remain here for any length of time, and their appearance is somewhat of a novelty. Our toilet occasioned us no small difficulty, now that we were again in polished cities, for you may imagine the condition of our trunks, which two mules had galloped with over ninety leagues of plain and mountain, and which had been opened every night. Such torn gowns, crushed collars, ruined pélérines! One carpet bag had burst and discharged its contents of combs, brushes, etc., over a barranca, where some day they may be picked up as Indian antiquities, and sent to the Museum, to be preserved as a proof that Montezuma's wives brushed their hair. However, by dint of a washer-woman and sundry messages to *peluqueros* (hairdressers), we were enabled to *turn out* something like Christian travellers. The first night we could not sleep on account of the innumerable ants, attracted probably by a small garden, with one or two orange-trees in it, into which our room opened.

The next morning we had a great many visitors, and though there is here a good deal of that provincial pretension one always meets with out of a capital, we found some pleasant people amongst them. The Señora H——o came in a very handsome carriage, with beautiful northern horses, and took us out to see something of the town. Its extreme cleanness after Mexico is remarkable. In that respect it is the Philadelphia of the republic; with wide streets, well paved; large houses of two stories, very solid and well built; magnificent churches, plenty of water, and withal a dulness which makes one feel as if the houses were rows of convents, and all the people, except beggars and a few business men, shut up in performance of a vow.

The house of Don A——o H——o is, I think, more elegantly furnished than any in Mexico. It is of immense size, and the floors beautifully painted. One large room is furnished with pale blue satin, another with crimson damask, and there are fine inlaid tables, handsome mirrors, and everything in very good taste. He and his wife are both very young—she not more than nineteen, very delicate and pretty, and very fair; and in her dress, neatness, and house, she reminds me of a Philadelphian, always with the exception of her diamonds and pearls. The ladies smoke more, or at least more openly, than in Mexico; but they have so few amusements, they deserve more indulgence. There are eleven convents of nuns in the city, and taking the veil is as common as being married. We dined at the Señora H——o's; found her very amiable, and heard a young lady sing, who has a good voice, but complains that there are no music-masters in Puebla.

The fine arts, however, are not entirely at a standstill here; and in architecture, sculpture, and painting, there is a good deal, comparatively speaking, worthy of notice. There used to be a proverb amongst the Mexicans, that "if all men had five senses, the Poblanos had seven." They are considered very reserved in their manners—a natural consequence of their having actually no society. Formerly, Puebla rivalled Mexico in population and in industry. The plague, which carried off fifty thousand persons, was followed by the pestilence of civil war, and Puebla dwindled down to a very secondary city. But we now hear a great deal of their cotton-factories, and of the machines, instruments, and workmen, brought from Europe here, already giving employment to thirty thousand individuals.

In the evening we drove to the new paseo, a public promenade, where none of the public were to be seen, and which will be pretty when the young trees grow.

19th.—C——n went out early, and returned the visit of the celebrated Don N. Ramos Arispe, now an old man, and canon of the cathedral, but formerly deputy in the Spanish Cortes, and the most zealous supporter of the cause of independence. It is said that he owed the great influence which he had over men of a middling character, rather to his energetic, some say to his domineering disposition, than to genius; that he was clear-headed, active, dexterous, remarkable for discovering hidden springs and secret motives, and always keeping his subordinates zealously employed in his affairs. C——n also visited the bishop, Señor Vasques, who obtained from Rome the acknowledgment of independence.

We set out after breakfast with several gentlemen, who came to take us to the cotton-factories, etc. We went first to visit the factory established at the mill of Santo Domingo, a little way out of the city, and called "La Constancia Mejicana" (Mexican Constancy). It was the first established in the republic, and deserves its name from the great obstacles that were thrown in the way of its construction, and the numerous difficulties that had to be conquered before it came into effect.

In 1831 a junta for the encouragement of public industry was formed, but the obstacles thrown in the way of every proposal were so great, that the members all abandoned it in despair, excepting only the Señor *Don Esteban Antuñano,* who was determined himself to establish a manufactory of cotton, to give up his commercial relations, and to employ his whole fortune in attaining this object.

He bought the mill of Santo Domingo for one hundred and seventy-eight thousand dollars, and began to build the edifice, employing foreign workmen at exorbitant prices. In this he spent so much of his capital, that he was obliged to have recourse to the Bank of *Avio* for assistance. The bank (*avio* meaning pecuniary assistance, or advance of funds) was established by Don Lucas Alaman, and intended as an encouragement to industry. But industry is not of the nature of a hothouse plant, to be forced by artificial means; and these grants of funds have but created monopolies, and consequently added to the general poverty. Machinery, to the amount of three thousand eight hundred and forty spindles, was ordered for Antuñano from the United States, and a loan granted him of one hundred and seventy-eight thousand dollars, but of which he never received the whole. Meanwhile his project was sneered at as absurd, impossible, ruinous; but, firmly resolved not to abandon his enterprise, he contented himself with living with the strictest economy, himself and his numerous family almost suffering from want, and frequently unable to obtain credit for the provisions necessary for their daily use.

To hasten the arrival of the machinery, he sent an agent to the north to superintend it, and to hire workmen; but the commercial house to which he was recommended, and which at first gave him the sums he required, lost their confidence in the agent, and redemanded their money, so that he was forced to sell his clothes in order to obtain food and lodging. In July, 1833, the machinery was embarked at Philadelphia, and in August arrived at Vera Cruz, to the care of Señor Paso y Troncoso, who never abandoned Antuñano in his adversity, and even lent him unlimited sums; but much delay ensued, and a year elapsed before it reached Puebla. There, after it was all set up, the ignorant foreign workmen declared that no good results would ever be obtained; that the machines were bad, and the cotton worse. However, by the month of January, 1833, they began to work in the factory, to which was given the name of "Mexican Constancy." A mechanist was then sent to the north, to procure a collection of new machinery; and, after extraordinary delays and difficulties, he embarked with it at New York in February, 1837.

He was shipwrecked near Cayo-Hueso, and, with all the machinery he could save, returned to the north in the brig Argos; but on his way there he was shipwrecked again, and all the machinery lost! He went to Philadelphia, to have new machines constructed, and in August re-embarked in the Delaware. Incredible as it may seem, the Delaware was wrecked off Cayo-Alcatraces, and for the third time the machinery was lost, the mechanist saving himself with great difficulty!

It seemed as if gods and men had conspired against the cotton spindles; yet Antuñano persevered. Fresh machinery was ordered; and though by another fatality it was detained, owing to the blockade of the ports by the French squadron, seven thousand spindles were landed, and speedily put in operation. Others have followed the example of Señor Antuñano, who has given a decided impulse to industry in Puebla, besides a most extraordinary example of perseverance, and a determined struggle against what men call *bad luck*, which persons of a feebler character sink under, while stronger minds oppose till they conquer it.

It was in his carriage we went, and he accompanied us all over the building. It is beautifully situated, and at a distance has more the air of a summer palace than of a cotton-factory. Its order and airiness are delightful, and in the middle of the court, in front of the building, is a large fountain of the purest water. A Scotchman, who has been there for some time, says he has never seen anything to compare with it, and he worked six years in the United States. Antuñano is unfortunately very deaf, and obliged to use an ear-trumpet. He seems an excellent man, and I trust he may be ultimately successful. We came out covered with cotton, as if we had been just unpacked, and were next taken to visit a very handsome new prison, which they are building in the city, but whether it will ever be finished, or not, is more doubtful. We also visited the Foundling Hospital, a large building, where there are more children than funds. They were all clean and respectable-looking, but very poor. Antuñano presented them with two hundred dollars, as a memorial, he said, of our visit.

C——n then went to the convent of El Carmen, to see the paintings of the Life of the Virgin, supposed to be original works of Murillo, particularly the Ascension and Circumcision; but which are ill-arranged, and have suffered greatly from neglect, many of them being torn. Indeed, in some of them are large holes made by the boys, who insisted that the Jewish priest was *the devil*. There is a Descent from the Cross, which is reckoned a fine painting; and it is a pity that these works should be shut up in this old convent, where there are about half-a-dozen old monks, and where they serve no purpose, useful or ornamental. Were they removed to the Mexican Museum, and arranged with care, they would at least serve as models for those young artists who have not the means of forming their taste by European travel. Zendejas as a painter, and Coro as a sculptor, both natives of Puebla, are celebrated in their respective arts, but we have not yet seen any of their works. C——n also visited the bishop, and saw his paintings and library, which we hope to do to-morrow; and from thence went to the college, the rector of which was *attaché* in Spain to the Minister Santa Maria.

We dined again in the house of Señor H——o. The manner in which his floors are painted is pretty and curious. It is in imitation of carpets, and is very rich in appearance and very cool in reality. A great many of the floors here are painted in this way, either upon canvas with oil colours, or upon a cement extended upon the bricks of which the floor is made, and prepared with glue, lime, or clay, and soap.

Señor H——o has four young and pretty sisters, all nuns in different convents. As there are no other schools but these convents, the young girls who are sent there become attached to the nuns, and prefer remaining with them for ever to returning home. After dinner, accompanied by Don N. Ramos Arispe, whom C——n formerly knew intimately in Madrid, and by various other ecclesiastics, we visited the boast of Puebla, the cathedral, which we did not do when we passed through the city on our arrival last year. To my mind, I have never seen anything more noble and magnificent. It is said that the rapid progress of the building was owing to the assistance of two angels, who nightly descended and added to its height, so that each morning the astonished workmen found their labour incredibly advanced. The name given to the city, "Puebla de los Angeles," is said to be owing to this tradition.

It is not so large as the cathedral of Mexico, but it is more elegant, simpler, and in better taste. Sixteen columns of exquisite marble, adorned with silver and gold, form the *tabernacle* (in Mexico called *el Ciprés*). This native marble, called Puebla marble, is brought from the quarries of Totamehuacan and Tecali, at two and seven leagues from the city. The floor of the cathedral is of marble—the great screens and high-backed chairs of richly-carved cedar. Everything was opened to show us; the tombs where the bishops are buried; the vault where a martyr lies, supposed to have been miraculously preserved for centuries, the gift of a pope to a bishop of Puebla. The figure appears to be of wax, enclosing the skeleton of the martyr, and has the most angelic countenance I ever beheld. It is loaded with false emeralds and diamonds.

We were also shown the jewels, which they keep buried, in case of a revolution. The *Custodia*, the gold stand in which they carry the Host, is entirely encrusted with large diamonds, pearls, emeralds, amethysts, topazes, and rubies. The chalices are equally rich. There are four sets of jewels for the bishop. One of his crosses is of emeralds and diamonds; another of topazes and diamonds, with great rings of the same, belonging to each.

In the evening we went with the M—— family, who have been very civil to us, to the theatre, where we saw a comedy better acted and more amusing than the tragedy which they murdered two nights before. We went early the next morning to the bishop's palace, to see his fine library and collection of paintings, where there were a few modern originals and many fine copies of the old masters. We then went with the Señora H——o, to return the visits of the ladies who had called on us. The young ladies invariably complain that they have neither music, nor drawing, nor dancing masters. There is evidently a great deal of musical taste among them, and, as in every part of Mexico, town or country, there is a piano (*tal cual*) in every house; but most of those who play are self-taught, and naturally abandon it very soon, for want of instruction or encouragement. We are now going to dine out, and in the evening we go to a concert in the theatre, given by the Señora Cesari and Mr. Wallace. As we must rise at three, to set off by the diligence, I shall write no more from this place. Our next letters will be from Mexico.

LETTER THE THIRTY-SIXTH

Concert—Diligence—Leave Puebla—Escort—View from the Cathedral Towers—Black Forest—History of the Crosses—Tales of Murder—An Alarm—Report of a Skirmish—Rio Frio—Law concerning Robbers—Their Moderation—Return to Mexico —Carnival Ball—Improvement in Dress.

MEXICO, 24th.

We went to the concert with our friends, the H——os. The music was better than the instruments, and the Señora Cesari looked handsome, as she always does, besides being beautifully dressed in white, with Paris wreaths. We took leave of our friends at the door of the hotel, at one in the morning, and lay down for two hours, in the full expectation of being robbed the following day, a circumstance which has now grown so common, that when the diligence from Puebla arrives in safety, it excites rather more sensation than when it has been stopped. The governor had ordered us an escort to Mexico, to be stationed about every six leagues, but last week the escort itself, and even the gallant officer at its head, were suspected of being the plunderers. Our chief hope lay in that well-known miraculous knowledge which they possess as to the value of all travellers' luggage, which no doubt not only makes them aware that we are mere pilgrims for pleasure, and not fresh arrivals, laden with European commodities, but also renders them perfectly familiar with the contents of our well-shaken portmanteaus; so that we trusted that a sarape or two, a few rings and earrings, and one or two shawls, would not prove sufficient to tempt them. We got into the diligence in the dark, half asleep, having taken all the places but three, which were engaged before we came; some sleepy soldiers on horseback, ready to accompany us, and a loaded gun sticking out of each window. Various beggars, who are here innumerable, already surrounded us; and it is, by the way, a remarkable circumstance, that notwithstanding the amazing numbers of the léperos in Puebla, the churches there are kept scrupulously clean, from which Mexico might take a hint with advantage.

Puebla is one of the few cities founded by the Spanish colonists, instead of being built upon the ruins of former greatness. It was founded in the sixteenth century, on the plains of Acajete, in a site occupied only by a few huts belonging to the Cholula Indians. It is surrounded by productive corn estates, and the landscape, when the light visited our eyes, was fertile though flat. The two finest views of Puebla may be seen from the towers of the cathedral, and from an azotea in the street of San Agustin. The landscape is extremely varied and very extensive.

To the north we see the mountain of Tlascala, the *Matlalcueyetl*, better known as the Malinchi; next it the hill and temple of Guadalupe and the mountain of the Pinar, crowned by its white church. Other churches and convents adorn the slopes of the mountains, the Church of Loreto, the Temple of Calvary, etc. The Malinchi is fertile, but these inferior mountains are sterile and bare.

To the south lie the great volcanoes, and between them we can distinguish the difficult and steep road by which Cortes undertook his first march to Mexico. We also see the city and pyramid of Cholula, the hill of San Nicolas, and that of San Juan, where General Bustamante encamped in 1832, when he went out against Santa Anna; near it the farmhouses of Posadas and Zavaleta, one celebrated by a battle, the other by a treaty.

To the east, but at a greater distance than the other mountains, rises the Peak of Orizava, the Star Mountain; the side now seen, that which rises over the table land of Mexico; its other side descends rapidly to the burning plains of Vera Cruz, and is the first distinguishable land discerned by those who approach these coasts. Even at this distance, its snowy summit is seen contrasting with its fertile woods and pleasant villages. It has, what mortals rarely possess united, a warm heart, with a clear, cold head.

We were awakened at a posada by their bringing us some hot coffee, and a man with a white nightcap on, having poked his head in at the window, in defiance of a loaded musket, I concluded he was a lépero, and sleepily told him I had nothing for him, in the phrase of the country to importunate beggars; "Perdone V. por Dios!" "Excuse me, for God's sake!"—but he proved to be a gentleman, who merely came to put himself and his property at our disposal, at that early hour of the morning.

When we entered the black forest, and passed through the

dark pine woods, then the stories of robbers began, just as people at sea seem to take a particular pleasure in talking of shipwrecks. Every cross had its tale of murder, and by the way, it seems to me, that a work written with *connaissance de cause*, and entitled "History of the Crosses," though it might not equal the "History of the *Crusades*," would be quite as interesting, and much more romantic, than the Newgate Calendar. The difficulty would consist in procuring authentic information concerning them. There were a lady and two gentlemen in the diligence, and the lady seemed to be very much *au fait* as to their purport and history. Under one her own servant was buried, and she gave rather a graphic account of his murder. He was sitting outside, on the top of the diligence. The party within were numerous but unarmed. Suddenly a number of robbers with masks on came shouting down upon them from amongst the pine trees. They first took aim at the poor *mozo*, and shot him through the heart. He fell, calling in piteous tones to a padre who was in the coach, entreating him to stop and confess him, and groaning out a farewell to his friend the driver. Mortal fear prevailed over charity both in priest and layman, and the coachman, whipping up his horses, passed at full gallop over the body of the murdered man, so that, the robbers being on foot, the remainder of the party escaped.

Whilst we were listening to tales of blood and murder, our escort took leave of us, supposing that we should meet another immediately, whereas we found that we had arrived at the most dangerous part of the road, and that no soldiers were in sight. We certainly made up our minds to an attack this time, and got ready our rings and watches, not to hide, but to give, for we womenkind were clearly of opinion, that in case of an attack, it was much better to attempt no defence, our party having only two guns amongst them.

There was a diligence some way behind us, full of people, and belonging to another line; driven by a Yankee coachman, so drunk that he kept his seat with difficulty, and, in defiance of all remonstrances, persisted in driving the coach at a gallop close by the brink of the great precipice along which the road wound; so that the poor passengers were exposed to a double danger.

Suddenly our escort appeared at the top of the hill, and the officer, riding up, excused himself to C——n for the delay, which had arisen from their having been engaged in a skirmish with the robbers in that very place. Two he said were taken, and he had marched them off to Puebla, where they will probably be let off in a few days, after a form of trial. Four had escaped, and had hid themselves amongst the trees and rocks, but could not, according to his calculations, be very far off. However, we were quite reassured by the arrival of the soldiers, and the sight of Rio Frio was very reviving. We got a very tolerable dinner from the Bordelaise in the forest-valley; and although the next part of the road is reckoned very insecure, we had no longer any apprehension, as besides having an escort, the fact that some of the robbers had been taken a few hours before, made it very unlikely that they would renew their attempts that day.

This pestilence of robbers, which infests the republic, has never been eradicated. They are in fact the growth of civil war. Sometimes in the guise of insurgents, taking an active part in the independence, they have independently laid waste the country, and robbed all whom they met. As expellers of the Spaniards, these armed bands infested the roads between Vera Cruz and the capital, ruined all commerce, and without any particular inquiry into political opinions, robbed and murdered in all directions. In 1824 a law was proposed in congress, which should subject all armed bands of robbers to military judges, in order to shorten proceedings, for many of those who had been apprehended and thrown into prison, found some opportunity to escape, while their trial was pending, and many had been imprisoned four or five times for the same offence, yet never brought to justice. In this law were included both robbers by profession and those bodies of insurgents who were merely extempore amateurs.

But whatever measures have been taken at different times to eradicate this evil, its causes remain, and the idle and unprincipled will always take advantage of the disorganized state of the country, to obtain by force what they might gain by honest labour. Count —— says gravely, that he cannot imagine why we complain of Mexican robbers, when the city of London is full of organized gangs of ruffians, whom the laws cannot reach; and when English highwaymen and housebreakers are the most celebrated in the world. Moreover, that Mexican robbers are never unnecessarily cruel, and in fact are very easily moved to compassion. This last assertion may, occasionally hold good, but their cruelties to travellers are too well known to bear him out in it as a general remark.

As a proof of their occasional moderation, I may mention, that the ladies of the F——a family, at the time of their emigration, were travelling from Mexico with a *padre*, when they were met by a party of robbers or insurgents, who stopped the coach, and commenced pillaging. Amongst other articles of value, they seized a number of silver dishes. The padre observed to them, that as this plate did not belong to the ladies, but was lent them by a friend, they would be obliged to replace it, and requested that one might be left as a pattern. The reasonable creatures instantly returned a dish and cover!

Another time, having completely stripped an English gentleman and his servant, and tied them both to a tree, observing that the man appeared particularly distressed at the loss of his master's spurs, they politely returned and laid the spurs beside the gentleman.

About four o'clock, though nearly blinded with dust, we once more looked down upon the valley of Mexico, and at five, during our last change of horses, we were met by Don M——l del C——o and the English courier Beraza, who had ridden out to meet us, and accompanied us on their fine horses as far as the Garita. Here we found our carriage waiting; got in and drove through Mexico, dusty as we were, and warlike as we seemed, with guns at the windows. In the Calle San Francisco, the carriage was stopped by Mr. ——, Secretary to the English Legation, who invited us to a grand masked and fancy carnival ball to be given on Monday, it being now Saturday. On our return home, we found everything in good order. Had some difficulty in procuring ball-dresses in time.

On Sunday we had a number of people to dinner, by chance, it being Spanish fashion to dine at a friend's house without invitation. This evening we go to the ball.

26th.—The ball was in the theatre, and very brilliant, but too many of the first people on these occasions keep their boxes, and do not dance; yet it was wonderfully select for so large an assembly. When we arrived, we were led upstairs by some of the commissioners, those who had charge of the ball, to the E——'s box, whom we found, as usual, elegantly dressed —the married ladies of the family with diamonds, the younger ones in white crape and gold. I had a black silk mask, but finding myself universally recognized, saw no particular advantage in keeping it on, and promptly discarded it. We took a few turns in the ball-room, and afterwards returned to the box. There were some capital figures in masks, and some beautiful ball-dresses, and though there were a number of dominoes and odd figures, I could not help remarking the great improvement in toilet which had taken place since the fancy ball of last year. One or two girls, especially the Señorita M——, wore ball-dresses which could only have proceeded from the fingers of a Parisian *modiste*. Madame de ——, dressed as a peasant, and with a mask, was known everywhere by her small foot and pretty figure. But it is impossible to look on at a ball very long, not mingling with it, without growing tired; and not even the numerous visitors to our box could prevent us from feeling much more sleepy than during many a moonlight ride through the lovely lanes of *tierra caliente*.

Next night there was a public masked ball, but we did not attend it. We feel much the better for our journey, and only hope that some day C——n may have leisure sufficient to enable us to take another ride through some other part of the country. This being near Lent, we shall have no *soirées* for six weeks, though balls are occasionally given during that time of fasting. The house has become very comfortable in the way of servants; our housekeeper a treasure, the coachman and footman excellent, the cook tolerable, the soldiers rarely tipsy more than once a week, and generally only one at a time, the others decent—so that we have nothing to complain of. —— has established a hen-house near the stable, and any old Indian woman who brings her a *manojo* (several hens tied together) is sure to be received with open arms.

One of our first visits on our return was to Tacubaya, where we were sorry to find the Countess C——a very much indisposed, and her courtyard filled with carriages, containing visitors making inquiries. I shall now send off my letters by the packet, that you may see we are safely re-established in Mexico.

LETTER THE THIRTY-SEVENTH

Distinguished Men—Generals Bustamante, Santa Anna, and Victoria—Anecdote—Señor Pedraza—Señor Gutierrez Estrada—Count Cortina—Señor Gorostiza—Don Carlos Bustamante—"Mornings in the Alameda"—Don Andrés Quintana Roo—Don Lucas Alaman—General Moran—General Almonte—Señor Cañedo—Señors Neri del Barrio and Casaflores—Doctor Valentin—Don Francisco Tagle—Eight Revolutions.

27th.

H—— in his last letter asks what distinguished men we have in Mexico? and with a tone of doubt as to their being very numerous. Distinguished in what way? As generals, as statesmen, as men of literature? It seems to me that a country where we have known Bustamante, Santa Anna, General Victoria, Posada, Gomez Pedraza, Gutierrez Estrada, Count Cortina, Gorostiza, Don Carlos Bustamante, Quintana Roo, General Moran, Don Lucas Alaman, General Almonte, Señor Cañedo, Don Francisco Tagle, Señor Neri del Barrio, Señor Fagoaga, Don José Valentin, the Count de Casaflores, etc., etc., is not so destitute of distinguished men as he supposes. The preceding are, I confess, strung together as they occur to me, without order or regularity; soldiers, statesmen, and literary men, some on one side of politics, some on another, but all men of note, and men who have acted, or suffered, or been distinguished in one way or another in the revolutions of the last thirty-two years. And there is not one amongst those I have mentioned, who, if he were to write merely his personal history, would not by so doing write the history of these civil wars. The three first, as principal figures in every revolution, are already historical; Bustamante as an honest man and a brave soldier; Santa Anna as an acute general, active and aspiring, whose name has a *prestige*, whether for good or for evil, that no other possesses; General Victoria, a plain, uneducated, well-intentioned man, brave and enduring. A passage in his life is well known, which ought to be mentioned as an *offset* to the doubtful anecdote of the two-headed eagle. When Yturbide, alone, fallen and a prisoner, was banished from

Mexico, and when General Bravo, who had the charge of conducting him to Vera Cruz, treated him with every species of indignity, Victoria, the sworn foe of the emperor during his prosperity, now, when orders were given him to see Yturbide embarked, surrounded him with attentions, and loaded him with respectful distinctions; so that Yturbide himself, moved with gratitude, after expressing his warm esteem for the General's consistent conduct, presented him with his watch as a memorial of his grateful admiration.

As for Don Manuel Gomez Pedraza, he has occupied too distinguished a place in the political occurrences of this country, not to be generally known. An officer in the time of the Spanish government, he was distinguished for his severe discipline and strict moral conduct. In the time of Yturbide he was military commandant of Huasteca, and supported the emperor, who afterwards made him commander-general of Mexico. In 1827 he was minister of war, during the presidency of Victoria, and was distinguished for his extraordinary activity, which quality was greatly wanting in that general. In 1828 he and Guerrero were announced as candidates for the presidency, and after a terrible political tempest, Gomez Pedraza was elected. The fermentation that succeeded, the fury of the two parties, the *Guerreristas* and *Pedrazistas*, which were mingled with *Yturbidistas*, was increased by the arrival of Santa Anna at Perote with eight hundred men, who, having shut himself up in the fortress, declared for Guerrero, and published a manifesto, which set forth that general as a hero, and his rival as a hypocrite. Then came the famous revolution of the *Acordada*, and both Pedraza and Guerrero disappeared. Pedraza left the Republic, and after another revolution, hearing that "the constitution and laws were re-established," returned to Vera Cruz; but was met by an order which prohibited him from disembarking. He then set sail for New Orleans. Another change brought him back; and at this present juncture he lives in tranquillity, together with his lady, a person of extraordinary talent and learning, daughter of the Lizenciado (jurisconsult) Señor Azcárate. Such are the disturbed lives passed by the "children of the soil."

Of Gutierrez Estrada, now far from his household gods, and languishing under unjust persecution, I have already spoken. Count Cortina is a gentleman and a scholar, a man of vast information, and a protector of the fine arts. His conversation is a series of electric sparks; brilliant as an ignis fatuus, and bewildering as a will-o'-the-wisp. I have seldom heard such eloquence even in trifles; and he writes with as much ease as he speaks. We have seen three clever pieces of his lately, showing his versatile genius; one upon earthquakes, one upon the *devil*, and one upon the holy fathers of the church!—the first in the form of a pamphlet, addressed to a lady, giving a scientific explanation of the causes of these phenomena, interspersed with compliments to her *beaux yeux;* the second is a burlesque poem; and the third a grave and learned dissertation.

Don José Eduardo Gorostiza, though a native of Vera Cruz, is the son of a Spanish officer, and when very young went to Spain, where he was known politically as a liberal. He was distinguished as a writer of theatrical pieces, which have been and still are very popular; and those which he merely translated, he had the merit of adapting to the Spanish stage, and *Castilianizing* in grace and wit. One of his pieces, which we saw the other evening at the theatre—*"Con tigo, pan y cebolla,"* (With thee, bread and onions,) is delightful. Besides occupying a place in the Cabinet of Mexico, he has been Chargé d'Affaires in Holland, and Minister at the Court of St. James. In conversation he is extremely witty and agreeable, and he has collected some good paintings and valuable books in the course of his European travels.

The reputation of Don Carlos Bustamante, deputy from Oajaca, is altogether literary. He has made many researches in Mexican antiquities; and has published a history of the "Discovery of America," written by Padre Vega, which was unknown before; also the "Gallery of Mexican Princes;" "Tezcoco in the last Days of its last Kings," etc. He lately sent me his "Mornings in the Alameda," a book intended to teach Mexican young ladies the history of their own country. I have read but a few pages of it, but was struck with the liberality of his remarks in regard to the Spaniards, which, coming from such a source, are so much more valuable and worthy of credit than any that can be made by a foreigner, that I am tempted to translate the passage to which I allude. "The Spanish government founded colleges and academies in the reign of the wise Charles the Third; it established that of fine arts, which it enriched with the most beautiful statues, which you can still see when you visit it. ("Their transportation," he says in a note, "cost seventy thousand dollars.") He sent excellent workmen, and imitated his predecessor Philip the Second, who sent to Mexico whatever could not find a place in the works of the Escurial. Of his wisdom, we have proofs in those magnificent temples which attract the attention of travellers, such as the

Cathedral of Mexico, San Agustin, Santo Domingo of Oaxaca, and others. Spain did no more, because she could do no more, and Spain gave to this America a constitution, which the Mexicans themselves, who pride themselves most on their learning, are unacquainted with; and whose analysis was formed by the learned Padre Mier, in the History of the Revolution, which he printed in London; a constitution, in which are made manifest the good intentions of the Austrian monarchs; and their earnest desire to render the Indians happy; especially in the case of the great Philip the Fourth, whose autograph law is preserved; and which I have read with respect and emotion, prohibiting the bad treatment of the Indians. In short, this America, if it were considered in a state of slavery under the Spanish dominion, was at least on a level with the peninsula itself. Read over the frightful list of taxes which oppressed the Spaniards, and compare it with those that were imposed upon us, and you will find that theirs is infinitely greater than ours. These truths being granted, remark the progress which the colonies had made in sciences and arts, and this truth which escaped from the light pen of the censor Beristain, will be confirmed. Mexico, he says, was the sunflower of Spain. When in her principal universities there were no learned men to fill the mathematical chairs, Mexico could boast of Don Carlos de Siguenza y Góngora: when in Madrid there was no one who had written a good epic poem, in Mexico the *Bernardo* was composed;" etc., etc.

The next on my list is Don Andrés Quintana Roo, the best modern poet of Mexico, a native of Yucatan, and who came to the capital when very young, to study law. He is said to possess immense learning, and was enthusiastic to fanaticism in the cause of independence; insomuch that he and his wife, Doña Leona Vicario, who shared in his ardent love of liberty, braved every danger in its cause, suffered imprisonment, escaped from the Inquisition, from the hands of robbers, endured every privation, so that their history would form a romance. He is now devoted to literature, and though he occasionally launches forth some political pamphlet, he is probably wearied of revolutions, and possesses all the calmness of a man whose first years have been spent in excitement and troubles, and who at length finds consolation in study alone; the well of science proving to him the waters of Lethe, in which he drinks the oblivion of all his past sorrows. And it is very much the case in Mexico at present, that the most distinguished men are those who live most retired; those who have played their part on the arena of public life, have seen the inutility of their efforts in favour of their country, and have now retreated into the bosom of their families, where they endeavour to forget public evils in domestic retirement and literary occupation.

Amongst these may be reckoned Don Lucas Alaman, who passed many years in Europe, and in 1820 was deputy to the Spanish Cortes. Shortly after his return he became minister of foreign relations, which high office he has filled during various seasons of difficulty.[1] He is a man of learning, and has always been a protector of art and science. In conversation he is more reserved, less brilliant, and more minute than Count Cortina, always expressing his opinion with caution, but very ready and able to give information on anything in this country, unconnected with politics. General Moran, now infirm, and long since retired from public service, is universally respected, both as a military man and a gentleman. He is married to a daughter of the late Marquis de Vivanco, general of division, who long held out against the independence, and when the colonial system was dissolved, would never go further than to desire a prince of royal birth in Mexico. General Moran has been exiled several times, and his health has not held out against bodily and mental suffering; but he is ending his days in a tranquil retirement in the midst of his family. Of General Almonte and of Señor Cañedo, who are figuring in public life in our own day, I have frequently written.

Señor Neri del Barrio and the Count de Casaflores, married to sisters, ladies of high birth, the eldest a countess in her own right, are, as well as their families, all that is most distinguished in Mexico. Señor Fagoaga, who is now in bad health, I know only by reputation. He is brother of the Marquis of Apartado, and of the celebrated Don José Maria Fagoaga, with whose family we have the pleasure of being very intimate. C——n says that he is a man of great taste and a thorough gentleman, and that his house, which is one of the handsomest in Mexico, possesses that ornament so rare in this country—well-chosen paintings. Don José Valentin, who has figured in the political world, and who was curate of Huamautla, is one of the kindest and best old men I have ever met with; so severe to himself, so indulgent to others—so simple in worldly matters, so learned in everything else—so sincere, good, and charitable. He is a universal favourite with

[1] He is now, September, 1842, once more filling the same situation under General Santa Anna.

young and old, being cheerful, fond of music, and of gay conversation, in proportion as he is wise and learned in his observations, and serious in his conversation when the occasion requires it. Doctor Valentin as an ecclesiastic, and Padre Leon as a monk, are models.

As for Don Francisco Tagle, he is a gentleman of the old school, and his name figures in all the political events which have taken place since the independence, of which he was one of the signers. He is very rich, possessing, besides a profitable maguey estate near Mexico, enormous property bounding Texas, and being also the keeper of the Monte Pio, formerly the house of Cortes, a palace, in which he and his family live. He is a man of great learning and information, and too distinguished not to have suffered personally in political convulsions. Whether he would choose the same path, with his present experience of a Mexican republic, he is too wise to mention. He and his family are amongst our most intimate friends, and with a few exceptions all those whom I have mentioned have been here since our return, which is one of the reasons why their names occurred first to my memory; for there are still many distinguished persons remaining.

Nearly all these, at least all who are married, have had the good fortune to unite themselves with women who are either their equals or superiors, if not in education,—in goodness, elevation of sentiment, and natural talent. They, as well as every Mexican, whether man or woman, not under forty, have lived under the Spanish government; have seen the revolution of Dolores of 1810, with continuations and variations by Morelos, and paralyzation in 1819; the revolution of Yturbide in 1821; the cry of Liberty (grito de Libertad) given by those generals "benemeritos de la patria," Santa Anna and Victoria, in 1822; the establishment of the federal system in 1824; the horrible revolution of the Acordada, in which Mexico was pillaged, in 1828; the adoption of the central system in 1836; and the last revolution of the federalists in 1840. Another is predicted for next month, as if it were an eclipse of the sun. In nineteen years three forms of government have been tried, and two constitutions, the reform of one of which is still pending in the Chambers. *"Dere is notink like trying!"* (as the old *perruquier* observed, when he set out in a little boat to catch the royal yacht, still in sight of Scottish shores, with a new wig of his own invention, which he had trusted to have been permitted to present to his most gracious majesty George the Fourth!).

LETTER THE THIRTY-EIGHTH

New Minister—San Angel—Profitable Pulque Estate—The Village—Surrounding Scenery—The Indians—The Padre—The Climate—Holy Week in the Country—Dramatic Representations—Coyohuacan—The Pharisees—Image of the Saviour — Music and Dresses — Procession — Catholicism amongst the Indians—Strange Tradition—Paul the Fifth—Contrast between a Mexican and a New England Village—Love of Fireworks—Ferdinand the Seventh—Military Ball—Drapeaux.

SAN ANGEL, March 30th.

It is a long while since I last wrote, but this week has been employed in moving into the country, and making arrangements for the sale of our furniture, in consequence of our having received official news from Spain of the nomination of a new envoy extraordinary and minister plenipotentiary to the republic of Mexico. As, on account of the yellow fever at Vera Cruz, we shall not wish to pass through that city later than May, it is necessary to be in readiness to start when the new minister arrives. On Thursday last we came out to this place, within three leagues of Mexico, where Don Francisco Tagle has kindly lent us his unoccupied country house. As we had an infinity of arrangements to make, much to bring out, and much to leave, and *all Mexico* to see, you will excuse this long silence. Our house in town we leave to the guardianship of the housekeeper; the other servants follow us here.

This house is very large, and has a fine garden and orchard full of fruit, with pretty walks all through it, and a sort of underwood of roses and sweet peas. It is a great pulque hacienda, and, besides what is sent into Mexico for sale, the court is constantly filled with the half-naked Indians from the village, who come to have their *jarros* filled with that inspiring beverage. Then there is Doña Barbara (the guardian of the pulque), a Spanish administrador, a number of good-looking Indian women, and babies *à discrétion*. There is a small chapel, a Piazza, with handsome pillars going all round the interior courtyard of the house, a billiard-table, and plenty of good rooms. In front of the house are the maguey-fields, and the azotea commands a beautiful view of the neighbouring villages, San Angel, Coyohuacan, Miscuaque, etc., with their woods and gardens, as well as of the city itself, with its lakes and volcanoes.

As C——n's affairs take him to Mexico nearly every day, we feel a little lonely in this large house, even though perfectly comfortable; and besides the extreme stillness and solitude, it is not considered safe for us to walk out alone; consequently the orchard must bound our wishes. And, of course, being prohibited from going further, we have the greatest desire to do so! In the evening, however, when our *caballeros* return, we frequently walk down to the village, where the English minister has also a house.

San Angel is pretty in its own way, with its fields of maguey, its scattered houses, that look like the *beaux restes* of better days, its market-place, parish church, church of El Carmen, with the monastery and high-walled gardens adjoining; with its narrow lanes, Indian huts, profusion of pink roses, little bridge and avenue, and scattered clusters of trees; its houses for *temperamento* (*constitution,* as they call those where Mexican families come to reside in summer), with their grated windows, and gardens and orchards; and then the distant view of Mexico, with the cathedral towers, volcanoes, and lofty mountains, scattered churches and long lines of trees; and nearer, the pretty villages of Coyohuacan and Miscuaque; and everywhere the old church, the broken arch, the ancient cross, with its faded flower-garlands, to commemorate a murder, or erected as an act of piety—all is so characteristic of Mexico, that the landscape could belong to no other part of the known world.

There is the Indian with his blanket, extracting the pulque from the maguey; the ranchero, with her reboso and broad-brimmed hat passing by upon her ass; the old lépero, in rags, sitting basking in the sun upon the stone seat in front of the door; the poor Indian woman, with matted hair and brown baby hanging behind her, refreshing herself by drinking three *elacos* (halfpence) worth of pulque from a *jarrito* (little earthen jar); the portly and well-looking padre prior del carden (the Carmelite friar), sauntering up the lane at a leisurely pace, all the little ragged boys, down to the merest urchin that can hardly lisp, dragging off their large, well-holed hats, with a *"Buenos dias, padrecito!"* (Good-morning, little father!)—the father replying with a benevolent smile, and a slight sound in his throat intended for a *Benedicite;* and all that might be dull in any other climate brightened and made light and gay by the purest atmosphere, and bluest sky, and softest air, that ever blew or shone upon a naughty world.

We are now approaching the holy week once more—in Mexico a scene of variety in the streets and of splendour in the churches; but in the country a play, a sort of melodrama, in which the sufferings, death, and burial of our Saviour are represented by living figures in pantomime. We have heard a great deal of these representations, and are glad to have the opportunity of seeing them, which we intend to do in the village of Coyohuacan, where they are particularly curious. Besides this, our friends the A——s have a house there for the season, and, as the city of Cortes's predilection, it is classic ground. Meanwhile, for the last few days, the country has been overrun with Pharisees, Nazarenes, Jews, and figures of the Saviour, carried about in procession; all this in preparation for the holy week, a sort of overture to the drama.

The first evening we arrived here there was a representation of the Pharisees searching for Christ. The Pharisees were very finely dressed, either in scarlet stuff and gold or in green and silver, with helmets and feathers, mounted upon horses which are taught to dance and rear to the sound of music, so that upon the whole they looked like performers at Astley's. They came on with music, riding up the lanes until they arrived in front of this house, which being the principal place hereabouts, they came to first, and where the Indian workmen and servants were all collected to see them. They rode about for some time, as if in search of Christ, until a full-length figure of the Saviour appeared, dressed in purple robes, carried on a platform by four men, and guarded on all sides by soldiers. It is singular, that after all there is nothing ridiculous in these exhibitions; on the contrary, something rather terrible. In the first place, the music is good, which would hardly be the case in any but a Mexican village; the dresses are really rich, the gold all real, and the whole has the effect of confusing the imagination into the belief of its being a true scene.

The next evening the same procession passed, with some additions, always accompanied by a crowd of Indians from the villages, men, women, and children. Bonfires were made before the door of the hacienda, which were lighted whenever the distant music was heard approaching, and all the figures in the procession carried lighted lamps. The Saviour was then led up to the door, and all the crowd went up to kiss his feet. The figure which is carried about this evening is called "Our

Saviour of the Column," and represents the Saviour tied to a pillar, bleeding, and crowned with thorns. All this must sound very profane, but the people are so quiet, seem so devout, and so much in earnest, that it appears much less so than you would believe. . . .

The cross was planted here in a congenial soil, and as in the Pagan East the statues of the divinities frequently did no more than change their names from those of heathen gods to those of Christian saints, and image-worship apparently continued, though the mind of the Christian was directed from the being represented to the true and only God who inhabits eternity, so here the poor Indian still bows before visible representations of saints and virgins, as he did in former days before the monstrous shapes representing the unseen powers of the air, the earth, and the water; but he, it is to be feared, lifts his thoughts no higher than the rude image which a rude hand has carved. The mysteries of Christianity, to affect his untutored mind, must be visibly represented to his eyes. He kneels before the bleeding image of the Saviour who died for him, before the gracious form of the Virgin who intercedes for him; but he believes that there are many Virgins, of various gifts, and possessing various degrees of miraculous power and different degrees of wealth, according to the quality and number of the diamonds and pearls with which they are endowed—one even who is the rival of the other—one who will bring rain when there is drought, and one to whom it is well to pray in seasons of inundation. Mexico owes much of its peculiar beauty to the religious or superstitious feelings of its inhabitants. At every step we see a white cross gleaming amongst the trees, in a solitary path, or on the top of some rugged and barren rock—a symbol of faith in the desert place; and wherever the footsteps of man have rested, and some three or four have gathered together, there, while the ruined huts proclaim the poverty of the inmates, the temple of God rises in comparative splendour.

It is strange, yet well authenticated, and has given rise to many theories, that the symbol of the cross was already known to the Indians before the arrival of Cortes. In the island of Cozumel, near Yucatan, there were several; and in Yucatan itself, there was a stone cross; and there, an Indian, considered a prophet among his countrymen, had declared that a nation bearing the same as a symbol, should arrive from a distant country! More extraordinary still was a temple dedicated to the Holy Cross by the Toltec nation in the city of Cholula.

Near Tulansingo also, there is a cross engraved on a rock, with various characters, which the Indians by tradition attribute to the apostle Saint Thomas. In Oajaca also there existed a cross which the Indians from time immemorial had been accustomed to consider as a divine symbol. By order of the Bishop Cervantes, it was placed in a sumptuous chapel in the cathedral. Information concerning its discovery, together with a small cross cut out of its wood, was sent to Rome to Paul the Fifth, who received it on his knees, singing the hymn, "*Vexilla Regis prodeunt,*" etc.

If any one wishes to try the effect of strong contrast, let him come direct from the United States to this country; but it is in the villages especially that the contrast is most striking. Travelling in New England, for example, we arrive at a small and flourishing village. We see four new churches, proclaiming four different sects; religion suited to all customers. These wooden churches or meeting-houses are all new, all painted white, or perhaps a bright red. Hard by is a tavern with a green paling, as clean and as new as the churches, and there are also various smart *stores* and neat dwelling-houses; all new, all wooden, all clean, and all ornamented with slight Grecian pillars. The whole has a cheerful, trim, and flourishing aspect. Houses, churches, stores, and taverns, all are of a piece. They are suited to the present emergency, whatever that may be, though they will never make fine ruins. Everything proclaims prosperity, equality, consistency; the past forgotten, the present all in all, and the future taking care of itself. No delicate attentions to posterity, who can never pay its debts. No beggars. If a man has even a hole in his coat, he must be lately from the Emerald Isle.

Transport yourself in imagination from this New England village to that of ——, it matters not which, not far from Mexico. "Look on this picture, and on that." The Indian huts, with their half-naked inmates, and little gardens full of flowers; the huts themselves either built of clay, or the half-ruined *beaux restes* of some stone building. At a little distance an hacienda, like a deserted palace, built of solid masonry, with its inner *patio* surrounded by thick stone pillars, with great walls and iron-barred windows that might stand a siege. Here a ruined arch and cross, so solidly built, that one cannot but wonder how the stones ever crumbled away. There, rising in the midst of old faithful-looking trees, the church, gray and ancient, but strong as if designed for eternity; with its saints and virgins, and martyrs and relics, its gold and silver and precious stones, whose value would buy up all the spare lots in the New England village; the lépero with scarce a rag to cover him, kneeling on that marble pavement. Leave the enclosure of the church, observe the stone wall that bounds the road for more than a mile; the fruit trees overtopping it, high though it be, with their loaded branches. This is the convent orchard. And that great Gothic pile of building, that stands in hoary majesty, surmounted by the lofty mountains, whose cloud-enveloped summits, tinged by the evening sun, rise behind it; what could so noble a building be but the monastery, perhaps of the Carmelites, because of its exceeding rich garden, and well-chosen site, for they, of all monks, are richest in this world's goods. Also we may see the reverend old prior riding slowly from under the arched gate up the village lanes, the Indians coming from their huts to do him lowly reverence as he passes. Here, everything reminds us of the past; of the conquering Spaniards, who seemed to build for eternity; impressing each work with their own solid, grave, and religious character; of the triumphs of catholicism; and of the Indians when Cortes first startled them from their repose, and stood before them like the fulfilment of a half-forgotten prophecy. It is the present that seems like a dream, a pale reflection of the past. All is decaying and growing fainter, and men seem trusting to some unknown future which they may never see. One government has been abandoned, and there is none in its place. One revolution follows another, yet the remedy is not found. Let them beware lest half a century later, they be awakened from their delusion, and find the cathedral turned into a meeting-house, and all painted white; the *railing* melted down; the silver transformed into dollars; the Virgin's jewels sold to the highest bidder; the floor washed (which would do it no harm), and round the whole, a nice new wooden paling, freshly done in green—and all this performed by some of the artists from the *wide-awake* republic farther north.

Just as I wrote these words, a shower of crackers startled me from the profane ideas in which I was indulging, and the prancing of the horses of Jews and Pharisees, and the crackling of bonfires, warn me that it is time to take an evening stroll, that the sun is down, and the air refreshing. However, as to crackers and rockets, the common people enjoy them by day as much as by night. It is their favourite method of commemorating any event, evil or religious. "What do you suppose the Mexicans will be doing now?" said King Ferdinand to a Mexican who was at the Spanish court, shortly after the final success of the Revolutionists. "Letting off rockets, your Majesty," answered the Mexican. "Well—I wonder what they are doing now in Mexico!" said the King in the afternoon. *"Tirando cohetes*—letting off rockets, your Majesty." His Majesty chose to repeat the question in the evening. "What will your countrymen be doing now?" "The same thing, your Majesty. Still letting off rockets."

Yesterday we drove into Mexico, to see how matters stood in our house, and received a number of visitors in our deserted apartments. Just before we left Mexico for this place, three very magnificent aides-de-camp brought us an invitation from General Valencia, to attend a ball to be given by him and other officers, in the theatre, to the president, on the occasion of his excellency's being declared "benemerito de la patria." We did not go, as we were setting off for the country, but C——n being requested, as were the other ministers, to send the colours of his nation, did so, and to-day there is much talk in Mexico, besides a paragraph in the newspapers, connected with these matters. It appears that the *drapeaux* whether by accident or design, were improperly placed, and these faults in etiquette are not uncommon here. The English minister having observed that his *drapeau* was placed in a subordinate rank, and finding that his warnings beforehand on the subject, and his representations on seeing it were neglected, cut it down and left the ballroom, followed by all the English who were there.

LETTER THE THIRTY-NINTH

Holy Thursday at Coyohuacan—Hernan Cortes—His Last Wishes—Padres Camilos—Old Church—Procession—Representation of the taking of Christ—Curate's Sermon under the Trees—A Religious Drama—Good Friday—Portable Pulpit—Heat—Booths—Religious Procession—Simon the Cyrenian—Coutumes—Curate's Sermon—Second Discourse—Sentence Pronounced by Pontius Pilate—Descent from the Cross—Procession of the Angels—Funeral Hymn—The Pesame to the Virgin—Sermon—"Sweet Kitty Clover"—Music in Mexico—Anecdote.

On Holy Thursday we went early in the morning to Coyohuacan (now pronounced Cuyacan), which is almost a continuation of the village of San Angel; but there are more trees in it, and every house has its garden, or at least its inner court, filled with orange-trees. Here, after the total destruction of the ancient Tenochtitlan, Cortes took up his residence for several months. Here he founded a convent of nuns, and in his testament he desired to be buried in this convent, "in whatever part of the world I may finish my days." The conqueror's last wishes in this respect were not held sacred. At the time of the conquest, Coyohuacan, together with Tacubaya, etc., stood upon the margin of the Lake of Tezcuco; most of the houses built within the water upon stakes, so that the canoes entered by a low door. This was undoubtedly the favourite retreat of Cortes, and it is now one of the prettiest villages near Mexico. Its church is wonderfully handsome; one of the finest village churches we have yet seen.

One of the prettiest places in the village belongs to an order of monks called the *Padres Camilos*. It consists of a house and garden, where the monks go by turns to enjoy the country air. Comfortable padres! There is one room looking into the garden, and opening into a walk bordered by rose-bushes, which is such a place for a siesta; cool, retired, fragrant. A hammock with a mattress on it is slung across the room, and here the good padre may lie, with one eye opened to the roses, and the other closed in inward meditation. However, its whole merit consists in being cleanly and neatly kept, for it is a large, empty house, and the garden, so called, is little more than a pasture-field, with nice gravel-walks cut through it, bordered with fine rose-bushes, and beautified by a clear fountain.

We went to the A——'s house, which is halfway between San Angel and Coyohuacan; the Señora A—— driving me herself in an open carratella with white *frisones* (northern horses), which, compared with the spirited little Mexican steeds, look gigantic. We went first to see the church, which was brilliantly illuminated, and ornamented with loads of flowers and fruit (especially oranges), and thronged with ragged lepéros and blanketed Indians. We then set off, to endeavour, if possible, to find a place in the crowd, who had hurried off to see *el prendimiento* (the taking of Christ), and to hear the curate preach an appropriate sermon in a portable pulpit, amongst the trees.

We made our way through the patient, bronzed and blanketed crowd, not without sundry misgivings as to the effects of *evil communication;* and at length reached the procession, all ranged on the grass under the trees, in a pretty and secluded little grove; in two long rows fronting each other; each person carrying a lamp surmounted by a plume of coloured feathers, very ingeniously made of coloured spun glass. They were all dressed in the costume of Pharisees, Jews, Romans, etc. The image of the Saviour was shortly after carried through on a platform, to the sound of music, followed by the eleven disciples, and was placed in a kind of bower amongst the trees, supposed to give a representation of the garden of Gethsemane. A portable pulpit, covered with shining stuff, was carried in, and placed beneath a tree just outside of this enclosure, and soon after, the curate arrived, and mounted into his place. A number of little ragged boys, who had climbed up on the very topmost branches of the trees, to have a good view, were *piked* down with lances by the Jews, notwithstanding their seemingly just remonstrances that they were doing no harm; but when the Jews observed in answer to their "Que hacemos?" "What are we doing?"—"The Señor Cura will be angry;" —they tumbled down one on the top of the other like ripe apples, and then stood watching for the first convenient opportunity of slipping up again.

The curate began his sermon by an account of the sufferings and persecution of Christ; of the causes and effects of his death, of the sinfulness of the Jews, etc. He talked for about half an hour, and his sermon was simple enough and adapted to his audience. He described the agony of Christ when in the garden to which he often resorted with his disciples, and the treachery of Judas who knew the place, and who *"having received a band of men and officers from the chief priests and pharisees, cometh thither with lanterns and torches and weapons."* As he went on describing the circumstances minutely, one who represented the spy, with a horrible mask like a pig's face, was seen looking through the trees where the Saviour was concealed; and shortly after, Judas, his face covered with a black crape, and followed by a band of soldiers, glided through stealthily. "Now," said the curate, "observe what the traitor does. He hath given them a sign, saying, *'Whomsoever I shall kiss, that same is he—hold him fast.'* He goes—he approaches the sacred person of the Lord." Here Judas went forward and embraced the Saviour. "It is done!" cried the preacher. "The horrible act of treachery is completed. *And forthwith he came to Jesus, and said, Hail, Master, and kissed him. But now, Jesus knowing all things that should come upon him, went forth and said unto them, Whom seek ye? They answered him, Jesus of Nazareth. Jesus saith unto them, I am he."* As the curate said these words, they all fell prostrate on the ground. "Mark," cried he, "the power of the Word! They came out to take him with swords and with staves, but at the sound of the Divine Word, they acknowledge the power of God, and fall at his feet. But it is only for a moment. Behold, now they bind him, they buffet him, they smite him with the palms of their hands, they lead him away to the high priest."

All this was enacted in succession, though sometimes the curate was obliged to repeat the same things several times before they recollected what to do. "And already, in anticipation of the iniquitous sentence, behold what is written." This alluded to a paper fastened upon a pole, which a man held above the heads of the crowd, and on which was written, "Jesus of Nazareth, King of the Jews, condemned to death by Pontius Pilate, President of Upper Galilee."

And now, escorted by Judas and the multitude, the Saviour was borne through the crowd, in conclusion of the *prendimiento.* The curate wound up his discourse by an exhortation to abstain from sin, which had been the cause of this awful event. I regret to state that at this very moment, a man poked his hand into A——'s pocket, who turned very sharply round, and asked him what he wanted; "Nada, Señorito," (Nothing, sir,) said he, with an innocent smile, showing two rows of teeth like an ivory railing, but at the same time disappearing pretty swiftly amongst the crowd, who now all began to move, and to follow the procession, the band striking up a *galope*. In the evening we returned to San Angel, and visited the lighted churches there. As it was late when we entered the *parroquia* (parish church), the lights were nearly all extinguished, and a few alone of the devout were still kneeling before a figure of our Saviour in chains. . . .

On Good Friday we set off early for Coyohuacan, though rather afraid of the sun, which at present, in the middle of the day, is insupportable, and even by ten o'clock disagreeable. The whole enclosure round the church, and to a great distance beyond it, was covered with people, and there were even a few carriages full of well-dressed persons, who had come from the different neighbouring haciendas; amongst others, the family of the Marquesa de Vivanco. The padre Yturalde, who has some reputation for eloquence, was expected to preach three sermons at Coyohuacan that day, besides one in the village of Mizcuaque. We found that one sermon was just concluded. By the time we arrived the sun was pouring down his beams like molten lead. Our carriage was open, and under every tree was a crowd, so there were small hopes of finding shade. Women were selling fruit; and booths with ices and *chia* were erected all down the lane leading from the church. At last, however, a little room was made, and seats were placed for us close to the pulpit, and under a tree.

The image of the Saviour was now carried forwards on a platform, with the heavy cross appearing to weigh him down; and on the same platform was Simon, the Cyrenian, assisting him to bear the weight. The Cyrenian was represented by an old man, with hair white as snow, dressed in scarlet cloth; who, in a stooping posture, and without once moving his body, was carried about for hours in the whole force of the sun, the rays pouring down upon his uncovered head. For a long while we had believed him to be a wooden figure dressed up, and when he came near he greatly excited our surprise and compassion. If he survives this day's work it will be a miracle. I can now almost give faith to ——'s assertion, that in some of the villages the man who represents Judas actually hangs himself, or is hanged upon a tree! The Saviour was dressed in crimson velvet, with the crown of thorns; and a figure of the Virgin, in deep mourning, was carried after him by Indian women.

The procession consisted of the same men on horseback as we had seen on foot the preceding day; of the Spy, the Pharisees, the Jews, the Betrayer, and the mob. Some had helmets and feathers, and armour. Some wore wreaths of green and gold leaves. One very good-looking man, with long curls and a gold crown, and a splendid mantle of scarlet and gold, was intended for a Roman. By his crown he probably meant to personify the Roman Cæsar. The sermon, or rather the discourse of the padre, was very good, and appeared to be extempore. He made an address to the Virgin, who was carried by and led up to the pulpit, and another to the Saviour, during which time the audience was breathlessly attentive, notwithstanding the crying of children and the barking of dogs. It was supposed that they were now leading Christ before the judgment-seat of Pilate, and the next scene was to be the delivery of the sentence.

When the curate's discourse was finished, the procession went on; the Indian women began to sell their nuts and oranges, and the band struck up an air in the distance, to which, when last I heard it, Ducrow's horses were dancing! We, in a fiery sun, which made its way through our mantillas, now proceeded to search for a convenient place from which to hear the padre's next sermon, and to see the next scene in the sacred drama. The padre, who was walking under the shade of a lilac silk parasol, insisted upon resigning it to me. The Señora —— did not seem to feel the heat at all. At last, in order to avoid the crowd, we got up on the low azotea of a house, beside which the pulpit was placed; but here the sun was overwhelming.

The padre's sermon was really eloquent in some passages, but lasted nearly an hour, during which time we admired the fortitude of the unhappy Cyrenian, who was performing a penance of no ordinary kind. The sun darted down perpendicularly on the back of his exposed head, which he kept bent downwards, maintaining the same posture the whole time, without flinching or moving. Before the sermon was over we could stand the heat no longer, and went in under cover. I felt as if my brains were melted into a hot jelly. We emerged upon hearing that the procession was again moving towards the pulpit, where it shortly after formed itself into two lines. In a few moments a man with a plumed helmet, mounted on a fiery horse, galloped furiously through the ranks, holding a paper on the point of his lance, the sentence pronounced by Pontius Pilate.

Arrived at the pulpit, he handed it up to the priest, who received it with a look of horror, opened it, tried to read it, and threw it on the ground with an air of indignation. The messenger galloped back more furiously than he came, and his horse bolting at the end of the lines, occasioned a laugh amongst the spectators. Then followed the parting address to the Saviour, whose bearers now brought him up to the pulpit, followed by the mournful figure of the Virgin. Reflections on the event concluded this act.

We returned in the afternoon, to see the descent from the cross, which was to be performed within the church. The church was crowded, and a black curtain hung before the altar. The padre now recapitulated all that had taken place, and described the Saviour's parting with his mother at the foot of the cross, addressing the Virgin who stood in her sable robes not far from the altar, and interrupting his sermon to pray for her intercession with her Divine Son. I observed all the women in tears as he described the Virgin's grief, the torments of the crucifixion, the indignities that the Saviour had suffered. All at once he exclaimed in a loud voice, "Draw back the veil, and let us behold him!" The curtain was drawn, and the Saviour crucified appeared. Then the sobs of the women broke forth. They clasped their hands, beat their breasts and groaned, while the soldiers who stood below the cross clashed their swords, and one of them struck the body with a lance. At the same time the Virgin bowed her head, as if in grief. Unfortunately I was near enough to see how this was effected, which peep behind the scenes greatly diminished the effect.

Then the soldiers mounted a ladder near the crucifix, and took down the body, to bear it away. As it came by the pulpit, the priest seized the hands, and showed the marks of the nails, at the same time breaking out into exclamations of grief. The soldiers stood below, impatiently clashing their swords; the women sobbed violently; the procession passed on, and we returned to the A——'s house.

In the evening the "Procession of the Angels" took place. Figures dressed in silk and gold, with silver wings, were carried by on platforms to the sound of music. The body of the Saviour lay in a sort of glass hearse, carried by men chanting a dirge, and followed by the Virgin. This procession was really pretty, but had an odd, unnatural effect amongst the fresh green trees, the smell of incense mingling with the fragrance of the flowers, and the gaudy silk and gold and plumes of feathers gilded by the soft setting sun, as they flashed along. I climbed up an old stone cross near the church, and had a good view. Everything looked gaudy when near; but as the procession wound along under the broken arches and through the green lanes, and the music came fainter upon the ear, and the beating of drums and the tolling of bells and the mournful chant were all blended into one faint and distant harmony, the effect was beautiful. I thought of the simple service of the Scottish kirk, and of the country-people coming out after the sermon, with their best Sunday gowns on, and their serious, intelligent faces, discussing the merits of their minister's discourse; and wondered at the contrasts in the same religion. . . .

As the evening was cool and pleasant we walked through the fields to the church of La Concepcion, where the procession was to pass, and sat down on the grass till we heard it coming. As the body was carried by, all went on their knees. At night commenced the *pesame*, or condolence to the Virgin, in the church. She stood on her shrine, with her head bowed down; and the hymns and prayers were all addressed to her, while the sermon, preached by another *cura*, was also in her honour. I plead guilty to having been too sleepy to take in more than the general tenour of the discourse. The musicians seemed to be playing "Sweet Kitty Clover," with variations. If Sweet Kitty Clover is genuine Irish, as who can doubt, how did these Indians get hold of it? Did Saint Patrick go round from the Emerald Isle by way of Tipperary? But, if he had, would he not have killed the *alacrans,* and *chicaclinos,* and *coralillos,* and *vinagrillos?* This requires consideration.

In the *Ora pro nobis,* we were struck with the fineness of the rustic voices. But music in this country is a sixth sense. It was but a few days before leaving Mexico, that, sitting alone at the open window, enjoying the short twilight, I heard a sound of distant music; many voices singing in parts, and coming gradually nearer. It sounded beautiful, and exactly in unison with the hour and the scene. At first I concluded it to be a religious procession; but it was not a hymn—the air was gayer. When the voices came under the window, and rose in full cadence, I went out on the balcony to see to whom they belonged. It was the *forçats*, returning from their work to the Acordada! guarded by soldiers, their chains clanking in measure to the melody, and accompanied by some miserable-looking women.

We left the church feeling very tired and sleepy, and walked towards the booths, where, in the midst of flowers and evergreens, they were still selling ices, and lemonade and *chia.*

We sat down to rest in the cleanest of these leafy bowers, and then returned to Coyohuacan. There was no drunkenness, or quarrelling, or confusion of any sort. An occasional hymn, rising in the silence of the air, or the distant flashing of a hundred lights, alone gave notice that the funeral procession of the Saviour had not yet halted for the night; but there was no noise, not even mirth. Everything was conducted with a sobriety befitting the event that was celebrated. That some of the curate's horses were stolen that night, is only a proof that bad men were out, and took the opportunity of his absence from home to plunder his stables. We were told an anecdote concerning Simon the Cyrenian, which is not bad. A man was taken up in one of the villages as a vagrant, and desired by the justice to give an account of himself—to explain why he was always wandering about, and had no employment. The man, with the greatest indignation, replied, "No employment! I am substitute Cyrenian at Coyohuacan in the Holy Week!" That is to say, he was to be substituted in the Cyrenian's place, should anything occur to prevent that individual from representing the character.

LETTER THE FORTIETH

Balloon—San Bartolo—Indian Women—A Beauty—Different Castes—Indians—Their Character, etc.—Those of Noble Race —Ball at the French Minister's—Abecilta—Danger of Walking Unattended—Shooting Party—A Murder—Robbery of a Farmhouse—Discomfited Robber Captain—The "Zambos"— Letters and Visitors—Country Life in Mexico.

23rd April.

We went to Mexico yesterday to see a balloon ascend from the Plaza de Toros, with an aëronaut and his daughter; French people, I believe. The scene was really beautiful. The plaza was filled with well-dressed people, and all the boxes crowded with ladies in full toilet. The president was there with his staff, and there were two bands of music. The day was perfectly brilliant, and the streets crowded with handsome carriages, many of them open. The balloon swayed itself up and down in the midst of the plaza like a living thing. Everything seemed ready for the ascent, when it was announced that there was a hole in the balloon, and that, consequently, there could be no ascent that day. The people bore their disappointment very good-humouredly, although it was conjectured that the *air traveller* had merely proposed to himself to get their money, without the slightest intention of performing his voyage. One amusing circumstance was, that some penny-a-line rhymer had written an account of it in verse beforehand, giving a most grandiloquent account of the ascent of the balloon; and when we came out, the plaza was full of men selling these verses, which the people were all buying and reading with roars of laughter.

The first of May being *San Felipe*, there will be a ball at the French Minister's, to which we shall probably go.

25th.—We have just returned from a ride to San Bartolo, an Indian village, four leagues from this, where we went with a large party, some on horses, some on asses, others on mules, and one adventurous Jehu driving himself in a four-wheeled carriage, with a pair of horses, over a road formed of ruts, stones, holes, and rocks, where, I will venture to say, no carriage ever made its appearance before. Even the horses and asses got along with difficulty. In spite of large straw hats and green veils, we were burnt the colour of red Indians. In the middle of the day we find the sun intolerable at present, and, owing to the badness of the roads, we did not reach our destination until twelve or one o'clock.

San Bartolo is a small, scattered Indian village, with a church, and is remarkable for a beautiful spring of water, that jets cold and clear from the hard rock, as if Moses had but just smote it; for its superb tall pine-trees; for the good looks and cleanness of the Indian women, who are for ever washing their long hair in the innumerable clear streamlets formed by the spring; and for a view of Mexico, which is particularly favourable, owing to the thick, dark screen of pine wood in the foreground, and the distinct view of the Laguna. Our dinner was carried by Indians, who had trotted off with it at daydawn; but who had taken the wrong road, and did not arrive till long after us. We dined under the pine-trees by the side of the stream, but surrounded by crowds of gaping Indians, in too close vicinity to be agreeable. Some of the young women were remarkably handsome, with the most beautiful teeth imaginable, laughing and talking in their native tongue at a great rate, as they were washing in the brooks, some their hair and others their clothes. The men looked as dirty as Indians generally do, and by no means on a level with these handsome damsels, who are so much superior to the common race of Indians near Mexico, that one would think they had some intermixture of Spanish blood in their veins. A sister of the woman who takes charge of the hacienda where we live, is one of the most beautiful creatures I ever beheld. Large eyes, with long dark lashes, black hair nearly touching the ground, teeth like snow, a dark but glowing complexion, a superb figure, with fine arms and hands, and small beautifully-formed feet. All that is best of Indian and Spanish, "of dark and bright," seems united in her. C––n says he has seen peasant women in Andalusia in the same style of beauty, and quite as handsome. She is only nineteen. Such beauties as these startle one every now and then in some remote village. She belongs, no doubt, to the *mestizos*—the descendants of whites and Indians, the handsomest race in Mexico.

You ask if the castes in Mexico are distinct. There are seven supposed to be so. 1st, the Gachupinos, or Spaniards born in Europe; 2nd, the Creoles, that is, whites of European family born in America; 3rd, the Mestizos; 4th, the Mulattoes, descendants of whites and negroes, of whom there are few; 5th, the Zambos, descendants of negroes and Indians, the ugliest race in Mexico; 6th, the Indians; and 7th, the remains of the African negroes.

Of pure Indians, Humboldt in his day calculated that there existed two millions and a half in New Spain (without counting mestizos), and they are, probably, very little altered from the inferior Indians, as Cortes found them. The principal families perished at the time of the conquest. The priests, sole depositaries of knowledge, were put to death; the manuscripts and hieroglyphical paintings were burnt, and the remaining Indians fell into that state of ignorance and degradation, from which they have never emerged. The rich Indian women preferred marrying their Spanish conquerors to allying themselves with the degraded remnant of their countrymen; poor artisans, workmen, porters, etc., of whom Cortes speaks as filling the streets of the great cities, and as being considered little better than beasts of burden; nearly naked in *tierra caliente,* dressed pretty much as they now are in the temperate parts of the country; and everywhere with nearly the same manners, and habits, and customs, as they now have, but especially in the more distant villages where they have little intercourse with the other classes. Even in their religion, Christianity, as I observed before, seems to be formed of the ruins of their mythology; and all these festivities of the church, these fireworks, and images, and gay dresses, harmonize completely with their childish love of show, and are, in fact, their greatest source of delight. To buy these they save up all their money, and when you give a penny to an Indian child, it trots off to buy crackers, as another would to buy candy. Attempts have been made by their curates to persuade them to omit the celebration of certain days, and to expend less in the ceremonies of others, but the indignation and discontent which such proposals have caused, have induced them to desist in their endeavours.

Under an appearance of stupid apathy they veil a great depth of cunning. They are grave and gentle and rather sad in their appearance, when not under the influence of pulque; but when they return to their villages in the evening, and have taken a drop of comfort, their white teeth light up their bronze countenances like lamps, and the girls especially make the air ring with their laughter, which is very musical. I think it is Humboldt who says that their smile is extremely gentle, and the expression of their eyes very severe. As they have no beard, if it were not for a little moustache, which they frequently wear on the upper lip, there would be scarcely any difference between the faces of men and women.

The Indians in and near the capital are, according to Humboldt, either the descendants of the former labourers, or are remains of noble Indian families, who, disdaining to intermarry with their Spanish conquerors, preferred themselves to till the ground which their vassals formerly cultivated for them. It is said that these Indians of noble race, though to the vulgar eye undistinguishable from their fellows, are held in great respect by their inferior countrymen. In Cholula, particularly, there are still caciques with long Indian names; also in Tlascala—and though barefoot and ragged, they are said to possess great hidden wealth. But it is neither in or near the capital that we can see the Indians to perfection in their original state. It is only by travelling through the provinces that we can accomplish this; and should the lateness of the season oblige us to remain here any time after another minister arrives, we may probably take a longer journey in some different direction from *tierra caliente*, where we may see some tribes of the indigenous Mexicans. Certainly no visible improvement has taken place in their condition since the independence. They are quite as poor and quite as ignorant, and quite as degraded as they were in 1808, and if they do raise a little grain of their own, they are so hardly taxed that the privilege is as nought.

May 2nd.—We returned from Mexico this morning, having gone in to attend the ball given at the French Minister's, on the day of Louis Philippe. It was very pretty, and we stayed till it was very late. We met with such a cordial reception from all our friends, whom we have not seen for a month, that we are tempted to believe ourselves as much missed in Mexico as they say we are. The Señora L—— and the E——s were amongst the best dressed Mexican ladies last night; the latter in white crape and diamonds, and the other in black blonde over rose-colour, also with diamonds. The Señora A——, who went with us, looked very pretty in a white blonde dress, with a small black velvet turban rolled round with large diamonds and pearls. There were a great number of small crimson velvet turbans, and an amazing number of black blonde dresses. There were certainly some very pretty women. The *corps diplomatique* went in uniform.

7th.—Abecilta, a favourite Spanish actor, died a few days ago, and, as C——n took several boxes on the night of a play given for the benefit of his widow, we went in to the theatre on Saturday last. We are now looking out for another house in Mexico, for when the rainy season begins we shall find this too far from the city for C——n, who is obliged to be there constantly.

We ventured to take a walk alone yesterday morning through the lanes, down to San Angel and Coyohuacan, for which piece of imprudence we were severely reprehended, and to-day it appears that two women had been robbed and ill-treated on the road near here; so we are too ready to subscribe to the renewal of our sentence of imprisonment in the house and orchard, when we have no gentlemen with us; but it must be confessed that it takes greatly from the charms of a country life, not to be able to walk out fearlessly. . . .

The quietness and stillness of this place is incredible. There is actually not a sound in the air; not a sight but a ragged Indian. The garden is in great beauty. The apricots are ripe and abundant. The roses are in full blow; and there is a large pomegranate-tree at the gate of the orchard, which is one mass of ponçeau blossom. It is much warmer in the middle of the day this summer than it was last.

We spent a pleasant day lately at a great hacienda a few leagues from this, belonging to a Spanish millionaire, on occasion of a shooting party. We went there to breakfast, and afterwards set off on horseback, sitting sideways on *men's* saddles, to see the sport. It would have been very agreeable but for the heat. The sportsmen were not very successful;—saw a flight of rose-coloured flamingoes, who sailed high over their heads, unhurt; killed some very handsome birds called *trigueros*, with beautiful yellow plumage, and some ducks. The trigueros are considered a delicacy. We rode with the administrador all round the estate, which is very productive and profitable. He told us that they sell in Mexico, annually, fifteen thousand dollars' worth of corn, and ten thousand dollars' worth of milk, sending in this produce in canoes, by the canal which passes this way. We dismounted from our horses in a green meadow covered with daisies and buttercups, which, from association, I prefer to the tuberoses and pomegranate blossom, which now adorn the gardens. The Señor —— gave us an excellent dinner *à l'Espagnole;* after which I made an attempt to fire at some birds which shook their tails, and flew away in the most contemptuous manner. . . .

The new Secretary of Legation, Señor T——, and the new attaché, Señor G——, have just arrived in Mexico.

10th.—The Baron and Madame de ——, with their secretary,

the Count de B——, came out yesterday morning unexpectedly to breakfast, and spent the day with us.

13th.—We went out with C——n last evening, to take a walk; when a man rushed by us in a state of great agitation, and on going further we met some workmen, who told us that an Indian labourer had stabbed a man in the next field, and that he had died before a padre could be procured. We heard the cries of his wife and children, and A——, crossing the ditch that bordered the field, went to see the man. He was a master-workman, or director, and had found fault with one of the men for his idleness. High words ensued, and the labourer (probably the man who had passed us) drew his knife and stabbed him. He was lying stone dead, with his hand half cut through in his efforts to defend himself. A—— asked an administrador, who was standing near, what would be done to the guilty man. "Probably nothing," said he, shrugging his shoulders; "we have no judges to punish crime." This rencounter, as you may believe, took away from us all inclination to pursue our rambles.

There is a pretty farmhouse in the village, in which we took shelter the other day from a shower of rain. The farmers are civil and respectful, a superior kind of people, with good manners rather above their station. The daughters are good-looking, and the house clean and neat. One of the girls gave me an account of a nocturnal visit which the robbers paid them last winter. She showed me the little room where she was alone and asleep, when her mother and sister, who slept in the chamber adjoining, being wakened by the breaking in of their door, sprang out of the window to make their escape, and she was left in the house alone. She jumped out of bed and bolted the door (her room had no other egress), and there she held a parley with these night visitors, promising to unlock every drawer and closet, if they would wait till she put on her clothes, and would do her no personal injury. The agreement was made, and they kept their word. They cleared the house of every article it contained, leaving nothing but the blanket in which the girl had wrapped herself. All their clothes, household utensils, money, everything was carried off with astonishing precision; and having made her swear not to move till they had time to leave the village, they paid her no further attention. The other women, who had given the alarm, found no one inclined to move in the middle of the night against a party whose numbers their fears had probably magnified.

The administrador gave us an amusing account this evening

of a visit which a band of no less than thirty robbers once ventured to pay this strong and well-defended hacienda. He was living there alone, that is, without the family, and had just barred and bolted everything for the night, but had not yet locked the outer gate, when looking out from his window into the courtyard by moonlight, he saw a band of robbers ride up to the door. He instantly took his measures, and seizing the great keys, ran up the little stair that leads to the azotea, locking the gate by which he passed, and, calling to the captain by name (for the robbers were headed by a noted chieftain), requested to know what he wanted at that hour of the night. The captain politely begged him to come downstairs and he would tell him; but the agent, strong in the possession of his great keys, and well knowing the solidity of the iron-barred windows, continued his parley in a high tone. The captain rode round, examined everything with a practised eye, and found that it would require a regular siege to make good his entry. He threatened, entreated, observed that he would be content with a small sum of money, but all in vain. There stood the sturdy administrador on the housetop, and there sat the captain on his horse below, something like the fox and the crow; but the agent with the keys was wiser than the crow and her cheese, for no cajoling would induce him to let them out of his grasp; and worse than all, shooting him would have done them no good. At last the captain, finding himself entirely outwitted, took off his hat, politely wished the agent a very good night, drew off his men and departed.

Another time, being also alone, he was attacked in broad daylight by two men who came under pretence of buying pulque; but having time to get hold of a sword, he overpowered one, which frightened the other, upon which they both began to laugh, and assured him it was mere experiment to see what he would do—a perfect jest, which he pretended to believe, but advised them not to try it again, as it was too good a joke to be repeated. Señor —— pointed out to us the other day a well-known robber captain, who was riding on the high road with a friend. He had the worst-looking, most vulgar, and most villainous face I ever saw; a low-lived and most unpoetic-looking ruffian; fat and sallow.

We saw a horribly ugly man to-day, and were told he was a *lobo*, the name given here to the *Zambos;* who are the most frightful human beings that can be seen. La Güera Rodriguez told us that on an estate of hers, one woman of that race was in the habit of attending church, and that she was so fearfully hideous, the priest had been obliged to desire her to remain at home, because she distracted the attention of the congregation!

We spent yesterday at the house of the —— minister at San Angel, where he gave us and the —— minister and his family a beautiful breakfast. How consistent everything looks in a good English house! so handsome without being gaudy—the plate so well cleaned, the servants so well trained.

June 8th.—We were sitting under an apple-tree the other day, trying to tame the fiercest little deer I ever saw, who was butting and kicking with all his might, when a large packet of letters was brought us, the reading of which insured us an agreeable afternoon. We continue to lead a very quiet life here, occasionally taking a short ride in the evening, and making acquaintance with the neighbouring villages, the prettiest of which is Tesapan, a most rural and leafy spot, where there are fine fruit trees, plenty of water, and good-looking peasant-girls. Sometimes we go to San Antonio to see the V——o family; occasionally to San Agustin, where they are preparing for the great fête. We are in treaty for a house in Mexico, having now given up all idea of passing through Vera Cruz this summer. We are in hopes of having that of the late Marquesa de San Roman, who died some time ago, but the delays that take place in any transaction connected with a house in Mexico, and the difficulty of obtaining a decisive answer, are hard trials of patience.

We generally have a number of visitors from Mexico on Sunday, and those who come in carriages may be considered as real friends, for they decidedly risk their necks, not to mention their carriage-springs at a *bad bit* on the road, which the owners, who are Indians, will not allow any one to mend for them, and will not mend themselves. When we reach it, we are obliged regularly to get out of the carriage, go about a hundred yards on foot, and then remain in much anxiety at the top of the hill, till we see whether or not the carriage arrives unbroken, which it rarely does. A few dollars would make it perfectly safe.

Our chief visitors during the week are from the Carmelite convent of San Angel. The old *padre guardian* is about eighty. Each convent has a prior, but the padre guardian exercises authority over all the convents of his order as well as over his own.

There are many excellent houses and fine gardens in San Angel, and a number of families from Mexico are now there for the season. Tacubaya and all the environs are beginning to be occupied, and Mexico looks warm and deserted. But there are so few incidents in our quiet life among the magueys, that I shall write no more till we return from San Agustin after the fête. If you wish to hear how we pass our time, you must know that we generally rise about six, and go out into the orchard and stroll about, or sit down with a book in a pleasant arbour at the end of one of the walks, which is surrounded by rose-bushes, and has a little stream of water running past it. Nor do we ever enter the orchard unarmed with a long pole, for its entrance is guarded by a flock of angry geese, hissing like the many-headed Hydra that watched over the golden apples of the Hesperides. At eight we breakfast, and by nine the sun is already powerful enough to prevent us from leaving the house. We therefore sit down to read or write, and do occasionally take a game at billiards. C——n generally rides to Mexico, but if not, goes up to the azotea with a book, or writes in his study until four o'clock, when we dine.

After dinner we walk into the village, if we have any attendant esquire; if not, we go to the azotea and see the sun set behind the volcanoes, or walk in the garden till it is dark, and then sit down in the front of the house, and look at the lights in Mexico. Then we have tea or chocolate—and the candles are lighted—and the last Indian workman has gone off to his village—and the house is barred in—and we sit down to read, or write or talk, or sometimes we play billiards by lamplight. And then indeed the silence and the solitude make us feel as if the world were completely shut out. I never experienced such perfect stillness. Even the barking of a dog sounds like an event. Therefore, expect no amusing letters from this place; for though we are very comfortable, there are no incidents to relate. The Indians come in the morning to drink pulque, (which, by the way, I now think excellent, and shall find it very difficult to live without!) a little child from the village brings us some bouquets of flowers, which the Indians have a pretty way of arranging in a pineapple or pyramidal form; the Chinese cook, with his little slits of eyes, passes by with meat and fruit which he has been buying at the market of San Angel; the prior saunters in to see how we are—a chance visitor comes on horseback from Mexico, with a long sword by his side, as if he were going to fight the Saracens. And excepting that a padre came last Sunday and said mass to us in the pretty little chapel of the hacienda, which saved us the trouble of going down to the village, and, moreover, took chocolate with us afterwards, there has been nothing to vary the usual routine of our country life.

LETTER THE FORTY-FIRST

*Gambling—Fête at San Agustin—Breakfast at San Antonio—
Report—Cock-fight—Ladies—Private Gambling—A* Vaca—
The Calvario—*Bonnets—Dinner—Evening Ball—Mingling of
Classes—Copper Tables—Dresses and Decorations—Indian
Bankers, Male and Female—Decorum—Habit—Holders of
Banks—Female Gambler—Robbery—Anecdote—Bet—*Casa de
Moneda—*Leave San Angel—Celebration—Address—Cross
and Diploma—Reply—Presentation of a Sword—Discourses
and Addresses—Reflections.*

10th June.

One year since I last wrote of San Agustin! An entire year has
fled swiftly away on rushing pinions, to add its unit to the rolling century. And again, on a bright morning in June, we set
off for the hospitable San Antonio, where we were invited to
breakfast and to pass the night on the second day of the fête.
We found a very brilliant party assembled; the family with all
its branches, the Ex-Minister Cuevas, with his handsome
sister-in-law, La Güera Rodriguez, with one of her beautiful
granddaughters (daughter of the Marquis of G——e), now
making her first appearance in Mexico, and various other
agreeable people. The first day of the fête, a rumour was
afloat that an attack was to be made on the banks by the
federal party; that they expected to procure the sinews of war
to the extent of a million of dollars, and then intended to raise
a *grito* in Mexico, taking advantage of the temporary absence
of the president and his officers. The plan seemed rather feasi-
ble, and the report, true or false, was current yesterday; but
if there was any truth in it, the discovery has been made in
time, for nothing has occurred. San Agustin appeared even
gayer and more crowded than it was last year. We spent the
day at the E——s, and went with them to a box in the plaza
to see the cock-fight, which I had no particular pleasure, I
must confess, in witnessing again, but went for the sake of
those who had not seen it before. The general *coup d'œil* was
exceeding gay, and the improvement in the dress of the ladies
since last year very striking. There were neither diamonds nor

pearls among the most fashionable. The bonnets were chiefly Parisian, as were many of the gowns. One box looked a veritable parterre of flowers. The ladies of our party wore dresses and bonnets as simple, fresh, and elegant as could be seen in any part of the world. A young and titled heiress, newly arrived from her distant estates, wore pink satin with a white hat and feathers, and we observed, that according to the ancient San Agustin fashion, she changed her dress four or five times a day. But the ladies may dress and may smile, and may look their very best; they are little thought of this day, in comparison with the one all-powerful, all-pervading object. It is even whispered that one cause of the more than usual crowd at San Agustin this year, is that many failures are expected in mercantile houses, and that the heads of these houses or their agents are here on the desperate hope of retrieving their falling fortunes.

A good deal of play on a small scale goes on in the private houses, among those who do not take much part in the regular gambling; but all are interested more or less; even strangers, even ladies, even ourselves. Occasional news is brought in, and received with deep interest of the state of the banks, of the losses or gains of the different individuals, or of the result of the *vacas,* (a sort of general purse into which each puts in two or three ounces,) by different stragglers from the gambling-houses, who have themselves only ventured a few ounces, and who prefer the society of ladies to that of the Monte players. These are generally foreigners, and chiefly English.

We found the road to the *Calvario,* where, as usual, there was a ball in the afternoon, blocked up with carriages, and the hill itself covered with gay figures; who were dancing as well as the tremendous crowd would permit. This was really tolerably republican. The women generally were dressed as the better classes of Mexicans used to be, years ago, and not so many years neither (and as many in the country, still are) in blonde dresses, with very short petticoats, open silk stockings and white satin shoes; and such a collection of queer bonnets has probably never been seen since the days when *les Anglaises pour rire* first set foot on Gallic shores. Some were like small steeples, others resembled helmets, some were like sugar-loaves, and most seemed to have been set on, for convenience-sake, all the way out. Amidst these there was a good sprinkling of pretty Herbaults and Paris dresses, but they belonged to the more fashionable classes. The scene was amusing from its variety, but we did not remain long, as it threatened rain. As we looked back, the crowd on the hill presented the appearance of a bed of butterflies dancing with black ants.

We returned to the ——'s to dinner, which was very handsome, and entirely French. There were about twenty-eight persons at table, some of them looked as if they had rather lost than otherwise. After dinner—music and conversation on the events and probabilities of the day, till it was time to dress for the ball at the Plaza. We, however, preferred going to a box, which saves the trouble of dressing, besides being "*de mucho tono*," very fashionable; but when we arrived, not a box was to be had, the crowd was so great, and there were so many people of *tono*, besides ourselves, who had preferred doing the same thing; so we were obliged to content ourselves with retreating to a third row of benches on the floor, after persuading at least a dozen of very good-natured women to turn out, in order to let us in. We were afterwards joined by the —— Minister and his wife. The ball looked very gay, and was prodigiously crowded, and exceedingly amusing.

There were people of all classes; *modistes* and carpenters, shop-boys, tailors, hatters, and hosiers, mingled with all the *haut ton* of Mexico. Every shop-boy considered himself entitled to dance with every lady, and no lady considered herself as having a right to refuse him, and then to dance with another person. The Señora de ——, a most high-bred and dignified person, danced with a stable-boy in a jacket and without gloves, and he appeared particularly gratified at the extraordinary opportunity thus afforded him of holding her white gloves in his brown paws. These fellows naturally select the first ladies as their partners, and, strange as it may seem, there is nothing in their behaviour that the most fastidious can complain of. They are perfectly polite, quiet, and well conducted; and what is more remarkable, go through a quadrille as well as their neighbours. The ball was quietness itself, until near the end, when the wind-instruments were suddenly seized with a fit of economy, the time they were paid for having probably expired, and stopped short in the midst of a waltz; upon which the gentlemen waltzers shouted "*Viento! Viento!*" at the full extent of their voices, clapping their hands, refusing to dance, and entirely drowning the sound of some little jingling guitars, which were patiently twanging on, until the hired sons of Æolus had to resume their labours.

There were some pretty faces among the secondary class of small shopkeepers; but their beauty is not striking, and takes a long time to discover; especially *fagotées* as they are in their overloaded dresses. Amongst the handsomest of the higher classes, were the Señora C——s, and a daughter of the Marquis G——e.

On the third night of the fête, C——n and I having left the ball-room, about ten o'clock, walked out in the direction of the copper-tables which filled the middle of the square, and were covered with awnings. It is a sight that, once seen, can never be forgotten. Nothing but the pencil of Hogarth, or the pen of Boz, could do justice to the various groups there assembled. It was a gambling *fête champêtre*, conducted on the most liberal scale.

On each table were great mountains of copper, with an occasional sprinkling of silver. There was a profusion of evergreens, small tin lamps dripping with oil, and sloping tallow candles shedding grease upon the board. Little ragged boys, acting as waiters, were busily engaged in handing round pulque and chia in cracked tumblers. There was, moreover, an agreeable tinkling produced from several guitars, and even the bankers condescended to amuse their guests with soothing strains. The general dress of the company consisted of a single blanket, gracefully disposed in folds about the person; so as to show various glimpses of a bronze skin. To this some added a pair of Mexican pantaloons, and some a shirt of a doubtful colour. There were many with large hats, most of which had crowns or parts of crowns, but all affording free entrance to the fresh air. Generally speaking, however, the head was uncovered, or covered only with its native thatching of long, bushy, tangled black hair.

This might be out of compliment to the ladies, of whom there were several, and who ought in politeness to have been mentioned first. Nothing could be simpler than their costume, consisting of a very dirty and extremely torn chemise, with short sleeves, a shorter petticoat, and a pair of shoes, generally of dirty satin: also a reboso, and the long hair hanging down as Eve's golden locks may have done in Paradise. "They call this place a Paradise," a Spanish soldier wrote to his father; "and so I think it is, it is so full of *Adams*."

There was neither fighting, nor swearing, nor high words. I doubt whether there be as much decorum at Crockford's; indeed, they were scrupulously polite to each other. At one table, the banker was an enormously fat gentleman, one half of whose head was bound up with a dirty white handkerchief, over which a torn piece of hat was stuck, very much to one

side. He had a most roguish eye, and a smile of inviting be-
nignity on his dirty countenance. In one hand he held and
tingled a guitar, while he most ingeniously swept in the copper
with the other. By his side sat two wretched-looking women,
with long matted hair, their elbows on the table, and their
great eyes fixed upon the game with an expression of the most
intense anxiety. At another, the *banker* was a pretty little Indian woman, rather clean, comparatively speaking, and who
appeared to be doing business smartly. A man stood near her,
leaning against one of the poles that supported the awning,
who attracted all our attention. He was enveloped in a torn
blanket, his head uncovered, and his feet bare, and was glaring upon the table with his great dark, haggard-looking eyes,
his brown face livid, and his expression bordering on despair.
It needed no one to tell us that on the table was his last stake.
What will such a man do but go upon the road?

I have heard it mentioned as a strong circumstance in favour of the Mexican character, that there is neither noise nor
disturbance in these reunions; none of that uproar and violence
that there would be in an English mob, for example. The fact
is certain, but the inference is doubtful. These people are degraded, and accustomed to endure. They are gentle and cunning, and their passions are not easily roused, at least to open
display; but once awakened, it is neither to uproar that these
passions will be excited, nor by fair fight that they will be as-
suaged. In England, a boxing-match decides a dispute amongst
the lower orders; in Mexico, a knife; and a broken head is
easier mended than a cut throat. Despair must find vent in
some way; and secret murder, or midnight robbery, are the
fatal consequences of this very calmness of countenance, which
is but a mask of Nature's own giving to her Indian offspring.

Another reason for this tranquillity is the *habit* of gambling,
in which they have indulged from childhood, and which has
taught them that neither high words nor violence will restore
a single dollar once fairly lost; and in point of fairness, everything is carried on with the strictest honour, as among gamblers of high degree.

While "high life below stairs" is thus enacting, and these
people are courting fortune in the fresh air, the gentlemanly
gamblers are seated before the green cloth-covered tables, with
the gravity befitting so many cabinet councils; but without
their mystery, for doors and windows are thrown open, and
both ladies and gentlemen may pass in and out, and look on
at the game, if they please. The heaps of ounces look tempt-

ingly, and make it appear a true El Dorado. Nor is there any lack of creature-comforts to refresh the flagging spirits. There are supper-spread tables, covered with savoury meats to appease their hunger, and with generous wines to gladden their hearts; and the gentlemen who surrounded that board seemed to be playing, instead of Monte, an excellent knife and fork.

You must not suppose that those who hold gaming-tables are the less considered on that account; on the contrary, as the banks generally win, they are amongst the richest, and, consequently, the most respected men in Mexico. These bankers are frequently Spaniards, who have found gambling the readiest stepping-stone to fortune. Señor —— explained to me one plan of those who hold the banks, a sort of *hedging*, by which it is next to impossible that they can lose. For example, one of these gentlemen proposes to his friends to take a share in a *vaca*, each contributing a few ounces. Having collected several hundred ounces, they go to play at *his bank*. If they win, he receives his share, of course; and if they lose his bank wins the whole. It is proceeding upon the principle of "Heads I win, tails you lose."

At the tables, few words are spoken. The heaps of gold change masters; but the masters do not change countenance. I saw but one person who looked a little out of humour, and he was a foreigner. The rich man adds to his store, and the poor man becomes a beggar. He is ruined, but "makes no sign."

The ladies who have collected ounces and made purses, send their friends and admirers to the tables to try their luck for them; and in some of the inferior houses, the Señoras of a lower class occasionally try their fortune for themselves. I saw one of these, who had probably lost, by no means "taking it coolly." She looked like an overcharged thunder-cloud; but whether she broke forth in anger or in tears, thunder or rain, we did not stay to see.

In short, it is an all-pervading mania, and as man is "a bundle of habits," the most moral persons in this country (always excepting one or two ladies who express their opinions strongly against it) see nothing in it to condemn, and are surprised at the effect it produces on a stranger; and, indeed, after a few years' residence here, a foreigner almost becomes reconciled to these abuses, by the veil of decorum with which they are covered.

We returned to San Antonio by the brightest possible moonlight, and in perfect safety, it being on the high-road to Mexico, and therefore guarded by soldiers. We heard the next morning, that a nephew of General B——s, who had ventured upon going by a cross-road to his house, at *Mizcuaque*, has been attacked and robbed of his winnings, besides being severely wounded. This being the natural consequence, the *morale* to the story can excite no surprise. The robbers who, in hopes of plunder, flocked down at the time of the fête, like sopilotes seeking carrion, hide themselves among the barren rocks of the *Pedregal*, and render all cross-roads insecure, except with a very strong escort.

An anecdote was related to us this morning, by a member of the cabinet, a striking one amongst the innumerable instances of fortune's caprices. A very rich Spaniard, proprietor of several haciendas, attended the fête at San Agustin, and having won three thousand ounces, ordered the money to be carried in sacks to his carriage, and prepared to return to Mexico along with his wife. His carriage was just setting off, when a friend of his came out of an adjoining house, and requested him to stay to breakfast, to which he agreed. After breakfast, there being a monte table in the house, at which some of his acquaintances were playing, he put down two ounces, and lost. He continued playing and losing, until he had lost his three thousand ounces, which were sent for and transferred to the winners. He still continued playing with a terrible infatuation, till he had lost his whole fortune. He went on blindly, staking one hacienda after another, and property of all sorts, until the sun, which had risen upon him a rich and prosperous man, set, leaving him a beggar! It is said that he bore this extraordinary and sudden reverse with the utmost equanimity. He left a son, whom we have seen at San Agustin, where he earns his livelihood as *croupier* at the gambling-tables.

29th.—No particular occurrence has taken place since the fête; a visit from the new Secretary of Legation and the Attaché, a diplomatic dinner at the —— minister's, much going and coming and writing on the subject of a house in Mexico, a correspondence concerning the sale of our furniture, mules, etc., etc., a good deal of interest excited by a bet between two English gentlemen, as to whether it were possible for one of them to ride from Mexico to San Angel in twenty minutes, which feat he performed, starting from the gate called "*El Niño Perdido*," and reaching the old church of San Angel within the given time; these I think are the most remarkable circumstances that have taken place. We are now in treaty for the furnished apartments of the director of the *Casa de Moneda* (the mint), a great building next the palace, from which upwards of one thousand three hundred millions of coined gold and silver have issued since the beginning of the sixteenth century. The house is a palace in extent and solidity; and the residence of the director is very spacious and handsome, besides having the great advantage of being furnished. We expect to return to Mexico in a few days.

CASA DE MONEDA, 6th July.

Here we are, re-established in Mexico, for a short time at least, and not without difficulty has it been accomplished. We left the country with some regret, as this is the pleasantest time of the year for being there, and everything was looking green and beautiful. We came in, ourselves, in a loaded carriage, and in advance, fourteen asses loaded with boxes, four Indians with ditto, and two enormous loaded carts, one drawn by four, and another by eight mules. We were a regular *caravan*, as our friend the alcalde called us. Imagine the days of packing and unpacking consequent thereupon! . . .

On the 1st of July, the victory gained by the government over the federalist party was celebrated with great éclat. The president was presented with a diamond cross, valued at six thousand dollars, and General Valencia with a splendid jewel-hilted sword of great value. "Yesterday morning," says the newspaper of the day, "a general pealing of the bells and the usual salutes announced to the capital that it was a day of rewards and of universal joy. At twelve o'clock, his Excellency the President of the Republic went to the palace, to fulfil the formality of closing the sessions, and to receive from the hands of the President of the Chamber of Deputies, the diploma and cross of honour mentioned in the decrees of the second of March and second of May of this year. An immense multitude occupied the galleries; and the President, Don J. M. Maria Bravo, addressed his Excellency General Bustamante, in the following speech:

"Citizen General, and illustrious President:—Nations never forget the distinguished services that are done to them, nor fail to reward those heroic actions performed for the common good. Sooner or later they show themselves grateful, and reward as they ought their good and valiant servants. The Mexican nation has not forgotten yours, and its congress has ever borne in mind those which you performed for it at that happy period when the unfortunate hero of Iguala, causing the voice of freedom to resound to the remotest lands of the Mexican territory, gave a terrible lesson to those who wish to subdue weak nations, with no other title than that of strength. You were one of the first and most valiant chiefs, who, placed by his side, assisted in this important and happy work; you it was who showed to the tyrant in the fields of Juchi, Aztcapozalco and others, that the sword of the Mexicans once unsheathed for liberty and justice, fights without softening or breaking; and knows how to triumph over its enemies, even when superior forces oppose it; you it was, in short, who with intrepid valour co-operated in re-establishing a liberty which, torn from the ancient children of the soil, was converted by their oppressors into a hard and shameful tyranny. History has already consecrated her pages to you: she will record to posterity your heroic deeds, and congress has already busied itself in rewarding such interesting services.

"If some Mexicans, erring in their opinions, by a fatality in this country, have disowned them, making an attempt against your personal liberty, notwithstanding the dignity of the first magistrate; trampling upon laws and overturning order; they have at length been obliged to respect you; and your valour, firmness, and decision, have made them preserve the consideration due to an ancient chief of our independence, and to a first magistrate who has known how to set an example of subordination to the laws, and to give with dignity lessons of valour and of honourable conduct.

"A diploma and a cross are the rewards which the sovereign congress has decreed for these services and merits. Do not regard in the one the effaceable characters in which it is written, nor be dazzled by the brilliancy of the other. See in both a proof of your country's gratitude, and engraving it in your soul, continue to give testimonies to your country that she is the first object of your care; that your watchings, fatigues, and labours are dedicated only to procure for her those benefits which may bring about the durable and solid peace that she so much desires, and for which you would, if necessary, sacrifice yourself on her altars.

"Do not forget that to-day she shows herself grateful, and that this is the day decreed by the august national representative body, to put you in possession of the title and insignia which manifests her gratitude. I, in the name of the congress, congratulate you on this fortunate event, and having the honour to fulfil the desire of the sovereign power, place in your hands this diploma of deserving reward from your country, and give you possession of this cross."

His Excellency having received the diploma and cross above mentioned, with his native modesty replied thus:

"In hearing, by the organ of the august national representation, the great encomiums with which it favours me, putting me at the same time in possession of these precious gifts, my soul overflows with ineffable pleasure, and is overwhelmed with the deepest gratitude. My satisfaction and my glory are immense. What could I have done, that thus the generous hand of the representatives of the Mexican people should load me with honours? Have my trifling services been able to fix the attention of the country, on whose altars have been sacrificed so many and such illustrious heroes of liberty? My glory would have been yet greater, had I, like them, descended to the sepulchre, when the sun of victory brightened the existence of this sovereign and independent nation, to the glory of the universe.

"The honours which I receive to-day are certainly great; but I should have preferred them before the never sufficiently mourned catastrophe of the immortal Yturbide. Let us throw a thick veil over so irreparable a loss. It is true that, surviving such great misfortunes, I have been enabled to consecrate my existence and my vigilance to the peace, order, and felicity of this beloved country. But how difficult is the conduct of those who govern in the midst of the conflict of civil dissensions! In these, my conscience has chosen, and my resolution has never vacillated between ignominy and honour. Do I, on this account, deserve the national gratitude and munificence manifested by such distinguished rewards? I return for them to the representatives of the nation my frankest gratitude; fixing my mind only on the grandeur and benevolence of the sovereign power which rewards me in the sacred name of the country. I shall preserve till death these precious objects which render my name illustrious as a soldier and as a supreme magistrate. They will stimulate me more and more every day to all kinds of sacrifices, even to the giving up my life should it be necessary; that I may not be unworthy of the favourable conception and of the recompence with which the worthy representatives of so magnanimous a nation have to-day honoured me. Receive, gentlemen, this frank manifestation of my sentiments, and of my fervent vows for the felicity of the republic, with the most sincere protestations of my eternal gratitude."

"The liveliest emotions of satisfaction" (I still quote from the *Diario*) "followed this expressive discourse. Joy was

painted on every countenance. The frank satisfaction which
every one felt gave to this act a solemnity which words are
incapable of describing. His Excellency, accompanied by the
corporations and by a brilliant and numerous concourse, then
passed to the hall of the court-martial, to put in possession of
his Excellency General D. Gabriel Valencia the sword of honour which the august national representation had granted him,
for his loyal and valiant conduct in the affair of July of 1840.
His Excellency the President began this ceremony by expressing his sentiments to his Excellency the *Gefe de la plana
mayor* (head of the staff), in these terms:

"Citizen General:—In this day, the most flattering of my
life, in which the august representatives of the nation have
just put me in possession of the rewards granted to my small
services, I fulfil the law which imposes upon me the grateful
task of presenting you with the sword of honour, with which
their munificence has also chosen to remunerate yours.

"Receive it as the distinguished reward of your loyalty, and
of the valour with which you fought at that memorable period,
from the 15th to the 26th of July, defending with bravery
the constitution and supreme powers of the Republic. I congratulate myself with you, not doubting that you will always
employ the edge of this steel in defence of the honour, of
the sacred rights, and of the laws of this country. Yes, general,
of this beloved country, to whom we owe all kinds of sacrifices;
yes, of this beloved mother, who now more than ever reclaims
the fraternal union of all her children, to conquer the internal
and external enemies who oppose her felicity and aggrandizement, let us pledge ourselves to correspond thankfully to the
generosity with which the representatives of the nation have
rewarded us, and let us march united in the same path which
honour and duty traced out for us, in that day of honourable
memory for the defenders of the laws. Eternal praise to the
brave soldiers and citizens who co-operated with us in the
establishment of order!"

To which General Valencia replied:—"That a correspond-
ent reward should follow an heroic action, nothing more natural; but to remunerate a service which does not go beyond
the sphere of ordinary things, such as mine in the affair of
the 15th to the 26th of July of 1840, by such a noble distinction as the sword of honour with which your Excellency has
deigned to gird me, in the name of the National Congress,
of this the magnanimity of the sovereignty is alone capable;
and so it is that I remain annihilated by a present worthy of

the ages of the Roman Senate and Republic. What did I do, your Excellency, in those days, that any one of my countrymen would not have done better? Nothing, sir; so that, in receiving this sword of honour, my confusion equals my doubt as to my place in the gratitude of the congress which has given it to me, of your Excellency who has deigned to present it to me, and of my worthy countrymen who bestowed it that I might wear it.

"In this condition, your Excellency, of content and satisfaction, I can say no more, but that I hope your Excellency will manifest to congress my eternal gratitude; that your Excellency will receive my noble acknowledgments, and my companions the assurance that every time I put it on I shall remember the names of all and each of them who accompanied me on the 15th of July of 1840, together with the pleasure that to them I owe so great a mark of respect."

Amongst the congratulations given to the president, the following "congratulation from his Excellency General Valencia to his Excellency the President, on his receiving the decoration of the cross of honour from congress," is very remarkable. "God said, the first day of the creation of the world, when it was in a state of chaos, '*Let there be light, and there was light.*' *And God saw his work and pronounced it good!* With how much more reason ought the garrison of Mexico to do so every day in which, by any action, the 15th of July 1840 is celebrated—in which, by their strength and heroic valour, that passage of Genesis was politically repeated in this capital. Society arose in chaos. Its president is taken. Authorities no longer exist, and those who ought to save them are converted into their oppressors. '*God said let there be light, and there was light!*' The honourable troops, reunited in the citadel, in the midst of chaos, said 'Let order be re-established—let the supreme magistrate be set at liberty, and let things resume their proper march.' Order *was* re-established, your Excellency was set free, and the political body followed the regular path, without which no society exists. So it is that those worthy troops who thus said, thus undertook, and thus accomplished, now also resemble the Creator of the world (*hoy tambien se asememejan al Criador del mundo*) in his content, when satisfied with his work.

"The cross which has been worthily placed on your Excellency's breast this day, reflects in such a singular manner upon the hearts of the valiant men of that period (*reflecta de un modo tan singular sobre los corazones de los valientes de aquella época*), that their souls are expanded in contemplating it, by the honour which results to them from it.

"May your Excellency be happy one and a thousand times, with such a noble and worthy decoration. Let your Excellency receive in it the sincere congratulations of the garrison of Mexico, which figures in each stone of this cross, like the stars in the firmament."

"This ceremony being concluded, the two rewarded generals presented themselves on the principal balcony of the palace, in front of which passed the brilliant column of honour; at its head marched the commandant-general, Don Valentin Canalizo; and the brilliancy, neatness, and elegance, which all the corps of the garrison displayed, is above all praise. When the regiment had passed, a sumptuous entertainment was served in one of the halls of the Minister of War, in which elegance, good taste, and propriety, rivalled one another; while repeated toasts showed the most sincere joy, united with the most patriotic and fraternal sentiments. Rain having begun to fall at about three in the afternoon, the paséo was on this account not so crowded as might have been expected; nevertheless, the military bands were present, and at six in the evening their Excellencies Generals Bustamante and Valencia having presented themselves there, were received with *vivas* and universal joy.

"At night the chiefs and officers of the *plana mayor* gave a ball in the college of the Mineria; and the theatre of New Mexico dedicated its entertainment to his Excellency the President. Nothing disturbed the joy of this day; one sentiment alone of union and cheerfulness overflowed in the capital, proving to those illustrious generals the unanimous applause with which Mexicans see their country reward the distinguished services of their children, who are so deserving of their love and gratitude."

Notwithstanding the ineffable joy which, according to the *Diario,* is generally felt on this occasion, there are many who doubt the policy of this celebration, at a time when the troops are unpaid—when the soldiers, wounded at the last *pronunciamiento,* are refused their pensions, while the widows and orphans of others are vainly suing for assistance. "At the best," say those who cavil on the subject, "it was a civil war—a war between brothers—a subject of regret and not of glory—of sadness and not of jubilee." As for General Valencia's congratulation to the president, in which he compares the "honourable troops" to the Supreme Being, the re-establishment of order in Mexico to the creation of the world from chaos, it is chiefly incomprehensible. Perhaps he is carried away by his joy and gratitude, and personal affection for Bustamante—perhaps he has taken a leaf from a translation of *Bombastes Furioso*.

One thing is certain: the whole affair had a brilliant appearance; and the handsome carriages, fine horses, gaily-dressed officers and soldiers, together with the military music and the crowds of people collected, produced an imposing effect.

LETTER THE FORTY-SECOND

Italian Opera—Artists, Male and Female—Prima Donna— Lucia de Lammermoor—Some Disappointment—Second Representation—Improvement—Romeo and Giulietta—La Ricci—La Señora Cesari—The Mint—False Coining—Repetition of Lucia—Procession by Night—A Spanish Beauty— Discriminating Audience—A little Too Simple—Gold Embroidery—Santiago—Pilgrims—Old Indian Custom—Soirée —Mexico by Moonlight—Mysterious Figure—Archbishop— Viceroy.

13th July.

We little expected to be still here at the opening of the new Italian opera, and had consequently given up our box. Señor Roca, who went to Italy to bring out the *requisites*, has arrived at the end of a wonderfully short period, with the singers, male and female, the new dresses, decorations, etc.; and the first opera, Lucia de Lammermoor, was given last week. The theatre is the former *Teatro des Gallos*, an octagonal circus, which has been fitted up as elegantly as circumstances would permit, and as the transition from the crowing of cocks to the soft notes of *Giulietta* rendered necessary. The *prima donna assoluta* is the Signora Anaide Castellan de Giampietro, born in Paris, bred in Milan. The *prima donna soprano* is the Signora de Ricci; and the second *donna* is called Branzanti. The first tenor is Signor Giampietro, husband to the prima donna; and the second tenor is the Signor Alberti Bozetti. The first bass is Signor Tomassi, and the buffo bass Signor Spontini. They have been so much *proné*, and public expectation has been so much excited, that we supposed it probable that the first evening at least would be a failure to a certain extent. Besides, the Mexican audience, if not very experienced, is decidedly musical; and they have already had a pretty good opera here, have heard Madame Albini, la Cesari, Garcia (the father of Malibran) and the *beux restes* of Galli; therefore can compare.

The first evening, the Castellan made her appearance as *Lucia*. She is about twenty; slight and fair, with black hair, graceful, and with a very sweet, clear, and pure young voice, also very correct. The tenor rests upon his wife's laurels. He looks well, but little more can be said in his praise. Tomassi has some good notes, and a fine figure. Of the others who sang that evening there is little to be said. The theatre is extremely well got up, the dresses are new and rich, and the decorations and scenery remarkably good. The public, however, were disappointed. They had prepared for wonders, and were not satisfied with a fair performance. The applauses were few and far between. The Castellan was not called for, and the following day a certain degree of discontent pervaded the aristocracy of the capital.

At the second representation of the same opera things mended. The voice of La Castellan was appreciated. Applauses were loud and long, and at the end of the opera she and the director were called for and received with enthusiasm. She seems likely to become a favourite.

Last evening we had Romeo and Giulietta, in which La Ricci and La Cesari made their appearance, the former as Giulietta, the latter as Romeo. The Ricci is a thin young woman, with a long, pale face, black eyes and hair, long neck and arms, and large hands; extremely pretty, it is said, off the stage, but very ineffective on it; but both on and off with a very distinguished air. Her voice is extensive, but wanting cultivation, and decidedly *pea-hennish;* besides that, she is apt to go out of tune. Her style of dress was excessively unbecoming to her style of beauty. She wore a tight white gown, a tight blue satin-peaked body, with long tight blue sleeves. The public were indulgent, but it was evident that they were disappointed.

La Cesari, highly married, and who for the last three years has not appeared upon the stage, came out as *Romeo*, with tunic and mantle, white silk stockings, hat, and feathers, etc. She was very much frightened and ill at ease, and it required all the applause with which the public greeted the *entrée* of their former favourite to restore her to self-possession. She looked remarkably well—tall, handsome, beautifully formed, rather pale, with fine dark eyes, dark hair, and *moustaches.* Her acting was greatly superior, as much so as was her beauty to any of the others. She has more knowledge of the theatre, more science, taste, and energy, than any of them; but her voice, a soft contralto, is out of use and feeble. The theatre, besides, is ill-constructed for the voice, and must have a bad effect upon the fulness and tone. On the whole, it seems doubtful whether the opera will endure long. Were we going to remain here, I should trust that it might be supported, for, with all its faults and drawbacks, it is decidedly the best public exhibition in Mexico. The *coup d'œil* was exceedingly pretty, as all the boxes were crowded, and the ladies were in full dress.

July 20th.—As we are living in the mint, the directors have called on us; and this morning they came to invite us to descend into the lower regions to see the silver coined. We went all over this immense establishment, a fine picture of decayed magnificence, built about one hundred and ten years ago by the Spaniards. Dirty, ill-kept, the machinery rude, the workmen discontented; its fine vaulted roofs, that look like the interior of a cathedral, together with that *grandiose* style which distinguished the buildings of the Spaniards in Mexico, form a strong contrast with the occupants.

We saw the silver bars stretched out, the dollars cut and whitened and stamped; and in one place we saw the machines for *coining false money*, which have been collected in such numbers that there is hardly room for them! We saw the place where the silver and gold is tested; and the room with the medals, amongst which are some ancient Roman, Persian, and English, but especially Spanish, and many of the time of Charles III.; when we were looking at which, an old gentleman exclaimed, "Would to Heaven those days would return!" without doubt the general feeling. This old man had been forty-four years in the Casa de Moneda, and had lived under several viceroys. He could remember, when a boy, being sent with a commission to the Viceroy Revillagigedo, and being very much frightened, but soon reassured by the kind reception of the representative of majesty. He spoke of the flourishing condition of the mint in those days, which coined twenty-seven millions annually, and was a royal house. He said that the viceroys used to praise them and thank them for their exertions; that the house was then kept in the most perfect order, the principal officers wearing a uniform, etc.

Hereupon another old gentleman took up the theme, and improved upon it; and told us, that, on one occasion, they had one million three hundred thousand dollars' worth of gold in the house; and described the visit of the vice-queen Yturriguary, who came to see it, and sat down and looked round her in amazement at the quantity of gold she saw accumulated. This old gentleman had been thirty years in the mint, and seemed as though he had never been anywhere else;

as if he were part and parcel in it, and had been coined, and beat out, and clipped there.

Hearing him, another fat man, rather unclipt-looking than otherwise, began to bewail the state of the times, till it was a chorus universal, where all sang in one key. One had a very large, underhanging lip, with a kind of tragi-comic countenance, and was constantly making lugubrious puns. Another, who seemed bred to the mint, (though by his account the mint was not *bread* to him,) was insatiably curious, as a man born in a mint might be. We passed about three hours in a mixture of admiration of the past and sorrow for the present, and were reconducted to our domicile by the poor *employés*, who seemed to think that a Spanish minister was the next best to a Spanish viceroy, or of anything they had seen for some time.

> "The Past is nothing; and at last,
> The Future will but be the Past,"

says Lord Byron. Here the past is everything; and the future? —Answer it who can.

We were assured, while wondering at the number of machines for false coining which had been collected, that there are twice that number now in full force in Mexico; but that they belong to such distinguished personages, the government is afraid to interfere with them. Besides this, there is now no sufficient punishment for this crime, a capital offence in the days of the Spanish government. A lady here is said to have exclaimed with much simplicity on hearing her husband accused of false coining, "I really wonder why they make so much noise about it. It seems to me that my husband's copper is as good as any other!"

24th.—We went last evening to the opera, which was a repetition of Lucia, as it appears they cannot venture, in the face of public disapprobation, to repeat Romeo and Giulietta at present. As we were passing through the square, the carriage suddenly drew up, the coachman and footman uncovered their heads, and an immense procession came passing along the cathedral, with lights and military music. There were officers in full uniform, with their heads uncovered, a long file of monks and priests, and a carriage carrying the host, surrounded by hundreds of people on foot, all bearing lighted torches. A band of military music accompanied the procession, all which astonished us, as it was no fête-day. When, at length, being able to pass along, we arrived at the opera, we were informed that they were carrying the *viaticum* to a rich acquaintance of ours, a general, who has been indisposed for some time, and whose illness has now exhibited fatal symptoms.

For him, then, these great cathedral bells are tolling heavily; for him, the torches and the pompous procession—the sandalled monks, and the officers in military array; while two bands of music are playing at his door and another in front of the cathedral, and in the midst of these sounds of monkish hymn and military music, the soul is preparing to wing its flight alone and unattended.

But the sweet notes of Lucia drown all other from our ears, if not from our thoughts. In a house not many hundred yards off, they minister the host to the dying man, while here, La Castellan, with her pretty French graces and Italian singing, is drawing tears from our eyes for fictitious sorrows.

The theatre was pretty well filled, though there were some empty boxes, sights more hideous in the eyes of actors than toothless mouths. We sat with Madame la Baronne de ——, and nearly opposite was Madame ——, related to the *"Principe de la Paz,"* a handsome woman, with a fine Bohemian cast of face, dark in complexion, with glittering teeth, brilliant eyes, and dark hair. La Castellan sang very well, with much clearness, precision, and facility. She is certainly graceful and pretty, but, except in her method, more French than Italian. Her style suits Lucia, but I doubt her having *l'air noble* sufficient for a Norma or a Semiramis. The bass improves upon acquaintance, but the handsome tenor is nought. The audience seemed to me both indulgent and discriminating. They applauded the pretty prima donna *con furor;* they praised the bass when he deserved it, the tenor when it was possible; but where he sang false, nothing could extort from them a solitary *viva.* This discrimination makes their applause worth having, and proceeds less from experience or cultivation, than from a *musical instinct.*

In a visit we made this morning, we were shown a piece of embroidery, which, from its splendour and good taste, is worthy of observation, though by no means uncommon here. We went to call on the wife of a judge, who showed us all through their beautiful house, which looks out on the Alameda. In one of the rooms, their daughter was engaged on a piece of embroidery for the altar of the chapel. The ground was the very richest and thickest white satin; the design was a garland of vine-leaves, with bunches of grapes. The vine-leaves were beautifully embroidered in fine gold, and the grapes were composed of amethysts. I can conceive nothing richer and more tasteful than the general effect. The gold embroidery done in Mexico is generally very beautiful, and there are many ladies who embroider in great perfection. There is an amazing quantity of it used in the churches, and in military uniforms. I have also seen beautiful gold-embroidered ball-dresses, but they are nearly out of fashion. . . . We hear that General ——, though still ill, is likely to recover.

25th.—This being the day of Santiago, the patron saint of Spain, C——n was invited by the padres to San Francisco to attend mass in the church there. We were shown to the tribuna (gallery) of the Countess de Santiago, where they gave us chairs, and put down a piece of carpet. C——n and the rest of the legation were in the body of the church, in velvet chairs, with lighted tapers in their hands. The saint was carried in procession, going out by the principal door, making a tour of the streets, and returning by a side door. The music was pretty good, especially one soprano voice. Twelve little boys were placed on crimson velvet benches, on either side of the altar, representing pilgrims of Galicia (of which Santiago is the capital), handsome little fellows, belonging to respectable families, dressed in robes of dark green or crimson, or violet-coloured velvet, with falling lace collars, and the neck ornamented with gold and silver shells; a large pilgrim's hat fastened on behind, and hanging down, and in their hands staffs with gold bells. They were beautiful children, and all behaved with becoming gravity and decorum during the ceremony, walking with much dignity in the procession.

After the *funcion,* we went out to Santiago, an old church near Mexico, where the Indians annually come in procession on this day, and sell their fruit, flowers, pulque, etc. All the waste ground near the church was covered with green booths, and there was a great crowd of carriages and horsemen, and people on foot. The troops were drawn out, escorting the procession to the church. But though the scene was curious, as the remnant of an old-established ceremony, and the Indians, with their booths and flowers, and great show of fruit, were all very picturesque, the sun was so intense, that after walking about a little while, and buying tunas and nuts and peaches, we returned home, together with the Güera Rodriguez, who was in the carriage with us, and giving us a lively description of what this fête used to be in former days. Had a visit the same morning from the Señora M——, whom I think even handsomer by daylight, than she appeared to be at the opera; not always the case with dark beauties.

26th.—Another representation of Vaccaj's Romeo and Giulietta, with the second appearance of La Ricci. Music and Ricci seem considered a failure. The Señora Cesari made the handsomest of Romeos, as usual, but was ill, and out of spirits. The opera as a whole was coldly received; the boxes and pit were nearly empty, and La Ricci seems unlikely to gain any favour with the public, though it must be confessed that she looked better, was more becomingly dressed, and both sang and acted better than the preceding night. Yesterday we went to a *soirée* at the —— minister's. Madame Castellan and her tenor were there, and had come from a dinner given by a rich curate to the whole *corps opératique*, from the prima donna down to the *joueur du fagote*, and even to the tailor who makes the opera dresses, and his wife. This rich padre, it is said, spends a great part of his fortune in entertaining actors and singers. La Castellan (permission to that effect having been obtained from the manager, for it is against their agreement to perform in private houses) sang several airs to the piano, with much expression, especially from *Robert le Diable;* and *Nina Pazza per Amore;* but I prefer her voice in the theatre. She is not at all beautiful, but has a charming face with a very musical expression.

We returned home by moonlight, the most flattering medium through which Mexico can be viewed; with its broad and silent streets, and splendid old buildings, whose decay and abandonment are softened by the silvery light; its ancient churches, from which the notes of the organ occasionally come pealing forth, mingled with faint blasts of music borne on the night wind from some distant procession; or with the soft music of a hymn from some neighbouring convent. The white-robed monk—the veiled female—even the ragged beggar, add to the picture; by daylight his rags are too visible. Frequently, as the carriages roll along to the opera, or as, at a late hour, they return from it, they are suddenly stopped by the appearance of the mysterious coach, with its piebald mules, and the *Eye* surrounded by rays of light on its panels; a melancholy apparition, for it has come from the house of mourning, probably from the bed of death. Then, by the moonlight, the kneeling figures on the pavement seemed as if carved in stone. The city of Mexico by moonlight—the environs of Mexico at daybreak—these are the hours for viewing both to advantage, and for making us feel how

"All but the spirit of man is divine."

In front of our house, I should say of *the Mint*, is the archbishop's palace, and in front of this palace an object which has greatly excited our curiosity. It is an old man, who, whether as a penance, or from some motive which we do not know, kneels, wrapt in his sarape, beside the wall of the *Arzobispado* from sunset till midnight, or later—for we have frequently gone out at nine in the evening, and left him kneeling there; and on our return at one in the morning have found him in the same position. He asks no alms, but kneels there silent and motionless, hour after hour, as if in the performance of some vow. . . .

We made a call this evening on the archbishop in his own palace, an enormously large building; a sort of street, like this Casa de Moneda. He received us very cordially, and looked very comfortable without his robes of state, in a fine cloth dressing-gown, lined with violet-coloured silk.

August 1st.—We had a visit last evening from one of the directors of the mint, a curious and most original genius, a Mexican, who has served nearly thirty years in that and other capacities, and who, after speaking of the different viceroys he had seen, proceeded to give us various anecdotes of the Viceroy Revillagigedo, the most honoured for his justice, renowned for his energy, and feared for his severity, of the whole dynasty. Our friend was moved to enthusiasm by the sight of an old-fashioned but very handsome musical clock, which stands on a table in the drawing-room, and which he says was brought over by this viceroy, and was no doubt considered a miracle of art in those days.

Some of the anecdotes he told us are already generally known here, but his manner of telling them was very interesting, and he added various particulars which we had not heard before. Besides, the stories themselves seem to me so curious and characteristic, that however much they lose by being tamely written instead of *dramatized* as they are by him, I am tempted to give you one or two specimens. But my letter is getting beyond all ordinary limits, and your curiosity will no doubt keep cool till the arrival of another packet.

LETTER THE FORTY-THIRD

Revillagigedo—The False Merchant and the Lady—The Vice-roy, the Unjust Spaniard, the Indian, and the Golden Ounces—Horrible Murder—Details—Oath—Country Family —The Spot of Blood—The Mother unknowingly denounces her Son—Arrest of the Three—Confession—Execution—The Viceroy fulfils his Pledge—Paving of the Streets—Severity to the Monks—Solitary Damsel—Box on the Ear—Pension— Morning Concert—New Minister—"Street of the Sad Indian"—Traditions—A Farewell Audience—Inscription on a Tomb.

August 3rd.

A lady of fortune, owing to some combination of circumstances, found herself in difficulties, and in immediate want of a small sum of money. Don —— being her *compadre,* and a respectable merchant, she went to him to state her necessities, and offered him a case of valuable jewels as security for repayment, provided he would advance her eight hundred dollars. He agreed, and the bargain was concluded without any written document, the lady depositing her jewels and receiving the sum. At the end of a few months, her temporary difficulties being ended, she went to her *compadre's* house to repay the money, and receive back her jewels. The man readily received the money, but declared to his astonished *comadre,* that as to the jewels, he had never heard of them, and that no such transaction had taken place. The Señora, indignant at the merchant's treachery, instantly repaired to the palace of the vice-king hoping for justice from this Western Solomon, though unable to conceive how it could be obtained. She was instantly received by Revillagigedo, who listened attentively to her account of the circumstances. "Had you no witnesses?" said the count. "None," replied she. "Did no servant pass in or out during the transaction?" "No one." The viceroy reflected a moment. "Does your compadre smoke?" "No, sir," said the lady, astonished at this irrelevant question, and perhaps the more so, as the count's aversion to smoking was so well known, that none of his smoking subjects ventured to approach him without having taken every precaution to deaden any odour of the fragrant weed which might lurk about their clothes or person. "Does he take snuff?" said the viceroy. "Yes, your Excellency," said his visitor, who probably feared that for once his Excellency's wits were wool-gathering. "That is sufficient," said the viceroy; "retire into the adjoining chamber and *keep quiet*—your jewels shall be restored." His Excellency then despatched a messenger for the merchant, who immediately presented himself.

"I have sent for you," said the viceroy, "that we may talk over some matters in which your mercantile knowledge may be of use to the state." The merchant was overwhelmed with gratitude and joy; while the viceroy entered into conversation with him upon various affairs connected with his profession. Suddenly the viceroy put his hand first in one pocket, then in the other, with the air of a man who has mislaid something. "Ah!" said he, "my snuff-box. Excuse me for a moment while I go to fetch it from the next room." "Sir!" said the merchant, "permit me to have the honour of offering my box to your Excellency." His Excellency received it as if mechanically, holding it in his hand and talking, till pretexting some business, he went out, and calling an officer, desired him to take that snuff-box to the merchant's house, asking his wife as from him, by that token, to deliver to the bearer a case of jewels which he had there. The viceroy returned to the apartment where he had left his flattered guest, and remained in conversation with him until the officer returned, and requesting private speech of the viceroy, delivered to him a jewel-case which he had received from the merchant's wife.

Revillagigedo then returned to his fair complainant, and under pretence of showing her some rooms in the palace, led her into one, where amongst many objects of value, the jewel-case stood open. No sooner had she cast her eyes upon it than she started forward in joy and amazement. The viceroy requested her to wait there a little longer, and returned to his other guest. "Now," said he, "before going further, I wish to hear the truth concerning another affair in which you are interested. Are you acquainted with the Señora de ——?" "Intimately, sir—she is my *comadre*." "Did you lend her eight hundred dollars, at such a date?" "I did." "Did she give you a case of jewels in pledge?" "Never," said the merchant, vehemently. "The money was lent without any security; merely as an act of friendship, and she has invented a story concerning some jewels, which has not the slightest foundation." In vain

the viceroy begged him to reflect, and not, by adding falsehood to treachery, force him to take measures of severity. The
merchant with oaths persisted in his denial. The viceroy left
the room suddenly, and returned with the jewel-case in his
hand; at which unexpected apparition, the astonished merchant changed colour, and entirely lost his presence of mind.
The viceroy ordered him from his presence, with a severe re-
buke for his falsehood and treachery, and an order never again
to enter the palace. At the same time he commanded him
to send him, the next morning, eight hundred dollars with
five hundred more; which he did, and which were, by the
viceroy's order, distributed amongst the hospitals. His Excellency is said to have added a severe reprimand to the lady,
for having made a bargain without writing.

Another story which I recollect, is as follows: A poor Indian
appeared before the viceroy, and stated that he had found in
the street a bag full of golden ounces, which had been ad-
vertised with the promise of a handsome reward to the person
who should restore them to the owner; that upon carrying
them to this Don —— ——, he had received the bag, counted
the ounces, extracted two, which he had seen him slip into
his pocket; and had then reproached the poor man with having stolen part of the money, had called him a thief and a
rascal, and, instead of rewarding, had driven him from the
house. With the viceroy there was no delay. Immediate action
was his plan. Detaining the Indian, he despatched an officer
to desire the attendance of Don —— —— with his bag of ounces.
He came, and the viceroy desired him to relate the circumstances, his practised eye reading his falsehood at a glance.
"May it please your Excellency, I lost a bag containing gold.
The Indian, now in your Excellency's presence, brought it to
me in hopes of a reward, having first stolen part of its contents. I drove him from the house as a thief, who, instead of
recompense, deserves punishment."

"Stay," said the viceroy, "there is some mistake here. How
many ounces were there in the bag you lost?" "Twenty-eight."
"And how many are here?" "But twenty-six." "Count them
down. I see it is as you say. The case is clear, and we have all
been mistaken. Had this Indian been a thief, he would never
have brought back the bag, and stolen merely two ounces. He
would have kept the whole. It is evident that this is not your
bag but another which this poor man has found. Sir, our interview is at an end. Continue to search for your bag of gold;
and as for you, friend, since we cannot find the true owner,

sweep up these twenty-six pieces and carry them away. They are yours." So saying, his Excellency bowed out the discomfited cheat and the overjoyed rustic. Mr. —— says that this story, he thinks, is taken from something similar in an oriental tale. However, it *may* have occurred twice.

A horrible murder took place in 1789, during the vice-royaltyship of Revillagigedo, which is remarkable in two particulars; the trifling circumstances which led to its discovery, and the energy displayed by the viceroy, contrasting strongly with the tardy execution of justice in our days. There lived in Mexico at that period, in the street of *Cordovanes*, No. 15, a rich merchant of the name of Don Joaquin Dongo. A clerk named José Joaquin Blanco, who had formerly been in his office, having fallen into vicious courses, and joined in companionship with two other young men, Filipe Aldama and Baltazar Quintero, gamblers and cock-fighters (with reverence be it spoken!) like himself, formed, in concert with them, a plan for robbing his former master.

They accordingly repaired to the house one evening when they knew that Dongo was from home, and imitating the signal which Blanco knew the coachman was in the habit of making to the porter when the carriage returned at night, the doors were immediately thrown open, and the robbers entered. The porter was their first victim. He was thrown down and stabbed. A postman, who was waiting with letters for the return of the master of the house, was the next, and then the cook, and so on, until eleven lay weltering in their blood. The wretches then proceeded to pick the locks of the different bureaux, guided by Blanco, who, in his former capacity, had made himself *au fait* of all the secrets of the house. They obtained twenty-two thousand dollars in specie, and about seven thousand dollars' worth of plate.

Meanwhile the unfortunate master of the house returned home, and at the accustomed signal the doors were opened by the robbers, and on the entrance of the carriage, instantly re-locked. Seeing the porter bathed in blood, and dead bodies lying at the foot of the staircase, he comprehended at once his desperate situation, and advancing to Aldama, who stood near the door, he said, "My life is in your hands; but for God's sake, show some mercy, and do not murder me in cold blood. Say what sums of money you want. Take all that is in the house, and leave me, and I swear to keep your secret." Aldama consented, and Dongo passed on. As he ascended the stairs, stepping over the body of the postman, he encountered

Quintero, and to him he made the same appeal, with the same success; when Blanco, springing forward, held his sword to Quintero's breast, and swearing a great oath, exclaimed, "If you do not stab him, I will kill you on the spot!" Conceive, for one moment, the situation of the unfortunate Dongo, surrounded by the murdered and the murderers in his own house, at the dead of the night, and without a hope of assistance! The suspense was momentary. Thus adjured, Quintero stabbed him to the heart.

The murderers then collected their spoil, and it being still dark, two of them got into Dongo's carriage, the third acting as coachman, and so drove swiftly out of the gates of the city, till, arriving at a deserted spot, not far from a village, they turned the carriage and mules adrift, and buried their treasure, which they transported afterwards to a house in the Calle de la Aguila (the street of the eagle), No. 23; and went about their avocations in the morning, as if nothing had occurred. Meanwhile, the public consternation may be conceived, when the morning dawned upon this bloody tragedy. As for the viceroy, he swore that the murderers should be discovered, and hanged before his eyes, that day week.

Immediately the most energetic measures were taken, and the gates of the city shut, to prevent all egress. Orders were given through all the different districts of the capital, that every guest, or visitor, or boarder, whether in inn or lodging, or private house, should have their names given up to the police, with an account of their condition, occupation, motives for living in Mexico, etc. Strict cognizance was taken in all the villages near the capital, of every person who had passed through, or entered, or left the village within a certain space of time. All the roads near the capital were scoured by parties of soldiers. Every hidden place was searched by the police; every suspected house entered. The funeral of the ill-fated Dongo and of the other victims, took place the following day; and it was afterwards remembered that Aldama was there amongst the foremost, remarking and commenting upon this horrible wholesale butchery, and upon the probabilities of discovering the murderers.

A country family from a neighbouring village, hearing of all these doings in Mexico, and with that love of the marvellous which characterizes persons uneducated, or unaccustomed to the world, determined to pay a visit to the capital, and to hear at the fountain head, all these wonderful stories, which had probably reached them under a hundred exaggerated forms.

No sooner had they entered their lodgings, than they were visited and examined by the police, and their deposition taken down as to their motives for visiting the capital, their place of birth, etc. As a gratuitous piece of information, one of them mentioned, that, passing by a barber's shop (probably with his eyes opened wide in the expectation of seeing horrible sights), he had observed a man talking to the barber, who had a stain of blood upon his *queue* (hair being then worn powdered and tied behind). Trifling as this circumstance appears to us, the viceroy ordered that the person who mentioned it should instantly conduct the police officers to the shop where he had observed it. The shop being found, the barber was questioned as to what persons he had been conversing with that morning, and mentioned about half-a-dozen; amongst others *Aldama*, who did not bear a very good reputation. Aldama was sent for, confronted with the man who gave the information, identified as the same, and the stain of blood being observed, he was immediately committed to prison upon suspicion. Being questioned as to the cause of the stain, he replied, that being at a cock-fight, on such a day, at such an hour, the blood from one of the dying cocks, which he held, had spirted up, and stained the collar of his shirt and his hair. Inquiries being made at the cock-pit, this was corroborated by several witnesses, and extraordinary as it is, it is most probable that the *assertion was true*.

But meanwhile, the mother of Blanco, deeply distressed at the dissolute courses of her son, took the resolution (which proves more than anything else Revillagigedo's goodness, and the confidence which all classes had in him) to consult the viceroy as to the means of converting the young man to better habits. It seems as if the hand of an avenging Providence had conducted this unfortunate mother to take a step so fatal to her son. She told the viceroy that she had in vain attempted to check him, that his days and nights were spent with profligate companions in gambling-houses and in cock-pits, and that she feared some mischief would come some day from his fighting and swearing and drinking; that but a few days since he had come home late, and that she had observed that his stockings were *dabbled in blood;* that she had questioned him upon it, and that he had answered surlily he had got it in the cock-pit. Her narration was hardly concluded, before Blanco was arrested and placed in a separate cell of the same prison with Aldama. Shortly after, Quintero, only as being the intimate friend and companion of both parties, was taken up on suspicion and lodged in the same prison; all being separately confined, and no communication permitted between them.

It seems as if Quintero, perhaps the least hardened of the three, was struck with the conviction that, in the extraordinary combination of circumstances which had led to the arrest of himself and his companions in villany, the finger of God was too distinctly visible to permit a doubt of ultimate discovery to rest upon his mind, for he confessed at once, and declaring that he saw all denial was useless, gave a circumstantial account of the whole. He begged for nine days' grace to prepare himself for death, but the viceroy would grant but three. When Aldama confessed, he made the avowal that he was guilty of a previous murder, when he was alcalde of a village near Mexico, which was before the time of Revillagigedo, and for which he had been tried and acquitted. He being alcalde, the postman of the village was in the habit of passing by his house, giving him an account of whatever money he had collected, etc. One evening this man stopped at Aldama's, and told him he was intrusted with a sum of fifteen hundred dollars to carry to a neighbouring village. At twelve o'clock he left Aldama's house, who, taking a short cut across the fields, reached the postman by this other direction, stabbed him, and carried back the money. Next day, when the murder was made known, the alcalde, in his robes of justice, visited the body, and affected to institute a strict search for the murderer. Nevertheless he was suspected and arrested, but escaped by bribery, and shortly after, leaving the village, came to the wider theatre of Mexico.

The murderers having thus made their confession, were ordered to prepare for death. A scaffold erected between the central gate of the palace, and that which is now the principal gate of the city guards, was hung with black to denote that the criminals were of noble blood. An immense crowd were assembled; and the viceroy, standing on the balcony of his palace, witnessed the execution in the great square, the *very day week* that the murders were committed.

The streets were then kept in perfect order, both as to paving and lighting; and on one occasion, having rode all through the city, as was his custom, to observe whether everything was in order for the holy week, he observed that several parts of the different streets were unpaved, and out of repair; whereupon, sending for the head of the police, he desired that these streets should be paved and in order before the holy week, of which it wanted but a few days. The officer declared the thing to be impossible. The viceroy ordered it to be done, on the penalty of losing his place. Early on the morning of Palm Sunday, he sent to know if all was in readiness; and as the bells tolled for early mass, the last stone was laid on the Calle San Francisco, which completed the work. . . .

It is said he frequently went about *incog.*, attended by one or two aides-de-camp, by which means, like another Haroun Al Raschid, he was enabled to discover and correct hidden abuses. By his orders, no monk could be out of his convent after vespers. Walking one evening along the streets, he encountered a monk in the Calle San Francisco, taking his pleasure long after the appointed hour. The viceroy walked directly to the convent; and on making himself known, was received by the abbot with all due respect. "How many monks have you in your convent, father?" asked the viceroy. "Fifty, your Excellency." "There are now only forty-nine. Call them over, see which is the missing brother, and let his name be struck out." The list was produced—the names called over, and only forty-five monks presented themselves. By order of the viceroy, the five who had broken through the rules, were never again admitted into the convent. Alas! could his Excellency have lived in these our degenerate days, and beheld certain monks of a certain order drinking pulque and otherwise disporting themselves! nay, seen one, as we but just now did from the window, strolling along the street by lamplight, with an *Yntida* (Indian girl) tucked under his arm! . . . .

One more anecdote of the "immortal Revillagigedo," and I have done. It was very late at night, when not far from the gate of the city called "The lost child," (in commemoration of that period when *"the child Jesus tarried behind in Jerusalem,"* and that his parents sought for him sorrowing,) his Excellency encountered a good-looking damsel, walking briskly and alone, at these untimely hours; yet withal quiet and modest in her demeanour. Wishing to try the temper of her steel (or brass) he left his officers a little way behind; and perhaps they were not astonished. . . . "Oh! by no means, certainly not!"—when they saw the grave and severe Revillagigedo approach the fair maiden somewhat familiarly, and request permission to accompany her in her rambles, a proposal which was indignantly rejected. "Anda!" (Come!) said his Excellency, "give over these airs—you, a *mugercilla,* strolling about in search of adventures." Imagine the feelings of his Excellency, on receiving in reply a tremendous and well-applied box on the ear! The staff rushed forward, and were astonished to find the viceroy with a smiling countenance, watching the retreating steps of the adventurous damsel. "What! your Excellency—such insolence! such audacity! such——" "Come, come," said the viceroy, "she has proved herself worthy of our favour. Let instant inquiry be made as to her birth and parentage, and as to her reasons for being on the streets at this hour. They must be honest ones." The result proved the viceroy correct in his opinion. She was a poor girl, supporting a dying mother by giving music lessons, and obliged to trudge on foot from house to house at all hours; and amongst her scholars was the daughter of an old lady who lived out of the gates of the city, and from whose house, being that of her last visited pupil, she had frequently to return late at night. On being informed of these particulars, his Excellency ordered her a pension of three hundred dollars per annum, to be continued to the day of her death, and it is said she is still alive, though very old. This is making one's fortune by a *coup de main,* or by a *lucky hit!*

August 6th.—This morning we had some very good music; Madame Castellan and the tenor, and Madame Cesari having passed some hours here, together with Madame la Baronne de —— and a few other gentlemen and ladies. La Castellan was very amiable, and sang beautifully, but looked pale and fatigued. She has been very effective lately in the Somnambula. Madame Cesari was in great beauty.

About an hour after they had gone, the new minister and his family made their *entrée* into Mexico. It is now, however, too late for us to return till the autumn, as there is a great deal of fever at Vera Cruz; nor do we entirely give up hopes, as soon as C——n shall be at leisure, of making another journey on horseback into the interior. There are, however, rumours of another pronunciamiento, and should this be the case, our present quarters next to the palace will be more distinguished than agreeable.

I have always had a curiosity to know why the Calle del Indio Triste (Street of the Sad Indian) was so called. We are on visiting terms with two or three *houses* in that street, and never pass those large black letters, which tell the passenger that this is the street of *"The Sad Indian,"* without my imagination figuring to itself that here some tragedy connected with the conquest must have taken place. It was therefore with great joy that I fell upon an article in the "Mosaico Mejicano," purporting to give an explanation of this melancholy title-page to an otherwise very tolerable (in the way of houses) but very ill-paved street, where, amongst other handsome edifices, is the house of a rich Spaniard (Señor R——o), remarkable for its beautiful entrance and elegant *salons*. It appears that there are different traditions respecting it. One, that shortly after the conquest, a rich cacique lived there, who acted as a spy on his Indian brethren, and informed the viceroy of all their plans and combinations against the government; but that on one occasion, having failed to inform his patrons of an intended mutiny, they seized this pretext for sequestrating his property:— that afterwards, poor, abandoned and despised, he sat down in the corner of the street, weeping his misfortune and meeting with no pity; until at length he abstained from all food for some days, and was found dead in the corner of the street, sitting in the same melancholy posture; that the viceroy declared his wealth crown property, and with the intention of striking terror into the hearts of the malcontents, caused a stone statue to be made representing the weeping Indian; that this statue was placed at the corner of the street, with its back to the wall, and so remained until, the house being pulled down, the statue was sent to the Museum, where it now is; the street retaining the name of the Sad Indian.

But there is another tradition mentioned concerning the origin of the name, more interesting and even more probable. It appears that the ground now occupied by this street is the site of the Palace of Axayacatl, the father of Montezuma, last Emperor of Mexico. In this spacious and magnificent palace the Spaniards were received and lodged, and, according to Torquemada, each in a separate apartment. There were a multitude of idols in this dwelling, and though they had no separate temple, various feasts were dedicated to them. After the conquest they were for the most part broken and destroyed, and it was only lately that, by accident, the head of the god of the waters, beautifully worked in serpentine marble, was discovered there; still, one statue had been preserved, that of an Indian, said to have been placed there by the Aztecs, as a memorial of their sorrow at the death of Montezuma, to whom, on account of his misfortunes, they gave the name of "*el Indio triste.*" This was afterwards placed at the corner of the new building erected there by the Spaniards, and gave its name to the street. It is a melancholy-looking statue, whomsoever it may represent, of an Indian in a sitting posture, with a most dejected and forlorn air and countenance. The material is basaltic stone.

11th.—C——n has just returned from seeing the general archives, which are all in confusion and going to ruin. Don

Ygnacio Cuevas, who has the charge of them, has written various works—the History of the Viceroys—the Californias, etc. —which were robbed or destroyed in the last pronunciamiento. He related the story of Revillagigedo and the jewels, only differing from *my* friend's narrative in that he says it was not a jewel-case, but a diamond bracelet. He assured C——n that Mexico in Indian means "below this," alluding to the population who, according to tradition, are buried beneath the *Pedregal.*

18th.—News has arrived that General Paredes *pronounced* in Guadalajara on the eighth of the month! Strange rumours are afloat, and it is generally supposed that Santa Anna is or will be the prime mover of the great changes that are predicted. By many, however, it is talked of as very trifling, as a mere movement that will soon be put down. The plan which Paredes has published is essentially military, but announces a congress, which renders it very popular in the departments. It has been adopted by the departments of Zacatecas, Durango, and Guanajvato. Meanwhile, everything continues here as usual. We have been several times at the opera; the *paseos* are very crowded, and we had a musical *soirée* the other evening, which was very gay, but from the signs of the times, will probably be our last in Mexico.

28th.—This morning C——n took his farewell audience of the president, and the new minister was received.

30th.—These few last days have chiefly been spent in paying visits of ceremony with the Señora ——. Nevertheless we spent an hour last evening in the beautiful cemetery a little way out of the city, which is rather a favourite haunt of ours, and is known as the *"Panteon de Santa Maria."* It has a beautiful chapel attached to it, where the daily mass is said for the dead, and a large garden filled with flowers. Young trees of different kinds have been planted there, and the sight of the tombs themselves, in their long and melancholy array of black coffins, with gold-lettered inscriptions, even while it inspires the saddest ideas, has something soothing in its effect. They are kept in perfect order, and the inscriptions, though not always eloquent, are almost always full of feeling, and sometimes extremely touching. There is one near the entrance, which is pathetic in its native language, and though it loses much in the translation, I shall transcribe it:

"Here lie the beloved remains of Carmen and José Pímentel y Heras. The first died the 11th of June, 1838, aged one year and eleven months; the second on the 5th of September of 1839, in the sixteenth month of his existence; and to their dear memory maternal love dedicates the following:—

"EPITAPH.

"*Babes of my love! my Carmen and José!*
Sons of your cherished father, Pímentel.
Why have you left your mother's side? for whom?
What motives have ye had to leave me thus?
But hark! I hear your voice—and breathlessly
I listen. I hear ye say—'To go to heaven!
Mother! we have left thee to see our God!'
Beloved shades! if this indeed be so,
Then let these bitter tears be turned to joy.
It is not meet that I should mourn for ye,
Since me ye have exchanged for my God.
To Him give thanks! and in your holy songs,
Pray that your parents' fate may be like yours."

LETTER THE FORTY-FOURTH

Agitation—Storm—Revolution—Manifesto—Resembling a Game of Chess—Position of the Pieces—Appearance of the City— Firing—State of Parties—Comparisons—"Comicios"—The People—Congress—Santa Anna—Amnesty offered—Roaring of Cannon—Proclamation—Time to look at home—*The Will of the Nation—Different Feelings—Judge's House destroyed— The Mint in Requisition—Preparations—Cannonading—*"Los Enanos."

31st.

This afternoon the clouds, gathered together in gloomy masses, announced a thunderstorm, and at the same time a certain degree of agitation apparently pervading the city was suddenly observable from our balconies. Shops were shutting up; people hurrying in all directions, heads at all the windows, and men looking out from the azoteas; but as these symptoms were immediately followed by a tremendous storm of thunder and lightning and splashing rain, we trusted that the cause had been very simple. But these elements of nature are wielded by the Hand that called them forth, and can stay them at His will, and the sun breaking forth smilingly and scattering the clouds, made us feel that the storm had but refreshed the parched earth and cleared the sultry atmosphere. Not so with the storm which has been brooding in the hearts of a handful of ambitious men, and which has burst forth at last, its bolts directed by no wise or merciful power, and by the hands of selfish and designing and short-sighted mortals.

The storm, though short, had not passed away, when news was brought us of a new *revolution in Mexico!* General Valencia, he who pronounced (but two short months ago!) the high-flown and flattering speech to the president, on receiving the sword of honour, has now *pronounced* in a very different and much clearer manner. Listen to him now:—

"Soldiers! The despotism of the Mexican government, the innumerable evils which the nation suffers, the unceasing remonstrances which have been made against these evils, and which have met with no attention, have forced us to take a step this evening, which is not one of rebellion, but is the energetic expression of our resolution to sacrifice everything to the common good and interest. The cause which we defend is that of all Mexicans; of the rich as of the poor; of the soldier as of the civilian. We want a country, a government, the felicity of our homes, and respect from without; and we shall obtain all; let us not doubt it. The nation will be moved by our example. The arms which our country has given us for her defence, we shall know how to employ in restoring her honour —an honour which the government has stained by not acknowledging the total absence of morality and energy in the actual authorities. The army which made her independent shall also render her powerful and free. The illustrious General Santa Anna to-day marches to Puebla, at the head of our heroic companions at Vera Cruz, while upon Queretaro, already united to the valiant General Paredes, the brave General Cortazar now begins his operations.

"In a few days we shall see the other forces of the republic in motion, all co-operating to the same end. The triumph is secure, my friends, and the cause which we proclaim is so noble, that conquerors, we shall be covered with glory; and, happen what may, we shall be honoured by our fellow-citizens."

In this manifesto, which is mere declamation, there is no plan. It appears that no one particularly counted upon General Valencia, and that, whether fearing to be left out in the events which he saw approaching, or apprehensive of being arrested by the government, who suspected him, he has thought it wisest to strike a blow on his own account. Pacheco, who commanded the citadel, together with Generals Lombardini and Sales, who had been ordered out to march with their respective regiments against the *pronunciados,* are now in the citadel, and in a state of revolt. The two last had but just received money for the payment of their troops on the preceding day.

8 o'clock.—Nothing further, but that the president has sallied forth on horseback from San Agustin; and was received with repeated *vivas* by the people collected in the square.

1st September.—This revolution is like a game at chess, in which kings, castles, knights, and bishops, are making different moves, while the pawns are looking on or taking no part whatever.

To understand the state of the board, it is necessary to explain the position of the four principal pieces—Santa Anna,

Bustamante, Paredes, and Valencia. The first move was made by Paredes, who published his plan, and *pronounced* on the eighth of August at Guadalajara. About the same time, Don F—— M——, a Spanish broker, who had gone to Manga de Clavo, was sent to Guadalajara, and had a conference with Paredes, the result of which was, that the plan of that general was withdrawn, and it was supposed that he and Santa Anna had formed a combination. Shortly after, the Censor of Vera Cruz, a newspaper entirely devoted to Santa Anna, pronounced in favour of the plan of Paredes, and Santa Anna, with a few miserable troops, and a handful of cavalry, arrived at Perote. Here he remains for the present, kept in check by the (government) General Torrejon. Meanwhile Paredes, with about six hundred men, left Guadalajara and marched upon Guanajuato; and there a blow was given to the government party by the defection of General Cortazar, who thought fit thus to show his grateful sense of having just received the rank of general of brigade with the insignia of this new grade, which the president put on with his own hands. Another *check to the president*. Once begun, defection spread rapidly, and Paredes and Cortazar having advanced upon Queretaro, found that General Juvera, with his garrison, had already *pronounced* there, at the moment that they were expected in Mexico to assist the government against Valencia. Paredes, Cortazar, and Juvera are now united, and their forces amount to two thousand two hundred men.

Meanwhile General Valencia, pressed to declare *his plan,* has replied that he awaits the announcement of the intentions of Generals Paredes and Santa Anna; and, for his own part, only desires the dismissal of General Bustamante.

This, then, is the position of the three principal *pronounced* chiefs, on this second day of September of the year of our Lord 1841. Santa Anna in Perote, hesitating whether to advance or retreat, and, in fact, prevented from doing either by the vicinity of General Torrejon. Paredes in Queretaro, with the other revolted generals. Valencia in the citadel of Mexico with his *pronunciados;* while Bustamante, with Generals Almonte and Canalizo, the *mark* against which all these hostile operations are directed, is determined, it is said, to fight to the last.

Mexico looks as if it had got a general holiday. Shops shut up, and all business is at a stand. The people, with the utmost apathy, are collected in groups, talking quietly; the officers are galloping about; generals, in a somewhat party-coloured dress, with large gray hats, striped pantaloons, old coats, and generals' belts, fine horses, and crimson-coloured velvet saddles. The shopkeepers in the square have been removing their goods and money. An occasional shot is heard, and sometimes a volley, succeeded by a dead silence. The archbishop shows his reverend face now and then upon the opposite balcony of his palace, looks out a little while, and then retires. The chief effect, so far, is universal idleness in man and beast,—the soldiers and their quadrupeds excepted.

The position of the president, however, is not so bad as at first sight it might appear, or as it will be, if his enemies are permitted to reunite. He has upwards of two thousand men, twelve pieces of ordnance, and, though his infantry are few, and he has little artillery, he has good cavalry. Valencia has twelve hundred men, twenty-six pieces of ordnance, with good infantry, and almost all the artillery. The rebels have possessed themselves of the Acordada, and given liberty to those who were imprisoned for political opinions—a good loophole for the escape of criminals.

Those who understand these matters say that the principal object of the government should be to reduce the rebels to the citadel only, and to occupy all the important points in its neighbourhood, San Diego, San Hipolito, San Fernando, etc.; but as yet this has not been done, and the *pronunciados* are gradually extending, and taking possession of these points. . . .

3rd.—They are now keeping up a pretty brisk fire between San Agustin and the citadel. This morning the streets were covered with coaches, filled with families leaving the city.

4th.—Things are becoming more complicated. The rebels now occupy San José, Salto de Agua, the college of Vizcaynas (from which all the poor girls and their teachers have fled), Regina, San Juan de la Penitencia, San Diego, and San Fernando—a long line of important points. The president's line begins at San Francisco, continuing by La Concepcion; but, without a map of the city, you will not understand the position of the two parties. However, every turret and belfry is covered with soldiers, and the streets are blocked up with troops and trenches. From behind these turrets and trenches they fire at each other, scarcely a soldier falling, but numbers of peaceful citizens; shells and bombs falling through the roofs of the houses, and all this for *"the public good."*

The war of July had at least a shadow of pretext; it was a war of party, and those who wished to re-establish federalism may have acted with good faith. Now there is neither principle, nor pretext, nor plan, nor the shadow of reason or legality. Disloyalty, hypocrisy, and the most sordid calculation, are all the motives that can be discovered; and those who then affected an ardent desire for the welfare of their country have now thrown aside their masks, and appear in their true colours; and the great mass of the people, who, thus passive and oppressed, allow their quiet homes to be invaded, are kept in awe neither by the force of arms, nor by the depth of the views of the conspirators, but by a handful of soldiers, who are themselves scarcely aware of their own wishes or intentions, but that they desire power and distinction at any price.

It is said that the federalists are very much elated, hoping for the eventual triumph of their party, particularly in consequence of a proclamation by Valencia, which appeared two days ago, and is called "the plan of the *Comicios*," said to be written by General Tomel, who has gone over to the citadel, and who, having a great deal of classical learning, talks in it of the Roman *Committees* (the *Comicios*). Since then the revolution has taken the name of liberal, and is supported by men of name, the Pedrazas, Belderas, Riva Palacio, and others, which is of great importance to Valencia, and has given force and consistency to his party. Besides this, the *pronunciados* have the advantage of a free field from the citadel out to Tacubaya, where it is said that certain rich bankers, who are on their side, are constantly supplying the citadel with cartloads of copper, which they send in from thence. . . .

Meanwhile, we pass our time very quietly. In the morning we generally have visitors very early, discussing the probabilities, and giving us the last reports. Sometimes we venture out when there is no firing, which is much less constant and alarming than it was last year. So far we continue to have visitors in the evening, and Señor B—— and I have been playing duets on the harp and piano, even though Mexico is declared "in a state of siege." The —— minister, who was here this morning, does, however, strongly recommend us to change our quarters, and to remove to Tacubaya; which will be so troublesome, that we are inclined to delay it until it becomes absolutely necessary. . . .

5th.—We went upon the azotea this afternoon, to have a good view of the city. There were people on almost all the balconies, as on a fête-day. A picturesque group of friars of the order of La Merced, in their white robes, had mounted up on the belfry of their church, and were looking out anxiously. The palace roof next our own had soldiers on it. Everything at that moment was still and tranquil; but the conduct of the people is our constant source of surprise. Left entirely uncurbed, no one to direct them, thousands out of employment, many without bread, they meddle with nothing, do not complain, and scarcely seem to feel any interest in the result. How easily might such a people be directed for their good! It is said that all their *apathetic sympathies* are in favour of Bustamante.

Some say that Santa Anna will arrive to-day—some that the whole affair will be settled by treaty; but neither reports nor bulletins can be depended on, as scarcely any one speaks according to his true feelings or belief, but according to his political party. . . .

It appears that the conduct of congress in this emergency has given little satisfaction. They affect to give a declaration of the national will, and are as ambiguous as the Delphic Oracle; and it is said that their half-measures, and determination not to see that public opinion is against them, and that a thorough change can alone undermine this military revolution, will contribute more than anything to its eventual triumph. . . .

The president has made use of the extraordinary powers which have been granted him by the *Poder Conservador* (conservative power, a singular and intermediate authority introduced into the Mexican constitution), to abolish the ten per cent. on consumption, and to modify the personal contribution, reducing it to the richer classes alone. This concession has apparently produced no effect. It is said that the government troops continue to desert, convinced that a revolution in which Santa Anna takes part must triumph. Four new generals have been made by the president. . . .

6th.—We went out to Tacubaya, and found it impossible to procure a room there, far less a house. This is also the case at Guadalupe, San Joaquin, in fact in every village near Mexico. We are in no particular danger, unless they were to bombard the palace. There was a slight shock of an earthquake yesterday.

10th.—On the 7th, the president offered an amnesty to the *pronunciados*. Whatever might have been the result, the evening concluded with a terrible thunderstorm, mingled with the roaring of cannon, which had a most lugubrious effect. Many people were killed on the street. We had gone out in the morning, but met the Ex-Minister H——a, who strongly advised us to return home directly, as balls were falling, and accidents happening all round.

Soon after a proclamation was issued by General Valencia, purporting that if the president did not yield, he would bombard the palace; and that if the powder which is kept there were to blow up, it would ruin half the city. This induced us to look at home, for if the palace is bombarded, the Casa de Moneda cannot escape, and if the palace is blown up, the Casa de Moneda will most certainly keep it company. When the proclamation came out in the morning, various were the opinions expressed in consequence. Some believed it to be a mere threat, and others that it would take place at eleven at night. An old supernumerary soldier who lives here (one of those who was disabled by the last revolution) assured us that we had better leave the house, and as we refused, on the plea of having no safer house to go to, he walked off to the azotea, telling us he would *let us know* when the first bomb fell on the palace, and that then we must go perforce. In the evening we went downstairs to the large vaulted rooms where they are making cannon balls, and where the vaults are so thick and solid, that it was thought we should be in safety, even if General Valencia really kept his word. We sat up that night till twelve o'clock, listening anxiously, but nothing happened; and now, in consequence of a deputation which has been sent to the citadel by certain foreigners of distinction (though unknown to the government), we are no longer afraid of any sudden assault of this kind, as General Valencia has promised, in consideration of their representations, not to proceed to these last extremities, unless driven to them for his own defence.

In listening to the different opinions which are current, it would seem that Bustamante, Santa Anna, and Valencia are all equally unpopular; and that the true will of the nation, which congress was afraid to express, was first for the immediate convocation of a Constitutional Congress; and secondly, that they should not be governed by Santa Anna, yet that Bustamante should renounce, and a provisional president should be named. . . .

Santa Anna writes, complaining that Bustamante, by assuming extraordinary powers, commanding the army and yet continuing president, is infringing the constitution. But as he is coming on to destroy it entirely, this is being rather particular. It is reported that the typhus fever is in the citadel, but there are many floating rumours which are not to be depended upon. . . . There is evidently a great deal of consternation beginning to be felt amongst the lower classes. Foreigners gen-

erally are inclined towards Santa Anna, Mexicans to Bustamante; but all feel the present evils. The léperos seem to
swarm in greater numbers than ever, and last evening two
small shops were broken into and robbed. In vain the president
publishes manifestos that the shops may be opened; they remain carefully shut, all commerce paralyzed, and every one,
who has the means to do so, leaving the city.

We hear that the shells from the citadel have destroyed
part of the beautiful house belonging to Judge Peña y Peñas,
in front of the Alameda.

11th.—We have just received private information from the
government, that they will shortly require this house for arms
and ammunition and troops; coupled with still more private
advice to provide for our safety by leaving it. We shall therefore gladly accept the kind invitation of the F——a family, to
remove to their hacienda of San Xavier, about three leagues
from this. We had at first declined this invitation, owing to its
distance from the city—inconvenient for us, who are only waiting for the first opportunity to leave it; but besides that after
the most diligent search in all the surrounding villages, we
cannot find a single unoccupied room, we are very glad to
spend our remaining days in Mexico with so distinguished a
family. I shall therefore write little more at present on the
subject of the revolution, which now that we have lived some
time in Mexico, and have formed friendships there, fills us
with feelings entirely different from those which the last produced; with personal sentiments of regret, private fears, and
hopes for the future, and presentiments of evil which owe
more than half their sadness to individual feelings.

12th.—We are now in the midst of all the confusion occasioned by another removal; surrounded by trunks and boxes
and *cargadores,* and at the same time by our friends (all
those who have not taken flight yet) taking leave of us. . . .

A great cannonading took place last night, but without any
important result. The soldiers, in the day-time amuse themselves by insulting each other from the roofs of the houses
and convents. Yesterday, one of the president's party singled
out a soldier in the citadel, shot him, and then began to dance
the *Enanos,* and in the midst of a step, *he* was shot, and
rolled over, dead. . . .

We shall write again from San Xavier.

LETTER THE FORTY-FIFTH

SAN XAVIER, 16th September.

After a morning of fatigue, confusion, bustle, leave-taking, etc., etc., a coach with four mules, procured with the utmost difficulty, drove up to the door; the coach old and crazy, the mules and harness quite consistent, and the postilions so tipsy that they could hardly keep their seats. But we had no time to be particular, and climbed in amidst bows and hand-shakings, and prophecies of breaking down and of being robbed by a band of *forçats* headed by a Spaniard, who are said to be scouring the country; who are *said* to be, for just now, seeing is believing, and few reports are worth attending to. However, we took two servants on horseback, by way of escort, and rattled off, the coach creaking ominously, the postilions swinging from side to side, and our worthy housekeeper, whom we had carried off from the smoking city, screaming out her last orders to the *galopina,* concerning a certain green parrot which she had left in the charge of that tenderhearted damsel, who, with her *reboso* at her eyes, surrounded by directors of the mint, secretaries of legation, soldiers and porters, had enough to do to take charge of herself. The city looked very sad, as we drove through the streets; with closed shops, and barred windows, and cannon planted, and soldiers riding about. At every village we passed, the drivers called for brandy, tossed off a glassful, which appeared to act like a composing draught, as they gradually recovered their equilibrium. We were glad to arrive at San Xavier, where we received a most cordial welcome, and to be removed, at least for a while, from sights and sounds of destruction. A great part of the road to *Tlanapantla,* the village near which San Xavier is situated, leads through traces of the ruins of the ancient Tenochtitlan.

This part of the country is extremely pretty, being a corn and not a maguey district. Instead of the monotonous and stiff maguey, whose head never bends to the blast, we are surrounded by fields of waving corn. There are also plenty of trees; poplar, ash, and elm; and one flourishing specimen of the latter species, which we see from the windows in front of the house, was brought here by Mr. Poinsett. The hacienda, which is about three leagues from Mexico, is a large irregular building in rather a low situation, surrounded by dark blue hills. It belongs to the Señoras de F——a, of the family of the Marquis de A——o; *millionaires*—being rich in haciendas and silver-mines; very religious, very charitable, and what is less common here, extremely learned; understanding French, English, German, and even Latin. Their education they owe to the care of their father, one of the most distinguished men in Mexico, who was banished twice, once for liberal opinions, and the second time for supporting the "Plan of Iguala," in fact for not being liberal enough. In these emigrations, his family accompanied him, travelled over a great part of Europe, and profited by their opportunities. They returned here when the independence was accomplished, hoping for peace, but in vain. Constant alarms, and perpetual revolutions have succeeded one another ever since that period.

The hacienda has the usual *quantum* of furniture belonging to these country houses; and it is certainly no longer a matter of surprise to us, that rich proprietors take little interest in embellishing them. A house which will in all probability be converted once a year into a barrack, is decidedly better in a state of nature, than encumbered with elegant furniture. This house has been entirely destroyed in that way more than once, and the last time that it was occupied by troops, was left like an Augean stable. We have here the luxury of books. My room opens into a beautiful chapel, covered with paintings representing saints and virgins holding lilies, where mass is said occasionally, though the family generally attend mass in the village church of Tlanapantla. Before the house is a small flower-garden filled with roses and peculiarly fine dahlias, pomegranate-trees and violets, which, though single, have a

delicious fragrance. This stretches out into an immense
vegetable-garden and orchard, terminating in a shrubbery,
through which walks are cut, impervious to the sun at noonday. There is also a large reservoir of water, and the garden,
which covers a great space of ground, is kept in good order.
There are beautiful walks in the neighbourhood, leading to
Indian villages, old churches, and farms; and all the lanes are
bordered with fruit-trees.

Tlanapantla, which means in Indian, *between lands,* its
church having been built by the Indians of two districts, is a
small village, with an old church, ruined remains of a convent,
where the curate now lives, a few shops, and a square where
the Indians hold market (*tangis* they call it) on Fridays. All
along the lanes are small Indian huts, with their usual mud
floor, small altar, earthen vessels, and collection of daubs on
the walls; especially of the Virgin of Guadalupe; with a few
blest palm-leaves in the corner; occupied, when the men are
at work, by the Indian woman herself, her sturdy, scantily-
clothed progeny, and plenty of yelping dogs. Mrs. Ward's
sketch of the interior of an Indian hut is perfect, as all her
Mexican sketches are. When the women are also out at their
work, they are frequently tenanted by the little children
alone. Taking refuge from a shower of rain yesterday, in one
of these mud huts, we found no one there but a little bronze-
coloured child, about three years old, sleeping all alone on
the floor, with the door wide open; and though we talked loud,
and walked about in the cottage, the little thing never wakened. A second shower drove us for shelter to a farmhouse,
where we entered a sort of oratorio attached to the house; a
room which is not consecrated, but has an altar, crucifix, holy
pictures, etc. The floor was strewed with flowers, and in one
corner was an old stringless violoncello, that might have
formed a pendant to the harp of Tara.

However, the most remarkable object of the rancho is its
proprietress, a tall, noble-looking Indian, Doña Margarita by
name, a mountaineer by birth, and now a rich widow, possessing lands and flocks, though living in apparent poverty. The
bulk of her fortune she employs in educating poor orphans.
Every poor child who has no parents, finds in her a mother
and protectress; the more wretched, or sick, or deformed, the
more certain of an asylum with her. She takes them into her
house, brings them up as her own children, has them bred to
some useful employment, and when they are old enough, married. If it is a boy, she chooses him a wife from amongst the

girls of the mountains, where she was born, who she says are "less corrupted" than the girls of the village. She has generally from twelve to twenty on her hands, always filling up with new orphans the vacancies caused in her small colony by death or marriage. There is nothing picturesque about these orphans, for, as I said before, the most deformed and helpless, and maimed and sick, are the peculiar objects of Doña Margarita's care; nevertheless, we saw various healthy, happy-looking girls, busied in various ways, washing and ironing, and sewing, whose very eyes gleamed when we mentioned her name, and who spoke of her with a respect and affection that it was pleasant to witness. Truly, this woman is entitled to happy dreams and soft slumbers! The remainder of her fortune she employs in the festivals and ceremonies of the church; in fireworks, in ornaments for the altars, etc.

19th.—Every day a messenger arrives from Mexico, bringing news of the *pronunciamiento*, which are eagerly waited for, and read with intense interest. It is probable, now, that affairs will soon come to a crisis. A step has been taken by the president, which is considered very imprudent by those who are looking on in this great game. General Torrejon, who with nine hundred good soldiers kept Santa Anna in awe at Perote, has been sent for to Mexico, Bustamante wishing to reunite his forces. These troops, together with those of Codallos (the Governor of Puebla) brings up his army to three thousand five hundred, or some say to four thousand men, all effective, and of which nine hundred are good cavalry. Bustamante being now at the head of the army, Hechavarria exercises the executive power, according to the constitution, in his capacity of president of the Council of State, (*Consejo de Estado*); the Mexicans having no vice-president.

Santa Anna, who had until now remained in Perote with his unorganized troops, no officers on whom he could depend, and a handful of miserable cavalry, has moved forwards to Puebla. Arrived there, his numbers were increased by one hundred men of the Tobacco customs, (brought him by Señor —— ——, who, with a rich Spanish banker went out to meet him,) forty horsemen seduced from the escort of Codallos, and a company of watchmen! As yet, no movement has taken place or seems likely to take place in his favour in Puebla. Señor Haro is named governor of that city in the place of Codallos, who was sent for to join the president in Mexico; and Puebla, which used to be the great theatre of revolutions, has remained on this occasion in the most perfect neutrality, neither declaring for one party nor the other; probably the wisest course to pursue at this juncture. Every one is of opinion that five hundred troops sent by Bustamante, would instantly put this mongrel army of Santa Anna's to flight; for though he has collected about a thousand men, he has not three hundred good soldiers. . . .

On the other hand, General Paredes is marching in this direction with General Cortazar, his orders from Santa Anna no doubt being to keep the president in play, and to divert his attention by treaties or preliminaries of treaties, whilst he continues to march with caution towards the capital. The great event to be dreaded by the government is a junction of the *pronunciado* forces. As long as they are separate, it is in no immediate danger; but like the bundle of rods, what can easily be broken separately, will assume strength when joined together. I make no further excuse for talking about politics. We talk and think of little else.

21st.—Yesterday (Sunday) we were startled by the intelligence, that Generals Canalizo and Noriega had arrived at the village in the middle of the night, with a large troop, and that General Bustamante himself had made his appearance there at five in the morning: so that the peaceful little Tlanapantla had suddenly assumed a warlike appearance. As it lies on the direct road to Guanajuato there could be no doubt that they were marching to meet Paredes. C——n immediately walked down to the village to pay his respects to the president, who was lodged at the curate's, and meanwhile General Noriega came to the hacienda to see the ladies. C——n found the president very much fatigued, having passed fourteen days and nights under arms, and in constant anxiety; General Orbegoso was with him.

After breakfast we went down to the village to see the troops, who were resting there for a few hours. The cavalry occupied the square, the horses standing, and the men stretched asleep on the ground, each soldier beside his horse. The infantry occupied the churchyard. Dreadfully fatigued, they were lying some on the grass, and others with their heads pillowed on the old tombstones, resting as well as they could with their armour on. Before they started, the curate said mass to them in the square. There was a good deal of difficulty in procuring the most common food for so many hungry men. Tortillas had been baked in haste, and all the hens in the village were put in requisition to obtain eggs for the president and his officers. We sat down in a porch to see them set off; a melancholy sight enough, in spite of drums beating and trumpets sounding. An old soldier, who came up to water his own and his master's horse, began to talk to us of what was going on, and seemed anything but enthusiastic at the prospects of himself and his comrades, assuring us that the army of General Paredes was double their number. He was covered with wounds received in the war against Texas, and expressed his firm conviction that we should see the Comanche Indians on the streets of Mexico one of these days; at which savage tribe he appeared to have a most devout horror; describing to a gaping audience the manner in which he had seen a party of them devour three of their prisoners. . . .

About four o'clock the signal for departure was sounded, and they went off amidst the cheers of the people.

22nd.—Great curiosity was excited yesterday afternoon, when news was brought us that Bustamante, with his generals and troops, had returned, and had passed through the village, on their way back to Mexico! Some say that this retrograde march is in consequence of a movement made in Mexico by General Valencia—others that it has been caused by a message received from General Paredes. We paid a visit in the evening to the old curate, who was pretty much in the dark, morally and figuratively, in a very large hall, where were assembled a number of females, and one tallow candle. Of course all were talking politics, and especially discoursing of the visit of the president the preceding night, and of his departure in the morning, and of his return in the afternoon, and of the difficulty of procuring tortillas for the men, and eggs for the officers.

23rd.—We have received news this morning of the murder of our porter, the Spaniard whom we had brought from Havana. He had left us, and was employed as porter in a *fabrica* (manufactory), where the wife and family of the proprietor resided. Eight of General Valencia's soldiers sallied forth from the citadel to rob this factory, and poor José, the most faithful and honest of servants, having valiantly defended the door, was cruelly murdered. They afterwards entered the building, robbed, and committed dreadful outrages. They are selling printed papers through the streets to-day, giving an account of it. The men are taken up, and it is said will be shot by orders of the general; but we doubt this, even though a message has arrived, requiring the attendance of the *padre* who confesses criminals; a Franciscan monk, who, with various of his brethren, are living here for safety at present.

The situation of Mexico is melancholy.

24th.—News have arrived that General Paredes has arrived at the *Lecheria*, an hacienda belonging to this family, about three leagues from San Xavier: and that from thence he sent one of the servants of the farm to Mexico, inviting the president to a personal conference. The family take this news of their hacienda's being turned into military quarters very philosophically; the only precaution on these occasions being to conceal the best horses, as the *pronunciados* help themselves, without ceremony, to these useful quadrupeds, wherever they are to be found.

26th.—This morning, General Bustamante and his troops arrived at Tlanapantla, the president in a coach. Having met C——n on the road, he stopped for a few moments and informed him that he was on his way to meet General Paredes at the *Lecheria*, where he hoped to come to a composition with him. We listened all day with anxiety, but hearing no firing, concluded that some arrangement had in fact been made. In the evening we walked out on the high-road, and met the president, the governor, and the troops all returning. What securities Bustamante can have received, no one can imagine, but it is certain that they have met without striking a blow. It was nearly dusk as they passed, and the president bowed cheerfully, while some of the officers rode up, and assured us that all was settled.

Sunday, 27th.—Cavalry, infantry, carriages, cannon, etc., are all passing through the village. These are the *pronunciados*, with General Paredes, following to Mexico. Feminine curiosity induces me to stop here, and to join the party who are going down to the village to see them pass. . . .

We have just returned after a sunny walk, and an *inspection* of the *pronunciados*—they are too near Mexico now for me to venture to call them *the rebels*. The infantry, it must be confessed, was in a very ragged and rather drunken condition—the cavalry better, having *borrowed* fresh horses as they went along. Though certainly not *point-device* in their accoutrements, their good horses, high saddles, bronze faces, and picturesque attire, had a fine effect as they passed along under the burning sun. The sick followed on asses, and amongst them various masculine women, with *sarapes* or *mangas* and large straw hats, tied down with coloured handkerchiefs, mounted on mules or horses. The sumpter mules followed, carrying provisions, camp-beds, etc.; and various Indian women trotted on foot in the rear, carrying their husbands' boots and clothes. There was certainly no beauty amongst these feminine followers of the camp, especially amongst the mounted Amazons, who looked like very ugly men in a semi-female disguise. The whole party are on their way to Tacubaya, to join Santa Anna! The game is nearly up now. *Check from two knights and a castle*—from Santa Anna and Paredes in Tacubaya, and from Valencia in the citadel. People are flying in all directions, some from Mexico, and others from Guadalupe and Tacubaya. . . .

It appears that Santa Anna was marching from Puebla, feeling his way towards the capital in fear and trembling. At Rio Frio a sentinel's gun having accidentally gone off, the whole army were thrown into the most ludicrous consternation and confusion. Near Oyotla the general's brow cleared up, for here he was met by commissioners from the government, Generals Orbegoso and Guyame. In a moment the quick apprehension of Santa Anna saw that the day was his own. He gave orders to continue the march with all speed to Tacubaya, affecting to listen to the proposals of the commissioners, amusing them without compromising himself, and offering to treat with them at *Mexicalsingo*. They returned without having received any decided answer, and without, on their part, having given any assurance that his march should not be stopped; yet he has been permitted to arrive unmolested at Tacubaya, where Paredes has also arrived, and where he has been joined by General Valencia; so that the three *pronunciado* generals are now united there to dispose of the fate of the republic. . . .

The same day General Almonte had an interview with Santa Anna, who said with a smile, when he left him, "*Es buen muchacho* (he is a good lad)—he may be of service to us yet." . . .

The three *allied sovereigns* are now in the archbishop's palace at Tacubaya, from whence they are to dictate to the president and the nation. But they are, in fact, chiefly occupied with their respective engagements and respective rights. Paredes wishes to fulfil his engagements with the departments of Guanjuato, Jalisco, Zacatecas, Aguas Calientes, Queretaro, etc. In his *plan* he promised them religious toleration, permission for foreigners to hold property, and so on—the last, in fact, being his favourite project. Valencia, on his side, has his engagements to fulfil with the federalists, and has proposed Señor Pedraza as an integral part of the regeneration —one whose name will give confidence now and ever to his party. General Santa Anna has engagements *with himself*. He has determined to command them all, and allows them to fight amongst themselves, provided he governs. Paredes is, in fact, furious with Valencia, accusing him of having interfered when not wanted, and of having ruined his *plan*, by mingling it with a revolution, with which it had no concern. He does not reflect that Valencia was the person who gave the mortal wound to the government. Had he not revolted, Santa Anna would not have left Perote, nor Paredes himself passed on unmolested. . . .

The conservative body has been invited to go to Tacubaya, but has refused. The majority desire the election of Paredes, or of any one who is not Santa Anna or Valencia; but Paredes himself, while drawing no very flattering portrait of Santa Anna, declares that he is the only man in the republic fit for the presidency—the only man who can make himself obeyed—in short, the only one capable of taking those energetic measures which the safety of the republic requires. He flatters himself that he, at the head of his division, will always keep Santa Anna in check; as if Cortazar, who deserted Bustamante in a moment of difficulty, could be depended on! . . .

Meanwhile they are fortifying Mexico; and some suppose that Bustamante and his generals have taken the rash determination of permitting all their enemies to unite, in order to destroy them at one blow. . . .

29th.—There being at present an armistice between the contending parties, a document was published yesterday, fruits of the discussion of the allied powers at Tacubaya. It is called *"las bases de Tacubaya,"* and being published in Mexico by General Almonte, many expected and hoped that a new *pronunciamiento* would be the consequence; but it has been quietly received, and the federalists welcome it as containing the foundations of federalism and popularity. There are thirteen articles, which are as follow:

By the first—It is the will of the nation that the supreme powers established by the constitution of '36 have ceased, excepting the judicial, which will be limited in its functions to matters purely judicial, conformably to the existing laws.

By the second—A *junta* is to be named, composed of two deputies from each department, elected by his Excellency the Commander-in-Chief of the Mexican army, Don Antonio Lopez de Santa Anna, in order that they may be entirely free to point out the person who is to hold the executive power provisionally.

By the third—This person is immediately to assume the executive power, taking an oath in the presence of the junta to set for the welfare of the nation.

By the fourth—The provisional executive power shall in two months convoke a new congress, which, with ample powers, shall engage to reconstitute the nation, as appears most suitable to them.

By the fifth—This congress extraordinary shall reunite in six months after it is convened, and shall solely occupy itself in forming the constitution.

By the sixth—The provincial executive shall answer for its acts before the first constitutional congress.

By the seventh—The provincial executive shall have all the powers necessary for the organization of all the branches of the public administration.

By the eighth—Four ministers shall be named, of foreign and home relations, of public instruction and industry, of treasury, and of war and marine.

By the ninth—Each department is to have two trustworthy individuals to form a council, which shall give judgment in all matters on which they may be consulted by the executive.

By the tenth—Till this council is named, the *junta* will fulfil its functions.

By the eleventh—Till the republic is organized, the authorities in the departments which have not opposed, and will not oppose the national will, shall continue.

By the twelfth—The general-in-chief and all the other generals promise to forget all the political conduct of military men or citizens during the present crisis.

By the thirteenth—When three days have passed after the expiration of the present truce, if the general-in-chief of the government does not adopt these *bases,* their accomplishment will be proceeded with; and they declare, in the name of the nation, that this general, and all the troops who follow him, and all the so-called authorities which counteract this national will, shall be held responsible for all the Mexican blood that may be uselessly shed, and which shall be upon their heads.

30th.—To the astonishment of all parties, Bustamante and his generals *pronounced* yesterday morning for the federal system, and *this* morning Bustamante has resigned the presidency. His motives seem not to be understood, unless a circular, published by General Almonte, can throw any light upon them.

"Without making any commentary," he says, speaking of the document of Tacubaya, "upon this impudent document, which proposes to the Mexican nation a military government, and the most ominous of dictatorships in favour of the false defender of public liberty, of the most ferocious enemy of every government that has existed in the country, I hasten to send it to you, that you may have it published in this state, where surely it will excite the same indignation as in an immense majority of the inhabitants of the capital, who, jealous of the national glory, and decided to lose everything in order to preserve it, have spontaneously proclaimed the re-establishment of the federal system, the whole garrison having followed this impulse. There is no medium between liberty and tyranny; and the government, relying on the good sense of the nation, which will not see with indifference the slavery that is preparing for it, puts itself in the hands of the states, resolved to sacrifice itself on the altars of the country, or to strengthen its liberty for ever.

"I enclose the renunciation which His Excellency Don Anastasio Bustamante makes to the presidency," etc.

3rd October.—Though a very democratic crowd collected, and federalism was proclaimed in Mexico, it appears that no confidence in the government was inspired by this last measure. Some say that had Bustamante alone declared for the federal system, and had sent some effective cavalry to protect the *pronunciados* of that party all through the country, he might have triumphed still. Be that as it may, General Canalizo pronounced for federalism on the second of October, but this is not followed up on the part of the Generals Bustamante and Almonte, while the vice-president, *Hechavarria,* has retired to his house, blaming Almonte for having published an official document without his knowledge. Everything is in a state of perfect anarchy and confusion. The léperos are going about armed, and no one remains in Mexico but those who are obliged to do so. It is said that in Tacubaya great uneasiness prevailed as to the result of this new movement, and Santa Anna offered an asylum there to the congress and conservative body, although, by the ultimatum from Tacubaya, published on the twenty-eighth, the constitution of '36 was concluded, and of course these authorities were politically dead.

I had hardly written these words when the roaring of cannon announced that hostilities have recommenced.

5th.—For the last few days, we have been listening to the cannon, and even at this distance, the noise reverberating amongst the hills is tremendous. The sound is horrible! There is something appalling, yet humbling, in these manifestations of man's wrath and man's power, when he seems to usurp his Maker's attributes, and to mimic his thunder. The divine spark kindled within him, has taught him how to draw these metals from the earth's bosom; how to combine these simple materials, so as to produce with them an effect as terrible as the thunderbolts of heaven. His earthly passions have prompted him so to wield these instruments of destruction, as to deface God's image in his fellow-men. The power is so divine—the causes that impel him to use that power are so paltry! The intellect that creates these messengers of death is so near akin to divinity—the motives that put them in action are so poor, so degrading even to humanity!

On the third, there was a shower of bombs and shells from the citadel, of which some fell into the palace, and one in our late residence, the mint. An engagement took place in the Virga; and though Bustamante's party were partially victorious, it is said that neither has much reason to boast of the result. General Espinosa, an old insurgent, arrived at the village last night, and sent to request some horses from the hacienda, which were sent him with all convenient speed, that he might not, according to his usual plan, come and take them. In exchange for some half-dozen farm horses in good condition, he sent half a dozen lean, wretched-looking quadrupeds, the bones coming through their skin, skeletons fit for dissection.

News have just arrived to the effect that last night, at three o'clock, Bustamante suddenly left the city, drawing off all his troops from the turrets, and leaving General Orbegoso in the palace, with one hundred men. It was generally reported, that he had marched into the interior, to bring about a federal revolution; but it appears that he has arrived at Guadalupe, and there taken up his quarters. A loud cannonading has been kept up since ten o'clock, which keeps us all idle, looking out for the smoke, and counting the number of discharges.

6th.—A messenger has brought the intelligence that there had been more noise and smoke than slaughter; the cannons being planted at such distances, that it was impossible they could do much execution. Numerous bulletins are distributed;

some violently in favour of Bustamante and federalism, full of abuse and dread of Santa Anna; others lauding that general to the skies, as the saviour of his country. The *allied* forces being in numbers double those of Bustamante, there is little doubt of the result.

7th.—*A capitulation.* Santa Anna is triumphant. He made his solemn entry into Mexico last evening, Generals Valencia and Canalizo being at the head of the united forces. Not a solitary *viva* was heard as they passed along the streets; nor afterwards, during his speech in congress. *Te Deum* was sung this morning in the cathedral, the archbishop in person receiving the new president. We have just returned from Mexico, where we went in search of apartments, and with great difficulty have found rooms in the hotel of the Calle Vegara; but we shall remain here a day or two longer. There is no great difference in the general appearance of the city, except that the shops are reopened, and that most of the windows are broken. Immediately after the morning ceremony, Santa Anna returned to the archbishop's palace at Tacubaya; which residence he prefers to the president's palace in Mexico. His return there, after his triumphant entry into the capital, was very much *en Rio*—a retinue of splendid coaches with fine horses, going at full speed; the general's carriage drawn by four beautiful white horses—(belonging to Don F—— M——; the very same that were sent to bring us into Mexico) brilliant aides-de-camp, and an immense escort of cavalry. Thus concludes the revolution of 1842, though not its effects.

The new ministry, up to this date, are Señor Gomez Pedraza for Foreign and Home Relations; Castillo, *un petit avocat* from Guadalajara, said to be a furious federalist and Latin scholar, for Public Instruction; General Tornel for War and Marine; and Señor Dufoo for the Treasury. Valencia proposed Paredes for the War Department; but he declined, saying, "No, no, General—I understand you very well. You want to draw me from off my division."

Those who know Bustamante best, even those who most blame him for indecision and want of energy, agree on one point; that the true motives of his conduct are to be found in his constant and earnest desire to spare human life.

LETTER THE FORTY-SIXTH

Santa Mónica—Solidity—Old Paintings—Anachronism—Babies and Nurses from the Cuna—Society—Funds—Plan—Indian Nurses—Carmelite Convent—Midnight Warning—Old Villages and Churches—Indian Bath—San Matéo—The Lecheria—Fertility—Nolino Viejo—Dulness—Religious Exercises —Return to Mexico—Mexican Hotel—New Generals—Disturbances—General Bustamante—Inconvenience—Abuses in the name of Liberty—Verses—Independence celebrated.

8th.

The Revolution has lasted upwards of thirty-five days; and during that time, though I have written of little else, we have been taking many rides in the environs of this hacienda, some of which were very interesting. We are also making the most of our last few days of Mexican country life. On Thursday we went on horseback with a large party to visit the mill of Santa Mónica, an immense hacienda, which tradition, I know not with what truth, supposes to have been in former days the property of Doña Marina; a gift to her from Cortes. At all events, at a later period it belonged to the Augustine monks, then to a Mexican family, who lost their fortune from neglect or extravagance. It was bought by the present proprietor for a comparatively trifling sum, and produces him an annual rent of thirty-five thousand dollars upon an average. The house is colossal, and not more than one-third of it occupied. The granaries, of solid masonry, contain fourteen thousand loads of corn—they were built about two hundred and fifty years ago. From all the neighbouring haciendas, and even from many distant estates, the corn is sent to this mill, and is here ground, deposited, and sold on account of the owner, a certain portion deducted for the proprietor of Santa Mónica. It seems strange that they should have no windmills here, in a country colonized by Spain, where, according to *Cervantes,* they were common enough. The house is in a commanding situation, and the views of the mountains, especially from the upper windows, are very grand. In some of the old, unoccupied apartments, are some good copies of old paintings, the copies themselves of ancient date. There is the Angel announcing to Elizabeth the birth of Saint John; a Holy Family, from Murillo; the destruction of Sodom and Gomorrah, which is one of the best; particularly the figures in the foreground, of Lot and his family. Lot's wife stands in the distance, a graceful figure just crystallized, her head turned in the direction of the doomed city. I looked into every dark corner, in hopes of finding some old daub representing Doña Marina, but without success. There is the strangest contrast possible between these half-abandoned palaces, and their actual proprietors. We had beautiful riding-horses belonging to the hacienda, and enjoyed everything but the exceeding heat of the sun, as we galloped home about one o'clock. . . .

As a specimen of rather a remarkable anachronism, we were told that a justice in the village of Tlanapantla, speaking the other day of General Bustamante, said, "Poor man—he is persecuted by all parties, just as Jesus Christ was by the *Jansenists*, the *Sadducees*, and the *Holy Fathers of the Church!*" What a curious *olla podrida* the poor man's brain must be!

In the midst of the revolution, we were amused by a very peaceful sight—all the nurses belonging to the *Cuna*, or Foundling hospital, coming from the different villages to receive their monthly wages. Amongst the many charitable institutions of Mexico, there appears to me (in spite of the many prejudices existing against such institutions) none more useful than this. These otherwise unfortunate children, the offspring of abject poverty or guilt, are left at the gate of the establishment, where they are received without any questions being asked; and from that moment, they are protected and cared for, by the best and noblest families in the country. The members of the society consist of the first persons in Mexico, male and female. The men furnish the money; the women give their time and attention. There is no fixed number of members, and amongst them are the ladies in whose house we now live. The *President* is the Dowager Marquesa de Vivanco. When the child has been about a month in the *Cuna*, it is sent, with an Indian nurse, to one of the villages near Mexico. If sick or feeble it remains in the house, under the more immediate inspection of the society. These nurses have a *fiadora*, a responsible person, who lives in the village, and answers for their good conduct. Each nurse is paid four dollars per month, a sufficient sum to induce any poor Indian, with a family, to add one to her stock. Each lady of the society has a certain number under her peculiar care, and gives their clothes, which are poor enough, but according to the *village fashion*. The child thus put out to nurse, is brought back to the *Cuna* when weaned, and remains under the charge of the society for life; but of the hundreds and tens of hundreds that have passed through their hands, scarcely has one been left to grow up in the *Cuna*. They are constantly adopted by respectable persons, who, according to their inclination or abilities, bring them up either as favoured servants, or as their own children; and the condition of a *"huerfano,"* an orphan, as a child from the hospital is always called, is perfectly upon a level with that of the most petted child of the house. The nurses in the *Cuna* are paid eight dollars per month.

Upwards of a hundred nurses and babies arrived on Sunday, taking up their station on the grass, under the shade of a large ash-tree in the courtyard. The nurses are invariably bronze; the babies generally dark, though there was a sprinkling of fair English or German faces amongst them, with blue eyes and blonde hair, apparently not the growth of Mexican land. Great attention to cleanliness cannot be hoped for from this class, but the babies looked healthy and contented. Each nurse had to present a paper which had been given her for that purpose, containing her own name, the name of the child, and that of the lady under whose particular charge she was. Such as—*"Maria Josifa—baby Juanita de los Santos—belonging to the Señora Doña Matilde F——, given on such a day to the charge of Maria Josefa."* Constantly the nurse had lost this paper, and impossible for her to remember more than her own name; as to who gave her the baby, or when she got it, was entirely beyond her powers of calculation. However, then stept forward the *fiadora* Doña Tomaso, a sensible-looking village dame, grave and important as became her situation, and gave an account of the nurse and the baby, which being satisfactory, the copper was swept into the nurse's lap, and she and her baby went away contented. It was pleasant to see the kindness of the ladies to these poor women; how they praised the care that had been taken of the babies; admired the strong and healthy ones, which indeed nearly all were; took an interest in those who looked paler, or less robust; and how fond and proud the nurses were of their charges; and how little of a hired, mercenary, *hospital* feeling existed among them all. . . .

A judge in the village, who comes here frequently, a pleasant and well-informed man, amused us this evening by recounting to us how he had once formed a determination to become a monk, through sudden fear. Being sent by government to Toluca, some years ago, to inquire into the private political conduct of a *Yorkino*, he found that his only means of remaining there unsuspected, and also of obtaining information, was to lodge in the convent of the Carmelite friars. The padres accommodated him with a cell, and assisted him very efficaciously in his researches. But the first night, being alone in his cell, the convent large and dreary, and the wind howling lugubriously over the plains, he was awakened at night by a deep sepulchral voice, apparently close to his ear, tolling forth these words:

> *"Hermanos, en el sepulcro acaba,*
> *Todo lo que el mundo alaba!"*

> *"My brothers, all must finish in the tomb!*
> *Of all that men extol, this is the doom."*

Exceedingly startled, he sprang up, and opened the door of his cell. A dim lamp faintly illuminated the long vaulted galleries, and the monks, like shadows, were gliding to midnight prayer. In the dreariness of the night, with the solemn words sounding in his ear like a warning knell, he came to the satisfactory conclusion that all was vanity, and to the determination that the very next day he would retire from the world, join this holy brotherhood, and bind himself to be a Carmelite friar for life. The day brought counsel, the cheerful sunbeams dispelled the gloom, even within the old convent, and his scruples of conscience melted away.

There are old villages and old churches in this neighbourhood that would delight an antiquary. In the churchyard of the village of San Andrés, is the most beautiful weeping ash I ever saw. We took shelter from the sun yesterday under its gigantic shadow, and lay there as under a green vault. We saw to-day, near another solitary old church, one of the Indian oven-baths, the *temezcallis*, built of bricks, in which there is neither alteration nor improvement since their first invention, heaven alone knows in what century.

9th.—We rode last evening to another estate belonging to this family, called *San Mateo*, one of the prettiest places on a small scale we have seen here. The road, or rather path, led us through fields, covered with the greatest profusion of bright yellow sunflowers and scarlet dahlias, so tall that they came up to our horses' ears. The house is built in the cottage style (the first specimen of that style we have seen here), with the piazza in front, large trees shading it, and a beautiful view from the height on which it stands. It has rather an English than a Spanish look. No one lives there but the agent and his wife—and a fierce dog.

11th.—This morning we rose at five, mounted our horses, and accompanied by Señor E——, together with the adminis- trador and the old gardener, set off to take our last long ride from San Xavier; for this evening we return to Mexico. The morning was fine and fresh, the very morning for a gallop, and the country looked beautiful. We rode first to the *Lecheria*, where Generals Bustamante and Paredes had their last event- ful conference, having passed on our way various old churches and villages, and another hacienda also belonging to this fam- ily, whose estates seem countless. The *Lecheria* is a large un- occupied house, or occupied only by the administrador and his family. It is a fine building, and its courtyard within is filled with flowers; but having neither garden nor trees near it, seems rather lonely; and must have been startled to find it- self the *rendezvous* of contending chieftains. It is surrounded by fertile and profitable fields of corn and maize. We staid but a short time in the house, and having observed with due re- spect the chamber where the generals conferred together, re- mounted our horses and rode on. I have no doubt, by the way, that their meeting was the most amicable imaginable. I never saw a country where opponent parties bear so little real ill-will to each other. It all seems to evaporate in words. I do not believe that there is any real bad feeling subsisting at this moment, even between the two rival generals, Bustamante and Santa Anna. Santa Anna usurped the presidency, partly because he wanted it, and partly because if he had not, some one else would; but I am convinced that if they met by chance in a drawing-room, they would give each other as cordial an *ambrazo* (embrace), Mexican fashion, as if nothing had hap- pened.

Our road led us through a beautiful track of country, all belonging to the Lecheria, through pathways that skirted the fields, where the plough had newly turned up the richest pos- sible soil, and which were bordered by wild flowers and shady trees. For miles our path lay through a thick *carpeting* of the most beautiful wild flowers imaginable: bright scarlet dahlias, gaudy sunflowers, together with purple and lilac, and pale straw-coloured blossoms, to all which the gardener gave but the general name of *mirasoles* (sunflower). The purple con- volvulus threw its creeping branches on the ground, or along whatever it could embrace; while all these bright flowers, some growing to a great height, seemed, as we rode by them, to be flaunting past us in their gay colours, like peasants in their holiday dresses. The ground also was enamelled with a little low inquisitive-looking blossom, bright yellow, with a peeping brown eye; and the whole, besides forming the gayest assemblage of colours and groups, gave to the air a delicious fragrance.

But at last we left these fertile grounds, and began to ascend the hills, part of which afford pasture for the flocks, till, still higher up, they become perfectly arid and stony. Here the whole landscape looks bleak and dreary, excepting that the eye can rest upon the distant mountains, of a beautiful blue, like a peep of the promised land from Mount Nebo. After having rode four leagues, the latter part over this sterile ground, affording but an insecure footing for our horses, we descried, low down in a valley, an old sad-looking building, with a ruined mill and some trees. This was the object of our ride; the *"Molino viejo"* (old mill), another hacienda belonging to these rich lady proprietors; and profitable on account of the fine pasture which some of the surrounding hills afford. Nothing could look more solitary. Magdalene might have left her desert, and ended her days there, without materially bettering her situation. The only sign of life is a stream that runs round a very productive small orchard in front of the house, while on a hill behind are a few maguey plants, and on the *mirador*, in front of the house, some creepers have been trained with a good deal of taste. There are bleak hills in front—hills with a scanty herbage behind it, and everywhere a stillness that makes itself felt: while, strange circumstance in this country! there is not even a church within a league and a half. There has been a chapel in the house, but the gilded paintings are falling from the walls—the altar is broken, and the floor covered with dried corn. The agent's wife, who sits here all alone, must have time to collect her scattered thoughts, and plenty of opportunity for reflection and self-examination. Certain it is, she gave us a very good breakfast, which we attacked like famished pilgrims; and shortly after took our leave.

The heat on the shadeless hills had now become intense. It is only on such occasions that one can fully appreciate the sufferings of *Regulus*. We returned by the *carriage-road*, a track between two hills, composed of ruts and stones, and large holes. On the most barren parts of these hills, there springs a tree which the Indians call *guisachel;* it resembles the savine, and produces a berry of which ink is made. The road was bordered by bushes, covered with white blossoms, very fragrant. We galloped as fast as our horses would carry us, to escape from the sun; and passed a pretty village on the high road, which is a fine broad causeway in good repair, leading to Guanaxuato. We also passed *San Mateo*, and then rode over the fields fast home, where we arrived, looking like broiled potatoes. . . .

We had a conversation with —— this morning, on the subject of the *"ejercicios,"* certain religious exercises, to which, in Mexico, men as well as women annually devote a certain number of days, during which they retire from the world to a religious house or convent, set apart for that purpose, of which some receive male and other female devotees. Here they fast and pray and receive religious instruction, and meditate upon religious subjects during the period of their retreat. A respectable merchant, who, in compliance with this custom, lately retired for a few days to one of these religious establishments, wrote, on entering there, to his head clerk, a young man to whom he was much attached, informing him that he had a presentiment that he would not leave the convent alive, but would die by the time his devotional exercises were completed; giving him some good advice as to his future conduct, together with his last instructions as to his own affairs. He ended with these words: *"hasta la eternidad!"* until eternity! The letter produced a strong effect on the mind of the young man; but still more, when the merchant died at the end of a few days, as he had predicted, and was carried from the convent to his grave.

MEXICO, Calle Vergara, 12th.

We reached Mexico last evening, and took up our quarters in an inn or hotel kept by an English woman, and tolerably clean, though of course not very agreeable. A number of *pronunciado* officers are also here—amongst others, General ——, who I hope will be obliged to go soon, that we may have his parlour; a mysterious English couple; a wounded Colonel, an old gentleman, a fixture in the house, etc. There is a *table d'hôte*, but I believe no ladies dine there. Invitations to take up our quarters in private houses have been pressed upon us with a kindness and cordiality difficult to resist. . . .

Though politics are the only topic of interest at present, I think you will care little for having an account of the Junta of

Representatives, or of the elections, with their chiefly military members. Considering by whom the members are chosen, and the object for which they are elected, the result of their deliberations is, as you may suppose, pretty well known beforehand. Military power is strengthened by every act, and all this power is vested in the commanders-in-chief. New batches of generals are made, in order to reward the late distinguished services of the officers, and colonels by hundreds. Eleven generals were created in the division of Paredes alone. Money has been given to the troops in the palace, with orders to purchase new uniforms, which it is said will be very brilliant. There appears, generally speaking, a good deal of half-smothered discontent, and it is whispered that even the revolutionary bankers are half repentant and look gloomy. The only opposition paper is "Un Periodico Mas;" one more periodical—the others are all ministerial.

In the south there has been some trouble with Generals Bravo and Alvarez, who wish that part of the country to govern itself until the meeting of congress. There was some talk of putting Valencia at the head of the troops which are destined to march against them, but there are now negotiations pending, and it is supposed there will be some agreement made without coming to bloodshed. It is said that orders were sent to General Almonte to leave the republic, and that he answered the despatch with firmness, refusing to acknowledge the authority of Santa Anna. General Bustamante, who is now in Guadalupe, intends to leave the scene of his disasters within a few months. C——n paid him a visit lately, and though scarcely recovered from his fatigues both of body and mind, he appears cheerful and resigned, and with all the tranquillity which can be inspired only by a good conscience, and the conviction of having *done his duty to the best of his abilities.* . . .

As for us personally, this revolution has been the most inconvenient revolution that ever took place; doing us all manner of mischief; stopping the sale of our furniture, throwing our affairs into confusion; overthrowing all our plans, and probably delaying our departure until December or January. But in these cases, every one must suffer more or less; and meanwhile, we are surrounded by friends and by friendly attentions. It will be impossible for us to leave Mexico without regret. It requires nothing but a settled government to make it one of the first countries in the world. Santa Anna has much in his power. *Reste à savoir* how he will use that power. Perhaps in these last years of tranquillity, which he has spent on his estate, he may have meditated to some purpose.

It is singular how, in trying to avoid small evils, we plunge into unknown gulfs of misery; and how little we reflect that it might be wiser to

> *"Bear those ills we have,*
> *Than fly to others that we know not of."*

Every one has heard of the abuses that produced the first revolution in Mexico—of the great inequality of riches, of the degradation of the Indians, of the high prices of foreign goods, of the Inquisition, of the ignorance of the people, the bad state of the colleges, the difficulty of obtaining justice, the influence of the clergy, and the ignorance in which the Mexican youth were purposely kept. Which of these evils has been remedied? Foreign goods are cheaper, and the Inquisition *is not;* but this last unchristian institution had surely gradually lost its power before the days of the last viceroy?—But in the sacred name of *Liberty,* every abuse can be tolerated.

> *"O fatal name, misleader of mankind,*
> *Phantom, too radiant and too much adored!*
> *Deceitful Star, whose beams are bright to blind,*
> *Although their more benignant influence poured*
> *The light of glory on the Switzer's sword,*
> *And hallowed Washington's immortal name.*
> *Liberty! Thou when absent how deplored,*
> *And when received, how wasted, till thy name*
> *Grows tarnished; shall mankind, ne'er cease to work thee*
>   *shame?*

> *"Not from the blood in fiercest battle shed,*
> *Nor deeds heroical as arm can do,*
> *Is the true strength of manly freedom bred,*
> *Restraining tyranny and licence too,*
> *The madness of the many and the few.*
> *Land, whose new beauties I behold revealed,*
> *Is this not true, and bitter as 'tis true?*
> *The ruined fane, the desolated field,*
> *The ruffian-haunted road, a solemn answer yield.*

> *"Where look the loftiest Cordilleras down*
> *From summits hoary with eternal snow*
> *On Montezuma's venerable town*
> *And storied vale, and Lake of Mexico,*

These thoughts the shade of melancholy throw
   On all that else were fair, and gay, and grand
As nature in her glory can bestow.
   For never yet, though liberal her hand,
So variously hath she adorned, enriched one land.

"What boots it that from where the level deep
   Basks in the tropic sun's o'erpow'ring light
To where yon mountains lift their wintry steep,
   All climes, all seasons in one land unite?
What boots it that her buried caves are bright
   With wealth untold of gold or silver ore?
While, checked by anarchy's perpetual blight,
   Industry trembles 'mid her hard-earned store,
While rapine riots near in riches stained with gore?

"O sage regenerators of mankind!
   Patriots of nimble tongue and systems crude!
How many regal tyrannies combined,
   So many fields of massacre have strewed
As you, and your attendant cut-throat brood?
   Man works no miracles; long toil, long thought,
Joined to experience, may achieve much good,
   But to create new systems out of nought,
Is fit for Him alone, the universe who wrought.

"But what hath such an hour of such a day
   To do with human crimes, or earthly gloom?
Far wiser to enjoy while yet we may,
   The mock-bird's song, the orange flower's perfume,
The freshness that the sparkling fountain showers.
   Let nations reach their glory or their doom,
Spring will return to dress yon orange bowers,
And flowers will still bloom on, and bards will sing of flowers."

21st.—In pursuance of the last-mentioned advice, we have been breakfasting to-day at Tacubaya, with the —— minister and his family, and enjoying ourselves there in Madame ——'s garden. We have also just returned from the Marquesa de ——'s, where we had a pleasant evening, and met General Paredes, whom I like very much; a real soldier, thin, plain, blunt, and all hacked with wounds.

23rd.—C——n has been dining at the —— minister's, where he met all the great actors in the present drama, and had an agreeable party. We are now thinking of making our escape from this hotel, and of taking a horseback journey into Michoacan, which shall occupy a month or six weeks. Meantime I am visiting, with the Señorita ——, every hospital, jail, college, and madhouse in Mexico!

26th.—To-day they are celebrating their independence. All the bells in all the churches, beginning with the cathedral, are pealing—cannon firing—rockets rushing up into the air—Santa Anna in the Alameda, speechifying—troops galloping—little boys running—Te Deum chanting—crowds of men and women jostling each other—the streets covered with carriages, the balconies covered with people—the Paséo expected to be crowded. I have escaped to a quiet room, where I am trying to find time to make up my letters before the packet goes. I conclude this just as the dictator, with his brilliant staff, has driven off to Tacubaya.

LETTER THE FORTY-SEVENTH

*Opera—Santa Anna and his Suite—His Appearance—*Belisario
—Solitary "Viva!"—Brilliant House—Military Dictatorship—
San Juan de Dios—*Hospital* de Jesus—Cuna—*Old Woman
and Baby—Different Apartments—Acordada—Junta—Female
Prisoners—Chief Crime—*Travaux Forcés—*Children—Male
Prisoners—*Forçats—*Soldier's Gambling—Chapel—Confes-
sional—Insane Hospital—Frenchmen—Different Kinds of In-
sanity—Kitchen—Dinner—Insane Monk—"Black Chamber"—
Soldiers—College—Santa Anna's Leg—Projects—All Saints—
Señora P——a—Leave-takings.*

4th November.

A great *funcion* was given in the opera in honour of his excellency. The theatre was most brilliantly illuminated with wax
lights. Two principal boxes were thrown into one for the president and his suite, and lined with crimson and gold, with draperies of the same. The staircase leading to the second tier
where this box was, was lighted by and *lined* all the way up
with rows of footmen in crimson and gold livery. A crowd of
gentlemen stood waiting in the lobby for the arrival of the
hero of the fête. He came at last in regal state, carriages and
outriders at full gallop; himself, staff and suite, in splendid
uniform. As he entered, Señor Roca presented him with a
librétto of the opera, bound in red and gold. We met the great
man *en face*, and he stopped, and gave us a cordial recognition. Two years have made little change in him in appearance.
He retains the same interesting, resigned, and rather melancholy expression; the same quiet voice, and grave but agreeable manner; and surrounded by pompous officers, he alone
looked quiet, gentlemanly, and high bred. The theatre was
crowded to suffocation; boxes, pit, and galleries. There was
no applause as he entered. One solitary voice in the pit said
"Viva Santa Anna!" but it seemed checked by a slight movement of disapprobation, scarcely amounting to a murmur. The
opera was Belisarius; considered *à propos* to the occasion, and
was really beautifully *montée;* the dresses new and superb—
the decorations handsome. They brought in real horses, and

Belisarius entered in a triumphal chariot, drawn by white steeds; but for this the stage is infinitely too small, and the horses plunged and pranced so desperately, that Belisarius wisely jumped out and finished his *aria* on foot. The two prima donnas acted together—the wife and daughter of the hero— both about the same age, and dressed very well. But the Castellan's voice is not suited to the opera, and the music, beautiful as it is, was the least effective part of the affair. The generals, in their scarlet and gold uniforms, sat like peacocks surrounding Santa Anna, who looked modest and retiring, and as if quite unaccustomed to the public gaze! The boxes were very brilliant—all the diamonds taken out for the occasion. His Excellency is by no means indifferent to beauty—*tout au contraire;* yet I dare say his thoughts were this night of things more warlike and less fair.

Let all this end as it may, let them give everything whatever name is most popular, the government is now a military dictatorship. Señor —— calls this revolution "the apotheosis of egotism transformed into virtue;" and it must be confessed, that in most of the actors, it has been a mere calculation of personal interests.

10th.—We went, some days ago, with our friends from San Xavier, to visit the hospital of San Juan de Dios, at San Cosmé. We found that, being at present under repair, it has but two occupants, old women—who keep each other melancholy company. The building is very spacious and handsome; erected, of course, during Spanish dominion, and extremely clean—an observation worthy of note, when it occurs in Mexican public buildings. There is a large hall, divided by square pillars, with a light and cheerful aspect, where the patients sleep; and a separate apartment for women. The rooms are all so clean, airy, and cheerful, that one forgets it is an hospital. In this respect, the style of building here is superior to all others, with large airy courtyards and fountains, long galleries and immense apartments, with every window open. There is no part of Europe where, all the year round, invalids can enjoy such advantages; but, also, there are few parts of Europe where the climate would permit them to do so.

The following day we visited another hospital; that known as the *Hospital de Jesus*—hallowed ground; for here the mortal remains of *Cortes* were deposited. And, though rescued from desecration by a distinguished individual, during a popular tumult, so that they no longer repose in the sanctuary of the chapel, there still exists, enshrined here, that over which time and revolutions have no power—his *memory*.

The establishment, as an hospital, is much finer, and the building infinitely handsomer than the other. The director, a physician, led us first into his own apartments, as the patients were dining, and afterwards showed us through the whole establishment. The first large hall, into which we were shown, is almost entirely occupied by soldiers, who had been wounded during the *pronunciamiento*. One had lost an arm, another a leg, and they looked sad and haggard enough, though they seemed perfectly well attended to, and, I dare say, did anything but *bless* the revolutions that brought them to that state, and with which they had nothing to do; for your Mexican soldier will lie down on his mat at night, a loyal man, and will waken in the morning and find himself a *pronunciado*. Each one had a separate room, or at least a compartment divided by curtains from the next; and in each was a bed, a chair, and a small table; this on one side of the long hall. The other was occupied by excellent hot and cold baths. We then visited the women's apartment, which is on a similar plan. Amongst the patients is an unfortunate child of eight years old, who in the *pronunciamiento* had been accidentally struck by a bullet, which entered her left temple and came out below the right eye, leaving her alive. The ball was extracted, and a portion of the brain came out at the wound. She is left blind, or nearly so, having but a faint glimmering of light. They say she will probably live, which seems impossible. She looks like a galvanized corpse—yet must have been a good-looking child. Notwithstanding the nature of her wound, her reason has not gone, and as she sat upright in her little bed, with her head bandaged, and her fixed and sightless eyes, she answered meekly and readily to all the questions we put to her. Poor little thing! she was shocking to look at; one of the many innocent beings whose lives are to be rendered sad and joyless by this revolution. The doctor seemed very kind to her.

A curious accident happened to Señor —— in this last *pronunciamiento*. He had already lost his leg in the first one; and was limping along the street, when he was struck by a ball. He was able to reach his house, and called to his wife, to tell her what had occurred. Her first impulse was to call for a doctor, when he said to her very coolly, "Not this time, —a carpenter will do better." He had been shot in his *wooden leg!*

At the end of the women's apartment in this hospital, there

is a small chapel where mass is said to the invalids. It is only remarkable as having over the altar an image of the *Purisima*, brought from Spain by Cortes. We went all through the building, even to the enclosure on the azotea, where dead bodies are dissected; and on which azotea was a quantity of wool, taken from the mattresses of those who die in the hospital, and which is left in the sun during a certain period before it is permitted to be used again. The whole establishment struck us as being healthy, cleanly, and well-conducted. We then visited the fine old church, which has but one broad aisle with a handsome altar, and near it is the small monument, under which the bones of the conqueror were placed. The sacristy of the church is remarkable for its ceiling, composed of the most intricately and beautifully carved mahogany; a work of immense labour and taste, after the Gothic style. The divisions of the compartments are painted blue and ornamented with gilding. In the centre of the apartment is an immense circular table, formed of one piece of mahogany; for which large sums have been refused.

We went in the evening to visit the *Cuna*, which is not a fine building, but a large, healthy, airy house. At the door, where there are a porter and his wife, the babies are now given in. Formerly they were put in at the *reja*, at the window of the porter's lodge; but this had to be given up, in consequence of the tricks played by boys or idle persons, who put in dogs, cats, or dead animals. As we were going upstairs, we heard an old woman singing a cheerful ditty in an awfully cracked voice, and as we got a full view of her before she could see us, we saw a clean, old body sitting, sewing and singing, while a baby rolling on the floor in a state of perfect ecstasy, was keeping up a sort of crowing duet with her. She seemed delighted to see these ladies, who belong to the *Junta*, and led us into a large hall where a score of nurses and babies were performing a symphony of singing, hushing, crying, lull-abying, and other nursery music. All along the room were little green painted beds, and both nurses and babies looked clean and healthy. The ——s knew every baby and nurse and directress by name. Some of the babies were remarkably pretty, and when we had admired them sufficiently, we were taken into the next hall, occupied by little girls of two, three, and four years old. They were all seated on little mats at the foot of their small green beds; a regiment of the finest and healthiest children possible; a directress in the room sewing. At our entrance, they all jumped up simultaneously, and surrounded us with the noisiest expressions of delight. One told me in a confidential whisper, that "Manuelita had thumped her own head, and had a pain in it;" but I could not see that Manuelita seemed to be suffering any acute agonies, for she made more noise than any of them. One little girl sidled up to me, and said in a most insinuating voice, "*Me llevas tu?*" "Will you take me away with you?"—for even at this early age they begin to have a glimmering idea that those whom the ladies choose from amongst them are peculiarly favoured. We staid some time with them, and admired their healthy, happy, and well-fed appearance; and then proceeded to the apartment of the boys; all little things of the same age, sitting ranged in a row like senators in congress, and, strange to say, much quieter and graver than the female babies; but this must have been from shyness, for before we came away, we saw them romping in great style. The directresses seem good respectable women, and kind to the children, who, as I mentioned before, are almost all taken away and brought up by rich people, before they have time to know that there is anything peculiar or unfortunate in their situation. After this adoption, they are completely on a level with the other children of the family—an equal portion is left them, and although their condition is never made a secret of, they frequently marry as well as their adopted brothers and sisters.

Those who are opposed to this institution, are so on the plea that it encourages and facilitates vice. That the number of children in the hospital is a proof that much vice and much poverty do exist, there is no doubt; that by enabling the vicious to conceal their guilt, or by relieving the poor from their burden, it encourages either vice or idleness, is scarcely probable. But even were it so, the certain benefits are so immense, when laid in the balance with the possible evils, that they cannot be put in competition. The mother who leaves her child at the *Cuna,* would she not abandon it to a worse fate, if this institution did not exist? If she does so to conceal her disgrace is it not seen that a woman will stop at no cruelty, to obtain this end? as exposure of her infant, even murder? and that, strong as maternal love is, the dread of the world's scorn has conquered it? If poverty be the cause, surely the misery must be great indeed, which induces the poorest beggar or the most destitute of the Indian women (whose love for their children amounts to a passion) to part with her child; and though it is suspected that the mother who has left her infant at the *Cuna,* has occasionally got herself hired as a nurse, that she may have the pleasure of bringing it up, it seems to me that no great evil can arise, even from that.

These orphans are thus rescued from the contamination of vice, from poverty, perhaps from the depths of depravity; perhaps their very lives are saved, and great sin prevented. Hundreds of innocent children are thus placed under the care of the first and best ladies in the country, and brought up to be worthy members of society.

Another day we devoted to visiting a different and more painful scene—the *Acordada,* or public jail; a great solid building, spacious, and well ventilated. For this also there is a *Junta,* or society of ladies of the first families, who devote themselves to teaching the female malefactors. It is painful and almost startling to see the first ladies in Mexico familiarly conversing with and embracing women who have been guilty of the most atrocious crimes; especially of murdering their husbands; which is the chief crime of the female prisoners. There are no bad faces amongst them; and probably not one who has committed a premeditated crime. A moment of jealousy during intoxication, violent passions without any curb, suddenly aroused and as suddenly extinguished, have led to these frightful results. We were first shown into a large and tolerably clean apartment, where were the female prisoners who are kept apart as being of a more *decent family* than the rest. Some were lying on the floor, others working—some were well dressed, others dirty and slovenly. Few looked sad; most appeared careless and happy, and *none* seemed ashamed. Amongst them were some of the handsomest faces I have seen in Mexico. One good-looking common woman, with a most joyous and benevolent countenance, and lame, came up to salute the ladies. I inquired what she had done. "Murdered her husband, and buried him under the brick floor!" Shade of Lavater! It is some comfort to hear that their husbands were generally such brutes, they deserved little better! Amongst others confined here is the wife, or rather the widow, of a governor of Mexico, who made away with her husband. We did not see her, and they say she generally keeps out of the way when strangers come. One very pretty and coquettish little woman, with a most intellectual face, and very superior-looking, being in fact a relation of Count ——'s, is in jail on suspicion of having poisoned her lover. A beautiful young creature, extremely like Mrs. ——, of Boston, was among the prisoners. I did not hear what her crime was. We were attended by a woman who has the title of *Presidenta,* and who, after some years of good conduct, has now the charge of her fellow-prisoners—but she also murdered her husband! We went up-stairs, accompanied by various of these distinguished criminals, to the room looking down upon the chapel, in which room the ladies give them instruction in reading, and in the Christian doctrine. With the time which they devote to these charitable offices, together with their numerous devotional exercises, and the care which their houses and families require, it cannot be said that the life of a Mexican señora is an idle one; nor, in such cases, can it be considered a useless one.

We then descended to the lower regions, where, in a great, damp, vaulted gallery, hundreds of unfortunate women of the lowest class, were occupied in *travaux forcés*—not indeed of a very hard description. These were employed in baking tortillas for the prisoners. Dirty, ragged, and miserable-looking crea-tures there were in these dismal vaults, which looked like pur-gatory, and smelt like—Heaven knows what! But, as I have fre-quently had occasion to observe in Mexico, the sense of smell is a doubtful blessing. Another large hall near this, which the prisoners were employed in cleaning and sweeping, has at least fresh air, opening on one side into a court, where poor little children, the saddest sight there, were running about—the chil-dren of the prisoners.

Leaving the side of the building devoted to the women, we passed on to another gallery, looking down upon an immense paved court with a fountain, where were several hundreds of male prisoners, unfortunately collected together without any reference to the nature of their crime; the midnight murderer with the purloiner of a pocket-handkerchief; the branded felon with the man guilty of some political offence; the debtor with the false coiner; so that many a young and thoughtless individual whom a trifling fault, the result of ignorance or of unformed principles, has brought hither, must leave this place wholly contaminated and hardened by bad example and vi-cious conversation. Here there were indeed some ferocious, hardened-looking ruffians—but there were many mild, good-humoured faces; and I could see neither sadness nor a trace of shame on any countenance; indeed they all seemed much amused by seeing so many ladies. Some were stretched full-length on the ground, doing nothing; others were making rolls for hats, of different coloured beads, such as they wear here, or little baskets for sale; whilst others were walking about alone, or conversing in groups. This is the first prison I ever visited, therefore I can compare it with no other; but the system must be wrong which makes no distinctions between different degrees of crime. These men are the same *forçats* whom we daily see in chains, watering the Alameda or Paséo, or mending the streets. Several hundreds of prisoners escaped from the Acordada in the time of the *pronunciamiento*—probably the worst amongst them—yet *half the city* appears to be here now. We were shown the row of cells for criminals whom it is necessary to keep in solitary confinement, on account of disorderly behaviour—also the apartments of the directors.

In passing downstairs, we came upon a group of dirty-looking soldiers, busily engaged in playing at cards. The alcalde, who was showing us through the jail, dispersed them all in a great rage, which I suspected was partly assumed for our edification. We then went into the chapel, which we had seen from above, and which is handsome and well kept. In the sacristy is a horrid and appropriate image of *the bad thief*. We were also shown a small room off the chapel, with a confessional, where the criminal condemned to die spends the three days preceding his execution with a padre chosen for that purpose. What horrid confessions, what lamentations and despair that small dark chamber must have witnessed! There is nothing in it but an altar, a crucifix, and a bench. I think the custom is a very humane one.

We felt glad to leave this palace of crimes, and to return to the fresh air.

The following day we went to visit *San Hipólito*, the insane hospital for men, accompanied by the director, a fine old gentleman, who has been a great deal abroad, and who looks like a French marquis of the *ancien régime*. I was astonished, on entering, at the sweet and solitary beauty of the large stone courts, with orange trees and pomegranates now in full blossom, and the large fountains of beautifully clear water. There must be something soothing in such a scene to the senses of these most unfortunate of God's creatures. They were sauntering about, quiet and for the most part sad; some stretched out under the trees, and others gazing on the fountain; all apparently very much under the control of the administrador, who was formerly a monk, this *San Hipólito* being a dissolved convent of that order. The system of giving occupation to the insane is not yet introduced here.

On entering, we saw rather a distinguished-looking, tall and well-dressed gentleman, whom we concluded to be a stranger who had come to see the establishment, like ourselves. We were therefore somewhat startled when he advanced towards us with long strides, and in an authoritative voice shouted out, "Do you know who I am? I am the Deliverer of Guatemala!" The *administrador* told us he had just been taken up, was a Frenchman, and in a state of furious excitement. He continued making a tremendous noise, and the other madmen seemed quite ashamed of him. One unhappy-looking creature, with a pale, melancholy face, and his arms stretched out above his head, was embracing a pillar, and when asked what he was doing, replied that he was "making sugar."

We were led into the dining-hall, a long airy apartment, provided with benches and tables, and from thence into a most splendid kitchen, high, vaulted, and receiving air from above, a kitchen that might have graced the castle of some feudal baron, and looked as if it would most surely last as long as men shall eat and cooks endure. Monks of San Hipólito! how many a smoking dinner, what viands steaming and savoury must have issued from this noblest of kitchens to your refectory next door.

The food for the present inmates, which two women were preparing, consisted of meat and vegetables, soup and sweet things; excellent meat, and well-dressed *frijoles*. A poor little boy, imbecile, deaf and dumb, was seated there cross-legged, in a sort of wooden box; a pretty child, with a fine colour, but who has been in this state from his infancy. The women seemed very kind to him, and he had a placid, contented expression of face; but took no notice of us when we spoke to him. Strange and unsolvable problem, what ideas pass through the brain of that child!

When we returned to the dining-hall, the inmates of the asylum, to the number of ninety or a hundred, were all sitting at dinner, ranged quietly on the benches, eating with wooden spoons out of wooden bowls. The poor hero of Guatemala was seated at the lower end of the table, tolerably tranquil. He started up on seeing us, and was beginning some furious explanations, but was prevented by his neighbour, who turned round with an air of great superiority, saying, "He's *mad!*" at which the other smiled with an air of great contempt, and looking at us said, "He calls *me* mad!" The man of the pillar was eyeing his soup, with his arms as before, extended above his head. The director desired him to eat his soup, upon which he slowly and reluctantly brought down one arm, and ate a few spoonfuls. "How much sugar have you made to-day?" asked the director. "Fifty thousand kingdoms!" said the man.

They showed us two men, of very good family, and one old

gentleman who did not come to dinner with the rest, but stood aloof, in the courtyard, with an air of great superiority. He had a cross upon his breast, and belongs to an old family. As we approached, he took off his hat, and spoke to us very politely; and then turning to the director, "Y *por fin*," said he, "*Cuando saldré?*" "When shall I leave this place?" "Very soon," said the director. "You may get your trunks ready." He bowed and appeared satisfied, but continued standing in the same place, his arms folded, and with the same wistful gaze as before. The director told us that the two great causes of madness here are love and drinking, (mental and physical intoxication); that the insanity caused by the former is almost invariably incurable, whereas the victims of the latter generally recover, as is natural. The poor old gentleman with the cross owes the overthrow of his mind to the desertion of his mistress. We saw the chapel, where a padre says mass to these poor creatures, "the Innocents," as they are called here. They do not enter the chapel, for fear of their creating any disturbance, but kneel outside, in front of the iron grating, and the administrador says it is astonishing how quiet and serious they appear during divine service.

As we passed through the court, there was a man busily employed in hanging up various articles of little children's clothes, as if to dry them—little frocks and trousers; all the time speaking rapidly to himself, and stopping every two minutes to take an immense draught of water from the fountain. His dinner was brought out to him (for he could not be prevailed on to sit down with the others), and he ate it in the same hurried way, dipping his bread in the fountain, and talking all the time. The poor madman of the *sugar-kingdoms* returned from dinner, and resumed his usual place at the pillar, standing with his arms above his head, and with the same melancholy and suffering expression of face.

The director then showed us the room where the clothes are kept; the straw hats and coarse dresses, and the terrible straight waistcoats made of brown linen, that look like coats with prodigiously long sleeves, and the *Botica* where the medicines are kept, and the secretary's room where they preserve the mournful records of entry and death—though often of exit. All round the court are strong stone cells, where the furious are confined. He took us into an empty one, where a Franciscan friar had been lodged. He had contrived to pull down part of the wall, and to make a large hole into his neighbour's cell adjoining. Fancy one madman seeing the head of another appear through a hole in his cell! The whole cell was covered with crosses of every description, drawn with a piece of coal. They had been obliged to remove him into another in the gallery above, where he had already begun a new work of destruction. I was afterwards told by the Padre P——n, the confessor of condemned criminals, and who is of the same order as this insane monk, that this poor man had been a merchant, and had collected together about forty thousand dollars, with which he was travelling to Mexico, when he was attacked by robbers, who not only deprived him of all he possessed, but gave him some severe wounds on the head. When somewhat recovered, he renounced the world, and took his vows in the convent of San Francisco. Shortly after, he became subject to attacks of insanity, and at last became so furious, that the superior was obliged to request an order for his admission to San Hipólito.

The director then led us to the gallery above, where are more cells, and the terrible *"Cuarto Negro,"* the Black Chamber; a dark, round cell, about twelve feet in circumference, with merely a slit in the wall for the admission of air. The floor is thickly covered with straw, and the walls are entirely covered with soft stuffed cushions. Here the most furious madman is confined on his arrival, and whether he throws himself on the floor, or dashes his head against the wall, he can do himself no injury. In a few days, the silence and the darkness soothe his fury, he grows calmer, and will eat the food that is thrust through the aperture in the wall. From this he is removed to a common cell, with more light and air; but until he has become tranquil, he is not admitted into the court amongst the others.

From this horrible, though I suppose necessary den of suffering, we went to the apartments of the administrador, which have a fine view of the city and the volcanoes, and saw a virgin, beautifully carved in wood, and dressed in white satin robes, embroidered with small diamonds. On the ground was a little dog, dying, having just fallen off from the azotea, an accident which happens to dogs here not unfrequently. We then went up to the azotea, which looks into the garden of San Fernando and of our last house, and also into the barracks of the soldiers, who, as —— observed, are more dangerous madmen than those who are confined. Some rolled up in their dirty yellow cloaks, and others standing in their shirt-sleeves, and many without either; they were as dirty-looking a set of military heroes as one would wish to see. When we came downstairs again, and had gone through the court, and were passing the last cell, each of which is only lighted by an aperture in the thick stone wall, a pair of great black eyes glaring through, upon a level with mine, startled me infinitely. The eyes, however, glared upon vacancy. The face was thin and sallow, the beard long and matted, and the cheeks sunken. What long years of suffering appeared to have passed over that furrowed brow! I wish I had not seen it. . . .

We afterwards went to the college of Bizcainos, that K—— might see it—my third and last visit. What a palace! What courts and fountains! We went over the whole building as before, from the azotea downwards, and from the porter's lodge upwards. Many of the scholars, who went out during the revolution, have not yet returned. K—— was in admiration at the galleries, which look like long vaulted streets, and at the chapel, which is certainly remarkably rich. . . .

Having stopped in the carriage on the way home, at a shoemaker's, we saw *Santa Anna's leg* lying on the counter, and observed it with due respect, as the prop of a hero. With this leg, which is fitted with a very handsome boot, he reviews his troops next Sunday, putting his *best foot foremost;* for generally he merely wears an unadorned wooden leg. The shoemaker, a Spaniard, whom I can recommend to all customers as the most impertinent individual I ever encountered, was arguing, in a blustering manner, with a gentleman who had brought a message from the general, desiring some alteration in the boot: and wound up by muttering, as the messenger left the shop, "He shall either wear it as it is, or review the troops next Sunday without his leg!"[1]

We have ordered *mangas* to wear in our intended journey, which is now nearly decided on—nothing tolerable to be had under seventy or eighty dollars. They are made of strong cloth, with a hole in the middle for putting the head through, with black velvet capes, fringed either with silk or gold, and are universally lined with strong calico. They are warm and con-

[1] Boston, November, 1842.—*A propos des bottes,* I copy the following paragraph from an Havana newspaper:

"Mexico, 28th September.—Yesterday, was buried with pomp and solemnity in the cemetery of Saint Paul, the foot which his Excellency, President Santa Anna, lost in the action of the 5th December, 1838. It was deposited in a monument erected for that purpose, Don Ignacio Sierra y Roso having pronounced a funeral discourse appropriate to the subject."

venient for riding in the country. I have seen some richly embroidered, which cost five hundred dollars.

It is as I prophesied—now that we are about leaving Mexico, we fancy that there still remain objects of interest which we have not seen. We have paid a visit, probably a last visit, to Our Lady of Guadalupe, and certainly never examined her cathedral with so much attention, or lingered so long before each painting and shrine, or listened with so much interest to the particulars of its erection, which were given us by Señor ——, whose authority in these matters is unimpeachable.

It appears that the present sacristy of the parochial church dates back to 1575, and was then a small chapel, where the miraculous image was kept, and where it remained until the beginning of the next century, when a new church was built, to which the image was solemnly transported. Even when enclosed in the first small sanctuary, its fame must have been great, for, by orders of the archbishop, six doweries of three hundred dollars each, to be given to six orphans on their marriage, were annually drawn from the alms offered at her shrine. But in 1629 Mexico suffered the terrible inundation which destroyed so large a part of the city, and the excellent archbishop, D. Francisco Manzo, while devoting his time and fortune to assist the sufferers, also gave orders that the Virgin of Guadalupe should be brought into Mexico, and placed in the cathedral there, then of very different dimensions from the present noble building, occupying, it is said, the space which is now covered by the principal sacristy. When the waters retired, and the Virgin was restored to her own sanctuary, her fame increased to a prodigious extent. Copies of the Divine Image were so multiplied, that there is probably not an Indian hut throughout the whole country where one does not exist. Oblations and alms increased a thousand fold; a silver throne, weighing upwards of three hundred and fifty marks, and beautifully wrought, chiefly at the expense of the viceroy, Count of Salvatierra, was presented to her sanctuary, together with a glass case (for the image), considered at that time a wonder of art. At the end of the century a new temple, the present sanctuary, was begun; the second church was thrown down, but not until a provisional building (the actual parish church) was erected to receive the image. The new temple was concluded in 1709, and is said to have cost from six to eight hundred thousand dollars, collected from *alms alone*, which were solicited in person by the viceregal archbishop, D. Juan de Ortega y Montanez. Two private individuals in Mexico gave, the one thirty, the other fifty thousand dollars, towards its erection.

The interior is of the Doric order, and has three aisles, divided by eight pillars, upon which with the walls are placed eighteen arches, the centre one forming the dome of the edifice. It runs from north to south, has three great gates, one fronting Mexico, and two others at the sides. Its length may be two hundred and fifty feet, and its width about one hundred and thirty. In the four external angles of the church are four lofty towers, in the midst of which rises the dome. Three altars were at first erected, and in the middle one, destined for the image, was a sumptuous tabernacle of silver gilt, in which were more than three thousand two hundred marks of silver, and which cost nearly eighty thousand dollars. In the centre of this was a piece of gold, weighing four thousand and fifty *castellanos* (an old Spanish coin, the fiftieth part of a mark of gold), and here the image was placed, the linen on which it is painted guarded by a silver plate of great value. The rest of the temple had riches corresponding. The candlesticks, vases, railing, etc., contain nearly fourteen thousand marks of silver, without counting the numerous holy vessels, cups and chalices adorned with jewels. One golden lamp weighed upwards of two thousand two hundred *castellanos*—another seven hundred and fifty silver marks.

In 1802 some part of the walls and arches began to give way—and it was necessary to repair them. But first, under the direction of the celebrated sculptor Tolsa, a new altar was erected for the image. His first care was to collect the most beautiful marbles of the country for this purpose—the black he brought from Puebla, and the white, gray and rose-coloured from the quarries of San José Vizarron. He also began to work at the bronze ornaments, but from the immense sums of money necessary to its execution, the work was delayed for nearly twenty years. Then, in 1826, it was recommenced with fresh vigour. The image was removed meanwhile to the neighbouring convent of the Capuchinas, and the same year the altar was concluded, and the Virgin brought back in solemn procession, in the midst of an innumerable multitude. This great altar, which cost from three to four hundred thousand dollars, is a concave hexagonal, in the midst of which rise two white marble pillars, and on each side two columns of rose-coloured marble, of the composite order, which support the arch. Between these are two pedestals, on which are the images of San Joaquin and Santa Anna, and two niches, containing San José and St. John the Baptist. Above the cornices are three other pedestals, supporting the three Saints, Michael, Gabriel, and Raphael; and above St. Michael, in the midst of cherubim and seraphim, is a representation of the Eternal Father. The space between the upper part of the altar and the roof, is covered with a painted crimson curtain, held by saints and angels. The tabernacle in the centre of the altar, is of rose-coloured marble, in which the image is deposited, and all the ornaments of the altar are of gilt bronze and zinc.

Besides the collegiate and the parish church, there are at Guadalupe the church of the Capuchin Nuns, and the churches of the Hill and the Well; all in such close conjunction, that the whole village or city, as it calls itself, seems altogether some religious establishment or confraternity, belonging to these temples and churches, united in the worship of the Virgin, and consequent upon the "Miraculous Apparition" manifested to the chosen Indian, Juan Diego.

I regret not having known till lately, that there exists in Mexico a convent of *Indian Nuns:* and that each nun, when she takes the veil, wears a very superb Indian dress—the costume formerly worn by the *cacicas*, or ladies of highest rank.

I went some days ago with the Señorita F——a to visit a house for insane women, in the *Calle de Canoa*, built in 1698, by the rich congregation of *el Salvador*. The institution is now in great want of funds; and is by no means to be compared with the establishment of San Hipólito. The directress seems a good kind-hearted woman, who devoted herself to doing her duty, and who is very gentle to her patients; using no means but those of kindness and steadiness to subdue their violence. But what a life of fear and suffering such a situation must be! The inmates look poor and miserable, generally speaking, and it is difficult to shake off the melancholy impression which they produce on the mind. We were particularly struck by the sight of one unfortunate woman of the better class, who, with her long hair all dishevelled, and eyes sparkling with a wild light, stood at the open window of her cell, where for the present they are obliged to confine her, and who poured forth the most piteous lamentations, and adjured every one who passed, in the most pathetic terms, to restore her husband and children to her. One girl was singing cheerfully—one or two women were sewing, but most of them were sitting crouched on the floor, with a look of melancholy vacancy. The poor are admitted gratis, and the richer classes pay a moderate sum for their board. . . .

To turn to a very different theme. We continue to go to the opera, certainly the most agreeable amusement in Mexico, and generally to the —— minister's box, in the centre. Last evening, *Belisario* was repeated, but with less splendour than on its representation in honour of Santa Anna.

We expect to leave this on the sixteenth, going·in a diligence as far as Toluca, where a Mexican officer, Colonel Y——, has kindly promised to meet us with mules and horses. M. le Comte de B—— and Mr. W——, secretaries of the French and English Legations, have made arrangements for accompanying us as far as Valadolid; with which agreeable travelling companions we may reasonably expect a pleasant journey.

Last Sunday was the festival of All Saints; on the evening of which day, we walked out under the *portales,* with M. and Madame de ——, —— minister and his wife, to look at the illumination, and at the numerous booths filled with *sugar skulls,* etc.; temptingly ranged in grinning rows, to the great edification of the children. In general there are crowds of well-dressed people on the occasion of this fête, but the evening was cold and disagreeable, and though there were a number of ladies, they were enveloped in shawls, and dispersed early. The old women at their booths, with their cracked voices, kept up the constant cry of "Skulls, *niñas,* skulls!"—but there were also animals done in sugar, of every species, enough to form specimens for a Noah's ark.

14th.—We leave this the day after to-morrow, and shall write from our first halting-place; and as on our return we shall do little more than pass through Mexico, we are *almost* taking leave of all our friends. Were I to tell you all the kindness and hospitality, and cordial offers of service that we receive, and the manner in which our rooms (albeit the rooms of an inn) are filled from morning till night, it would seem an exaggeration. One acquaintance we have made lately, whom we like so much, that we have been vociferously abusing the system of *faire part* in this city, since, owing to the mistake of a servant, we have until now been deprived of the pleasure of knowing her. The mistake is rectified at the eleventh hour. The lady is the Señora de G——z P——a, one of the most accomplished and well-informed women in Mexico; and though our friendship has been short, I trust it may be enduring.

Two evenings since, we went with the Señora de C——s to

an amateur concert; and I question whether in any capital of Europe, so many good amateur voices could be collected. I do not speak of the science or cultivation, though the hostess, the Señora A——, has a perfect method. But yesterday we spent a most agreeable evening in a delightful family reunion, at the house of Señor N——i del B——o. It was strictly limited to the family relations, and was, I believe, his *jour de fête*. If all Mexican society resembled this, we should have too much regret in leaving it. The girls handsome, well educated, and simple in their manners and tastes—the Countess a model of virtue and dignity. Then so much true affection and love of home amongst them all! So much wealth and yet good taste and perfect simplicity visible in all that surrounds them! Mexico is not *lost* as long as such families exist, and though they mingle little in society, the influence of their virtues and charities is widely felt.

This morning C——n had an audience of the new president. He also paid a visit to General Bustamante, who is still at Guadalupe, and preparing for his departure. He will probably sail in the Jason, the man-of-war which brought us to Vera Cruz, and it is probable that we shall leave the republic at the same period. The Dowager Marquesa de Vivanco, who in consequence of ill health has not left her house for months, was among our visitors this morning.

To-day Count C——a dined here, and brought for our inspection the splendid sword presented by Congress to General Valencia, with its hilt of brilliants and opals; a beautiful piece of workmanship, which does credit to the Mexican artificers. He was particularly brilliant and eloquent in his conversation to-day—whether his theories are right or wrong, they are certainly *entrainant*.

Our next letters will probably be dated from Toluca.

LETTER THE FORTY-EIGHTH

TOLUCA, 16th.

In vain would be a description with the hopes of bringing
them before you, of our last few days in Mexico!—of the confusion, the bustle, the visits, the paying of bills, the packing
of trunks, the sending off of heavy luggage to Vera Cruz, and
extracting the necessary articles for our journey; especially yesterday, when we were surrounded by visitors and *cargadores*,
from half-past seven in the morning till half-past eleven at
night. Our very last visitors were the families of C——a and
E——n. The new president, *on dit*, is turning his sword into a
ploughshare. Preferring a country to a city life, nearly every
Sunday he names the house in which he desires to be *fêted*
the following week—now at the villa of Señor —— at Tacubaya
—now at the hacienda of Señor —— at San Agustin. As yet the
diplomatic corps do not attend these assemblies, not having
been officially received; but we hear that there is singing and
dancing, and other amusements, and that his excellency is
extremely amiable and *galant*.

By six o'clock this morning several of our friends were assembled to accompany us to the diligence (Señors C——o,
M——e, R——s, A——e, etc.), which, unfortunately, we had not
been able to secure for ourselves; for at this moment, the
whole world is in motion, going to attend the great annual
fair of San Juan de los Lagos; which begins on the fifth of
December, and to which Toluca is the direct road. Fortunately, the diligence had broken down the preceding evening,
and it was necessary to repair it; otherwise we should have

left behind various important articles, for in the confusion of our departure, every one had left some requisite item at the hotel;—C——n his gun; K—— her bag; I *everything*—and more especially the book with which I intended to beguile the weary hours between Mexico and Toluca. Our servant-boy ran— Señor R——s mounted his horse, and most good-naturedly gal- loped between the diligence office and the hotel, until, little by little, all the missing articles were restored. We climbed into the coach, which was so crowded that we could but just turn our heads to groan an adieu to our friends. The coach rattled off through the streets, dashed through the Alameda, and gradually we began to shake down, and, by a little ar- rangement of cloaks and sarapes, to be less crowded. A *padre* with a very Indian complexion sat between K—— and me, and a horrible, long, lean bird-like female, with immense red goggle-eyes, coal-black teeth, fingers like claws, a great goitre, and drinking brandy at intervals, sat opposite to us. There were also various men buried in their sarapes. Satisfied with a cursory inspection of our companions, I addressed myself to *Blackwood's Magazine,* but the road which leads towards the Desierto, and which we before passed on horseback, is dread- ful, and the mules could scarcely drag the loaded coach up the steep hills. We were thrown into ruts, horribly jolted, and sometimes obliged to get out, which would not have been dis- agreeable but for the necessity of getting in again. The day and the country were beautiful, but impossible to enjoy either in a shut coach. We were rather thankful when the wheels, sticking in a deep rut, we were forced to descend, and walk forwards for some time. We had before seen the view from these heights, but the effect never was more striking than at this moment. The old city with her towers, lakes, and vol- canoes, lay bathed in the bright sunshine. Not a cloud was in the sky—not an exhalation rose from the lake—not a shadow was on the mountains. All was bright and glittering, and flooded in the morning light; while in contrast rose to the left the dark, pine-covered crags, behind which the Desierto lies.

At Santa Fé we changed horses, and found there an escort which had been ordered for us by General Tornel; a necessary precaution in these robber-haunted roads. We stopped to breakfast at *Quajimalpa,* where the inn is kept by a French- man, who is said to be making a large fortune, which he de- serves for the good breakfast he had prepared for us by orders of the Count de B—— and Mr. W——, who had preceded us early in the morning on horseback; (enviable fate!). We had white fish from the river of Lerma, which crosses the plains of Toluca, fresh and well dressed, and without that taste of *mud* which those from the Mexican Laguna occasionally have; also hot cutlets, potatoes, coffee, etc.

After leaving this inn, situated in a country formed of heaps of lava and volcanic rocks, the landscape becomes more beautiful and wooded. It is, however, dangerous, on account of the shelter which the wooded mountains afford to the knights of the road, and to whose predilection for these wild solitudes, the number of crosses bore witness. In a woody defile there is a small clear space called *"Las Cruces,"* where several wooden crosses point out the site of the famous battle between the curate Hidalgo and the Spanish General Truxillo. An object really in keeping with the wild scenery, was the head of the celebrated robber *Maldonado*, nailed to the pine-tree beneath which he committed his last murder. It is now quite black, and grins there, a warning to his comrades and an encouragement to travellers. From the age of ten to that of fifty, he followed the honourable profession of free-trader, when he expiated his crimes. The padre who was in the coach with us, told us that he heard his last confession. That grinning skull was once the head of a man, and an ugly one too, they say; but stranger still it is to think, that that man was once a baby, and sat on his mother's knee, and that his mother may have been pleased to see him cut his *first tooth*. If she could but see his teeth now! Under this very head, and as if to show their contempt for law and justice, the robbers lately eased some travellers of their luggage. Those who were robbed, however, were false coiners, rather a common class in Toluca, and two of these ingenious gentlemen were in the coach with us (as we afterwards learnt), and were returning to that city. These, with the brandy-drinking female, composed our select little party!

The scenery without was decidedly preferable to that within, and the leathern sides of the vehicle being rolled up, we had a tolerable view. What hills covered with noble pines! What beautiful pasture-fields, dotted with clumps of trees, that looked as if disposed for effect, as in an English park!— firs, oaks, cedars, and elms. Arrived at the town or village of Lerma, famous for its manufacture of spurs, and standing in a marshy country at the entrance of the valley of Toluca, all danger of the robbers is passed, and with the danger, much of the beauty of the scenery. But we breathed more freely on another account, for here she of the goggle-eyes and goitre, descended with her brandy-bottle, relieving us from the oppressive influence of the sort of *day*-mare, if there be such a thing, which her presence had been to us.

The valley of Toluca was now before us, its volcano towering in the distance. The plains around looked cold and dreary, with pools of transparent water, and swamps filled with various species of water-fowl. The hacienda of San Nicolas, the property of Señor Mier y Teran, a Spaniard, was the only object that we saw worthy of notice, before we reached Toluca. This hacienda, formerly the property of the Carmelite monks, is a valuable estate. Not a tree is to be seen here, or in the valley, a great extent of which is included in it; but it is surrounded by vast fields of maguey and maize; it is traversed by a fine river, and is one of the most profitable estates in the country. The labourers here are in general the Ottomie Indians, a poor and degraded tribe. Here we dismissed our escort, which had been changed every six leagues, and entered Toluca about four o'clock, passing the *Garrita* without the troublesome operation of searching, to which travellers in general are subject. We found tolerable rooms in an inn; at least there were two or three wooden chairs in each, and a deal table in one; and Mr. W—— and the Count de B—— looking out for us. Colonel Y—— had not yet made his appearance.

Toluca, a large and important city, lies at the foot of the mountain of San Miguel de *Tutucuitlalpico;* and is an old, quiet, good-looking, respectable-seeming place, about as sad and solitary as Puebla. The streets, the square, and the churches are clean and handsome. To the south of the city lie extensive plains covered with rich crops; and about ten miles in the same direction is the volcano. We walked out in the afternoon to the Alameda, passing under the *portales;* handsomer and cleaner than those of Mexico; and sat down on a stone bench beside a fountain, a position which commanded a beautiful view of the distant hills and of the volcano, behind which the sun was setting in a sea of liquid flame, making it look like a great pearl lying amongst melted rubies. The Alameda has not been much ornamented, and is quite untenanted; but walks are cut through the grass, and they were making hay. Everything looked quiet and convent-like, and a fine fresh air passed over the new-mown grass, inclining to cold, but pleasant. The volcano is scooped out into a natural basin, containing, in the very midst of its fiery furnace, two lakes of the purest, coldest and most transparent water. It is said that the view from its summit, the ascent to which is very fatiguing, but has been accomplished, is beautiful and extensive. On the largest lake travellers have embarked in a canoe, but I believe it has never been crossed, on account of the vulgar prejudice that it is unfathomable, and has a whirlpool in the centre. The volcano is about fifteen thousand feet above the level of the sea, and nine thousand above Toluca. It is not so grand as Popocatepetl, but a *respectable* volcano for a country town—"*muy decente*" (very decent), as a man said in talking of the pyramids that adorn the wonderful cavern of Cucuhuamilpa.

We ordered supper at the inn, and were joined by the *Comandante* of Toluca, Don M—— A——, the officer who came out to meet us when we arrived in Mexico. I regret to state that such a distinguished party should have sat down, six in number, to fowl and frijoles, with only three knives and two forks between them. The provident travellers had, however, brought good wine; and if our supper was not very elegant, it was at least very gay. Colonel Y—— arrived about ten o'clock; but it is agreed that the animals require one day's rest, and we shall consequently spend to-morrow at Toluca.

17th.—We have spent this day in arranging our route, in which we are guided not by the most direct, but the most agreeable; in walking through the city, which, in the time of federalism, was the capital of the state, in climbing some of the steep roads cut through the hills, at whose base it lies; and in admiring the churches and convents, and broad, well-paved streets with their handsome houses, painted white and red. It is decided that the first night of our pilgrimage, we shall request hospitality at the hacienda of the ex-minister Hecha-varria—*La Gabia*, which is about ten leagues of very bad road from Toluca—which is sixteen from Mexico. All these important arrangements being made, and a sketch of our journey traced out, we are about retiring to rest, in the agreeable prospect of not entering any four or two wheeled vehicle, be it a cart, carriage, coach, or diligence, till we return here.

LA GABIA, 19th.

To get *under weigh* the first morning was a work of some difficulty. Mules to be loaded, horses to be fitted with saddles; and one mule lame, and another to be procured, and the trunks found to be too heavy, and so on. We rose at five, dressed by candlelight, took chocolate, put on our mangas, and then planted ourselves in the passage looking down upon the *patio,* to watch the proceedings and preparations. Colonel A—— arrived at seven with a trooper, to accompany us part of the way; and we set off while it was cool, without waiting for the rest of the party. Toluca looked silent and dignified as we passed through the streets—with its old convents and dark hills. The road, after leaving the city, was stony and mountainous; and having reached a small *rancho* with an old oratorio beside it, we halted to wait for our travelling companions. Colonel A—— amused us with an account of his warfare against the Comanches, in which service he had been terribly wounded. Singular contrast between these ferocious barbarians and the mild Indians of the interior! He considers them an exceedingly handsome, fine-looking race; whose resources, both for war and trade, are so great, that were it not for their natural indolence, the difficulties of checking their aggression would be formidable indeed. Colonel A—— being obliged to return to Toluca, left us in charge of his trooper, and we waited at the rancho for about half an hour, when our party appeared with a long train of mules and *mozos;* the gentlemen dressed Mexican fashion as well as their men; the best dress. in the world for a long equestrian journey. Colonel Y—— had staid behind to procure another mule, and there being two roads, we, as generally happens in these cases, chose the worst; which led us for leagues over a hilly country, unenlivened by tree, shrub, bush, or flower. The sun was already high, and the day intensely hot. We passed an occasional poor hut—a chance Indian passed us—showed his white teeth, and, in spite of the load on his back, contrived to draw his hat off his matted locks, and give us a mild good morrow—but for the rest, from Dan to Beersheba, from Toluca to La Gabia, all was barren. By twelve o'clock we might have fancied ourselves passing over the burning plains of Mesopotamia, notwithstanding an occasional cold breeze which swept across us for a moment, serving only to make us feel the heat with greater force. Then barranca followed barranca. The horses climbed up one crag, and slid down another. By two o'clock we were all starving with hunger, but nothing was to be had. Even Nebuchadnezzar would have found himself at a nonplus. The Count de B—— contrived to buy some granaditas and parched corn from an Indian, which kept us quiet for a little while; and we tried to console ourselves by listening to our arrieros, who struck up some wild songs in chorus, as they drove the wearied mules up the burning hills. Every Indian that we met assured us that La Gabia was *"cerquita,"* quite near—"*detras lomita*," behind the little hill; and every little hill that we passed presented to our view another little hill, but no signs of the much-wished-for dwelling. A more barren, treeless, and uninteresting country than this road (on which we have unanimously revenged ourselves by giving it the name of "the road of the three hundred barrancas") led us through, I never beheld. However, "it's a long lane that has no turning," as we say in Scotland; and between three and four, La Gabia was actually in sight; a long, low building, whose entrance appeared to us the very gates of Eden. We were all, but especially me, who had ridden with my veil up, from a curiosity to see where my horse was going, burnt to the colour of Pawnee Indians.

We were most cordially welcomed by Señor Hechavarria and his brothers-in-law, and soon refreshed by rest and an excellent dinner. Fortunately K—— and I had no mirrors; but each gave such a flattering description of the other's countenance, that it was quite graphic.

This beautiful hacienda, which formerly belonged to the Count de Regla, whose possessions must have been royal, is thirty leagues in length and seventeen in width—containing in this great space the productions of every climate, from the fir-clad mountains on a level with the volcano of Toluca, to the fertile plains which produce corn and maize; and lower down, to fields of sugar-cane and other productions of the tropics.

We retired to rest betimes, and early this morning rode out with these gentlemen, about five leagues through the hacienda. The morning was bright and exhilarating, and our animals being tired, we had fresh, strong little horses belonging to their stud, which carried us delightfully. We rode through beautiful pine-woods and beside running water, contrasting agreeably with our yesterday's journey; and were accompanied by three handsome little boys, children of the family, the finest and manliest little fellows I ever saw, who, dressed in a complete Mexican costume, like three miniature rancheros, rode boldly and fearlessly over everything. There was a great deal of firing at crows and at the wild duck on a beautiful little lake, but I did not observe that any one was burdened with too much game. We got off our horses to climb through the wooded hills and ravines, and passed some hours lying under the pine-trees, listening to the gurgling of the little brook, whose bright waters make music in the solitude; and, like the soldiers at the *pronunciamiento*, but with surer aim, pelting each other from behind the parapets of the tall trees, with fir

tops. About ten o'clock we returned to breakfast; and Colonel
Y—— having arrived, we are now preparing to continue our
journey this afternoon.

ANGANGUEO, 20th.

We left La Gabia at four o'clock, accompanied by our hospitable hosts for some leagues, all their own princely property,
through great pasture-fields, woods of fir and oak, hills clothed
with trees, and fine clear streams. We also passed a valuable
stone-quarry; and were shown a hill belonging to the Indians,
presented to them by a former proprietor. We formed a long
train, and I pitied the mistress of *El Pilar,* our next halting-
place, upon whom such a regiment was about to be unexpectedly quartered. There were C——n, K——, and I, and a
servant; the Count de B—— and his servant; Mr. W—— and
his servant; Colonel Y—— and his men; mules, arrieros, spare
mules, and lead horses; and all the *mozos* armed, forming altogether a formidable gang. We took leave of the Hechavarria
family when it was already growing dusk, and when the moon
had risen found we had taken a great round; so that it was
late at night when we arrived at *El Pilar,* a small hacienda,
situated in a wild-looking, solitary part of the country. A servant had been sent forward to inform the lady of the establishment of our approach, and we were most kindly received. The
house is clean and pretty, and, tired as we were, the *sala,*
boasting of an old piano, tempted us to try a waltz while they
were preparing supper. The man who waited at table, before
he removed the things, popped down upon his knees, and recited a long prayer aloud. The gentlemen had one apartment
prepared for them—we another, in which, nay, even in the
large four-posted and well-curtained bed allotted to us, Madame Yturbide had slept when on her way to Mexico before
her coronation. The Señora M—— also showed us her picture,
and spoke of her and the emperor with great enthusiasm.

This morning we rose by candlelight, at five o'clock, with
the prospect of a long ride, having to reach the *Trojes of
Angangueo,* a mining district (*trojes* literally mean granaries),
fourteen leagues from El Pilar. The morning was cold and raw,
with a dense fog covering the plains, so that we could scarcely
see each other's faces, and found our *mangas* particularly
agreeable. We were riding quickly across these ugly marshy
wastes, when a curious animal crossed our path, a *zorillo,* or
epatl, as the Indians call it, and which Bouffon mentions un-

der the generic name of *mouffetes*. It looks like a brown and white fox, with an enormous tail, which it holds up like a great feather in the air. It is known not only for the beauty of its skin, but for the horrible and pestilential odour with which it defends itself when attacked, and which poisons the air for miles around. Notwithstanding the warnings of the *mozos* as to its peculiar mode of defence, the gentlemen pursued it with guns and pistols, on horseback and on foot, but fired in vain. The beast seemed bullet-proof; turning, doubling, winding, crossing pools, hiding itself, stopping for a moment as if it were killed, and then trotting off again with its feathery tail much higher than its head; so that it seemed to be running backwards. The fog favoured it very much. It was certainly wounded in the paw, and as it stopped and seemed to hesitate, the sportsmen thought they had caught him; but a minute afterwards away went the waving tail amongst the pools and the marshy grass, the zorillo, no doubt, accompanying it, though we could not see him, and fortunately without resorting to any offensive or defensive measures. While they were chasing the zorillo, and we had rode a little way off, that we might not be accidentally shot in the fog, an immense wolf came looming by in the mist, with its stealthy gallop, close to our horses, causing us to shout for the sportsmen; but our numbers frightened it; besides which, it had but just breakfasted on a mule belonging to the hacienda, as we were told by the son of the proprietress of El Pilar, who, hearing all this distant firing, had ridden out to inquire into its cause, supposing that we might have lost our way in the fog, and were firing signals of distress.

We continued our journey across these plains for about three leagues, when the sun rose and scattered the mist; and after crossing a river, we entered the woods and rode between the shadows of the trees, through lovely forest scenery, interspersed with dells and plains and sparkling rivulets. But by the time we left these woods, and made our way up amongst the hills, the sun was riding high in the heavens, the pastures and green trees disappeared, and, though the country was still fertile and the soil rich, its beauties lay hid in the valleys below. K——'s horse received a sort of *coup de soleil*, shivered and trembled, and would not go on; so she mounted another, and one of the *mozos* led hers slowly by a different road to a village, to be watered. About one o'clock we began to wish for breakfast, but the mules which carried the provisions had taken a different path, and were not in sight; so that, arriving at an Indian hut close by a running stream, we were unanimous in dismounting, and at least procuring some *tortillas* from the inmates. At the same time, the Count de —— very philanthropically hired an old discoloured-looking horse, which was grazing peaceably outside the hut, and mounting the astonished quadruped, who had never, in his wildest dreams, calculated upon having so fine a chevalier on his back, galloped off in search of more solid food, while we set the Indian women to baking *tortillas*. He returned in about half an hour, with some bones of boiled mutton, tied up in a handkerchief! some salt, and thick tortillas, called *gorditas*, and was received with immense applause. Everything vanished in an incredibly short space of time, and we resumed our journey with renewed vigour. Towards the afternoon we entered the state of Michoacan, by a road (destined to be a highway) traced through great pine-forests, after stopping once more to rest at *Las Millas*, a few huts, or rather wooden cages, at the outskirts of the wood. Nothing can be more beautiful or romantic than this road, ascending through these noble forests, whose lofty oaks and gigantic pines clothe the mountains to their highest summits; sometimes so high, that, as we look upwards, the trees seem diminished to shrubs and bushes; the sun darting his warm, golden light between the dark-green extended branches of these distant forest pyramids, so that they seem to be basking in the very focus of his rays. Untrodden and virgin as these forests appear, an occasional cross, with its withered garland, gives token of life, and also of death; and green and lonely is the grave which the traveller has found among these Alpine solitudes, under the shadows of the dark pine, on a bed of fragrant wild-flowers, fanned by the pure air from the mountain-tops. The flowers which grow under the shade of the trees are beautiful and gay in their colours. Everywhere there are blue lupins, marigolds, dahlias, and innumerable blossoms with Indian names. Sometimes we dismounted and walked up the steepest parts, to rest our horses and ourselves; but, as it was impossible to go fast on these stony paths, it became entirely dark before Angangueo was in sight; and the road, which, for a great part of the way, is remarkably good, now led us down a perpendicular descent amongst the trees, covered with rocks and stones, so that the horses stumbled, and one, which afterwards proved to be blind of one eye, and not to see very clearly with the other, fell and threw his rider, who was not hurt. It was near eight o'clock (and we had been on horseback since six in the morning), when, after crossing a shallow stream, we saw the fires of the furnaces of Angangueo, a mining village, at the foot of some wild hills. We rode past the huts, where the blazing fires were shining on the swarthy faces of the workmen, the road skirting the valley, till we reached the house of Don Carlos Heimbürger, a Polish gentleman at the head of the German mining establishment. This house, the only one of any consequence at Angangueo, is extremely pretty, with a piazza in front, looking down upon the valley, which at night seems like the dwelling of the Cyclops, and within a very picture of comfort. We were welcomed by the master of the house, and by Madame B——n, a pretty and accomplished German lady, the wife of a physician who resides there. We had already known her in Mexico, and were glad to renew our acquaintance in this outlandish spot. One must have travelled fourteen leagues, from morning till night, to know how comfortable her little drawing-room appeared, with its well-cushioned red sofas, bright lights, and vases of flowers, as we came in from the cold and darkness, and how pretty and *extra*-civilized she looked in her black satin gown, not to mention the excellent dinner and the large fires, for they have chimneys in this part of the world. In a nice little bedroom, with a cheerful fire, the second time I have seen one in two years, I indite these particulars, and shall continue from our next place of rest.

LETTER THE FORTY-NINTH

Leave Trojes—*Beautiful Territory—Tarrascan Indians—Taxi-maroa — Distressed Condition — An Improvement — Cold Morning—Querendaro—Fine Breed of Horses—San Bartolo —Produce—Country Proprietors—Colear—Ride to Morelia— Wild Ducks—Sunset—Cathedral Bell—Cuincho—Curates Morelos, Matamoros and Hidalgo—Warm Baths—Handsome Girls—Starving Travellers—Lost Mules—Lancers— Night on a Heap of Straw—Mules Found—Tzintzontzan— King Calsonsi—Pascuaro—Kind Reception—Bishop—Robbers —Curu—Night in a Barn—Mountain—Uruapa—Enchanting Scenery—Pleasant Family—Jorullo.*

VALLADOLID, 25th.

As the house was so agreeable, and our next day's journey short, we could not prevail upon ourselves to leave the *Trojes* before nine o'clock; and even then, with the hopes of spending some time there on our return to see the mining establishment; the mills for grinding ore, the horizontal water-wheels, etc., etc.; and still more, the beautiful scenery in the neighbourhood.

That you may understand our line of march, take a map of Mexico, and you will see that Michoacan, one of the most beautiful and fertile territories in the world, is bounded on the north by the river Lerma, afterwards known by the name of Rio Grande; also by the department of Guanajuato; to the east and north-east it bounds that of Mexico, and to the west, that of Guadalajara. It lies on the western slope of the Great Cordillera of Anahuac. Hills, woods, and beautiful valleys diversify its surface; its pasture-grounds are watered by numerous streams, that rare advantage under the torrid zone, and the climate is cool and healthy. The Indians of this department are the Terascos—the Ottomi and the Chichimeca Indians. The first are the most civilized of the tribes, and their language the most harmonious. We are now travelling in a north-westerly direction, towards the capital of the state, Valladolid, or Morelia, as it has been called since the independence, in honour of the curate Morelos, its great supporter.

We had a pleasant ride of nine leagues through an open pasture-country, meeting with nothing very remarkable on our journey, but an Indian woman seated on the ground, her Indian husband standing beside her. Both had probably been refreshing themselves with pulque—perhaps even with its homœopathic extract *mezcal;* but the Indian was sober and sad, and stood with his arms folded, and the most patient and pitying face, while his wife, quite overcome with the strength of the potation, and unable to go any further, looked up at him with the most imploring air, saying repeatedly—*"Matame, Miguel, matame"* (Kill me, Miguel—kill me)—apparently considering herself quite unfit to live.

About five o'clock we came in sight of the pretty village and old church of *Taximaroa;* and riding up to the *meson,* or inn, found two empty dark rooms with mud floors—without windows, in fact without anything but their four walls—neither bench, chair, nor table. Although we travel with our own beds, this looked rather uninviting, especially after the pleasant quarters we had just left; and we turned our eyes wistfully towards a pretty small house upon a hill, with a painted portico, thinking how agreeably situated we should be there! Colonel Y—— thereupon rode up the hill, and presenting himself to the owner of this house, described our forlorn prospects, and he kindly consented to permit us all to sup there, and moreover to receive the ladies for the night. For the gentlemen he had no room, having but one spare apartment, as one of his family was a great invalid, and could not be moved. Accordingly, our travelling luggage was carried up the hill; the horses and mules and servants were quartered in the village, the gentlemen found lodging for themselves in a bachelor's house, and we found ourselves in very agreeable quarters, on a pretty piazza, with an extensive view, and one large room, containing a table and some benches, at our service. Meanwhile, M. de B—— rushed through the village, finding eggs and hens and tortillas, and then returning, he and Mr. W—— produced the travelling stores of beef and tongue, and set about making mustard and drawing bottles of wine, to the great wonderment and edification of the honest proprietor. Even a clean tablecloth was produced; a piece of furniture which he had probably never seen before, and now eyed wistfully, doubtless taking it for a *sheet.* We had a most amusing supper, some performing dexterously with penknives, and others using tortillas as forks. We won the heart of the *bourgeois* by sending a cup of tea to his invalid, and inviting him to partake of another, which he seemed to consider a rare and medicinal beverage. About nine o'clock the gentlemen departed to their lodgings, and our beds were erected in the large room where we had supped; the man assuring us that he was quite pleased to have us under his roof, and liked our company extremely well; adding, "*Me cuadra mucho la gente decente*" (I am very fond of decent people).

We left Taximaroa at six o'clock, having spent rather a disturbed night, in consequence of the hollow coughs with which the whole family seemed afflicted, at least the poor invalid on one side of our room, and the master of the house on the other. The morning was so cold, that every manga and sarape was put in requisition. Our ride this day was through superb scenery, every variety of hill and valley, water and wood, particularly the most beautiful woods of lofty oaks, the whole with scarcely a trace of cultivation, and for the most part entirely uninhabited. Our numbers were augmented by Colonel Y——'s troop, who rode from Morelia to meet him. We had a long journey, passed by the little village of *San Andrés*, and stopped to eat *tortillas* in a very dirty hut at Pueblo Viejo, surrounded by the dirtiest little Indian children. Throughout the whole ride, the trees and flowering shrubs were beautiful, and the scenery so varied, that although we rode for eleven hours in a hot sun, we scarcely felt fatigued, for wherever there are trees and water and fresh green grass, the eye is rested. In this and in our last few days' journey, we saw a number of blue birds, called by the common people *guardia-bosques*, wood guardians. About half-past five we entered a winding road, through a natural shrubbery, leading to *Querendaro*, the fine hacienda of Señor Pimentel, a senator. When we arrived the family were at dinner, and we were invited to join them, after which we went out to see the hacienda, and especially the handsome and well-kept stables, where the proprietor has a famous breed of horses, some of which were trotted out for our inspection—beautiful, spirited creatures—one called "*Hilo de Oro*" (golden thread)—another, "*Pico Blanco*" (white mouth), etc. In the inner courtyard are many beautiful and rare flowers, and everything is kept in great order.

At nine o'clock the following morning we left Querendaro, and rode on to *San Bartolo*, a vast and beautiful property, belonging to Señor Don Joaquin Gomez, of Valladolid. The family were from home, with the exception of his son and nephew, who did the honours of the house with such cordial and genuine hospitality, that we felt perfectly at home before the day was over. I think the Mexican character is never seen to such advantage as in the country, amongst these great landed proprietors of old family, who live on their own estates, engaged in agricultural pursuits, and entirely removed from all the party feeling and petty interests of a city life. It is true that the life of a country gentleman here is that of a hermit, in the total absence of all society, in the nearly unbroken solitude that surrounds him. For leagues and leagues there is no habitation but his own; the nearest miserable village may be distant half a day's journey, over an almost impassable road. He is "monarch of all he surveys," a king amongst his farm servants and Indian workmen. Nothing can exceed the independence of his position; but to enjoy this wild country life, he must be born to it. He must be a first-rate horseman, and addicted to all kinds of country sport; and if he can spend the day in riding over his estate, in directing his workmen, watching over his improvements, redressing disputes and grievances, and can sit down in the evening in his large and lonely halls, and philosophically bury himself in the pages of some favourite author, then his time will probably not hang heavy on his hands.

As for the *young master* here, he was up with the lark—he was on the most untractable horse in the hacienda, and away across the fields with his followers, chasing the bulls as he went—he was fishing—he was shooting—he was making bullets—he was leagues off at a village, seeing a country bull-fight —he was always in a good humour, and so were all who surrounded him—he was engaged in the dangerous amusement of *colear*—and by the evening it would have been a clever writer who had kept *his* eyes open after such a day's work. Never was there a young lad more evidently fitted for a free life in the country.

There was a generous, frank liberality apparent in everything in this hacienda, that it was agreeable to witness; nothing petty or calculating. Señor ——, lame through an accident, and therefore unable to mount his horse, or to go far on foot, seemed singularly gentle and kind-hearted. The house is one of the prettiest and most cheerful we have seen yet; but we passed a great stone building on the road, which the proprietor of San Bartolo is having constructed for one of his family, which, if it keep its promise, will be a palace when finished. The principal produce of this hacienda is *pimiento,* the capsicum. There is the *pimiento dulce* and the *pimiento picante,* the sweet fruit of the common capsicum, and the fruit of the bird pepper capsicum. The Spaniards gave to all these peppers the name of *chile*, which they borrowed from the Indian word *quauhchilli,* and which, to the native Mexicans, is as necessary an ingredient of food as salt is to us. At dinner we had the greatest variety of fine fruit, and pulque, which is particularly good in this neighbourhood. They also make here a quantity of excellent cheese.

After dinner they proceeded to amuse us with the *colear* of the bulls, of which amusement the Mexicans throughout the whole republic are passionately fond. They collect a herd, single out several, gallop after them on horseback; and he who is most skilful, catches the bull by the tail, passes it under his own right leg, turns it round the high pummel of his saddle, and wheeling his horse round at right angles by a sudden movement, the bull falls on his face. Even boys of ten years old joined in this sport. It is no wonder that the Mexicans are such *centaurs,* seeming to form part and parcel of their horses, accustomed as they are from childhood to these dangerous pastimes. This is very dangerous, since the horse's legs constantly get entangled with those of the falling bull, which throws both horse and rider. Manifold are the accidents which result from it, but they are certainly not received as warnings; and after all, such sports, where there is nothing bloody, nor even cruel, saving the thump which the bull gets, and the mortification which he no doubt feels, but from both of which he soon recovers; and which are mere games of skill, trials of address—are manly and strengthening, and help to keep up the physical superiority of that fine race of men—the Mexican *rancheros.*

The next day we parted from our travelling companions, the Count de B—— and Mr. W——, who are on their way to the fair of San Juan, and are from thence going to *Tepic,* even to the shores of the Pacific Ocean. Unfortunately, our time is limited, and we cannot venture on so distant an expedition; but we greatly regretted separating from such pleasant *compagnons de voyage.* We spent the morning in walking about the hacienda, seeing cheese made, and visiting the handsome chapel, the splendid stone granaries, the great mills, etc. We also hope to spend some time here on our return. By letters received this morning from Mexico, we find that Señor Gomez Pedraza has left the ministry.

As we had but six leagues to ride in order to reach Morelia, we did not leave San Bartolo till four in the afternoon, and enjoyed a pretty ride through a fertile and well-wooded country, the road good and the evening delightful. As the sun set, millions and tens of millions of ducks, in regular ranks and regiments, darkening the air, flew over our heads, changing their quarters from one lake to another. Morelia is celebrated for the purity of its atmosphere and the exceeding beauty of its sky; and this evening upheld its reputation. Toward sunset, the whole western horizon was covered with myriads of little lilac and gold clouds, floating in every fantastic form over the bright blue of the heavens. The lilac deepened into purple, blushed into rose-colour, brightened into crimson. The blue of the sky assumed that green tint peculiar to an Italian sunset. The sun himself appeared a globe of living flame. Gradually he sank in a blaze of gold and crimson, while the horizon remained lighted as by the flame from a volcano. Then his brilliant retinue of clouds, after blazing for a while in borrowed splendour, melted gradually into every rainbow hue and tinge; from deep crimson to rose-colour and pink and pale violet and faint blue, floating in silvery vapour, until they all blended into one soft gray tinge, which swept over the whole western sky. But then the full moon rose in cloudless serenity, and at length we heard, faintly, then more distinctly, and then in all its deep and sonorous harmony, the tolling of the cathedral bell, which announced our vicinity to a great city. It has a singular effect, after travelling for some days through a wild country, seeing nothing but a solitary hacienda, or an Indian hut, to enter a fine city like Morelia, which seems to have started up as by magic in the midst of the wilderness, yet bearing all the traces of a venerable old age. By moonlight, it looked like a panorama of Mexico; with a fine square, portales, cathedral, broad streets, and good houses. We rode through the city, to the house of Colonel Y——, where we now are; but as we intend to continue our journey to its furthest limits without stopping, we are now, after a night's rest, preparing to resume our ride. They are saddling the horses, strapping on the sarapes behind the saddles, taking down and packing up our *lits de voyage*, and loading the mules, all which is a work of time. On our return we hope to remain here a few days, to see everything that is worthy of notice.

PASCUARO.

Accompanied by several gentlemen of Morelia, who came early in the morning to see C——n, we set off for the warm baths of *Cuincho*; and as we rode along, the hill of *Las Bateas* was pointed out to us, where, by order of the Curate Morelos, two hundred Spaniards were murdered in cold blood, to revenge the death of his friend, the Curate Matamoros, who was taken prisoner and shot by orders of Yturbide. Horrible cruelty in a Christian priest! It is singular, that the great leaders of the independence should have been ecclesiastics; the Curate Hidalgo its prime mover, the Curates Morelos and Matamoros the principal chiefs. Hidalgo, it is said, had no plan, published no manifesto, declared no opinions; but rushed from city to city at the head of his men, displaying on his colours an image of the Virgin of Guadalupe, and inciting his troops to massacre the Spaniards. Morelos was an Indian, uneducated, but brave and enterprising, and considered the mildest and most merciful of these soldier priests! Matamoros, equally brave, was better informed. Both were good generals, and both misused the power which their position gave them over the minds of the unenlightened populace. When Morelos became generalissimo of the revolutionary forces, he took a step fatal to his interests, and which led to his ultimate ruin. He formed a congress, which met at Chilpansingo, and was composed of lawyers and clergymen; ignorant and ambitious men, who employed themselves in publishing absurd decrees and impossible laws, in assigning salaries to themselves, and giving each other the title of *Excellency*. Disputes and divisions arose amongst them; and, in 1814, they published an absurd and useless document in the village of Apatzingan, to which they gave the name of the "Mexican Constitution." The following year, Morelos was defeated in an engagement which took place in the environs of Tesmelaca, taken prisoner, led to Mexico, and, after a short trial, degraded from his ecclesiastical functions, and shot in the village of San Cristobal Ecatepec, seven leagues from the capital. The revolutionary party considered him as a martyr in the cause of liberty, and he is said to have died like a true hero. The appellation of Morelia, given to the city of Valladolid, keeps his name in remembrance, but her blood-stained mountain is a more lasting record of his cruelty.

A vile action is recorded of a Spaniard, whose name, which deserves to be branded with infamy, escapes me at this moment. The soldiers of Morelos having come in search of him, he, standing at his door, pointed out his brother, who was in a room inside the house, as the person whom they sought; and escaped himself, leaving his brother to be massacred in his place. We contrasted the conduct of this miserable wretch with the noble action of the Prince de Polignac, under similar circumstances.

At half-past ten, after a pleasant ride of about five leagues, we arrived at the natural hot springs of Cuincho. The place is quite wild, the scenery very striking. The building consists of two very large baths, two very damp rooms, and a kitchen. The baths are kept by a very infirm old man, a martyr to intermitting fever, and two remarkably handsome girls, his daughters, who live here completely alone, and, except in summer, when the baths are resorted to by a number of *canónigos* and occasional gentlemen from Morelia, "waste their sweetness on the desert air." The house, such as it is, lies at the foot of rocky hills, covered with shrubs, and pouring down streams of hot water from their volcanic bosoms. All the streams that cross your path are warm. You step by chance into a little streamlet, and find the water of a most agreeable temperature. They put this water in earthen jars to cool, in order to render it fit for drinking, but it never becomes fresh and cold. It contains muriatic acid, without any trace of sulphur or metallic salt. I think it is Humboldt who supposes that in this part of Mexico there exists, at a great depth in the interior of the earth, a fissure running from east to west, for one hundred and thirty-seven leagues, through which, bursting the external crust of the porphyritic rocks, the volcanic fire has opened itself a passage at different times, from the coasts of the Mexican Gulf, as far as the South Sea. The famous volcano of Jorullo is in this department, and boiling fountains are common in various parts of it.

We stopped here to take a bath, and found the temperature of the water delicious, about the ordinary temperature of the human body. The baths are rather dark, being enclosed in great stone walls, with the light coming from a very small aperture near the roof. A bird, that looked like a wild duck, was sailing about in the largest one, having made its entry along with the water when it was let in. I never bathed in any water which I so much regretted leaving. After bathing, we waited for the arrival of our mules, which were to follow us at a gentle pace, that we might have breakfast, and continue our journey to *Pascuaro,* a city nine leagues farther.

But several hours passed away, and no mules appeared; and at length we came to the grievous conviction that the arrieros had mistaken the road, and that we must expect neither food nor beds that night; for it was now too late to think of reaching Pascuaro. In this extremity, the gentlemen from Morelia, suf-

fering for their politeness in having escorted us, the two damsels of the bath, naiads of the boiling spring, pitying our hungry condition, came to offer their services; one asked me if I
should like "to eat a *burro* in the mean time?" A *burro* being
an *ass*, I was rather startled at the proposition, and assured
her that I should infinitely prefer waiting a little longer before
resorting to so desperate a measure. "Some people call them
pecadoras," (female sinners!) said her sister. Upon this, the
gentlemen came to our assistance, and burros or pecadoras
were ordered forthwith. They proved to be hot tortillas, with
cheese in them, and we found them particularly good. It grew
late, but no mules arrived; and at length the young ladies and
their father rushed out desperately, caught an old hen that was
wandering amongst the hills, killed, skinned, and put it into a
pot to boil, baked some fresh tortillas, and brought us the spoil
in triumph! One penknife was produced—the boiling pan
placed on a deal table in the room off the bath, and every one,
surrounding the fowl, a tough old creature, who must have
chuckled through many revolutions, we ate by turns, and concluded with a comfortable drink of lukewarm water.

We then tried to beguile the time by climbing amongst the
hills at the back of the house—by pushing our way through
the tangled briers—by walking to a little lake, where there
were ducks and waterfowl, and close to the margin a number
of fruit trees. We returned to the baths—the mules had not
been heard of—there was no resource but patience. Our
Morelian friends left us to return home before it should grow
dusk; and shortly after, an escort of twenty-three lancers, with
a captain, arrived by orders of the governor, Don Panfilo
Galiudo, to accompany us during the remainder of our journey.
They looked very picturesque, with their lances, and little
scarlet flags, and gave a very formidable aspect to the little
portico in front of the baths, where they deposited all their
military accoutrements—their saddles, guns, sarapes, etc. The
captain had with him his wife and daughter, and a baby of
about two years old, which, during all the time they were with
us, was constantly carried by one of the soldiers, with the utmost care, in front of his horse.

Meanwhile, the moon rose, and we walked about discon-
solate, in front of the baths—fearing greatly that some accident
might have overtaken our unescorted mules and servants; that
the first might be robbed—and that the drivers might be killed.
But it was as well to try to sleep if it were only to get over
the interminable night; and at length some clean straw was

procured, and spread in a corner of the damp floor. There K—— and I lay down in our mangas. C——n procured another corner—Colonel Y—— a third, and then and thus, we addressed ourselves seriously to repose, but in vain. Between cold and mosquitoes and other animals, we could not close our eyes, and were thankful to rise betimes, shake the straw off, and resume our march.

The road was pretty and flowery when the light came in, and we gradually began to open our eyes, after taking leave of our fair hostesses and their father. When I say *the road* you do not, I trust, imagine us riding along a dusty highway. I am happy to say that we are generally the discoverers of our own pathways. Every man his own Columbus. Sometimes we take short cuts, which prove to be long rounds:

> *"Over hill, over dale,*
> *Through bush, through brier;"*

through valley and over stream; and this kind of journey has something in it so independent and amusing, that with all its fatigues and inconveniences, we find it delightful—far preferable even to travelling in the most commodious London-built carriage, bowling along the queen's highway with four swift posters, at the rate of twelve miles an hour.

Arrived at the huts, we stopped to make inquiries concerning the mules. Two loaded mules, the peasants said, had been robbed in the night, and the men tied to a tree on the low road leading to Pascuaro. We rode on uneasy enough, and at another hut were told that many robbers had been out in the night, and that amongst others, a woman had been robbed and bound hand and foot. The road now became bleak and uninteresting, the sun furiously hot, and we rode forward with various misgivings as to the fate of the party; when at a cluster of huts called *el Correo*, we came up with the whole concern. The arrieros had forgotten the name of Cuincho, and not knowing where to go, had stopped here the previous night, knowing that we were bound for Pascuaro, and must pass that way. They had arrived early, and missed the robbers.

We stopped to breakfast at some huts called La Puerta de Chapultepec, where we got some tortillas from a half-caste Indian, who was in great distress, because his wife had run off from him for the fourth time with "another gentleman!" He vowed that though he had taken her back three times, he never would receive her more; yet I venture to say, that when the false fair one presents herself, she will find him placable;

he is evidently in such distress at having no woman to take care of his house.

After leaving Chapultepec, the scenery improves, and at length we had a beautiful view of the hills, at the foot of which lies the ancient city of *Tzintzontzan*, close by the opposite shore of the Lake of Pascuaro; formerly capital of the independent kingdom of Michoacan, an important city, called at the time of Cortes, *Hurtzitzila*. It was formerly the residence of the monarch, King *Calsonsi*, an ally of Cortes, and who, with his Indian subjects, assisted him in his Mexican war. It is now a poor Indian village, though it is said that some remains of the monarch's palace still exist. A *propos* to which, we have several times observed, since we entered this state, large stones lying in fields, or employed in fences, with strange hieroglyphic characters engraved on them, some of which may be curious and interesting.

The view as we approach Pascuaro with its beautiful lake studded with little islands, is very fine. The bells were tolling, and they were letting off rockets for some Indian festival, and we met parties of the natives who had been keeping the festival upon *pulque* or *mezcal* (a strong spirit) and were stumbling along in great glee. We came up to an old church, that looks like a bird's-nest amongst the trees, and stands at the outskirts of the city. Here, it is said, his Majesty of Michoacan came out to meet his Spanish ally, when he entered this territory.

Pascuaro is a pretty little city with sloping roofs, situated on the shores of the lake of the same name, and in front of the little Indian village of Janicho, built on a beautiful small island in the midst of the lake. C——n says that Pascuaro resembles a town in Catalonia. It is entirely unlike any other Mexican city. We made a great sensation as we entered with our lancers and mules, tired and dust-becovered as we were, and brought all the *Pascuaranians* to their balconies. We passed churches bearing the date of 1580! We went to the largest and best house in the town, that of Don Miguel H——a (a friend of Colonel Y——'s). He was from home, but we were most hospitably entertained by his wife, who received us without any unnecessary ceremony or compliments, and made us quite at home. We walked out with her by moonlight to see the Square and the Portales, which is a promenade in the evening, and were followed by crowds of little boys; strangers being rather an uncommon spectacle here. The only foreign lady, Doña —— says, whoever was here in her recollection, was a Frenchwoman, to whom she was very much attached, the daughter of a physician, and whose husband was murdered by the robbers.

This morning, the weather being cold and rainy, and our quarters too agreeable to leave in any violent haste, we agreed to remain until to-morrow, and have spent a pleasant day in this fine large house, with Doña ——, and her numerous and handsome children. We have not been able to visit the lake, or the Indian islands on account of the weather, but we hope to do so on our return from *Uruapa,* our next destination. Our hostess is a most agreeable person; lively, kind-hearted, and full of natural talent. We did not expect to meet such a person in this corner of the world.

The first bishop of Michoacan, Vasco de Quiroga, who died in Uruapa, was buried in Pascuaro, and the Indians of this state still venerate his memory. He was the father and benefactor of these Tarrascan Indians, and went far to rescue them from their degraded state. He not only preached morality, but encouraged industry amongst them, by assigning to each village its particular branch of commerce. Thus one was celebrated for its manufacture of saddles, another for its shoes, a third for its *bateos* (painted trays), and so on. Every useful institution, of which some traces still remain amongst them, is due to this excellent prelate; an example of what one good and zealous and well-judging man can effect.

We have been taking another stroll by moonlight, the rain having ceased; we have lingered over a pleasant supper, and have wished Doña —— good-night. Yet let me not forget, before laying down my pen, to celebrate the excellence of the white fish from the lake! so greatly surpassing in excellence and flavour those which we occasionally have in Mexico. These no doubt must have constituted *"the provisions,"* which according to tradition, were carried by regular running posts, from Tzintzontzan to Montezuma's palace in Mexico, and with such expedition, that though the distance is about one hundred leagues, they were placed, still smoking, on the Emperor's table!

URUAPA, 30th.

We went to mass at six o'clock; and then took leave of the Señora H——a, who gave us a cordial invitation to spend some days with her on our return. It was about eight o'clock when we left Pascuaro, and mounted the hills over which our road lay, and stopped to look down on the beautiful lake, lying like a sheet of silver in the sun, and dotted with green islands.

Two disagreeable personages were added to our party. Early in the morning, intelligence was brought that a celebrated robber, named *Morales*, captain of a large band, had been seized along with one of his companions; and permission was requested to take advantage of our large escort, in order that they may be safely conducted to Uruapa, where they are to be shot, being already condemned to death. The punishment of hanging is not in use in Mexico.

The first thing therefore that we saw, on mounting our horses, was the two robbers, chained together by the leg, guarded by five of our lancers, and prepared to accompany us on foot. The companion of Morales was a young, vulgar-looking ruffian, his face livid, and himself nearly naked; but the robber-captain himself was equal to any of Salvator's brigands, in his wild and striking figure and countenance. He wore a dark-coloured blanket, and a black hat, the broad leaf of which was slouched over his face, which was the colour of death, while his eyes seemed to belong to a tiger or other beast of prey. I never saw such a picture of fierce misery. Strange to say, this man began life as a shepherd; but how he was induced to abandon this pastoral occupation, we did not hear. For years he has been the scourge of the country, robbing to an unheard of extent, (so that whatever he may have done with them, tens of thousands of dollars have passed through his hands,) carrying off the farmers' daughters to the mountains, and at the head of eighty ruffians, committing the most horrible disorders. His last crime was murdering his wife in the mountains, the night before last, under circumstances of barbarity too shocking to relate, and it is supposed, assisted by the wretch now with him. After committing the crime, they ran to hide themselves in an Indian village, as the Indians, probably from fear, never betray the robbers. However, their horror of this man was so great, that perfect *hate* cast out their fear, and collecting together, they seized the ruffians, bound them, and carried them to Pascuaro, where they were instantly tried, and condemned to be shot; the sentence to be executed at Uruapa.

The sight of these miserable wretches, and the idea of what their feelings must be, occupied us, as they toiled along, each step bringing them nearer to their place of execution; and we could not help thinking what wild wishes must have sometimes throbbed within them, of breaking their bonds, and dashing away from their guards—away through the dark woods, over mountain and river, down that almost perpendicular precipice, over the ravine, up that green and smiling hill, and into these gloomy pine woods, in whose untrod recesses they would be secure from pursuit—and then their despair when they felt the heavy, clanking chain on their bare feet, and looked at the lances and guns that surrounded them, and knew that even if they attempted to fly, could they be insane enough to try it, a dozen bullets would stop their career for ever. Then horror and disgust at the recollection of their savage crimes took the place of pity, and not even ——'s suggestion, that the robber-chief might have killed his wife in a transport of jealousy, could lessen our indignation at this last most barbarous murder of a defenceless woman.

But these thoughts took away half the pleasure of this most beautiful journey, through wild woods, where for leagues and leagues we meet nothing but the fatal *cross;* while through these woods of larches, cedars, oaks, and pines, are bright vistas of distant pasture-fields, and of lofty mountains, covered with forests. Impossible to conceive a greater variety of beautiful scenery—a greater *waste* of beauty, if one may say so— for not even an Indian hut was to be seen, nor did we meet a single passing human being, nor a trace of cultivation. As we came out of the woods we heard a gun fired amongst the hills, the first token of human life that had greeted us since we left Pascuaro. This, Señor —— told us, was the signal-gun usually fired by the Indians on the approach of an armed troop, warning their brethren to hide themselves. Here the Indians rarely speak Spanish, as those do who live in the neighbourhood of cities. Their language is chiefly the harmonious Tarrascan.

Towards the afternoon we came to a path which led us into a valley of the most surpassing beauty, entirely carpeted with the loveliest blue, white, pink, and scarlet wild flowers, and clothed with natural orchards of peach- and apricot-trees in full bloom, the grass strewed with their rich blossoms. Below ran a sparkling rivulet, its bright gushing waters leaping over the stones and pebbles that shone in the sun like silver. Near this are some huts called *Las Palomas,* and it was so charming a spot, that we got off our horses, and halted for half-an-hour; and while they prepared breakfast for us, a basket of provisions from Pascuaro having been brought on by the provident care of Doña ——, we clambered out amongst the rocks and luxuriant trees that dipped their leafy branches in the stream, and pulled wild flowers that would grace any European garden.

Having breakfasted in one of the huts, upon fowl and tortillas, on which memorable occasion two penknives were produced (and I still wonder why we did not bring some knives and forks with us, unless it be that we should never have had them cleaned), we continued our journey: and this mention of knives leads me to remark, that all common servants in Mexico, and all common people, eat with their fingers! Those who are rather particular, roll up two tortillas, and use them as a knife and fork, which, I can assure you from experience, is a great deal better than nothing, when you have learnt how to use them.

Our road after this, though even wilder and more picturesque, was very fatiguing to the horses—up and down steep rocks, among forests of oak and pine, through which we slowly wended our way; so that it was dark when we descended a precipitous path, leading to a small Indian village, or rather encampment, called *Curu*. It was now too late to think of reaching Uruapa, or of venturing to climb by night the series of precipices called the *Cuesta de Curu*, over which we should have had to pass. But such a place as *Curu* for Christians to pass the night in! A few miserable huts filled with Indians, and not, so far as we could discern, even an empty shed, where we might rest under cover. However, there was no remedy. The *arriero* had already unloaded his mules, and was endeavouring to find some provender for them and the poor horses. It was quite dark, but there was a delicious fragrance of orange-blossoms, and we groped our way up to the trees, and pulled some branches by way of consolation. At length an old wooden barn was discovered, and there the beds of the whole party were put up! We even contrived to get some boiling water and to have some tea made—an article of luxury which, as well as a teapot, we carry with us. We sat down upon our trunks, and a piece of candle was procured and lighted, and, after some difficulty, made to stand upright on the floor. The barn, made of logs, let the air in on all sides, and the pigs thrust their snouts in at every crevice, grunting harmoniously. Outside, in the midst of the encampment, the soldiers lighted a large fire, and sat round it roasting maize. The robbers sat amongst them, chained, with a soldier mounting guard beside them. The fire, flashing on the livid face of Morales, who, crouched in his blanket, looked like a tiger about to spring— the soldiers, some warming their hands at the blaze, some lying rolled in their sarapes, and others devouring their primitive supper—together with the Indian women bringing them hot tortillas from the huts—the whole had a curious and picturesque effect. As for us, we also rolled ourselves in our mangas, and lay down in our barn, but passed a miserable night. The pigs grunted, the mosquitoes sung, a cold air blew in from every corner, and, fortunately, we were not until morning aware of the horrid fact, that a whole nest of scorpions, with their tails twisted together, were reposing above our heads in the log wall. Imagine the condition of the unfortunate slumberer on whose devoted head they had descended *en masse!* In spite of the fragrant orange-blossom, we set off early the next morning.

URUAPA.

On leaving the fascinating village of Curu, we began to ascend *La Cuesta;* and travelled slowly four leagues of mountain-road, apparently inaccessible; but the sure-footed horses, though stepping on loose and nearly precipitous rocks, rarely stumbled. The mountain of Curu is volcanic, a chaos of rent rocks, beetling precipices, and masses of lava that have been disgorged from the burning crater. Yet from every crag and crevice of the rock spring the most magnificent trees, twisted with flowering parasites, shrubs of the brightest green, and pale delicate flowers, whose gentle hues seem all out of place in this savage scene. Beside the forest oak and the stern pine, the tree of the white blossoms, the graceful *floripundio,* seems to seek for shelter and support. Creepers that look like scarlet honeysuckles, and flowering vines of every variety of colour, hang in bright garlands and festoons, intwining the boughs of the trees; adorning, but not concealing the masses of bare rock and the precipitous crag that frowns amidst all this luxury of vegetation. The whole scene is "horribly beautiful."

As we wound through these picturesque paths, where only one can go at a time, our train stretched out to an immense distance, and the scarlet streamers and lances of the soldiers looked very picturesque, appearing and then vanishing amongst the rocks and trees. At one part, looking back to see the effect, I caught the eye of the robber Morales, glaring with such a frightful expression, that, forgetful of his chains, I whipped up my horse in the greatest consternation, over stones and rocks. He and the scene were in perfect unison.

At length we came to the end of this extraordinary mountain-forest, and after resting the tired horses for a little while, in a grove of pines and yellow acacias, entered the most lovely little wood, a succession of flowers and shrubs, and bright green grass, with vistas of fertile cornfields bordered by fruit trees—a peaceful scene, on which the eye rests with pleasure, after passing through these wild, volcanic regions.

On leaving the woods, the path skirts along by the side of these fields, and leads to the valley where Uruapa, the gem of the Indian villages, lies in tranquil beauty. It has indeed some tolerable streets and a few good houses; but her boast is in the Indian cottages—all so clean and snug, and tasteful, and buried in fruit trees.

We rode through shady lanes of trees, bending under the weight of oranges, *chirimoyas, granaditas, platanos,* and every sort of delicious fruit. We found that, through the kindness of Señor Ysasaga, the principal person here, the curate's house had been prepared to receive us—an old unfurnished house next the church, and at present unoccupied, its owner being absent. We found the whole family extremely kind and agreeable; the father a well-informed, pleasant old gentleman, the mother still beautiful, though in bad health; and all the daughters pretty and unaffected. One is married to a brother of Madame Yturbide's. They made many apologies for not inviting us to their own house, which is under repair; but as it is but a few steps off, we shall spend most of our time with them. It seems strange to meet such people in this secluded spot! Yet, peaceful and solitary as it appears, it has not escaped the rage of civil war, having been burnt down four different times by insurgents and by Spaniards. Señor Ysasaga, who belongs to Valladolid, has taken an active part in all these revolutions, having been the personal friend and partisan of Hidalgo. His escapes and adventures would fill a volume.

I could not help taking one last look of the robbers, as we entered this beautiful place, where Morales at least is to be shot. It seemed to me as if they had grown perfectly death-like. The poor wretches must be tired enough, having come on foot all the way from Pascuaro.

31st.—This place is so charming, we have determined to pitch our tent in it for a few days. Our intention was to proceed twenty leagues farther, to see the volcano of Jorullo; but as the road is described to us as being entirely devoid of shade, and the heat almost insupportable—with various other difficulties and drawbacks—we have been induced, though with great regret, to abandon the undertaking, which it is as tantalizing to do, as it is to reflect that yesterday we were but a short distance from a hill which is but thirty leagues from the Pacific Ocean.

In 1813, M. de Humboldt and M. Bonpland, ascended to the crater of this burning mountain, which was formed in September 1759. Its birth was announced by earthquakes, which put to flight all the inhabitants of the neighbouring villages; and three months after, a terrible eruption burst forth, which filled all the inhabitants with astonishment and terror, and which Humboldt considers one of the most extraordinary physical revolutions that ever took place on the surface of the globe.

Flames issued from the earth for the space of more than a square league. Masses of burning rock were thrown to an immense height, and through a thick cloud of ashes, illuminated by the volcanic fire, the whitened crust of the earth was gradually seen swelling up. The ashes even covered the roofs of the houses at Querétaro, forty-eight leagues distance! and the rivers of San Andres and Cuitumba sank into the burning masses. The flames were seen from Pascuaro; and from the hills of Agua-Zarca was beheld the birth of this volcanic mountain, the burning offspring of an earthquake, which bursting from the bosom of the earth, changed the whole face of the country for a considerable distance round.

> "And now, the glee
> Of the loud hills shakes with its mountain mirth,
> As if they did rejoice o'er a young earthquake's birth."

Here the earth returned the salutation, and shook, though it was with fearful mirth, at the birth of the young volcano.

In a letter written at the time of the event to the bishop of Michioacan by the curate of the neighbouring village, he says, that the eruption finished by destroying the hacienda of Jorullo, and killing the trees, which were thrown down and buried in the sand and ashes vomited by the mountain. The fields and roads were, he says, covered with sand, the crops destroyed, and the flocks perishing for want of food, unable to drink the pestilential water of the mountains. The rivulet that ran past his village was swelled to a mighty river, that threatened to inundate it; and he adds, that the houses, churches, and hospitals are ready to fall down from the weight of the sand and the ashes—and that "the very people are so covered with the sand, that they seem to have come out of some sepulchre." The great eruptions of the volcano continued till the following year, but have gradually become rarer, and at present have ceased.

Having now brought our journey to its furthest limits, I shall conclude this letter.

LETTER THE FIFTIETH

*Indian Dresses—Saints—Music—Union of Tropical and Euro-
pean Vegetation—Old Customs—Falls of the Sararaqui—
Silkworms — Indian Painting — Beautiful Heroine — Leave
Uruapa—Tziracuaratiro—Talkative Indian—Alcalde's House
—Pascuaro—Old Church—Mosaic Work—The Lake—The
Cave—Fried Fish—Rich Indians—Convent—Cuincho—Dark-
ness — Morelia — Alameda — Cathedral — Silver — Wax-
works—College—Wonderful Fleas.*

URUAPA, 31st.

The dress of the Indian women of Uruapa is pretty, and they
are altogether a much cleaner and better-looking race than we
have yet seen. They wear *"naguas,"* a petticoat of black cotton
with a narrow white and blue stripe, made very full, and
rather long; over this, a sort of short chemise made of coarse
white cotton, and embroidered in different coloured silks. It
is called the *sutunacua*—over all is a black reboso, striped with
white and blue, with a handsome silk fringe of the same colours. When they are married, they add a white embroidered
veil, and a remarkably pretty coloured mantle, the *huepilli,*
which they seem to pronounce *guipil*. The hair is divided,
and falls down behind in two long plaits, fastened at the top
by a bow of ribbon and a flower. In this dress there is no
alteration from what they wore in former days; saving that
the women of a higher class wore a dress of finer cotton with
more embroidery, and a loose garment over all, resembling a
priest's surplice, when the weather was cold. Among the men,
the introduction of trousers is Spanish—but they still wear the
majtlatl, a broad belt, with the ends tied before and behind,
and the *tilmatli* or *tilma* as they now call it, a sort of square
short cloak, the ends of which are tied across the breast, or
over one shoulder. It is on a coarse *tilma* of this description
that the image of the Virgin of Guadalupe was found painted.

Yesterday, being the festival of San Andres, the Indians
were all in full costume and procession, and we went into the
old church to see them. They were carrying the saint in very
fine robes, the women bearing coloured flags and lighted ta-

pers, and the men playing on violins, flutes, and drums. All had garlands of flowers to hang on the altars; and for these lights and ornaments, and silk and tinsel robes, they save up all their money. They were playing a pretty air, but I doubt its being original. It was not melancholy and monotonous, like the generality of Indian music, but had something wild and gay in it; it was probably Spanish. The organ was played by an Indian. After mass we went upstairs to try it, and wondered how, with such miserable means, he had produced anything like music. In the *patio*, between the curate's house and the church, are some very brilliant large scarlet flowers, which they call here *"flor del pastor,"* the shepherd's flower; a beautiful kind of *euphorbia;* and in other places, *"flor de noche buena,"* the flower of Christmas-eve.

Last evening we walked out in the environs of this garden of Eden, by the banks of the river *Marques,* amidst a most extraordinary union of tropical and European vegetation; the hills covered with firs, and the plains with sugar-cane. We walked amongst bananas, shaddock, chirimoyas, and orange-trees, and but a few yards higher up, bending over and almost touching them, were groves of oak and pine. The river pursues its bright unwearied course through this enchanting landscape, now falling in cascades, now winding placidly at the foot of the silent hills and among the dark woods, and in one part forming a most beautiful natural bath, by pouring its waters into an enclosure of large, smooth, flat stones, overshadowed by noble trees.

A number of the old Indian customs are still kept up here, modified by the introduction of Christian doctrines, in their marriages, feasts, burials, and superstitious practices. They also preserve the same simplicity in their dress, united with the same vanity and love of show in their ornaments, which always distinguished them. The poorest Indian woman still wears a necklace of red coral, or a dozen rows of red beads, and their dishes are still the *gicalli,* or, as they were called by the Spaniards, *gicaras,* made of a species of gourd, or rather a fruit resembling it, and growing on a low tree, which fruit they cut in two, each one furnishing two dishes; the inside is scooped out, and a durable varnish given it by means of a mineral earth, of different bright colours, generally red. On the outside they paint flowers, and some of them are also gilded. They are extremely pretty, very durable and ingenious. The beautiful colours which they employ in painting these *gicaras* are composed not only of various mineral productions, but of the wood, leaves, and flowers of certain plants, of whose properties they have no despicable knowledge. Their own dresses, manufactured by themselves of cotton, are extremely pretty, and many of them very fine.

December 1st.—We rode out early this morning, and passing through the lanes bordered with fruit trees, and others covered with blossoms of extraordinary beauty, of whose names I only know the *floripundio*, ascended into the pine woods, fragrant and gay with wild thyme, and bright flowers; the river falling in small cascades among the rocks. After riding along these heights for about two leagues, we arrived at the edge of a splendid valley of oaks. Here we were obliged to dismount, and to make our way on foot down the longest, steepest, and most slippery of paths, winding in rapid descent through the woods; with the prospect of being repaid for our toil, by the sight of the celebrated Falls of the *Sararaqui*. After having descended to the foot of the oak-covered mountain, we came to a great enclosure of lofty rocks, prodigious natural bulwarks, through a great cavern in which the river comes thundering and boiling into the valley, forming the great cascade of the Sararaqui, which in the Tarrascan language means *sieve*. It is a very fatiguing descent, but it is worth while to make the whole journey from Mexico, to see anything so wildly grand. The falls are from fifty to sixty feet high, and of great volume. The rocks are covered with shrubs and flowers, with small jets of water issuing from every crevice. One lovely flower, that looks as if it were formed of small white and rose-coloured shells, springs out of the stones near the water. There are rattlesnakes among the woods, and wild boars have occasionally been seen. The Señoritas Y——, when children, two or three years ago, wandering among these mountain-paths, saw an immense rattlesnake coiled up, and tempted by its gaudy colours, were about to lift it, when it suddenly wakened from its slumber, uncoiled itself, and swiftly glided up the path before them, its rattles sounding all the way up amongst the hills.

We sat beside the falls for a long while, looking at the boiling, hissing, bubbling, foaming waters, rolling down headlong with such impetuous velocity that one could hardly believe they form part of the same placid stream, which flows so gently between its banks, when no obstacles oppose it; and at all the little silvery threads of water, that formed mimic cascades among the rocks; but at length we were obliged to recommence our toilsome march up the slippery mountain. We were accompanied by several officers—amongst others, by the commandant of Uruapa.

Señor —— says that they are at present occupied here at the instigation of a Frenchman, named *Genould*, in planting a large collection of mulberry-trees, (which prosper wonderfully well in this climate) for the propagation of silkworms. But they have no facilities for transport, and at what market could the silk be sold? There are a thousand improvements wanting here, which would be more profitable than this speculation. They have sugar, corn, maize, minerals, wood, cotton, water for machinery; every valuable and important produce, all requiring their more immediate attention. We had a pleasant ride home, and when we got back amongst the lanes leading to the village, stopped every moment to admire and wonder at the rare and beautiful blossoms on the trees; and pulled branches of flowers off them, more delicate and lovely than the rarest exotics in an English hothouse.

2nd.—This morning, the weather was damp and rainy, but in the afternoon we took a long walk, and visited several Indian cottages, all clean, and the walls hung with fresh mats, the floors covered with the same; and all with their kitchen utensils of baked earth, neatly hung on the wall, from the largest size in use, to little dishes and *jarritos* in miniature, which are only placed there for ornament. We also went to purchase *gicaras,* and to see the operation of making and painting them, which is very curious. The flowers are not painted, but inlaid. We were fortunate in procuring a good supply of the prettiest, which cannot be procured anywhere else. We bought a very pretty *sutunacua,* and a black reboso. The women were not at all anxious to sell their dresses, as they make them with great trouble, and preserve them with great care.

We had a beautiful walk to the Magdalena, about a mile from the village. Every day we discover new beauties in the environs. And one beauty we saw on entering a small rancho, where they were painting gicaras at a table, while a woman lay in the shaking fever in a bed adjoining, which was quite consistent with the place. This was a lady, the proprietress of a good estate some leagues off, who was seated on her own trunk, outside the door of the rancho. She was a beautiful woman in her prime, the gentlemen said *passée,* and perhaps at eighteen she may have been more charming still; but now she was a model for a Judith—or rather for a Joan of Arc, even though sitting on her own luggage. She was very fair, with large black eyes, long eyelashes, and a profusion of hair as black as jet. Her teeth were literally dazzling—her lips like the reddest coral —her colour glowing as the down upon a ripe peach. Her figure was tall and full, with small, beautifully-formed hands, and fine arms. She rose as we came in, and begged us to be seated on a bench near the door; and with the unceremoniousness of travellers who meet in outlandish places, we entered into conversation with her. She told us her name, and her motives for travelling, and gave us an account of an adventure she had had with the robbers, of which she was well fitted to be the heroine. It appears that she was travelling with her two sons, lads of fifteen and sixteen, when they arrived at this rancho to rest for the night; for by this time you will understand that those who travel hereabouts must trust to chance or to hospitality for a night's lodging. To their surprise, they found the farmers gone, their dogs gone, and the house locked. They had no alternative but to rest as they could, among their luggage and mules, in the yard in front of the house. In the middle of the night they were attacked by robbers. The boys instantly took their guns, and fired, but without effect. Still, in the darkness, the robbers probably imagined that there were more people and more arms, and when she, dragging a loaded musket off one of the horses, prepared to join in the engagement, the cowardly ruffians took flight—a good half dozen before a woman and two boys. She was particularly indignant at the farmers, these "*malditos rancheros*," as she called them, who she said had been bribed or frightened into withdrawing their dogs and themselves.

We returned home after a long walk in the dark, and in the midst of all the howling, yelping, snarling, barking dogs, which rushed out as we went by, from every cottage in Uruapa.

After supper they sent for a clever Indian girl, who understands Spanish as well as her native idiom, and who translated various Castilian words for us into the original Tarrascan, which sounds very liquid and harmonious. To-morrow we shall leave Uruapa and this hospitable family, whose kindness and attention to us we never can forget. It seems incredible that we have only known them a few days. We have, however, the hopes of seeing them again as we pass through Valladolid, where they intend removing in a few days.

PASCUARO, 4th December.

We left Uruapa yesterday morning at eleven o'clock, accompanied part of the way by Señor Ysasaga and another gentleman, amongst whom was Madame Yturbide's brother. We are now returning to Morelia, but avoided *Curu* and the rocks, both to save our animals, and for the sake of variety. We rode through large tracts of land, all belonging to the Indians. The day was agreeable and cloudy, and the road, as usual, led us through beautiful scenery, monotonous in description, and full of variety in fact. Though nearly uninhabited, and almost entirely uncultivated, it has pleased nature to lavish so much beauty on this part of the country, that there is nothing melancholy in its aspect; no feeling of dreariness in riding a whole day, league after league, without seeing a trace of human life. These forest paths always appear as if they must, in time, lead to some habitation; the woods, the groves, the clumps of trees, seem as if they had been disposed, or at least beautified by the hand of art. We cannot look on these smiling and flowery valleys, and believe that such lovely scenes are always untenanted—that there are no children occasionally picking up these apricots—no village girls to pluck these bright, fragrant flowers. We fancy that they are out in the fields, and will be there in the evening, and that their hamlet is hid behind the slope of the next hill; and it is only when we come to some Indian hut, or cluster of poor cabins in the wilderness, that we are startled by the conviction that this enchanting variety of hill and plain, wood and water, is for the most part unseen by human eye, and untrod by human footsteps.

We had no further adventure during this day's journey, than buying bread and cheese from sheer hunger, at a little wooden tavern by the road-side, whose shelves were covered with glittering rows of bottles of brandy and *mezcal*. At some of the Indian huts also we bought various branches of *platanos*, that most useful of fruits, and basis of the food of the poor inhabitants of all the tropical climates. It has been said that the banana is not indigenous in America, and that it was brought over by a friar to Santo Domingo. If so, its adopted country agrees with it better than its native land; but I believe there are many traditions which go to prove that it did already exist in this hemisphere before the sixteenth century, and that the Spaniards did no more than increase the number of the already indigenous species. Its nutritive qualities, and the wonderful facility with which it is propagated, render it at once the most useful of trees, and the greatest possible incentive to indolence. In less than one year after it is planted the fruit may be gathered and the proprietor has but to cut away the old stems and leave a sucker, which will produce fruit three months after. There are different sorts of bananas, and they are used in different ways; fresh, dried, fried, etc. The dried plantain, a great branch of trade in Michoacan, with its black shrivelled skin and flavour of smoked fish or ham, is exceedingly liked by the natives. It is, of all Mexican articles of food, my peculiar aversion.

About four o'clock we arrived at the small village of Tziracuaratiro, a collection of Indian cottages, with little gardens, surrounded by orange and all manner of fruit trees. As we had still one or two hours of daylight, and this was our next halting-place, we wandered forth on foot to explore the environs, and found a beautiful shady spot, a grassy knoll, sheltered by the surrounding woods, where we sat down to rest and to inhale the balmy air, fragrant with orange-blossoms. We were amused by a sly-looking Indian, of whom C——n asked some questions, and who was exceedingly talkative, giving us an account of his whole *ménage*, and especially praising beyond measure his own exemplary conduct to his wife, from which I infer that he beats her, as indeed all Indians consider it their particular privilege to do; and an Indian woman who complained to a padre of her husband's neglect, mentioned, as the crowning proof of his utter abandonment of her, that he had not given her a beating for a whole fortnight. Some one asked him if he allowed his wife to govern him. "Oh! no," said he, "that would be the mule leading the arriero!"

There was nothing to be seen in the village, of which it hardly deserves the name, but a good-looking old church, which two old women were sweeping out; but they told us they rarely had mass there, as the padre lived a long way off. The alcalde permitted us and our escort to occupy his house, consisting of three empty rooms with mud floors; and about seven the next morning we were again on horseback, and again *en route* for Pascuaro; a pretty ride of eleven or twelve leagues. We breakfasted at the village of *Ajuna*, in a clean hut where they gave us quantities of tortillas and chile, baked by some very handsome *tortilleras*. A number of women were carrying about a virgin all covered with flowers, to the sound of a little bell.

It was about four o'clock when we arrived at the hills near

Pascuaro. Here we dismounted from our horses, and remained till it was nearly dusk, laying on the grass, and gazing on the lake, as the shadows of evening stole slowly over its silver waters. Little by little the green islands became indistinct; a gray vapour concealed the opposite shores; and like a light breath spread gradually over the mirrored surface of the lake. Then we remounted our horses, and rode down into Pascuaro, where we found the Señor H——a as before, ready to receive us, and where, our mules being disabled, we proposed remaining one or two days.

5th.—We have been spending a quiet day in Pascuaro, and went to mass in the old church, which is handsome and rich in gilding. At the door is printed in large letters—"For the love of God, all good Christians are requested not to spit in this holy place." If we might judge from the observation of one morning, I should say that the better classes in Pascuaro are fairer and have more colour than is general in Mexico; and if this is so, it may be owing partly to the climate being cooler and damper, and partly to their taking more exercise (there being no carriages here), whereas in Mexico no family of any importance can avoid having one.

We were very anxious to see some specimens of that mosaic-work which all ancient writers upon Mexico have celebrated, and which was nowhere brought to such perfection as in Pascuaro. It was made with the most beautiful and delicate feathers, chiefly of the *picaflores*, the humming-birds, which they called *huitzitzilin*. But we are told that it is now upwards of twenty years since the last artist in this branch lived in Pascuaro; and though it is imitated by the nuns, the art is no longer in the state of perfection to which it was brought in the days of Cortes. We are told that several persons were employed in each painting, and that it was a work requiring extraordinary patience and nicety, in the blending of the colours, and in the arrangement of the feathers. The sketch of the figure was first made, and the proportions being measured, each artist took charge of one particular part of the figure or of the drapery. When each had finished his share, all the different parts were reunited, to form the picture. The feathers were first taken up with some soft substance with the utmost care, and fastened with a glutinous matter upon a piece of stuff; then, the different parts being reunited, were placed on a plate of copper, and gently polished, till the surface became quite equal, when they appeared like the most beautiful paintings, or, according to these writers, more beautiful from the splendour and liveliness of the colours, the bright golden, and blue, and crimson tints, than the paintings which they imitated. Many were sent to Spain, and to different museums both in Europe and Mexico; but the art is now nearly lost, nor does it belong to the present utilitarian age. Our forefathers had more leisure than we, and probably we have more than our descendants will have, who, for aught we know, may, by extra high-pressure, be able to

"Put a girdle round about the earth in forty minutes."

We, however, saw some few specimens of saints and angels, very defective in the sketch, but beautiful in the colouring, and quite sufficient to prove to us that there was no exaggeration in these accounts.

7th.—We rode yesterday to the shores of the lake, where we embarked in a long canoe, formed of the hollow trunk of a tree, and rowed by Indians, a peculiarly ugly race, with Tartar-looking faces. The lake was very placid, clear as one vast mirror, and covered with thousands of wild ducks, white egrets, cranes, and herons—all those waterfowl who seem to whiten their plumage by constant dipping in pools and marshes and lakes. On the opposite shore, to the right, lay the city of Tzinzunzan; and on a beautiful island in the midst of the lake the village of *Janicho,* entirely peopled by Indians, who mingle little with the dwellers on the mainland, and have preserved their originality more than any we have yet seen. We were accompanied by the prefect of Pascuaro, whom the Indians fear and hate in equal ratio, and who did seem a sort of Indian *Mr. Bumble;* and, after a long and pleasant row, we landed at the island, where we were received by the village alcalde, a half-caste Indian, who sported a pair of bright blue merino pantaloons! I suppose to distinguish himself from his blanketed brethren. The island is entirely surrounded by a natural screen of willow- and ash-trees, and the village consists of a few scattered houses, with small cultivated patches of ground, the alcalde's house, and an old church.

We walked, or rather climbed, all over the island, which is hilly and rocky, and found several great stones entirely covered with the ancient carving. Moved by curiosity, we entered various caverns where idols have been found, and amongst others one large cave, which we had no sooner groped our way into than I nearly fell down suffocated by the horrible and most pestilential atmosphere. It appears that it is the sleeping-place of all the bats in the island; and heaven forbid that I should ever again enter a bat's bedchamber! I groped my way out again as fast as possible, heedless of idols and all other antiquities, seized a *cigarito* from the hand of the astonished prefect, who was wisely smoking at the entrance, lighted it, and inhaled the smoke, which seemed more fragrant than violets, after that stifling and most unearthly odour.

The chief food of these islanders, besides the gourds and other vegetables which they cultivate, is the white fish, for which the lake is celebrated; and while we were exploring the island, the Indians set off in their canoes to catch some for us. These were fried at the alcalde's and we made a breakfast upon them which would have rejoiced the heart of an epicure.

We then went to visit the church; and, though the cottages are poor, the church is, as usual, handsome. Amongst other curiosities there is a Virgin, entirely covered with Indian embroidery. The organist's place is hereditary in an Indian family, descending from father to son. The long-haired Indian who played it for us has such a gentle expression and beardless face, that he looks like a very young woman. Some of the Indians here are very rich, and bury their money; and one, called Agustin Campos, who has beautified the church, as we read on an inscription carved on a stone outside, has thirty thousand dollars, is much respected, and has the addition of *Don* to his name, yet wears a coarse blanket like his fellowmen. We staid some hours on the island, and went into some of the huts, where the women were baking tortillas, one Indian custom, at least, which has descended to these days without variation. They first cook the grain in water with a little lime, and when it is soft peel off the skin; then grind it on a large block of stone, the *metate*, or, as the Indians (who know best) call it, the *metatl*. For the purpose of grinding it, they use a sort of stone roller, with which it is crushed, and rolled into a bowl placed below the stone. They then take some of this paste, and clap it between their hands till they form it into light round cakes, which are afterwards toasted on a smooth plate, called the *comalli* (*comal* they call it in Mexico), and which ought to be eaten as hot as possible.

On our return, we had the variety of a slight storm, which ruffled the placid surface of the lake, and caused the rowers to exert all their strength to bring the canoe to port before it should become more violent.

This morning we walked all through Pascuaro, which can boast of many good houses, a square and portales, and ended by going to visit the convent of Santa Catarina. We saw some of the nuns, who wear white dresses, and, instead of veils, the black Indian reboso. They were common-looking women, and not very amiable in their manners; but we did not go further than the outside entry. On our return we met a remarkable baby in arms, wearing an enormous white satin turban, with a large plume of white feathers on one side, balanced on the other by huge bunches of yellow ribbons and pink roses. It also wore two robes, a short and a long one, both trimmed all round with large plaitings of yellow satin ribbon. It was evidently very much admired as it passed along. To-morrow, our mules having recovered, we set off for Valladolid.

VALLADOLID, 9th.

About half-past seven we left Pascuaro, which, considering that we had a long day's journey before us, was scarce early enough. We regretted very much taking leave of the Señora H——a, who has been so kind to us, and whom we can certainly never hope to see again. I observe that in these long days' journeys we generally set off in silence, and sometimes ride on for hours without exchanging a word. Towards the middle of the day we grow more talkative, and again towards evening we relapse into quiet. I suppose it is that in the morning we are sleepy, and towards evening begin to grow tired—feeling sociable about nine o'clock, a.m., and not able to talk for a longer period than eight or ten hours. It was about four in the afternoon when we reached Cuincho, where we were welcomed by the damsels of the baths, whose father is now still more of an invalid than before. It is a lonely life that these poor girls lead here, nor should I think their position a very secure one. Their poverty, however, is a safeguard to a certain extent, and there are few robbers in this country in the style of Morales. We were tempted to stop here and take a bath, in consequence of which it was dark when we set off for Morelia. The horses, unable to see, took enormous leaps over every little streamlet and ditch, so that we seemed to be riding a steeple-chase in the dark. Our gowns caught upon the thorny bushes, and our journey might have been traced by the tatters we left behind us. At length we rode the wrong way, up a stony hill, which led us to a wretched little village of about thirty huts, each having ten dogs on an average, according to the laudable custom of the Indians. Out they all rushed simultaneously, yelping like three hundred demons, biting the horses' feet, and springing round us. Between this canine concert, the kicking of the horses, the roar of a waterfall close beside us, the shouting of people telling us to come back, and the pitch darkness, I thought we should all have gone distracted. We did, however, make our way out from amongst the dogs, re-descended the stony hill, the horses leaping over various streamlets that crossed their path, turned into the right road, and entered the gates of Morelia without further adventure, between nine and ten o'clock.

MORELIA, 11th.

We have passed the last few days very agreeably in this beautiful city, seeing everything worthy of notice, and greatly admiring the wide and airy streets, the fine houses, the handsome public buildings, but especially the cathedral, the college, and the churches. It has also a fine square, with broad piazzas occupying three of its sides, while the cathedral bounds it to the east. There is a crowded market in the plaza, and a fine display of fruit and vegetables. The population is said to be a little upwards of fifteen thousand, but one would suppose it to be much greater. Living and house-rent is so cheap here, that a family who could barely exist upon their means in Mexico, may enjoy every luxury in Valladolid. The climate is delightful, and there is something extremely cheerful in the aspect of the city, in which it differs greatly from Toluca. We received visits from various *Morelians*, amongst others from Don Cayetano Gomez, the proprietor of San Bartolo.

We went one evening to the alameda, a broad, straight walk, paved with flat stones, shaded by fine trees, under which are stone benches, and bounded by a low stone wall. Several ladies were sitting there, whom we joined, and amongst others, a remarkably pretty *Poblana*, married into the Gomez family. The alameda is crossed by a fine aqueduct of solid masonry, with light and elegant arches. We drove to the *paséo*, a broad, shady road, where we met but few carriages; and the same evening we went out on foot to enjoy the music of a very good military band, which plays occasionally for the amusement of the citizens. It is not to be supposed that, when Mexico can boast of so little society, there should be much in a provincial town; besides, this city has the pretension of being divided into *cliques*, and there are "first people," and "second-rate people," and "families in our set," and so on; so that some of the ladies being musicians, one set will get up a concert, another a rival concert, and there not being a sufficient musical society to fill two concerts, both fall to the ground. There is a neat little theatre, but at present no company. Some of the houses are as handsome as any in Mexico, but there is no city which has fallen off so much since the Independence as Morelia, according to the accounts given us by the most respectable persons.

We had a visit from the bishop, Señor Portugal, one of the most distinguished men here, or in fact in the whole republic of Mexico, a man of great learning, gentle and amiable in his manners, and in his life a model of virtue and holiness. He was in the cabinet when Santa Anna was president, concerning which circumstance an amusing story was told us, for the correctness of which I do not vouch, but the narrator, a respectable citizen here, certainly believed it. Señor Portugal had gone, by appointment, to see the president on some important business, and they had but just begun their consultation, when Santa Anna rose and left the room. The minister waited—the president did not return. The time passed on, and still the minister continued expecting him, until at length he inquired of an aide-de-camp in waiting, if he could inform him how soon the president might be expected back. "I hardly know," said the officer, "for his excellency has gone to visit *Cola de plata*" (silver tail). "And who may *Cola de plata* be?" said the minister. "A favourite cock of his excellency's, wounded this morning in a fight which he won, and to whose care he is now personally attending!" The bishop soon after sent in his resignation.

Accompanied by several of our friends, including one of the canons of the cathedral, we visited that splendid building the second day of our arrival. It is still wonderfully rich, notwithstanding that silver to the amount of thirty-two thousand marks has been taken from it during the civil wars. The high altar is dazzling with gold and silver; the railing which leads from it to the choir is of pure silver, with pillars of the same metal; the two pulpits, with their stairs, are also covered with silver; and the general ornaments, though numerous and rich, are disposed with good taste, are kept in order, and have nothing tawdry or loaded in their general effect. The choir itself is extremely beautiful; so also is the carved screen before the organ, the doors of the first being of solid silver, and those of the other of richly-carved wood. There is also an immense silver font, and superb lamps of silver. We particularly admired some fine paintings, chiefly by Cabrera, and especially a Madonna and child, in which there is that most divine expression in the face of the Virgin, the blending of maternal love with awe for the divinity of the child. Four of these paintings, it is said, were sent here by a Spanish king, as far back as Philip II. These four are colossal in size, and are finely painted, but little cared for or appreciated, and placed in a bad light.

We were shown two saints, sent from Rome, loaded with false jewels, but carefully preserved in their respective shrines. All the holy vessels and priests' dresses and jewels were taken out for our inspection. The sacramental *custodia* cost thirty-two thousand dollars, and the richest of the dresses eight thousand. There is a lamb made of one pearl, the fleece and head of silver; the pearl of great size and value.

We toiled up through winding staircases to the belfry; and it required the beautiful and extensive landscape spread out before us, to compensate us for this most fatiguing ascent. The bells are of copper, and very sonorous. The *canonigo* pointed out to us all the different sites which had been the scenes of bloody battles during the revolutionary war. The facilities for obtaining provisions, and the mountainous character of the country, are amongst the causes that have rendered this province the theatre of civil war. The padre afterwards took us into a large apartment, a sort of office, hung round with the portraits of all the bishops of Michoacan; one bearing so striking a resemblance to our friend, Don Francisco Tagle, that we were not surprised to find that it was in fact the portrait of one of his family, who had occupied the episcopal see of Michoacan; and below it were the Tagle arms, referring to some traditionary exploit of their ancestors. They represent a knight killing a serpent; and the motto is—"Tagle que la serpiente mató y con la Princesa casó" (Tagle who killed the serpent, and married the Princess).

The same evening, we visited a lady who possesses a most singular and curious collection of works in wax; and more extraordinary still, they are all her own workmanship. Every fruit and every vegetable production is represented by her with a fidelity, which makes it impossible to distinguish between her imitations and the works of nature. Plates with bread, radishes, and fish; dishes of fowls, and chile, and eggs; baskets full of the most delicious-looking fruit; lettuces, beans, carrots, tomatoes, etc.; all are copied with the most extraordinary exactness. But her figures show much greater talent. There are groups for which an amateur might offer any price, could she be prevailed upon to offer these masterpieces for sale. There is a Poblana peasant on horseback before a ranchero, looking back at him with the most coquettish expression; her dress perfection, from the straw hat that half shades her features, to the beautiful little ankle and foot in the white satin shoe, the short embroidered petticoat, and the reboso thrown over one shoulder; a handsome Indian, selling pulque and brandy in her little shop, with every variety of liquor temptingly displayed in rows of shining bottles, to her customers; the grouping and colouring perfect, and the whole interior arrangement of the shop, imitated with the most perfect exactness. There is also a horrid representation, frightfully correct, of a dead body in a state of corruption, which it makes one sick to look at, and which it is inconceivable that any one can have had pleasure in executing. In short, there is scarcely anything in nature upon which her talent has not exercised itself.

Yesterday we visited the *Seminario,* or college, a fine spacious old building, kept in good repair. The rector conducted us over the whole establishment. There is a small well chosen library, containing all the most classic works in Spanish, German, French, and English; and a larger library, containing Greek and Latin authors, theological works, etc., a large hall, with chemical and other scientific apparatus, and a small chapel where there is a beautiful piece of sculpture in wood: the *San Pedro,* by a young man, a native of Valladolid, so exquisitely wrought, that one cannot but regret that such a genius should be buried here, should not at least have the advantage of some years' study in Italy, where he might become a second Canova.

One must visit these distant cities, and see these great establishments, to be fully aware of all that the Spaniards bestowed upon their colonies, and also to be convinced of the regret for former times which is felt amongst the most distinguished men of the republic; in fact, by all who are old enough to compare what has been with what is.

I ought not to omit, in talking of the natural productions of Valladolid, to mention that it is famous for *fleas.* We had been alarmed by the miraculous stories related to us of these vivacious animals, and were rejoiced to find ourselves in a house, from which, by dint of extreme care, they are banished. But in the inns and inferior houses they are said to be a perfect pestilence, sometimes literally walking away with a piece of matting upon the floor, and covering the walls in myriads. The nuns, it is said, are or were in the habit of harnessing them to little carriages, and of showing them off by other ingenious devices.

We rode out in the evening to meet our friends from Uruapa, who were expected to arrive yesterday; I upon a very formidable and handsome cavalry-horse, rather above his work, which some expected to run away, and others to throw me off, and which might have done both, but being a noble creature did neither. We did not meet our friends, who, having been delayed on the road, only arrived this evening. We have therefore decided to remain here till to-morrow afternoon, when we shall continue our journey homewards by San Bartolo.

LETTER THE FIFTY-FIRST

San Bartolo—Mass—Market—Rancheros—San Andrés—Insanity —Rancho—House of Don Carlos Heimbürger—Wild Scenery —German Songs—Las Millas—Leave-taking—Storm—Rainbow—El Pilar—La Gabia—Toluca—News—Copper Pronunciamiento—Return to Mexico—General Moran—Funeral Obsequies—New Theatre—Cock's Mass—Santa Clara—Santa Fé Prisoners—New Year.

ANGANGUEO, 14th.

After taking leave of all our hospitable friends in Morelia, we set off in the afternoon, and had a delightful ride to San Bartolo. Fortunately the following day (Sunday) was that of the Virgin of Guadalupe, one of the greatest festivals here; so that we had an opportunity of seeing all the people from the different villages, who arrived in the courtyard by daybreak, and held a market in front of the hacienda. Various were the articles for sale, and picturesque the dresses of the sellers. From cakes, chile, atole, and ground-nuts, to rebosos and bead rosaries, nothing was omitted. In one part of the market the sturdy rancheros were drinking pulque and devouring hot cakes; in another, little boys were bargaining for nuts and bananas; countrywomen were offering low prices for smart rebosos; an Indian woman was recommending a comb, with every term of endearment, to a young country-girl, who seemed perfectly ignorant of its use, assuring her customer that it was an instrument for unravelling the hair, and making it beautiful and shining, and enforcing her argument by combing through some of the girl's tangled locks.

Before breakfast we went to mass in the large chapel of the hacienda. We and the family went to the choir; and the body of the chapel was filled with rancheros and their wives. It is impossible to see anywhere a finer race of men than these rancheros—tall, strong, and well made, with their embroidered shirts, coarse sarapes, and dark blue pantaloons embroidered in gold. After mass, the marketing recommenced, and the rebosos had a brisk sale. A number were bought by the men for their wives, or *novias*, at home; which reminds me of a story of ——s of a poor Indian woman in their village, who desired her husband to buy a *petticoat* for her in Mexico, where he was going to sell his vegetables. She particularly impressed upon him that she wished it to be *the colour of the sky,* which at sunrise, when he was setting off, was of a flaming red. He returned in the evening, bringing, to her great indignation, a petticoat of a dusky gray, which happened to be the colour of the sky when he made his purchase.

In the evening we rode through the fields, the servants and the young master of the house amusing themselves as they went, by the chasing and *colear* of the bulls. They have one small, ugly, yellow-coloured bull, which they call tame, and which the *mozos* ride familiarly. They persuaded me to try this novel species of riding, a man holding the animal's head with a rope; but I thought that it tossed its horns in a most uncomfortable and alarming manner, and very soon slipped off. We stopped during our ride, at a house where the proprietors make a small fortune by the produce of their numerous beehives; and walked along the banks of a fine clear river, winding through beautiful and verdant groves.

The next morning by six o'clock we were again on horseback, and took leave of San Bartolo. We rode by *Yndaparapeo,* a considerable village, with sloping shingle roofs; and about ten reached Querendaro, breakfasted with Señor Pimentel, and then continued our journey towards San Andrés, where we were to pass the night. We had a horse with us which occasionally fell down on the road, shivering all over, groaning, and apparently dying; but which had twice recovered from these fits. But this day, having stopped beside a running stream to water our horses, the unfortunate beast fell again, and when we had remounted, and were riding forward, a servant galloped after us, to tell us that the horse was dead at last; so we left him to his lonely grave by the river's side. Great, therefore, was our amazement, when, some time after, we perceived him trotting along the road at a great rate, in pursuit of his party, apparently quite recovered.

We passed the night at San Andrés, a poor *venta,* but clean, consisting of three empty rooms, a spirit-shop, and a kitchen. Our escort slept in the piazza, rolled in their sarapes. Our beds were stuck up in the empty rooms, and we got some supper upon fowl and tortillas. We were interested by the melancholy air of a poor woman, who sat aloof on the piazza, uncared for, and noticing no one. We spoke to her, and found that she was insane, wandering from village to village, and subsisting on charity. She seemed gentle and harmless, but the very picture of misery, and quite alone in the world, having lost all her family. But "God tempers the wind to the shorn lamb." We saw her again in the morning before we set off, and saw her get some breakfast in the kitchen. The poor people of the *venta* seemed kind to her. They who dwell in comfortable houses, surrounded by troops of friends, and who repine at their lot, would do well to compare it with that of such a being.

This morning we left San Andrés, and have had a pleasant ride, in spite of a hard-trotting horse, which fell to my lot. Impossible to conceive more beautiful scenery than that which we passed through to-day. Some of the hills have a singular formation, each large hill appearing composed of a variety of smaller ones, of a pyramidal shape. We rode through Taximaroa without stopping, and breakfasted at a rancho, where the whole family were exceedingly handsome. The ranchero himself was a model for a fine-looking farmer, hospitable and well-bred; knowing his place, yet without any servility. The rancherita, who was engaged in the kitchen, was so handsome, that we made every possible excuse for going to look at her.

About four o'clock we once more crossed the hills and came down upon the plains by which we left Angangueo; and passed over a river as red as blood, that looked as if hostile armies had been engaged in fierce combat by its banks, and their bodies rolled in the tide. This ensanguined hue is, however, caused, not by warlike steel, but by peaceful copper; not peaceful in its effects, by the way, at this moment, for the whole country, more or less, is in commotion on the subject of copper coin.

You must know, that some few years ago, the value of copper was suddenly reduced by law to one half, causing a great loss to all, but much distress to the poor. The intrinsic value of the copper, however, bore so little relation to the value given to it, that it was a very productive business to counterfeit it, of which many unprincipled individuals availed themselves to such an extent, that it had almost become an openly exercised branch of industry all through the republic. When Santa Anna became provisional president, he ordered that all the copper coin, whose currency was now reduced to six or eight per cent. below par, should be given in to certain deposits which he named, promising to repay it in genuine coin of real value. But this naturally caused a still greater depreciation, bringing it down as low as sixty per cent.; and still greater discontent, the people having little faith in the promise, and, in fact, the pay-

ment could not be made at the appointed time, because there
were not sufficient coining machines; and as the few new cents
that did circulate, were said not to contain their real value, the
distress became greater than ever. The merchants refused to
receive copper, and there was no silver or small change. In
the mean time, in many of the large haciendas, the proprietors
have given checks to the workmen, with which they have been
able to buy what they required at the shops, which are attached to these haciendas.

The amount of the copper in circulation cannot be calculated, for it is almost all counterfeit. It is supposed, however,
to be at least from eight to nine millions of dollars. You may
easily imagine the fortunes that will be made (and as they
say are being made) by those of the government party, who
are buying up for sixty, what will be paid them by favour of
the government at the rate of a hundred.

We rode up the hills that lead to the house of Don Carlos
Heimbürger, and were again hospitably received by him and
his German friends. Nothing can have a finer effect than the
view from the piazza of his house in the evening, looking down
upon the valley. The piazza itself has a screen of green creepers, which have the effect of a curtain of a theatre half drawn
up. Behind the house rises a dark frowning hill, in the form of
a pyramid. In front is the deep ravine, with the huts of the
workmen, and while the moon throws her quivering beams
over the landscape, the metallic fires of livid blue light up the
valley. There is something wild and diabolic in the scene; and
as the wind howls round the valley with a dismal sound, it
seems as if one were looking on at some unholy, magical incantation; so that it is pleasant to return after a while to the
comfortable rooms and cheerful fires within, which have so
homely and domestic an air. We hope to spend to-morrow
here, and the following day to go on to Toluca, from whence
I shall continue my letter.

TOLUCA, 19th.

The next day we visited the works, which are like all others,
excepting that here they do not use quicksilver to extract the
silver from the lead, but do so by the process of oxidation, by
the means of a reverberatory furnace. The people generally
have an unhealthy appearance, as nearly all have who are engaged in these works—the air being loaded with particles of
metal. After visiting the mills and the sheds where the process

of oxidation is carried on, and admiring the metallic riches of these mountains, we left the hot and poisoned atmosphere, and walked up the mountains clothed with a hardy vegetation—with every noble tree and flowering shrub—and pursued our course till we came to a fine waterfall, which plunges from a great height over the gigantic rocks.

The scenery here is rude and wild. The great rocks are covered with hardy trees—the pine, the cedar, the oak, and the flowering laurel. The river, after dashing down in this noble cascade, runs brawling amongst the forest-clothed hills, till it reaches the plains, and flows on placidly. We spent an agreeable day, wandering amongst the mountains; and when we returned sat on the piazza to watch the moon as her broad disk rose over the valley, and the fierce blue lights that made her mild fires grow pale.

All Germans are musical, and the gentlemen in this house did not belie the national reputation. After dinner, a bright fire blazing, doors and windows shutting out the cold air that whistled along the hills, they struck up in chorus some of the finest national airs, particularly the Hymn to the Rhine—so that it seemed an illusion that we were in this wild, mining district, inhabited only by the poorest Indians; and we were transported thousands of miles off, across the broad Atlantic, even to the land where

> "The castled crag of Drachenfels
> Frowns o'er the broad and winding Rhine."

We also amused ourselves by examining Madame B——'s Album; and if those milk-and-water volumes, belonging to young ladies, where young gentlemen write prettinesses, be called Albums, some other name should be found for a book where some of the most distinguished artists in Germany have left proofs of their talent, and where there is not one page which does not contain something striking and original. Nothing pleased me so much as the fanciful illustration of the beautiful legend of *Lorelei*, which Madame B—— read to us with great feeling. We became too comfortable here for hardy equestrian travellers, and had we staid much longer should have begun to complain of tough fowls, beds in barns, and other inconveniences, which we had hitherto laughed at; but we tore ourselves away from our Capua, and on the morning of the sixteenth set off for *El Pilar*.

Don Carlos Heimbürger, M. and Madame B——, etc., accompanied us for seven leagues, all through the woods. We had a delightful ride, the day was cool and cloudy, and we were besides, constantly shaded by the noble forest trees. But we had not reached Las Millas before the sky was overcast, the clouds became black and gloomy, and at length broke out in rain. We galloped fast, for the day, besides being rainy, was cold; and in the afternoon reached Las Millas. Here we breakfasted in the little portico, which we preferred to the interior of the cottage, chiefly upon tortillas and boiled *tejocotes*, a fruit which grows in great abundance, and resembles a small apple. Here again were two Indian girls of admirable beauty, *dans leur genre*, baking tortillas. We were now obliged to part from our kind German friends, and to ride across the plains. But had not gone more than halfway, when the clouds burst forth in torrents, pouring their fury on our devoted heads, so that in five minutes we were all drenched as if we had fallen into a river. We took shelter for a little while under a solitary spreading tree, but the storm increased in violence, and it was advisable to gallop forwards, in order to arrive at El Pilar before it became dark. Suddenly, the most beautiful rainbow I ever beheld smiled out from amongst the watery clouds. It formed a complete and well-defined arch of the most brilliant colours in the heavens, reflected by another on the plains, which, uniting with it, blended its fainter hues with the light of the heavenly bow.

We arrived at El Pilar tired and drenched, and greatly in need of the hospitable reception which was given to us by its mistress.

The following morning we set off early for *La Gabia*, feeling some regret that our journey was drawing to a close. Some of us, who rode in front, found ourselves surrounded by several suspicious-looking, well-armed men on horseback, who, under pretence of asking some questions, rode very close to us, and then stopped and faced round on their horses—but there was no danger, our escort being at a short distance, and when they observed its approach, they bestowed no further attention upon us. Don Xavier Hechavarria had returned to Mexico, but we were cordially welcomed by his brother-in-law, Don Manuel Gorospe, and so kindly pressed to remain some days, that nothing but our limited time would have induced us to set off next morning for Toluca. Here we arrived last night, having performed our journey by a different and more agreeable road than that of the "three hundred barrancas." We entered Toluca by moonlight, and found that respectable city all in commotion on the subject of copper; presenting a

very different aspect from the quiet and conventual air of repose which distinguished it little more than a month ago. Yesterday Colonel Y——, who has accompanied us during all this
journey, left us, to return to Michoacan, having thus brought
us back in safety to the point from which we started.

We are spending a very tiresome day in the inn, which,
however, is a more decent place, and belongs to a better line of
coaches than the other. We have been enlivened by several
visits, amongst others, from the commandant, and from an
aide-de-camp of General Valencia's. For the first time since we
left it, we have news from Mexico. Santa Anna, *dit-on,* is now
Dictator or King, in all but the name; affecting more than
royal pomp, yet endeavouring by his affability to render himself popular. Above all, he has made known his determination
of not seizing an inch of ground belonging to the clergy;
which seizure of church property was the favourite idea of
Paredes and the *progresistas.* This resolution he has not
printed, probably in order not to disgust that party, but his
personal declaration to the archbishop and the padres of the
Profesa, and in a letter to the bishop of Puebla, is, that he will
not only leave their property untouched, but that, were he out
of power, he would draw his sword in their defence—for that,
good or bad, he is a sincere Catholic. This has done much to
re-establish him in the good opinion of the clergy, and it is
said that in every convent in Mexico, monks and nuns are now
wearying Heaven with prayers in his behalf. In short, the conquerors and the conquered, those of the Progress, and those
of the Dictatorship, seem all, barring a few noble exceptions,
actuated by one motive; personal interest.

Count C——a is restored to the command of his battalion *del
Comercio,* which has been re-established (it having deserted
to the federalists in the last revolution). It appears that the
president's favourite plan is to have thirty thousand men under arms; and there is little doubt that he will bring this about.
Sixteen new generals have been created; and General Tornel
is made a General of Division. The Señora V——a has given a
ball, at which she and other ladies appeared with trains, rehearsing, as it would seem, before the court drawing-rooms. I
was told, and by good authority, that the present sent by
Santa Anna to the lady of the commander-in-chief on her
birthday, was a box containing three general's belts, with a
request that she would bestow them on those whom she considered most deserving of them; and that the lady herself
buckled the sashes on her favoured knights, in her own bou-

doir. Thus was valour rewarded by the hand of beauty; and

"Thus should desert in arms be crowned."

Meanwhile the master of the house presents himself with a disturbed and gloomy countenance, and doubts much whether we can have any dinner to-day, because no one will sell anything, either for copper or silver; moreover hints darkly that they expect a *copper pronunciamiento* to-morrow; and observes that the shops are shut up.

Since we could get no dinner, we went out to take a walk; and methinks the Tolucanos have a fierce and agitated aspect. We attempted to go to mass this morning, but there was a congregation of léperos, who filled not only the church, but the whole enclosure and the street beyond, so that we could not even approach the church door. Unfortunately we cannot get a diligence until the 21st.

They have brought us at last, I will not say dinner—but something to eat.

20th.—This morning, the firing of squibs, the beating of drums, the shouting and confusion on the streets, announced that the ragamuffin population of Toluca had turned out; and going to the balcony, I very nearly received the salutation of

"A sky-
Rocket in my eye."

Orders have been given out by the alcalde, that copper shall be received in payment by the merchants, some of whom have declared they will only receive silver. A large mob has collected before the alcalde's door, with shouts of "Viva la plata! Muerta al cobre!" (Long live silver! Death to copper!)—apostrophizing these useful metals, as if they were two generals.

The merchants have issued a declaration, that during three days only, they will sell their goods for copper (of course at an immense advantage to themselves). The Indians and the poorer classes are now rushing to the shops, and buying goods, receiving in return for their copper about half its value. If Santa Anna keeps his word, the *patriotism* of the merchants will be rewarded.

C——n has just had a visit from one of the merchants, who wishes his conduct to be represented in a proper light in Mexico.

MEXICO, 22nd.

With much joy we stepped into the diligence early yesterday morning, accompanied by the commandant of Toluca, and
retraced our road to Mexico; for though Toluca is a fine city,
with clean, airy houses, wide, well-paved streets, and picturesque in its situation, there is something sad and deserted in
its appearance, an air of stagnation that weighs upon the
spirits; and the specimens we have seen of its lower orders are
not inviting. We had rather an agreeable journey, as the day
was cool, and we had the diligence to ourselves. We breakfasted again at Cuajimalpa, took leave of the interesting
itzcuin tepotzotli, still hanging from its hook—and again ascended the eminence from which Mexico suddenly bursts
upon the view, and after a short absence, with all the charms
of novelty. Before we arrived at Tacubaya, we were met by a
carriage containing Señor A—— and his lady, who insisted on
our leaving the diligence; and carried us off to their own house,
where we now are. On the second of January we expect to take
our final departure from the "great city of the lake."

December 28th.—Another old year about to chime in! Another Christmas past away! But during these last few days it
has been all in vain to attempt finishing my letter, between
making arrangements for our journey, receiving and returning
visits, going to the opera, and seeing and revisiting all that we
had left unseen or wished to see again before leaving this. People seem determined that we shall regret them, and load us
with kindness and attentions, the more flattering, that now at
least they are entirely personal, and cannot proceed from any
interested motive. We have reason to think them both steady
and sincere in their friendship.

General Moran has died, universally regretted. He has been
embalmed according to the system of *Ganal,* and his funeral
was performed with extraordinary magnificence, the troops
out, the foreign ministers and the cabinet following on foot,
the former in full uniform, and a great train of carriages reaching along the whole Calle San Francisco, from the church to
the square. The body, dressed in a general's uniform, was carried upon a splendid bier, and was so perfectly embalmed,
that he seemed not dead, nor even asleep, but lying in an at-
titude of repose. The expense of this operation will probably
prevent its ever becoming very common; and certainly there
are but few cases where it can be advisable to adopt it. An

embalmed dynasty might be a curious sight. To trace the features of a royal line, from Charlemagne to Charles X.—from Alfred to William IV., would be a strange study. Mary of Scotland and Elizabeth, lying in the repose of death, yet looking as they lived and hated centuries back, might be a curious piece of antiquity. A Hernan Cortes—a Washington—a Columbus—a Napoleon; men, whose memory for good or for evil, will survive time and change—it would be a strange and wondrous thing, if we could look on their features as they were in life. But it is to be trusted that this method of successfully wrestling with the earth for what it claims as its due, will not generally prevail; or, at the end of a few centuries, the embalmed population would scarce leave room for their living and breathing descendants: nor is it an agreeable idea that one might, in a lapse of ages, grace the study of an antiquary, or be preserved amongst the curiosities of a museum. I would stuff birds and beasts, and preserve them in cabinets, but not the remains of immortal man. *Dust unto dust;* and the eye of faith turned from the perishing remains to the spirit which has gone to the God who gave it.

The *funcion* performed in the general's honour, within the church, was as magnificent as ecclesiastic and military splendour could render it. We were in the gallery above. The bier, placed on a lofty scaffolding, covered with black velvet and lighted with wax tapers, was placed near the altar. The music was solemn and impressive. Every respect has been shown to the deceased general, by Santa Anna's orders. Excepting the *corps diplomatique* and the officers, all within the church were in deep mourning. . . .

The chief difficulty we have in arranging our affairs here, consists in the perfect impossibility of persuading any tradesman to keep his word. They name the day, the hour, the minute, at which they are to be with you, or at which certain goods are to be sent to you. They are affronted if you doubt their punctuality, and the probability is, you never hear of them or their goods again. If they are not exact for their own interest, they will not be so for yours; and although we have had frequent proofs of this carelessness, we are particularly annoyed by it now that we are within a few days of our departure. During our residence here we have had little to do with shops and shopkeepers, having found it more convenient and economical to send to Paris or even to the United States for all articles of dress. Now, though everything must still be comparatively dear, the *bad times* have caused a great reduction in prices; and dear as all goods are, they would be still dearer, were it not for the quantity that is smuggled into the republic. There are an amazing number of French shop-keepers; French tailors, hatters, shoemakers, apothecaries, etc.; but especially French modistes and perruquiers. The charges of the former are exorbitant, the latter are little employed except by gentlemen. There are also many Spanish shops, some German, and a few English; but I think the French preponderate.

We went some time ago to see the *Monte Pio*, which is under the auspices of Señor Tagle; and it is melancholy enough to see the profusion of fine diamonds and pearls that are displayed in these large halls. After a certain time has elapsed without their being redeemed, the pledged articles are sold; gold and silver, in whatever form, by the weight, but jewels for their intrinsic value. There is a sale once a week. We were shown privately the jewels of the Virgen de los Remedios; which are very superb.

There is a small theatre lately established, called the Theatre of *New Mexico*, where there is a Spanish company, the same whom we saw two years ago in Vera Cruz. They are drawing away various persons from the principal theatre. Their object seems to be to make people laugh, and they succeed. On Christmas eve we went there to see the *gracioso* (harlequin) in a woman's dress, dance *Tripili*, an old Spanish dance, accompanied with singing. They introduced some appropriate lines concerning the late troubles about the *copper*, which were received with great applause. Just as they were concluding the Tripili, a young gentleman in the pit, I do not know whether Mexican or Spanish, rose, and waving his hand after the manner of a man about to make an address, and requesting attention, kindly favoured the audience with some verses of his own, which were received with great good-nature; the actors bowing to him, and the pit applauding him. It seemed to me a curious piece of philanthropy on his part.

At midnight we went to the church of Santa Clara, to attend what is called the *Misa del Gallo*, the Cock's Mass; which is private,—only respectable persons being admitted by a private entrance; for midnight mass in Mexico takes place with shut doors, as all nightly reunions are dreaded. Santa Clara being attached to the convent of that name, we remained after mass to see the white-robed sisters receive the sacrament from the hands of a priest, by the small side-door that opens from the convent to the church. The church was lighted, but the convent was in darkness; and looking in through the grating, we could only distinguish the outline of their kneeling figures, enveloped in their white drapery and black veils. I do not think there were a dozen persons in the church besides ourselves.

A good deal of interest has been excited here lately about the Texian prisoners taken in the Santa Fé expedition, the first detachment of whom have arrived, after a march of nearly two thousand miles, and are now lodged in the convent of Santiago, about two miles from the centre of the city. As their situation is represented to be very miserable, and as it is said that they have been stripped of their hats, shoes, and coats; some of the Mexican families, and amongst others, that of Don Francisco Tagle, regardless of political enmity, have subscribed to send them a supply of linen and other necessary articles, which they carried out there themselves. Being invited to accompany them to Santiago, I did so; and we found the common men occupying the courtyard, and the officers the large hall of the convent. So far they have been treated as prisoners of war generally are; but it is said to be the intention of Santa Anna to have them put in chains, and sent out to sweep the streets, with the miserable prisoners of the Acordada. Colonel C——, who was presented to me, seemed to treat the whole affair very lightly, as the fortune of war; and had evidently no idea that any such fate was in store for them; seeming rather amused by the dress of the monks, whom he now saw for the first time. In the Mexicans generally, there seems very little if any vindictive feeling against them; on the contrary, a good deal of interest in their favour, mingled with some curiosity to see them. The common men appeared more impatient and more out of spirits than the officers. We shall probably know nothing more of their fate, before leaving Mexico.

We had some intention of paying a last visit to the Museum before we went; and Don José Maria Bustamante, a friend of ours, professor of botany, and considered a man of learning, was prepared to receive us; but we were prevented from going. I must, however, find time to answer your question as to the population. The Mexican republic is supposed to contain upwards of seven millions of inhabitants; the capital, two hundred thousand. Their number cannot be exactly fixed, as there has been no general census for some time; a labour in which a commission, with Count Cortina at its head, has been employed for some time past, and the result of which will be published shortly. All other questions must be replied to *de vive voix*.

I must now conclude my last letter written from this place; for we are surrounded by visitors, day and night; and, to say the truth, feel that it is only the prospect of returning to our family, which can counterbalance the unfeigned regret we feel at leaving our friends in Mexico. My next letter will most probably be dated from Vera Cruz.

LETTER THE FIFTY-SECOND

Last Day in Mexico—Theatre—Santa Anna—French Minister's —Parting—Diligence—Last Look of Mexico—Fatigue—Robbers—Escort—Second Impressions—Baths at Jalapa—Vera Cruz—Some Account of San Juan de Ulua—Siege of 1825—Siege of 1838—General Bustamante—Theatre—Of the North Winds.

VERA CRUZ, 6th January, 1842.

Having concluded our arrangements for leaving Mexico on the 2nd of January, we determined, as the diligence started long before daybreak, not to attempt taking any rest that night. We went out early, and took leave of the Dowager Marquesa de Vivanco, who was confined to the house by illness, and whose kindness to us has been unremitting ever since our arrival. It is a sad thing to take leave of a person of her age, and in her delicate state of health, whom there is scarcely a possibility of our ever seeing again. Some days before we parted also from one of our oldest friends here, the Countess C——a. The last day, besides the Spaniards who have been our constant friends and visitors ever since we came here, we had melancholy visits of adieu from Señor Gomez Padraza and his lady, from the families of Echavarri, of Fagoaga, Cortina, Escandon, Casa-flores, and many whose names are unknown to you. Amongst others was the Güera Rodriguez.

About eight o'clock, accompanied even to the door of the carriage by a number of ladies who were with us to the last, and amongst these were P——a C——a and L——z E——n, we broke short all these sad partings, and, with the A——s and the family of the French minister, set off for the theatre of New Mexico. I can imagine your surprise at such a *finale,* but it was the only means left us of finishing a painful scene, and of beguiling the weary hours yet remaining before the diligence started, for it was in vain to think of rest or sleep that night. The theatre was very crowded, the play an amusing piece of *diablerie,* called the *"Pata de Cabra"* (the goat's foot), badly got up, of course, as its effect depends upon scenery and machinery. I believe it was very entertaining, but I cannot say

we felt inclined to enter into the spirit of it. The family of
General V——a were there, and, this being the day of a great
diplomatic dinner given by Santa Anna, various officers and
diplomates came in late and in full dress. I was informed by
one of the company, that six colonels stood the whole time of
dinner behind his Excellency's chair! I wonder what French
officer would do as much for Louis Philippe! *Vogue la galère!*
From the theatre, which concluded about one, we drove to
the house of the —— minister, where we spent a very grave
half-hour, and then returned home with a very splendid
brioche, of generous proportions, which Madame la Baronne
de —— had kindly prepared for our journey.

Arrived at the A——'s, we sat down to supper, and never
was there a sadder meal than this, when for the last time we
sat at the hospitable board of these our earliest and latest
Mexican friends. We were thankful when it was all over and
we had taken leave, and when, accompanied to the inn by
Señor A——d and other gentlemen, we found ourselves fairly
lodged in the diligence, on a dark and rather cold morning,
sad, sleepy, and shivering. All Mexico was asleep when we
drove out of the gates. The very houses seemed sunk in slumber. So terminated our last Mexican *New Year's Day*.

When we reached the eminence, from which is the last view
of the valley, the first dawn of day was just breaking over the
distant city; the white summits of the volcanoes were still enveloped in mist, and the lake was veiled by low clouds of
vapour, that rose slowly from its surface. And this was our
last glimpse of Mexico!

The diligence is now on a new and most fatiguing plan of
travelling night and day, after leaving Puebla; so that, starting
from Mexico at four o'clock on the morning of the 2nd of January, it arrives in Vera Cruz early on the morning of the 5th,
saving a few hours, and nearly killing the travellers. The government had granted us escorts for the whole journey, now
more than ever necessary. It was five in the afternoon when
we reached Puebla, and we set off again by dawn the next
morning.

We had just left the gates, and our escort, which had rode
forward, was concealed by some rising ground, when, by the
faint light, we perceived some half-dozen mounted cavaliers
making stealthily up to us across the fields. Their approach
was first discerned by a Spanish lady who was with us, and
who was travelling with strings of pearl and valuable diamonds concealed about her person, which made her peculiarly

sharp-sighted on the occasion. *"Ladrones!"* said she, and every one repeated *"Ladrones!"* in different intonations. They rode across the fields, came up pretty close to the diligence, and reconnoitred us. I was too sleepy to be frightened, and reconnoitred them in return with only one eye open. The coachman whipped up his horses, the escort came in sight, and the gentlemen struck into the fields again. The whole passed in a minute or two. The soldiers of the escort came riding back to the diligence; and the captain, galloping up to the window, gave himself great credit for having "frightened away the robbers."

We arrived at Perote when it was nearly dusk, supped, and started again at eleven o'clock at night. We passed a horrible night in the diligence, and were thankful when daybreak showed us the beautiful environs of Jalapa. It is singular that on a second impression, returning by this road, the houses appear handsomer than they did before, and nature less beautiful. I conclude that this is to be accounted for simply from the circumstance of the eye having become accustomed both to the works of nature and of man, which characterize this country. The houses, which at first appeared gloomy, large, and comfortless, habit has reconciled us to, and experience has taught us that they are precisely suited to this climate of perpetual spring. The landscape, with its eternal flowers and verdure, no longer astonishes and bewilders us, as when we first arrived from a country where, at that season, all nature lies buried in snow. Besides, in our last journey through Michoacan, we have passed among scenes even more striking and beautiful than these. Then the dresses, which at first appeared so romantic; the high, Morrish-looking saddle, the gold-embroidered manga, the large hat, shading the swarthy faces of the men, the coloured petticoat and reboso, and long black hair of the women, though still picturesque, have no longer the charm of novelty, and do not attract our attention. The winter also has been unusually severe for Mexico, and some slight frosts have caused the flowers of this natural garden to fade; and, besides all this, we were tired and sleepy and jolted, and knew that we had but an hour or two to remain, and had another day and night of purgatory in prospect. . . .

Still, as we passed along the shady lanes, amongst the dark chirimoyas, the green-leaved bananas, and all the variety of beautiful trees, intwined with their graceful creepers, we were forced to confess that winter has little power over these fertile regions, and that in spite of the leveller, *Habit*, such a landscape can never be passed through with indifference.

Arrived at Jalapa, we refreshed ourselves with the luxury of a bath, having to pass through half the city before we reached the bathing establishment, from which there is the most beautiful view of wood, water, and mountain that it is possible to behold. The baths are the property of a lady who has a cotton factory and a good house in the city, and fortunate she is in possessing a sufficient portion of worldly goods; since, as she informed us, she is the mother of twenty children! She herself, in appearance, was little more than thirty. We then returned to breakfast, and shortly after left Jalapa.

I will not inflict upon you a second description of the same journey; of Plan del Rio, with its clear river and little inn—of Puerto del Rey, with its solid majestic bridge thrown over the deep ravine, through which rushes the impetuous river Antigua —or of how we were jolted over the road leading to Paso de Oveja, etc. Suffice it to say, that we passed a night, which between suffocating heat, horrible jolting, and extreme fatigue, was nearly intolerable. Stopping to change horses at Santa Fé, we saw, by the light of the torches which they brought to the door, that we were once more among bamboo-huts and palm-trees. Towards morning we heard the welcome sound of the waves, giving us joyful token that our journey was drawing to a close; yet when we entered Vera Cruz and got out of the diligence, we felt like prisoners who have been so long confined in a dungeon, they are incapable of enjoying their liberty, we were so thoroughly worn out and exhausted. How different from the agreeable kind of fatigue which we used to feel after a long day's journey on horseback!

Breakfast, and a fresh toilet had, however, their due influence. We were in an hotel, and had hardly breakfasted when our friend, Don Dionisio Velasco, with some other gentlemen, arrived, and kindly reproaching us for preferring an inn to his house, carried us and our luggage off to his fine airy dwelling, where we now are, and where a good night's rest has made us forget all our fatigues.

As we must remain here for one or two days, we shall have time to see a little more of the city; and already, upon a second survey, sad and dilapidated as it now appears, I can more readily imagine what it must have been in former days, before it was visited by the scourge of civil war. The experience of two Mexican revolutions, makes it more easy for us to conceive the extent to which this unfortunate city must have suffered in the struggle made by the Spaniards, to preserve the castle, their last bulwark in this hemisphere. San Juan de Ulua, in spite of the miserable condition in which it now is, remains a lasting memorial of the great works which, almost immediately after their arrival on these shores, were undertaken by the Spanish conquerors.

In 1682, sixty-one years after they had set foot on Aztec soil, they began this fortress, in order to confirm their power. The centre of the space which it occupies is a small island, where the Spaniard, Juan de Grijalva arrived, one year before Cortes reached the Mexican continent. Having found the remains of two human victims there, they asked the natives why they sacrificed men to their idols, and receiving for answer that it was by orders of the kings of *Acolhua,* the Spaniards gave the island the name of Ulua, by a natural corruption of that word.

It is pretended that the fortress cost four millions; and though this immense sum is no doubt an exaggeration, the expense must have been very great, when we consider that its foundations are below the water, and that for nearly three centuries it has resisted all the force of the stormy waves that continually beat against it. Many improvements and additions are gradually made to the castle; and, in the time of the viceroys, a first-rate engineer paid it an annual visit, to ascertain its condition, and to consider its best mode of defence, in case of an attack. In 1806, however, Vera Cruz was sacked by the English corsair, Nicholas Agramont, incited by one Lorencillo, who had been condemned to death for murder in Vera Cruz, and had escaped to Jamaica. Seven millions of dollars were carried off, besides three hundred persons of both sexes, whom the pirates abandoned on the Island of Sacrificios, when they re-embarked.

In 1771 the viceroy, then the Marquis de la Croix, remitted a million and a half of dollars to the governor, in order that he might put the castle in a state of defence; and the strong bulwarks which still remain, attest the labour that has been bestowed upon it. The outer polygon, which looks towards Vera Cruz, is three hundred yards in extent; to the north it is defended by another of two hundred yards; whilst a low battery is situated as a rear-guard in the bastion of Santiago; and on the opposite front is the battery of San Miguel. The whole fortress is composed of a stone which abounds in the neighbouring island, a species of coral, excellent for building, *piedra mucara.*

In 1822 no stronghold of Spanish power remained but this castle, whose garrison was frequently reinforced by troops from

Havana. Vera Cruz itself was then inhabited by wealthy and
influential Spaniards. Santa Anna then commanded in the
province, under the orders of Echavarri, the captain-general,
and with instructions from Yturbide, relative to the taking of
the castle. The commandant was the Spanish General Don
José Davila. It was not, however, till the following year, when
Lemaur succeeded Davila in the command of the citadel, that
hostilities were begun by bombarding Vera Cruz.

Men, women, and children then abandoned the city. The
merchants went to Alvarado, twelve leagues off, whilst those
who were driven from their houses by a shower of balls, sought
a miserable asylum amongst the burning plains and miserable
huts in the environs. Some made their way to Jalapa, thirty
leagues off; others to Cordova and Orizava, equally distant.
With some interruptions, hostilities lasted two years, during
which there was nearly a constant firing from the city to the
castle, and from the castle to the city.

The object of General Barragan, now commander-in-chief,
was to cut off all communication between the garrison of the
castle and the coasts, and to reduce them to live solely upon
salt provisions, fatal in this warm and unhealthy country. In
1824 the garrison, diminished to a mere handful, was replaced
by five hundred men from the peninsula; and very soon these
soldiers, shut up on the barren rocks, surrounded by water,
and exposed to the dangers of the climate, without provisions
and without assistance, were reduced to the most miserable
condition. The next year, Don José Copinger succeeded
Lemaur, and continued hostilities with fresh vigour.

This brave general, with his valiant troops, surrounded by
the sick and the dying, provisions growing scarcer every day,
and those that remained corrupt and unfit to eat, yet resolved
to do his duty, and hold out to the last. No assistance arrived
from Spain. A Mexican fleet was stationed off the Island of
Sacrificios and other points, to attack any squadron that might
come from thence; while the north winds blew with violence,
keeping back all ships that might approach the coasts. "Gods
and men," says a furious republican (Zavala), "the Spaniards
had to contend with; having against them, hunger, sickness,
the fire and balls of the enemies, a furious sea covered with
reefs, a burning atmosphere, and above all, being totally ignorant as to whether they should receive any assistance."

The minister of the treasury, Esteva, then came from Mexico, and proposed a capitulation; and the Spanish general
agreed that should no assistance arrive within a certain time,

he would give up the fortress; evacuating it with his whole garrison, and with the suitable honours. The Spanish succours arrived a few days before the term was expired, but the commander of the squadron, seeing the superiority in point of numbers of the Mexican fleet, judged it prudent to return to Havana to augment his forces. But it was too late. On the fifteenth of September, the brave General Copinger, with the few troops that remained to him, marched out of the fortress, terminating the final struggle against the progress of revolution, but upholding to the last the character for constancy and valour which distinguished the sons of ancient Spain.

Of its last assault by the French squadron in 1838, there is no need to say anything. Every newspaper, as you will remember, gave an account of the capitulation of what the French gazettes called "San Juan de Ulua, the St. Jean d'Acre of the new world, which our mariners saluted as the Queen of the Seas, *vierge sans tache*," etc.

6th.—We have just had a visit from General Bustamante, who, with his aide-de-camp, a son of General Calderon (formerly governor of Jalapa), intends shortly to sail in the Jason for Havana. We have also had a visit from the commander of that vessel, Captain Puente, who succeeded our friend Captain E——a; and who has been kindly endeavouring to make arrangements for taking us also, not having before been aware of our intentions of leaving Vera Cruz at this period. But although we should have much pleasure in returning by the vessel that brought us, we fear that, without putting the officers to great inconvenience, it will be impossible for them to accommodate so many, for we know the *carte du pays*. It is therefore probable that we shall go by the English packet, which sails on the eighth, but unfortunately goes round by Tampico, not very agreeable at this season.

We went to mass this morning, which was said to be particularly crowded in consequence of the general desire to catch a glimpse of the ex-president. . . .

I find, personally, one important change in taste if not in opinion. Vera Cruz cookery, which two years ago I thought detestable, now appears to me delicious! What excellent fish! and what incomparable *frijoles!* Well, this is a trifle; but after all, in trifles as in matters of moment, how necessary for a traveller to compare his judgments at different periods, and to correct them! First impressions are of great importance, if given only as such; but if laid down as decided opinions, how apt they are to be erroneous! It is like judging of individuals

by their physiognomy and manners, without having had time
to study their character. We all do so more or less, but how
frequently we find ourselves deceived!

7th.—We went to the theatre last evening. In the boxes
there were only a lady and gentleman, besides our party. The
pit, however, was full; but there are no good actors at present.
We have been walking about to-day, notwithstanding the heat,
purchasing some necessary articles from French modistes and
French perfumers, most of whom, having got over the fever,
are now very well satisfied to remain here and make their
fortune. We afterwards walked down to the Mole, and saw
the pleasantest sight that has met our eyes since we left Mexico—the sea covered with ships. It was refreshing to look again
on the dark blue waves, after so long an absence from them.
Commodore ——, of Mexico, who was present, pointed out the
Jason, and the Tyrian, Captain Griffin, lying out in the harbour, and strongly recommended us to go in the latter, as did
the English consul, with proper patriotism. We have requested
him to take our berths, when he goes to visit the captain on
board this evening. . . .

No sooner has this been done beyond recall, than we find
that comfortable arrangements have been made for taking us
in the Jason, which goes direct to Havana. It is now too late, so
we can only regret our precipitation. There is another beautiful Spanish vessel just arrived, the *Liberal*, Captain Rubal-
cava, who, with Captain Puente, of the Jason, has been to see
us this evening. If the wind holds fair, the packet sails to-
morrow; but the experienced predict a norther.

The symptoms of this terrible wind, which blows in the
Mexican Gulf, from the autumnal to the vernal equinox, are
known not only to the sailors, but to all those who have lived
some time in this city. The variation in the barometer is the
surest sign. A land breeze from the north-west first blows
gently, then varies to the north-east, then changes to the south.
The heat is then suffocating and the summits of all the great
mountains appear cloudless and distinct against the deep blue
sky, while round their base flows a veil of semi-transparent
vapour.

Suddenly the tempest bursts forth; and all are instanta-
neously relieved—all but the poor mariners! The air becomes
refreshed—clouds of dust come sweeping along the streets,
driving away, as it were, the pestilential atmosphere. Then
there is no fever in Vera Cruz.

All communication is cut off between the castle and the

city, and between the city and all foreign shipping. Sometimes the norther lasts three or four days, sometimes even twelve. If it turns to a southerly breeze, the tempest generally returns; if it changes to the east or north-east, the breeze generally lasts three or four days, and the ships in the port take advantage of the intervals to escape, and gain the high seas. These gales are particularly dreaded off the coasts of Tampico.

8th.—We sail in a few hours, the *norte* not having made its appearance, so that we expect to get clear of the coast before it begins. The Jason sails in a day or two, unless prevented by the gale. We only knew this morning that it was necessary to provide mattresses and sheets, etc., for our berths on board the packet. Fortunately, all these articles are found ready made in this seaport town. We have just received a packet of letters, particularly acceptable as bringing us news of home before our departure. I have also received two agreeable *compagnons de voyage* in the shape of books; Stephen's "Central America," and Washington Irving's "Life of Margaret Davison," opportunely sent me by Mr. Prescott. . . .

Our next letters will be written either at sea, or from Tampico.

LETTER THE FIFTY-THIRD

Sail in the Tyrian—Norther off Tampico—The Bar—The River Panuco—The Pilot—The Shore—Alligator—"Paso de Doña Cecilia"—Tampico—Spanish Consul's House—Society—Navigation—Banks of the Panuco—Extraordinary Inoculation—The "Glorieta"—Leave Tampico—Furious Norther—Voyage—Arrival at Havana.

ON BOARD H. B. M. PACKET TYRIAN, 15th.

On the 8th, having taken leave of the family of our friend, Señor Velasco, and of General Bustamante, whom we hope to see again in Havana, we went out in a little boat, accompanied as far as the packet by several gentlemen, and in a short time were standing on deck, looking our last at Vera Cruz and its sandbanks, and sopilotes, and frowning castle, as the shores gradually receded from our view, while the Tyrian was making the best of her time to get clear of reefs and rocks, before the arrival of the norther. We regretted to find, that instead of being one of the new line of English packets, the Tyrian was the last of the old line; small, ancient, and incommodious, and destined to be paid off on her return to England. Captain Griffin, the commander, who looks like an excellent, gentlemanly man, is in wretched health, and in a state of acute suffering. There were no passengers but ourselves, and a young Mexican, guiltless of any acquaintance with salt water, up to this date.

The very next morning out burst the norther, and with loud howling swept over the ocean, which rose and tossed to meet the coming storm. Surely no wind ever had a voice so wildly mournful. How the good ship rolled, and groaned, and creaked, and strained her old timber joints! What rocking, thumping, falling, banging of heads at the low entry of the cabin! Water falling into berths, people rolling out of them. What fierce music at night, as the wind, like a funeral dirge, swept over the ocean, the rain falling in torrents, and the sky covered with one dark, lugubrious pall! And how lonely our ship seemed on the world of waters!

But the next day, the storm waxed fiercer still, and the night was worse than the day. The waves that dashed over the deck made their way into the cabin. At one time, we thought the ship had struck, and even the captain believed that a mast had fallen. It was only a huge wave that broke over the deck with a sound like thunder, drowning the wretched hens and ducks, who little thought, when they left their comfortable English poultry-yard, they were destined to be drowned off Tampico —and drenching the men. Our little lamp, after swinging to and fro for some time went out, and left the cabin in darkness. Impossible to sleep of course, and for the *first time* at sea, I confess to having felt afraid. Each time that the ship rolled upon her side on the slope of a huge billow, it seemed impossible that she could ever right again, or that she could avoid receiving the whole contents of the next great watery mountain that came roaring on.

On the morning of the eleventh there was still no abatement of the storm. All was dark and dreary. The norther continued to blow with unrelenting fierceness, and the ship to rock and roll amongst a tumult of foaming billows. The nights in this pitch darkness seemed interminable. The berths being constantly filled with water, we dragged our mattresses on the floor, and lay there wishing for the dawn. But the dawn brought no relief. The wind howled on like a fierce wild beast roaring for its prey. I had made my way every day upstairs, and by dint of holding on, and with a chair tied with strong ropes, had contrived to sit on deck. But this day I retreated under cover behind the helmsman, when, lo! a large wave burst over the ship, found me out in my retreat, and nearly throwing down several stout sailors in its way, gave me the most complete salt-water bath I have had since I left New York. All that night we were tossed about in storm and darkness.

On the thirteenth the wailing of the norther grew fainter, and towards night died away. On the fourteenth it veered round, and the coast of Tamaulipis appeared in sight faintly.

This morning opened with a slight norther; nevertheless they have hung out the packet flag and cast anchor, in expectation of the pilot boat. Meanwhile, all is at a stand-still, *morally* speaking, for we are rolling so that it is scarce possible to write comprehensibly. We see the sad-looking shores of Tampico, long, low, and sandy, though to the south stretching out into gloomy, faintly-seen woods. We can distinguish the distant yellow sand and the white surf breaking furiously over the *bar*. The day is gloomy but not cold. A slight rain accompanies the light north wind. Sea-gulls are flying in circles round the ship and skimming the surface of the waves. The master looks impatient and anxious, and prognosticates another week of northers. Vessels, they say, have been detained here thirty days, and some even three months! No notice is taken of our signal—a sign that the bar is impassable.

16th.—The ship has rolled and pitched all night, and to-day we remain in the same predicament.

TAMPICO, 18th.

Yesterday morning the wind was much lighter, and a pilot-boat came out early, in which the captain set off with his despatches; and we being assured that we might cross the ominous bar in safety, hired a boat for forty dollars, with ten sailors and a pilot, too glad at the prospect of touching the solid earth even for one day. Having got into this boat, and being rowed out to the bar, we found that there the sea was very high, even though the day was calm. The numerous wrecks that have taken place here have given this bar a decidedly bad reputation. Great precaution is necessary in crossing it, constant sounding, and calm weather. It is formed by a line of sandhills under the water, whose northern point crosses that to the southward, and across which there is a passage, whose position varies with the shifting sands, so that the pilots are chiefly guided by the surf.

Perched upon a sandbank was a regiment of enormous white pelicans of thoughtful and sage-like physiognomy, ranged in a row, as if to watch how we passed the bar. Over many a drowning crew they have screamed their wild sea dirge, and flapped their great white wings. But we crossed in safety, and in a few minutes more the sea and the bar were behind us, and we were rowing up the wide and placid river Panuco—an agreeable change. We stopped at the house of the *commandant*, a large, tall individual, who marched out and addressed us in English, and proved to be a native of the United States.

We stopped at a collection of huts, to let our sailors breakfast, where there is the house of a celebrated character, Don Leonardo Mata, a colossal old pilot, but who was from home at present. We amused ourselves by wandering along the beach of the river and making a collection of beautiful shells, which we left at the old pilot's house, to be kept there till our return. A sort of garden, attached to the house, is appropriately ornamented with the figure-head and anchor from a wreck. We got into our boat again and glided along the shores, on one side low and marshy, with great trees lying in the water; on the other also low, but thickly wooded and with valuable timber, such as logwood and ebony, together with cedars, India-rubber trees, limes, lemons, etc. On the bare trunk of a great tree, half-buried in the water, sat an amiable-looking alligator, its jaws distended in a sweet, unconscious grin, as if it were catching flies, and not deigning to notice us, though we passed close to it. A canoe with an Indian woman in it, was paddling about at a very little distance. All these beautiful woods to the right contain a host of venomous reptiles, particularly the rattlesnake. Cranes and herons were fluttering across the surface of the river, and the sportsmen brave the danger of the reptiles, for the sake of shooting these and the beautiful rose-coloured spoonbills and pheasants that abound there.

The approach from Tampico is very pretty, and about two miles from it on the wooded shore, in a little verdant clearing, is a beautiful *ranchito*—a small farmhouse, white and clean, with a pretty piazza. In this farm they keep cows and sell milk, and it looks the very picture of rural comfort, which always comes with double charm when one has been accustomed to the sight of the foaming surges and the discomforts of a tempest-tossed ship. The sailors called it "El Paso" (the pass) "de Doña Cecilia;" which sounded delightfully romantic. The proprietress, this Doña Cecilia, who lives in such peaceful solitude, surrounded by mangroves, with no other drawbacks to her felicity but snakes and alligators, haunted my imagination. I trusted she was young, and lovely, and heartbroken; a pensive lay nun who had retreated from the vanities and deceits of the world to this secluded spot, where she lived like a heroine upon the produce of her flocks, with some "neat-handed Phillis," to milk the cows and churn the butter, while she sat rapt in contemplation of the stars above or the snakes below. It was not until after our arrival at Tampico that I had the mortification to discover that the interesting creature, the charming recluse, is seventy-eight, and has just buried her seventh husband! I accept the account doubtingly, and henceforth shall endeavour to picture her to my mind as an ancient enchantress, dwelling amongst serpents, and making her venomous charms of

> "Adder's fork, and blind-worm's sting,
> Lizard's leg, and owlet's wing."

As you approach Tampico, the first houses that meet the eye, have the effect of a number of coloured bandboxes; some blue, some white, which a party of tired milliners have laid down amongst the rushes. On leaving the boat, and walking through the town, though there are some solid stone dwellings, I could have fancied myself in a New England village. Neat "shingle palaces," with piazzas and pillars; nothing Spanish, and upon the whole, an air of cleanness and cheerfulness astonishing to me who have fancied Tampico an earthly purgatory. We afterwards heard that these houses were actually made in the United States and sent out here. There are some good-looking *stores;* and though there is certainly little uniformity in the architecture of the houses, yet considering the city was built only sixteen years ago, I consider it a slandered place. In 1825 there were but a few Indian huts here, and any little commerce there was, concentrated itself in *Pueblo Viejo,* which stands on the shores of a lake some miles off. We were taken to the house of a Spanish consul, a fine, airy, stone building with a gay view from the windows;—the very first house that was built in the place.

Its owner, Don Juan de la Lastra, Spanish vice-consul, is not here himself, but we were kindly received by Don José de Comez Mira, the consul. In the evening all the principal Spaniards in the place came to see C——n; and having arrived here yesterday morning as perfect strangers, without the probability of finding any one whom we knew, we find ourselves surrounded by the most unexpected and gratifying attentions. As to what is called society, there is literally none in Tampico. Those who live here, have come in the hope of making their fortune; and the few married men who are amongst them have been unwilling to expose their wives to the unhealthy climate, the plague of mosquitoes and *xins-xins,* the intermittent fevers, which are more to be dreaded here than the yellow fever, and the nearly total deprivation of respectable female society. The men, at least the Spaniards, unite in a sort of club, and amuse their leisure evenings with cards and billiards; but the absence of ladies' society must always make it dull. Riding and shooting in the neighbourhood are their out-of-door amusements, and there is excellent sport along the river, which may be enjoyed when the heat is not too intense.

Our captain, who has paid us a visit this evening, with several Englishmen, expects to get off to-morrow. We staid at home in the morning on account of the heat, and wrote letters, but in the afternoon we made the most of our time, walking about the city, in which there is not much to see. There are many comfortable-looking large houses, generally built according to the customs of the country whereof the proprietor is a native. Were it not for the bar, which is a terrible obstacle, not only from the danger in crossing it, but the detention that it causes, vessels having been stopped outside for months, Tampico would become a most flourishing port. Besides that the depth of water can permit vessels of burden to anchor near the town, there is an interior navigation up the country, for upwards of forty leagues.

The banks of the river are described as being very beautiful, which we can easily believe from what we have already seen; but for its beauties after passing Tampico, its wooded shores dotted with white ranchos, its large cattle farms, and its picturesque old Indian town of Panuco, we must trust to hearsay. The country in the vicinity is described as being a wilderness of rare trees, matted together with graceful and flowering creepers, the wild haunts of birds of bright and beautiful plumage; but our ardour to visit these tangled shrubberies was damped by the accounts of myriads of *xins-xins* and *garrapatos;* little insects that bury themselves in the skin, producing irritation and fever; of the swarming mosquitoes,—the horrid caimans that bask on the shore; and worse than all, the venomous snakes that glide amongst the rank vegetation. Parrots and butterflies and fragrant flowers will not compensate for these.

We have just been hearing a curious circumstance connected with poisonous reptiles, which I have learned for the first time. Here, and all along the coast, the people are in the habit of inoculating themselves with the poison of the rattlesnake, which renders them safe from the bite of all venomous animals. The person to be inoculated is pricked with the tooth of a serpent, on the tongue, in both arms and on various parts of the body; and the venom introduced into the wounds. An eruption comes out, which lasts a few days. Ever after, these persons can handle the most venomous snakes with impunity; can make them come by calling them, have great pleasure in fondling them; and the bite of these persons is poisonous! You will not believe this; but we have the testimony of seven or eight respectable merchants to the fact. A gentleman who breakfasted here this morning, says that he has been vainly endeavouring to make up his mind to submit to the operation, as he is very much exposed where he lives, and is obliged to travel a great deal on the coast; that when he goes on these expeditions, he is always accompanied by his servant, an inoculated negro, who has the power of curing him, should he be bit, by sucking the poison from the wound. He also saw this negro cure the bite given by an inoculated Indian boy to a white boy with whom he was fighting, and who was the stronger of the two. The stories of the eastern jugglers, and their power over these reptiles, may perhaps be accounted for in this way. I cannot say that I should like to have so much *snaky* nature transferred into my composition, nor to live amongst people whose bite is venomous. . . .

We have just returned from a moonlight walk to the *Glorieta*, a public promenade which they are making here, where there are some stone benches for the promenaders, close to which some public-spirited individuals had dragged the carcase of a horse, which obliged us to retrace our steps with all convenient speed.

As for provisions in this place, if we may judge by the specimens we have seen in this house, they are both good and abundant. We had especially fine fish, and a variety of vegetables. To-morrow, alas! we return to our packet, much refreshed, however, by two pleasant days on shore, and consoling ourselves for our prolonged voyage by the reflection, that had we gone direct to Havana, we should not have seen Tampico; and, as La Fontaine's travelling pigeon says,

> "Quiconque ne voit guère
> N'a guère à dire aussi. Mon voyage depeint
> Vous sera d'un plaisir extrême.
> Je dirai: j'étais là; telle chose m'avint:
> Vous y croirez être vous-même."[1]

Once more on board our floating prison. A *norte* is expected this evening, but at least it will now be in our favour, and will drive us towards Havana. Our Spanish friends concluded their cordial and disinterested kindness, by setting off with us by daybreak this morning, in a large boat with Spanish colours unfurled, crossing the bar with us, coming on board, and running no small risk in recrossing it, with every prospect of a norther before their eyes. We stopped at the house of the

---

[1] *He who sees little, little can he say;*
And when my travels I describe some day,
And say, "That chanced to me—there I have been"—
The pleasure you will feel will be so great,
You will believe, while hearing me relate,
That all these wonders you yourself have seen.

"Marine Monster," Don Leonardo Mata, before crossing the bar, took up our shells, and had the felicity of making his acquaintance. He is a colossal old man, almost gigantic in height, and a Falstaff in breadth—gruff in his manners, yet with a certain clumsy good-nature about him. He performs the office of pilot with so much exclusiveness, charging such high prices, governing the men with so iron a sway, and arranging everything so entirely according to his own fancy, that he is a complete sovereign in his own small way—the *tyrant of Tampico*. He has in his weather-beaten face such a mixture of bluffness and slyness, with his gigantic person, and abrupt, half-savage manners, that, altogether, I conceive him to be a character who might have been worthy the attention of Walter Scott, had he chanced to encounter him. Old and repulsive as he is, he has lately married a pretty young girl—a subject on which he does not brook raillery. One amiable trait the old tyrant has in his character—his affection for his old mother, who is upwards of ninety, and who resides at Mahon, and to whom he is constant in his attentions. At one time he was in the habit of sending her small sums of money; but as they were frequently lost, he sent her five hundred dollars at once by a safe conveyance. The old woman, he said, was so frightened by seeing such a quantity of money in her hut, that she could not sleep, and at length entrusted it to a *friend*, who carried it off altogether. Since then he has assigned her fifteen dollars a month, upon which the old woman lives in what she considers great luxury.

We took leave of our friends an hour or two ago, but do not expect to set sail till the afternoon, as they are discharging the quicksilver which our vessel brought, and loading the silver which we carry away. Three young Englishmen came on board this morning, to see the packet, and are making a disagreeable visit, being perfectly overwhelmed by sea-sickness.

20th.—Last night arose a furious norther. To-day it continues; but as it is driving us towards our desired haven, and away from these dangerous coasts, we need not complain. As usual on these occasions, I find myself alone on the deck, never suffering from the universal prostrator of landsmen. By way of variety, I have been sitting in the cabin, holding on to the leg of a table, and trying to read Stephens, with as much attention as circumstances will permit. All further attempts at *writing* must be delayed!

30th.—On the 21st the norther continued with unabated

violence, the wild wind and the boiling waves struggling on the agitated bosom of the ocean, great billows swelling up one after the other, and threatening to engulf us; the ship labouring and creaking as if all its timbers were parting asunder, and the captain in such a state of intense suffering, that we were in great apprehension for his life. Horrible days, and yet more horrible nights! But they were succeeded by fine weather, and at length we had the consolation of seeing the moon, smiling placidly down upon us, like a harbinger of peace. On the evening of the twenty-sixth the full moon rose with a troubled countenance, her disk obscured by angry clouds. She shook them off, but still looked turbid and superb. A gloomy cloud, black as night, still stretched over her like a pall, thickly veiling, yet not entirely obscuring her light, and soon after she appeared, riding serenely in the high heavens, mildly triumphant. Of all who sing the praises of the moon, who should love her blessed beams from his inmost heart like the seaman? Then the angry clouds dispersed;—the north wind blew freshly, but not fiercely, as if even his blustering fury were partly soothed by the influence of her placid light;— the studding-sails were set, and the Tyrian bounded on her course eight knots an hour.

The next day the wind died away, and then blew lightly from the opposite quarter. We were about two hundred and fifty miles from Havana, but were then driven in the direction of Yucatan. The two following days we had contrary wind, but charming weather. We studied the chart, and read, and walked on deck, and played at drafts, and sat in the moonlight. The sea was covered with flying fish, and the "Portuguese men of war," as the sailors call the independent little nautilus, sailed contemptuously past us in their fairy barks, as if they had been little steamers. A man fell overboard, but the weather being calm, was saved immediately. We have been tacking about and making our way slowly towards Havana, in a zigzag line. Yesterday evening the moon rose in the form of a large heart, of a red gold colour. This morning, about four o'clock, a fine fresh breeze sprung up from the north-east, and we are going on our course at a great rate, with some hopes of anchoring below the Morro this evening. To-day being Sunday, we had prayers on deck, which the weather had not before permitted;—the sailors all clean and attentive, as English sailors are. Last night they sang "Rule Britannia," with great enthusiasm.

Last evening we once more saw the beautiful bay of Havana, once more passed the Morro, and our arrival was no sooner known, than the captain-general, Don Geromino Valdés, sent his *falua* to bring us to the city, and even wished us to go to his palace; but Don B——o H——a, who gave us so hospitable a reception on our first visit, came on board, and kindly insisted on taking us to his house, where we found everything as elegant and comfortable as before, and from whence I now write these few lines.

In the midst of our pleasure at being once more on dry land, surrounded by our former friends, and at receiving letters from home, we were shocked and distressed to hear of the unexpected death of our friend, the Señora de Gutierrez Estrada, who had followed her husband to Havana in his exile. What a blow to him, to her mother, to all her friends! . . .

I shall send off this letter by the first opportunity, that you may know of our safe arrival.

LETTER THE FIFTY-FOURTH

Havana—The Carnival—The Elssler—La Angosta—Ingenio of Count V——a—General Bustamante—Lord Morpeth—Leave Havana—Voyage in the Medway—Old Friends—Return to the United States.

It has been very agreeable for us to return here as private individuals, and to receive the same attentions as when we came in a public situation, but now with more real friendliness. Having arrived at the time of the carnival, we have been in the midst of masked balls, which are curious to see for once; of operas, dinners, and every species of gaiety. But returning so soon, I shall enter into no details. The weather is beautiful, and this house, situated on the bay, receives every sea-breeze as it blows. The Elssler is still attracting immense and enthusiastic crowds; and is now dancing at the theatre of Tacon, where she is seen to much more advantage than in the other. We have been breakfasting in the luxurious *Quintas* in the neighbourhood, driving in the Paseo every evening in an open volante, attending the opera; in short, leading so gay a life, that a little rest in the country will be agreeable;—and we have accepted with pleasure the invitation of Count and Countess F——a, to spend some time at *La Angosta,* one of his country places; a sugar and coffee estate. General Bustamante arrived in the Jason, a few days after us, they having sailed later. They had been very anxious concerning the fate of the Tyrian, in these northern gales off Tampico. We have received letters from our Mexican friends, and learn, with great sorrow, the death of the Dowager Marquesa de Vivanco, and of the Señora H——a of Pascuaro—also the *murder* of a Spanish physician, with whom we were intimately acquainted,—at his distant hacienda.

LA ANGOSTA, 13th March.

We have spent a most agreeable fortnight at La Angosta, and have also visited the Count and Countess V——a, in their plantation near this. General Bustamante was here for a day or two. Lord Morpeth also passed a few days with us; so that altogether we have had a pleasant party. We have been delighted with the elegant hospitality, without ostentation or etiquette, which we have met with here. But we shall now return so soon, that I shall reserve all particulars till we meet.

ON BOARD THE STEAM-SHIP MEDWAY, April 28th.

With a warning of only three hours, we came on board this splendid steamer, eight days ago, after taking a hurried leave of our kind friends, at least of all those who are now in Havana; for the Count and Countess de F——a, and the Count and Countess de V——a are still in the country. Don B——o H——a and his family accompanied us to the ship in the government *falua*. General Bustamante, with his young aide-de-camp, together with Señor de Gutierrez Estrada, and various other gentlemen, hearing of our sudden departure, came out in boats to take leave of us. Alas! those leave-takings.

We had the agreeable surprise of finding that we were acquainted with all our fellow-passengers. There are our particular friends the E——s, the padre F——n, and Mr. G——s, all from Mexico; M. D——s de M——s, who was attached to the French legation in Mexico, and is now returning from a mission to California; Mr. and Miss —— of Boston, etc. We came on board on the evening of the twentieth, but did not leave the harbour till the morning of the twenty-first. The day was beautiful, and as we passed out, we could distinguish the waving of many handkerchiefs from the balconies. In this floating palace, with large airy berths, a beautiful cabin, an agreeable society, books, a band of music, ices, etc.; not to mention that important point, an excellent and good-hearted captain, we have passed our time as pleasantly as if we were in the most splendid hotel.

On the twenty-third we went out in a little boat, in the middle of the night, to Nassau, in New Providence, to buy some of those beautiful specimens of shell-flowers, for which that place is celebrated. We set off again at three in the morning of the twenty-fourth, on which day, being Sunday, we had prayers on board. The weather was beautiful, and even with contrary wind, the Medway went *steaming* on her course at the rate of nine knots an hour.

On the twenty-fifth we lay off Savannah. A pilot came on board, and we went up the river in a boat to the city, where we passed an agreeable day, and in the evening returned to the ship. Crowds of people from Savannah went out to see the steamer. The next day we cast anchor off Charleston, and again a pilot came on board; but the day was stormy and gloomy, and only two of the passengers went on shore. We have now had several days of bad weather; wind and rain; and one night a storm of thunder and lightning; yet down in the cabin there is scarce any motion, and we have been sitting reading and writing as quietly as if we were in our own rooms. After two years and a half of spring and summer, we feel the cool very much.

29th.—We are now passing the Narrows. Once more the green shores of Staten Island appear in sight. We left them two years and six months ago; just as winter was preparing to throw his white shroud over the dolphin hues of the dying autumn; the weather gloomy and tearful. Now the shores are covered with the vegetation of spring, and the grass is as green as emeralds. I shall write no more, for we must arrive to-day; and I shall be the bearer of my own despatches.

The day is bright and beautiful. The band is playing its gayest airs. A little boat is coming from the Quarantine. In a few minutes more we shall be *at home!*

THE END